WATER GARDENING
Water Lilies and Lotuses

WATER GARDENING
Water Lilies and Lotuses

PERRY D. SLOCUM
and
PETER ROBINSON
with Frances Perry

TIMBER PRESS
Portland, Oregon

Grateful acknowledgment is hereby made to
Dr. John H. Wiersema of the Systemic Botany and
Mycology Laboratory, USDA-ARS, Beltsville,
Maryland, for permission to reprint illustrations from
his *A Monograph of Nymphaea Subgenus Hydrocallis
(Nymphaeaceae)*, volume 16 of *Systematic Botany
Monographs*, published in 1987 by the American Society
of Plant Taxonomists, Ann Arbor, Michigan.

Mention of trademark, proprietary product, or vendor
does not constitute a guarantee or warranty of the
product by the publisher or authors and does not imply
its approval to the exclusion of other products or
vendors.

ISBN 0-88192-335-4

Printed in Hong Kong

TIMBER PRESS, INC.
The Haseltine Building
133 S.W. Second Avenue, Suite 450
Portland, Oregon 97204, U.S.A.

Library of Congress Cataloging-in-Publication Data

Slocum, Perry D.
    Water gardening : water lilies and lotuses / Perry
D. Slocum and Peter Robinson with Frances Perry.
        p.   cm.
    Includes bibliographical references (p.   ) and
index.
    ISBN 0-88192-335-4
    1. Water gardens. 2. Water lilies. 3. Aquatic
plants. I. Robinson, Peter, 1938–   . II. Perry,
Frances. III. Title.
SB423.S58   1996
635.9'674—dc20   95-9495
                                          CIP

Contents

Color plates follow pages 144 and 208

Preface

The range of opportunities for including water in the garden is surpassed only by the amazing variety of plants that will thrive there, from the zones of deeper water to the moist soil near the water's edge. This two-part book is intended to inspire and inform the professional or keen amateur gardener, in both subtropical and temperate climates, with complete details on creating and stocking a successful water or bog garden.

The content begins with an overview of how water has figured in garden history and how its presence has influenced contemporary design. Advice on siting and construction follows, with special attention to the styles of creative planting that may be achieved through good construction and management. The impact and versatility of flexible liners is noted—how they simplify construction and how they prevent excessive water loss through drainage, thereby saving one of the world's most precious resources. The critical role water plays in nature's balance by attracting wildlife to the garden is also explored. Not only floating and submerged aquatics and marginals but also moisture-loving plants more commonly associated with drier soil regimes are covered extensively, to encourage greater exploitation of this zone by the gardener. The detail offered in the plant descriptions across the numerous habitats encountered in and around water makes this book unique, particularly the specifics gathered in Part Two on the dramatic water lilies and lotuses.

I write as a horticulturist; my background in a botanic garden has underpinned my specialism in designing and planting water and bog gardens. Throughout the creation of Part One, I was guided by Frances Perry, who before her death in 1993 was one of the foremost international authorities on water plants. Despite failing health, Frances maintained a close interest in the development of this portion of the book; the expert knowledge she passes on is gleaned from her years of growing and propagating many of the marginals and moisture-lovers at Perry's Hardy Plant Farm in North London. Her nephew Mr. David Everett of Anglo Aquarium Plant Co. Ltd. was involved throughout as well, always ready with both technical support and the loan of slides.

Part Two provides a wealth of firsthand experience from one of the most respected North American authorities on *Nymphaea* and *Nelumbo*, including species and cultivars, both the old favorites and the newer commercially available hybrids. Many of the plants formally and meticulously described are products of Mr. Slocum's own internationally recognized breeding efforts, and his many splendid photographs amount to a second generous act of creation from which the reader is sure to benefit.

Peter Robinson

PART ONE

Water and Bog Gardens

by

PETER ROBINSON

with FRANCES PERRY

Chapter 1

History of Water Plants and Gardens

Water is an essential element, without which life cannot be long sustained. Accordingly, since the dawn of time, mankind has striven to live within reasonable reach of a river, lake, or similar body of fresh water, as is revealed by the geographical situations of so many cities. Water was necessary not only for the needs of the human population but also for stock animals. Fairly soon, various aquatic and bog plants were recognized, directly or indirectly, as a source of food and shelter for a wide variety of creatures, including waterfowl, some mammals, and economically important fish. Certain aquatic plants also provided food, such as rice, which is the most important crop species in the world. Others provided raw materials for industrial purposes, medicine, and building materials and even benefited humans in the maintenance of clear water or assisted in the recovery of polluted water.

Nevertheless, in freshly constructed waterways, some species of aquatic plants prove troublesome by a rapidity of growth which impedes navigation or water intake. *Salvinia* (a water fern) and *Eichhornia* (water hyacinth) are prime examples of such rampant colonizers, often interfering with crops on irrigated land, fish production, and free navigation for boats.

Aquatics may also create conditions suitable for pests and diseases affecting humans, domestic animals, and crop plants—their uniquely advantageous position rendering them largely resistant to climatic extremes of heat, cold, or drought. In the past, some aquatics were even singled out as having religious significance. In the Orient, appreciation of water plants for their usefulness and aesthetic appeal followed the rise of the great Asiatic cultures, particularly in China, where from around 2700 B.C., nelumbos especially had religious connotations and were esteemed for their medicinal properties. Later, nelumbos spread to Egypt, probably through the agency of ancient Roman spice-traders who regularly visited the East in a two-way bartering system (Figure 1).

The title "lotus" also confuses since several plants have been known by this name. Thus in addition to *Nelumbo nucifera* (syn. *N. speciosa*), also termed the sacred lotus of India, the appellation was applied by Egyptians to certain water lilies (*Nymphaea* species), especially the day-blooming *N. caerulea* (the blue lotus of the Nile) and the nocturnal white *N. lotus* (Figure 2). The name can also refer to *Lotus corniculatus*, the bird's foot trefoil, grown in various parts of the world as food for livestock. The lotus of Homeric legend relates to *Ziziphus lotus*, a small North African tree with edible fruits, consumption of which was supposed to make peo-

FIGURE 1. A decorative frieze from Allahabad, India, 250 B.C., has a lotus motif.

11

FIGURE 2. The blue lotus (*Nymphaea caerulea*) was a favorite flower of the Egyptians and valued for its beauty. From *The Waterlilies: A Monograph of the Genus Nymphaea* by Henry S. Conard (1905).

ple forget their homes and friends and yearn to live in idleness in Lotus-land. Both *Nymphaea caerulea* and *N. lotus* are maintained in Sanskrit literature and may have had religious associations.

We have no knowledge of how water plants were cultivated in those faraway days, but it was probably with care and respect since Hindus, and the ancient peoples of Tibet and Nepal particularly, held *Nelumbo* in veneration, believing that Buddha was born in its heart. Buddhism, a religion inaugurated in India in the 6th century B.C., holds that the world is a transient reflection of the deity, with human souls held fast in life until their owners have been sufficiently purified by divine contemplation to be taken into the sacred presence. Thus the *Nelumbo*, illustrated as a support of Buddha, can claim a place of high esteem in the association of plants to early cultures (Figure 3).

Indian Brahmins, who also claim that from a nelumbo's mystic blossom sprang Brahma, the Absolute and Creator of the Universe, belong to a religious movement of high priestly rank, inaugurated in 1828 by Ram Mahan Roy, a wealthy Hindu whose aim was to found a purified national church that was free from superstition and idolatry. He called it Brahma Somaj, the Society of Believers in One God.

Yet some Orientals were evidently appreciative of water plants for purely aesthetic reasons. Chou Tun-I, a Chinese writer of the 11th century A.D., penned this little gem:

Since the opening days of the T'ang dynasty (A.D. 600) it has been fashionable to admire the peony; but my favorite is the water lily. How stainless it rises from its slimy bed! How modestly it reposes on the clear pool—an emblem of purity and truth! Symmetrically perfect, its subtle perfume is wafted far and wide; while there it rests in spotless state, something to be regarded reverently from a distance, and not to be profaned by familiar approach. (H. Giles, *Gems of Chinese Literature*)

In spite of its miniature size and scarcely discernible perfume, Dr. Henry S. Conard, in his landmark *The Waterlilies: A Monograph of the Genus Nymphaea* (1905), considered that this eulogy referred to the pygmy water lily, *Nymphaea tetragona* (Figure 4).

At some period in their history, Indian poets have likened many parts of the human body to the *Nelumbo*. To the Chinese it typified female beauty, while the Japanese considered the plant an emblem of purity since the splendid flowers grew unsullied by the muddy waters of its habitat. Images of Oriental deities are often

FIGURE 3. Buddha is seated on a lotus blossom.

seen reclining on huge nelumbo leaves. An ancient prayer heard in Tibet and other regions of the Himalayas includes the phrase *Om mani padme hum*, which can be translated as "Oh, the jewel in the heart of the lotus! Amen." This benediction is unceasingly repeated on prayer wheels—extraordinary devices peculiar to that part of the world and reputedly invented for easy multiplication of this prayer. W. J. Hooker, writing in *Curtis's Botanical Magazine* in 1808, stated that "a native of Nepal, who entered Sir William Jones' study, made prostrations before a lotus, the flowers of which happened to be there for examination."

Widespread though reverence for the lotus has been, most of our knowlege concerning the early uses of water plants has come from ancient Egypt, where nymphaeas, nelumbos, and papyruses in particular are widely represented on tomb wall paintings, found as dried blossoms in sarcophagi, and reproduced as decorative elements on pillars and columns in architecture (Figures 5 and 6). In his *Grammar of the Lotus* Professor W. H. Goodyear (1891) ascribes to the lotus a high place in the arts of 30 centuries before Christ. He likens the twisted sepals of the lotus to the Ionic capital (one of the three Greek orders of architecture), and from that the Greek meander (an ornamental pattern composed of twisted lines used for bordering pottery and similar decorations). Doubled again, the meander becomes a swastika, earliest of all symbols, representing life and darkness, good and evil, male and female, life and death, according to the angle at which it is presented. The swastika was used on many Egyptian artifacts and pottery as well as on temple facades. All these were probably derived from *Nymphaea lotus*, the native water lily, whereas the cornucopia or horn-of-plenty spilling out its contents is believed to be linked with the well-filled seed pods of *Nelumbo nucifera*.

FIGURE 4. The white flower of the pygmy water lily (*Nymphaea tetragona*) is scarcely larger than a silver dollar. PERRY SLOCUM

Opinions differ as to which plant the Greek historian Herodotus (who visited Egypt around 460 B.C.) had in mind when he wrote:

> When the Nile is full and has made the plains like a sea, great numbers of lilies spring up in the water; these they gather and dry in the sun, then having pounded the middle of the lotus, which resembles a poppy, they make bread of it and bake it. The root also of this lotus is fit for food, and is tolerably sweet, and is round and the size of an apple.

Conard believed this description must have referred to a nymphaea, probably *N. lotus*, especially as Herodotus goes on to describe other lilies, "like roses, with fruits like a wasp's nest and edible seeds the size of an olive stone." This probably referred to the Oriental lotus (*Nelumbo*), since nymphaea seeds do not grow as large as olive stones.

Undoubtedly both plants were a source of food. Pliny (A.D. 23–79) relates how Egyptian bakers kneaded the milletlike seed with milk or water to make bread. There was no bread in the world, he declared, "more wholesome and lighter as long as it is hot; but being once cold, it is harder of digestion and becometh weighty and ponderous" (Caius Pliny Secundus, *Historie of the World*, 2nd translation [Holland: Philemon, 1601]).

This description obviously refers to nymphaeas, but nelumbo seeds were also ground into flour for bread-

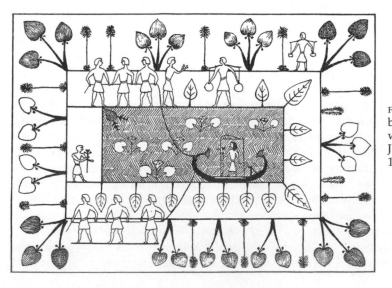

FIGURE 5. An Egyptian wall painting depicts a boat being drawn across a lake covered with water lilies. From *The Ancient Egyptians* by Sir J. Gardner Wilkinson (London: John Murray, 1854).

FIGURE 6. King Amenhotep offers lotuses to the Egyptian god Amon. From *The Grammar of the Lotus* by W. H. Goodyear (1891).

making. In fact, the propagation method of separately enclosing the large seeds in balls of clay and dropping them into the Nile at sowing time is thought to be the origin of the Biblical phrase "Cast thy bread upon the waters, for thou shalt find it after many days."

The use of flowers for social purposes was tremendously important to the ancient Egyptians. It seems to have been particularly significant during the 19th to 21st dynasties when, according to Sir J. Gardner Wilkinson (1854), following the anointing ceremony at a nobleman's reception, servants presented each guest with a lotus flower which was then either held in the hand or attached to the head before visitors entered the reception rooms. These rituals probably indicated that the guests came with peaceable intent. That the fragrant *Nymphaea lotus* was constantly used for this purpose is clear from mural paintings and hieroglyphics of around 2600–2100 B.C.

In those far-off days, scented plants owed their importance to the fact that unpleasant odors were invariably associated with evil. Clean, sweet scents, on the other hand, were symbolic of purity and goodness. This was the thinking that led upper-class Egyptians of the time to fumigate their homes regularly with incense and pleasantly fragrant flowers—partly for enjoyment and partly to counteract the unpleasant odors of humanity (Figure 7). It was also the underlying reasoning behind embalming, when the viscera were removed, corpses cleansed with sweet-smelling herbs, and mummies strewn with fragrant plants and spices. Wreaths and circlets of flowers were often laid on the breasts of mummies, sometimes in such quantities that the sarcophagus was practically filled with floral tributes. These were particularly common on the mummies of females, placed there to represent purification and regeneration. Conard relates that long-stalked blooms of *Nymphaea caerulea* were attached to the swaddling bands around the mummies of Ramses II and his priest Nighan and that odd flowers were scattered on their bodies (Figure 8).

Schweinfurth, in *The Flora of Ancient Egypt* (1883), believed the wreaths of Amenhotep were probably older than the Trojan War, dating—along with those of Ramses II and other mummies found at Thebes in 1881—from around 2000 B.C. Ramses's flowers, however, were renewed around 1100 B.C. because of the damage sustained by the coffin during its removal "to a safer place" in the Valley of the Temple of the Kings. Schweinfurth also soaked some of the wreaths, reconstituted them, and found them to be as perfectly preserved as any herbarium specimens in British and continental museums. Perhaps more importantly, he was unable to detect any structural differences between these ancient plant relics and the nymphaeas found growing in Egypt at that time, suggesting that the climate had scarcely changed in the intervening centuries.

The fact that nelumbos are no longer widespread in Egypt seems to bear out the belief that they were originally imported from the East and subsequently cultivated for food and ornamental purposes. Another plant associated with ancient Egypt—reputedly the "bulrush" which hid the infant Moses—is the paper reed, *Cyperus papyrus* (syn. *Papyrus antiquorum*), a 6–15 ft (2–4.5 m) reed with huge, moplike heads of floral

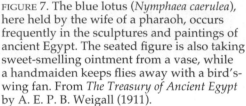

FIGURE 7. The blue lotus (*Nymphaea caerulea*), here held by the wife of a pharaoh, occurs frequently in the sculptures and paintings of ancient Egypt. The seated figure is also taking sweet-smelling ointment from a vase, while a handmaiden keeps flies away with a bird's-wing fan. From *The Treasury of Ancient Egypt* by A. E. P. B. Weigall (1911).

spikelets. It was cultivated by the Egyptians as a source of food and medicine as well as to provide papyrus, the first writing paper known to mankind. This was made quite simply, by peeling the stems and cutting the inner pith lengthwise into thin strips. These were then laid closely side by side, sprinkled with gummy water, and covered with heavy presses, which caused them to stick together. After drying into broad sheets, the "paper" was cut to the required size.

Papyrus had other uses. At one time it was important to Egyptian pharaohs as representing the king's authority over Lower Egypt. In *De Historia Plantarum*, published in Amsterdam in 1644, the Greek philosopher Theophrastus wrote,

> They [the Egyptians] use the roots instead of wood, not only for burning, but they make boats of it and from the rind they weave sails, mats, a kind of cloth, coverlets, ropes, and other things. . . . Above all the plant is of a very great use in the way of food. For all the natives chew the papyrus raw, boiled, and roasted; they swallow the juice and spit out the quid.

Seemingly, when large temples or tombs were built, huge papyrus rafts, made from the stalks, were employed to transport the enormous obelisks, such as those erected at Karnak and Luxor. In recent years, rafts and boats built of *Cyperus papyrus* have proved to be not only navigable but quite manageable. Although scarce in present-day Egypt, the plant is still plentiful in Uganda and other parts of tropical Africa.

GARDENS OF THE MIDDLE EAST AND INDIA

It is understandable that gardens with water features should appeal to people living in hot, dry countries, and we know they were highly esteemed by the Persians (Iranians) as far back as the 5th century B.C. At that time, gardens were apparently constructed in four sections, a simulation perhaps of the world, which Mid-

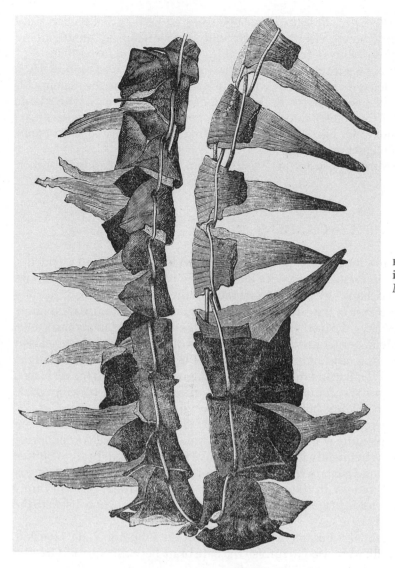

FIGURE 8. Wreaths of lotus petals were found in the tomb of the pharaoh Ramses II. From *Nature* (1883).

dle Eastern peoples believed to be similarly quartered. To this end the garden was split into four by means of crossing canals. Then, if there was sufficient water pressure from a lake, stream, or reservoir at a sufficiently high elevation beyond, water was guided to jets installed either in the canals or alongside the banks in order to produce rows of fountains.

Following the conquest of Persia by Islamic Arabs in the 7th century A.D., these four-part designs were widely copied by Muslims of other nations, particularly in central Asia and India—where the Taj Mahal (Plate 1) remains a well-known example—and later in Mediterranean regions. It was Islamic gardeners who pioneered fountains and controlled jets of water, passing on these techniques to North Africa and Spain. Their expertise is still splendidly evident in the 15th-century Moorish gardens of the Alhambra and the Generalife (Plate 2) in Granada, Spain, and in the great gardens of France, Germany, and England, where the designs later spread.

The people of India, with their wealth of water lilies, including both day- and night-blooming species and hybrids, must have been interested in pool construction for many centuries. Where water did not occur naturally, it was often channeled into lakes and reservoirs from distant sources. This occurred not only in Egypt, where the Nile was tapped during the annual rising of the waters from sources farther south, but also in India and Afghanistan in the Mogul era. The Moguls, Oriental adventurers and reputedly descendants of Ghengis Khan and Tamburlaine, came into prominence in the 16th and 17th centuries.

The first Mogul leader of historical importance was a bandit called Bābur, who, having conquered Kabul (now the capital of Afghanistan), set his sights on the rich lands north of the Khyber Pass near the borders of present-day Pakistan. This entailed bitter fighting, but eventually force prevailed, and Bābur set up an empire based in Agra, in northern India. Although a despot, he must be admired for his great architectural ability. He was responsible for the building of many charming gardens with aquatic features, often bringing water from far-distant sources for the purpose. Many of these memorable gardens are still in existence.

An outstanding example of a formal Oriental garden is the Taj Mahal at Agra, which was built by Shāh Jahān—a descendant of Bābur—as a mausoleum for his favorite wife, Mumtaz Mahal. Before the main building of this exquisite edifice is a wide canal, intersected halfway along its length by a cross canal with a large square pool, usually filled with water lilies, at the point of intersection. In the center of this pool, a square marble platform supports a tank with four white water lilies—apparently floating, yet in reality carved of marble, with a small jet of water rising from the center of each bloom.

The Shalamar Bagh in Kashmir and the Museum Garden at Gwalior, India, are also outstanding for their lavish use of water features.

CHINESE GARDENS

Water has long played a significant role in Chinese gardens. This is revealed by paintings and woodcuts, some dating back to the 13th century. Also in existence are still older frescoes painted by Buddhist monks of the 7th to 9th centuries on the walls of cave chapels along the desert route of the ancient "silk road" leading to the West. These have probably survived because of the extremely dry atmosphere of their unusual situation.

Probably most Chinese water features have derived from garden builders of the Han dynasty (206 B.C.–A.D. 220), a period when palatial gardens were constructed on vast areas of farmland forcibly enclosed for the purpose. This practice may have been significant in the development of Chinese gardens, but at the time it seriously impaired agricultural development and must have brought great suffering to the displaced peasants. The imperial garden of the Emperor Wu, for example, was constructed as a huge pleasure park, seven miles (11 km) around with 12 ornamental lakes, only one of natural origin.

The concepts of the imperial gardens were widely copied by wealthy Chinese landowners, who constructed lakes and islands in many designs, planting willows and other trees along the shores in order to provide water reflections and shade. The gardens frequently included decorative moon (arched) bridges built of stone or wood linking the shore to teahouses and islands, from which visitors could view lotuses growing in the water. So obsessed did the Chinese become with these plants that the withered leaves were rarely removed, even in autumn, one poet recommending, "Keep the remaining lotus leaves, that I may listen to the sound of the rain."

Later in the Sui dynasty (A.D. 589–618), flowers became more popular. In the Emperor Yang's garden, flowers and leaves fashioned from colored silk were used to furbish the bare branches of shrubs and trees in autumn and winter, while water plants, also of silk, graced the ponds.

Although some of these fine gardens have survived (Plate 3), many were unfortunately destroyed during the wars involving Japan in comparatively recent times.

JAPANESE GARDENS

In Japan the Indian lotus (*Nelumbo nucifera*), known by the Japanese as *Hasu*, is the seasonal flower of August and the symbol of life since all parts of it can be eaten, including the roots. It has come to typify sincerity and nobility in the legends and religious development of past eras, partly because of the plant's usefulness to mankind but also due to its annual emergence from the still waters.

Sima Eliovson, the South African horticulturist and traveler, suggests in her book *Gardening the Japanese Way* (London: George G. Harrap & Company, Ltd., 1971) that styles of garden-making in Japan derived originally from Korea and that the chief period in the early history of garden design was A.D. 646–794, when Nara was the capital of Japan. Just prior to that, in A.D. 612, a Japanese emissary called Ono no Imoko, having seen the Chinese imperial garden built for the Emperor Wu, was so impressed that Korean craftsmen were retained to build similar features in the imperial garden of the Empress Suiko. Like the Chinese designs, this Japanese garden featured a lake and an island, a combination that has persisted as a theme for Japanese gardens ever since.

The Heian period which followed (795–1195) is significant because a treatise written toward the end of this term offered suggestions for garden-making that reproduced the natural beauty of the countryside as well as ideas regarding the diversion of streams and the correct manner of placing rocks. A so-called pond built at this time at Osawa is still used for boating, although no actual gardens survive.

The next period of importance in garden design, the Momoyama (1573–1603), has been likened to the Renaissance period in Europe. The period is noteworthy on account of the many tea gardens built at this time, often with stone water basins in which visitors could rinse their hands and stepping stones which made for easy passage across lakes containing water plants.

The Edo period (1603–1867) was named after a new town called Edo, built on an expanse of flat ground by wealthy aristocrats, who constructed fine estates with large lakes and islands. Later, great numbers of smaller gardens were built as merchants moved into the city, which in 1869 changed its name to Tokyo. In 1853, however, after being sealed off from the outer world for two centuries, Commodore Matthew Perry of the United States Navy arrived and prevailed upon the Emperor to open up Japan for trade with the Western world. It was then the turn of the Japanese to import ideas from the West, including notions of flower gardens and wide stretches of lawn. Other features developed, but the traditional use of water is as important in Japan today as it ever was in the past (Plate 4).

EUROPEAN GARDENS

Many types of garden design reached southern Europe in medieval times, long before they were seen farther north. Most of these were of a basic nature rather than ornamental, designed to provide fruit, vegetables, and herbs for food and medicinal purposes, and usually enclosed within walls or hedges to ensure privacy. Flowers were normally grown only for decorative purposes.

Greece and Rome undoubtedly adopted ideas culled from those of the Moguls and Persians as well as the ancient Egyptians. Unfortunately, few traces remain of gardens created prior to the Renaissance period, with the exception of a notable example excavated at Pompeii, Italy, from the ashes of Mount Vesuvius, a rare survival.

In almost every case, early Italian gardeners apparently built an elaborate marble fountain in a prominent central position. Leading from this, they installed small open channels, marble-edged or faced with marble slabs, normally bridging these over at the intersections of avenues or paths. Water was of special importance and was utilized in every conceivable manner, including trickling springs, brooklets, channels, pools, and waterfalls. The characteristic central placement of fountains and walkways continued until the Renaissance.

Enough written treatises survive from that period onward for us to realize that gardens then ceased to be isolated features and became part of the surrounding landscape and view. Also, from that time forward, gardeners made lavish use of statuary.

The most outstanding example of a Roman design of the 16th century was the Villa d'Este gardens at Tivoli, Italy, built by Pirro Ligorio. This marvelous achievement embraced all the inventions of the new art of water gardening, with everything in unison, the most diverse elements finding perfect fulfillment in an overall picture of cascades, waterfalls, fountains, water jets, fish ponds, grottoes, and terraces, each dependent upon its neighbor, and all linking up to the villa itself. Flowers were relegated to secluded spots, with any plants grown in the main area limited in number and of an evergreen nature, such as pines, laurels, cypresses, and holly oaks.

The Villa d'Este gardens, which attract thousands of visitors annually, also contain such elaborate features as a water theater; the Fountain of the Organ, which resembles a huge pipe organ with many small waterfalls (Plate 5); and the Pathway of the One Hundred Fountains, a promenade walk running alongside three rows of small fountains.

The success of the Villa d'Este was immense, and all over Italy in the 17th century, sumptuous villas sprang up in the midst of splendid gardens. It was a period of great wealth and luxurious display, and soon the new fashion spread into Lombardy, Piedmont, and Liguria. Naturally, these developments did not go unnoticed by neighboring countries, particularly Spain, France, and later, Britain.

In 16th-century Europe, water garden jokes were also popular. Some of these could be triggered by a hidden operator, who, by turning a tap, caused jets of water to rise out of the paving and shoot up ladies' garments or caused seats to suddenly soak an unsuspecting sitter. In other cases, grottoes became showery; artificial trees dripped; or statues suddenly sprayed spectators from various parts of their anatomy. One of the best examples of this coarse sense of humor is at Augsburg, Germany.

Some of these eccentricities spread to England, notably at Chatsworth in Derbyshire, which Dr. Charles Leigh in 1700 described as containing

Neptune, with his sea-nymphs from whence, by the turning of a cock, immediately issue forth several columns of water, which seem'd to fall upon sea-weeds. Not far from this is another pond where sea-horses continually roll and near to this stands a tree which exactly resembles a willow; by the turn of a cock each leaf distils continually drops of water and lively represents a shower of rain.

At first the French tended to adopt Italian designs, although with less emphasis on statuary. François I apparently recruited Italian architects and workmen to rebuild and decorate the palace at Fontainebleau after the style of the Italian Renaissance, turning a huge marshy area adjoining the palace into a large lake.

Many wealthy landowners copied this idea, with the result that the major French gardens were largely built on flat sites and made almost exclusive use of still pools rather than the cascades and fountains favored in Italy. These long, narrow, and symmetrical layouts were designed to provide vistas of the surrounding countryside, usually from a specific vantage point. Beds were divided by clipped hedges, with topiary features planted parallel to the pools.

In 1662 the architect André Le Nôtre began his greatest masterpiece, the magnificent garden at Versailles, which he designed for Louis XIV, the Sun King. The garden at Vaux-le-Vicomte (Plate 6), which was actually Le Nôtre's first triumph, aroused the king to such jealousy that he spirited the architect away to design Versailles. Although Le Nôtre went on to build Fontainebleau, Meudon, and Saint-Cloud—all of which relied heavily on water features—Versailles remains his pièce de résistance, attracting thousands of visitors annually to this day.

The Versailles estate was originally a small hunting lodge used by Louis XIII. Le Nôtre's brief was to create the greatest garden the world had ever known—a vast palace outdoors which would accommodate thousands of people. Trees were arranged in geometric patterns some distance from the house, but glass beads, colored sand, or porcelain in complex parterres were more important ingredients of this unique style. The wide central vista stretched from the courtyard to the far distance, reinforced by the cruciform canal, its arms extending 5900 ft (1800 m) from east to west and 4920 ft (1500 m) from north to south. It accommodated a flotilla of excursion boats and was decorated with classical statues. The canal, artificial lakes, and the hundreds of fountains were supplied with water from distant sources through feats of hydraulic engineering. Throughout the reign of Louis XIV the gardens continued to be enlarged and made more elaborate at incalculable costs both in money and human life. The gardens were replenished with 1.9 million flowerpots filled with flowers brought by the navy from warmer climes, and the three giant parterres contained 150,000 plants. Much of the glory of Versailles remains today, a striking testimonial to André Le Nôtre, the greatest engineer and artist with water features ever seen in Europe.

Meantime in England, this age of grandeur seems to have taken the form of constructing canals or long, rectangular stretches of water. In 1703 the long canal at Chatsworth in Derbyshire was built, a great stretch of water into which the Emperor Fountain now plays.

At Studley Royal in Yorkshire lived John Aislabie, landowner and landscape architect, one-time Chancellor of the Exchequer in Walpole's government, and the man who sponsored what became known as the South Sea Bubble. In 1722, after that vast financial empire collapsed and Aislabie was found guilty of "most notorious, dangerous, and infamous corruption with a view to his own exorbitant profit," he retired to his property in Yorkshire and there built a series of pools, canals, and water cascades, overlooked by a temple in the classical style on a group of ponds known as the moon pools, so called because Aislabie intended them to be seen by moonlight. Later his son extended the garden to take in Fountains Abbey, a nearby, recently acquired, ruined Gothic abbey (actually a Cistercian monastery); so today the garden can be viewed as a whole, in parts bordering the River Skell, backed by dramatic, heavily wooded slopes, with a curving lake leading to Huby's 170-ft (52-m) tower which still dominates the Cistercian ruins. The two Aislabies must therefore be credited with creating one of the most prodigious formal water designs still to be seen in Britain.

Among the few ornamental fountains of this period which still remain are Cibber's fountain of sea horses on the lawn in front of Chatsworth erected in the 1690s, the Duke of Marlborough's Bernini Fountain at Blenheim Palace (1710), and the Dragon Fountain at Holkham Hall, Norfolk (1720).

During the remainder of the 18th century, fountains and water features went out of fashion, until with Queen Victoria on the throne after 1837 they came flooding back. Sir Joseph Paxton (1803–1865), the great

English gardener and architect, was outstanding in this sphere. To understand his prodigious energy, character, and achievements, it is worth relating his own description of his first day as head gardener at Chatsworth, seat of the 6th Duke of Devonshire, where he remained until the duke's death in 1858. Said Paxton,

> I left London by the Comet Coach for Chesterfield and arrived at Chatsworth at half-past four o'clock in the morning of the ninth of May 1826. As no person was to be seen at that early hour, I got over the green-house gate by the old covered way, explored the pleasure grounds and looked around the outside of the house. I then went down to the kitchen gardens, scaled the outside wall and saw the whole of the place, set the men to work at six o'clock, then returned to Chatsworth and got Thomas Weldon to play me the water works and afterwards went to breakfast with poor dear Mrs. Gregory and her niece, the latter fell in love with me and I with her, and thus completed my first morning's work at Chatsworth, before nine o'clock. (Miles Hadfield, Robert Harling, and Leonie Highton, eds., *British Gardeners: A Biographical Dictionary* [London: Zwenner Ltd., 1980])

It must be remembered that Paxton was only 23 at this time, but his inventiveness and industry would result in the building of the great Emperor Fountain in 1843, rising 289 ft (88 m) and at that time the highest jet in the world, and his ingenuity as an engineer would enable him to master the intricacies of building the greenhouses in the gardens between 1836 and 1840, including the Great Stove or Conservatory, the greatest area of glass in the world (Figure 9). It was there that in 1849 he grew the giant water lily *Victoria amazonica*, originally called *V. regia* in honor of the sovereign. This experience led to his success in 1851 in designing for Prince Albert the Crystal Palace, a great iron and glass exhibition center in Hyde Park, London. Later this edifice was removed to Sydenham Hill and elaborated with gardens, lakes, terraces, cascades, and statuary. Paxton was also elected to Parliament and knighted, but he died of overwork and ill health at the early age of 62.

FIGURE 9. Joseph Paxton's greenhouse, which he built at Chatsworth for the first flowering in Britain of the giant water lily *Victoria amazonica*, was inspired by the ribs in the leaves of the water lily itself. From *Gardener's Chronicle* (1850).

In the 20th century came another great urge to create water gardens. To this period belong Bodnant in Gwynedd, Wales (Plate 7); Waddesdon Manor, Buckinghamshire; Blenheim Palace, Oxfordshire; Sheffield Park, Sussex; Compton Acres, Dorset; Hidcote Manor Garden, Gloucestershire; Longstock Water Gardens, Hampshire; and the development of water features at Kew and Wisley as well as outstanding bog gardens at the Savill Garden, Windsor Great Park, Berkshire. In Scotland, water gardens appeared at Stranraer; the small garden of Inverewe near Wester Ross; Benmore in Argyll; Logan on the western edge of Galloway; and many more.

This period was important to horticulture in Britain in still other respects. The Prince Consort became president of the Royal Horticultural Society in 1858 and remained in this office until his death in 1861. It was the era of great gardening writers such as William Robinson, the Loudons, Shirley Hibberd, Gertrude Jekyll, and Ellen Willmott, all of whom fostered a widespread interest in gardening. And it was also the era of Robert Fortune, William Lobb, Frank Ludlow, and Reginald Farrer, who searched the world for new plants to grace British gardens.

NORTH AMERICAN GARDENS

Not surprisingly, the first gardens in the United States were modeled on those of Europe, the settlers' native continent, and particularly those of Britain. Most of the early plant collectors in North America were British. North Americans have always been indefatigable travelers, however, and very soon their gardens were influenced by other civilizations.

Noteworthy in the United States is Longwood, the magnificent garden of the late Pierre S. Du Pont at Kennett Square in Pennsylvania (Plate 8). This garden is unique, containing everything the most dedicated gardener would wish to see—a thousand acres of beauty spreading out from a huge indoor conservatory that is always in character due to constantly changing displays, even in winter. Beyond is a vast fountain garden possessing an elaborate underwater lighting system that, when turned on at dusk, illuminates the evening sky with red, blue, yellow, green, and white arcs of color. Longwood also has beautifully kept pools of hardy and tropical water lilies, as well as nelumbos and outstanding hybrid victorias.

The Missouri Botanical Garden in St. Louis is of special importance to growers of water lilies, for it was here that George H. Pring worked for many years on the hybridization of tropical nymphaeas. The first of the great North American botanical gardens, it was established by Henry Shaw in 1859. Here he built his country home, Tower Grove House, on a site reputedly almost treeless, except for a few sassafras trees.

Now the garden is a treasury of plants and features of many kinds, including the huge Climatron, 175 ft (53 m) in diameter and 70 ft (21 m) high at the center, which was built without interior props. This impressive construction was the world's first air-conditioned, moisture-controlled greenhouse.

Biltmore House at Asheville, North Carolina, belonged to the late George Vanderbilt and is noteworthy because the gardens were designed by Frederick Law Olmsted (1822–1903), a landscape architect whose work has been compared to that of the French architect André Le Nôtre. Certainly it appears to have been based on Vaux-le-Vicomte and has a variety of pools containing lotuses and water lilies as well as some fine fountains.

Today, water plants are a feature of most large American gardens, at the New York Botanical Garden; the Denver Botanic Gardens, Colorado; the Chicago Botanic Garden, Illinois; Cypress Gardens, Winter Haven, Florida; Bellingrath Garden, near Mobile, Alabama; and Kenilworth Aquatic Gardens, Washington, D.C.

During the past century and a half, North Americans—like the British and French—have taken an increasing interest in their gardens, so that today there are more of them, both public and private, as well as more horticultural books and magazines and more flower shows than ever before. This renewal of interest has naturally extended to water gardening, as outstanding gardens with water plants and aquatic features are now firmly established in most countries of the world.

Chapter 2

The Hybridizers

Considering the long years and many places in which water lilies and lotuses have been grown as ornamental plants, it seems highly probable that mutations occasionally occurred. Some may have been sufficiently striking to warrant propagation, probably by division of the root tubers, since seed propagation often proves an unreliable method for perpetuating plant variants.

Although pure conjecture, it is possible, for example, that *Nymphaea tetragona*, the pygmy water lily, produced divergences from the norm over a very long period. This small species with its tiny, white, fragrant flowers and dark green, purple-backed leaves is a prolific seeder, producing young flowering plants the second season from sowing. This prodigality has led to much confusion and independent naming based on such divergencies as flower size, petal markings, or country of origin. Thus, even in the present century we have had a *N. tetragona* var. *himalayense* from India, introduced by Sprenger in 1902 (now probably extinct); a *N. tetragona* var. *angusta* f. *orientalis* from China; *N. tetragona* var. *grandiflora*, a large-flowered variety introduced by Lagrange in 1900; and various others.

Indeed, things became so confused that in 1935 Amos Perry, a pioneer of hardy water lily cultivation, wrote:

> For many years I have tried every reliable source at home and abroad to procure plants or seeds of the true *N. tetragona*. In the spring of 1896 I purchased from T. Smith of Newry [Ireland] a pretty, small-flowered form as *N. pygmaea*. This proved identical to the plants distributed by Latour-Marliac of France, who claimed his stock was of Chinese origin. Both stocks however were identical to *Nymphaea candida*, which I had earlier received from correspondents in the Himalayas and Bohemia and had myself seen flowering in Finland. My stock of the true *N. tetragona* was raised from seed collected in Yunnan. The flowers are tetragonal [four-angled], snow white, and about one inch across.

Among the many variants of *Nymphaea tetragona* available before World War II, Amos Perry always considered *N. tetragona* var. *georgii*, raised at the Göteborg Botanical Garden in Sweden in 1938 to be the finest, although it was known to be a rather difficult plant, slow to increase, which finally disappeared during the war years. Undoubtedly the most outstanding *N. tetragona* derivative is 'Joanne Pring', a pink cultivar with flowers 3–4 in (8–10 cm) across, which appeared as a sport in the Missouri Botanical Garden in St. Louis in 1942 and was subsequently developed and named by George Pring.

Curiously, the first deliberate attempt to hybridize water lilies in Britain occurred at Chatsworth, Derbyshire, where in 1851 Joseph Paxton pollinated the tropical, night-blooming *Nymphaea rubra* with *N. lotus*, naming the resultant hybrid, a brilliant rose-pink with blooms 12 in (30 cm) across, 'Devoniensis', in honor of his employer, the 6th Duke of Devonshire.

In 1852, a similar cross was deliberately repeated at the Van Houtte Nurseries at Ghent, Belgium, using *Nymphaea rubra* as seed parent, pollinated by *N. ×ortgiesiana* (a *N. lotus* derivative). The resultant hybrid was named *N. ×ortgiesiana* 'Rubra'. The following year (1853) at the Royal Botanical Garden, Berlin, Herr Bouche also tried a cross, using *N. rubra* and a different form of *N. lotus*, producing *N. ×boucheana*.

In 1989, however, Charles Otto Masters surmised in an article in the *Water Garden Journal* that similar crosses had long occurred naturally between *Nymphaea rubra* and *N. lotus* in India, suggesting that Paxton's 'Devoniensis' and presumably the other hybrids were self-pollinated seedlings of *N. rubra* and well duplicated in India.

All these hybrids were still available in Europe at the turn of the century, although they attracted little attention in Britain where severe winters and cold winds did not encourage the cultivation of tender plants. Indeed, for many years even hardier water plants were rarely grown, except by owners of a pond or natural lake, although old baths, cisterns, lead troughs, sawn-down casks, and similar watertight receptacles were sometimes used to house the odd nymphaea and a few fish.

In Elizabethan times, Francis Bacon (*Of Gardens* 1625) had written, "Fountains are a great beauty and refreshment; but ponds mar all, and make the garden unwholesome and full of flies and frogs." Nor were the 19th-century writers particularly encouraging. The *Gardener's Chronicle* in 1848, responding to a reader's enquiry as to where *Nymphaea alba*, the common white water lily of central Europe, could be obtained, replied that "the roots of these things may sometimes be had in the nurseries, but they are not usually kept."

The water garden was further denigrated in 1883 by William Robinson, who in *The English Flower Garden* wrote, "Unclean and ugly ponds deface our gardens; some have a mania for artificial water, the effect of water . . . pleasing them so well that they bring it near their houses, where they cannot have any of its good effects. But they have instead the filth that gathers in stagnant water, and its evil smell on many a lawn." In 1907, England's greatest authority on rock gardening, Reginald Farrer, wrote, "Advice to those about to make a water garden—don't!"

Three things changed these defeatist ideas—concrete, which proved to be a reliable material for building garden ponds; a French nurseryowner named Joseph Bory Latour-Marliac; and biological research that revealed the interdependence of plant and animal life and showed how to effect the necessary balance between the two in order to ensure water clarity.

Joseph Bory Latour-Marliac was born at Granges (a department of Lot-et-Garonne) in 1830 and due to the encouragement of his father and other relations—all botanists and naturalists of some distinction—took an interest in natural history from a very early age. Educated in Paris, he then returned to his family home at Temple-sur-Lot in southern France and later took charge of his father's estate, where the family grew a variety of trees, bamboos, and eucalyptus species as well as Japanese lacquer trees (*Rhus verniciflua*), Japanese persimmons (*Diospyros kaki*), and other tropical fruits. According to an article that appeared in 1894 in *The Garden* (an English magazine founded by William Robinson), these were grown in the main grounds of the estate, an area of 62 acres (25 ha). It seems, however, that there was also a propagating section of about 2.5 acres (1 ha), laid out in a series of subdivisions, where "17 sprays emerge from the ground and carry a good supply of warm water (50°F) [10°C] throughout the year. It has been estimated," the article continued, "that three of the principal springs supply an average of 25,000 gal [95 kl] per day directed into approximately 40 ponds divided into more than 600 compartments and used for the cultivation of all sorts of aquatic plants."

This latter venture was undoubtedly due to an article that the young Marliac had read in *La Revue du Jardin des Plantes de Paris*. This appeared in 1858 and was written by a Professor Leveque who described some of the exciting tropical nymphaeas growing in tanks at the Paris Museum of Natural History. The 28-year-old Marliac was entranced and thought how wonderful it would be if some of the brilliant blues, reds, and yellows of these tropical water lilies could be bred into hardy species to beautify the waters of the Seine. From then on it became his life's ambition to achieve this goal.

Few hardy water lilies were known in Europe at this time; *Nymphaea alba* was widespread on the continent, and the dwarf white *N. candida* could be found in northern lakes. Then in 1878, Otto Froebel of Zurich introduced into England (and presumably France) a pink sport of *N. alba*, recently discovered in a lake in Sweden. This sport deepened with age to deep red. (After many years of painstaking breeding, Froebel developed the deep red 'Froebeli' [1898], which, despite its origins in the cold lakes of Switzerland, thrives particularly well in the warmer waters of southern North America.) About the same time *Harper's* magazine carried an article by Mary Treat describing her experiences with a semihardy canary-yellow species studied during a winter in Florida. This plant, later known as *N. mexicana* (syn. *N. flava*), has a running habit like a strawberry plant and was introduced to Britain in 1881.

Marliac presumably welcomed both the Swedish *Nymphaea alba* var. *rubra* and *N. mexicana* and also acquired from the United States the sweetly scented, small, white *N. odorata* and a number of geographical variants. These included one called *N. odorata* var. *rosea*, the Cape Cod pink water lily discovered by Millspaugh in 1893 under unusual circumstances. According to his account, "On a plat of low bottom land near Buffalo, Putnam County [West Virginia], the plough turns up a large number of small tubers each season that the soil is cultivated. These, planted in tubs, produce, much to the astonishment of the neighbourhood, beautiful deep pink water lilies. How long this bottom has been drained is not known, but the evidence adduced, by the fact above stated of the existence of a pond here, certainly over a century ago, is very interesting." All the plants subsequently in cultivation are reputed to have been derived from a single tuber.

Undoubtedly these plants must have reached Marliac sooner than this, for while some of his first hybrids— *Nymphaea* ×*marliacea* 'Rosea' in 1879 and *N.* ×*marliacea* 'Chromatella' and *N.* ×*marliacea* 'Carnea' in 1887— may have obtained their color from the tropical nymphaeas with which he was experimenting, their stamina and shape indicate a hardier background. When Amos Perry visited Temple-sur-Lot early in the century, he was amazed at the range of hybrids Marliac had already produced. They grew, he said, in a curious combination of large tanks and containers that had to be cooled in summer with cold water applied by an elderly woman helper to prevent overheating. Marliac's hybridizing techniques were never revealed and his methods died with him. He did, however, tell Amos Perry that he would reveal his secret for £1000, or it would take him (Perry) 40 years to find out. Since neither option was taken up, the world is none the wiser. Nor apparently did Marliac reveal his methods to his successors. Yet in a long and rewarding life, Marliac left a legacy of about 70 first-class *Nymphaea* hybrids, all of which are still widely grown throughout the world's water gardens.

Marliac's successes were followed by a spate of cultivars from a variety of sources. Amos Perry, being particularly unfortunate, eventually gave up hybridizing. He wrote, "The hybridization of water lilies is generally so much fruitless labor, and the results are far from encouraging. Out of 159 recorded crosses we made in 1927, only one pod set seed, and the offspring were no better, and indeed, not as good as many of the existing varieties." Amos Perry obtained a number of awards of merit from the Royal Horticultural Society for exhibits of 'James Brydon' (1906), *Nymphaea tetragona* 'Rubra' (1928), *N. tetragona* (1935), and several tropical cultivars. The only original Perry introductions were 'Princess Elizabeth' (1935), 'Perfield' (1938), and 'Perfield White' (1942), all of which appeared in a batch of seedlings from *Nymphaea* 'Brackleyi Rosea', a fragrant, rose-pink-to-white cultivar introduced around 1909. Other hybridizers have laid claim to the introduction of 'Princess Elizabeth', but bearing in mind that in 1935 Queen Elizabeth was a princess and that permission would have had to have been sought before naming plants after members of the royal family, it is unlikely that foreign growers would depart from protocol in order to honor another country's royalty.

'Princess Elizabeth', a miniature cultivar, is described by Philip Swindells (*Waterlilies*, 1983) as having "blooms of a delicate cyclamen-pink which intensify with age, held well above the water and are very fragrant."

The Gardener (September 1904), describing a recent Perry exhibit of water lilies in Manchester, wrote, "The use of the water lily is one of the features of the day, and Mr. Amos Perry's collection of 32 species and cultivars of nymphaeas was surrounded by an eager crowd. They were shown in shallow tanks along the front of a long stand, a happy idea, which earnt them a Gold Medal and Commemorative Diploma." The catalog of 1905 then listed 45 species and varieties.

New cultivars also came in the early years from growers in the United States, most of them through chance seedlings or cross-pollination by insects rather than deliberate hybridization programs. In 1881 Edmund D. Sturtevant of New Jersey issued probably the first water garden catalog in the United States, entitled *Rare Water Lilies*. Although he was originally given credit for seven cultivars, only one day-blooming tropical ('Rose Star') is still listed in catalogs.

George Richardson of Lordstown, Ohio, introduced *Nymphaea tuberosa* 'Richardsonii' as early as 1894. This huge, very double, white hardy variety has never been surpassed for beauty. Unfortunately, its large leaves, wide leaf spread, and only moderate flowering habits make it unsuited to the average water garden.

Henry A. Dreer and his Dreer Nurseries of Philadelphia, one of the first nurseries to grow and sell aquatics at the beginning of the 20th century, offered the following hybrids that have stood the test of time: 'James Brydon' (1900), 'William B. Shaw', and 'William Falconer' (1899).

In 1913 Helen Fowler, daughter of W. B. Shaw, owner of the Shaw Water Gardens, now the Kenilworth Aquatic Gardens in Washington, D.C., introduced 'Rose Arey', one of the most beautiful of all pink hardy water lilies.

William Tricker came to the United Sates in 1885 after having worked at Kew Gardens in England. While working as a private gardener on an estate on Staten Island, he experimented for several years growing water lilies in pools and tubs and started his own business in 1895 under the name of William Tricker Inc., which still continues trading as the oldest supplier of aquatics in America. He was one of the first hybridizers of tropical water lilies, many of which, such as 'Panama Pacific' and 'Blue Beauty', are still offered. He died in 1916 and will be remembered for his contribution to the range of tropicals.

Undoubtedly the greatest tropical water lily hybridizer of them all was George H. Pring. He came to the United States from England as quite a young man. He was associated with the Missouri Botanical Garden for 63 years, much of that time as head of horticulture. For several decades in the early part of the 20th century he hybridized and introduced some of the finest tropical day- and night-blooming cultivars known today. Many carry his name, and any collection would be enhanced by 'Director George T. Moore', 'Emily Grant Hutchings', and 'General Pershing', to name but a few.

In the early 1920s August Koch of the Chicago Parks Department forwarded a seed pod of one of his crosses to Pring, who called the resulting viviparous lavender-blue seedling 'August Koch' (1922) after its donor. Koch also developed the well-known, tender, blue cultivar 'Pamela', which was later listed by Johnson Water Gardens of Hynes, California. This establishment also developed several cultivars independently, including 'Blue Triumph'.

In 1918 Martin E. Randig established Randig Water Lily Gardens at San Bernardino, California. Martin Randig was also a great hybridizer of tropical water lilies. Many of his cultivars are comparable and in some cases superior to Pring's finest. What collection could be without 'Afterglow', 'Evelyn Randig', 'Red Flare', and 'Ted Uber', just some of Randig's introductions?

John A. Wood of Thermal, California, introduced many beautiful cultivars. He operated a wholesale nursery near the northern end of the Salton Sea, which is 235 ft (72 m) below sea level. In this ideal climate for tropical water lilies beautiful introductions appeared such as 'Janice C. Wood', 'Wood's Blue Goddess', and 'Wood's White Knight'. Van Ness Water Gardens of Upland, California, now lists many of Jack Wood's introductions.

Charles Thomas of Lilypons Water Gardens, Buckeystown, Maryland, has two excellent introductions to his credit listed in what must be the most beautiful catalog of water lilies available. These two cultivars, 'Louise' (red) and 'Virginia' (white), have plant patents. George L. Thomas, founder of Lilypons in 1917, introduced 'Mrs. C. W. Thomas' in 1931—the first water lily for which a plant patent was applied. George L. Thomas, Jr., received Plant Patent No. 2453, the sixth water lily patented, for the viviparous tropical 'Margaret Mary', an all-time favorite for the small pool or tub garden.

In 1969 Dr. Kirk Strawn of Texas A & M University introduced a superb yellow hardy cultivar called 'Charlene Strawn' and other hybrids such as 'Marian Strawn'. Another Texan, Kenneth Landon, must be credited with several fine introductions made in the 1980s and 1990s. Two of the more recent are 'Catherine Marie' and 'Jennifer Rebecca', both night-blooming tropicals.

In 1969 Dr. Monroe Birdsey of the University of Miami in Coral Gables, Florida, introduced a day-blooming tropical named 'Albert Greenberg', which has beautifully mottled leaves and pink, orange, and yellow flowers. It was named after Albert Greenberg, who is widely considered the "father" of aquarium plants.

Other more recent American hybridizers include Joseph Lingg of Ardsley, New York; Patrick Nutt of Longwood Gardens, Kennett Square, Pennsylvania, renowned also for his work on *Victoria*; Bill Frase of Orlando, Florida; and Rolf Nelson, the manager of the Texas branch of Lilypons Water Gardens.

Development of water lilies has not been entirely restricted to America. In recent years Charles Winch of Sydney, Australia, has introduced several magnificent day-blooming tropicals, including 'Black Prince' (deep violet), 'Mary Mirgon' (lavender-purple), and the very fine 'Charles Winch' (white). Hardy water lily hybridizer Reginald Henley of Odiham in Hampshire, England, has produced (according to Bill Heritage in his masterly article on water lily hybrids in *The Garden* of April 1990) many seedlings of which 'Regann', 'Ballerina', 'Fiesta', and 'Peach Blossom' are due to be seen in the near future. As Bill Heritage says, "So it can be done, even in the English climate."

Perhaps the most successful introductions, however, have come from the talented American co-author of this book, Perry D. Slocum. With a wizardry matched only by Marliac, his prolific introductions have included several outstanding cultivars of both tropicals and hardies. Many are the results of planting known seed producers close to choice cultivars or species and letting Mother Nature do the rest; others are the results of planned crosses by hand. Both systems have combined to produce some of the most exciting introductions in this century. Of the extensive list, cultivars such as 'American Star', 'Pearl of the Pool' (the first hardy nymphaea to be patented), 'Pink Sensation', and 'Ray Davies' cannot fail to be appreciated for their form and color. Nor has his magic been limited to water lilies. No summer visitor to his charming water gardens could forget the amazing variety of *Nelumbo* cultivars, again many being the results of his particular talent for harmonizing with nature.

Chapter 3

Design and Construction of Water and Bog Gardens

Water continues to make a major contribution to contemporary landscape and garden design as the trend for softer and more natural-looking planting gains ever-increasing momentum. Modern architecture makes extensive use of water, reflecting strength of line and adding life through sound and movement. The use of water in interior landscaping, once restricted to large private conservatories and botanic gardens, is now commonplace in atriums, shopping malls, airport lounges, and restaurants. These interior water features have a refreshing and therapeutic effect on weary travelers and shoppers, and enlightened planners are making more and more use of water in nursing and retirement homes, where there is time to spend on reflection at the water's edge.

Most modern architectural water features make little use of plants, however; so it is in the relative calm of private gardens that the present phenomenon of water gardening as a creative leisure interest has unfolded. Thanks to some farsighted nurseryowners and hybridizers, the range of plants now readily available for water gardens and bogs is far greater than at any time in our history. Such a wealth of material can bring frustration to the plant enthusiast with only limited garden space, particularly in attempts to achieve good plant balance and mixing. Care in the design stage is therefore paramount, particularly in the informal water garden where the planting can extend far beyond the water's edge.

Water gardens offer a lushness of plant growth that can be refreshing in high summer, particularly when there is adequate planting near the water. The lush growth is almost entirely herbaceous material, offering limited interest in the winter. Thus plants that give some break from dead brown stalks and wet soil are especially valuable, and the designer should give special consideration to the form and color of woody stems, tree outlines, and branch patterns. Whether the surroundings of a water garden dictate a formal or informal style, the gardener must decide whether the water feature provides the opportunity to grow the maximum number of plants and thereby create or extend a plant collection, or whether it is best designed for simplicity and a strong visual effect. With the constant availability of moisture, the problems of rapid plant growth and consequent overcrowding are exaggerated in water gardens, and enormous discipline in density of planting is required in order to achieve the maximum impact of water. Japanese gardens illustrate restraint with waterside planting without any loss of impact.

One of the most powerful design elements in the water garden is the water surface. Constantly changing with the light, wind, and angle of sun, the area devoted to clear water should be the first consideration when deciding the scale of a new water garden. Examples of too little water in relation to the scale of the surroundings are all too common. When this valuable element is then cluttered with ill-chosen varieties of water lilies, their flowers choked by enormous leaves thrusting from the surface of the water, the effect is lost and the water feature becomes a muddle.

There are no hard and fast rules on the area that should be devoted to water surface in relation to the total size of the site, but it is better to be generous in the initial space afforded to water. In addition, larger water volumes are easier to manage, as long as there is adequate depth in relation to area. An extensive shallow pool often suffers from excessive growth of algae caused by rapid and frequent temperature fluctuations.

Guidelines for siting are more specific. The role water will play in a garden should determine its position. It is a mistake, for instance, to place a reflective pool where there is only an ugly wall to reflect. Formal pools have fewer siting possibilities than informal ones since their geometric shapes sit more comfortably within main axis lines or viewpoints in the garden. Frequently, formal water gardens are near the house, set into a paved area where they either provide a dominant focal point or lead the eye to one. The long, canal-like pool lends itself to reflecting a special feature along its length or highlighting a fountain (Plate 9). The effect of the whole can be enhanced by symmetrical balance along the pool sides and by constrained groups of water lilies occasionally breaking the water surface.

Just as the choice of water lilies can improve or spoil the effect of the water surface, so a fountain influences the success of a formal pool. Too many settings use the geyser jet, which by the introduction of air near its outlet creates a noisy, gushing mixture of air and water, quite out of place when a peaceful atmosphere is desired. In a water garden designed for simplicity and restfulness, any fountain should reflect this mood rather than intrude noisily upon the scene. A simple spout of water may provide sufficient interest. Fountains are powerful features in their own right, and their design must be considered very carefully in planning a water garden.

Informal pools can be sited with greater freedom. In a small garden, shade and overhanging trees may eliminate the most desirable position for a pool with water lilies since these plants require a liberal ration of sun. But where water lilies are not essential, an attractive pool can be made in a woodland setting. Such a pool should be planted with the amount of shade in mind, and the debris from tree cover must be removed frequently. Dense, permanent shade from buildings is more difficult to accommodate in pool planning as it causes water temperatures to remain cold and the plants to become spindly and weak.

In contrast, partial shade, or shade for only a part of the day, may well be advantageous as several extremely choice plants for the waterside flourish under such conditions. Dry shade certainly limits plant choices, but the construction of a water garden enables moisture to reach the plants and thus creates an environment with enormous potential for a range of foliage plants too sensitive to thrive in hot sun.

The soft, turgid growth of aquatic and moisture-loving plants makes them vulnerable to wind damage. In choosing a site for these plants, avoid windswept positions or situations where wind funnels between buildings or dense masses of vegetation. It is no accident that many of the finest gardens displaying stands of lush foliage are in valleys protected from wind and planted with a good mixture of deciduous and evergreen trees. If a sheltered area cannot be found for the water garden, protect the plantings with natural, semipermeable windbreaks. Many moisture-loving shrubs and trees are suitable for this purpose, enhancing the water garden by framing the herbaceous foliage.

If a site has existing undulations, there is much sense in creating a pool where water would collect naturally. As this is generally a low-lying area, one must anticipate certain problems. Frost, which is likely to accumulate and linger in shallow pockets, could damage flowers at the water's edge. In an area prone to flooding, chemicals introduced by flood water could damage the water balance and harm any ornamental fish. In areas that have a high water table, groundwater sometimes exerts such pressure on flexible pool liners that they billow up into the water.

Outlining the proposed pool and adjacent bog areas with rope, lengths of bamboo cane, or a garden hose is a valuable exercise when considering the design. If the proposed water garden area can be seen from the house, view it from the main windows, particularly from the rooms used for relaxation (Plate 10). Try to imagine the features that will be reflected in the water from the favorite window and adjust the pool's position accordingly. If the garden is small and neighboring buildings are likely to be reflected, consider using specimen plantings to enhance the reflected images and subdue the effect of any unattractive walls.

In a small garden, it is often extremely difficult to find the perfect site for a water feature. Site considerations, important though they are, should not become so constraining that a pool is located where it will not be fully enjoyed. Good plant selection is the key to making a success of a compromise in siting.

Additional technical refinements that pool owners may need to consider before construction include automatic refilling systems, pipework to handle overflows, and drains at pool bottoms to allow for emptying. The siting, climatic situation, and the particular style of pool management have a bearing on the need for these features. A low-lying pool subjected to heavy, prolonged downpours in an area of high rainfall, for instance, may collect considerable surface water from surrounding land, making an overflow to a substantial drainage system a virtual necessity. In a dry, sunny climate, a pool containing bog and marginal plants may require frequent replenishment. If a pool is not closely managed in the dry season—if, for example, the owner is away for long periods—it is wise to install a small tank discreetly hidden near the pool edge that, by an integral ball cock valve at the same level as the pool, can replenish the water from the domestic water supply. Any automated supply should also incorporate an overflow drain in case of faulty operation of the ball cock valve. The overflow pipe should be connected where possible to the rainwater drains of the house, and if this is impracticable, a soakaway drain should be constructed if no other drain outlet can be found. A pool with a large fountain is a prime candidate for an automatic water replenishment and overflow facility. Unless close watch is kept over it in blustery weather, considerable volumes of water can be lost in spray over the sides of the base pool.

The need for a drain at the bottom of a pool depends on how often it will be emptied. In cold, northern climates, concrete pools may have to be drained in the fall to prevent them from cracking due to ice pressure and the fish and plants overwintered indoors. In more temperate climates good management should keep the need for emptying a pool to an absolute minimum. In a pool to be drained infrequently, renting a pump to empty the system as needed may be more economical than installing a drainage system. Pools with flexible or rigid liners need not be drained for winter. On the contrary, liner materials should not be exposed to the sun in either winter or summer. Also, one may be reluctant to make a hole for a drain pipe in a flexible liner as it is difficult to seal the material around the hole. There are, however, special watertight adaptors available that simplify the operation by trapping the liner between two large washers as they are tightened around the pipework passing through. Such valves may have to be used if air, water, or methane is trapped underneath the liner and needs to be vented out.

NATURAL POOLS

Most formal pools are constructed with flexible membranes, rigid, preformed containers, or concrete. For informal pools, the situation may sometimes allow a natural pond to be created without a liner in areas with a high water table. Many ponds on private estates have been created from excavations for clay or gravel for use in building the residence. With time, plants naturalized themselves in and around the water, culminating in a haven for wildlife.

The small garden pool seen in the average backyard is more manageable when lined, but for large informal water gardens, construction by compaction or "puddling" as described below can produce considerable savings by eliminating the cost of the liner (Plate 11). Pools without liners have their problems, however, since they provide such good bottom anchorage for vigorous roots that they are prone to being quickly overrun and the water surface swamped by foliage. Compared to lined pools, they are also more prone to seasonal changes in water level, risking the margins to flooding in winter and prolonged exposure to sunshine in summer, which in turn can cause severe cracking in certain heavy soils. Unlined pools are made more waterproof by lining them with a 6-in (15-cm) layer of clay that is compacted by any heavy implement that can be manhandled into the excavation. In small pools, a heavy hammer weighing a minimum of 7 lb (3.5 kg) is a useful tool for tamping the surface. On very large pools the action of heavy mechanical equipment is normally adequate to help compaction. Unlined pools, which can be prone to a certain amount of seepage, are ideal when a local stream or spring is available for replenishing the water. Another advantage of the unlined over the lined pool is the greater range of shapes that may be achieved. No doubt one can overdo serpentine edges, but the creation of promontories, islands, and irregular outlines that prevent the water from being seen in total from any one point adds a great deal to a pool's attraction. When the plants are allowed to intermingle and their selection is dominated by indigenous species, such pools are extremely suitable as wildlife pools. They need more management than might appear, however. Totally uncontrolled and random planting neither attracts a wide variety of visiting wildlife nor pleases aesthetically. On the contrary, a wildlife pool is a form of water gardening that requires skill in the selection and grouping of plants. When executed sensitively, it makes a very positive contribution to wildlife conservation.

To construct an unlined pool through the process called puddling, thoroughly examine the soil profile beforehand. First, preferably in the summer, dig boreholes to a depth of 3–4 ft (1–1.2 m) to reveal the current level of the water table. From this observation, it should be possible to determine whether the water is high enough to create a pool without excessive excavation. The land contours should also be thoroughly examined so that the proposed excavation sits naturally in the surroundings. Boreholes, as they fill with water, may signal the presence of a subterranean flow. If a spring or source of water appears from surrounding land, it can be exploited to create a spur of water resembling a stream as an adjunct to the main pool, which then appears to be the water source when the landscaping is complete.

If the subsoil is so heavy and impervious that it holds water when compacted, determining the summer height of the water table may not be so critical. The basin created by excavation and compaction will act in the same way as a liner. For pools constructed by this simple method, any work is better done in the summer using the heaviest machine it is practical to maneuver on the site. The machine should track and retrack over the area in different directions to compact the earth as much as possible. The contours of the pool should allow for a maximum depth of 30–36 in (75–90 cm). In climatic areas with extremes of heat or cold, it is advantageous to increase this depth by a minimum of 1 ft (30 cm), particularly if fish are to be introduced.

Grading toward the sides should take into account the planting design for the water. In areas where a clear water surface is desired, the grading of the edge can be a simple slope. Where planting in the water is to be undertaken, the contours should allow for the creation of shallow side shelves, approximately 9 in (23 cm) in depth, with the width determined by the scale of the proposed planting. Lateral seepage of water can be reduced by digging out a trench around the entire perimeter of the water area and refilling the trench with compacted impervious soil. If the line of the trench is varied to include quite large areas between water and trench, moisture-loving trees included in the garden design will pick up any moisture that seeps through the clay lining at the water's edge.

In areas with a high summer water table, construction of an unlined pool requires excavating at two depths: a deeper area of 2 ft (0.6 m) for the water and a shallower area of 12 in (30 cm) for any surrounding bog plants. Here the water level in the pool depends totally on the water table, which in periods of severe drought can be low enough to cause such water stress that surrounding plants suffer and certain deciduous trees defoliate prematurely. Conversely, the low-lying land created for bog plantings around the pool will be prone to flooding after heavy rain in winter. If machinery is available for large-scale earth moving, this is nonetheless one of the simplest of all water systems to create, and some very fine natural ponds have been created by this technique.

Any surplus soil from the excavation of an unlined pool can be used for damming or edging. Occasionally, it can be used to create mounds that add interest to land contours. Mounding the soil around a small-scale garden pool, for instance, allows the introduction of rocks and alpines and extends the possibilities of a small space. This technique is rarely appropriate for large-scale pools, however, as they are nearly always sited in low-lying areas. Artificial mounds may completely spoil the natural land form, which is enhanced when low-lying water nestles comfortably within it.

Both construction systems for natural pools lend themselves to the creation of islands if the water area is large enough. Islands allow scope for imaginative planting and design. Their size and position in the water relate to the site, but they must not look like contrived humps in the middle. Plantings will have a large impact on the success of an island. Some trees lend height and architectural appeal. Birch and pine stand out as classic examples of such trees for temperate zones, whereas palm species are more effective amid subtropical vegetation and also create magnificent reflections. Features such as boat moorings, rustic boats or punts, and pebble beaches can then be added, building on the sense of invitation and escape that water so easily inspires.

CONCRETE POOLS

For many years, concrete was the main material used in water garden construction. When used carefully with ample reinforcement, it remains a viable option for formal pools, particularly in public areas such as parks and shopping malls or commercial plazas. Concrete has the advantage of withstanding the pressures of heavy pedestrian traffic and even vandalism at pool edges. In the main it is frost resistant, although in very severe conditions it may need protection of some type. Its disadvantages include the length of time required for building and curing and the labor-intensive nature of the construction process. Large, formal concrete pools with vertical sidewalls require foundations and wooden forms—expensive undertakings in themselves—to contain the freshly made concrete during the curing process.

Concrete continues to be used in the construction of many lily pools in America, but it is being used less in Britain, where flexible liners have generally superseded concrete in both formal and informal pool construction. The following guidelines summarize construction techniques for concrete pools with sloping or vertical sidewalls. Both systems of construction are very time consuming and require considerable manual effort, particularly the vertical sidewall pool with its wooden molds. This may be an operation that is sensible to pass to an experienced contractor.

Pools with sloping sidewalls

In concrete pools with sloping bottoms (see Figure 10), the sidewalls need an approximately 45° slope for stability during the construction process. This significantly reduces the surface area of the pool bottom, which may prompt an increase in the size of the pool outline. If shallow-water plants are to be included around the pool perimeter, it is best to incorporate a shelf 9 in (23 cm) deep and 9 in (23 cm) wide. Since the finished pool should be a minimum of 24 in (60 cm) deep (in colder northern climates 30 in [75 cm] would be better), excavate to a depth of 30 in (75 cm) to allow for the 6-in (15-cm) thickness of concrete. It is very important to level the excavation after digging the hole. Place a level on a two-by-four or straight plank laid over the hole. Then smooth the earth and spread a waterproofing membrane such as 4 mil (0.1 mm) polyethylene over the entire excavation. Place concrete reinforcing mesh over the polyethylene sheeting wherever the concrete is to be poured. If a drainage system has been installed and a drain hole is required, pierce the sheeting for a coupling about 2 in (5 cm) in diameter (to hold a removable overflow pipe) and 6 in (15 cm) long to be positioned at the pool bottom that will later allow water to empty into the piped drain or soakaway. A removable stopper of cloth or burlap placed in the top of the coupling prevents the wet concrete from filling the pipe during the construction process. This drainage hole may be omitted if a pump will be used to pipe water into a surface drain to empty the pond. Mix or order a concrete mix composed of three parts 20 mm aggregate, two parts washed sand, and one part cement. Mix or specify the mixture to be on the dry side so that it will not slump away from the sloping walls.

Once a 3-in (8-cm) thickness of the mix is spread over the bottom and sides, pull the reinforcing mesh through the concrete to the top of this first layer with a rake or other toothed tool, then spread a second layer of equal thickness over it. Smooth the final surface and use a level to make sure that the top is even around the entire edge of the pool. On the following day, brush a mixture of equal parts sand and portland cement over the surface to seal any tiny pores or crevices. If the construction work is being done in very sunny and dry conditions, sprinkle the concrete surface with water occasionally to prevent it from drying too rapidly.

Copestones to enhance the edges may now be added. The choice of coping is particularly important for formal pools. Paving slabs or bricks can be used, and if the slab or brick is large enough, a slight overhang on the inside edge is recommended. In mortaring the coping to the top of the concrete, it is useful to incorporate under the section of coping nearest an electical outlet a short length of pipe or conduit to be used later for housing any electrical wiring for a submersible pump or lighting.

After three to four days, fill the pool with water and leave it for a day. Then thoroughly scrub the concrete

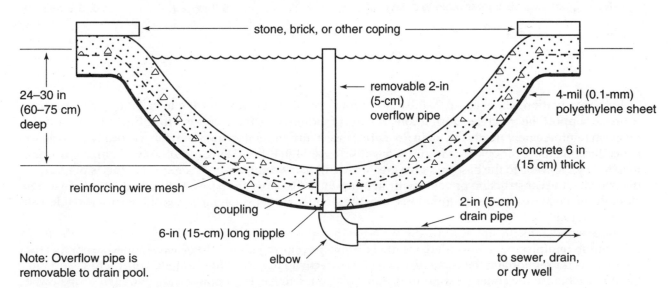

FIGURE 10. Cross section of a concrete pool with sloping sidewalls.

surface to remove any free lime that may have effervesced from the fresh concrete. After scrubbing, drain the pool, allow it to dry out again for three or four days, then refill, this time adding household vinegar diluted with water at a ratio of 1:200. Allow this mixture to remain in the pool for several days. Then empty the pool and scrub the surface again with a solution of 1 gal (4.5 l) of vinegar mixed with 4 gal (18 l) of water. Refill the pool a third time and test the pH level. If the pH is close to neutral (7), it is safe to begin planting, and after a further 7 to 10 days, ornamental fish may be introduced. If the water still appears heavily alkaline, drain the pond, and when the surface is thoroughly dry, brush the concrete surface clean and paint with a proprietary sealant. Allow the necessary drying time given with the sealant's instructions before refilling with water.

Pools with vertical sidewalls

Much of the construction information and curing techniques described for pools with sloping sidewalls apply to pools with vertical sidewalls. The latter, however, differ in requiring the use of wooden forms to support the wet concrete in the sidewalls. Moreover, the concreting is undertaken in two stages: the base is allowed to harden for three to four days before the walls are poured (see Figure 11).

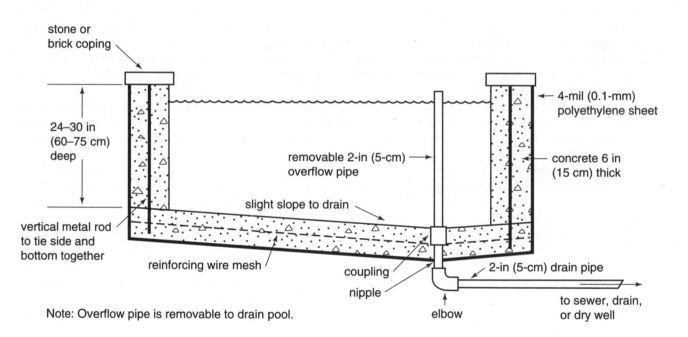

FIGURE 11. Cross section of a concrete pool with vertical sidewalls.

In the excavation, allow about 2 ft (0.6 m) beyond the planned walls for the installation of the wooden forms to support the concrete. During construction of the 6-in (15-cm) thick base, in addition to the horizontal mesh reinforcement inside the main floor area, insert further reinforcing steel rods vertically into the wet concrete along the position of the future sidewalls. These 24-in (61-cm) long rods planted 12 in (30 cm) apart help to key the walls to the base and give greater strength. If a drainage hole is required, this is prepared as described in the construction of pools with sloping sidewalls. After the base has dried out, it is time to consider the extensive carpentry required to create the wooden forms into which the concrete for the sidewalls will be poured.

These wooden forms are built to allow a 6-in (15-cm) width of concrete to be poured inside the mold. Rigid mesh reinforcement or rods are inserted during the pouring process to provide added strength. Horizontal rods for reinforcing the concrete can be tied directly to the 24-in (61-cm) long vertical rods and must be in place before the concrete is poured. After the concrete has been poured, the wooden forms can be removed after two days and the surrounding soil replaced behind the walls.

In Europe, particularly England, a planting area for marginal and bog plants is frequently built behind and adjoining the main pool (see Figure 12). It can be a channel several feet long, 24 in (60 cm) wide, and 12 in (30 cm) deep running along the main pool. If this area is constructed at the same time as the main pool, it can be tied directly to it with reinforcing rods and wires. If the bog planter is built at a later time, it will be necessary to frame up and pour all four walls—not just three walls as when the main pond is poured. The walls and floor of the bog pond should be 6 in (15 cm) thick and reinforced with rods and wires. Install a 1.5–2 in (4–5 cm) overflow pipe between the two pools before the concrete is poured. The overflow pipe, whose purpose is to supply the bog garden with water and to drain off surplus rainwater, should be installed near the top of the pools just below where the coping will be placed.

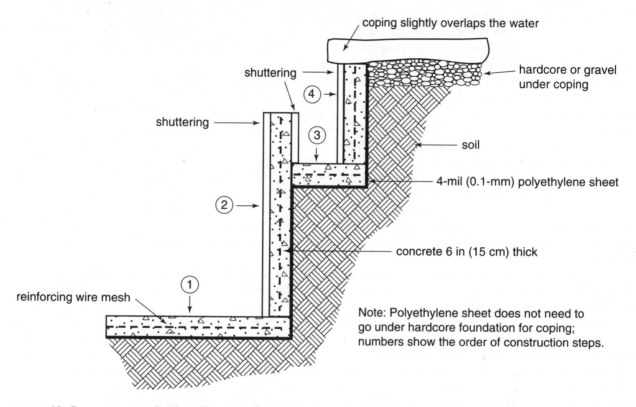

FIGURE 12. Concrete vertical-sidewall pool with adjoining bog planter.

RIGID PREFORMED POOLS

The retail display areas of aquatic and garden centers are frequently dominated by rigid pools in an ever-increasing array of sizes, shapes, and colors. Their attraction is in the speed of installation, which requires no more than digging a hole to conform to the shape of the mold. The size of these pools can be deceptive since they look much larger when displayed on their sides than when positioned in the soil. In making a choice, remember that adequate depth in relation to water surface is important in water management, and preformed pools less than 18 in (45 cm) deep can lead to problems, particularly in the overwintering of fish in areas prone to prolonged frosts.

Rigid pools are fabricated in a range of materials. Fiberglass offers the greatest rigidity and strength, while some of the cheaper plastic forms are prone to cracking at the edges. Molded pools frequently incorporate marginal shelves and planting areas.

To install a preformed pool, first mark out the outline by inverting the pool onto the proposed site. (If the pool is asymmetrical in outline, keep the pool upright and mark the edges with bamboo canes or string. The lip of the pool should sit 1–2 in (2.5–5 cm) above the level of the surrounding soil. Remove the soil to the necessary depth, allowing for a 2-in (5-cm) layer of sand beneath the pool. Remove any sharp stones that may be exposed and spread a 2-in (5-cm) layer of soft sand across the bottom of the hole. Insert the pool form, checking that the sides are level all the way around. When satisfied that it fits snugly and is level, put 4 in (10 cm) of water into the pool to give it stability and fill in with sand around the outside of the mold, adding more water as the work progresses. Once installed, try to disguise the hard edge of the plastic or fiberglass with paving or creeping plants as appropriate to the garden design. Plants can be introduced as soon as the pool is full of water.

POOLS WITH FLEXIBLE LINERS

The development and introduction of strong, flexible liners has made an enormous impact on water garden construction, particularly for informal water areas. The versatility of these liners allows for the construction of pools of any shape and for the relatively easy incorporation of bog gardens. Flexible liners are basically membranes for lining holes in order to make a pool. They are manufactured from polyethylene, PVC (polyvinyl chloride), or rubber-based EPDM and butyl.

In the late 1950s, polyethylene started the transition from concrete pool construction to the use of flexible liners. It was cheap, transportable, and versatile, giving rise to the present rash of brand names advertised for pool lining. Its susceptibility to puncturing and rapid deterioration in ultraviolet light, resulting in hardening and cracking, were its chief disadvantages. The area near the water's edge exposed to sunlight was especially prone to leaking, so continued use of the material was limited to situations where the liner was completely shielded from sunlight.

A new generation of polymers was developed in the early 1960s from which PVC emerged as a distinct improvement on polyethylene. PVC took longer to break down in ultraviolet light and could be made more durable by the incorporation of a screen mesh of fiberglass. Today many similar compounds are available, the strongest of which is a laminated material sandwiching nylon mesh between the layers instead of fiberglass. This double-ply material lasts 10 to 15 years and has become very popular for pool building in North America.

Later in the 1960s the introduction of a synthetic rubber material known as butyl constituted the real breakthrough in the manufacture of liners. At last there was a tough material that would not break down in ultraviolet light and that boasted a long life expectancy, thus giving permanence to water features built with it. Butyl liners have become enormously popular in Britain, with suppliers offering long guarantees on the lifespan of the material. Its popularity has led to inferior grades being manufactured internationally, so care must be taken to avoid cheaper brands that may have toxic residues. Extensive commercial reservoirs are constructed with butyl in Britain where its resistance to ultraviolet deterioration is seen as a major advantage.

On both sides of the Atlantic, numerous new plastic and synthetic rubber-based materials claim all the advantages of butyl, including environmental friendliness. Unless any of the new generation of compounds becomes substantially cheaper, the ideal liner for informal water gardens remains a top-quality butyl liner about 32 mil, or 0.032 in (0.8 mm), thick.

In choosing a material, be sure that it is possible to repair any holes in the liner. For an independent bog garden with no link to the main pool, there is little justification for using anything more expensive than polyethylene or a single-ply PVC liner.

Construction of a lined pool

To build a pool with a flexible liner, first mark out the outline of the pool with a garden hose or rope. As one is seldom lucky enough to construct a pool on a completely level site, it is best to identify the desired level of the water surface on a stout peg on the edge of the area to be dug. By adding several other pegs around the proposed outline at the same level, it is possible to see any sloping ground more clearly.

Calculate the size of liner required by adding twice the depth of the pool to the maximum length and then again to the maximum width of the shape required. Add an extra 12 in (30 cm) to both the width and the length to allow for possible overlap or for minor modifications during construction. For example, assuming the depth of the desired pool to be 2 ft (0.6 m), a pool 10 ft (3 m) by 8 ft (2.5 m) would require a liner 15 ft (4.5 m) by 13 ft (4 m). Certain irregular shapes may require an extra flap of liner to be welded at the supplier's or joined on site by means of a portable welder.

When the liner can be obtained readily from a local source, there is an advantage to excavating the hole before measuring and ordering the liner. There is no substitute for actually seeing the prepared hole in order to visualize the finished scheme. Sometimes at this late stage, changes are made in the planned shape or an adjacent bog garden is added, increasing the overall size of the liner needed. Once the liner is in place it is much more difficult to make such modifications.

If a liner has been ordered, begin the excavation inside the proposed outline. The sides of the excavation should slope slightly to reduce the risk of the edges crumbling as the digging progresses. The design should provide a shelf for shallow-water plants about 10 in (25 cm) below the surface of the pool and 10–12 in (25–30 cm) wide.

After the shelf has been created and leveled, dig out the remaining dirt to a final depth of 2 ft (0.6 m) for most small-to-medium-sized pools in temperate areas and 3 ft (1 m) for areas with either long, hot summers or very cold winters. Check that the pool is level by placing a carpenter's level on a two-by-four or a sturdy plank laid across the excavation. Remove any sharp protrusions, add a layer of sand about 1 in (2.5 cm) deep on the bottom (Figure 13), then put a layer of polyester matting or carpet padding on the bottom and sides of the excavation to protect the liner (Figure 14). This padding is a precaution against any sharp objects that might puncture the liner when it is under water pressure.

The liner can now be draped into the hole and anchored loosely by large stones and bricks at the edges (Figures 15–17). Liners made of materials such as butyl stretch a little under pressure and do not need to be tucked into every corner initially. Fill the pool with water. The weight of the water will settle the liner into corners, and provided it has been placed evenly in the hole, only gentle tugging will be necessary to eliminate most wrinkles or folds. As the water level nears the finished height, make adjustments to achieve a level bank by adding loose soil behind the edges of the liner. Trim off surplus liner to within 6 in (15 cm) of the final water level. The remaining liner can be hidden under soil, grass, or stones at the water's edge. Plants should be added as soon as possible.

Edging pools with flexible liners

The method used for edging the pool should be carefully considered and executed as it has a large impact on the success of the pool. The simplest edging is created by mortaring paving stones on top of the liner at the pool's edge (Plate 12). For areas that will experience heavy traffic, this method is a practical necessity. Ideal in a formal setting, this edging is rather unnatural in an informal one. Also, it is frequently overdone so that many small, informal pools are completely surrounded by paving. In cold northern climates, mortar breaks up more rapidly and it is better to leave stones loose.

Grass, if allowed to meet the water's edge, is particularly pleasant and simple in a casual setting. Some form of reinforcement may be necessary where the grass meets the water to prevent the soil under the grass from washing away (Plate 13). This can be achieved very satisfactorily with stone. For such a stone support around pool edges, natural facing stone, which greens with algae, is a good choice. Installation requires a small wall about 9 in (23 cm) high built on top of the liner on the shelf at the edge of the pool. The small stone wall, which is built before the pool is filled, should be no higher than the level of the surrounding grass, enabling the mower to cut right up to the pool edge. The grass soon creeps over the top of the stone and disguises it. In order not to affect the pH of the water, the mortar used in making the submerged wall should be painted with a proprietary sealant after drying.

Objections to grass edges around pools are often raised on two counts: first, lawn clippings flying loose land in the water, and second, grass tends to grow into the water and along the shallow sides that mowers cannot reach. In many settings, however, extra care in collecting and disposing of clippings and keeping the grass contained is well worthwhile in achieving a more natural edge.

Washed pebbles or cobbles of various grades and colors are becoming increasingly popular as pool edging (Plate 14). In addition to lending a natural appearance to the waterside, especially when used in combination with other types of edging, they have the advantage of disguising the liner both above and below the water level. Further, they may remedy a problem of construction if the final water level is difficult to fix. Running the cobbles some distance above and below the waterline makes any change in the level of the water less apparent. The pebble or cobble beach area must have only a slight incline to prevent the pebbles from rolling into the deeper water. Bear in mind that the pool edging will look contrived if the pebbles are all the

FIGURE 13. Soft sand spread over the excavation for a new pool protects the liner from punctures. The terraces are shelves for marginal plants. PETER ROBINSON

FIGURE 14. A layer of polyester matting further cushions and protects the liner. PETER ROBINSON

FIGURE 15. The butyl rubber liner is unfolded and draped over the excavation. PETER ROBINSON

FIGURE 16. The liner has been pressed into place and boxes have been constructed to serve as planters for water lilies or as holders for filter medium. A stream with waterfall (at left) will feed the pool. PETER ROBINSON

FIGURE 17. Flat-topped stones anchor the liner and form the edge of the pool. PETER ROBINSON

same size and shape. A more interesting and natural appearance is created by using a smaller and flatter pebble on the waterline, then gradually increasing pebble size and variety farther away from the water. In mild climates it may be best to bed the cobbles in mortar for greater stability.

Rocks, too, are useful in pool edging (Plate 15). When partially submerged they look especially attractive, and they provide an excellent means of holding back soil for a bog garden. Rather than run the risk of piercing the liner when positioning the rocks, it is best to bed them in mortar. This approach ensures that they are securely placed at the correct angle. Flat-topped stones with their tops in parallel, whether level or at a slight angle, look much better than irregular stones with points and angles uncoordinated. Leave the stones loose in cold northern climates as the mortar will quickly break up.

Whenever possible, choose rocks that occur naturally in the area and are not too porous. Impervious granite is a good choice in colder regions, particularly if partially submerged. Compared with certain sandstones, which are very absorbent, granite is less susceptible to damage in severe frost. In very hot, dry regions, the softer rocks will increase water loss by evaporation from their surface. In temperate regions, however, sandstone encourages rapid surface growth of moss and lichens, which quickly gives a very established appearance. Other forms of plant life evolve on sandstone with time, and soon a community of ferns and other native flora will almost totally cover the rock.

The materials most commonly used for formal pool edges are paving slabs or crazy paving. If a sitting area borders the pool, the paving edge can be extended into a patio or terrace that continues the same stone and pattern. The surface of natural stone is prone to the growth of algae, which should be removed with an algicide to prevent someone's slipping near the water's edge. Certain brands of concrete paving incorporate nonslip surfaces.

Resin-bonded gravel, used extensively for surfacing around swimming pools, can also be used around formal water gardens. This consists of a thin layer of small pebbles mixed in a specially formulated resin and skimmed over a concrete base. The mixture hardens and becomes a nonslip, porous surface that resists frost damage. The pebbles are available in a variety of colors that blend with building textures, making the material attractive to architects.

RAISED POOLS

Raised or semiraised pools have many advantages, particularly if the coping is of a suitable height and width to be used for seating. Ledges that provide a resting place are a special boon to the elderly or disabled, who appreciate being able to touch and observe the water close up. A raised pool surrounded by paving, which in turn is flanked by a border, can form a pleasant centerpiece in a small rectangular backyard.

A sloping site makes it necessary for a major part of any pool to be raised and provides an opportunity for some interesting materials to be used in building the sidewalls. Figure 18 shows a raised pool on a sloping site with a rockery to disguise the lower wall. Raised pools may be constructed completely above ground, or they may be partially raised, no more than a few inches above ground level. Both types are more susceptible to freezing than below-ground pools, and if fish are to be considered, the minimum water depth must be 24–30 in (60–75 cm).

With additional bracing and modification, raised pools can be constructed in concrete much as described above for sunken concrete pools with vertical sides. Raised sidewalls, however, need some form of covering or cladding to make them look attractive. Combining a flexible or rigid liner with a covering of brick, stone, timber, or a mixture of materials can be successful. Old railroad crossties or sleepers can perform the dual function of providing the rigidity needed against the water pressure and making a pleasing exterior.

If bricks or walling stones are used for raised pools, in order to give the structural strength to resist the internal water pressure and to provide adequate support for coping, they should be built with inner and outer sidewalls of brick or walling stone on the "cavity wall" principle with wire ties bedded into the soft mortar during construction. A flexible liner lines the inside, making the pool watertight. As the pool is lined, concrete is not required as a base, and only the walls will require concrete foundations, which should be 4–6 in (10–15 cm) deep and 15 in (38 cm) wide. As the outer wall will be constructed of a decorative brick or walling stone, the foundations should not be exposed on a sloping site and should therefore be buried at the lowest point of the gradient. As a safeguard against punctures, spread a layer of sand 1 in (2.5 cm) thick over the base before inserting the liner. A layer of concrete may be poured over the liner if there is a risk of damage by vandalism.

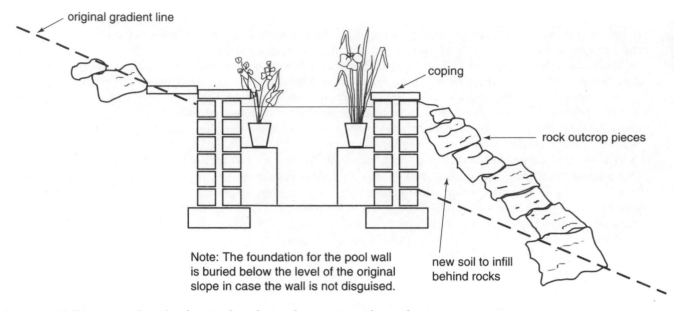

original gradient line

coping

rock outcrop pieces

Note: The foundation for the pool wall
is buried below the level of the original
slope in case the wall is not disguised.

new soil to infill
behind rocks

FIGURE 18. Disguising the side of a raised pool on a sloping site with a rockery.

Figure 19 shows two ways of incorporating the liner so that it cannot be seen near the waterline. This is a desirable effect, since water seen against brick or stone is far more attractive than water seen against a black liner. In method 1 most of the liner is draped inside the sidewalls, and a few inches below the water surface it is tucked behind the inner wall, which is covered from that point upward with attractive facing stone or brick that will be visible at the water surface. This technique enables the builder to use a cheaper brick or building block for the lower portion of the inner wall. In method 2 the liner is sandwiched between the inner and outer walls of the pool.

In a raised pool where no provision has been made for a marginal-plant shelf, shallow-water plants in containers can be supported by underwater blocks. Alternatively, a shelf 9 in (23 cm) wide could be formed before the liner is inserted by building up walling blocks or bricks from the bottom of the pool to within 9–12 in (23–30 cm) of the proposed water surface. In order to cushion the sharp surfaces, it is vital to cover the top and side of the shelf with protective matting before draping the liner into place.

Figure 20 shows how in a partially raised pool, where the proposed water level would be no higher than 12 in (30 cm) above the existing ground, a plant shelf can be easily constructed by digging out only the deeper zone of the pool 12 in (30 cm) inside the inner wall. On a sloping site, the foundations for the pool's walls should be buried at the lower level of the slope as recommended earlier for the raised pool. Alternatively, if any foundations are exposed, they can be disguised by creating a soil bank or rockery.

When inserting the liner into a raised pool, drape it evenly over the sidewalls with a little to spare. Rectangular pools require the liner to be folded at the corners. With circular pools, folds are more difficult to hide, and it may be worth ordering a specially shaped liner that has been prefabricated to eliminate folds when inserted.

Preformed molded pools can be used as raised pools, with facing stone, brick, timbers, or rockery stone forming the outside wall. The sidewall should provide good anchorage for the coping to overlap the edge of the PVC or fiberglass mold. Any space between the outside wall and the preformed pool can be filled with sand, and where the mold outline has an irregular base to accommodate marginal-plant shelves, brick supports can be placed under the mold to give extra stability.

The complete success of any raised pool is affected by the choice and construction of the coping, which should be in harmony with the texture of the sidewalls and other garden components. Many paving materials are suitable for the purpose. An overhang above the water's edge creates a useful shadow that helps to hide any mortar bedding the copestones. If brick is used to build the pool, the last course can be turned at right angles to the underlying courses to straddle the two walls if no more appropriate coping material can be found. If possible, the coping should be wider than the length of a brick, since the sides of a raised pool are interesting places on which to sit and relax.

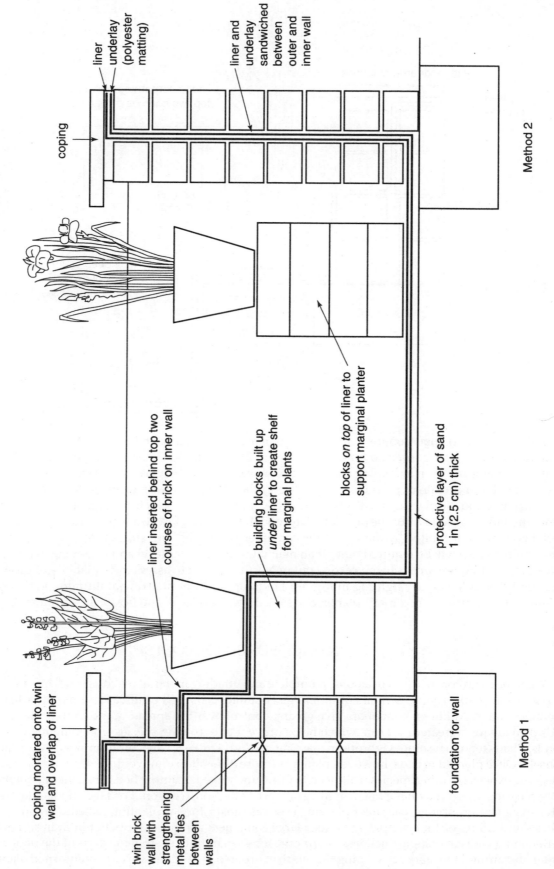

FIGURE 19. Two methods of incorporating the liner in a raised pool.

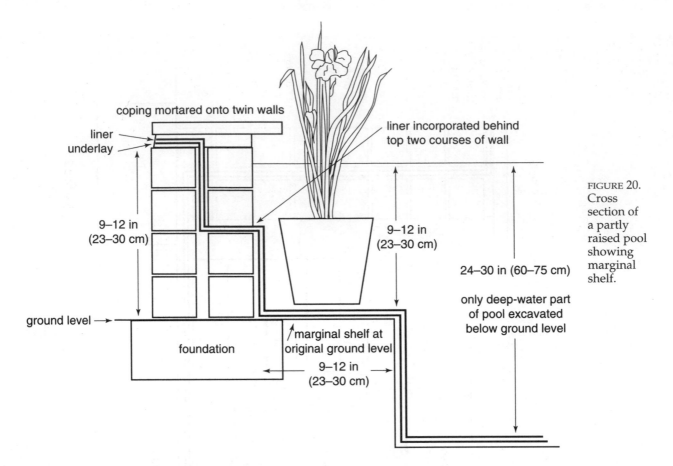

coping mortared onto twin walls

liner
underlay

liner incorporated behind
top two courses of wall

9–12 in
(23–30 cm)

9–12 in
(23–30 cm)

24–30 in (60–75 cm)

FIGURE 20.
Cross
section of
a partly
raised pool
showing
marginal
shelf.

only deep-water part
of pool excavated
below ground level

ground level →

foundation

marginal shelf at
original ground level

9–12 in
(23–30 cm)

Half barrels, sandstone troughs, washtubs, and many other ornamental containers can be used to create miniature raised water gardens outdoors (see Figure 21). In addition, small water features can be created indoors by using any of an increasing number of large waterproof fiberglass and plastic containers. Many are designed to build up into a composite arrangement, allowing scope for creative indoor planting and some intermixing of aquatic plantings with other features. Unlike aquaria, which are explained in Chapter 6, these miniature indoor gardens must be positioned in good light not too close to a wall, particularly a north-facing wall. Plant choice is limited by the size of the container, but water lilies suitable for any size are available. Little maintenance will be required other than maintaining the water level and removing dead or damaged leaves. Interesting research is being carried out in North America to assess the suitability of growing water lilies under supplementary lighting in interior landscapes. Without artificial illumination, permanently planted interior displays of aquatic plants soon look drawn and weak and flowering is minimal.

PLANTING BEDS INSIDE POOLS

When the main construction of a pool is complete and building materials such as sand, blocks, bricks, and face stones are still on hand, permanent submerged planting beds can be built as an alternative to planting in containers later. Although containers give greater control over the spread of individual species, planting beds provide for a greater root run, which helps prevent tall-growing species from blowing over in strong winds. Plants tend to be more vigorous in planting beds, and mixed plant communities can be planted more densely. Once planted in beds, however, plants are more difficult to remove, and vigorous plants can multiply at the expense of other species if allowed to grow unchecked. Planting beds are generally more aesthetically pleasing when they have been an integral part of the construction. For large pools that incorporate extensive plant groupings, container planting is not as satisfactory as planting in beds. Vigorous water lily species and cultivars, for example, need such large containers that these are better built in situ beforehand.

Retaining walls of a single thickness of brick or stone can be built at strategic parts of the pool, both in the center and around the margins, varying the width in order to give added variety for informal planting. Beds

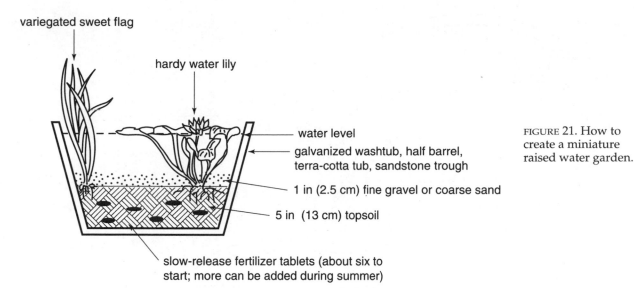

variegated sweet flag

hardy water lily

water level

galvanized washtub, half barrel,
terra-cotta tub, sandstone trough

1 in (2.5 cm) fine gravel or coarse sand

5 in (13 cm) topsoil

slow-release fertilizer tablets (about six to
start; more can be added during summer)

FIGURE 21. How to create a miniature raised water garden.

for vigorous water lilies in ponds whose depth is 30 in (75 cm) or more should be made 18 in (45 cm) deep and 24 in (60 cm) square. Medium and small varieties will have ample space in beds 12 in (30 cm) deep and 18 in (45 cm) square. Marginal or bog plants are best contained in beds 9 in (23 cm) deep. If the retaining walls around the beds are built to the height of the water level, fish such as koi are prevented from disturbing the soil and damaging the plants (see Figure 22). Good garden soil free from any residual weedkiller can be used to fill the beds, which are top-dressed with gravel or rock chips before the pool is filled with water.

STREAMS

A stream, either in association with a pool or as a feature in its own right, brings an extra dimension to the pleasure of water and introduces the element of movement. An existing pond may provide a stream's source or outlet and extend the range of plants in the water garden. A natural stream or watercourse may already be running through the property, providing the gardener a rare opportunity to make artful changes in its course and width without the expense of liners and pump. The nature of the garden and the undulations and levels of the terrain influence the style. A stream may be equally successful as a gentle slow-moving thread of water meandering through a lush landscape (Plate 16) or as a lively, high-spirited brook noisily babbling over rocks and waterfalls (Plate 17). In either case, water highlights the mood of the garden, enhancing foliage and texture on the one hand and contributing life and movement on the other.

Slow-moving streams

Although many gardeners relish the challenge of executing complex designs or growing the most difficult plants, they had best refrain from importing quantities of soil to create a fast-moving stream with waterfalls on a flat site. It is far better to plot a slow meandering course for the water, creating the impression of gradual erosion and silting over the years. Specimen plants with bold foliage are aesthetically pleasing on promontories created at bends, and less spectacular plants can be comfortably grouped along the gentler curves. With a little ingenuity, a stream can be constructed even on nearly flat sites, the size of the pump dictating the speed at which the water flows.

Artificially constructed streams are, in essence, elongated pools, and they should be constructed in such a way that they hold water when the pump is not operating. In a perfectly flat garden, therefore, constructing dams and rills at changes in level along the watercourse would be unnecessary. It is more common, however, to site the length of the stream along a natural gradient, no matter how small. Then it becomes necessary to select points at which to break the slope by one or several small waterfalls, or rills.

The origin of the stream, which in many cases is the end of the delivery pipe from a pump, can become a small header pool with the pipework disguised by rocks or cobbles arranged to draw maximum effect from

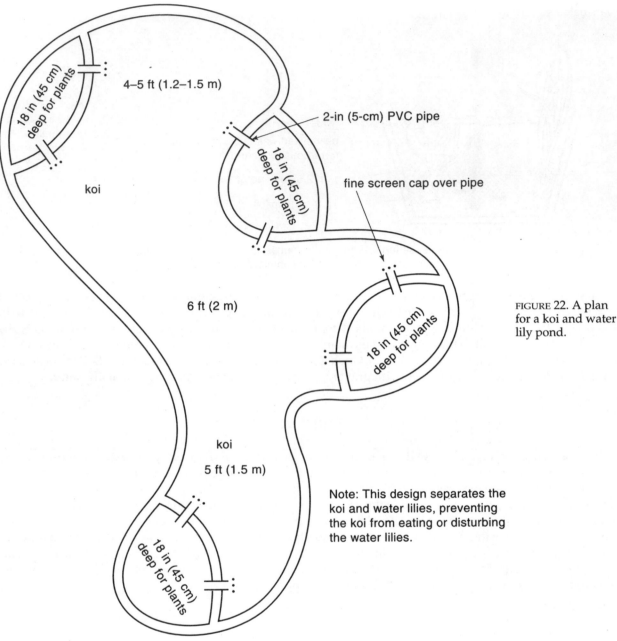

4–5 ft (1.2–1.5 m)

18 in (45 cm) deep for plants

koi

2-in (5-cm) PVC pipe

18 in (45 cm) deep for plants

fine screen cap over pipe

6 ft (2 m)

18 in (45 cm) deep for plants

FIGURE 22. A plan for a koi and water lily pond.

koi

5 ft (1.5 m)

Note: This design separates the koi and water lilies, preventing the koi from eating or disturbing the water lilies.

18 in (45 cm) deep for plants

the water's sound. Alternatively, the stream's source can be hidden behind foliage or rocks positioned to suggest that the water is flowing from a natural spring (Figure 23). A pool also makes an excellent culmination to the stream, but if a pool is not possible, a sump will still be necessary to provide a reservoir for the water circulating around the system. If a submersible (or sump) pump is used, it can be housed in this reservoir. Make sure the volume of water in the pond or sump is sufficient to charge the system, particularly when the pump is used intermittently. Depending upon the type of construction along the stream margins, water loss from evaporation and transpiration can be considerable. If only a small pond acts as the reservoir, the stream's effect will be diminished by a low water level after a day or two of hot, sunny weather.

If a sump is used, its outline and depth will be determined by the size of the stream and the amount of surface area available. The deeper the sump can be excavated, the less area it will occupy, always ensuring that it is adequately covered for safety and easy access to the submersible pump. The sides of the sump will not require marginal shelves as a pool would, and it should be lined with good-quality PVC or butyl.

One way of disguising the sump is to support cobbles or pebbles on a grating into which the stream spills (Figures 24 and 25). This attractive cover to the water is easily removed when access to the submersible pump

FIGURE 23. Carefully arranged rocks disguise the origin of a stream. PETER ROBINSON

is required. Water can be added to the system manually by hose as needed or automatically by means of a ball cock valve installed in the reservoir and an intake pipe linked to the domestic water supply.

At the design stage, first settle on the shape and style of the reservoir or bottom pool, then plot the route of the water upstream. At the point at which the water enters the reservoir, make a sill to prevent the water from draining out of the system completely when the pump is off. From this ledge, gradually slope the excavation toward the proposed stream bottom. The maximum water depth need be no more than a few inches.

For a slow-moving, meandering stream, which allows for considerable planting of marginal or bog plants, the excavation should be deeper and wider than the actual area allocated to water. This allows soil to be placed on top of the liner and held back with rocks, later to become the waterlogged banks of the stream. The soil can later be dressed with cobbles or small stones to give a more natural appearance. The width of the liner needs to be at least 6–8 ft (2–2.5 m) to allow for adequate and varied side planting. Too often streams are constructed in such a way that the associated plantings along the sides never thrive because they are too dry and beyond the reach of the water. A liner that is wider than the course of the stream also permits flexibility in making gentle changes in the stream's direction, since the excess material can be folded at the curves.

When there are few changes in direction and the stream sides are to be enhanced with lush foliage, one long piece of liner is adequate, provided it is of sufficient width. As the edges of the liner will be covered with soil and rock, there is little risk of ultraviolet deterioration. A good-quality PVC or butyl is recommended, however, in case the stream bottom becomes dry in summer and any small area is then exposed to sunshine.

Dig out the stream bed with a flat bottom of varying width, and when the design calls for a rill or waterfall, slope the stream bed away from the falls so that some of the water will be contained in that section when the pump is not running (see Figure 26). Make the sides of the watercourse shallow and sloping. Once the

FIGURE 24. Large stones outline the bed of a slow-moving stream that drains into a sump. The cover for the sump is a grating that will support decorative cobbles. PETER ROBINSON

FIGURE 25. With cobbles in place and a gushing fountain, the system makes a delightful addition to the garden. PETER ROBINSON

excavation is complete, rake the surface to remove any sharp stones and spread a layer of soft sand or poly-ester matting over the area before setting the liner in place.

The next step is to place the rocks forming the sides of the stream on the liner. In temperate climates set them in a mortar base for rigidity and for the protection of the liner. The rocks should vary in size to prevent the edge from looking too regular and should be large enough to hold back a sufficient depth of soil for planting. Most rocks have one flat side, which should be used as the top, since this makes it easier to walk on them and gives the stream a more natural appearance. Keep the flat tops level and tilt them all in the same direction. Otherwise, the final effect will be spoiled by a haphazard ribbon of rock that is unlikely to occur in nature beside a slow-moving stream.

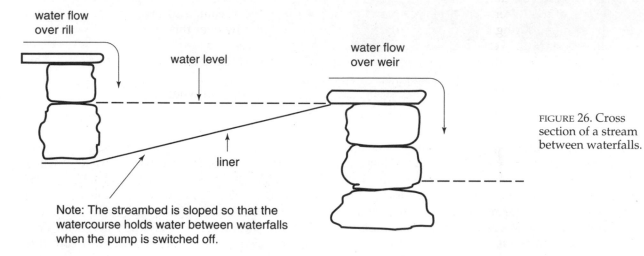

water flow over rill

water level

water flow over weir

liner

Note: The streambed is sloped so that the watercourse holds water between waterfalls when the pump is switched off.

FIGURE 26. Cross section of a stream between waterfalls.

Fast-moving streams

Faster-moving streams are best suited to sloping sites and may require a number of rills, waterfalls, or cascades to accommodate changes in elevation or in the direction of flow. Before excavation begins, carefully plan the stream's route. For a natural effect, the distance between rills should vary. A longer section of stream may lend itself to widening and to the introduction of large stones or boulders in the water. In planning the watercourse, return to one main viewpoint to visualize the scheme. The viewpoint, which may well be a patio or window, will give you a better sense of the stream than looking down on it from the top of the system. If a steep slope is to be covered in a short distance, waterfalls with drops of several feet may be necessary. Mixing small rills with one or two larger waterfalls adds considerable interest to the scheme.

Construction techniques for a fast-moving stream differ in two fundamental ways from those for a slow-moving stream. First, the varying stream widths, waterfalls, and rock pools in the system require the use of several pieces of liner of different lengths and widths that can overlap at the height changes. This approach also permits sharp changes of direction at these points, allowing the stream to be more jagged and angular than would be appropriate for a flatter site (Figure 27). Second, the edges of a fast-moving stream, which should be less lushly planted than the edges of the meandering type, are more likely to have rocky or grassy sides with creeping or tufted plants. The stream should appear as an integral part of a rocky landscape; thus, the builder relies heavily on the use of rock, preferably of an indigenous type. For natural-looking waterfalls, a good proportion of the stone used for construction should be flat and fairly regular in outline.

To build a fast-moving stream that culminates in a waterfall, first construct a base or reservoir pool, lining it with butyl to ensure maximum flexibility and resistance to ultraviolet deterioration. Make sure that the liner at the proposed waterfall area extends well above the pool's water level.

Butyl should also be used for lining the stream sections and header pool at the top of the stream. The width of the streambed liner is determined by the flow rate of the pump and the size of the waterfall. For smaller systems with a 6-in (15-cm) curtain of water, the liner would need to be a minimum of 3 ft (1 m) wide to allow for building up the stream sides with rocks to direct the water over the falls. Larger systems will require wider liners pro rata; a waterfall 12 in (30 cm) in diameter requires a 6-ft (2-m) width of liner.

Prepare the ground along the proposed route of the stream carefully, making steps in the soil where any waterfalls will be sited. Excavate the route of the stream to about 12 in (30 cm) in depth in level sections between the waterfalls, ensuring that no sharp surfaces are exposed. Spread a layer of sand or matting over the stream bed to protect the liner.

Lay the first piece of stream liner over the bottom pool liner and along the first section of the stream bed. The stream liner should overlap the pool liner below the water level of the bottom pool. This section underlies the waterfall and lines the stream bed up to and including the vertical drop for the next waterfall.

As the next step, select substantial rocks to position in the bottom pool on the marginal shelf to hide the liner at the waterfall and act as the support for the flat piece of rock over which the water will fall. Bed these rocks in a layer of mortar about 1–2 in (2.5–5 cm) thick to protect the liner and give greater rigidity to the rocks. Build up the rocks vertically to the height of the waterfall.

At the top of the waterfall, place large pieces at either side of the stream, then put a thinner, flat piece between them, mortaring these on top of the liner. The water will flow over this center stone, which also determines the water level of the section of stream above the waterfall. Spread the liner under the center stone and fold it against the inside surfaces of the taller side stones just above the proposed waterline. This ensures that no water will be lost laterally at the falls. Similarly, turn up a small fold of liner behind the center stone and secure it with mortar. This prevents the seepage that can occur when mortar alone is used for waterproofing. (See Figures 28–30.)

FIGURE 27. On a steep site a waterfall makes a radical change in the direction of a stream. PETER ROBINSON

FIGURE 28. To prevent water loss from seepage at a waterfall, a fold of the liner is pulled up against the center stone, over which the water will fall, and secured with mortar. PETER ROBINSON

FIGURE 29. Flat stones are mortared over the fold of liner behind the center stone. The stream bed slopes away from the waterfall to ensure that this section of the stream will hold an adequate amount of water when the pump is turned off. PETER ROBINSON

FIGURE 30. The liner is pulled up high on the side stones of the waterfall to prevent the lateral loss of water. Additional stones are mortared into place to cover the liner. PETER ROBINSON

Stabilize the liner above the waterfall with rocks to act as stream banks, extending the edges of the liner beyond the rocks to create planting areas. Mortar the rocks in place to give greater stability and protect the liner. Bed small pieces of rock into the freshly made mortar to give a more natural appearance. For mortar used to prevent seepage, waterproofing powder should be added to a stiff mixture of one part cement to three parts sand.

One by one, build the upstream waterfalls in the same way. For each section of the stream, the edge of the liner behind the rocks at the stream sides should be slightly higher than the top of the center waterfall stone.

The pipe used to circulate the water from the bottom pool to the stream's origin should be buried in a shallow trench at the side of the watercourse and protected from accidental punctures by tiles placed over the pipe in the trench. If the end of the delivery pipe is to be hidden in a small header pool, unless a nonreturn valve has been fitted, be sure that the pipe outlet is above the water level of the pool. Otherwise, when the pump is turned off, water will return to the reservoir through the pipework and pump.

After the mortar has hardened and the system tested for leaks, drain the water and wash out any debris. A small amount of lime from the mortaring may affect the water, and the system should be rinsed with a dilution of household vinegar as described earlier. If the initial use shows that the pump is too powerful for the job, fit a gate valve on the delivery pipe to adjust the system to the desired pressure. To improve the flow or level of the waterfalls, allow the cement to harden thoroughly, then use a hammer and chisel to fine-tune the stones over which the water spills.

BOG GARDENS

The term "bog garden" conjures up so many images that a clear definition is vital at the outset. For the purposes of this book, a bog garden can be defined as an area of saturated soil that is never allowed to dry out in the summer. A good many gardens contain soil areas that become waterlogged in winter but dry out in summer and would thus be of little value to true bog plants. The bog garden described here is most commonly an extension of the zone of shallow water at the pool side, best suited to the plants known in water-garden literature as marginals or water's edge plants. These plants have the ability to thrive with their roots under the waterline. They must not be confused with the large group of plants commonly known as moisture-loving plants—plants that cannot thrive with their roots constantly under the waterline and that grow best in the first transition area between wet conditions and ordinary soil. While many marginals or bog plants can cross the waterline and survive in conditions that are hardly ever waterlogged, the same cannot be said of the moisture-lovers, which would soon succumb if their roots were waterlogged for any length of time. In creating a bog garden, this important distinction must be considered at both design and construction stages, since the fine line between conditions below and above the water level can make the difference in the success or failure of moisture-loving plants.

By varying the height of the soil level, it is possible to construct beds or borders that house both types of plants. Marginals or true bog plants grow in the lower zone, and the moisture-loving plants grow in the higher zone, where the bulk of their roots are in soil containing air kept moist by capillary action from the waterlogged soil below. As this method of construction gives the effect of mounds around pool edges, it may look too contrived on a level site. If moisture-loving plants, as distinct from true bog plants, are desired at the water's edge, then a completely separate bed, with its water content regulated independently, must be constructed for them adjacent to the main pool. This approach is described later in the section on moisture-loving plants.

A true bog garden can be created in association with a pool or as an independent feature. Such a garden forms a natural partnership with a pool and makes an ideal complement to an informal water garden.

The most natural-looking bog garden is created by simply extending the pool liner beyond the pool itself (see Figure 31). Most liners, particularly butyl, are able to contain the roots of bog plants on the inside of the liner and prevent invasion of neighboring species on the outside. There are a few exceptions to this, such as *Typha*, whose sharp piercing root tip has been known to puncture even the strongest of liners. During construction, excavate the bog area to a depth of 18–24 in (45–60 cm) in the desired shape. The outer edge should slope upward to a point higher than the water level of the pool. As a next step, build a retaining wall along the edge of the pool. The wall should hold back the soil but allow water to pass through. Flat-bottomed rocks set into mortar make an ideal informal retaining wall. Other materials are suitable so long as they look natural and will not decompose underwater. Try to disguise the top of the retaining wall as much as possible,

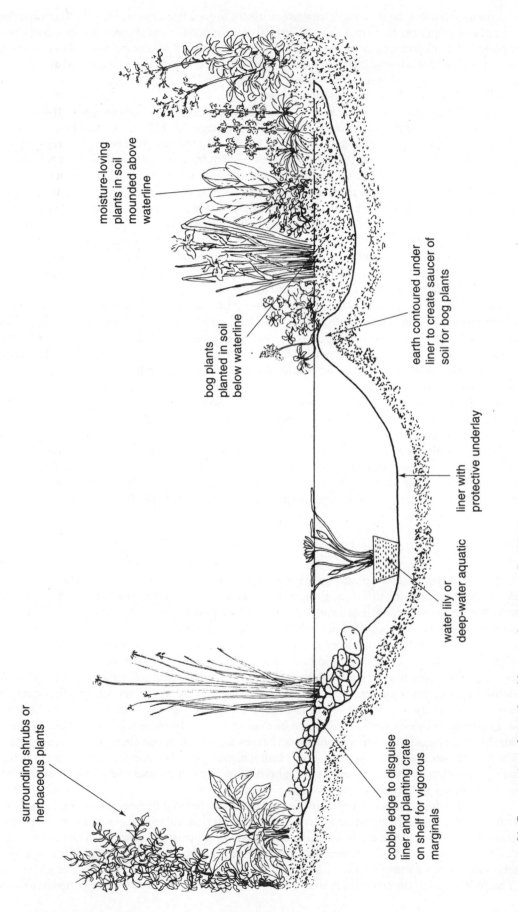

moisture-loving
plants in soil
mounded above
waterline

bog plants
planted in soil
below waterline

earth contoured under
liner to create saucer of
soil for bog plants

liner with
protective underlay

surrounding shrubs or
herbaceous plants

water lily or
deep-water aquatic

cobble edge to disguise
liner and planting crate
on shelf for vigorous
marginals

FIGURE 31. Cross section of a pool and bog garden using a flexible liner.

and if rocks are used, be sure their tops are not a lot higher than the soil level beyond the bog area to avoid an unnatural appearance. When the wall is complete, place the excavated soil on top of the liner, covering it completely. Check frequently to see that the edge of the liner does not get buried below the pool's waterline, or seepage over the edge will occur. If the pool has been constructed in a natural dip, it may be a good idea to continue the liner well above the water level of the pool, thus creating moist conditions alongside the bog area that will be ideal for moisture-loving plants.

Remember that this system of construction causes considerable water loss through evaporation from the soil and further water loss through transpiration from the leaves of the bog plants. The water level of a small shallow pool adjacent to the bog garden will drop rapidly, and the pool will require frequent replenishment. This is undesirable if fish are present, since the introduction of fresh water alters the water chemistry and adversely affects their health. Therefore, it is important not to have the bog area larger than a quarter of the pool's volume to minimize changes in water chemistry when water is added. Rainwater, which can sometimes be drawn from a drainage system, is generally better than tap water because its dilute acidity is closer to that of pool water. In areas known to have very acid rainfall, the domestic water supply may be more suitable.

To construction an independent bog garden one simply creates a waterproofed basin of soil (Figure 32). In this case the liner need be no more than a heavy-gauge polyethylene, as there is no risk of deterioration due to ultraviolet light. In the event of accidental puncturing, the water-loss rate would not normally be sufficient to prevent the bed's remaining almost completely waterlogged.

While the construction of such a bed is relatively simple, its successful integration into the garden setting is much more complex. An oval-shaped bed full of bog plants would look out of place if not sited naturally and coordinated into the overall planting. Likewise, one would not expect to see bog plants on a raised mound, as in nature they grow largely in low-lying spots. Careful integration into the garden design, imaginative shaping of the bed, and an adventurous choice of plants for the bog and surrounding areas make the most of such a garden feature.

Adding water in dry periods can be done either manually or by soaker hose or automatically through an adjacent cistern with a ball cock valve connected to the waterline. As the soil will be almost permanently waterlogged, it should not contain too much organic matter, which causes acidity and releases methane as it decays. Although a natural bog is often peaty, it supports very limited plant life. The decorative bog garden is not intended to recreate such an extreme ecosystem but to provide a wet environment for a wide range of decorative plants. The ideal soil is good loam free of residual chemicals and deep-rooted perennial weeds. It is not necessary to introduce specially formulated composts into the bog garden.

BEDS FOR MOISTURE-LOVING PLANTS

Construction of beds for plants requiring ample moisture is very similar to the construction of a bog garden with one important difference: the beds must have drainage. Moisture-loving plants cannot tolerate waterlogging for any length of time and, unlike bog plants, require an oxygenated soil. As moisture will seep from these beds, be careful not to site them too close to the thirsty roots of nearby trees as these roots could play havoc with the moisture levels in the bed and damage the membrane.

Considerations of design and siting are also similar, though beds for moisture-loving plants must be positioned to provide increased protection from wind. Many moisture-loving plants grow so rapidly that their lush foliage becomes more and more vulnerable to wind damage as the summer progresses. The only remedy may be to remove and cut back the damaged foliage, but this expedient so spoils the effect of these plants that their appearance by late summer can be disappointing. In planning for wind protection, remember that natural windbreaks in the form of shrubs and trees are always more attractive than artificial windbreaks and can serve the additional purpose of providing a backdrop to the bed. Nearby trees give another important benefit: partial shade, which serves to heighten color perception and to provide a degree of frost protection needed by many moisture-loving plants.

Like bog gardens, beds for moisture-loving plants can be built in association with a pool or as independent features in the garden. When beds are constructed exclusively for moisture-loving plants, the method is almost the same whether the bed is adjacent to the pond or free-standing. The successful bed becomes an independent system with its own moisture regime, and even when sited at the edge of a pool, it is not dependent on the pool's water supply.

The first step in construction is to dig out the bed to the required shape and size to a depth of 15–18 in

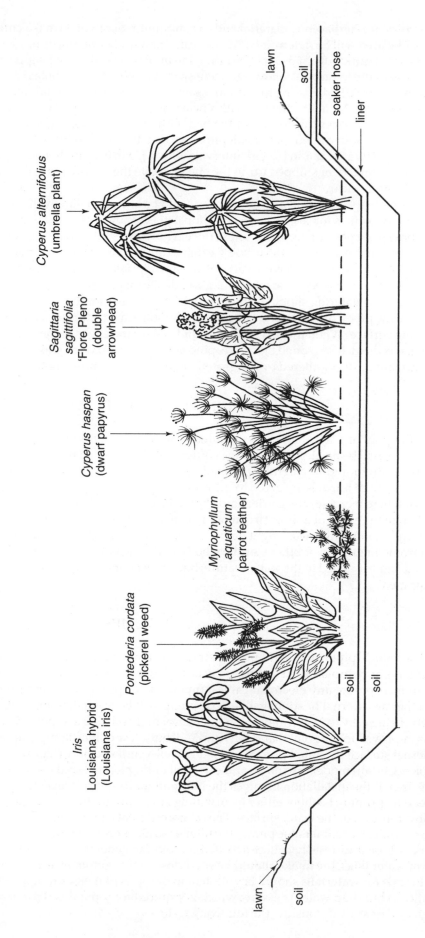

FIGURE 32. How to plant an independent bog garden.

(38–45 cm) for herbaceous material and to a minimum depth of 30 in (75 cm) for vigorous shrubs and small trees. The area will be determined by the scale and number of moisture-loving plants to be grown and will need to be a minimum of 5–6 ft (1.5–2 m) wide in parts in order not to appear too ribbonlike. If excavating a bed close to the main pool, allow sufficient space between the two holes to prevent the side of the pool from collapsing. If the bed is being made at the same time as the pool, a retaining wall can be used to give rigidity to the pool side. Next, line the bed with a heavy sheet of polyethylene that has had small seep holes punched in the bottom. Cover the bottom of the bed with gravel or rock chips to prevent the holes from becoming clogged. Add soil to about half the depth of the bed, then lay a reinforced or rigid pipe for water supply that has been perforated at 6-in (15-cm) intervals with 0.125 in (0.3 cm) holes along the length of the bed. The pipe should be bunged, or stopped up, at the end opposite the supply connection and surrounded with gravel to keep the holes clear.

Alternatively, a proprietary soaker hose could be buried shallowly. If the bed is more than 3 ft (1 m) wide, then use two pipes in parallel joined by simple plastic junction pieces that will reduce the system to one vertical pipe that sticks up from the soil surface. This pipe is fitted with a hose connector to allow for frequent, easy watering. As described for bog gardens, this system can be automated by the construction of a submerged cistern with a ball cock valve at the appropriate height and connected to the waterline. An automated system is especially useful as a good deal of water is lost by evaporation, transpiration, and slow drainage. No watering should be necessary in the winter months.

Once the pipework is installed, the remaining soil can be returned. Ample organic matter should be added near the surface. When the bed is filled, simply cover the edges of the liner with soil. Make certain that perennial weeds such as ground elder, creeping buttercup, and couch grass are not present in the soil as they will be rampant until smothered by the growth of the vigorous moisture-loving species.

BRINGING ELECTRICITY TO THE POOL

If the pool or water feature is intended to include water movement, a system of filtration, or lighting, electricity will be needed to power the equipment. The route of the electrical wiring from domestic source to the pool site should be carefully planned, and preferably, the cable itself installed by a qualified electrician before the final touches are given to the project. The supply cable should be encased in a protective armored sleeve where it crosses the garden and should be connected to the source by a safety device that cuts off the current in the event of a short circuit or break in the cable. Likewise, it should be connected to the water garden equipment with a watertight device in compliance with the regulations of the Institute of Electrical and Electronic Engineers or other statutory body in the appropriate state or country. This junction can be integrated and concealed in the water feature, but it must remain accessible in order to disconnect and service the equipment.

PUMPS

The pump, pipework, and housing should be made part of the basic design of the water garden. Small fountains or pump-assisted features may be added later with no disturbance to the original pool, but it is better to incorporate any electrical cables, pipework, or pump housing into the initial construction. Decide whether an external or submersible-type pump will be needed. Submersible pumps are growing in popularity, being easy to install and becoming increasingly reliable and powerful. In the 1980s, this type of pump was improved to the point that it can handle all but a few domestic applications. For large public installations, external surface-mounted pumps housed in well-ventilated and secure chambers are still the most popular choice. Certain models are noisy and can spoil one's pleasure in the water movement if sited too near a sitting area. If the installation involves the intermittent running of an external pump, it is important to ensure adequate priming facilities either by installing nonreturn foot valves in the intake pipe or by siting the pump below the level of the water surface. The reinforced intake pipe should be kept as short as possible. For either an external or a submersible pump, the filter or strainer on the intake should not be on the very bottom of the pond where it can easily collect debris. To avoid the generation of water currents and turbulence that can harm water lilies, the intake should be sited close to the bottom of any waterfall.

Pumps for waterfalls should be selected on the basis of their output in water volume rather than on their ability to build up water pressure, which is required for fountains. To assess the size of pump needed for a waterfall or stream, consider the following factors:

1. The distance above pool level to which the water must be pumped. This is known as the "head"—the vertical distance between the pool's surface and the discharge point at the top of the waterfall.

2. The length and bore of the delivery pipe. The bore should be as wide as is practical to the scheme in order to cut down loss of flow through friction of the pipe walls. For every 10-ft (3-m) length of hose, the loss of flow is roughly equal to 1 ft (0.3 m) of vertical rise, or head.

3. The rate at which the water is required to fall over the rills or waterfalls. Large, flat stones in a waterfall designed to give the effect of a weir or low dam would look odd if only a trickle of water spilled over their surface. As a rule, a flow rate of 300 gal (1362 l) per hour is required to produce a 6-in (15-cm) curtain of water over a weir.

4. The volume of the base pool. As mentioned above, the pump's intake should be close to the bottom of the waterfall at the water's point of entry to the pond. In addition to the benefits of preventing currents in the water and reducing pond turbulence, this keeps the required length of pipework to a minimum. Water lilies do best if the system's hourly water change rate is not greater than the pool's capacity.

Armed with this information, pay a visit to a pump supply store and refer to any available charts giving the performance capacities of various pumps. If possible, seek advice from the pump supplier, who can draw from experience with similar installations. When exact specifications are difficult to obtain, it is better to err on the side of overcapacity than undercapacity. To remedy a slight overcalculation, a gate valve can always be fitted to the delivery pipe to reduce the water flow.

Choosing a pump for a fountain is not quite so complex. In this case, the desired height of the water and the number and size of the fountain jets determine the pressure required. Here, too, it is wise to refer to available charts and seek specialist advice. For a small installation with a simple fountain ornament 2–3 ft (0.6–1 m) high—a popular water garden feature—a vast range of relatively cheap pumps is available. Numerous low voltage pumps and transformer kits help to ensure safety in such installations.

FOUNTAINS

The skills needed to design and construct a fountain are those of the engineer rather than the gardener. The keeper of fancy fish will use a fountain to oxygenate the water on hot summer nights. The garden designer will use the fountain as a focal point. The plant lover, on the other hand, may find little use for a fountain, since the turbulence produced by its spray can prevent the successful development of water lilies and other plants with floating leaves.

When used as a focal point, a vigorous fountain may be the dominant and vibrant hub of a set piece in formal garden architecture. Indeed, a successfully executed fountain is like a magnet and is the perfect complement to a long formal pool. A simple fountain jet enhances both formal and informal pools (Plates 18 and 19). The simplicity of a thin vertical spout can be extremely eye-catching, particularly when surrounded by a rich mixture of foliage. While fountains that send up strong jets are most effective when seen from a distance, jets producing fine sprays of water can be appreciated only at close quarters and are ideally suited to small intimate pools in walled gardens. A water feature that adjoins building or retaining walls provides a good opportunity for the use of gargoyles or wall fountains (Plate 20).

Too often fountains fall into some ill-defined category, and a partly clogged jet spouting from a listing plastic fountainhead is a far cry from the idealized concept of a splashing, refreshing column of water breaking into points of light. When considering a fountain for garden design, begin with this basic guideline: fountains must be done well or not at all.

In many temperate areas, wind restricts the use and effectiveness of fountains. Wind may so affect a fountain's performance that its potential is never fully realized for the most of the year. Where persistent strong winds are a consideration, jets that lift short, heavy columns of water have become increasingly popular.

One simple fountain that can find a snug place in a plant enthusiast's garden is the cobble fountain (Plate 21). This delightful little feature can integrate plants quite successfully almost to the edge of the fountain jet. Construction is simplicity itself (Figure 33). First sink a receptacle such as a plastic trash can or a half barrel into the ground to house a submersible pump. The receptacle should be large enough to prevent too frequent replenishment as water is lost by evaporation from the cobble surfaces in hot weather. Then take a circular piece of pool liner or polyethylene approximately 5 ft (1.5 m) in diameter and cut a hole out of the cen-

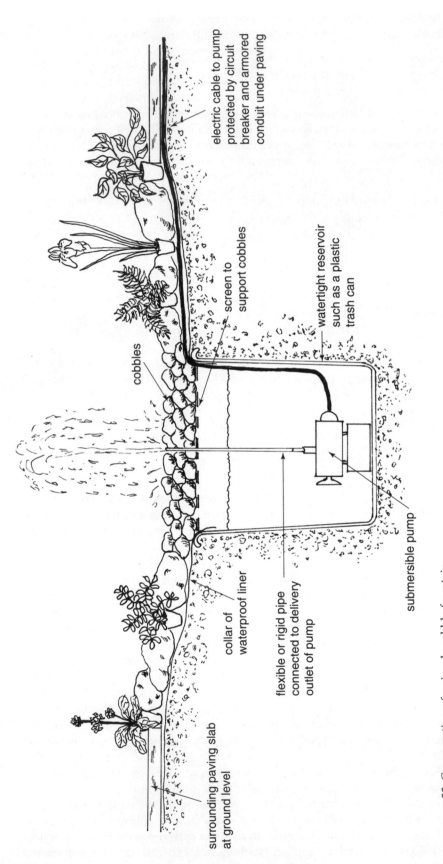

electric cable to pump
protected by circuit
breaker and armored
conduit under paving

screen to
support cobbles

watertight reservoir
such as a plastic
trash can

cobbles

collar of waterproof liner

flexible or rigid pipe
connected to delivery
outlet of pump

submersible pump

surrounding paving slab
at ground level

FIGURE 33. Cross section of a simple cobble fountain.

ter slightly smaller than the opening of the receptacle. Spread the liner over the receptacle. The liner should extend about 18 in (45 cm) all around the receptacle. It helps if the ground slopes into the rim of the receptacle to catch and return the splashing water to the reservoir. Cover the receptacle with a wire or plastic screen sturdy enough to support the weight of the cobbles. Next, attach a length of hose or extension pipe to the outlet of the pump at the bottom of the container and push it upward through the mesh covering the top of the container. Finally, arrange the cobbles on the mesh and surrounding liner and cut the pump's delivery pipe to the height of the cobbles. Different arrangements of the cobbles yield various effects. Similarly, the sound of the water falling through tends to change as the water level drops in the reservoir. The changing sound can be an important cue that more water is needed, since the pump may be damaged if the reservoir dries out. As a last step, certain small marginal plants can be introduced by plunging them in small soil-filled containers into the cobbles near the edge of the liner. The effects of water movement and sound, the subtle colorings of the wet cobbles, and a few well-selected surrounding plants are a very pleasing combination.

To vary this simple design, incorporate a stone millstone into the cobbles, feeding the delivery pipe from the pump upward through the center of the stone. If the flow pressure is correctly adjusted, the water forms interesting concentric ripples on the stone's surface then spills over the edge and returns through the cobbles to the reservoir. Where a stone millstone is difficult to obtain, kits are available that incorporate pump, pipework, reservoir, and liner as well as a simulated fiberglass millstone and support.

Many ornamental fountains and preformed arrangements of fountain jets are available from specialist suppliers. In the end, choosing a fountain is largely a matter of personal taste. Exercise caution in adding a fountain to the garden plan, however, as a fountain introduced merely to justify the expense of a pump can spoil rather than improve an otherwise restful scene.

FILTRATION

An ornamental pool with adequate depth, sufficient water volume, and suitable plantings should have no need for filtration to maintain clear water. Extreme temperature fluctuations, prolonged periods of midsummer sunshine, insufficient plantings, or heavy fish populations, however, can individually or collectively upset the water balance and cause a rapid upsurge in algae growth, which will cloud the water. When a pool becomes out of balance, the use of a filter can ameliorate if not correct the situation. In a pool that will sustain a large fish population, some form of filter should be installed in any case.

There are two types of filter—mechanical and biological—and they are designed to be used either in the pool or outside it. A pump is required to move the pool water through the filter, and if a pump is already in service for a stream, waterfall, or fountain, it will be relatively inexpensive to install an underwater filter. General-purpose external and ultraviolet filters are extremely effective and may be added to a pond as appropriate.

Mechanical filters

Mechanical filters, which are submerged in the pool or mounted externally, remove algae and other particulate matter from the water mechanically. The active principle varies greatly from manufacturer to manufacturer. Filters can rely upon fine netting, fine gravel, charcoal, sand, replaceable filter pads, sponges, or foam to trap debris. All serve the same purpose of removing undesirable suspended particles from the pool. Because the filtering action depends upon physically trapping the particles, the filter must be opened and cleaned periodically to prevent clogging. Thus, an out-of-the-water filter with replaceable filter pads may be the most convenient to operate and clean.

Biological filters

A biological filter system requires the intake pipe on a pump to draw water through a permeable medium that is housed either in the pool or outside it. After a few weeks of running, beneficial bacteria develop on this medium, converting toxic ammonia, which is the product of decomposing plants and fish waste and the food supply of algae, to nitrites and later nitrates, the food supply of the plants. The concept for this sort of filter has been successfully used for many years by water treatment plants and fish hatcheries to clarify and purify the water running through them. If the system is turned off during the winter, it will require a few weeks of reestablishment in the spring before it becomes effective again. The medium used to filter the water can be gravel, sand, foam, pan scourers, or any material that has a large surface area for the growth of the bacteria a well as ample spaces for the water to pass through. Several excellent proprietary submersed or external biological filters are available at aquatic centers (see Appendix B).

A substantial submersed biological filter can be built during pool construction by creating an enclosure of bricks or building stones on the pool bottom to hold the filter medium. In planning the size of the filter, follow this rule of thumb: one cubic yard of medium will support 50 lb of fish (one cubic meter for 27 kg of fish). For heavily stocked koi carp pools, the quantity of filter medium should be as much as one-eighth the volume of the pool.

When building the retaining wall for the filter bed, leave a gap in the bricks near the bottom of the wall. Before filling the bed with filter medium, place a coiled length of perforated plastic or PVC pipe on the bottom. Seal one end and feed the opposite end through the gap left in the wall to be connected later to the intake of the submersible pump outside the filter bed. The filter medium can then be put on top of the perforated pipe. Since the effectiveness of the filter is linked to the rate at which water is drawn through the filter medium, the pump's output should be approximately one quarter of the pool's capacity each hour. (A pool of 8000 gallons would require a pump of 2000 gallons per hour.) The delivery pipe of the pump then supplies any stream, waterfall, or fountain with freshly filtered water.

It must be remembered that with this type of integral biological filter the pump must be run constantly if the bacteria are to be kept alive. If the pump is turned off for only a day or two in the summer the bacteria will decay, resulting in less oxygen being available to the fish.

LIGHTING

When a source of electricity must be provided to power a pump in the water garden, there is a strong case for installing a lighting system at the same time. Water movement from fountains or waterfalls is an interesting feature to enhance with lighting, and many low-voltage systems are available for above or below the water. Resist the temptation to overdo, however. A large number of colored lights can create an effect more appropriate to a fairground than a garden.

A small number of features well illuminated can be very effective, particularly when illuminated from below. Submerged lights are a good choice for use in the turbulent water under fountains or waterfalls. They can be mounted under ledges to avoid a direct view of the lights. The cobble fountain is particularly effective when highlighted with a soft amber light, which gives the gentle dancing of the water the flickering effect of a fire. Spotting surrounding trees with underlighting may bring a new dimension to the form and shape of each tree. One of the most dramatic effects of lighting is to highlight the beautiful intense colors of night-blooming tropical water lilies thrusting above the dark water.

SAFETY

Many parents or grandparents of young children are reluctant to include open water in their gardens for fear of accidental drowning. One method of making the pool safer without spoiling the aesthetic effect is to install a grating just beneath the water's surface. Construct the grating of wooden cross-supports with 2–3 in (5–8 cm) black plastic mesh in between. The color black is specified for the mesh since this considerably reduces the grating's visual impact. Support the grating around the edges with a shallow submerged shelf and in the center with a brick or stone pier. On windy sites, such a grating offers the bonus of providing support for stems growing through the mesh, and the structure has been a considerable frustration for at least one very hungry heron.

Electrical safety is considerably increased by the addition of contact breaker units fitted to the supply of any pumps or lighting. This is a sensible precaution whether or not children are at risk.

Chapter 4

Planting Water and Bog Gardens

The care exercised in good planning and construction of a water garden can now be rewarded in the most exciting stage of all: the planting. No other type of gardening presents such a challenge in combining color, texture, and form. No other type of gardening provides such a range of growing situations, from slightly damp to completely submerged. No other group of plants offers such a range of leaf size, from the breathtaking *Victoria* to the humble duckweeds. Faced with such a daunting challenge, some gardeners find it difficult not to overcrowd the planting with uncoordinated groups of plants. The choice and arrangement of plants affords enormous scope to reflect the style, taste, and skill of the gardener (Plate 22).

While the plants for each zone of planting are selected from separate groups, they must be coordinated to give a satisfying picture. The surrounding framework planting is therefore as important to consider as the water surface because it provides a vital element: year-round interest. If there is room to consider trees near the water's edge, they should be one of the first priorities (Plate 23).

Most ornamental trees suited to moist or wet soil are deciduous, even the conifers, and their winter outline may be the characteristic that influences the choice, particularly for a specimen tree. In a large garden the mixing of species makes a rich background, but it is important to provide enough space so that the shapes of the individual silhouettes are not spoiled (Plate 24). There is a strong case for treating the main waterside trees as specimens with ample space between them and filling the gaps behind them with species more suited to foliage mixing. Although the shade and leaf fall created by trees make strong arguments for restricting their use near water, their contribution far outweighs the disadvantage. If trees are planted on the northern side of the water, their shadows will not affect sun-loving aquatic plants, and if leaves are prevented from sinking to the pool bottom in large quantities, no harmful superabundance of nutrients will develop. In a small layout with space only for one medium-sized specimen, the yellow-leaved alder with its magnificent catkins makes a good choice. A tree for temperate zones, it remains in scale with modest layouts. Palm trees, whether tropical or temperate, bring a quality of escapism to a large water garden. Pines conjure up a totally different mood, particularly the dark foliage of the Austrian pine, whose somber colors make a fine background for more colorful plantings. A well-grown weeping willow (Plate 25) has a soft, graceful appearance and is best suited to a sheltered position in a romantic garden. The silhouettes of bald cypress trees, such as those found in southern Florida with their incredible roots, evoke associations of heat and lushness (Plate 26).

Continuing down the scale in framework planting, woody shrubs make a good link to the trees. There is no shortage of interest in the water garden during the summer months, but shrubs with colored winter bark have a special value in providing year-round interest. There are several species of willow and dogwood whose stems have brilliant colorings in winter. Cutting these plants back hard in spring assures a bushy quantity of them for the coming winter. As well as aesthetic value, shrub growth also provides some protection from wind. Although certain shrubs can be treated as specimen plantings, they are frequently better when planted in groups.

As plant choice widens with the introduction of marginal herbaceous plants, the gardener must exercise greater care, particularly when considering variegated foliage. Water has such beauty when surrounded with contrasts that allow different viewpoints to reflect different moods. Variegated foliage can look attractive when highlighted by a restful frame of greens but can be lost if introduced into an exuberant and dynamic mix of color. Reflections of pastel shades exaggerate distance and tend to stretch the water.

When moisture-loving herbaceous plants are introduced, the challenge becomes even greater to achieve a successful plant mix (Plate 27). It is not simply a matter of positioning according to height and spread of the material. There is such variance in the style and speed of growth among moisture-loving, bog, and marginal plants that the basic principles are not adequate. Even the most knowledgeable plant enthusiasts must also possess imagination and ability in order to successfully combine form and color. Good planting schemes in and around water require artistic confidence to provide areas of gentle and subdued colorings to contrast with the areas where strong colors are given their chance at summer splendor (Plate 28). Subdued colors work well in humid temperate climates where their paleness and subtle textures look in harmony (Plate 29). The same colors would have much less impact in an area subject to prolonged and intense sunshine.

It helps to visit as many gardens as possible, absorbing the ambience of the surroundings and studying the plant associations. Similarly, observing natural plant associations while walking near countryside pools and streams will be of great value in the creation of a "wildlife" pool. Such observations can be inspiring, filling one with incentive to achieve a similar combination of plant husbandry and artistry. Each garden has its own unique character, and what might have been a highly successful grouping in one garden may be difficult to achieve in another.

A useful start is to make a list of one's favorite plants, noting conditions of light, aspect, exposure, flowering time, height, color, and soil type. If the gardens where the plants are noted can be visited at different times, it helps enormously to observe their characteristics before and after flowering. One visit invariably leads to a list of plants in flower at their peak and has no reference to their appearance at other times. From these visits one can build a unique catalog relating to one's own perception of plant characteristics and how each plant relates to neighboring plants. Taking into consideration the limitations of one's own site will narrow the range of choice. Creating a coordinated water garden takes into account a blending of one's favorite ingredients and at the same time keeps plants from the same habitat together. Plant associations will allow for the ample variation in foliage shapes to act as links between dominant colors.

When several favorite species are in flower at the same time, pay particular attention to the basic rules of color combination, which have to be considered throughout all the garden seasons. Color harmony is difficult to describe, and it may be useful to refer to a color wheel. Those colors that are adjacent or analogous to one another harmonize because they share a pigment. The opposite, or complementary, colors contrast or intensify each other. In a garden, however, texture and tonal variations allow the gardener to use a much broader palette than is apparent from the simplified color wheel. White flowers are useful in breaking any possible clashes of color harmony since white, like gray, has the property of reflecting light.

In the saturated-soil and shallow-water areas, the rapid and prolific growth of some species may swamp neighboring plants. The gardener, therefore, must take into account the level of maintenance anticipated in the garden. If this proves to be very limited, the choice must be kept to the less invasive species. Determine at the outset whether attitudes toward plant growth are restrained or informal and relaxed. Certain bog plants require considerable space after flowering to accommodate their enormous leaves. If these are removed or reduced to fit into a confined space, the effect is lost and the plant gradually weakens.

In planting beds that extend into the water, try to avoid placing plants in a line parallel to the edge of the pool. Even in formal situations, it is not imperative to achieve complete symmetry, least of all with bog plants. These plants are best planted in groups and not confined to straight edges. When any rock edging the water predominates, plant both sides of the rock to give an immediate informal effect and soften the hardness characteristic of so many overmanicured pools.

Choosing plants which emerge from or float on the water surface requires the same care and thought. The essence of success in this dimension is restraint. The ease of reproduction of free-floating aquatic plants necessitates discretion in the choice and quantity of material, as certain species can soon get out of hand and become unwelcome. This is particularly the case in large pools where netting off excess surface cover is much more difficult than in a small pond. A prevailing wind is likely to blow plant communities to one end of the pond where they may become compacted and provide too much shade for submerged species. On the surface of still ponds, the floating leaves and flowers of rooted aquatics such as water lilies should be given a special opportunity to show off their unique qualities. Not least of these is their delicacy and impeccable but fleeting beauty. Their presence seldom goes unnoticed and unadmired, not only for their colors and shape but for their intrinsic softness and vulnerability as well.

Plants that grow vertically from the water surface are among the most beautiful in the plant kingdom. Many European aquatic gardeners envy the ease with which their North American counterparts can grow *Nelumbo*, a plant that is unsurpassed in form, texture, and flower delicacy. Such a plant is magnificent in its impact as a specimen planting. When overgrown and massed it can become another aquatic weed with little to commend it. Other specimen water and marginal plants with vertical leaves such as cannas and taros provide striking accents. As with *Nelumbo*, they should be used with restraint or their impact will be lost.

When the water surface is skillfully planted, it complements the whole water feature. Such a composition requires the size and quantity of leaves to be in proportion to the area of water. One could be forgiven for mixing flower colors at random, but to dominate such a unique canvas with masses of coarse leaves of unsuitable varieties could spoil an otherwise perfect picture.

The placement of the submerged aquatic plants may not require the same artistic sensitivity, but what they lack in aesthetic value they more than compensate in their contribution to clear water. Algae, whether suspended and microscopic or floating and filamentous, is the bugbear of many a good water garden. It may be beyond the control of the gardener if the water source is from neighboring land and is highly charged with nitrogen and phosphorous. Sometimes green water is a temporary condition caused by microscopic algae feeding on mineral salts present in tap water when filling up the pool.

To wage battle against algae with plants rather than a filtration system requires that plants compete with the algae for resources. There are many submerged aquatics, such as *Callitriche hermaphroditica*, *Ceratophyllum demersum*, *Eleocharis acicularis*, *Lagarosiphon major*, and *Ranunculus aquatilis*, that are champion warriors in this respect. These and other suitable oxygenators are further described in Chapter 6. Enough oxygenating plants and the algae are suppressed; too few and the algae dominate. It may be advantageous to slightly overstock a new pool with oxygenators to combat the initial greening stage in the pool's development. Some genera may be prohibited in your area; check with the relevant state authority if in doubt.

PLANTING OXYGENATORS AND FLOATING PLANTS

The planting priority of a new pool, therefore, is to plant oxygenators and floating plants to compete with the algae for food and light. In concrete or lined ponds, plant the oxygenators in aquatic containers of planting soil in the form of bunches of unrooted cuttings gathered together with a piece of lead gently clasped around the base of the stems. Planting in containers, where they will later take root, is preferable to planting in soil on the pool bottom in that it gives a measure of control over growth. An average-sized container of 12-in (30-cm) diameter could accommodate five or six bunches. The planting soil simply provides anchorage and does not need to contain much nutrient or organic matter. It should, however, be free of fertilizer or any other chemical residue such as weedkiller or pesticide. Simply push the plants into a narrow hole dug into the planting medium with a finger or very thin trowel. After gently firming the bunches in, cover the soil with gravel before submerging the container. This prevents the soil from clouding the water. Any position will be appropriate for the containers as long as they are not submerged deeper than 3–4 ft (1–1.2 m). Use one bunch of oxygenating plants for every 2 sq ft (0.2 sq m) of water surface.

Planting the floating species is simplicity itself: simply scatter the plants on the surface of the pool. Once between a third and half of the water surface is covered, the only maintenance is to net off excess plants as necessary. Since many of the floaters reproduce by producing dormant buds or spores that live in the mud on the pool bottom, remember that any winter cleaning may result in their loss.

PLANTING WATER LILIES AND OTHER DEEP-ROOTED AQUATICS WITH SURFACE-FLOATING LEAVES

The main group of plants to dominate the water surface is the water lilies, either the tropicals with their exotic flower colors thrusting above the water or the hardies with their more delicate, usually floating flowers. (Several of the new hardy water lilies rise several inches above the water.) The second part of this book lists and describes their characteristics in detail. Many other genera of hardy and tropical plants share the deeper water, and any basic planting techniques fundamentally different from the methods described here for water lilies will be included in their descriptions in Chapter 6. Figure 34 shows how to plant a pool with plants in containers.

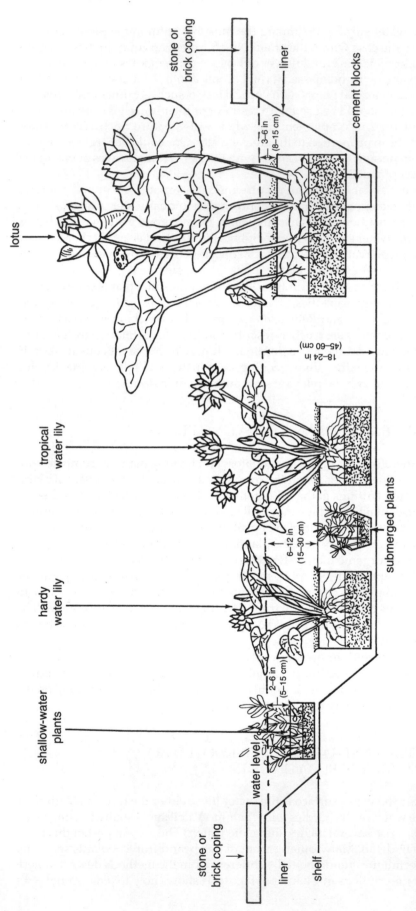

FIGURE 34. How to plant a pool.

In addition to flower color, most catalogs describe the optimum water depth and foliage spread for each cultivar and species. Armed with this information, the gardener can calculate the number of plants required to cover approximately half the water's surface. It is most important to choose cultivars appropriate to the depth of water available, as shallow-water selections will soon succumb if planted too deeply. Vigorous deep-water cultivars will soon thrust their leaves above the water surface if planted in too shallow conditions. The initial establishment, particularly of the smaller cultivars, can be successful only when the young leaves are able to reach the water surface quickly and not exhaust the plant's reserves in an attempt to reach light and air in deep water. Too many water lilies die at this vulnerable stage of their lives by being plunged into deep cold water at planting time. The timing of planting should coincide with water temperatures warm enough for growth as well as sufficient light intensity and day length for food manufacture through the young leaves.

When the plants have been purchased by mail order, one must trust the supplier's selection of material, and buying from nurseries with a reputation to lose may be worth the extra premium paid for their plants. When buying material from a local nursery, choosing containerized plants allows early establishment if the plants look vigorous and healthy. If they are already weak and spindly-looking, the young rootstock freshly cut from a healthy, sturdy specimen is a much better buy. Good aquatic nurseries have the parent stock on display so that the vigor and cleanliness of the material can be assessed. Stagnant containers full of algae, snails, and duckweed often indicate stock that is not well maintained and prone to disease. Vacuum-packed plants must be treated with great caution, particularly if there is no clear indication of how long they have been out of the water. Water gardening is such a specialized form of growing that one must have confidence in the grower. Treat with caution the retailer who claims to be an aquatic supplier but whose knowledge is in the realm of tropical fish.

Whether buying locally or ordering plants by mail, it is generally better to include planting containers in the purchase than trust to planting in soil covering the bottom of the pond. Planting in loose soil can result in the rampant and uncontrolled growth of excess leaves at the expense of flowers. The size of the container is related to the vigor of the variety, ranging from permanent planting tubs 2–3 ft (0.6–1 m) square with capacities of 30 qt (34 l) or more to pails or crates 6–8 in (15–20 cm) square with a capacity of no more than 5 qt (5.6 l). Containers with lattice sides allow greater gas exchange and penetration of the roots into the water. Lining such a planter with close-weaved permeable material, such as burlap or Hessian cloth, contains soil and roots more effectively.

Include aquatic planting soil in your purchase if there is no reliable source of material at home. Good loam or garden soil free of residual pesticide and herbicide and not recently treated with nitrogenous fertilizer makes an adequate planting medium for water lilies. There is little point in using soil formulated for terrestrial potted plants as these mixtures usually contain peat and ground styrofoam, which have no value in an underwater planter and are apt to float away. Prepared aquatic planting soil is ideal as it is composed of a heavy loam containing small quantities of the major, minor, and trace elements. Organic matter in the mixture will rot, and if the resultant gases cannot escape easily in the confined space of the planting tub, the reabsorbed gas can be harmful to roots. Prepared soil mixtures for potted plants are charged with nutrients that, in an aquatic situation, would cause the water to go green quickly. There is, nevertheless, a case for adding a pinch of superphosphate or bonemeal to the planting medium to help initial establishment. Alternatively, specially formulated tablets of slow-release fertilizer can be added at planting time.

The hardy water lilies have special planting requirements. With all types it is imperative to plant the crown or growing point shallowly. With the Marliac, pygmy, tuberosa, and odorata types, the technique requires that their fleshy rhizomatous roots be laid horizontally under approximately 1 in (2.5 cm) of soil. With the upright, or pineapple, group, the more rounded rootstocks should be planted vertically or at a slight angle in the soil with the top or crown almost exposed at the surface. Before planting, trim off fibrous roots and examine carefully for any sign of infected tissue. Any suspicious material should be cut out and the exposed tissue dusted with a fungicide. Frequently the foliage is damaged in shipping, and it is far better to remove this before planting than to leave it to rot off. Even if all the foliage is dead or damaged, the plant can still survive at planting time. During the planting operation, keep the rootstock and foliage cool and damp and never leave plants exposed to sun or drying wind, no matter how briefly.

When planting in tubs or pans it is most important to thoroughly firm the soil around the rootstock. Once all the air is expelled and the soil saturated, the volume shrinks considerably. When the soil has been inadequately firmed, containers end up only half full after submergence. It is therefore a good practice to water thoroughly before planting and add any extra soil that may be required. Finally, when the soil has been satisfactorily firmed, top dress the container with pea gravel to prevent nosy fish from disturbing the soil. Figure 35 shows a planter in cross section.

Once planted, the containers should be submerged to only a shallow depth. This is achieved by temporarily elevating the containers with stones or bricks. Once growth starts and new leaves are being actively formed, remove the supports in stages until the container is at the final planting depth recommended for that species. When the plants are planted in permanent planting beds, lower the depth of the water in the pool at planting and gradually raise it as the plants gain vigor.

The overall technique for planting tropical water lilies is similar to that for the hardies but varies in a few important ways. The tropicals are, in the main, more vigorous and faster growing than the hardies, and the size of the container and feeding regime should be adjusted for this. In temperate climates they are planted later than the hardies, usually in late May or early June, which is nearly one month later than the beginning of the hardy planting season. Their rate of growth is so fast that there is little to be gained from planting them earlier.

While the hardies are sold as rootstocks of the parent plant, tropical water lilies are sold as complete young plants. The tropicals will develop a tuberous root, which in temperate areas will need overwintering out of the water in damp sand in a frost-free situation. Since the lifting and overwintering of the tubers is often unsuccessful, the amateur gardener would be better advised to pay the premium for young plants from a specialist grower each spring and grow them as annuals. Otherwise, look for a smaller, walnut-sized tuber at the base of the leaves that is more likely to be successfully overwintered than older and larger tubers. The night-blooming varieties produce several smaller tubers, while the day-blooming forms produce single ones. The young plants are planted into containers as described for the hardies but with a tablet of slow-release fertilizer added to the planting medium. They are planted shallowly and unlike the hardies do not need to be gradually introduced to deeper water. They flourish in the surface water, which warms quickly in the sun. In certain temperate areas their cultivation is best restricted to heated greenhouses. Water temperatures of 75–85°F (24–29°C) are ideal for tropicals. Below 70°F (21°C) young tropicals frequently go dormant. See Part Two of this book for general planting timetables.

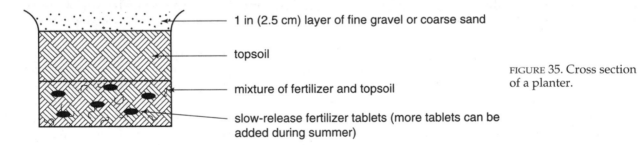

1 in (2.5 cm) layer of fine gravel or coarse sand

topsoil

mixture of fertilizer and topsoil

slow-release fertilizer tablets (more tablets can be added during summer)

FIGURE 35. Cross section of a planter.

PLANTING HYBRID LOTUSES

The planting technique for the decorative lotus hybrids (*Nelumbo*) also deserve special mention. Like the tropical water lilies, they thrive in warm water in baking sunshine and with liberal feeding. They can only survive frost if their extensive root system has built up a network of rhizomes below the frost line, and for this reason they need deep containers that can be given winter protection in nontropical areas. Such containers should be round to allow the rapidly expanding root system to curve with the sides of the container rather than get stuck in the corner of a square crate where the root tip may grow up and out of the planter. The container should be a minimum of 16–20 in (40–50 cm) in diameter and 9–10 in (23–25 cm) deep. Try to obtain plants with thick fleshy roots from the supplier early in the spring planting season while the roots still have adequate food reserves. Later in the season as the plants become more active, the roots will be in a vegetative state and less suitable for container planting. The planting medium should be a rich, heavy loam well supplemented with a root-promoting fertilizer such as bonemeal and six to eight tablets of slow-release water lily fertilizer. A container of the size described would take 4–6 oz (113–170 g) of bonemeal, and a large planting barrel would require 1 lb (0.45 kg). The tuberous roots, 8–16 in (20–40 cm) long, should be planted horizontally 2 in (5 cm) deep. Ensure that the vulnerable and delicate tip of the root just protrudes from the soil surface. A flat stone laid over the long root will help secure this shallow planting. Treat the tip of the root with great care in any subsequent movement; if damaged, growth may well be prevented. Firm the soil carefully and cover the surface but not the root tip with gravel. Water well, then lower into the pool so that 6 in (15 cm) of water covers the root tip. In pools deeper than 2 ft (0.6 m), plants can be lowered later to 9–12 in (23–30 cm) beneath the surface as growth occurs. If the pool temperature falls no lower than 68°F (20°C), growth will soon begin. Light levels and sunshine play an enormous part in the successful summer growth of lotuses by helping develop the fleshy roots in the warm soil, which further ensures their survival over the next winter. Containerized plants grown in greenhouses in temperate areas should be gradually dried off in the autumn and the roots carefully lifted and stored in damp sand in a frost-free place. See Part Two for general planting timetables.

PLANTING MARGINALS

Planting the marginal plants for the water's edge and bog garden is a much simpler process. The ideal time for planting these is spring, after danger of frost has passed, when growth has just started. Avoid planting in the dormant season as plants are more susceptible then to rotting. The plants are easier to plant and establish when they have been grown in pots and already have a good root system. Plant either in containers or in planting beds as described in Chapter 3. The size of the container will be related to the vigor of the plant and can give considerable control over its spread and height. In choosing the container, take into account how much constraint is required and the depth of the water in which the container is to be positioned. Many of the plants referred to as marginals, growing in very shallow water, have varying tolerance of the depth of water above the root system, and this is another factor to consider when choosing a container. Containerized planting follows broadly the technique described for water lilies, ensuring very firm planting and covering the soil with gravel if it is to be submerged. Mixing plants of different species in the same container can lead to a tangled mess of foliage, but two or three plants of the same species, particularly the dwarfer carpeting plants, can be quite effective. The plants for containers or prepared beds are generally so vigorous and easy to grow that their planting follows the basic principles applied to the vast majority of cultivated plants: do not bury too deeply and if bare rooted, spread the root system adequately. As the soil is waterlogged, one of the main problems in their initial establishment is wind blowing the plant or container over. Therefore, tall plants should be planted in containers large enough that the wind will not blow them over. Firm planting coupled with cutting back aerial growth are also helpful. There is often great reluctance to reduce or prune leaves and stems in a newly acquired plant. In an aquatic situation, however, growth is so rapid that the plant's establishment is more successful when there is less foliage to be damaged by wind.

PLANTING MOISTURE-LOVERS

Any particular planting operations associated with specific moisture-loving plants, shrubs, or trees will be given in the notes relating to the species in Chapter 8.

Chapter 5

Floating Plants

The floating plants flourish on or near the surface of the water without a root system anchored in soil. Most species absorb their nutrition from dissolved mineral salts and other nutrients in the water, making a valuable contribution to the surpression of algae. Since they also inhibit the growth of algae by reducing light levels in the water, they are an ideal group of plants to include in the planting of new pools that have little or no shade from the leaves of established water lilies or other submerged aquatics with floating leaves.

They are also valuable assets to the fancy fish keeper. Their roots, particularly of genera like *Pistia* and *Eichhornia*, can provide a safe home for the eggs or nests of certain tropical fish and goldfish. Bubbles of oxygen can frequently be found trapped under floating leaves, which, when reabsorbed during the hours of darkness, help to maintain reserves of oxygen.

Most floaters are tropical, and in temperate regions material has to be removed in the autumn to overwinter in shallow trays in good light at a minimum temperature of 50–55°F (10–13°C). Even in tropical areas it is a good idea to keep a separate small stock in case of unforeseen loss.

Much emphasis has been placed on introducing floaters for their value in helping to achieve a successful water balance. Many of the species are truly beautiful plants that are normally seen only from above. Planting in an aquarium brings a new dimension to the appreciation of this group, particularly in the display of their roots and underwater arrangement. *Pistia stratiotes* (water lettuce) is a case in point. The marvelous subtle shades of color that change along the length of its intriguing roots can seldom be appreciated to the full in any other setting. Some of the plants described in this section may spend part of their life cycle in a submerged, dormant state.

Certain genera, such as *Eichhornia*, *Salvinia*, *Stratiotes*, and *Trapa*, may be prohibited in some areas. It is advisable to seek further information from the relevant state authority before introducing any prolific floating plant.

AZOLLA. Mosquito fern, water fern, fairy moss. Azollaceae. The name is derived from the Greek *azo*, meaning to dry, and *ollo*, meaning to kill—killed by drought. This genus comprises eight species of small dainty green floating plants with pinnately branched two-lobed scalelike leaves. The upper leaf lobe is aerial, the lower lobe submerged. The leaves assume reddish brown tints toward autumn when they produce overwintering bodies that sink to the bottom. As they reproduce rapidly by self-division, they can quickly blanket the surface of a small pool with growth that has the advantage of helping to reduce algae. Use caution in introducing it to large pools because it can be difficult to net off if growth becomes too rampant. Colonies of the blue-green alga *Anabaena* thrive symbiotically in the cavities of the lower surfaces of the leaves.

A. caroliniana. Mosquito plant, fairy moss. Native to subtropical America, this species has become naturalized in shallow ponds, ditches, and sluggish streams from New England to the Pacific Coast. In Britain, where it has also been naturalized, its common name is fairy moss. The delicate lacy pale green fronds turn red toward autumn and are 0.5–1 in (1.3–2.5 cm) long with fine roots underneath. In cooler temperate zones overwinter some plants in shallow pans of water or wet soil in a frost-free place with good light. If the plant is introduced into the water garden be sure to keep it in check as it can become a real pest.

A. filiculoides. A species native to western South America, it has been found in shallow ponds in California and Long Island, New York. The fronds are much divided and longer than those of *A. caroliniana*, being about 0.5–2 in (1.3–5 cm) long, pale green, and tinted pink.

A. pinnata. A lesser-known species native to tropical regions of southeastern Asia and southern Africa, it has firm-textured reddish brown fronds, 0.5–1 in (1.3–2.5 cm) long, and masses of feathery roots.

A. pinnata var. *africana*. Native to tropical Asia and Africa, it is smaller than *A. pinnata* and is often difficult to find in the trade.

A. rubra. An attractive but little-known species native to Australia, it has very dainty, firmly textured reddish crimson fronds about 0.5–1 in (1.3–2.5 cm) in length.

CERATOPTERIS. Water fern, floating fern, floating stag's horn fern. Parkeriaceae. The name is derived from the Greek *kera*, meaning a horn, and *pteris*, meaning a fern. A genus of four species, these floating ferns are distributed in all tropical regions. They can sometimes be found submerged, rooting in the mud of shallow ponds. The lobed or feathery leaves are arranged in rosettes, with the leaf stalks buoying up the plants with internal air pockets. All the species are viviparous, with the smaller fronds covered with many bulbils that, when pegged onto moist soil, produce new plants quite quickly if the temperature is no lower than 75°F (24°C).

C. pteridoides. Floating fern. A species native to South America, it is also found in Florida and along the Gulf Coast of Mississippi and Louisiana. In the northern United States the fern is grown indoors in aquaria and conservatories because survival is unlikely outdoors in winter. Often referred to as the floating fern, the foliage can be gathered and eaten. Growth is in the form of a rosette, with the tall, much-divided larger fertile fronds standing erect in the middle of the pale green floating sterile fronds. Buds of new plants form in the notches of the leaf margins. It spreads rapidly and can be a potential nuisance in man-made lakes. Plate 30.

C. richardii [*C. deltoidea*]. Enjoying a wide tropical distribution, this is the largest species, with thick and succulent barren fronds lying just underneath the water surface. The finely divided fertile fronds stand quite erect above the water surface.

C. thalictroides. Water fern, water sprite, water horn-fern. A free-floating species sometimes rooted in mud, it is found in eastern Asia and Madagascar. This species grows about 21–30 in (53–75 cm) above the water with very attractive delicate pale green foliage. There is a marked distinction between the deeply segmented fertile fronds and the parsleylike foliage of the sterile fronds. Flourishing in acid water, it is cultivated in Japan as a spring vegetable.

EICHHORNIA. Pontederiaceae. Named after Prussian politician J. A. F. Eichhorn (1779–1856), this genus of tropical, mainly floating plants comes from South America. Seven species are found rooted in the mud of stagnant and slow-moving freshwater ponds, lagoons, and water courses, occasionally persisting on saturated soils. It is easily killed by salt water. Water hyacinth spreads vegetatively with alarming speed in warm and tropical areas, sometimes becoming a major weed.

E. azurea. Blue water hyacinth. This rapid-growing floating plant displays considerable variation in leaf size and shape, from ribbonlike, about 4 in (10 cm) long and 0.3 in (0.8 cm) wide, to rounded spoon shapes, about 3 in (8 cm) in diameter. Unlike the more common *E. crassipes*, the petioles do not have spongy balloonlike swellings. The bright pale blue, funnel-shaped flowers have a dark blue throat and are slightly hairy on the outside. They grow in pairs on erect stems.

E. crassipes [*E. speciosa*]. Water hyacinth. This lovely, showy plant requires plenty of sunlight and warmth if it is to flourish. Balloonlike petioles, swollen with spongy tissue, enable the petioles to float and support pale green shiny rounded leaves in perfect rosettes. These attractive features are supplemented with superb flowers of delicate pale bluish to lilac with very marked peacock eyes of yellow held high on 6-in (15-cm) spikes. Long feathery dangling roots, purplish black in color, provide a perfect medium for spawning goldfish. It spreads by means of stolons so rapidly that in warm climates the plant has become a nuisance on navigable waterways; it is prohibited in some areas. In temperate climates the plant is best overwintered indoors until all danger of frost has passed. The species has two cultivars: 'Major', which is slightly larger than the norm with pinky lilac flowers, and 'Aurea' with yellow flowers. Plate 31.

HYDROCHARIS. Hydrocharitaceae. The name is derived from the Greek *hydor*, meaning water, and *chara*, meaning grace. A genus of two temperate and subtropical free-floating or submerged species inhabiting the shallow water of pools, lakes, and the wetter part of marshes, it is distributed across Europe, Asia, Africa, and Australia.

H. morsus-ranae. It is sometimes called frogs-bit because frogs, which enjoy the same habitats, are reputed to bite the leaves when trying to catch insects. A native of Europe and western Asia, this delightful and graceful floating plant is like a small water lily. Borne on long petioles, the beautifully veined kidney-shaped green shiny leaves, about 1 in (2.5 cm) across, rest on the water in the form of a rosette. The small white flowers with a yellow center are unisexual. During the summer, the plant increases by means of stolons that arise in the leaf axils and grow to produce new rosettes. As autumn approaches, turions (terminal overwintering buds that are rich in starch), drop to the bottom of the pool where they overwinter. In spring they rise to the surface and grow into new plants. Snails, particularly *Limnaea*, are very fond of their succulent leaves and can soon spoil their appearance.

LEMNA. Duckweed. Lemnaceae. The name is derived from a Greek name for a water plant. A genus of 13 temperate and tropical small floating species that are almost cosmopolitan, these plants are usually gregarious and form green floating mats on the surface of still or slowly moving water. They reproduce almost exclusively by asexual means, enabling them to spread at a prodigious rate with populations reaching pest proportions. The flattened or globular plant body is without a clearly defined leaf or stem. Although they provide food for fish and waterfowl and help to obscure light and subsequent algae growth in a new pond, they should be introduced with great caution.

L. gibba. Thick duckweed. Distributed widely across the Northern Hemisphere, this species has spongy leaves that are thickened and almost round, about 0.3 in (0.8 cm) across, with one rootlet attached to each leaf. The fronds are gray on the underside and bright green on the top.

L. minima. Native to California and Florida, this species is almost identical to *L. minor*.

L. minor. Lesser duckweed. A common species occurring worldwide with the exception of the polar regions, this is the most widespread species of all the lemnas. These very small plants have light green ovate leaves with a single rootlet hanging down from each one. It can become a nuisance, requiring frequent skimming off the pool. Goldfish love it, and it can be a valuable food source for them. Plate 32.

L. perpusilla. Widespread in the New and Old Worlds, this species grows in clusters of three to five with thick, unsymmetrical leaves.

L. polyrrhiza [*Spirodela polyrrhiza*]. Great duckweed. A species native to tropical America and Europe, this is the largest of the duckweeds with leaves of a dark

green color on the upper side and purplish red underneath, nearly round in shape, and about 0.5 in (1.3 cm) across. Attached to each leaf are several rootlets.

L. trinervis. A native of New Jersey, this species has leaves that are round and thin with one rootlet attached to each leaf.

L. trisulca. Star duckweed, ivy-leaved duckweed. This species is perhaps the easiest to control since it reproduces more slowly than the other duckweeds. The light green transparent leaves are elliptical in shape, about 0.5 in (1.3 cm) long, with the young plants growing at right angles to the old ones. Usually submerged, the plants only float to the surface during flowering. They make an excellent water purifier.

L. valdiviana. Native to the southern United States and South America, this species has many pitted stomata on small green leaves.

LIMNOBIUM. Hydrocharitaceae. The name is derived from the Greek *limne*, meaning a marsh, and *bios*, meaning life. This genus of two species of floating rosette plants that sometimes root in pond bottoms is found in the warmer lowlands along the south Atlantic Coast of North America and the lower Mississippi Valley. If water levels are low and the roots penetrate the mud, the plant's appearance alters markedly with elongated petioles sending the leaves erect above the shallow water.

L. sinclairii. Native to South America, this stolon-producing floating plant has oval to rounded leaves about 0.5–1 in (1.3–2.5 cm) long that are carried on short petioles. Male and female flowers, which have no great merit, are produced on the same plant.

L. spongia. American frogs-bit. A floating species found from Lake Ontario to the southern United States, this plant is very like *Hydrocharis morsus-ranae*, having small floating loosely arranged heart-shaped leaves, 1–2 in (2.5–5 cm) long, that are green above and tinted with purple beneath, especially near the margins. It spreads easily by stolons that bear beautiful purplish feathery trailing roots. Certain fish in tropical aquaria like to anchor their bubble nests to it.

L. stoloniferum [*L. laevigatum, Trianea bogotensis*]. Amazon frogs-bit. A species native from Mexico southward to Central and South America, this little rosette plant has overlapping floating leaves about 1 in (2.5 cm) across that are thick, smooth, and almost round, with spongy tissue underneath for buoyancy. The flowers are white and insignificant with the male and female on separate plants. At the slightest hint of cold, the leaves turn brown and die.

NEPTUNIA. Leguminosae. The name is derived from Neptune, god of the sea, but the members of this genus of 12 species from the warmer regions of the world mostly inhabit dry areas. A few, however, are found in wet conditions and withstand frequent flooding. One species, a floating plant, is often found as a weed in irrigation ditches.

N. plena. Water sensitive. Native to tropical Asia, this warm-water plant has finely pinnate leaves not unlike those of *Mimosa pudica*, the sensitive plant, exhibiting the same sensitivity to touch. The undersurfaces of the floating stems are white, spongy, and full of air cells that provide great buoyancy. Fringed flowers grow in heads with bright yellow female flowers on top and brown male flowers beneath.

PHYLLANTHUS. Euphorbiaceae. The name is derived from the Greek *phyllon*, meaning a leaf, and *anthos*, meaning a flower, a reference to many of the species whose flowers develop on flattened shoots that resemble leaves. A large, diverse genus from all tropical and subtropical regions, the species described below varies considerably from the others, which range from trees and shrubs to small herbs.

P. fluitans. This tender floating species from northern South America bears a superficial resemblance to *Salvinia*. A small colorful floating aquatic, it has delicate horizontal stems bearing orbicular leaves up to 1 in (2.5 cm) in diameter that grow in two rows and overlap one another. Two swellings, one on either side of the midrib, give the leaf an inflated appearance and help the buoyancy of the plant. The young leaves start off bright crimson and become paler with age, until on maturity they are a subtle shade of green, giving the plant a delightful color combination, made more interesting by an additional red pigment in the hanging roots. The whitish unisexual flowers are very small and insignificant.

PISTIA. Araceae. The name is derived from the Greek *pistos*, meaning watery. This single-species genus of floating rosette plants, sometimes rooted in bogs and sending out several runners, has a cosmopolitan tropical and subtropical distribution. Radiating stolons terminate in new plantlets, each in turn producing further plantlets, which can result in the plant's becoming a nuisance in certain tropical waters.

P. stratiotes. Water lettuce. A common plant in Florida and along the Gulf Coast, its long roots can be seen to great effect in an aquarium. Use with caution in a varied planting scheme as the large surface leaves reduce light to the submerged species. (It is this feature, however, that makes it useful for starving out algae in pools.) The velvety, sessile, parallel-veined leaves grow to 10 in (25 cm) long and 4 in (10 cm) wide. These slightly overlapping pubescent leaves have somewhat crenated tips and are a soft shade of pale green on the upper surface and whitish green on the underside. The leaves vary in shape from shell-like to wedgelike and are arranged in spirals or rosettes. Inconspicuous white flowers enclosed by a delicate greenish spathe, 1–2 in (2.5–5 cm) long, grow in the leaf axils. Long slender feathery rootlets of exquisite coloring—white when young, turning purplish, then indigo, and finally black—hang down in the water as much as 18 in (45 cm) and are excellent for collecting goldfish spawn. Plate 33.

RICCIA. Ricciaceae. Named after an 18th-century Italian senator, Pietro Francisco Ricci, this worldwide genus of 200 species of mostly terrestrial liverworts has colonized a wide range of habitats. Only two or three are floating species, generally favoring eutrophic conditions.

R. fluitans. Crystalwort. Native to Europe, America, and Asia, this tiny plant, about 0.1 in (0.3 cm) long, undifferentiated between leaf, stem, and root, is called a thallus. Pale green in color, the much-segmented foliage either forms cushions or spreads out loosely on or just below the water surface. Crystalwort makes a good surface oxygenator in aquaria and provides shelter for fish fry.

RICCIOCARPUS. Ricciaceae. A single-species genus with a wide distribution, this aquatic liverwort often occurs on the surface of the water in association with *Azolla* or *Lemna*.

R. natans. With nearly worldwide distribution, this small plant has closely compacted star-shaped bodies with serrated edges and has the same usefulness in aquaria as *Riccia fluitans*.

SALVINIA. Salviniaceae. Named after Antonio Mario Salvini (1633–1729), professor of Greek at Florence, Italy, this is a cosmopolitan genus of 14 species of free-floating ferns with a tropical and subtropical distribution. Found mainly in Central and South America, Africa, and southern India, it has also become acclimatized in some temperate regions. The enormous growth rate of some of the species, second only to *Eichhornia*, has made it capable of covering large areas and becoming a serious pest in southeastern Africa, Sri Lanka, and southern India. On Lake Kariba on the Zambesi River in Africa, it makes blankets of plants and decaying debris up to 10 in (25 cm) thick. The rootless plants have slender floating irregularly branched stems that bear leaves in whorls of three—two floating and one submerged. The floating leaves are very soft to the touch with a covering of fine silky hairs. The submerged one is finely divided into linear segments resembling roots. Fruiting bodies (sporocarps) develop among the submerged leaves and sink to the bottom in autumn when the old plant dies. These rise to the surface again in spring and start to grow. In warmer areas of the world the sporocarps have no winter resting period.

S. auriculata. Butterfly fern. Native to tropical America, this species has become acclimatized in some temperate regions. A perennial floating fern growing to about 10 in (25 cm), it has firm fronds about 1 in (2.5 cm) long and 2 in (5 cm) wide covered with hairy leaflets. It can become a nuisance, requiring frequent skimming off the pool, and is prohibited in some areas. Plate 34.

S. minima. Little salvinia. A native of southern Brazil, this species has nearly round green leaves, 0.2–0.5 in (0.5–1.3 cm) long, slightly downy on the upper surface. It is an ideal species for the aquarium because of its small leaves.

S. natans. A floating fern with a wide distribution throughout the warm temperate regions of the Northern Hemisphere with the exception of North America, it bears attractive roundish green leaflets up to 1 in (2.5 cm) long with shiny brown hairs underneath.

SESBANIA. Leguminosae. A genus of 70 species from the warmer parts of the world, the majority of these plants grow in wetlands prone to flooding, and only a few species are true aquatics.

S. aculeata. An annual native to the East Indies, this plant's floating roots are covered with a spongy tissue for buoyancy. The flowers are yellow and sweet-pea-like, and the leaflets are pale green and smooth.

STRATIOTES. Hydrocharitaceae. The name is derived from the Greek *stratiotes*, meaning a soldier, a reference to the plant's swordlike leaves. A single-species genus, it is native to Europe and northwestern Asia.

S. aloides. Water soldier, water aloe. As the common name suggests, this unusual plant resembles a floating aloe. During the summer the plant rises to the water surface to flower. After flowering, it descends to produce many axillary shoots, which, when the plant rises to the surface again in later summer, grow into new plants with winter buds, or turions. These turions separate from the parent plant and sink to the bottom to overwinter. The male and female flowers, which are produced on short stems on separate plants, are white and about 1.5 in (4 cm)

across. The plant is the last extant species in the genus. Eight extinct species have been identified to date from fossil remains. It is prohibited in some areas. Plate 35.

TRAPA. Water chestnut. Trapaceae. The name is derived from the Latin *calcitrappa*, which means a calthrop, a device with four spikes, one of which points up to damage the hooves of cavalry horses (or tires). The eight species in this genus of floating aquatic plants from Europe, Asia, and Africa form rosettes of mottled diamond-shaped dentate leaves with pinkish petioles, 2–4 in (5–10 cm) long, that are spongy and inflated. The flowers are white, short-stemmed, and inconspicuous, producing fruits that are like black thorny chestnuts with four spikes. Rich in fat and starch, they are eaten in continental Asia, Malaysia, and India.

T. bispinosa. Singhara nut plant. A native of India, this species has very long woolly petioles, 4–6 in (10–15 cm) in length, bearing wide black-margined leaves, 2 in (5 cm) long and 2–3 in (5–8 cm) wide, that are hairy beneath. The fruits may have two or four spikes. This is the better species for aquarium culture.

T. natans. Water chestnut. A native of Europe, this floating species is an attractive addition to an ornamental pond. The diamond-shaped leaves form rosettes 24–30 in (60–75 cm) across with shiny pale green surfaces, conspicuous veins, and serrated edges. The reddish spongy petioles are 1.5–8 in (4–20 cm) long. For propagation the fruits should be collected in the autumn and stored for the winter in water or wet sphagnum moss. If allowed to dry out they will not germinate. This plant is prohibited in the United States. Plate 36.

UTRICULARIA. Bladderwort. Lentibulariaceae. The name is derived from the Latin *utriculus*, meaning bladder, the insect-catching organ of the plant. This large genus of over 200 species of floating, sometimes terrestrial, rootless aquatics with a cosmopolitan distribution is distinguished by the presence of small bladders, which in some species are capable of trapping small aquatic animals. Having no roots, the stems and leaves of these species are modified to act as anchoring or absorbing organs with some stems being entirely submerged and producing erect linear leaves. Others have leafy stems that are free-floating or anchored loosely at the base by a rootlike appendage. Small crustaceans and water insects are trapped in bladders positioned on their leaves with an opening that is closed by a hinged flap. The loose end of the flap lies against a base of thickened tissue, and the exposed face carries stiff projecting bristles. When something touches the bristles, the flap opens inward, and water, containing the organism, rushes into the bladder. The flowers, yellow or purple, are usually held above the water, sometimes supported by a whorl of spongy floating leaves. Most species, being tropical, are mainly used in aquaria. Temperate species overwinter by winter buds. They are reasonably easy to grow in still shallow water.

U. inflata. Swollen bladderwort, big floating bladderwort. Found throughout United States and Nova Scotia, this species is free floating with submerged alternate leaves and four to nine inflated floating leaves that are whorled like the spokes of a wheel with four to twelve yellow flowers 0.75 in (2 cm) wide on scapes up to 16 in (40 cm) long.

U. minor. Lesser bladderwort. This species has become naturalized in shallow water and along the edges of ponds and streams in the northeastern United States and the Great Lakes region. The pale yellow flowers are held on very slender stems. In an aquarium its olive-green foliage and translucent bladders are shown off to their full effect.

U. purpurea. Purple bladderwort. This purple-flowered species is found in acid lakes and ponds in the southeastern United States, west to Texas and as far north as Minnesota and southern Canada.

U. resupinata. Reversed bladderwort. Found in the eastern United States, this species was named for the reversed structure of the bladders. The flowers are purple.

U. vulgaris. Common bladderwort. A widespread species, it is found extensively in Europe, Asia, and throughout the United States except in the extreme South. The rich golden yellow flowers in groups of six or eight are carried on strong stems well above the water surface. The bladders, which measure up to 0.2 in (0.5 cm) long, are held in a network of bright green finely divided foliage. Demanding high light but being rather slow-growing, it gradually forms a carpet across the surface of an aquarium but is prone to invasion by algae.

WOLFFIA. Water meal. Lemnaceae. Named in honor of German physician J. F. Wolff (1778–1806), this is a genus of eight species of floating aquatics from all tropical and subtropical regions that are reputed to be the smallest flowering plants in the world. Scarcely visible individually, they are prolific enough to form a solid carpet on the surface of the water. They can survive on damp vegetation at the bottom of dried-up ponds.

W. arrhiza. Rootless duckweed. Distributed in eastern Brazil, Africa, Europe, and western Asia, this species is only local and temporary in temperate zones. It has a dark green egg-shaped plant body up to 0.005 in (0.013 cm) long that is an attractive food to certain species of fish.

Chapter 6

Submerged Aquatic Plants for Ponds and Aquaria

Many submerged aquatic plants play an important decorative role, particularly when used in aquaria, but their function is far more fundamental in that they provide the biological and chemical balance necessary to achieve a successful water garden. Like the floating plants, they compete for light and food in the form of dissolved mineral salts, thereby starving out the algae. In addition, they produce oxygen in daylight, a vital element if fish are present. In providing shelter, shade, and habitats for fish fry and eggs, they receive in return the waste products from the fish that, instead of contaminating the water, are filtered out through absorption by the plants. So finely tuned is the healthy balance between these organisms that the overstocking of one type of life can have noticeable effects on the other. Submerged plants, for instance, that have gotten completely out of hand can produce so much carbon dioxide during the hours of darkness in warm water that a heavily stocked fish population can suffer.

The inclusion of submerged plant material is paramount to the success of a natural water garden. Although largely unseen, their effect is to bring health and life to the water in which their more decorative plant partners can excel. The following list of hardy and tender submerged aquatics suitable for aquaria and ponds illustrates the diversity of foliage and growth patterns that make such an important contribution to the success of a planting.

The following species, which are described on later pages, act as good pool oxygenators and are generally commercially available:

Cabomba caroliniana	Fontinalis antipyretica
Callitriche hermaphroditica	Hydrilla verticillata
Ceratophyllum demersum	Lagarosiphon major
Crassula helmsii	Myriophyllum heterophyllum
Egeria densa	Potamogeton crispus
Eleocharis acicularis	Ranunculus aquatilis
Elodea canadensis	Vallisneria spiralis

Certain rampant submerged aquatic species may be prohibited in some areas:

Alternanthera philoxeroides	Lagarosiphon major
Cabomba aquatica	Myriophyllum heterophyllum
Hydrilla verticillata	Myriophyllum hippuroides
Hygrophila polysperma	Myriophyllum spicatum

Check with the relevant state authority if in doubt over the prohibition of any aquatic species.

SETTING UP AN AQUARIUM

The habit, color, and leaf characteristics of submerged plants are appreciated to the full in an aquarium. Cultivating submerged plants in a bright interior environment increases the scope of water gardening and allows the varied and interesting structure of plants to be viewed at close quarters and at eye level. The enchantment of a secret underwater world, whose rich wealth of form is enhanced by a sense of weightless freedom, is extremely restful and captivating.

The interior furnishings of a home or office may dictate the siting of an aquarium, but it should not be placed too near a sunny window. Artificial lighting will provide the necessary light energy for the plants, and if too much natural light reaches the tank, the problem of green water occurs in much the same way as it does in a very small garden pool without adequate surface leaves. The similarity to a small garden pond does not end there, and the parallel guideline of greater water volume resulting in easier management is particularly relevant. In order to have enough scope for effective landscaping and plant variety, an aquarium 24 in (60 cm) deep, 24 in (60 cm) wide, and 50 in (130 cm) long is ideal. While many aquaria are smaller than this, an environment devoted to plant interest requires adequate room for diversity. If the aquarium must be smaller than the size described, length should be reduced rather than depth or width. The height of the tank must be comfortable for viewing, as much of the appeal of an aquarium lies in being able to see the detail in an environment that is normally difficult to observe in nature.

An aquarium designed principally for the appreciation of plants is called a dutch tank, named after the Dutch, whose passionate love for interior plants led them to start the trend for such tanks. One of the main requirements of a dutch tank over a traditional aquarium is a deeper planting medium, or substratum, resulting in increased weight and the need for adequate reinforcing of the base frame.

The capacity of an aquarium in gallons (liters) can be calculated by multiplying length in inches (centimeters) by the height and then by the width and dividing by 231 (838). In an aquarium measuring 50 in (130 cm) by 24 in (60 cm) by 24 in (60 cm), the capacity would be 127 gal (577 l). This amount of water would weigh approximately 1150 lb (520 kg), and some floors, particularly in upstairs apartments, cannot safely support more than 300 lb (136 kg) per sq yd (0.8 sq m).

The substratum should be about 3 in (8 cm) deep at the front of the tank and 4–5 in (10–13 cm) deep at the back. It should be chemically neutral and look as natural as possible. Lime-free sand, 0.08–0.2 in (2–5 mm) in diameter, that has been thoroughly washed makes a good material, both as a medium that encourages the quick penetration of roots and also as a good base color for the planting. A two-gallon bucketful (8 l) of sand is required for every sq ft (0.09 sq m) of tank floor area, more if the tank is to be landscaped. Certain specimen plants such as *Cryptocoryne* and most of the *Aponogeton* and *Echinodorus* species obtain their nutrients through the roots rather than the leaves, and they are planted in small nutrient-containing pots in the sand.

Although cold-water aquaria containing hardy plants will provide considerable interest, the full potential of an aquarium is realized when a wide variety of tropical species can be introduced. This is achieved by heating the aquarium with thermostatically controlled heating cables buried in the substratum. This system diffuses the heat much better than other types of aquarium heaters, and most plant species particularly enjoy such a heat source near their roots. A further advantage of heating cables is the exchange of heat between the substratum and the cooler water above it, resulting in well-oxygenated water being spread by conduction. The ideal water temperature for most tropical aquatic species is 73–79°F (23–26°C).

A tropical aquarium should ideally have 12 hours of light, simulating a typical tropical day. The intensity must be adequate for a wide range of species, particularly the dwarf carpeting plants on the floor of the aquarium such as *Echinodorus tenellus*. A guideline for the amount of light required in a tank 24 in (60 cm) deep is 0.4–0.7 watts per quart (0.95 l) of water. Fluorescent tubes directly above the water make a good light source, particularly if one of them is a wide-spectrum growth tube. Light sources that produce specific parts of the light spectrum can be experimented with, particularly those that display the red and blue colors. The arrangement of the lighting is also important; a very restful effect can be achieved when the back of the aquarium appears slightly darker than the front. The combination of an opaque back wall and subdued back lighting also creates the illusion of greater depth. Aquaria deeper than 24 in (60 cm) will need specialist high-intensity discharge lamps suspended over them.

A water filter should be considered if pristine water clarity is required. In a dutch tank, chamber and turbine-type filters are ideal when fitted outside the tank. Plants dislike fast currents, and with no fish present, the strong suction associated with certain filters is unnecessary. Alternatively, a decanting filter requiring a small part of the aquarium sectioned off for its use could be used. Internally fitted molded-polyurethane backgrounds that incorporate a space for a decanting filter are particularly useful.

Once the essential equipment has been chosen, there are accessories to consider that make the submerged landscape more interesting. Small pieces of rock provide a good framework for the substratum, and genera such as *Microsorum* and *Fontinalis* take root in the open water when loosely anchored to rock with a small stone. Avoid calcareous, semisoluble, or ore-bearing rocks, particularly those with vivid, garish colors. Pieces of igneous and reddish brown porous lava rock are excellent. If the aquarium is large enough, group the rocks together to form interesting outcrop formations. If submerged pieces of wood are used, they must similarly be chosen with care. Avoid resinous woods, such as pine, and sea-washed wood, but beech, oak, and willow are suitable, provided they are boiled first to clean and saturate the timber. Fossilized or petrified wood is ideal and is often available at aquatic suppliers. Cork bark in the background and small lengths of bamboo grouped closely together to simulate reed beds are imaginative additions to a landscape.

As with terrestrial plants, the choice of genera will be influenced by the acidity of the water, although most will succeed if extremes of acidity or alkalinity are avoided. Slightly acid water suits genera like *Cabomba*, *Cryptocoryne*, *Echinodorus*, and *Marsilea*, while *Vallisneria*, *Elodea*, *Sagittaria*, and *Myriophyllum* prefer more alkaline conditions.

Sketching a planting plan before purchasing the plants is helpful in designing a harmonious mixture that will not only provide variety in form, size, and color but also will be happy with the water chemistry and not appear overcrowded. The overall effect is better when planting is undertaken in groups rather than singly.

The taller species such as *Vallisneria spiralis* and *Sagittaria graminea* are best used at the back; bushier species such as *Hygrophila difformis* and *Ludwigia natans* make good corner groups. Shorter plants such as *Eleocharis acicularis* are particularly interesting in front of rocky outcrops, and ample clearing should be left for specimen plants such as *Echinodorous cordifolius* or *Aponogeton boivinianus*. *Cryptocoryne cordata* is attractive in dense clumps over open spaces.

Planting is easier when the tank is only partially filled beforehand. Damaged or browning leaves should be removed, and a few small stones, glass tubes, or lead weights can be placed around the plants initially to combat buoyancy. When filling the aquarium, slowly pour the water over a rock or piece of wood to reduce disturbance of roots and substratum. In the absence of fish, whose excreta would normally feed the plants, it will be neccessary to add fertilizer if the substratum is composed of inert sand. Long-lasting slow-release feeding tablets specially formulated for use in aquaria are recommended. Certain plants such as *Cryptocoryne cordata* appreciate extra iron, which is also available in tablet form. If fertilizer tablets are used regularly, change approximately one third of the water in the aquarium each time they are added to prevent the buildup of concentrated salts. If plants become very stunted, carbon dioxide may be deficient, and this condition can be remedied by using pressurized bottles to release the gas into the water. Many seed-setting species such as *Aponogeton* benefit from a winter rest period in a cooler aquarium, and their transfer is made easier when they are grown in small pots.

ALTERNANTHERA. Amaranthaceae. The name is derived from the Latin *alterno*, meaning alternate, and the Greek *anthera*, meaning stamens. This genus of 200 species is sometimes known as *Telanthera* and is distributed in most of the warm and hot regions of the world, particularly tropical South America. The genus is more commonly known for its carpet-bedding plants, whose unusual foliage colorings form excellent contrasts in massed plantings. More recently, those species found in marshy environments have been tried in aquaria, some with considerable success. The flowers are mainly inconspicuous, normally densely clustered in the leaf axils of any aerial shoots. Although creeping when in a terrestrial habitat, the stems become erect when submerged.

A. ficoidea. This is sometimes offered in the trade as the cultivar 'Sessilis'. A widely distributed species growing in tropical marshes, it is one of the most attractive and vigorous species for aquarium use and suitable for group planting. Its narrow leaves on a very short leaf stalk are up to 3 in (8 cm) long and 0.6 in (1.5 cm) wide, olive green on the upper side and reddish underneath. The plant is not long-lived in a submerged condition and should be replaced every six months or so. Cultivars with stronger foliage colors can be found in the trade such as 'Rubra', whose leaves are red on both sides, and 'Lilacina', which has reddish portions on the upper side with dark red underneath.

A. philoxeroides. Alligator weed. A tender species naturalized in the southeastern United States, it has become abundant in ponds, ditches, and sluggish streams. In some cases it crowds out other plants.

The medium green leaves are 2–5 in (5–13 cm) long and 0.25–0.75 in (0.6–2 cm) wide. In areas where it has become invasive, the stems can stand nearly 12 in (30 cm) above the water surface and be covered with white flowers 0.5 in (1.3 cm) in diameter. Because it will not thrive outside in temperate areas, it is only suitable for aquarium use.

A. reineckii [*Telanthera osiris*]. This tropical species from southern Brazil and Paraguay, where it grows above the waterline, has been found to tolerate a subaquatic existence. The short-stemmed leaves are long, narrow, and almost elliptical, up to 1.5 in (4 cm) long and up to 0.6 in (1.5 cm) wide. The upper side is light to olive green when in a bright position, turning brown when placed in darker surroundings. The leaf edges are sometimes pale red with the underside of the leaf blades pale green to slightly reddish.

AMMANNIA. Lythraceae. A genus of 30 subtropical and tropical amphibious marsh-loving species, it has a wide distribution in warmer countries. Many species are weeds in rice crops, and a few are worthwhile as aquarium specimens, although they are difficult to locate in the trade.

A. senegalensis. This tropical amphibious species from Senegal justifies its inclusion in an aquarium through having fine brown grasslike leaves, up to 1.25 in (3 cm) long and 0.4 in (1 cm) wide, with folded margins. When not submerged, the leaves are a much greener color. The flowers appear in clusters in the leaf axils of aerial shoots with small pale violet petals.

ANUBIAS. Water aspidistra, African cryptocoryne. Araceae. The name is derived from the Egyptian god Anubis, god of the shadows. The members of this genus of seven tropical species from West Africa are usually found in shallow shady streams in hot humid areas growing either at the water's edge or with rhizomes in the water and leaves projecting above the surface. Some species are capable of being totally submerged, making them suitable for aquarium culture. The shape and habit of the thick, long, and flat leaves are very similar to those of the common Victorian houseplant *Aspidistra*, and the more common aquarium plant *Cryptocoryne*, giving rise to the common names. They have the ability to survive in poor light, and their tough leaves are resistant to nibbling fish.

A. afzelii. The most northerly species of the genus, it is found in Senegal and Sierra Leone along streams. This species is suitable as a specimen plant for large aquaria that can accommodate its handsome leaves, 14 in (35 cm) long and 5 in (13 cm) wide, arising

from a thick rhizome often 0.5 in (1.3 cm) in diameter. A slow-growing species, particularly when submerged, the largest specimens tend to be found as bog plants. The rhizomes, which should never be buried too deeply, are capable of attaching themselves to pieces of wood or rock. The attractive aroidlike flowers, which are more generously produced when the plant is not submerged, are spathes that are green at the base with white tips.

A. heterophylla. An amphibious species found over a wide area of tropical rainforest in the Congo, Zaire, and Angola, it has flat, sometimes wavy, dark green leaves, growing to 6 in (15 cm) long and 1.5 in (4 cm) wide when submerged but reaching much larger proportions when used as a bog plant. The species makes a good specimen plant for large aquaria.

APONOGETON. Aponogetonaceae. A genus of 44 temperate and tropical species of submerged aquatics from Africa, Madagascar, Southeast Asia, and northern and eastern Australia, the majority inhabit rivers, lakes, and slow-moving waterways. Nearly all the species have a tuberous or rhizomatous root, which is thought to be why many can survive drops in water level or even drought. In cultivation these tubers can simply be dropped into loam-filled containers or planted into the soil at the bottom of the pond. They are generous with their flowers, which take the form of a spike protected by a spathe when submerged. Generally, the Asian and Australian species have a single spike, the African two, and species from Madagascar a minimum of two. An exception to this generalization is *A. distachyos*, an Australian species that carries two spikes instead of one. *Aponogeton* is an important genus to the water gardener in both temperate and tropical climates. The liberal display of attractive and scented flowers held above some of the loveliest of aquatic leaves, some of which have skeletonized leaf blades, makes them very worthy of planting.

A. bernerianus. A tropical Madagascan species, it has a thick tuberous rootstock 0.5–1.25 in (1.3–3 cm) in diameter. The pointed leaf blades, which have rounded bases and crinkled edges, are 10 in (25 cm) long and 1.5 in (4 cm) wide. The crisscross leaf venation exhibits small, almost square windows that become translucent between the veins. These areas of tissue resemble the skeletonized leaves of the more familiar *A. madagascariensis* but are smaller. The flower spike splits into two opposed spikes bearing white or rosy pink flowers.

A. boivinianus. A tropical species from Madagascar, sometimes confused with *A. bernerianus*, it has submerged dark green linear leaves with indented or wavy surfaces, sometimes reaching nearly 30 in (75 cm) in length. A successful plant for aquaria, its tolerance to hard water and handsome appearance make it a good centerpiece. The flower spike is made up of two, sometimes three, white flowers.

A. crispus. A tender species from Sri Lanka, it is very popular for aquarium culture. The submerged light green to reddish leaves are narrow with crinkled edges up to 12 in (30 cm) long and 1.5 in (4 cm) wide, making it an attractive centerpiece in larger-sized aquaria. The flower is white or cream-colored with reddish anthers, 4–6 in (10–15 cm) long, growing in a single spike 2–3 in (5–8 cm) above the water.

A. distachyos. Water hawthorn. A hardy, robust species from southern Africa that has become naturalized in northern Australia, western South America, and western Europe, it makes a superb decorative pool plant, tolerant of wide variations in light levels, water depth, and water temperature. The surface leaves are straplike, up to 8 in (20 cm) long by 3 in (8 cm) wide, green with occasional mottling, and almost evergreen in mild temperate winters. The flowers are white, 2–3 in (5–8 cm) long, with contrasting black anthers and are held on a double spike. Each spike has large white bracts from which the flowers are tightly arranged in two rows. The scent resembles hawthorn blossom, giving the plant its common name. A notoriously floriferous species, the plant flowers in early summer and again in autumn. Plate 37.

A. longiplumulosus. A tropical species from Madagascar, it provides interest in the aquarium through its long undulating leaves, 12–16 in (30–40 cm) long by 4 in (10 cm) wide, which are brownish to bright green with conspicuous longitudinal veins. It is robust and easily grown with pinkish to mauve flowers.

A. madagascariensis. Madagascar lace plant, lattice leaf plant. A tropical species from Madagascar, this unique and delicate plant is one of the most intriguing and unusual aquatics. It has an almost skeletonized submerged leaf formation in a dark olive-green color. The crisscross tracery of veins occasionally exhibits an area where the spaces are filled with green tissue. The leaves when fully grown are long and elliptical in shape, up to 18 in (45 cm) long and 2–4 in (5–10 cm) wide, with prominent veins parallel to the midrib. The small flowers are borne just above the water. The delicate leaves attract algae and are prone to rotting, making them a challenging species to cultivate. Filtered and circulating water at a minimum temperature of 60–65°F (16–18°C) in winter and 70–75°F (21–24°C) in summer is paramount. They are best cultivated out of bright light. 'Henkelianus', a commercially available white-flowered cultivar, has similar skeletonized leaves but with noticeably crenate tips. The leaves grow up to 10 in (25 cm) long and 3.5 in (9 cm) wide. Figure 36.

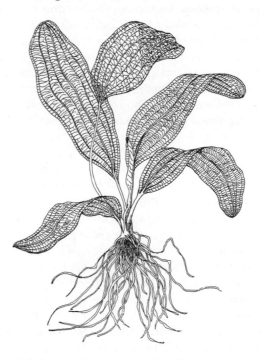

FIGURE 36. *Aponogeton madagascariensis.*

A. ulvaceus. A tender species from Madagascar, it makes a good aquarium plant through its attractive membranous bright green submerged leaves that are narrowed at the base, wavy-edged, and slightly curled, 12–15 in (30–38 cm) long and 1.5–2.5 in (4–6 cm) wide. It makes an attractive centerpiece in aquaria where its fast-growing, charming, thin, almost translucent leaves can be fully appreciated. The small sulfur-yellow flowers are borne slightly above the water.

BACOPA [*HERPESTIS*]. Water hyssop. Scrophulariaceae. A genus of approximately 56 species of amphibious aquatics found worldwide, particularly in the Americas, inhabiting wet and periodically flooded places, it consists of scrambling plants with hairy leaves. A few species are worthwhile for aquarium culture.

B. caroliniana [*B. amplexicaulis*, *Herpestis amplexicaulis*]. This half-hardy species is found in coastal areas of southern and central North America. The round stem is stiff, covered with fine hairs, rarely branched, and 24 in (60 cm) long. The submerged leaves have hairs on the underside, are sessile, fleshy, and egg-shaped, almost clasp the stem, and are up to 1 in (2.5 cm) long and 0.8 in (2 cm) wide. The light blue tubular flower, about 0.5 in (1.3 cm) long, appears above the water in the axils of the upper leaves.

B. monnieri. Found extensively in all tropical and subtropical regions including the southern United States, Mexico, and Madagascar, this is the easiest *Bacopa* species to maintain in an aquarium. The firm, pale green leaves are wedge-shaped, up to 0.6 in (1.5 cm) long, and up to 0.3 in (0.8 cm) wide, with longer internodes than *B. amplexicaulis*. The flowers are a pale violet color. This is a good plant for group planting toward the back or in the corners of an aquarium.

BARCLAYA [*HYDROSTEMMA*]. Nymphaeaceae. Named after G. W. Barclay, the English gardener and plant collector, this genus of four submerged aquatics occurs in tropical Southeast Asia in pools and streams, usually in forested regions. Members of this genus are not readily available in the trade but are worth seeking as collector's items. *Barclaya* is also discussed in Chapters 11 and 18.

B. longifolia. This tropical species found in southern Thailand, Burma, and Malaysia has leaves with olive-green to brown upper surfaces and reddish purple undersides, making it a useful aquarium specimen plant and a contrast to green foliage. The leaves are at first narrow and lanceolate, later becoming oblong and arrow-shaped, up to 20 in (50 cm) long and up to 1.5 in (4 cm) wide, attractively colored in red and green with a transparent bluish shade. They are also very soft and fragile with distinct corrugations along their length and an attractive red and brown venation. The flowers, which are rarely produced and only fully open when above the water, have petals that are green on the outside and pink or red on the inside. Plate 444; Figure 37; see also Figure 74 in Chapter 18.

BIDENS. Compositae. The name is derived from the Latin *bis*, meaning twice, and *dens*, meaning a tooth, a reference to the twin-toothed appearance of the plant's seeds. This large North American genus includes 200 species, but only a very few occur in water.

B. beckii [*Megaladonta beckii*]. Water marigold. Found in North America from Quebec and New Jersey to British Columbia and Oregon, this tall hardy aquatic species, extending to 6 ft (2 m), occurs in ponds, lakes, and slow-moving streams and is capable of growing above the water in moist areas. It is becoming increasingly rare due to water pollution. The submerged leaves, which occur in twos and threes, are opposite, sessile, lanceolate, and finely divided into forked hairlike segments. The

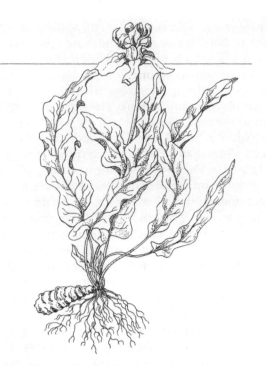

FIGURE 37. *Barclaya longifolia.*

beautiful yellow marigold-like flowers stand high above the water, making an attractive pool plant.

BLYXA. Hydrocharitaceae. The name is derived from the ancient Greek *blyzein*, meaning to flow. It is a genus of 10 tropical species found in Africa, Madagascar, Southeast Asia, New Guinea, and northern Australia. These little-known stoloniferous submerged annuals or perennials are rather grasslike in appearance, having rooted tufts of radical leaves. They appear frequently as a weed in rice fields and irrigation ditches.

B. aubertii. A tropical species from India, Southeast Asia, and Madagascar, it has submerged spirally arranged long, pointed leaves with triangular bases and sharp edges. The flowers are in the form of a membranous spathe, 1.5–4 in (4–10 cm) long, with little color. The grasslike appearance makes it an attractive addition to the aquarium, where the leaves can reach a height of 12 in (30 cm).

B. echinosperma. This tropical species is widely distributed in southern Asia. Its long, fine, grasslike pointed leaves up to 20 in (50 cm) long with rounded bases are a brighter green and narrower than those of *B. aubertii*, being only 0.1–0.2 in (0.3–0.5 cm) wide. It is sometimes referred to as hedgehog blyxa.

BRASENIA. Cabombaceae. A widely distributed subtropical single-species genus of aquatics with floating leaves, at first glance it may give the impression of certain *Potamogeton* species, but on closer examination its peltate leaves make it quite distinct. The distribution is almost worldwide with the exception of Europe, growing in pools and lakes, preferring acid water. Plants can be grown in an aquarium that is not too warm.

B. schreberi. Water shield, water target. Found quite extensively in eastern North America, this submerged species has a trailing rootstock, floating oval leaves 2.5 in (6 cm) in diameter, borne on long petioles, and erect elongated shoots. The underside and submerged portions of the leaves are coated with a thick gelatinous substance. The purple three-petaled flowers are about 0.5 in (1.3 cm) across and lie on the water surface, closing at night. In its native habitat the plant grows in a wide range of water depths, from 1 in (2.5 cm) to 6 ft (2 m). It is not a showy plant but makes an interesting subject for the water's edge where there is good light and ideally 8–10 in (20–25 cm) of water.

CABOMBA. Cabombaceae. This genus of seven species of delicate submerged aquatics comes from South America and southeastern North America. They have slender branched stems with finely dissected leaves that are frequently whorled or opposite. They generally grow rooted in stagnant or slow-moving water, ultimately developing floating leaves and flowers. The species' attractive leaves, which may be green or reddish purple, are similar looking, making them difficult to tell apart. The flowers, which are borne on the surface, are the best clues for identification. It is a genus that is deservedly very popular for aquarium use.

C. aquatica. A tropical species from southern Mexico and Brazil, the opposite, coarsely cut submerged leaves are up to 2 in (5 cm) in diameter, and the round floating leaves are 0.4–0.8 in (1–2 cm) in diameter. The submerged leaves are divided into five parts at the base, and every part divides four to five times again. It can grow in its native habitat to 4 ft (1.2 m), but as it requires reasonable light levels, the plant is unlikely to succeed in aquaria over 24 in (60 cm) in depth. Flowers, which are borne above the surface of the water, are yellow on the inside and green on the outside.

C. caroliniana. This subtropical species from the southeastern United States has bright green fan-shaped, coarsely segmented leaves up to 1.5 in (4 cm) in diameter. These attractive leaves grow quickly, making it a suitable aquarium background plant. The surface leaves are linear with pointed tips up to 0.8 in (2 cm) in length. The flowers are white with yellow spots. The plant is a common oxygenator, referred to in the trade as fish grass for goldfish bowls. Plate 38.

C. piauhyensis. A tropical species from northern South America, it has submerged segmented reddish-colored leaves growing in a round or kidney-shaped fan up to 1.5 in (4 cm) in diameter. The floating leaves are linear, up to 1.25 in (3 cm) in length. The flowers are reddish purple with yellow spots. It needs high light intensity and fairly shallow water.

C. pulcherrima. Purple fanwort. A tropical species from northern Florida and southern South Carolina, it has submerged finely divided, reddish-streaked leaves and stems. The reddish purple surface leaves are circular to kidney-shaped 0.6–0.8 in (1.5–2 cm) in diameter. The flowers, which also grow above the water, are 0.4 in (1 cm) in diameter and have white-to-cream centers with purple-tinged tips.

CALLITRICHE. Water starwort. Callitrichaceae. The name is derived from the Greek *kallos*, meaning beauty, and *thrix*, meaning hair, a reference to the plant's style of growth. This genus of 25 species is distributed worldwide with the exception of South Africa. They are small, slender plants that generally grow in a tight mass and occur in a wide variety of habitats, most frequently in temperate areas. They are recognizable by their terminal rosettes of leaves, which, when floating on the water surface, give rise to the common name starwort. The intertwined mass of stems provides homes for abundant minute life, and the young leaves are a particular delicacy for goldfish. They are excellent oxygenating plants and, when submerged in outdoor pools, are quite hardy.

C. hermaphroditica [*C. autumnalis*]. A hardy species, it is found extensively in Europe and North America, mostly in the northern United States. The small light green linear leaves are 0.4–0.75 in (1–2 cm) long, opposite, on thin branching stems. The upper leaves form a bright green rosette on the water surface. It is an excellent oxygenating plant, sold extensively for that purpose, often under the name *C. autumnalis*.

C. intermedia subsp. *hamulata* [*C. hamulata*]. Hooked starwort. An amphibious subspecies scrambling either on mud or more commonly submerged in depths up to 18 in (45 cm), its submerged leaves are deeply notched at the apex, 0.2–1.25 in (0.5–3 cm) long, and 0.02–0.05 in (0.05–0.1 cm) wide. The fruit bears a very narrow wing, giving the common name of hooked starwort.

C. stagnalis. This hardy species has slender branching stems which root at the nodes. The leaves are obovate or nearly circular, forming rosettes at the tips. The average leaf size is 0.3–0.5 in (0.8–1.3 cm) long and 0.2–0.3 in (0.5–0.8 cm) wide but can achieve lengths of 1 in (2.5 cm) in certain conditions. It is a luxuriant plant with stems frequently intertwining and forming a tight mass that is particularly attractive to small fish.

C. verna. A common hardy species, it has submerged linear leaves, 0.8 in (2 cm) long and 0.4 in (1 cm) wide, and conspicuous rosette leaves at the water surface that are orbicular and taper into a wide petiole about 0.4 in (1 cm) long and 0.1–0.2 in (0.3–0.5 cm) wide. Like other submerged *Callitriche* species, it grows into a mass of dense vegetation attractive to fish.

CARDAMINE. Cruciferae. The name is derived from the Greek *kardmon*, meaning cress. The genus contains approximately 150 species with a wide distribution in temperate zones. Most species are bog plants, but some are found growing submerged. Other *Cardamine* species are discussed in Chapter 8.

C. lyrata. A temperate species from Asia, it has stems 6–12 in (15–30 cm) high and bright green translucent alternate leaves up to 2 in (5 cm) long, rounded or slightly kidney-shaped, with thin petioles. The flowers are small with white petals. It makes quite an attractive cold-water aquarium plant if temperatures are 60–68°F (16–20°C) and the light is good.

CERATOPHYLLUM. Coontail, hornwort. Ceratophyllaceae. The name is derived from the Greek *ceratos*, meaning a horn, and *phyllon*, meaning a leaf. This genus of 30 hardy species of submerged rootless aquatics is found worldwide. The plants are usually 12–24 in (30–60 cm) long with whorls of stiff and slender dark green leaves crowding toward the apex, giving the appearance of a raccoon's tail. They grow only in submerged conditions, unable to tolerate even short periods of emergence, acting as good oxygenators in cold water and where shade may inhibit other species. They are frequently found free-floating or loosely anchored in the mud in both still and moving water. The plants overwinter by the tips of the shoots becoming shortened and thickened then breaking off and sinking to the bottom as buds.

C. demersum. A hardy species found worldwide and widespread in the United States, its bare stalks, which grow 12–24 in (30–60 cm) long, support submerged whorled leaves that are brittle, dark green, 0.6–1.5 in (1.5–4 cm) long, and forked. The inconspicuous flowers are borne within the axil of a leaf in a whorl.

C. echinatum. A hardy species found chiefly in the United States, the long branching stems are slightly more forking in the whorls than those of *C. demersum*.

C. submersum. A hardy species found in Europe and central and Southeast Asia, it is very similar to *C. demersum* but differs in having the leaves forked three to four times, a rather softer texture, and a brighter green color. It also lacks the spiky horns on the fruit present in *C. demersum*.

CRASSULA [*TILLAEA*]. Crassulaceae. The name is derived from the Latin *crassus*, meaning thick or swollen, a reference to the succulent aerial parts of most species. It is a genus of around 300 species of herbs and shrubs mostly from South Africa with a few that are cosmopolitan. Composed mainly of desert plants, the genus is unusual in containing a vigorous aquatic species that can quickly colonize large areas of water. The creeping submerged habit and small submerged leaves of the genus make the plants good oxygenators.

C. helmsii. Widely distributed in Europe, America, and Australia, this vigorous submerged aquatic has much-branched stems that creep or float and are capable of rooting from the lower nodes. The small opposite narrow leaves are 0.25–1 in (0.6–2.5 cm) long and united at the base to form a cylindrical collar around the stem. It prefers shallow water, but in deeper water of 3 ft (1 m), masses of stems float to the surface, forming dense growths of intertwined stems with small axillary white flowers. These flowers can also form on damp soils beside fresh water. Plants must be introduced with caution in situations where they are not confined or cut back by severe winters. It is an excellent oxygenating plant and is useful to starve out algae.

CRYPTOCORYNE. Araceae. The name is derived from the Greek *kryptos*, meaning hidden, and *koryne*, meaning a club. A genus of 50 or more species of marsh and submerged aquatics from Southeast Asia, it includes some of the most popular plants for aquaria. Their relative small size, tolerance of low light, and interesting stiff leathery leaf forms make them invaluable. They have the characteristic flower of the Araceae—a spathe that in certain species is highly colored. They are often slow to become established; in some cases, it may be many weeks before any growth occurs.

C. aponogetifolia. A submerged tropical species from the Philippines, it has long reddish brown leaf petioles and lanceolate leaf blades up to 30 in (75 cm) long, the upper side dark green with a paler shade underneath. The flower spathe is slightly twisted with purplish spots. Because of its size this species is only suitable for large aquaria where it makes an elegant specimen plant.

C. balansae. A submerged tropical species from Thailand, Vietnam, and southern China, it is similar to *Aponogeton undulatus* but has longer and narrower leaves. Its great charm is in the beautiful long crinkled foliage growing 12–16 in (30–40 cm) in cultivation and almost twice that size in the wild. The inflorescence is nearly 4 in (10 cm) long, purple, and folded over several times with red spots inside.

C. beckettii **var.** *petchii.* A tropical submerged form from Sri Lanka, it was one of the first aquarium plants to be successfully cultivated. The almost lanceolate wavy-edged leaves with violet petioles are olive green to brown on the upper side and reddish underneath, 4–8 in (10–20 cm) long, and 0.75–1.5 in (2–4 cm) wide.

C. ciliata. A tropical species from Southeast Asia, its identifying characteristic is the fringe of fine hairs on the outer edge of the spathe, which is purplish inside with a yellow spot. It grows to about 14 in (35 cm) high. Its narrow leaves have sheathed petioles that are slightly wavy at the edges. It is one of the most beautiful of the cryptocorynes.

C. cordata. A tropical submerged species from Borneo, Sumatra, and Thailand, it is commonly grown in aquaria. It has reddish leaves 3–6 in (8–15 cm) long with pale red veins and wavy margins.

C. lutea [*C. walkeri*]. A submerged medium-sized tropical species from Sri Lanka, it has wavy-edged elongated, rather egg-shaped leaves with olive-green to red-brown petioles and plain medium green leaf blades. The yellowish spathe has a reddish violet tube and is slightly twisted.

C. nevillii [*C. willisii*]. A medium-sized amphibious species from Sri Lanka, it has long egg-shaped leaves that are 1.5–3 in (4–8 cm) long and 0.4–0.6 in (1–1.5 cm) wide with a pulpy, leathery texture, midgreen on the upper side, and pale reddish underneath. The slightly twisted flower spathe is brown with a yellow ring.

C. wendtii. A medium-sized species from Sri Lanka, its leaves are so variable in size and color as to make the plant difficult to distinguish. The corrugated and wrinkled leaves with brownish to reddish petioles are 3–6 in (8–15 cm) long and 1 in (2.5 cm) wide, are sometimes heart-shaped at the base, and taper regularly toward a point. The dark brown spathe is more constant, however, growing 5–6 in (13–15 cm) long with a slight twist, a curve to one side, and a violet ring. Figure 38.

ECHINODORUS. Alismataceae. The name is derived from the Greek *echinos*, meaning a hedgehog, and *doros*, meaning a tube, a reference to the plant's spiny fruits. A genus of about 50 species of mostly subtropical aquatics from the warmer regions of the Americas and Africa, it grows in a wide variety of habitats. Many species are referred to as Amazon sword plants and serve as decorative marginal and bog plants. Some of the smaller species can be used as aquarium plants. They resemble sagittarias in shape, and identification is difficult when the plants have only the young long ribbonlike leaves.

E. berteroi. Cellophane plant. Found throughout much of North America, especially the southern United States and Mississippi Valley, and Mexico and the West Indies, it propagates readily from seed and develops a rosette of thin, ribbonlike, nearly translucent leaves up to 15 in (38 cm) long. If there are no exuberant fish to tear apart the rather fragile leaves, it makes a fine center plant for the aquarium.

E. cordifolius [*E. radicans*]. Honduras radicans. One of the oldest cultivated aquarium species, it is found in southern and central North America, particularly in the Mississippi Valley, and has been reported from Venezuela. The pale green submerged leaves are initially egg-shaped but later turn heart-shaped with reddish brown markings. Once emersed, broad oval egg-shaped leaves develop while the submerged leaves perish, changing the entire plant's form. A striking species, it is best used as a specimen plant in an aquarium or in the back-

FIGURE 38. *Cryptocoryne wendtii.*

ground of a pool. The leaves remain submerged only when there are fewer than 12 hours of daylight.

E. major. Ruffled sword plant. A species from South America and Brazil, it has wavy-edged pale green leaves, 17–18 in (43–45 cm) long and up to 2 in (5 cm) wide, which are slightly wider at the apex. The leaf form gives rise to the common name ruffled sword plant. It grows only in submerged conditions.

E. osiris. A species from South America, it is found growing in marshes or cool shallow water in the lower reaches of mountain streams. It is a tolerant species that adapts to aquarium life easily. The prolific wavy-edged foliage, 12–16 in (30–40 cm) long and 1.5–2.5 in (4–6 cm) wide, can turn reddish (so-called 'Rubra') under bright aquarium light conditions from its normal olive-green color.

E. paniculatus. Amazon sword plant. A popular aquarium plant from central South America, it forms a rosette of short-petioled submerged leaves up to 15 in (38 cm) long. The pale green leaf blade is lanceolate, pointed, and up to 2.75 in (7 cm) wide.

E. tenellus. Originating in Central and South America, this small species produces extensive carpeting runners and is known in the trade as pygmy chain swordplant. The leaves are narrow and linear, 2–2.5 in (5–6 cm) long, and less than 0.1 in (0.3 cm) wide. The habit of growth makes it an excellent foreground aquarium plant.

EGERIA. Water weed, water thyme. Hydrocharitaceae. The members of this genus of two species were originally native to the warm and temperate zones of South America and are now established in many countries worldwide where, in some cases, they have become pests.

E. densa [*Elodea densa*]. Argentinian waterweed. A South American temperate species, it has become naturalized widely in Central and North America, Europe, and Australia. It is a vigorous submerged plant with multibranched stems carrying whorls of midgreen sessile leaves that are linear with pointed tips, usually bent backward, 1 in (2.5 cm) long, and up to 0.1 in (0.3 cm) wide. The brittle branchlets easily break off the parent plant and later form clumps of dense floating vegetation, very much enjoyed by fish. The stems become spindly in tropical aquaria and the plant should only be used in cold-water aquaria that have good light and a water temperature that does not exceed 73°F (23°C). The inconspicuous flower protrudes above the water and is about 1 in (2.5 cm) long. The plant makes an excellent aquarium oxygenator.

ELEOCHARIS. Spike rush. Cyperaceae. The name is derived from the Greek *helos*, meaning a marsh,

and *charis*, meaning grace or beauty, a reference to the plant's attractive cover of marshy conditions. It is a cosmopolitan genus of approximately 150 species of temperate grasslike aquatic and marsh-dwelling plants, having rhizomatous roots, spreading quickly, and adapting well to varying water depths. Although they generally grow best in water no deeper than 4 in (10 cm), some species make charming little aquarium plants.

E. acicularis. Hair grass. A variable temperate species from North America, Europe, and Asia, the submerged pale green leaves are needlelike, up to 8 in (20 cm) long, and less than 0.02 in (0.05 cm) thick. The blossoms are small egg-shaped brown spikes that grow on a four-sided stem that is sheathed at the base. The neat small grassy spikes are an attractive addition to the foreground of a cold-water aquarium. It is a good oxygenating species and is available in the trade for that purpose. In a natural pond it may become a terrible pest.

E. dulcis [*E. tuberosa*]. Chinese water chestnut. Native to tropical East Asia, Pacific islands, Madagascar, and West Africa, the water chestnut is a fine plant for the water garden with its graceful cylindrical stems 1–3 ft (0.3–1 m) in height. The tubers or corms are eaten raw or cooked and are used in many Chinese dishes.

E. montevidensis [*E. palustris*]. Spike rush. This rush native to eastern North America produces clumps about 12 in (30 cm) high and grows in moist soil to 3 in (8 cm) of water. The leaves are round, narrow, and quill-shaped with a tuft of tiny light brown flowers at the tip.

ELODEA. Hydrocharitaceae. The name is derived from the Greek *helos*, meaning marsh or bog. A genus of 12 submerged temperate species distributed in North and South America, it has become widespread in many temperate regions worldwide. It is widely used as an oxygenating plant in ornamental pools where it combines vigorous growth with an ability to subdivide and spread rapidly. It has become a pest in many regions.

E. canadensis. Canadian pondweed. A native of North America that has spread to Europe, Asia, and Australia, this temperate species is one of the finest oxygenating plants for garden ponds. It can become invasive but is only likely to be a problem in large pools where it cannot be trimmed back. After its early introduction to Europe, where its invasive tendency caused considerable alarm, it has now settled down to being more beneficial, probably because the present population is mainly female. It has multibranched stems covered in sessile curving midgreen whorls of pointed leaves up to 0.4 in

(1 cm) long and 0.1 in (0.3 cm) wide. If used in an aquarium, the water temperature should not exceed 73°F (23°C) or the plant becomes spindly.

EURYALE. Prickly water lily, Gorgon plant. Nymphaeaceae. A single-species genus of aquatic plants from India, Bangladesh, and China, it has thorny floating leaves and was named after the mythological snake-haired Gorgon. *Euryale* is also discussed in Chapters 11 and 18.

E. ferox. This species was introduced into Europe in 1809 by William Roxburgh, director of the Calcutta Botanic Garden. The spectacular large circular puckered leaves are 2–3 ft (0.6–1 m) in diameter. These impressive leaves are olive green on the upper side with prominent veins and spines and exhibit an incredible purply blue hue underneath with dull red spiny veins. The small violet-magenta flowers are rarely more than 2 in (5 cm) across and have a stiffly spined calyx. The fruit is a berry, 2–4 in (5–10 cm) in diameter, containing seeds about the size of large peas. The seeds, when ripened on the plant and then baked, are much esteemed in India. Although it requires only marginally more heat than hardy water lilies, in temperate areas it is best grown in a warm greenhouse. It enjoys the same conditions and cultural requirements as described later in this chapter for *Victoria*. Plates 441–443; see also Figure 71 in Chapter 18.

FONTINALIS. Fontinalaceae. The name is derived from the Latin *fontinalis*, meaning living in fountains. This genus of nearly 60 species of aquatic mosses is distributed throughout the Northern Hemisphere and North Africa. They grow attached to boulders, logs, or tree roots, which adds to their decorative value in cold-water aquaria.

F. antipyretica. A hardy species of submerged moss having variable characteristics, it is distributed in Europe, Asia, North America, and Algeria and is found on stones in cold flowing water in association with algae and other mosses. It has branched triangular stems 8–20 in (20–50 cm) long, bearing dark olive-green to brownish leaves 0.3 in (0.8 cm) long and 0.1 in (0.3 cm) wide. The plant makes an attractive addition to the unheated aquarium.

HERPESTIS. See *Bacopa*.

HETERANTHERA. Pontederiaceae. The name is derived from the Greek *heteros*, meaning different, and Latin *anthera*, meaning anthers. This genus contains about 10 species of tender submerged or shallow-water aquatics, mostly native to tropical America and now widespread in the eastern and midwest-

ern United States. A few species are commercially available for aquarium use. Another species of *Heteranthera* is discussed in Chapter 7.

H. dubia. Water stargrass. This tropical submerged species from the southern United States, Mexico, and Cuba makes a good background plant for aquaria. The stems can reach 28–30 in (70–75 cm) long, bearing pale green grasslike leaves about 4 in (10 cm) long and solitary yellow flowers about 0.8–2.75 in (2–7 cm) long.

H. zosterifolia. A tropical submerged species from South America, it has trailing or branching stems growing up to 3 ft (1 m) high. The bright green leaves are 0.8–1.5 in (2–4 cm) long and 0.2 in (0.5 cm) wide. The small blue flowers, 0.02 in (0.05 cm) long and 0.05 in (0.1 cm) wide, grow in pairs just above the water surface. It is somewhat similar in appearance and function to *Egeria densa*, being a good oxygenator, but the leaves are ranked alternately rather than in whorls.

HIPPURIS. Hippuridaceae. The name is derived from the Greek *hippos*, meaning a horse, and *oura*, meaning a tail, a reference to the plant's resemblance to a horse's tail. This single-species genus of hardy aquatics is almost cosmopolitan.

H. vulgaris. Mare's-tail. This marsh plant has extensive runners and forms erect shoots with pale green narrow leaves, 2 in (5 cm) long and up to 0.1 in (0.3 cm) wide, arranged in whorls. It is of aesthetic value only in aquaria, but precautions should be taken to prevent its excessive invasion of the growing medium. Many variants of the species may be cataloged with separate-species status.

HOTTONIA. Featherfoil, water violet. Primulaceae. Named in honor of Dutch botanist P. Hotton (1648–1709), this is a genus of two temperate species of submerged aquatics found in bright clear pools in the Northern Hemisphere.

H. inflata. This species has interesting inflated stems and flower stalks, hence the specific name. The submerged thin leaves are very finely divided, bright green on the surface with grayish tints underneath. The rather inconspicuous pale lilac erect flowers are held above the water in whorls on clustered leafless flower stalks.

H. palustris. Water violet. A temperate European species, this attractive plant is a prized asset if it settles down in an ornamental pool. It is very similar to *H. inflata* but has showier pale lilac or white flowers that are borne on a stalk that is not inflated. The plant can reach a height of over 3 ft (1 m), and the crowded flower spike can be held as much as 14 in (35 cm) above the water surface. The leaves are finely divided and borne, like those of *H. inflata*, on stems that are sometimes inflated. In autumn it produces overwintering buds, or turions, that sink to the pool bottom, making the plant difficult to keep in containers. Figure 39.

FIGURE 39. *Hottonia palustris.*

HYDRILLA. Hydrocharitaceae. The name is derived from the Greek *hydor*, meaning water, and *illein*, meaning to turn. A single-species genus of submerged aquatics, it is found in the warmer areas of Europe, Africa, Asia, Australia, and North America in slow-moving streams and lakes to a depth of 10–16 ft (3–5 m).

H. verticillata. A species closely resembling *Elodea*, the much-branched stem, 6–12 in (15–30 cm) long, carries whorled light green linear to lanceolate leaves, 0.4–0.8 in (1–2 cm) long and 0.08–0.2 in (0.2–0.5 cm) wide. The leaves have fine translucent teeth and often small reddish brown dashes. It can be grown as an attractive oxygenator in pools and aquaria but may become a menace in large stretches of deep warm water. The plant is troublesome in parts of Florida. In the fall white corms develop on the stolons in the soil that enable it to survive the winter in cooler cliamtes.

HYGROPHILA. Acanthaceae. The name is derived from the Greek *hygros*, meaning wet or moist, and *philos*, meaning friend. This genus of approximately 100 species of moisture-loving aquatics comes from many warm regions worldwide, particularly Africa and Southeast Asia. Some species have been found suitable for aquarium culture.

H. difformis [*Synnema triflorum*]. Water wisteria. A tender species from Southeast Asia, the submerged branched stems grow 16–32 in (40–80 cm) long and bear a variety of pale green leaves that range from egg-shaped to lanceolate, some deeply lobed. Any aerial leaves produced are simpler and darker in color. Purplish flowers are borne in the leaf axils. The charming and indented submerged leaves make a good cluster of interesting foliage at the back of an aquarium.

H. polysperma. When submerged, this half-hardy creeping species from Southeast Asia grows erect on green stems up to 20 in (50 cm) long sparsely clad with bright green to brownish egg-shaped leaves, 1.5 in (4 cm) long and 0.6 in (1.5 cm) wide. The sessile bluish white flowers are confined to the axils of aerial leaves. It makes a good background plant in an aquarium.

H. salicifolia. Distributed widely in Southeast Asia, this tropical species has long thin pale green submerged leaves, 4–8 in (10–20 cm) long and 0.5–0.8 in (1.3–2 cm) wide, slightly curved on one side. It is one of the more vigorous species for aquarium use, growing 30–40 in (75–100 cm), and should be planted on its own to show off its attractive reddish-tinged leaves and violet flowers.

ISOETES. Quillwort. Isoetaceae. The name is derived from the Greek *isos*, meaning equal, and *etos*, meaning year, relating to its ability to maintain foliage throughout the year. This genus of 75 temperate and tropical aquatic and amphibious species is found in a wide variety of wet habitats. The corm-like stems are attractive food for water birds and rodents. The tapered linear leaves rise from the short corm, making it resemble a small tufted sedge rather than a fern. While a few species are capable of growing in depths of 13 ft (4 m) or more, most species grow in shallow water and are able to withstand periods above the water surface if the water recedes.

I. echinospora. A temperate species widespread in North America, it lives on the sandy or gravelly bottoms of lakes, ponds, and slow-moving streams. The pale green leaves are 14 in (35 cm) long and form a needlelike rosette 2–3 in (5–8 cm) in diameter.

I. lacustris. Quillwort. A temperate species from Europe, Asia, and North America, it has submerged awl-shaped olive-green leaves 6–12 in (15–30 cm) long. It can be grown in good light in a cold aquarium.

LAGAROSIPHON. Hydrocharitaceae. The name is derived from the Greek *lagaros*, meaning thin, and *siphon*, meaning tube. A genus of nine species of tender, submerged aquatics from central Africa and Madagascar, it has established itself in Europe and New Zealand. A plant similar to *Elodea*, it is an excellent oxygenator for fish bowls, pools, and aquaria.

L. major. African elodea. A tender submerged species from southern Africa, it differs in appearance from *Elodea* by its leaves, which are not in whorls but single in flat spirals and strongly recurved. Otherwise, the habit of growth with fragile stems up to 3 ft (1 m) long and dark green color are very similar. As it is not entirely hardy, the species is used in aquaria for its oxygenating properties. The plant is often wrongly called *Elodea crispa*. In natural ponds and lakes it may become a pest.

LILAEOPSIS. Umbelliferae. Some members of this genus of 20 wetland and aquatic species from North and South America, Australia, and New Zealand grow submerged. They occur mainly on the shores of freshwater lakes, with some species able to survive brackish or alkaline conditions. They have slender creeping rhizomes that bear two or more cylindrical or tapered leaves at each node. The habit of growth makes them suitable for carpeting plants in aquaria.

L. novae-zelandiae. A tender submerged creeping species from New Zealand and Australia, it reaches no more than 1.5–2 in (4–5 cm) in height. The white flowers generally occur only when the plants creep above the water level. This species is used as a foreground carpeting species in aquaria with good light levels and a water temperature no lower than 77°F (25°C).

LIMNOPHILA. Scrophulariaceae. The name is derived from the Greek *limne*, meaning a bog or pond, and *philos*, meaning a friend. A genus of 36 tropical aquatics, these plants grow in marshes, rice fields, and pools and along river banks mainly in Asia, Africa, and the East Indies. Nearly half the species have been found to be suitable as decorative aquarium plants. They may be initially mistaken for *Vallisneria*, but if allowed to flower, they are identifiable by their stalked and showy flowers.

L. aquatica [*L. indica*]. A tropical submerged species from Asia, the finely divided submerged leaves are 2 in (5 cm) long in whorls of six or eight and are so densely forked that they take on the appearance of rosettes. The stems bearing the thickly whorled pale green leaves normally grow to 20 in (50 cm) with adventitious white rootlets frequently seen at the nodes. Any leaves produced above the surface are totally different in appearance, being dark green, lanceolate, and up to 1 in (2.5 cm) long with finely serrated edges. The pale blue flower tube is nearly 1 in (2.5 cm) long. It is very handsome, suitable for use as an aquarium background plant.

LOBELIA. Campanulaceae. Named after the Dutch botanist Matthias de L'Obel (1538–1616), this is a large cosmopolitan genus of over 365 species, the majority exhibiting a desire for wet or moist soil. Only one species is a true aquatic, but a terrestrial form, *Lobelia cardinalis*, is sold by the trade for aquarium use.

L. dortmanna. Water lobelia. A cold-water submerged species from North America and western Europe, it is found in shallow water, mostly in acid pools and lakes in the northeastern United States, the Great Lakes region, and the Pacific Northwest. It is a low-growing species, only 1–2 in (2.5–5 cm) high, bearing clusters of stubby dark green leaves that form a dense carpet. The attractive light blue flowers are held in loose terminal racemes on stems above the water level.

LUDWIGIA. Onagraceae. Named in honor of Professor C. G. Ludwig (1709–1773) of Leipzig, Germany, this cosmopolitan genus includes 75 temperate and subtropical species of moisture-loving and wetland plants. Approximately 15 species are capable of being submerged and are suitable for aquarium cultivation. Some confusion over foliage characteristics may exist, and positive identification is only possible when flowers are present. Other *Ludwigia* species are discussed in Chapter 7.

L. arcuata. A tender species from the southeastern United States, the submerged leaves are narrow, pointed, sessile, and lanceolate, 0.4–1 in (1–2.5 cm) long and up to 0.08 in (0.2 cm) wide, olive green with reddish undersides. If the stems are allowed to grow above the water, it can quickly choke the surface. The small golden yellow sessile flowers are borne on aerial stems.

L. natans. Native to the United States, especially Florida, and the West Indies, this plant is grown extensively for aquaria as its red leaves provide a striking and pleasing contrast to the green plants.

L. sidioides. Native to South America, this semihardy plant with its square leaves, deep yellow blooms, and unique swirling pattern provides an attractive new addition to the water garden.

LYSIMACHIA. Loosestrife. Primulaceae. The name is derived from the Greek *lysis*, meaning loosening, and *mache*, strife, a reference to the alleged soothing qualities of the genus. This cosmopolitan genus of 150 species grows mainly in swamps and shallow water. One species can be used as a decorative submerged plant for aquaria, but *Lysimachia* is normally confined to the boggy edges of garden pools where it happily romps in and out of the water. Other species are discussed in Chapter 8.

L. nummularia. Creeping Jenny, moneywort, creeping Charlie. This hardy European species, which has been naturalized in eastern North America, scrambles between submerged and moist conditions at the water's edge. The four-cornered stems, which can produce long shoots up to 3 ft (1 m) in length, root easily at the nodes and produce small rounded leaves, 0.5–1 in (1.3–2.5 cm) long, growing in opposite pairs. The solitary golden yellow flowers with dark red dots inside are positioned in the leaf axils of aerial shoots. While used extensively as a decorative plant for softening the hard edges of pools, it is also successful in cold-water aquaria in high light conditions.

MARSILEA. Water clover, four-leaf clover. Marsileaceae. Named after Count L. F. Marsigli (1656–1730), an Italian botanist who specialized in ferns, this genus of 65 species consists of mainly tropical aquatic ferns, occurring frequently in Australia. They are often found in pools, irrigation ditches, and rice fields where they can become troublesome weeds. When submerged in deep water, the leaf petioles, which branch from extensive rhizomes, can extend to 3 ft (1 m). As marsh plants, however, they produce clusters of short-petioled leaves resembling four-leaf clovers and bearing fruiting bodies that are more numerous when the plant is out of the water. There are several very similar species, distinguishable only by their fruiting bodies. Some are successful in aquaria and water gardens.

M. drummondii. Common nardoo. Originating in Australia, this submerged or trailing species is reputed to have been used as a food plant by the Aborigines, who ground the fruiting bodies into a powder and mixed it with water. The leaves, which closely resemble *Oxalis* (sorrel) or a four-leaf clover, are soft and downy when mature, distinguishing it from the other species described.

M. quadrifolia. Water clover. A temperate species with origins in subtropical and temperate latitudes, it has been introduced to North America from Britain and Europe, where it has become quite rare. Now well established in several northern states, it is frequently grown in garden pools. The characteris-

tic soft green leaves, which in submerged plants float on the surface, resemble a four-leaf clover and sometimes fold in over each other with the veins forking repeatedly. When young, the leaves are downy, later becoming bare.

MICRANTHEMUM. Scrophulariaceae. The name is derived from the Greek *mikros*, meaning small, and *anthemon*, meaning flower. This is a genus of three species of very small creeping tender aquatics from Central America that form mats of vegetation in conditions of varying water levels.

M. umbrosum. Found in Central America and southeastern North America, this tiny, creeping aquatic suitable for aquarium use has opposite round pale green leaves up to 0.4 in (1 cm) long with creeping stems up to 12 in (30 cm) in length.

MICROSORUM. Polypodiaceae. The name is derived from the Greek *micros*, meaning small, and *soros*, meaning cluster, a reference to the clusters of fruiting bodies on the undersides of the plant's leaves. In this genus of 40 subtropical ferns that colonize shady, damp to aquatic habitats, one species is suitable for submerged culture in aquaria. They are generally categorized as terrestrial plants that will withstand flooding.

M. pteropus [*Polypodium pteropus*]. Java fern. A tropical submerged or terrestrial fern from Southeast Asia, this species has become popular as an aquarium plant because of its high tolerance to low light levels and very attractive appearance. It has a strong green scaly rootstock that should not be planted but placed on a piece of wood or rock. The submerged bright green lanceolate leaves are 2 in (5 cm) wide and 4–12 in (10–30 cm) long.

MYRIOPHYLLUM. Water milfoil. Haloragidaceae. The name is derived from the Greek *myrios*, meaning innumerable, and *phyllon*, meaning a leaf. This cosmopolitan genus of 40 species of submerged aquatics comes mainly from the Southern Hemisphere. The submerged stems are often long, bearing finely divided leaves that are extremely attractive. The genus exhibits a great diversity of habit, from species growing only 1 in (2.5 cm) high to some nearly 10 ft (3 m) long, making it a valuable addition as a decorative oxygenator to either the garden pool or the aquarium.

M. aquaticum [*M. brasiliense, M. proserpinacoides*]. Parrot feather. A popular, slightly tender submerged species from Brazil, Argentina, Chile, Australia, New Zealand, and Java, it is extensively used in aquaria and pools where its graceful foliage is capable of taking root in wet soil above the water and decorating the edges of both formal and informal water features. In temperate pools the foliage is prone to frost damage in severe winters. The stems can grow 20–60 in (50–150 cm) long with leaves 1–2 in (2.5–5 cm) long in whorls of four to six divided into four to eight bright green segments. Aerial parts of the stem develop a much deeper bluish green color with shorter, stiffer leaves that have a velvety shine. Plate 39.

M. filiforme. Frill. This Australian species has very finely divided bright green leaves and has become a popular aquarium plant in recent years.

M. heterophyllum. This hardy species is found widespread in the United States in ponds and sluggish streams. The plant can develop two types of submerged leaves, depending on the temperature. In cooler water 65–70°F (18–21°C), each whorl consists of four to six leaves that divide into nearly 20 segments, reaching a length of 2 in (5 cm). In warmer temperatures, 72–77°F (22–25°C), the leaf length is reduced to 0.75 in (2 cm) long. In conditions of bright light, the leaves can take on a bronze tint. If aerial leaves develop, they are lance-shaped and not divided.

M. hippuroides. Western milfoil, red water milfoil. A tender submerged species from the western United States and Mexico, the very attractive leaf colorations range from olive green to reddish brown, particularly at the tips, depending on the level of illumination. The finely divided leaves occur in whorls of four to six, up to 2 in (5 cm) long, with the petioles at different levels on the stalk. The fragile foliage is a little prone to attracting algae and should be cultivated in a well-filtered pool or aquarium.

M. spicatum. Eurasian water milfoil. A species native to Europe, Asia, and North Africa and widely naturalized, this myriophyllum grows very fast and can reach lengths of 6–10 ft (2–3 m). The plant can grow in fresh to brackish waters, tolerating salt up to 33 percent of sea-water strength. The stems are reddish to brown with olive-green leaves in whorls of three to six. The spikes of white flowers are found in the axils of several leaflike bracts. In the United States, where it is outlawed, thick growths prevent fishing, adversely affect shellfish, interfere with boat traffic, and give an unsightly appearance.

NAJAS. Naiad, water-nymph. Najadaceae. Named after the Naiads, nymphs of rivers or lakes in classical mythology, this genus of 35 cosmopolitan submerged aquatics is characterized by elongated slender stems and the ability to grow in a large variety of underwater conditions, often in depths of up to 16 ft (5 m). The genus has become a nuisance in irrigation ditches and rice fields and is not recommended for outdoor pools. It is a reasonable oxygenator and makes an excellent aquarium plant.

N. guadalupensis [*N. microdon*]. This submerged tender species from North and South America has brittle, slender stems that branch frequently. The dark green wavy leaves are also slender, no more than 0.06 in (0.15 cm) wide and up to 1 in (2.5 cm) long with intermittent toothed edges. The plant makes a good background in aquaria and is attractive to certain fish species for spawning.

NUPHAR. Nymphaeaceae. The name is derived from the Arabic *nailufar*, meaning water lilies. It is a genus of an uncertain number of submerged species (see the discussion in Chapter 11) found in temperate latitudes of the Northern Hemisphere in still or slowly moving water up to 5 ft (1.5 m) deep. Sometimes referred to as pond lilies, their tough, floating leaves bear some similarity to water lilies. They should be regarded as an alternative, however, only when the more decorative water lilies would not succeed because of factors such as acid water, deep water, water movement, or shade. Nuphars have both submerged and floating leaves growing from their stout creeping rootstocks. The submerged leaves are thin, delicate, and curly, justifying their consideration for a large cold-water aquarium. The floating leaves are tough, leathery, and extensively produced, affording refuge and shade in vast areas of natural lakes where they are often seen in association with the common white water lily. The yellow flowers, which stand well above the water, are bowl-shaped, embracing an urn-shaped ovary. The rootstocks can grow to 4 in (10 cm) thick and up to 6 ft (2 m) long with prominent leaf scars. *Nuphar* is also discussed in Chapter 18.

N. japonica. Japanese pond lily. This hardy species from Japan is one of the better choices for aquarium use, having attractive wavy heart-shaped submerged leaves, 3.5 in (9 cm) long and 2.5 in (6 cm) wide, which are a delicate reddish purple color. The cultivar 'Rubrotincta' is possibly the most decorative of all the nuphars, carrying erect surface leaves that are a dark green to coppery color and orange-scarlet flowers. Plate 431.

N. lutea. Yellow water lily. A common hardy species from Europe and western Asia, it has almost transparent alternate submerged leaves, 4–12 in (10–30 cm) long, oval in shape, with a deep sinus. The green floating leaves are 16 in (40 cm) long and 12 in (30 cm) wide, are more pointed than their submerged counterparts, and have a thick leathery texture. The bowl-shaped flower is yellow, about 2 in (5 cm) in diameter, with five yellow sepals and a faint smell of apple. This species will survive in deep and slow-moving water.

N. lutea subsp. *macrophylla* [*N. advena*]. American spatterdock. A North American hardy and variable plant, widespread in the eastern and central United States, Mexico, and the West Indies, it is robust with round yellow flowers with six sepals about 3 in (8 cm) across and bright coppery red stamens. The tough leathery leaves are round to oblong in shape, about 12 in (30 cm) long, standing well above the water. Plate 432.

N. lutea subsp. *polysepala*. A hardy North American plant found mainly in the Northwest from the northern Rocky Mountains to the Pacific Coast, it is a larger-than-average subspecies found in shallow bays, sluggish streams, and backwaters. The plant grows well in shallow water where its long lance-shaped leaves stand erect above the water. The yellow flowers reach 4–5 in (10–13 cm) in diameter.

N. lutea subsp. *pumila* [*N. microphylla*]. This hardy European subspecies is smaller than *N. lutea* and is the easiest of the nuphars to accommodate in a garden pool. The floating leaves generally do not exceed 6 in (15 cm) in either length or width. The flower is also smaller than that of *N. lutea* being 1–1.5 in (2.5–4 cm) across.

N. lutea subsp. *sagittifolia*. Cape Fear spatterdock. A temperate plant from the southeastern United States, particularly the Atlantic coastal states, the submerged foliage—narrow, almost transparent, and lance-shaped—makes it an attractive choice for aquarium use. It produces a few floating green leaves of the same shape and yellow flowers.

NYMPHOIDES. Floating heart. Menyanthaceae. The name is derived from *Nymphaea* and the Greek *eidos*, meaning form, a reference to the similarity of this genus to nymphaeas, or water lilies. A cosmopolitan genus of 20 species of temperate and subtropical submerged aquatics, its members resemble miniature water lilies in their mode of growth. They produce floating leaves with small flowers at the ends of the shoots, and in outdoor ponds they should be contained because of their strong runners.

N. aquatica. Underwater banana plant. Found in the eastern and southern United States, it produces miniature dahlialike tubers resembling a hand of bananas on petioles just below the floating leaves. Its flowers are 0.4–0.75 in (1–2 cm) in diameter. This is the banana plant used extensively in the aquarium trade.

N. cordata. From Newfoundland to Florida, this plant is similar to *N. aquatica* but produces longer, narrower, and more pointed tubers.

N. cristata. White water snowflake. From Java with abundant white flowers about 0.75 in (2 cm) in diameter, this is an excellent plant for water gardens.

N. germinata. Yellow water snowflake, yellow water fringe. From southern Asia, this plant has fuzzy yellow flowers that are about 0.75 in (2 cm) in diameter and are borne freely.

N. humboldtiana. A submerged species from tropical America, it has shiny pale green kidney-shaped floating leaves no wider than 6 in (15 cm) with reddish undersides that arise from runners and erect shoots. Where winters are cold but the pool is in a warm sunny position, it is frequently treated as an annual. In an aquarium it is of value only if surface cover is required. The white flowers have a central yellow tube and five fringed petals that are held above the water surface.

N. hydrocharioides. Orange water snowflake. Found in southern Asia, Africa, northern Australia, and New Guinea, this species is similar to *N. germinata* but rich orange in color instead of yellow. The fuzzy orange-petaled flowers are about 0.75 in (2 cm) in diameter and are freely produced.

N. indica. Water snowflake. From many tropical regions worldwide, this submerged species is slightly hardier than *N. humboldtiana* but almost identical in appearance with the same clusters of white fringed flowers arising from the junction of the leaf and the leaf stalk. Like *N. humboldtiana*, it is also frequently treated as an annual where there are cold winters and sunny summers. The floating leaves are 2–8 in (5–20 cm) in width, roundish, with a heart-shaped base. The plant can survive in water up to 3 ft (1 m) deep by the elongation of the thin petioles. It sometimes carries a bud and cluster of fleshy spurlike roots near the upper part of the petioles, especially during the cooler months in the southern United States.

N. peltata. Yellow floating heart, water fringe, yellow fringe. A hardy submerged species from Europe and introduced to North America, it has naturalized rapidly in rivers such as the Hudson. It is happiest in water 6–18 in (15–45 cm) deep, where it spreads widely by runners carrying the floating mottled heart-shaped leaves, which are about 2 in (5 cm) across. The flowers, held 2–3 in (5–8 cm) above the water, are yellow and fringed. The plant can quickly take over a shallow-water area with a muddy bottom, making an ideal situation for wildlife, but can be too invasive in a decorative setting. Plate 40.

OTTELIA. Hydrocharitaceae. A genus of 21 tropical and subtropical, submerged aquatics from slightly shaded forest locations in Africa and Southeast Asia, its members are very attractive plants grown mainly in aquaria where their interesting leaves can be seen to full advantage.

O. alismoides. A tropical submerged species from North Africa, tropical Asia, and Australia, it has become naturalized in Europe. The long thin round-to-heart-shaped pale green leaves are 4–8 in (10–20 cm) long. The translucent and bulging leaf blades, which are borne on long triangular petioles, have wavy edges and as the leaf matures, turn almost funnel-shaped. The white flowers, which float on the water surface, are held within distinctive winged spathes. Figure 40.

FIGURE 40. *Ottelia alismoides*.

PILULARIA. Pillwort. Marsileaceae. The name is derived from the Latin *pilula*, meaning pill, a reference to the shape of the plant's small fruiting bodies. This genus of six species of temperate aquatic ferns is distributed throughout Europe, the Americas, Australia, and New Zealand. They are mainly wetland species rather than true aquatics but will grow in submerged conditions and are suitable for cold-water aquaria.

P. globulifera. A temperate species from Europe, North Africa, and Australia, it bears, like the genus *Marsilea*, erect strictly sterile fronds and hard hairy fruiting bodies along a long thin rhizome. The slender threadlike leaves, 0.4–3 in (1–8 cm) long, are ta-

pered and do not have the flat leaf blade of *Marsilea*. The general appearance is that of a small grasslike plant, making the plant an interesting contrast in both pools and aquaria, where it is able to withstand a wide range of temperatures.

POTAMOGETON. Potamogetonaceae. The name is derived from the Greek *potamos*, meaning river, and *geiton*, meaning neighbor. This is a genus of 80 to 100 submerged species of temperate regions worldwide. They frequently colonize ditches and waterways, providing a valuable food for waterfowl. Only a few are suitable as decorative pond or aquarium plants as they quickly choke out other growth.

P. crispus. Curled pondweed. This hardy European species makes an excellent oxygenator. The stems can grow to 13 ft (4 m) or more, bearing narrow sessile leaves about 3 in (8 cm) long and 0.2–0.4 in (0.5–1 cm) wide. The leaves are extremely decorative, being almost translucent and wavy-edged, varying from green to reddish brown. This species has become naturalized in North America, where it is widespread in muddy or polluted streams, ponds, and small lakes in the northeastern and north central United States.

P. gayii. This subtropical species from South America is one of the few suitable for aquarium use. The plant bears only long delicate submerged leaves that are olive green to brownish, up to 2.5 in (6 cm), long and 0.1 in (0.3 cm) wide. It is an undemanding plant that is useful as a background to the aquarium, provided its runners are contained.

P. octandrus. A subtropical species from Africa and Asia, it is also suitable for aquaria, where its delicate pale green lanceolate submerged leaves grow to 3 in (8 cm) long and 0.5 in (1.3 cm) wide. Occasionally, floating leaves, which are elliptical in shape and slightly wider and shorter than the submerged leaves, are produced.

P. pectinatus. Fennel-leaved pondweed. A temperate species from Europe and Australia, its long submerged stems can grow 10 ft (3 m) or more and branch liberally to bear very narrow linear green to brownish leaves 0.5–6 in (1.3–15 cm) long and 0.02–0.08 in (0.05-0.2 cm) wide. The rhizomes form underground tubers that are eaten by waterfowl.

RANUNCULUS. Buttercup, crowfoot. Ranunculaceae. The name is derived from the Latin *rana*, meaning little frog, a reference to the plant's preferred habitat's being generally inhabited by frogs. *Ranunculus* is a large cosmopolitan genus of 400 temperate and tropical moisture-loving and aquatic species, of which nearly 40 grow in water. Waterfowl generally enjoy the aquatic species and are responsible for their extensive distribution, some having become invasive. *Ranunculus* is also discussed in Chapters 7 and 8.

R. aquatilis. Water crowfoot, water buttercup. A hardy European and North American submerged species, it grows in still freshwater lakes and swift-flowing streams and rivers in depths up to 2 ft (0.6 m). It can grow at altitudes as high as 3000 ft (900 m). The plant forms dense clumps, 2–3 ft (0.6–1 m) across, with submerged lower leaves divided into numerous fine segments and flatter, almost kidney-shaped, three-lobed floating leaves. In flowing water the stems trail downstream, carrying the attractive white flowers with yellow throats both below and on the surface. It is an excellent oxygenator for pools and cold-water aquaria, where it must have sufficient light to survive the winter. Plate 41.

ROTALA. Lythraceae. The name is thought to be derived from the Latin *rota*, meaning wheel, a reference to the leaf whorls in several species. It is a genus of 45 aquatic species from nearly all tropical regions. As aquarium plants, their beautiful and often highly colored leaves make an impressive display when grouped together. Many species have become a nuisance in rice fields and irrigation channels.

R. macrandra. A tropical species from Southeast Asia and Sri Lanka, its wavy-edged submerged leaves are egg-shaped and highly colorful, olive green to reddish on the upper side and pink to purple on the underside. These colorations vary with the light intensity. It is a very popular aquarium plant.

R. rotundifolia. A tropical species that is widespread throughout Southeast Asia, the submerged leaves occur in pairs and are small and lanceolate, up to 0.5 in (1.3 cm) long and 0.2 in (0.5 cm) wide, pale green on the upper side, and whitish green to reddish on the underside. Any aerial leaves are rounder and greener on both sides. The shoots, when grouped together, make good background clumps growing to about 8 in (20 cm) high.

SAGITTARIA. Arrowhead, swamp potato. Alismataceae. The name is derived from the Latin *sagitta*, meaning an arrow, as many of the species have arrow-shaped leaves. This cosmopolitan genus of 20 species of aquatics is found in a wide variety of habitats but mainly occurs in shallow water in marshes and along muddy shores. Sagittarias are among the best-known and most-popular aquatics for both outdoor and aquarium use. The submerged species are similar in general appearance to *Echinodorus* and *Vallisneria*, with thread- or ribbon-like submerged leaves arising from a basal rosette. Acting as good oxygenators, they place no great de-

mands on special cultivation. The tubers of several species are a rich source of starch. *Sagittaria* is also discussed in Chapter 7.

S. graminea. A temperate species from the eastern United States and Mexico, the submerged leaves make it a very good aquarium subject. The ribbon-like leaves up to 10 in (25 cm) long and 0.5 in (1.3 cm) wide arise from a rosette. Any aerial leaves produced are elliptic to lanceolate and narrowed toward the tip. The flowers are white, usually in groups of five to seven, and are held in a clusterlike inflorescence above the water.

S. lancifolia. Narrow-leaved sagittaria. A large, narrow-leaved plant 3–5 ft (1–1.5 m) in height, it is suitable for the background of a pool. The white flowers are arranged along a spike. Form *ruminoides* (red-stemmed sagittaria) is an interesting natural variation of *S. lancifolia.*

S. latifolia. Duck potato, wapato. A temperate species from North America to northern South America, it was an important food source for Native Americans. Although principally used by the water gardener as a marginal or bog plant, this robust and variable species also performs well in the aquarium, where as a young plant its submerged linear leaves are the attraction. The aerial leaves are lanceolate to arrow-shaped.

S. montevidensis. This striking new species from South America grows about 2 ft (0.6 m) high with 1-in (2.5-cm) three-petaled flowers and three brilliant red spots in the center of each bloom.

S. natans [*S. subulata*]. A temperate species from North America, it is common along the Atlantic Coast from Maine to Florida, growing in brackish tidal mud or silt. It is variable in form but makes an excellent plant for the aquarium on account of its dark green grassy foliage, often crooked, obtuse at the tip. The leaves are 2–12 in (5–30 cm) long but seldom achieve their ultimate length in well-lit aquaria. Young plants appear on runners from the short rootstocks, resulting in a quick carpet of foliage on the aquarium floor. Vigorous plants can produce small egg-shaped floating leaves and sometimes linear aerial leaves with obtuse tips. The white flowers float on the water surface. The variability of the species has led to many forms.

SAMOLUS. Water pimpernel, brookweed. Primulaceae. The members of this cosmopolitan genus of 10 temperate and subtropical amphibious species grow in shallow water, with several species found in brackish water. One or two species are suitable for the aquarium.

S. parviflorus [*S. floribundus*]. Water rose, water cabbage. A temperate amphibious species from North and South America and the West Indies, it is a small fragile plant, reaching only 4 in (10 cm) in height. The bright green leaves form a rosette of 7 to 14 oval leaves with a narrow base 2.5–4 in (6–10 cm) long and 1–1.5 in (2.5–4 cm) wide. The rosette-type growth has given it its common names. In submerged conditions it does not flower unless the day length exceeds 10 to 12 hours.

TILLAEA. See *Crassula*.

VALLISNERIA. Eel grass, tape grass. Hydrocharitaceae. Named after the Italian botanist Antonio Vallisneri (1661–1730), this is a cosmopolitan genus of 10 submerged tropical species that are very popular as decorative oxygenating plants for aquaria in view of their availability and ease of cultivation. Most species cultivated have ribbon- or tapelike leaves with rounded tips that form an attractive green curtain for the back of the tank. Several cultivars and species can give variation in planting. 'Torta', for example, has shorter and broader leaves twisted in close spirals for their entire length.

V. americana has large spirally twisted leaves growing over 36 in (90 cm) long and 0.75 in (2 cm) wide. The female spathe is on a stout scape that is spirally twisted. Although frequently sold for aquaria, *V. americana* does not hold up well.

V. spiralis. Tape grass, Italian vallisneria. A tropical submerged species native to southern Europe and North Africa, it is now widespread in many tropical and subtropical areas. The specific name refers to the spiraling nature of the flower stalk, not to the leaves, as is sometimes thought. One of the most popular aquarium plants, its ribbonlike leaves, growing from rosettes, are 8–32 in (20–80 cm) long and 0.2–0.5 in (0.5–1.3 cm) wide. These leaves can, on first sight, be taken for *Sagittaria* or *Ottelia*, but the parallel leaf venation and a tiny dentation on the tip of the leaf identifies *Vallisneria*. The species has an interesting means of pollination, having separate male and female plants. The male flowers disconnect from the plant to swim on the surface and release their pollen. The female plants elongate their spiral flower stalks so that the flowers can reach the surface and be pollinated. The spiral stem then contracts and the seeds ripen below the surface.

VICTORIA. Nymphaeaceae. Named in honor of Queen Victoria (1819–1901), this is a genus of two species of very large aquatic herbs native to tropical America. *Victoria* is also discussed in Chapters 11 and 18.

V. amazonica [*V. regia*]. Giant water lily, Amazon water lily. First discovered in Peru by German botanist Thaddaeus Haenke in 1801 and subsequently rediscovered on a number of occasions. Plates 42, 433–436.

This extraordinary plant became known to the world only in 1838 when John Lindley, a British botanist, wrote a descriptive account. Seeds were sent to Kew Gardens in the early 1840s, and although a few germinated, they never flowered. The first cultivated flowers were produced in 1849 by Joseph Paxton, head gardener to the 6th Duke of Devonshire at Chatsworth in Derbyshire, England, in the estate's greenhouses.

The almost circular floating glossy green leaves have a netted appearance from above and are usually 4–6 ft (1.2–2 m) across with edges that are turned up vertically 2–8 in (5 and 20 cm) high. Where the leaf stalk joins the leaf blade and again directly opposite, there are gaps in the vertical edge to allow water from tropical storms to drain away quickly. The underside of the leaf is coppery red, heavily veined, and covered with sharp awl-shaped prickles. Prickles also cover the strong leaf stalk that grows from a thick rhizome anchored to the muddy riverbed 4–6 ft (1.2–2 m) below. Great buoyancy is given to the leaves by the projecting veins on the underside, making them strong enough to support an adult provided a thin board is used to distribute the weight evenly. The large fragrant nocturnal flower has a diameter of 10–16 in (25–40 cm) and opens a creamy white, changing to pink then purplish red through successive nights, finally sinking below the water surface on the third day.

Pollination is carried out by beetles, and the resulting fruit, about 6 in (15 cm) in diameter, is thickly covered with spines and contains many pea-sized olive-green seeds that later turn black. In Britain and Europe victorias are treated as annuals and grown in greenhouses. Seed is sown in February or March in small pots of soil which are submerged 2–3 in (5–8 cm) deep at a minimum temperature of 85°F (29°C) in as light a position as possible. As the seedlings grow, they are transplanted into larger pots with the same minimum water temperature and depth over the crown maintained and the air temperature lowered to 75°F (24°C). In April or May they are planted into a container 6 ft (2 m) in diameter and 2 ft (0.6 m) deep in a rich organic soil, 15–18 in (38–45 cm) below the water, at a minimum water temperature of 75–80°F (24–27°C). In order to provide adequate room for the rapid growth of the huge leaves, the planting pool should have an overall diameter of 25 ft (7.5 m). Approximately 3 lb (1.36 kg) of compound fertilizer is added to the container on planting, and 1-lb (0.45-kg) dressings are applied at 14-day intervals during the growing season. If seed is required from the plant for the following year, pollination should be undertaken by hand and a muslin bag tied around the spent flower to prevent the seed from dispersing as the fruit ripens. The ripe fruits are removed in autumn as the plant dies down, and the seed stored in distilled water.

V. cruziana [*V. cruciata*, *V. trikeri*]. Santa Cruz water lily. Named by M. d'Orbigny in 1840 in honor of General Santa Cruz of Bolivia, this species is native to northern Argentina and Paraguay and was introduced into North American gardens around 1894. It succeeds in slightly lower temperatures and flowers earlier than *V. amazonica*. It also differs from *V. amazonica* by having smaller foliage that is a lighter green with purple undersurfaces. Plate 437; see also Figure 70 in Chapter 18.

'Longwood Hybrid' (Plates 438–440) is a cultivar raised at Longwood Gardens, Pennsylvania, in 1961 by crossing *V. amazonica* and *V. cruziana*. In comparison to either parent, this hybrid displays more vigor, larger and stronger leaves, and increased hardiness. The upturned leaf margins are taller, exposing much brighter surfaces on the outer sides. The flowers are larger and more plentifully produced.

Chapter 7

Marginal and Bog Plants

The marginal and bog plants add more interest to a water garden by providing a lush variety of foliage emerging from the shallow water or the muddy pool surrounds. Marginal planting should not crowd or enclose the water, and some margins should be left clear to give variation and highlight the planted areas as well as to allow better access for certain species of wildlife. Varying the space allocated to the different plant groups gives pool margins more appeal. Such planting is better than filling pool margins with uncoordinated individuals. Formal gardens are more likely to require specimen or symmetrical planting. Informal pools, although intended to look as natural as possible, require good composition in the planting scheme to avoid an overgrown mass of foliage or a ribbonlike artificiality.

Many marginal or bog plants are extremely invasive, and their roots should be contained to prevent them from outgrowing their space or spoiling adjacent plants. Container planting on shallow shelves helps to alleviate this problem and also allows easier removal or repositioning. The optimum depth of water over root systems is quite critical for certain species, and container planting makes this easier to achieve.

Greater density of planting is required in wildlife pools as the rampant, intermingling growth gives cover for nesting or feeding. Planting beds, as described in Chapter 3, may be more appropriate in this situation because they give a degree of control over the planting and at the same time allow a mat of vegetation to form near the water. Choosing the right species is important, planting not only those that will attract the particular type of wildlife desired but also those that will provide a restful plant mix rather than a chaotic one.

The plants listed in this group must not be confused with the bog plants sometimes found in aquatic catalogs. These catalogs frequently combine moisture-loving plants with bog plants, and their tolerance of water around the roots is quite different. Bog plants and marginal plants, unlike moisture-loving plants, thrive in totally saturated or submerged soils, a condition that would cause the extensive range of moisture-lovers to quickly succumb. Generally, the marginal plant will not tolerate a deep covering of water over the roots: 12 in (30 cm) is the maximum tolerance before the plant is categorized as a deep-water aquatic. The vast majority of marginal plants appreciate shallow water 2–6 in (5–15 cm) deep.

The appeal of foliage emerging from the water is difficult to resist, and visiting as many water gardens as possible to note successes and mistakes will aid in the selection of species. Marginal planting provides a unique opportunity to use the reflection at the base of the foliage. Such an opportunity for enhancing color, form, and variegation should not be wasted.

Certain genera such as *Sparganium* may be prohibited in some states, and it is advisable to seek further information from the relevant state authority before introducing any prolific marginal aquatic species.

ACORUS. Araceae. A name used by Theophrastus for a plant with an aromatic rhizome. A genus of two hardy species originating in eastern Asia and widespread in the Northern Hemisphere, it grows in the shallow margins of lakes and ponds. The swordlike leaves, which bear a strong resemblance to iris, have a quite distinctive and not unpleasant smell when bruised.

A. calamus. Sweet flag. A hardy, vigorous species from Southeast Asia naturalized in Europe and North America, it makes a good cover for waterfowl in a wildlife pond. The vigorous but plain leafy growth can be kept within bounds much easier than the typhas (reedmaces or cattails). The plant grows 2–3 ft (0.6–1 m) high with long glossy swordlike leaves that have a distinct midrib and crinkling along part of one edge. The unusual flower is a conical spadix that resembles a small horn emerging laterally just below the tip of a leaf. The rhizomatous and aromatic root has been used extensively for medicinal purposes.

'Variegatus' (variegated sweet flag) is a much superior plant for ornamental pools, where its cream-striped swordlike foliage, about 2–3 ft (0.6–1 m) high, makes a striking impact in the pool margin, particularly in spring. This cultivar is much more slow-growing and compact than *A. calamus*, carrying the same small flower spike, but the foliage is not so highly scented when bruised. Plate 43.

A. gramineus. Japanese rush, grassy-leaved sweet flag. This hardy species from Japan and eastern Asia grows in very shallow water at the edges of streams and pools. The grassy pointed dark green foliage grows in two quite distinct angled ranks about 8–12 in (20–30 cm) high. The flower is inconspicuous.

'Aureovariegatus', an attractive variegated cultivar of the Japanese rush, makes an excellent decorative plant for the margins of small pools in shallow water no more than 2–3 in (5–8 cm) deep. It also makes a good subject for sink or tub gardens. The grassy leaves grow to 9 in (23 cm) high with liberally striped cream or yellow markings.

'Albovariegatus' (syn. 'Argenteostriatus') is almost identical to 'Aureovariegatus' but has a white stripe in the variegation rather than cream or yellow. It is a very attractive low-growing plant for water gardens.

ALISMA. Water plantain. Alismataceae. A genus of nine species of hardy aquatics found mainly on the muddy edges of lakes and marshes, it has a worldwide distribution mainly in the Northern Hemisphere. The leaves have long petioles and spoonlike blades resembling the common terrestrial plantain. The flowers are borne in a pyramidal inflorescence.

A. gramineum. Narrow-leaved water plantain. This is a hardy aquatic species from Europe, North Africa, Asia, and central North America that when submerged has long narrow pointed leaves. When the plant grows above the water, they become more oblong or spoon shaped. The flowers are pinkish white and form a tight spike.

A. lanceolatum. A hardy species from Europe, North Africa, and central and southwestern Asia, it has attractive blue-green long petiolate and lanceolate leaves about 16 in (40 cm) in length with pointed tips, narrowing gradually at the base and growing from a basal rosette. The flowers are pinkish white. It is less rampant than *A. plantago-aquatica* var. *parviflorum*.

A. plantago-aquatica [*A. plantago*]. Water plantain. A widespread hardy species found in most temperate latitudes, it prefers very shallow water but is capable of surviving when submerged to 18 in (45 cm) and persisting in drying mud after the water level falls. It is a striking plant with bold long-stalked leaves growing up to 2 ft (0.6 m) long from a basal rosette. The rounded to cordate leaf blades have prominent ribbed longitudinal veins similar to the common terrestrial plantain. The pinkish white flowers grow in pyramidal panicles that yield masses of seeds that are capable of floating and spreading for some distance. If grown on muddy shores of ponds, young seedlings can become invasive.

The variety *parviflorum* (syn. *A. parviflora*) from North America thrives best with only 0.5 in (1.3 cm) of water above the crown. It is an attractive, hardy variety with neat pyramidal panicles of small whitish pink flowers. The leaves are slightly smaller and rounder than those of *A. plantago-aquatica*, frequently taking on a skeletonized appearance after falling in the water. The plant grows 15–18 in (38–45 cm) high.

ALOCASIA. Elephant's ear. Araceae. This genus of 70 species of tropical moisture-loving plants with short underground stems originates in tropical Asia. The genus is closely related to *Caladium* and *Colocasia*. A few species thrive in shallow water and along the boggy margins of tropical pools, creating bold, striking foliage displays and an occasional show of their typical aroid flowers which closely resemble *Zantedeschia*.

A. macrorrhiza [*A. indica*]. A native of Sri Lanka and India to Malaysia, this vigorous species has stout stems growing to 6 ft (2 m) or more. The deep green arrow-shaped leathery leaves have leaf blades 2 ft (0.6 m) long and petioles 3 ft (1 m) long. The green to yellowish aroidlike flower is 6–9 in (15–23 cm) long. The species thrives only if the water depth is no more than 3–4 in (8–10 cm).

ANUBIAS. See *Anubias afzelii*, Chapter 6.

BIDENS. See *Bidens beckii*, Chapter 6.

BUTOMUS. Butomaceae. The name is derived from the Greek *bous*, meaning an ox, and *temno*, meaning to cut, a reference to the reputed capability of the leaves to cut the mouths of grazing stock. A single-species genus of hardy shallow-water or bog plants, it is found widely distributed in Europe, western Asia, and North Africa and has naturalized in North America along the St. Lawrence River near Montreal. The plant is often found solitary in the water in association with typhas (reedmaces, cattails). It is an elegant species that is widely used as a decorative marginal plant.

B. umbellatus. Flowering rush. This attractive species has very long dark green pointed narrow leaves, sometimes twisted, that are up to 3 ft (1 m) long and 0.5 in (1.3 cm) wide with sheathed triangular bases. The round flower stalks are borne in leaf axils up to 5 ft (1.5 m) high with large individual umbels of conspicuous reddish white flowers. An extremely elegant plant, it thrives best in rich mud or shallow water no deeper than 3–5 in (8–13 cm). Plate 44.

CALLA. Araceae. The name is derived from the Greek *kallos*, meaning beauty. A single-species genus of hardy shallow-water plants from central and northern Europe, northern Asia, and North America, it occurs in wet woods, swamps, and bogs.

C. palustris. Bog arum. A charming creeping plant for the very edge of the water, its long conspicuous creeping rhizome drapes neatly over the boggy surrounds. The rhizome grows 6–20 in (15–50 cm) long and bears roundish shiny heart-shaped pointed leaves that are firm and leathery. The aroidlike white flowers resemble small arum lilies but are much smaller and rather flattened. The flowers, which are pollinated by water snails, develop into bright spikes of scarlet berries. The plant thrives only with no more than 2 in (5 cm) of water over its crown. Plate 45.

CALTHA. Marsh marigold. Ranunculaceae. This is a widespread, temperate genus of 10 marsh or bog-loving species that are extremely popular as decorative bog plants.

C. leptosepala. A lesser-known hardy species from western North America, it has great potential as a decorative plant for pool margins. The solitary silvery white flowers emerge from leafless flower stalks carried above deep green radical leaves.

C. palustris. Marsh marigold, kingcup, cowslip. A widespread species found in marshy meadows and along the margins of streams and ditches in temperate and cold regions of the Northern Hemisphere, it ranks justifiably as one of the most popular decorative aquatics for the side of an ornamental stream or pool. The plants normally reach 6–12 in (15–30 cm) high with long-stalked lower leaves and sessile upper leaves. The nearly round leaves are heart-shaped at the base and have dentate margins.

The beautiful waxy yellow buttercuplike flowers can be produced as early as February in mild winters but generally are at their peak in April, when their five petaloid sepals brighten the spring scene, particularly when contrasted with dwarf blue waterside bulbs. They look best in groups at the very edge of the water, withstanding waterlogged or even slightly submerged conditions in winter and a degree of drying out in the summer. Plate 46.

The variety *alba* (white marsh marigold) is a most attractive plant from the Himalayas, varying from the type in having white flowers with bright yellow centers and more compact growth. It is very prone to mildew. Plate 47.

'Flore Plena' (double marsh marigold), a double form of the type, covers the foliage with a mass of double yellow flowers, often producing a second flush later in the summer.

The variety *palustris* (giant marsh marigold) is a much more vigorous form for the larger pool. The plant can send its large yellow flowers on long stems up nearly 3 ft (1 m). The dark green leaves are as much as 10–12 in (25–30 cm) across, forming strong hummocks of foliage that can flourish in shallow water up to 4–5 in (10–13 cm) deep.

CANNA. Cannaceae. This genus of nine species native to tropical and subtropical America is made up of terrestrial plants with certain species cultivated and hybridized for use as partially submerged decorative plants.

C. americanallis var. *variegata*. Variegated canna. This canna grows to 6 ft (2 m) in height and has large green leaves striped with yellow. The flowers are a brilliant orange. It grows in moist soil or in as much as 6 in (15 cm) of water.

C. glauca. A native of Brazil, this species has been hybridized for use in decorative water displays. It has long slender stems growing 4–6 ft (1.2–2 m) with grayish lanceolate pointed leaves with whitish margins up to 18 in (45 cm) long. The flowers are yellow in a simple raceme, intermittently produced throughout the summer. Longwood Gardens in Pennsylvania has produced cultivars that are an improvement in density of flower and variation in color. Cultivars include 'Endeavor' (bright red), 'Erebus' (salmon-pink), 'Ra' (yellow), and 'Taney' (burnt orange). These are best grown in a sunny position in containers of rich soil and submerged no deeper than 12 in (30 cm). They make striking, colorful specimen plants.

CAREX. Sedge. Cyperaceae. The name is derived from the Greek *keiro*, meaning to cut, a reference to the plant's minutely toothed leaf margins, which are capable of cutting a hand. A large cosmopolitan genus of 1000 species of mainly temperate marsh plants preferring slightly acid conditions, it includes some species capable of thriving in shallow water. They are rhizomatous perennials with grasslike linear narrow leaves often finely serrated with triangular flower stalks bearing flowers in brownish spikes.

C. elata [*C. stricta*] **'Aurea'**. Bowles' golden sedge. One of the most decorative sedges of all for the water garden, this plant is for lovers of graceful yellow foliage at the water's edge. Growing to a height of 15 in (38 cm), it has tufts of bright grassy foliage. The brownish flower spikes, interspersed in the foliage, are rather inconspicuous. Although happy in very shallow water, it also succeeds in moist soil that is never allowed to dry out. Plate 48.

'Variegata', a variegated grasslike plant for shallow water up to 4 in (10 cm) in depth, grows 1–2.5 ft (0.3–0.8 m) tall and has attractive leaves striped in white and green.

C. pendula. Pendulous sedge. A native of west central and southern Europe, this elegant plant requires space to exhibit its delightful long spikes of pendulous flowers held on stems 3 ft (1 m) long, which are particularly effective when seen against the water. The rather straplike grassy foliage forms tufts 2–3 ft (0.6–1 m) high from which emerge the handsome drooping spikes of brown flowers. The plant thrives with no more than a very shallow covering of water over the roots.

C. pseudocyperus. A hardy species from Europe, North America, Asia, and Australia, this is one of the better and more graceful species for ornamental planting with its bright green grassy leaves 2–3 ft (0.6–1 m) long and interesting flowers in the form of drooping dark green spikelets that bloom in June. The plant is similar to *Cyperus alternifolius*, commonly known as umbrella plant.

C. riparia. Great pond sedge. A coarse plant growing nearly 60 in (150 cm) high, it has an acutely triangular stem and leaf blades with a deep midrib. A vigorous species, it often forms dense masses of foliage supporting a further cluster of leaves and flowers above. Although not a species for cultivation in the ornamental water garden, exceptional cultivars have been derived from it. Plate 49.

COLOCASIA. Taro. Araceae. A genus of seven tropical species from Asia, it consists of striking plants, often large, with thick erect stems and radical heart-shaped leaves. Like the alocasias, which they resemble, certain species thrive in shallow water and make bold architectural specimen plants.

C. affinis. From the tropical eastern Himalayas (Sikkim to Burma), this species has slender yellow flowers and ovate leaves with purple markings between the veins. The variety *jenningsii* 'Black Princess' has dark green foliage overlaid with black.

C. esculenta. Green taro. The plant forms an erect tuberous rootstock with ringlike scars on the surface where the leaves have fallen off. This species occurs wild in Burma and Assam and has been cultivated for its roots for 2000 years in Southeast Asia. It is a variable species that produces long-stalked heart-shaped to arrow-shaped leaves that resemble elephant ears. The leaf stalks are 3–10 in (8–25 cm) long and the leaf blade is up to 3 ft (1 m) in length. The leaves vary in color, often having prominent veins, giving an ornamental value. The flowers are insignificant spathes in the summer. Plate 50.

'Fontanesii' is a striking cultivar with heart-shaped leaves with dark green veining and leaf margins and violet leaf stalks. 'Hilo Beauty' (variegated taro) has white mottling on green leaves. 'Illustris' (imperial taro, black caladium) has attractive spots on its large leaves and violet leaf stalks.

C. violacea. Violet-stemmed taro. This species reaches 3–5 ft (1–1.5 m) in height and has deep violet stems.

COTULA. Compositae. The name is derived from the Greek *kotule*, meaning a small cup, a reference to the bases of the plant's leaves, which form a cup. A cosmopolitan genus of 75 mainly terrestrial species found mostly in the Southern Hemisphere, it has one species that can be considered a true aquatic.

C. coronopifolia. Water buttons, golden buttons, brass buttons. A hardy species from southern Africa, it has been widely introduced into Europe and North America. Essentially a swamp species, it can be found growing submerged in water up to 18 in (45 cm) deep, forming large dense floating masses on the surface with long roots reaching the mud below. The plant is more attractive when grown in shallow water where its smooth almost succulent stems, 6–12 in (15–30 cm) high, bear clasping, smooth, strongly scented toothed leaves, 0.5 in (1.3 cm) across, and masses of round bright disclike yellow flowers, 0.5 in (1.3 cm) in diameter. In temperate areas it dies down in winter, producing masses of seeds that regenerate easily and colonize large areas. It makes a cheerful, bright display along ornamental pool edges in water no deeper than 3–4 in (8–10 cm). Plate 51.

CRINUM. Crinum lily, spider lily. Liliaceae. The name is derived from the Greek *krinon*, meaning lily. This genus of 130 attractive bulbous species occurs widely in tropical areas. A few species are aquatic and make striking specimen plantings in shallow water around decorative tropical pools.

C. americanum. Southern swamp lily, southern swamp crinum. Native of wet places in Florida and along the Gulf Coast to Texas, this species has narrow leaves up to 2 in (5 cm) wide and 18–24 in (45–60 cm) long. The flowers are long petaled, white, and very fragrant. It will grow in up to 12 in (30 cm) of water.

C. purpurascens. Native to tropical Africa, this striking and attractive plant has a bulbous, truncated stem bearing a rosette of straplike leaves up to 18 in (45 cm) long and 0.75 in (2 cm) wide. The tubular flowers, which are white and tinged with red, are held in a large umbel. The plant flourishes in a rich soil with 4–6 in (10–15 cm) of water over the bulb.

CYPERUS. Umbrella sedge. Cyperaceae. A genus of 600 predominantly tropical species of wide distribution, it has just a few temperate species. They are cultivated for their decorative value in the bog garden and shallow-water areas.

C. alternifolius. Umbrella plant, umbrella palm. A tender species from Madagascar, it is frequently sold as a decorative pot plant. In warm sheltered pools in subtropical and tropical gardens it makes an elegant marginal plant growing 1–3 ft (0.3–1 m) high, crowned with numerous dark green radiating leaves. There are two cultivars of decorative merit: 'Gracilis', dwarfer and more slender, and 'Variegatus', with creamy white striping running lengthwise along the stems and leaves.

C. eragrostis [*C. vegetus*]. A hardy species from Chile, it has broad grasslike foliage with green spikelets. Plant it in 2–4 in (5–10 cm) of water.

C. haspan. Dwarf papyrus. This dwarf from tropical central Asia resembles a miniature *C. papyrus* but is much more manageable, growing 12–18 in (30–45 cm). This species makes an attractive specimen plant for both formal and informal pools, where it thrives with 2 in (5 cm) of water over the crown. The very interesting and attractive viviparous form of *C. haspan* produces young plantlets on the mophead umbels of flowers.

C. longus. Sweet galingale. This hardy European and North American native is an attractive colonizer of muddy banks. Its solitary, almost triangular stems grow 2–4 ft (0.6–1.2 m) and bear interesting bright green stiffly ribbed leaves that radiate from the top like umbrella ribs interspersed with brown spikelets. It grows best in water 2–4 in (5–10 cm) deep.

C. papyrus. Egyptian paper reed, giant papyrus. A native of tropical Africa, it forms huge stands of vegetation alongside rivers in the African interior. This species makes a tall elegant plant when grown in sheltered tropical situations or in a high-roofed conservatory in temperate areas. It produces an exten-

sive thick rhizomatous rootstock with long triangular pithy stems growing 12–15 ft (3.5–4.5 m) tall bearing mop-head tufts of fine long pendulous leaves and an umbel of greenish brown flower spikelets. The plant can become very straggly in areas of poor light, and its graceful elegance is easily spoiled by wind. Plate 52.

DACTYLORHIZA. Orchidaceae. The name is derived from the Greek *daktylos*, meaning finger, and *rhiza*, a root. It is a genus of 30 species of deciduous terrestrial orchids from Europe, Asia, North America, and North Africa. Other *Dactylorhiza* species are discussed in Chapter 8.

D. maculata. Heath spotted orchid. Growing 6–24 in (15–60 cm) tall, this member of the orchid family is native to Great Britain. The flower spike is dense with large flowers that vary from pale pink to pale purple and white with crimson blotches. The green linear to lanceolate leaves are often spotted. It requires an acid soil and boggy conditions.

DAMASONIUM. Alismataceae. A genus of six temperate species of shallow-water aquatics from Europe, North Africa, southern Australia, and western North America, it resembles *Alisma* with its long-stalked floating leaves with elliptic to ovate blades and heart-shaped base emerging from a cormlike rootstock.

D. alisma. Star fruit. A marginal species that only flourishes in shallow water less than 6 in (15 cm) deep, it can survive temporary drying out in the summer. The long-petioled leaves have lanceolate to ovate blades up to 4 in (10 cm) long. The attractive whorled inflorescence consists of white or pink flowers with a yellow spot at the base of each petal. The interesting fruit forms a starlike shape comprising six pointed carpels. The plant is not widely available in the trade, but when it can be obtained it makes a good marginal for the small informal pool.

DECODON. Lythraceae. The name is derived from the Greek *deka*, meaning ten, and *odous*, meaning a tooth, a reference to the plant's 10-toothed calyx. A single-species genus of vigorous marginal aquatics from North America, it has long angular recurving stems that produce spongy bark tissue on the submerged parts. The stems are normally 3–6 ft (1–2 m) long, often rooting at their tips as they grow and bend over.

D. verticillatus. Swamp loosestrife, water willow. A common species of North American water plant, it is found growing in the margins of ponds and streams, particularly in the eastern United States. The almost sessile lanceolate leaves, 2–5 in (5–13 cm) long, are borne on long arching stems, which make it very suitable for wildlife cover in the margins of a large informal pool. The whorls of pink tubular flowers are held in the leaf axils. The foliage is particularly dramatic in the autumn when the leaves turn a brilliant crimson before defoliating in the first frosts. It is prohibited in many areas.

DULICHIUM. Cyperaceae. This one-species genus of the sedge family occurs in North America.
D. arundinaceum. Water bamboo. Not a true bamboo but a fine, hardy plant for the background or corners of a pool, it produces 1–3 ft (0.3–1 m) stalks that somewhat resemble bamboo. The flowers are tiny and insignificant. It will grow in up to 8 in (20 cm) of water.

EQUISETUM. Horsetail, scouring rush. Equisetaceae. This genus of about 25 species of perennial herbs is widely distributed in wet places except in Australia and New Zealand. The stems are sometimes used in polishing.
E. hyemale. Common scouring rush, horsetail. An evergreen, staying green all winter, this species grows to 4 ft (1.2 m) in height. The hollow leafless stems are furrowed with 14 to 40 ridges. Native to Eurasia and western North America, it grows in moist soil to 8 in (20 cm) of water. A brownish pollen cone, somewhat resembling that of some of the mosses, is produced at the tip of the spikes. Great care must be taken in its introduction to gardens as it can spread prolifically and is not easy to control. Plant it in a container.

ERIOPHORUM. Wool grass, cotton grass. Cyperaceae. The name is derived from the Greek *erion*, meaning wool, and *phoreo*, meaning to bear, a reference to its common name of wool grass or cotton grass. A genus of 20 species, it is characteristically found in bogs, marshes, and the shallow-water margins of pools and lakes in most North Temperate regions. The plants have flat grasslike leaves and creeping rootstocks.
E. angustifolium. Cotton grass. A widespread temperate species, it is conspicuous when carrying tassels of white cottonlike flowers on short leafy stems usually no more than 12 in (30 cm) high. Common on acid moorland, it prefers to be cultivated on acid soil and covered by shallow water no deeper than 2 in (5 cm). Plate 53.
E. latifolium. A less-common species with rough flattened leaves that are wider than those of *E. angustifolium*, its drooping flower spikelets have dark purplish green scales.

E. russelianum [*E. russeolum*]. A distinctive and most attractive species found in North America, it grows to about 18 in (45 cm) tall with bright reddish brown bristles carried on solitary purplish brown spikelets.

GLYCERIA. Manna grass, sweet grass. Gramineae. The name is derived from the Greek, *glykys*, meaning sweet, a reference to the flavor of the seeds in some species. A widespread genus of 16 temperate species of aquatic grasses that quickly colonize the edges of streams, ponds, and waterways, it spreads rapidly and needs to be kept in check. One variegated species is worthy of consideration for ornamental planting.
G. maxima var. variegata. Variegated water grass. One of the most striking and easily grown variegated waterside grasses, it reaches a height of 2 ft (0.6 m). The leaves are striped green, white, and cream with pink flushes in spring and autumn. It grows in water up to 5 in (13 cm) deep and is very invasive if not confined in containers. Plate 54.

HETERANTHERA. Mud plantain. Pontederiaceae. The name is derived from the Greek *heteros*, meaning different, and the Latin *anthera*, meaning anthers. It is a genus of 10 species of small aquatics from tropical and subtropical America and Africa that grow in shallow water. The hardier forms make good marginal plants for small ponds while the tender species are used in aquaria (see *Heteranthera* in Chapter 6).
H. reniformis. Mud plantain. A tender species from South and tropical North America north to Texas and Connecticut, its scrambling habit makes it useful as a marginal plant for the edges of informal pools. Long branching stems bear smooth petiolate kidney-shaped leaves about 1 in (2.5 cm) across. Bunches of insipid pale blue flowers are occasionally produced.

HIBISCUS. Mallow, rose mallow, giant mallow. Malvaceae. This genus consists of about 250 species of herbs, shrubs, and trees in temperate and tropical regions. Two species are suitable for the water garden.
H. militaris. Soldier rose mallow, halberd-leaved rose mallow. Found in wet woods from Pennsylvania to Minnesota, south to Florida and west to Texas, it grows 5–7 ft (1.5–2.2 m) high with flowers 4–6 in (10–15 cm) across that are pink with red centers.
H. moscheutos. Common rose mallow, swamp rose mallow, mallow rose, swamp hibiscus. Found in marshes in the eastern United States from Massachusetts to Michigan and south to Florida and

Alabama, it grows 4–8 ft (1.2–2.5 m) high with flowers 6–10 in (15–25 cm) across in red, pink, or white.

HOUTTUYNIA. Saururaceae. Named after the Dutch naturalist Martin Houttuyn (1720–1794), it is a single-species genus of temperate aquatics from eastern Asia that flourishes in the wet marginal soils of pools and streams.

H. cordata. A hardy marginal or bog plant, it grows to a height of 18–20 in (45–50 cm). The broadly ovate bluish green leaves with heart-shaped bases grow on red stems that give off a very pungent scent of orange when crushed. Four white bracts subtend its sturdy terminal spike of small white flowers. The invasive rhizomes spread rapidly in moist soil at the edge of a pond. Any covering of water should be no deeper than 1–2 in (2.5–5 cm). 'Plena', a double-flowered cultivar, is showier and slightly easier to keep in bounds than the single form.

'Variegata' (syn. 'Chameleon') is striking, with vividly colored leaves splashed with crimson, green, and cream. The plant requires full sun to show off its full potential and has become popular through its ability to grow in ordinary border conditions. Severe winters are apt to take their toll if the root run is not deep enough for roots to escape prolonged freezing. Plate 55.

HYDROCLEYS. Limnocharitaceae. The name is derived from the Greek *hydor*, meaning water, and *kleis*, meaning key. It is a genus of nine tropical species from South America that are usually partly floating and partly rooted in still shallow water.

H. nymphoides. Water poppy. A tender decorative species from Brazil, it is widely cultivated in outdoor pools in tropical and subtropical areas and in greenhouses in temperate areas. The plant has thick, shiny, deep green broadly heart-shaped oval leaves 2–4 in (5–10 cm) across on long trailing stems up to 3 ft (1 m) long. The prolific but short-lived attractive flowers are light yellow with a red-and-brown center, 2–2.5 in (5–6 cm) across, and stand well above the water surface. Although it survives in up to 12–15 in (30–38 cm) of water, it does best in shallow conditions of 6 in (15 cm) of water in a rich soil. Plate 56.

HYDROCOTYLE. Water pennywort. Umbelliferae. The name is derived from the Greek *hydor*, meaning water, and *cotyle*, meaning a cavity, a reference to the plant's leaves' being hollowed out like cups. It is a cosmopolitan genus of 75 species of temperate and subtropical slender creeping marginal plants that sometime bear small tubers.

H. americana. A semihardy species found in ditches, streams, and along the edges of ponds in the southern United States, it can be used in the water garden or aquarium. In pools with natural bottoms it can be invasive.

H. vulgaris. Pennywort. A hardy species from Europe and North Africa, it has a thin trailing rooting stem 4–16 in (10–40 cm) long. The leaves, which have hairy undersides, are about 0.3–1.5 in (0.8–4 cm) in diameter, and the petiole joins the leaf blade in the center of the leaf. The small inconspicuous flowers are whitish or pink and are held on small stalks. Although not an outstandingly decorative plant, it can be used as an effective cover plant for wildlife in muddy margins. It is frequently used as an aquarium plant.

HYMENOCALLIS. Amaryllidaceae. The name is derived from the Greek *hymen*, meaning membrane, and *kallos*, meaning beauty, a reference to the membrane that unites the stamens. It is a genus of 40 tropical species of bulbous plants from North and South America with one species from West Africa. Most species enjoy moist terrestrial conditions, and one has been found to thrive in shallow water.

H. caribaea **'Variegata'**. Variegated spider lily. This spider lily from the West Indies has impressive green-and-white striped foliage and grows up to 2 ft (0.6 m) in height. It grows in moist soil or up to 6 in (15 cm) of water.

H. caroliniana [*H. occidentalis*]. Spider lily. A tender American bulbous aquatic, it grows to 24 in (60 cm), thriving in shallow water. This species has thick straplike leaves and an umbel of three to six interesting spiderlike white flowers that are strongly scented.

H. crassifolia [*H. liriosme*]. Spider lily. Native to the Gulf Coast states from Florida to Texas, this member of the amaryllis family generally grows to about 18 in (45 cm) in height but can reach up to 4 ft (1.2 m) when conditions are ideal. The impressive white flower has a cuplike center with six narrow radiating lobes comprised of three petals and three petal-like sepals. It grows in moist soil or up to 6 in (15 cm) of water.

HYPERICUM. St. John's wort. Guttiferae. The name is derived from the Greek *hyper*, meaning above, and *eikon*, image. A genus of 400 cosmopolitan species, it includes one aquatic species suitable for shallow pool margins.

H. elodes. Marsh hypericum. Native to western Europe, this is the one hypericum species that is not only tolerant of temporary flooding but is habitually found in water. The reddish stems, which grow 6–12 in (15–30 cm) long, form an attractive mat of small round perfoliate leaves that are thickly covered with soft hairs, creating an overall glaucous appearance. The small soft yellow saucer-shaped flowers, about 0.5 in (1.3 cm) across, are borne in clusters. An excellent carpeting plant for the pool edge, it can withstand as much as 2–3 in (5–8 cm) of water above its crown.

IRIS. Iris, flag, fleur-de-lis. Iridaceae. The name is derived from the Greek messenger Iris, who came to earth via a rainbow. It is a large, widely distributed genus of mainly temperate moisture-loving plants. The genus is one of the most important plant groups in the water garden: their leaves form the framework of formal and informal schemes alike. They have a wide range of moisture requirement, and only a few species (discussed here) are capable of thriving in shallow water. Other species are described in Chapter 8.

I. laevigata. A native of Japan and eastern Siberia, this species is one of the finest marginal irises for shallow water. The plant blooms in early summer with blue flowers, grows 2–3 ft (0.6–1 m) in height, and forms clumps of sword-shaped smooth green leaves that lack a distinct midrib. It must not be allowed to dry out. Although at home in shallow water of 3–4 in (8–10 cm), it also thrives in permanently wet soil. Plate 57.

There are several excellent cultivars available: 'Alba', with white flowers; 'Albo-purpurea', white flowers with purple-red streaks on the falls; 'Colchesterensis', with large white flowers heavily mottled with dark blue on the edges of the falls; 'Cowee', with very pale blue, almost white flowers; 'Mottled Beauty', with white flowers mottled with blue; 'Queen of Violets', with deep violet flowers; 'Semperflorens', with cobalt blue flowers; 'Snowdrift', with white flowers with pale yellow petal bases; and 'Variegata', with pale lavender-blue flowers and lovely cream-and-white-striped foliage, making it one of the most sought-after marginal aquatics.

I. pseudacorus. Yellow flag. A native of Britain, North Africa, and Asia Minor, this species is one of the most common marginal aquatics for large ponds. The strong, stiff bluish green swordlike leaves emerge from a vigorous rhizome, are 1 in (2.5 cm) wide, and grow to 3 ft (1 m). The flowers are yellow, 3–3.5 in (8–9 cm) across, with radiating brownish veins and a deeper orange spot in the throat. An ideal species for the margins of wildlife ponds, it grows in 6–9 in (15–23 cm) of water. The following cultivars represent improved selections: 'Bastardii',

with creamy yellow flowers, not as vigorous as the type; 'Flore Pleno', with double flowers, also slightly less vigorous than the type; 'Golden Queen', which produces golden yellow flowers in greater quantity and with more restrained leaf growth than the type; 'Sulphur Queen', which freely produces sulfur-yellow flowers; and 'Variegata', an excellent cultivar that can be justified even in a small pool because of its striking creamy-striped variegation that appears in the spring and gradually fades as summer advances. The flowers are similar to the type but growth is more subdued.

I. versicolor. A North American native, this free-flowering species is similar in vigor to *I. laevigata* and requires either permanently wet soil or up to 4 in (10 cm) of water above the crown. The flowers are violet-blue with yellow patches at the petal bases. The swordlike leaves grow about 24 in (60 cm) high. 'Kermesina', an outstanding cultivar with beautiful rich purple-and-white flowers, is very suitable for small ponds.

JUNCUS. Rush, bog rush. Juncaceae. A cosmopolitan genus of 225 species, it is more common in the Northern Hemisphere, mainly occurring in marshes and bogs. A few species occur in water. They prefer very damp, mostly wet banks where they grow in groups. Commonly referred to as rushes, they have a habit and general appearance similar to grasses, often with flattened leaves sheathed at the base. The majority have little justification for inclusion in an ornamental garden, but a few species have interesting or decorative features that warrant their consideration.

J. effusus. Soft rush, Japanese mat rush. Forming ornamental tufts or clumps of green spikes up to 3 ft (1 m) tall, this species is used in naturalized landscapes. It produces brown flower spikes and tolerates 3–5 in (8–13 cm) of water. In Japan the dried stems of this species are woven into tatami, the ubiquitous floor mats of Japanese houses.

'Spiralis' (corkscrew rush) is a hardy cultivar with dark green needlelike leaves that are contorted and corkscrewlike, growing to 18 in (45 cm) high. It is less invasive than the parent species, and its curious form of growth makes it striking on the verges of a small pond. It should have no more than 3–5 in (8–13 cm) of water over its crown.

'Vittatus' is an attractive variegated cultivar that grows to about 30 in (75 cm) with long thick needlelike leaves striped with yellow. It is rather prone to reverting to ordinary green leaves, which should be removed as soon as they are noticed.

J. ensifolius. A charming small hardy species, it grows 12–18 in (30–45 cm), producing neat tufts of grassy foliage and attractive round brown flower spikes. It will not tolerate water deeper than 2–3 in (5–8 cm).

LUDWIGIA. Onagraceae. Named in honor of Professor C. G. Ludwig (1709–1773) of Leipzig, Germany, it is a cosmopolitan genus of 75 temperate and subtropical species of moisture-loving and wetland plants, including several species suitable for aquarium cultivation. The species listed below are suitable for marginal planting of wildlife ponds. Other *Ludwigia* species are discussed in Chapter 6.

L. longifolia. Primrose willow. A Brazilian and Argentinian species, it has yellow flowers and glaucous green lanceolate leaves growing on erect red stems reaching 4–6 ft (1.2–2 m) high. The plant grows with up to 6–12 in (15–30 cm) of water above the crown.

L. palustris. Water purslane, creeping water primrose, primrose creeper. This hardy species departs from the usual use of ludwigias in aquaria. This species is found in Europe, North America, Asia, and Africa, forming mats of partially submerged vegetation along the margins of shallow ponds, streams, and marshes. The creeping or floating branched stems range 2–12 in (5–30 cm) in length, rooting at the nodes and producing shiny oval short-stalked leaves, up to 1 in (2.5 cm) long and 0.6 in (1.5 cm) wide with soft-textured pale green upper sides and whitish green undersides. Above the water the leaves are slightly tougher, deeper green, and smaller, often taking on a reddish tint. The cup-shaped flowers are yellow. The dense mass of foliage provides an excellent home for wildlife.

LYSICHITON. Skunk cabbage. Araceae. The name is derived from the Greek *lysis*, meaning loosening, and *chiton*, a cloak, a reference to the casting off of the spathe. It is a genus of two temperate species of bog plants from North America, Siberia, and Japan. They are on the borderline of tolerance to shallow water over their roots, but provided the water covering is very shallow and they have a deep root run, they should succeed at the waterside. They are frequently called skunk cabbages, which also refers to the distantly related *Symplocarpus foetidus* of eastern North America.

L. americanum. Found in western North America, this impressive hardy waterside plant provides a spring display of its aroidlike unpleasantly scented yellow flowers, 6–8 in (15–20 cm) tall. These are followed by the rapid development of huge, architectural, almost sessile leaves, capable of reaching 4 ft (1.2 m) high if the conditions are right. The finest specimens are grown in deep, rich soil, copiously supplied with water, and protected from wind and late frosts.

L. camtschatcense. An Asian species, it is very similar in habit and cultivation needs to *L. americanum* but has slightly shorter leaves and white flowers, which are similarly malodorous and marginally later to bloom. Plate 58.

MENTHA. Mint. Labiatae. Named after Xaverio Manetti (1723–1785), botanist and director of the botanic garden in Florence, Italy, this genus of 25 temperate species of aromatic plants prefers moist conditions and spreads rapidly by underground rhizomes. The genus includes one variable species from a limited number that thrive in aquatic conditions and is now widely available in the trade as a marginal plant.

M. aquatica. Water mint. A native of Europe, Asia, and North Africa, this species occurs in marshes, ditches, and alongside running water. Submerged nonflowering forms can occur to a depth of 6 ft (2 m). The plant has a thin rhizomatous root with long segments, grows to a height of 24–36 in (60–90 cm), and forms crossed pairs of hairy egg-shaped leaves with serrated margins. The lilac-colored globular flowers are produced in terminal whorls. This heavy-scented plant is useful for binding the edges of a shallow pool because it scrambles in and out of the water, rooting as it goes. Like terrestrial mints, it should be planted in containers to confine its rapid spread. Plate 59.

MENYANTHES. Buckbean, bogbean. Menyanthaceae. A single-species genus of temperate aquatics, it is distributed throughout North America, northern Asia, Europe, and northwestern India. Common in shallow pools and acid bogs, its thick, spongy, creeping rootstocks quickly colonize the edges.

M. trifoliata. Marsh trefoil, bogbean, buckbean. A charming marginal plant, it is suitable for the edges of decorative pools with its attractive foliage and interesting fringed flowers. It can spread to form extensive clumps 3 ft (1 m) or more in diameter on the creeping rhizome, which sometimes floats out into the water. The shiny cloverlike olive-green leaves are made up of three leaflets with a long petiole that clasps the rhizome with a broad sheath. The flower stalk can reach 10–16 in (25–40 cm) high with a dense spike of dainty frilled white to purplish flowers that emerge from attractive pink buds.

MIMULUS. Monkey flower. Scrophulariaceae. This genus of widespread temperate and subtropical species does not occur in Europe but is well concentrated in North America. Most of its species appreciate moisture-rich conditions, and a few make striking marginal plants for the decorative water garden.

M. cardinalis. A western North American species, it brings a vivid display to the poolside with its large scarlet flowers. It grows 1–3 ft (0.3–1 m) with soft gray-green hairy ovate leaves with serrated edges.

M. cupreus. A Chilean species, it is very similar to *M. guttatus* but more compact in habit, growing 6–8 in (15–20 cm) high and with fiery red flowers. It is a parent of the excellent cultivar 'Whitecroft Scarlet', one of the finest *Mimulus* cultivars, with bright green mats of neat foliage surmounted by vivid scarlet flowers.

M. guttatus. Monkey musk, monkey flower. A hardy species from western North America, it is very common in streams, ditches, and spring-fed pools throughout the western United States and Canada. It grows submerged in the winter and produces aerial shoots in the summer. The plant ranges 14–40 in (35–100 cm) in height and produces stout stems with ovate toothed leaves and an abundance of yellow flowers, each marked with a pair of reddish brown hairy ridges. Plate 60.

M. ×hybridus. An excellent range of garden hybrids derived primarily from *M. luteus* and *M. guttatus*, these plants are slightly more compact than their parents.

M. lewisii [*M. bartoniensis*]. A western North American species, this one is more delicate than *M. cardinalis*. It thrives in the same conditions and enjoys shade, growing to a height of 15–24 in (38–60 cm) with rosy pink to crimson flowers and hairy lanceolate sessile leaves with serrated edges.

M. luteus. Yellow monkey flower. A robust species originating in Chile and naturalized in North America and parts of western Europe, it has prostrate smooth, hollow stems growing 4–12 in (10–30 cm) high, rooting at the nodes, and carrying numerous yellow flowers with deep red or purple spots. Orange forms are also sometimes found.

M. ringens. Lavender musk. A hardy aquatic species from eastern North America, it has many branching square stems growing to 18 in (45 cm) and narrow dark green oblong leaves. The blue to bluish violet snapdragonlike flowers are about 1 in (2.5 cm) long with a very narrow throat. The plant is capable of growing in shallow water 3–5 in (8–13 cm) deep.

MYOSOTIS. Forget-me-not. Boraginaceae. The name is derived from the Greek *mys*, meaning mouse, and *ous*, ear, a reference to the appearance of the plant's leaves. A genus of 50 temperate species most commonly found in Europe and Australia and naturalized in North America, it includes a few aquatic forms of considerable value to the water gardener.

M. scorpioides [*M. palustris*]. Water forget-me-not. A hardy species native to Europe and Asia and naturalized in North America, it is found on the shallow banks of still and slow-moving water and in marshy meadows, ditches, and ponds. The plant has a creeping rhizome that supports an angular stem growing 9–12 in (23–30 cm) in length that tends to be prostrate on the lower portion and becomes erect toward the tip. The leaves are alternate, oblong, blunt at the top, tapering into the stalk below with short rough hairs. Flowering between May and July, the beautiful light blue flowers with yellow eyes are held in loose racemes. The species' semi-prostrate habit of growth in water up to 3 in (8 cm) deep and its delicate colorings make it an ideal edging plant for both the ornamental and wildlife pool. This valuable marginal produces several variants, among them 'Alba' (white), 'Semperflorens' (more compact), and 'Mermaid', a more free-flowering cultivar that is otherwise similar to the species. Plate 61.

NARTHECIUM. Bog asphodel. Liliaceae. A genus of eight temperate rushlike marsh plants, it has a wide distribution over the Northern Hemisphere. One species makes a good contribution by adding variety to the boggy margins of a small wildlife pool.

N. ossifragum. Bog asphodel. Often found in bogs among sphagnum, where its roots are covered with no more than 0.4 in (1 cm) of water, the slender, rigid, irislike leaves grow 6–12 in (15–30 cm) tall. The attractive flowers are rich yellow and starlike, standing stiffly erect.

NASTURTIUM. Watercress. Cruciferae. A genus of about six species of glabrous herbs of running water or wet soils, it is found in temperate regions worldwide.

N. officinale. Watercress. This species grows about 12 in (30 cm) tall and sends out white runners that root at every node. Excellent for streamside planting, it produces white flowers and prefers running water. The peppery-tasting leaves are often used in salads.

ORONTIUM. Araceae. A single-species genus of temperate plants from eastern North America, it grows in bogs or shallow water. It makes an attractive plant growing in the shallow margins of a decorative pool.

O. aquaticum. Golden club. This hardy species produces large bluish green velvety lance-shaped leaves with a silvery sheen on the undersides. The contrasting shades of the leaves, which grow to 18 in (45 cm), can be better appreciated when the plant is grown as a marginal. In water deeper than 12 in (30 cm), the leaves float on the surface, growing 5–12 in (13–30 cm) long and 5 in (13 cm) wide with a waxy covering. The unusual pencil-like flowers emerge from the water surface tipped with yellow, resembling small golden pokers. Plate 62.

PELTANDRA. Arrow arum. Araceae. The name is derived from the Greek *pelte*, meaning a shield, and *andreia*, meaning manliness, a reference to the stamen's shape. A genus of two temperate species from North America, it is closely related to the arums, which have proved successful as decorative marginal plants for shallow water.

P. sagittifolia [*P. alba*]. White arrow arum. A hardy North American species, it has strong, bright green, sagittate, conspicuously veined leaves growing from a short rhizome. The arumlike flower is white, about 3–4 in (8–10 cm) in length, and grows to 18 in (45 cm) above the water followed by fleshy red berries enclosed in the persistent leathery base of the spathe. Plate 63.

P. virginica. Green arrow arum. This hardy North American species is distinguished from *P. sagittifolia* by having a narrower and greener flower spathe that produces green rather than red berries. The firm leaves are narrowly sagittate, growing up to 30 in (75 cm) long and 3–8 in (8–20 cm) wide with conspicuous veining.

PETASITES. Butterbur, sweet coltsfoot. Compositae. The name is derived from the Greek *petasos*, meaning a broad-brimmed hat, a reference to the plant's large leaves. It is a genus of about 14 species of moisture-loving perennial herbs with thick rhizomes and stems native to Europe, Asia, and North America. Their large foliage is very effective by the waterside, particularly in the wild garden, but the plants are difficult to eradicate and can become a nuisance once established. One species is suitable for use in damp conditions around ponds; others are discussed in Chapter 8.

P. hybridis. Bog rhubarb, butterbur. Dense clusters of lilac-pink flowers appear close to the ground in winter and spring before the leaves come out. The leaves, which somewhat resemble those of *Gunnera*, grow to 2 ft (0.6 m) in diameter. The plant reaches a height of 3 ft (1 m) and prefers damp soil.

PHRAGMITES. Reed. Gramineae. The name is derived from the Greek *phragma*, meaning a fence, a reference to the plant's hedgelike mode of growth in ditches. A genus of three common perennial grasses widely distributed over temperate and trop-

ical regions, it is too invasive for the ornamental pool but may be useful in providing cover for wildlife around extensive lakes.

P. australis [*P. communis*]. Common reed. Native to most temperate regions, including both Americas, this widespread reed grows 6–10 ft (1.8–3 m) tall with broad glossy leaves and feathery heads of purplish maroon flowers. The hungry rootstock seeks vast areas of space and is therefore not a plant for the garden. The strong erect stems make it a valuable plant for thatching, and where extensive binding of sandy soil is required, it is a useful species. The less vigorous cultivar 'Variegatus', with creamy variegated leaves, if carefully controlled, may have a place on the moist banks of the water garden.

POLYGONUM. Smartweed, knotweed, fleece flower. Polygonaceae. The name is derived from the Greek *polys*, meaning many, and *gonu*, joint, a reference to the stems' having conspicuously swollen nodes. In this large genus of 150 species with worldwide temperate and tropical distribution, many are decorative moisture-loving plants. The amphibious species *P. amphibium* is a good plant for the shallow margins of an informal wildlife pool. Other *Polygonum* species are discussed in Chapter 8.

P. amphibium. Amphibious bistort. A hardy species from the North Temperate Zone, it occurs in slow-moving water and is particularly suitable for ponds with fluctuating water levels. When aquatic, it has a floating stem nearly 3 ft (1 m) long containing air spaces. The lanceolate emergent leaves clasp the stem and are rounder when floating, with long petioles that emerge from a papery sheath. The leaf blades are dark green, glossy, and leathery, bluntly tapering with dark markings near the top. The attractive flowers are neat pink spikes that are complemented in the autumn by some striking foliage tints. Plate 64.

PONTEDERIA. Pontederiaceae. Named after Giulio Pontedera (1688–1757), a professor of botany in Padua, Italy, it is a genus of five temperate and subtropical species of shallow-water plants from North and South America. The genus provides one of the most decorative blue-flowered marginal plants available in commerce.

P. cordata. Pickerel weed. A common hardy species found in shallow water throughout eastern North America, it forms a robust, tidy plant growing 18–24 in (45–60 cm) high. The thick creeping rootstock supports both radical leaves and single-stem cordate leaves that are erect, shiny, and olive green with exquisite swirling. A delightful soft blue flower spike appears from a leaf bract at the top of the stem. The species succeeds with up to 5 in (13 cm) of water above its crown. Plate 65.

The variety *lanceolata* (syn. *P. lanceolata*), a slightly tender species from the southeastern United States, grows 4–5 ft (1.2–1.5 m) high with narrow lanceolate leaves and longer flower spikes than *P. cordata*. The variety *alba* is white-flowered and was discovered in northern Florida. The form *angustifolia*, found in the southeastern United States, is similar to the type with lanceolate to linear-lanceolate leaves.

P. rotundifolia. Tropical pickerel weed. This Central and South American native has obovate to cordate green leaves 2–4 in (5–10 cm) long and 1.25–3 in (3–8 cm) wide. The light blue flower consists of six lobes and appears as a rounded flowerhead rather than a long spike as in *P. cordata* and its variations. It is illegal in Florida as it is very fast growing and can grow emersed, submerged, floating, or creeping, and, therefore, has become a real pest in lakes and streams.

POTENTILLA. Cinquefoil. Rasaceae. The name is derived from the Latin *poteus*, meaning powerful, a reference to the medicinal qualities of some species. It is a genus of 500 species found in the temperate and boreal regions of the Northern Hemisphere with a few occurring in the South Temperate Zone.

P. palustris [*P. comarum*]. Potentilla, marsh cinquefoil. Native to Great Britain and preferring marshy conditions, this species has long creeping rhizomes and pinnate leaves with serrated margins. The flowers, which grow to 18 in (45 cm) high, are dark purple and 1.5 in (4 cm) across.

RANUNCULUS. Buttercup, crowfoot. Ranunculaceae. The name is derived from the Latin *rana*, meaning little frog, a reference to the plant's preferred damp habitat. It is a large cosmopolitan genus of 400 temperate and tropical moisture-loving and aquatic species, of which nearly 40 grow in water. Other *Ranunculus* species are discussed in Chapters 6 and 8.

R. flammula. Lesser spearwort. This temperate European species is suitable as a decorative marginal plant for the informal edges of a wildlife pool. This species produces semiprostrate reddish stems, dark green oval leaves, and bright yellow flowers and is a smaller version of the greater spearwort (*R. lingua*).

R. lingua. Greater spearwort. A widespread temperate species from Europe and western Asia, it is normally found growing singly in wetlands and ditches. The hollow reddish stems grow to 5 ft (1.5 m) with long-stalked heart-shaped leaves on the nonflowering shoots and pointed, narrow to linear lance-shaped leaves with short stalks on the flowering shoots. The large golden flowers are 1–2 in (2.5–5 cm) across. The sappy stems are inclined to be blown over in strong winds when the plant is grown as a solitary specimen in exposed situations. The cultivar 'Grandiflorus' is sold in the trade as an improved, more vigorous form. Plate 66.

SAGITTARIA. Arrowhead, swamp potato. Alismataceae. The name is derived from the Latin *sagitta*, meaning an arrow, as many of the species have arrow-shaped leaves. A cosmopolitan genus of 20 species of aquatics, it is found in a wide variety of habitats but mainly in shallow water, on muddy shores, and in marshes. There are a number of decorative species suitable for marginal planting. They usually produce overwintering walnut-sized tubers at the ends of subterranean runners that become detached in the autumn. These tubers are rich in starch and attractive to waterfowl, necessitating some protection where birds are kept or encouraged. In deep running water it produces only ribbonlike submerged leaves, but in the shallow water at the sides of ponds, its characteristic arrow-shaped leaves have great charm. Other *Sagittaria* species are discussed in Chapter 6.

S. latifolia. Duck potato. A widespread North American species, it is suitable as an aquarium as well as a marginal plant (see Chapter 6). This species is generally more vigorous than *S. sagittifolia* with extremely variable leaf blades frequently reaching 32 in (80 cm) in length.

S. sagittifolia. Common arrowhead. A hardy, rampant native of Europe and Asia, the plant produces fine shiny arrow-shaped leaves up to 18 in (45 cm) long from which the white flowers are borne on three-angled stems in whorls of three. The attractive flowers have three large white petals with a purple blotch at the base. A very handsome double cultivar, 'Flore Pleno' (or double arrowhead, sometimes sold as *S. japonica*), has magnificent round double white flowers about 1 in (2.5 cm) in diameter arranged around a spike. The plant is easier to contain in the decorative pond and is described in nursery catalogs as Japanese double-flowering arrowhead. Plate 67; Figure 41.

SAURURUS. Saururaceae. The name is derived from the Greek *sauros*, meaning lizard, and *oura*, meaning tail, a reference to the similarity of the inflorescence to a lizard's tail. It is a genus of two hardy species of shallow-water plants from North America and east Asia.

S. cernuus. American swamp lily, lizard's tail. This

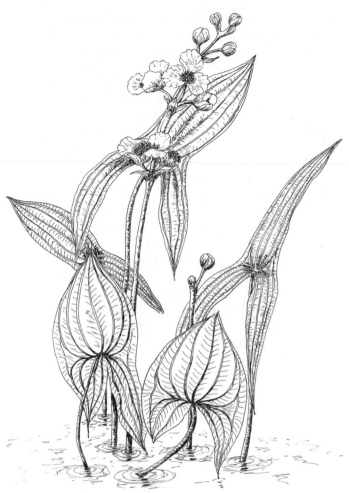

FIGURE 41. *Sagittaria sagittifolia*.

the base measures 0.75–1.25 in (2–3 cm). Brown flowers are carried at the tips of long drooping round stems. Reproduction is by seed and vegetatively from rootstocks. It is found growing in much of the southern United States, Mexico, and South America in water up to 30 in (75 cm) deep.

S. cyperinus. Woolgrass bulrush. Another tall rush reaching up to 6 ft (2 m) in height, it is characterized by large fluffy brown flower heads. Found in eastern Canada and the eastern and midwestern United States, it prefers moist or boggy soils.

S. lacustris [*Schoenoplectus lacustris*]. Bulrush. A widespread hardy species from Europe, North America, and Asia, it grows in large beds in lakes, ponds, and slow-moving water. The plant has a strong-growing rhizome that creeps along the soil surface. The erect stems, which are dark green and cylindrical, can reach up to 9 ft (2.7 m) with a diameter of 0.6 in (1.5 cm). The flower is a brown terminal spikelet. There are many more decorative forms, but this species provides useful cover for waterfowl in large lakes.

S. lacustris subsp. *tabernaemontani*. A taller subspecies with a more glaucous appearance to the leafless stems and an attractive farina. The variegated cultivars 'Zebrinus' and 'Albescens' are most used in decorative ponds. 'Zebrinus', a dwarfer Japanese plant for very shallow water, has a unique cream banding on the stems like porcupine quills and reaches a height of 3–6 ft (1–2 m). 'Albescens', with tall stems growing 3–4 ft (1–1.2 m) in height, has creamy vertical banding that makes a bold and bright display when planted against a dark background.

S. validus [*Schoenoplectus validus*]. Soft-stemmed bulrush. Similar to *S. californicus* in many ways, this species is smaller, growing up to 8 ft (2.5 m) in height, with a soft, spongy stem about 1 in (2.5 cm) in diameter at the base. It grows in mud or several feet of water and is found throughout the southeastern United States and the rest of temperate North America. Brown flower heads are at the tips of the rushes.

SCROPHULARIA. Figwort. Scrophulariaceae. A widely distributed genus of 200 species of temperate and subtropical plants mainly from the Northern Hemisphere, it includes one species used by the water gardener for planting in shallow water at the edge of a pool.

S. auriculata [*S. aquatica*]. Water figwort. A native of Europe and the Caucasus, this species grows 2–3 ft (0.6–1 m) tall with smooth cordate almost nettlelike leaves borne on stiff square stems. The small fig-shaped flowers, which are much loved by bees, are

hardy North American species is rampant in swamps and shallow water in the southeastern United States. In cultivation it grows 12–24 in (30–60 cm) high with attractive bright green cordate foliage and nodding spikes of fragrant white flowers that are 4–6 in (10–15 cm) long. Plate 68.

S. chinensis. A hardy species from Asia and much less commonly seen in cultivation than *S. cernuus*, it grows 12–16 in (30–40 cm) high, has pale green oval leaves 4–5 in (10–13 cm) long, and carries erect creamy white flower spikes.

SCIRPUS. Bulrush. Cyperaceae. A widely distributed genus of 100 temperate and tropical species found in marshes and shallow water, it is characterized by stems that are often very long, growing from a rampant stolon that necessitates the plants' being kept in check. They are most effective when grown in bold groups at the water's edge.

S. californicus. Giant bulrush. At 6–10 ft (2–3 m) in height, the giant bulrush can be used in the background of large ponds. The diameter of the spikes at in loose panicles, brown and greenish purple in color. The variegated cultivar 'Variegata' is the one worth growing at the water's edge. The leaves take on creamy margins to a light green center portion. The smaller leaves are sometimes almost entirely cream in color.

SPARGANIUM. Bur-reed. Sparganiaceae. The name is thought to be derived from the Greek *spargan*, meaning a ribbon. A genus of 21 mainly temperate species from the Northern Hemisphere, it is common on the edges of large lakes, ponds, streams, and ditches, sometimes in muddy ground, forming large clumps in association with reeds and reedmaces. They are much liked by waterfowl as nest-building sites and winter food.

S. americanum. American bur-reed. This species occurs sporadically throughout the eastern United States. The leaves can be erect, partially floating, or completely submerged. The erect leaves are rigid, while the submerged leaves, usually found in water depths up to 3 ft (1 m), are ribbonlike and soft. These underwater leaves may reach 1.25 in (3 cm) in width, while the erect leaves are usually about 0.5 in (1.3 cm) wide. The 0.75-in (2-cm) greenish white round flowers are borne on sturdy stalks with lateral rigid leaves above the water. An attractive plant for the background of a water garden, it can become a pest in natural ponds and canals. Water fowl and several species of marsh birds eat the seeds.

S. emersum. Unbranched bur-reed. A less-common species than *S. erectum*, it has unbranched flower stems and narrow leaves, giving it the appearance of a much more slender plant.

S. erectum [*S. ramosum*]. Bur-reed. A hardy species found in Europe and northern Asia, it has rhizomatous roots that have strong pointed tips and bear rosettes of long swordlike leaves that are triangular at the base and grow 3–4 ft (1–1.2 m) long and 0.5–1 in (1.3–2.5 cm) wide. The inflorescence is branched, exceeded in height by the basal leaves, and has conspicuous leaves at its base. The globular female flowers occur on the flower spike below several smaller male flowers. It tolerates a water depth up to 18 in (45 cm). This plant is prohibited in Florida.

STACHYS. Betony, hedge nettle, woundwort. Labiatae. This genus consists of about 300 species of herbs and subshrubs of temperate and subtropical regions and tropical mountains. One species found in Great Britain can be used in or around the water garden.

S. palustris. Marsh betony. This marsh plant with whorls of reddish purple flowers has narrow nettlelike leaves and flowers from June into September in Great Britain. It grows to a height of 12 in (30 cm) and prefers up to 3 in (8 cm) of water.

THALIA. Marantaceae. Named in honor of Johann Thal (1542–1583), a German botanist, this is a genus of 12 swamp-loving species from tropical and subtropical America and Africa. Certain species make architecturally striking plants for the shallow water's edge of tropical pools.

T. dealbata. A tropical species from the southern United States and Mexico, it grows to 6 ft (2 m) high with thick, striking, ovate to lanceolate glaucous blue leaf blades edged in purple, 20 in (50 cm) long and 10 in (25 cm) wide, dusted with white powder. The unusual small violet flowers are on branching panicles about 8 in (20 cm) long and carried high above the leaves. It makes an excellent conservatory plant in temperate areas, resembling cannas in habit. The plant will usually survive the winter in northern climates when planted in 12–18 in (30–45 cm) of water. Plate 69.

T. geniculata [*T. divaricata*]. A tropical and semitropical species native to Florida, tropical America, and the West Indies, it is somewhat similar to *T. dealbata* but grows larger leaves reaching up to 30 in (75 cm) long with a splotch of purple at the base. The tall flower stalks with zigzag spikes of small purple flowers hanging from panicles similar to those of *T. dealbata* may reach 8 ft (2.5 m) in height. This tender plant can be used for background planting in large pools in tropical or semitropical settings, including conservatories. It can become a pest in natural ponds. The form *ruminoides* (syn. *T. divaricata* var. *rubra*) is similar to *T. divaricata* except that it has very attractive red stems.

TYPHA. Cattail, reedmace. Typhaceae. A worldwide tropical and temperate genus of 10–15 species of marsh-loving aquatics, it spreads extensively in the silty margins of ponds and lakes. Most species must be introduced with great caution as they are extremely invasive and capable of puncturing pool liners. Their flower clusters are popular as dried decorations.

T. angustifolia. Lesser reedmace, narrow-leaved cattail. A hardy species from North America, Europe, Asia, and tropical America, it is slender and dark-leaved and grows to about 4 ft (1.2 m) high with leaves 0.4 in (1 cm) wide. The brown flower spikes are 0.5–0.8 in (1.3–2 cm) thick, with the male and female flowers separated by a gap of about 1 in (2.5 cm).

T. latifolia. Great reedmace, cattail. The common hardy species from Europe and North America, it has bluish green straplike leaves up to 1 in (2.5 cm) wide and 6–8 ft (2–2.5 m) long. The dark brown flower spike is 6–9 in (15–23 cm) long and about 1 in (2.5 cm) in diameter. The lighter brown male flowers are immediately above the dark brown females, not separated on the spike as are those of *T. angustifolia*. They make valuable cover for waterfowl but are almost impossible to control when their invasive rhizomes have an unlimited run, creating an extensive network of thick hungry roots.

'Variegata' is an attractive creamy variegated cultivar that is gradually becoming more available in the trade. Not so vigorous as *T. latifolia*, it is more suitable for decorative pool planting.

T. laxmannii [*T. stenophylla*]. Graceful cattail. A hardy species from southeastern Europe and Asia Minor, it has narrow grayish green half-round leaves that are grooved on one side and rounded on the other and grow to 4 ft (1.2 m) high. The flower spike has the lighter brown male flowers above and separated from the dark brown females underneath. Of the vigorous reedmaces, this species is slightly less invasive and more suitable for decorative pool planting with its narrow foliage. Plate 70.

T. minima. A hardy species from Europe, the Caucasus, and Asia and unlike its close relatives, it is suitable for even the tiniest pool. Growing no more than 12–18 in (30–45 cm) high, it has narrow needlelike leaves and interesting small round chocolate-brown flower spikes, making it an ideal choice to provide variety in a small layout.

VERONICA. Speedwell, brooklime. Scrophulariaceae. A large, variable genus of about 250 species mainly of the Northern Hemisphere, it includes a few hardy marsh species suitable for planting in the decorative pool margins. Another species of *Veronica* is discussed in Chapter 8.

V. americana. American brooklime. A hardy North American species, it has succulent creeping stems growing 24–30 in (60–75 cm) long. The smooth lanceolate leaves have acutely toothed edges and bear small violet or lilac flowers in their axils.

V. beccabunga. Brooklime. A hardy species native to Europe, Asia, and North Africa, where it grows half-submerged in ditches and streams, it is a scrambling, rather succulent plant, growing up to 12 in (30 cm) high with fleshy cylindrical hollow stems. The short-stalked elliptical leaves bear small blue flowers with white centers, 0.3 in (0.8 cm) across, in their axils. It can get a little straggly, and young growth can be used to replace old plants by reinserting the shoots as cuttings. It makes an excellent plant for softening any hard edges to a pond.

XANTHOSOMA. Malanga, tannia. Araceae. The name is derived from the Greek *xanthos*, meaning yellow, and *soma*, meaning a body, a reference to the yellow inner tissue of some species. It is a genus of 40 species of handsome moisture-loving or bog plants from tropical America, a few of which are so attractive as to justify their use as specimen marginal plants in tropical pools or as conservatory plants in temperate areas. They closely resemble the colocasias with their long arrow-shaped leaves.

X. violaceum. A tropical species from the American tropics, it is grown as a marginal aquatic for its handsome foliage that measures 2 ft (0.6 m) long and 18 in (45 cm) wide with purple petioles and leaf margins. It is most effective when grown in a rich, saturated soil and treated as a specimen.

ZANTEDESCHIA. Arum. Araceae. Named after Italian botanist Giovanni Zantedeschi (1773–1846), it is a genus of six species of tender South African marsh-loving plants with thick rhizomes and arrow-shaped leaves, often with white transparent dots. Many hybrids have been developed as decorative pot plants, and their potential as marginal pool plants has yet to be fully exploited.

Z. aethiopica. Arum lily, calla lily. A slightly tender species from southern Africa, it survives in temperate climates if adequately submerged in 12 in (30 cm) of water. This species grows 2–3 ft (0.6–1 m) tall with the familiar large fragrant white aroid flower 3–10 in (8–25 cm) long with a central yellow poker, or spadix, surrounded by shiny arrow-shaped leaves. There are several colored forms with spotted leaves. 'Green Goddess' has a yellow spadix and a green-and-white spathe. Plate 71.

'Crowborough', a smaller and reputedly hardier cultivar of the species, grows to 2 ft (0.6 m) high and is frequently available in specialist aquatic catalogs. It has a white flower similar to *Z. aethiopica* with a central yellow spadix. It makes an excellent softening plant for pool edges.

ZIZANIA. Wild rice, water oats. Gramineae. This genus consists of two or three species of tall annual or perennial grasses, reaching 4–7 ft (1.2–2.2 m) in height, found in North America and East Asia. One perennial species is used in water gardens.

Z. latifolia. Perennial rice, water rice, Manchurian wild rice. This species grows 4 ft (1.2 m) tall and makes a showy specimen for the background of the pool.

Chapter 8

Moisture-Loving Trees, Shrubs, Herbaceous Perennials, Ferns, and Ornamental Grasses

The moist soil surrounding the water provides an interesting area for planting a selection of coordinated species that relish these conditions. While many of the plants listed in this chapter also grow in ordinary garden soil, their full beauty can be appreciated only when they benefit from constantly available water. "A well-drained but moist soil" may seem at first a contradiction in terms, but it summarizes the particular condition of having available water near the roots but not surrounding them and denying them air. Many moisture-loving plants draw upon such reserves in large quantities; others are happier for their roots to sip rather than gulp. The method by which these moist areas can be created has been described in Chapter 3. The simplest and cheapest schemes require no more than lining a soil area with a punctured membrane.

The presence of moisture-loving plants in an informal design makes a restful and natural transition from the lush marginal growth to the surrounding landscape or garden, particularly when there is no identifiable or distinct boundary between the moist areas and the other soil conditions.

The moisture-loving planting area provides the framework for an informal water garden. The middle distance and background plantings play an important part in the integration of water into the landscape. Without good coordination of the surrounding trees, shrubs, and herbaceous plants, water may stick out like a sore thumb rather than be the jewel in the crown. The moist perimeter is a particularly exciting area for the artistic gardener, as it allows the fine tuning of a composition in a wider dimension than simply the area devoted to water. Herbaceous plants, which change almost daily in size and color, require that the gardener be restrained as well as confident in choosing them. With such a rich palette available the colors could run riot. The careful use of color and the good mixing of subdued tones, plant forms, and foliage textures are without doubt some of the great arts of the gardener.

The following list of plants is not intended to be exhaustive or rigidly encyclopedic. It dips into the relevant range of plants with a view to clothing the water garden with a good basic plant collection that should satisfy most situations and temperature zones. A selection of plants from the following list will not only cosset the informal water but create a garden in its own right. Searching for improved forms of the basic genera listed may broaden the water gardener's pleasure as much as seeking the elusive water lily that will complete the composition.

ACHILLEA. Yarrow. Compositae. Named after Achilles, who is reputed to have discovered the medicinal properties of the plant, this genus of approximately 100 temperate species from Europe, western Asia, and North America enjoys sun and well-drained soils. Two species thrive in sunny, moist soils by the water's edge.

*A. **ageratum** [A. decolorans]*. Originating in Switzerland, this species grows 12–24 in (30–60 cm) high and bears many white-petaled green-eyed flowers in loose flat clusters on thin stems, which look very fragile, with brightish green finely serrated leaves. 'W. B. Child', a particularly neat cultivar, makes an attractive cut flower.

A. ptarmica. Sneezewort. A European species naturalized in eastern North America, it can be invasive, growing to 2 ft (0.6 m) high, bearing narrow toothed lanceolate leaves and white flowers in terminal corymbs. 'The Pearl' is a double form, with neat buttonlike flowers in branching heads.

ACONITUM. Monkshood, aconite, helmet flower, wolfsbane. Ranunculaceae. The name is derived from the Greek *akonitum*, a name applied to poisonous plants of uncertain identity. This is a genus of 110 temperate species native to Europe, Asia, and North America that are particularly beautiful when massed and exceptional in flower when well supplied with water. Aconitums are deadly poisonous.

A. carmichaelii [*A. fischeri*]. A temperate species from China, it has erect divided foliage growing to 4 ft (1.2 m) with light blue hooded blooms. There is a fine cultivar, 'Arendsii', of the same height but with darker colorings that flowers in late summer. The variety *wilsonii* is a Chinese form producing rigid stems growing 5–6 ft (1.5–2 m) tall with large violet-blue flowers.

A. lycoctonum subsp. *vulparis*. Wolfsbane. A tall plant from Europe and northern Asia, it has deeply divided dark green leaves and yellow flowers borne on branching spikes. It grows to 5 ft (1.5 m).

A. napellus. Helmet flower, Turk's cap, friar's cap. The more common monkshood native to Europe and Asia, it grows to 4 ft (1.2 m) on erect stems with bright green foliage and hooded navy-blue flowers.

ACTAEA. Baneberry, cohosh, necklace weed. Ranunculaceae. The name is derived from the Greek *aktara*, meaning elder, a reference to the similarity of the plant's leaves to the common elderberry (*Sambucus*). It is a genus of 15 temperate species of vigorous and graceful shade and moisture-loving perennials. All have poisonous berries, giving rise to the common name baneberry.

A. alba. White baneberry. Originating in the moist woods of eastern North America, this elegant species grows to a height of 3 ft (1 m) on stiff stems bearing fresh green leaves and fluffy white flowers that later turn into white berries supported on conspicuous scarlet stalks.

A. rubra. Red baneberry. Native to North America, this shade-loving species has showy red berries held above fernlike leaves.

A. spicata. Herb Christopher, cohosh. A European native, it thrives in damp soil under evergreens. Growing to 24 in (60 cm), the plant bears small white flowers that are followed by purplish black poisonous berries.

ADIANTUM. Maidenhair fern. Adiantaceae. The name is derived from the Greek *adiantos*, meaning dry, a reference to the fronds of the fern reputedly remaining dry after being plunged underwater. Most species in this genus of over 200 widely distributed tropical and temperate ferns require moist soils and reasonable light levels but not direct sun. Very few are totally hardy unless sufficient cover over the underground rhizomes is provided in severe weather.

A. pedatum. American maidenhair fern, hardy maidenhair fern. A deciduous, temperate species from North America, northern India, China, and Japan, it is an extremely handsome fern, growing 15–18 in (38–45 cm) high with shiny black wiry stems bearing delicate green kidney-shaped fronds. Plate 72.

A. venustum. Kashmir maidenhair. A temperate species from the Himalayas, it is a small deciduous plant growing to 9 in (23 cm). Its extremely handsome young filigree fronds are tinted with brown and change in delightful soft green shades throughout the summer, finally turning reddish brown after the first frosts. Maidenhair ferns must not be planted too deeply or receive heavy top dressings.

AGERATINA. Compositae. A genus of 230 species from the eastern United States and central and western South America, it consists mainly of herbs and shrubs suited to wildflower gardens and the fringes of large wildlife pools.

A. altissima [*Eupatorium rugosum*]. White snake root. Growing 1–4 ft (0.3–1.2 m) tall, this late-flowering plant from North America has nettlelike leaves on stiff stems and flat heads of fuzzy white flowers.

AJUGA. Bugleweed. Labiatae. Many species in this genus of 40 temperate and subtropical perennial creeping plants love the damp conditions near water.

A. pyramidalis. Pyramid bugle. A temperate species found in damp meadows across central Europe and Asia, it grows up to 6 in (15 cm) high with plain green leaves and spreads by means of stolons. A useful carpeter in moist soils, it produces vivid gentian-blue flowers in a dense pyramidal spike in midsummer.

A. reptans. Carpet bugle. A common species native to Europe, this rather invasive creeper, which inhabits wet meadows, can make a good ground cover plant with blue flowers and dark green leaves 2–3 in (5–8 cm) long. There are some attractive cultivars that grow 4–5 in (10–13 cm) tall and are less invasive: 'Atropurpurea', with dark bronzy leaves; 'Burgundy Glow', with light blue flowers 5–6 in (13–15 cm) high above varying shades of wine red foliage with creamy leaf margins; and 'Multicolor', with foliage variegated in pink and cream. Plate 73.

ALCHEMILLA. Lady's mantle. Rosaceae. The name is derived from the Arabic *alkemelych*, a reference to the plant's use in alchemy. It is a genus of 30 temperate species from Europe, Asia, and America. Many are of easy cultivation and thrive in ordinary or poor soils but achieve a lush vigor when grown in damp pool margins.

A. mollis. Lady's mantle. One of the more common and larger species of the genus, it grows to 18 in (45 cm) high and is found in damp alpine meadows of Europe and Asia. The roundish leaves are downy, 4–5 in (10–13 cm) across, and hold onto droplets of moisture, adding to the plant's attraction. The tiny flowers are yellowish green and held in feathery sprays in early summer. The flowers and foliage soften edges and make good foils for stronger midsummer colors.

ALNUS. Alder. Betulaceae. The name is derived from the Latin name for alder. It is a genus of 30 temperate, deciduous trees and shrubs widely distributed in the Northern Hemisphere. They tolerate extremely wet soils and form attractive architectural landscape trees, particularly beautiful in late winter. The flowers are segregated into male and female catkins on the same tree, the males cylindrical, 2–6 in (5–15 cm) long, and the females shorter and woody, resembling conifer cones.

A. cordata. Italian alder. A hardy and most handsome species from Corsica and southern Italy, it forms a pyramidal tree growing to 80 ft (24 m). Its bright green finely toothed leaves are rounded, 2–4 in (5–10 cm) long, and have an abrupt point. The male catkins, which tend to grow in threes, are 2–3 in (5–8 cm) long. The conelike fruits, also in threes, are ovoid, erect, and 1–1.25 in (2.5–3 cm) long.

A. glutinosa. Common alder, European alder, black alder. A hardy species from Europe, western Asia, and North Africa and naturalized in eastern North America, it is a rather slender deciduous tree with a central trunk and small horizontal branches. The dark green leaves are broad and pear-shaped, coarsely toothed, 2–4 in (5–10 cm) long with a pointed apex, and sticky on the upper surface. It makes an impressive sight in early spring when the naked stems produce long yellow catkins among

the sticky buds and twigs. Not the most decorative of the species, it is suitable for naturalizing in extensive plantings and breaking the endless use of willow and poplar alongside water. Three cultivars are worthy of note: the yellow-leaved 'Aurea'; 'Imperialis', with deeply divided fine leaf lobes that are slender and pointed but not toothed; and 'Laciniata', sturdy and rather stiff, with leaves not so finely divided as those of 'Imperialis'.

A. incana. Gray alder, American speckled alder. A species from Europe and the Caucasus, it is one of the hardiest and most tolerant, generally growing to 30 ft (9 m), sometimes reaching 50 ft (15 m), in a cluster of small erect trunks bearing many small spreading branches in a broadly pyramidal shape. The oval leaves are matte green above and downy and grayish on the undersides, 2–4 in (5–10 cm) long, with a tapered base and an abrupt point. The male catkins grow 2–4 in (5–10 cm) long in groups on downy gray shoots, and the fruits are also found in clusters. 'Aurea' is an extremely decorative smaller tree, particularly in the spring, when the attractive reddish yellow shoots carry the most delightful orange catkins, 3–4 in (8–10 cm) long. The yellow leaves fade to green as the summer progresses. 'Pendula', clothed with grayish green leaves, makes an excellent small weeping tree for the waterside.

A. rubra [*A. oregana*]. Red alder. A medium-sized tree from western North America, it grows to 65 ft (20 m) in a pyramidal shape with slender, slightly pendulous branches and resinous red buds. The leaves, which are dark green on the upper side and grayish beneath, are 3–6 in (8–15 cm) long and broadly oval with a roundish base and double-toothed edges. The male catkins are 4–6 in (10–15 cm) long in groups.

A. rugosa. Smooth alder, speckled alder. A hardy shrub or small tree from the eastern United States, it grows 6–12 ft (2–3.5 m) tall with sticky shoots in spring and roundish or egg-shaped leaves, 2–4 in (5–10 cm) long, that are similar to those of *A. incana* but green on the underside.

ANAGALLIS. Pimpernel. Primulaceae. The name is derived from the Greek word meaning to delight, or possibly from a fable ascribing to the pimpernel the ability to alleviate melancholy. It is a widely distributed genus of 20 species of small herbs with one species suitable for moist almost bog conditions.

A. tenella. Bog pimpernel. This hardy perennial species from western Europe has creeping masses of small light green roundish leaves, 0.25 in (0.6 cm) long, and grows 2–4 in (5–10 cm) high. The delightful small bright pink flowers are produced in midsummer. Bog pimpernel makes a charming dwarf subject for the waterside.

ANEMONE. Windflower. Ranunculaceae. The name is derived from the Greek *anemos*, meaning wind, and *mone*, meaning a habitation, a reference to the preference of some species for windy places, hence its common English name. It is a genus of 120 species of mostly small perennials from the cooler parts of the Northern Hemisphere with a few in South America and South Africa.

A. rivularis. A hardy species from northern India and Sri Lanka, this handsome plant has loose umbels of snow white flowers with violet anthers and grows to 2 ft (0.6 cm) high. The stiff stems bear divided, freely branched dark green slightly hairy leaves. The species is very suitable for naturalizing in groups at the waterside.

A. virginiana. Thimbleweed. A hardy species from eastern North America, it tolerates a degree of flooding. The plant grows 2–3 ft (0.6–1 m) high and bears white or greenish flowers, 1.5 in (4 cm) across, above clumps of hairy leaves.

ANEMOPSIS. Saururaceae. The name is derived from the Greek and refers to the plant's resemblance to *Anemone*. This tender single-species genus from California and Mexico lives in shallow water or muddy sites.

A. californica. Apache beads. An erect-growing perennial with aromatic roots, it reaches 15–18 in (38–45 cm) tall with rounded to oblong radical leaves with long petioles that clasp the flower stem. The white flowers are in the form of a conical spadix, somewhat resembling *Anemone*, surrounded by a whorl of petaloid bracts below. Like *Anemone* it prefers alkaline situations.

ANGELICA. Umbelliferae. The name is derived from the Latin, alluding to the genus's valuable healing properties. It is a genus of 50 temperate species from the Northern Hemisphere and New Zealand.

A. archangelica. Garden angelica, archangel. A very statuesque addition to any bog garden, this handsome plant may attain 6 ft (2 m) in height. It is not a true perennial in that it may flower and seed within a three-year span. The large deeply indented leaves are carried on thick heavy stems, while the small creamy white flowers are clustered together in large round umbels on top of short stems. The tender young stems are boiled and candied for cake decoration. It seeds itself very easily.

ARETHUSA. Orchidaceae. Named after the Greek fountain nymph Arethusa, a reference to the habitat of the plant. It is a small genus of two species of temperate terrestrial orchids.

A. bulbosa. Swamp pink, dragon's mouth. A hardy species from Newfoundland west to Minnesota, it grows 5–10 in (13–25 cm) tall and flowers in May and June with a very attractive solitary rosy purple flower with a bearded crest running down the center of the lip, which is recurved at the apex. The plant likes a shady, moist, north-facing position and does best in a soil mix of leaf mold, rough loam, and sphagnum.

ARISAEMA. Araceae. The name is derived from the Greek and refers to the blood-red blotched leaves of some species. It is a genus of over 150 species mostly from Asia with a few from tropical Africa. The genus is in the *Arum* family and is valued for its interesting foliage, flowers, and berries.

A. candidissimum. A species from western China, it was first identified by George Forrest on the sides of the Yangtze Gorge in Yunnan. This handsome aroid does not appear until June and does best in retentive soil in semishade and sheltered from the wind. Bare pink stems carry white-veined spathes that are about 6 in (15 cm) long and blushed with pink and green on the outside and striped pink and white on the inside. The pointed tip of the spathe curves over the spadix to protect it from rain. Wrapped around the base of the stem is a large three-lobed leaf, 3–9 in (8–23 cm) long and wide, that turns a delightful creamy color in the autumn.

A. triphyllum. Jack-in-the-pulpit. A temperate species from North America, it thrives in cool, shady situations. The greenish spathe bears purplish markings that vary in intensity. The stripes inside range from light to dark purplish brown highlighted with pale green, enhancing the very dark spadix, which is protected by the overhanging spathe tip. The large leaves are trifoliate and long-stalked. An added bonus is the appearance of brilliant scarlet-orange berries that seed themselves in favorable situations. The plant flowers in June and July and is about 12 in (30 cm) tall.

ARISARUM. Araceae. The name is probably derived from the Greek *arista*, meaning a bristle or awn, and *Arum*, to which the genus is allied. The plants in this genus of three species from the Mediterranean region make good ground covers in shady, moist places.

A. proboscideum. Mouse plant. The mouse-tailed arum from the Apennines, it grows only about 4–5 in (10–13 cm) high. This well-named plant produces large clusters of small, very shiny green leaves among which are hidden small flowers with grayish white brown-backed spathes with long thin curved tips like mice tails.

ARNICA. Compositae. The origin of the name is uncertain but is probably from the Greek *arnakis*, meaning a lamb's skin, a reference to the leaves' soft texture. It is a genus of about 32 species from the North Temperate and Arctic regions.

A. chamissonis. Lamb's skin. This attractive species has hoary leaves and bright deep yellow flowers and flourishes in moist, sunny positions.

A. montana. Mountain tobacco. A hardy species from the mountains of central Europe, southern Scandinavia, and western Asia, it produces a flat rosette of leaves in the first year and stems bearing pleasantly aromatic bright orange daisylike flowers in the second year. The plant grows about 12 in (30 cm) high and requires a moist soil in a sunny position. A tincture of arnica soothes bruises and aching feet.

ARUM. Araceae. A very ancient name, it is possibly derived from the Arabic *ar-fire*, a reference to the burning taste of the plant. The genus is now limited to 12 species from Europe and the Mediterranean regions.

A. dioscoridis. This species is difficult to establish but produces magnificent purple-and-black-marbled spathes. The variety *smithii* has larger hastate leaves and more black coloring on the spathe.

A. italicum. A temperate species with a wide distribution, it is mainly found in southeastern Europe, as far south as the Canary Islands. The plant has glossy green arrow-shaped leaves, followed by greenish white spathes and cream-colored spadices. By autumn, columns of vermilion-colored berries are supported on stout stalks.

ARUNCUS. Goatsbeard. Rosaceae. A genus of two temperate species, it occurs from central Europe to China and Japan and also in North America. A distinguished genus for streamsides, it is appreciative of rich soils in semishaded positions and grows 6–7 ft (2–2.2 m) high.

A. dioicus [*A. sylvester*]. Goatsbeard. An elegant plant for the waterside, it produces masses of deeply cut green leaves above which rise waving spires of creamy white flowers. The male plants are usually the more feathery looking, but the females produce long-lasting chestnut-brown ornamental seed heads that are useful for drying. 'Kneiffi', a dwarf cultivar that flowers slightly later, grows 2.5–3 ft (0.8–1 m) high and is an exact miniature of the species with leaves so finely divided that they take on a fernlike appearance. Plate 74.

ARUNDINARIA. Bamboo cane. Gramineae. The name is derived from the Latin *arundo*, meaning a reed. This formerly large genus contains many species from China, Japan, and the Himalayas, some of which are described later in this chapter under *Pleioblastus*, *Pseudosasa*, *Sasa*, *Sinarundinaria*, and *Thamnocalamus*. They are generally referred to as bamboos and have a place near the water garden where their elegant architectural forms give substance to a mixed planting. As certain species spread quickly by their creeping, rambling rootstocks, they should be selected with care. They require a moist, retentive soil that must not be waterlogged and a partially shaded position sheltered from wind. Occasional pruning by cutting out very old and damaged canes is advisable.

ARUNDO. Gramineae. The name is derived from the Latin *arundo*, meaning a reed. It is a genus of three species of reedy grasses from the warmer parts of the Old World. These decorative grasses carry large feathery flower panicles and appreciate plenty of sunlight and moisture in the growing period.

A. donax. Giant reed. A slightly tender species from southern Europe to Iran, India, China, and Japan, it is a magnificent plant that can grow to 20 ft (6 m) in its natural habitat but only reaches about 10 ft (3 m) in the colder parts of North America and Britain. The thick-jointed, slender stems produce very ornamental long glaucous leaves at regular intervals and large panicles of flowers that are reddish at first then later turn white. As it is not fully hardy, some winter protection around the base of the plant should be given. The variety *versicolor* (syn. var. *variegata*), variegated Mediterranean weed, is smaller and less hardy than the type and produces attractive green-and-ivory-white-striped leaves. It is essential to provide winter protection where frosts occur.

ASCLEPIAS. Milkweed, butterfly flower. Asclepiadaceae. Named after Asklepios, the Greco-Roman god of medicine, it is a genus of over 100 species mostly from southern Africa and the New World except two species that grow in Arabia and the Orient and two that are naturalized in Australia.

A. incarnata. Swamp milkweed. An excellent plant for the waterside, it grows about 3 ft (1 m) high in a sunny position and produces stout stems and masses of rosy pink flowers in umbels.

ASPLENIUM. Spleenwort. Aspleniaceae. The name is derived from the Greek *a*, meaning without, and *splen*, a spleen, a reference to the supposed medicinal efficacy of many of the species. It is a genus of

700 widely distributed species of mainly tropical and subtropical ferns.

A. scolopendrium. Hart's-tongue fern. One of the few temperate species native to Europe, it has delightful undulating straplike fronds that provide an unusual contrast to the more usual deeply cut fern frond. The ideal planting niche is in shaded vertical crevices of rocky outcrops near waterfalls or streams. There are several cultivars that produce more undulating, crested, or frilled margins available from specialist nurseries.

ASTER. Compositae. The name is derived from the Greek *aster*, meaning a star. The genus contains 250 species, mostly from the Northern Hemisphere, especially North America, with several from the Old World and some from South Africa.

A. lanceolatus [*A. tradescantii*]. A North American species that is thought to have been introduced to Europe by John Tradescant in 1633, it grows to about 4 ft (1.2 m). One of the last to flower in autumn, this erect pyramidal plant produces masses of tiny white yellow-centered flowers.

A. nemoralis. Bog aster. This North American species grows 6–24 in (15–60 cm) tall and produces large violet-purple to rosy pink flowers in August and September.

A. novae-angliae. New England aster. From the northeastern and north central United States and Canada, this very tough species grows 5–6 ft (1.5–2 m) high with mauvey pink flowers and is the parent of many garden hybrids, including 'Harrington's Pink', a clear pink, and 'Andenken an Alma Pötschke', a salmon-tinged bright cherry-pink cultivar with branching heads and a more compact habit only 2.5 ft (0.8 m) high.

A. novi-belgii. Michaelmas daisy. A hardy species from the eastern United States, this rather slender aster grows up to 4 ft (1.2 m) high and produces large pyramidal heads of violet-blue flowers. The plant is excellent for holding banks of pools and streams because of its dense rooting system. Unfortunately, the large modern named varieties have flowers that are so heavy, the stems need support. The colors, however, are delightful, ranging from white through shades of pale to deep pink, crimson to dark purple, and pale to dark lavender-blue.

A. puniceus. Red-stalked aster. Native to Newfoundland west to southern Manitoba, south to Georgia and Alabama, the plant grows 3–5 ft (1–1.5 m) high with rigid reddish stems and roughish leaves that produce spreading heads of small lilac-colored flowers. This useful species is quite hardy and tolerates wet conditions but must not be too wet in the winter.

ASTILBE. Saxifragaceae. A genus of about 12 temperate species, it contains both tall and dwarf handsome herbaceous perennials that contribute greatly to waterside planting. Their attractive foliage makes good undergrowth from which rise tapering feathery panicles of white, pink, and crimson flowers. The rusty brown seed heads should never be cut down until spring as they provide a tremendous autumn and winter bonus. Although not particular as to soil, the plants do need plenty of water during the growing season and are at their best in partial shade.

A. ×arendsii. A group name commemorating European hybridizer Georg Arends, it covers a series of many garden hybrids raised since 1907 between the Chinese *A. chinensis* var. *davidii* and three Japanese species, *A. astilboides*, *A. japonica*, and *A. thunbergii*. These hybrids possess a tremendous range of characteristics and colors not only in their flowers but also in some magnificent mahogany-tinted foliage. Plate 75.

A. chinensis. This species from northern China has given rise to the dwarf 'Pumila', a garden selection that produces dense carpets of leaves and stiffly branched spikes of mauvey pink flowers 15–18 in (38–45 cm) high with a spread of about 2 ft (0.6 m). The variety *tacquetii*, also from northern China, has given rise to the cultivar 'Superba', which has dark-tinted roundish leaves topped by long dense spires of fluffy purply mauve flowers on dark mahogany stems about 4 ft (1.2 m) tall.

A. ×crispa **'Perkeo'**. This choice hybrid produces very low-growing dark crinkled leaves and masses of stumpy intense deep pink flower spikes no more than 6 in (15 cm) high.

A. rivularis. A species from western China and the Himalayas, it is a magnificent foliage plant for large-scale plantings. Making a large basal clump of deeply divided leaves, its arching plumes reach nearly 6 ft (2 m) tall with tiny greenish white flowers that become long-lasting brown seed heads.

A. simplicifolia. This dwarf species from Japan grows about 8 in (20 cm) tall and bears attractively arched short panicles of creamy colored flowers above glossy foliage. It is one of the several parents used by Arends for raising many dwarf hybrids that are ideal for the pool and streamside. One of the most popular plants is 'Bronze Elegans', which has extremely attractive dark foliage topped by short arching sprays of pink-tinged creamy salmon flowers about 12 in (30 cm) high. 'Sprite' is a charming *A. simplicifolia* hybrid growing 15–18 in (38–45 cm) high with chocolate-bronze leaves that become dark green as the season progresses. Wide pyramidal sprays of shell-pink flowers that produce reddish brown seed heads rise above the foliage.

ASTILBOIDES. Saxifragaceae. The name is derived from *Astilbe* and the Greek *eides*, meaning resembling. It is single-species genus of moisture-loving herbs from northern China.

A. tabularis [*Rodgersia tabularis*]. A distinctive species, it grows to 3 ft (1 m) tall with almost round lotuslike pale green leaves that are borne on a central leaf stalk. The equally distinctive creamy white clustered flowers are held well above the leaves on strong stems. It is hard to resist including this most attractive plant in any collection of distinctive waterside species.

ASTRANTIA. Masterwort. Umbelliferae. The name is derived from the Greek *aster*, meaning a star, a reference to the plant's starlike flower umbels. A genus of about 10 species from Europe and Asia, it has to be viewed at close quarters to be fully appreciated for its unique charm. From attractive lobed foliage, slender branching stems display an inflorescence made up of a rufflike circle of white or rose. Green-veined chafflike bracts carry a cluster of tiny rosy pink fertile flowers in the center. Astrantias require plenty of moisture in either semishade or open situations.

A. carniolica. This small plant from southeastern Europe grows 6–12 in (15–30 cm) high and has green-and-white bracts with pale pink flowers. 'Rubra' is the more usual garden form, about 18 in (45 cm) high with burgundy-red flowers.

A. involucrata 'Shaggy'. Also known as 'Margery Fish', this interesting plant produces large narrow white green-tipped "petals" more than 2 in (5 cm) across.

A. major. Greater masterwort. A European species that grows to 2 ft (0.6 m) high, it has five-lobed leaves and pink-and-green flowers. It prefers semishade and does very well by running water. 'Sunningdale Variegated' is an absolute stunner growing about 2.5 ft (0.8 m) high and providing two periods of interest: one in spring when the handsome maplelike foliage, variegated with two shades of green—one dark and the other pale near the margin mixed with cream—appears. The other is in high summer, when the flowers, which are not unlike those of *A. involucrata* 'Shaggy', bloom and the foliage loses its variegation and becomes dark green.

A. maxima. This species from southern Europe and the Caucasus grows 1.5–2.5 ft (0.5–0.8 m) tall and has smaller three-lobed leaves with pink flowers and bristly bracts.

ATHYRIUM. Dryopteridaceae. The name is derived from the Greek *athoros*, meaning good at breeding.

It is a genus of nearly 100 species of ferns from widely diverse parts of the world.

A. filix-femina. Lady fern. This hardy fern from Europe, North America, and Asia must be one of the most attractive hardy ferns with elegant arching vivid green lacy fronds rising to 3 ft (1 m). It prefers a shady, moist situation. This beautiful species has numerous cultivars of various sizes and shapes: 'Minor', about half the height of the lady fern and readily increased; 'Minutissimum', even smaller than 'Minor', slowly forming a mass of small crowns 4–6 in (10–15 cm) high; 'Percristatum', an interesting plant growing about 2–2.5 ft (0.6–0.8 m) with reddish brown stems that are heavily crested; 'Plumosum', a smaller cultivar producing daintily divided feathery light green fronds making it extremely attractive and well worth looking for; and 'Victoriae', perhaps the most lovely, with long elegant finely divided crested fronds that seem to form a latticework up the entire stem, growing to about 2.5–3 ft (0.8–1 m) high.

A. nipponicum. This Japanese species grows to 12 in (30 cm) high with coarsely divided green fronds and maroon-colored stalks. 'Pictum' (Japanese painted fern) is outstanding for its coloring. Purplish-tinted stalks seem to flush the pale gray coloring of the delicate fronds. The plant requires a sheltered position.

BETULA. Birch. Betulaceae. The name is the Latin for birch. It is a genus of about 60 species from the North Temperate and Arctic regions. These graceful, decorative trees, often with pendulous branches carrying dainty leaves and swinging catkins in spring, are a great asset to the garden. Most of the species prefer moist, sandy soil, but some, including *B. pendula* and *B. nana*, are adaptable and seem happy in both wet and dry situations.

B. maximowicziana. Monarch birch. A Japanese species, this is the largest-leaved of all the birches, growing 80–90 ft (24–27 m) high and making a good background tree with pale orange or gray branches and bark. This birch has long attractive hanging catkins in spring.

B. nana. Dwarf birch. A tough species from the Arctic, North America, northern Europe, and Siberia, it grows 2–4 ft (0.6–1.2 m) high with a low spreading habit.

B. nigra. River birch, red birch. This North American species grows 50–80 ft (15–24 m) tall with a graceful pyramidal shape. Noted for its remarkable reddish brown bark that takes on a ribboned look as it becomes slit and ragged with age, it is at its best at the sides of pools and streams so that its roots can run down to the water.

B. pendula. Silver birch, white birch, common birch. An elegant species from Europe and Asia Minor, it grows about 60 ft (18 m) high with a silvery peeling bark that eventually becomes dark and rough at the base. The dainty leaves are carried on pendulous branches. There are many cultivars of this species, including 'Dalecarlica' (Swedish birch) with deeply lobed leaves; 'Fastigiata', a slender columnar tree; 'Purpurea', a Hungarian species with purple leaves; and 'Youngii' (Young's weeping birch), which is very pendulous and dome-shaped with no leading shoot.

BLECHNUM. Blechnaceae. The name is derived from the Greek *blechnon*, meaning a fern. This genus of about 200 species is widely distributed throughout the world but mainly occurs in the Southern Hemisphere.

B. penna-marina. A charming dwarf species from the Antarctic and New Zealand, it has attractively cut almost erect evergreen fronds, 4–6 in (10–15 cm) long, that are dark olive green in color with a bristlelike texture.

B. spicant. Common hard fern, deer fern. From the North Temperate Zone, this attractive hardy evergreen fern makes a good clump with two kinds of fronds. The slender fertile fronds, 1–3 ft (0.3–1 m) long, grow massed together in the center of the plant. The sterile deep green shining fronds spread flat and are about 18 in (45 cm) long.

BUPHTHALMUM. Ox eye. Compositae. The name is derived from the Greek *bous*, meaning an ox, and *ophthalmos*, meaning an eye. A genus of two species from southern Europe, it is useful for large-scale planting.

B. salicifolium. This Austrian species grows 18–24 in (45–60 cm) tall with large masses of dark green leaves that make a good base for the slender stems carrying deep yellow daisylike flowers.

CAMASSIA. Camass, camas. Liliaceae. The name is derived from *quamash*, a Native American word. It is a genus of five or six species of moisture-loving bulbous plants from North America. They naturalize well in the wild garden but produce finer spikes of bloom under cultivated conditions.

C. cusickii. From Oregon, these large bulbs produce 3-ft (1-m) flower stems with approximately 30 to 100 pale blue narrow-petaled starlike flowers and slightly wavy glaucous leaves about 15 in (38 cm) long and 1.5 in (4 cm) wide.

C. leichtlinii. From western North America, it is perhaps the finest garden species, 3 ft (1 m) in height, with large slender stems carrying starry blooms

varying in color from creamy white (the usual color) to shades of blue. As the flowers die, the segments of the perianth converge and twist together. 'Plena' is a double cultivar that increases slowly, having well-packed long-lasting rosettelike creamy yellow flowers.

C. quamash [*C. esculenta*]. A species found growing along streambanks from British Columbia to Utah and central California, it was a staple in the diet of Native Americans. In gardening circles there has been confusion over this plant and *C. cusickii*, both having blue flowers varying in intensity.

CARDAMINE. Cruciferae. The name is derived from the Greek *kardmon*, meaning cress. The 150 species in this genus are natives of cool regions and damp ground, and some are found growing submerged. Another species of *Cardamine* is discussed in Chapter 6.

C. pratensis. Lady's smock, cuckoo flower, mayflower, meadow cress. Native to the Northern Hemisphere, it grows 1–1.5 ft (0.3–0.5 m) high. Rosy lilac flowers grow above cresslike leaves that may be used in salads. 'Flore Pleno', the double cultivar, is much superior with rosettes of small cresslike leaves and masses of small double pale lilac flowers, about 9–12 in (23–30 cm) tall, in May. This seedless form reproduces by the leaves taking root and developing new plantlets. Plate 76.

C. raphanifolia [*C. latifolia*]. Native to the Pyrenees, this plant grows in spreading rich green mats of foliage to a height of 18–24 in (45–60 cm), producing flower stems with blooms not dissimilar in size and coloring to honesty (*Lunaria biennis*).

C. trifolia. This smaller species grows about 6 in (15 cm) high and forms a slow-spreading mat of evergreen leaves that in winter become tinged with purple. Naked stems produce small white flowers in early spring.

CHELONE. Turtlehead. Scrophulariaceae. The name is derived from the Greek *kelone*, meaning a turtle. A genus of four species native to North America, it thrives in moist conditions and flowers in September and October, giving autumn interest to the garden.

C. glabra. Turtlehead. This species grows to about 2 ft (0.6 m) with white or rose-tinged flowers.

C. obliqua. From copious basal leaves, dark green leafy stems grow 2–2.5 ft (0.6–0.8 m) long and produce richly colored reddish purple flowers that are reliably weather-resistant.

CIMICIFUGA. Bugbane. Ranunculaceae. The name is derived from the Latin *cimex*, meaning a bug, and *fugio*, meaning to run away. The plant was once used to deter fleas, hence its common name. It is a showy genus of about 15 perennial species from Europe, central and eastern Asia, and North America. They thrive in moist soil in semishade and produce leaves at irregular intervals up wiry stems terminating in branching bottlebrush racemes of white or cream flowers.

C. americana. American bugbane, mountain bugbane. This tall species grows to 5 ft (1.5 m) with handsome broad-cut leaves, not unlike those of the Japanese anemone. Flowering in August, stiff stems carry spires of brownish buds that open to lightly fragrant fluffy flowers of pale cream with a hint of green.

C. dahurica. From the Far East, this rather rare species has blackish stems with more widely spaced fluffy creamy white flowers above much-divided and toothed foliage. It grows about 6 ft (2 m) high.

C. foetida. Fetid bugbane. A tall handsome plant from northeastern Asia, it grows 5–6 ft (1.5–2 m) tall with deeply veined much-divided dark green leaves. The flowers have a distinctly yellowish appearance because the sepals around the white stamens are yellow. The resulting green pods in arching sprays are very attractive and an added bonus.

C. racemosa. Black cohosh, black snakeroot. From northeastern North America, this handsome species grows about 5 ft (1.5 m) high and produces, earlier than the other species, densely covered spikes of pure white flowers above divided green leaves.

C. ramosa. An October-flowering species, it grows about 6 ft (2 m) tall with very large divided leaves supporting slender branching stems that produce pure white narrow spires of flowers. 'Brunette' is a very striking and desirable cultivar with perhaps the darkest purplish black leaves of all the cimicifugas. Growing to 6 ft (2 m), the slender purple stems bear spires of pinkish white fragrant flowers. 'Atropurpurea' is also an outstanding plant, growing to 6 ft (2 m) with dark purplish leaves and stems with ivory white flowers. Plate 77.

C. simplex. A late-flowering species from Russia to Japan, it provides two garden cultivars that are worthy of note. 'Elstead Variety', a cultivar that grows about 4 ft (1.2 m) high, has an extremely graceful habit with irregularly arching stems clothed with purplish buds that open to pure white with pink stamens. 'White Pearl', growing about 4 ft (1.2 m) high, has greenish brown leaves and spires of tiny ivory-tinted pale green buds that open to purest white flowers followed by pale green seed pods.

CLAYTONIA. Spring beauty. Portulacaceae. A genus of about 15 species, it is named in honor of John Clayton (1686–1773) of Virginia, one of the earliest American botanists.

C. virginica. From moist woods in North America, this erect slender little plant grows 2–6 in (5–15 cm) in height and produces loose racemes of pink flowers and rather linear leaves.

CLETHRA. Summersweet, white alder. Clethraceae. The name owes its origin to the Greek name for alder because of the similarity between the leaves of the two genera. A genus of about 30 species of compact bushes or small trees that appreciate a sheltered position in peaty moist soil, it provides suitable subjects for streamside planting. In late summer fragrant white flowers are produced in spikes.

C. alnifolia. Sweet pepperbush. This species, from eastern North America grows to 10 ft (3 m) high and produces erect panicles of fragrant flowers from July to September. 'Paniculata', a quite vigorous grower, is hardier and produces very long panicles of flowers and narrower smooth less-serrated leaves. 'Rosea' is pink-flowered.

COPTIS. Goldthread. Ranunculaceae. The name is derived from the Greek word meaning to cut, probably because of the much-divided leaves. A genus of about eight species, it is distributed over the North Temperate and Arctic regions.

C. trifolia. Goldthread. Native to northeast Asia and Alaska, this unusual and attractive small evergreen plant for cool, moist situations grows 3–6 in (8–15 cm) high. The plant makes low mats of shiny trifoliate leaves that in March are covered with single saucer-shaped small white flowers. The bitter roots produce a yellow dye and a valuable tonic medicine.

CORNUS. Dogwood. Cornaceae. The name is derived from the Latin *cornus*, meaning a horn, a reference to the plant's hard wood. It is a genus of about 45 species distributed over temperate parts of the Northern Hemisphere. The genus provides a wide range of decorative and useful trees and shrubs with some species thriving in wet situations, making them ideal subjects for waterside planting. Perhaps their greatest attraction is the brightly colored stems, which in winter enhance the landscape. These species should be cut back hard after spring flowering to encourage new wood, which has the most vivid coloration.

C. alba. Tartarian dogwood. Originating in Siberia and northern China, this rampant species grows to 10 ft (3 m) with branches becoming blood red in winter. It bears white, tinged blue, oval fruits. 'Elegantissima Variegata' (syn. 'Argenteomarginata') is a rich silver-variegated cultivar with foliage turning pink in autumn. Red stems that can grow up to 6 ft (2 m) tall brighten the winter garden. 'Gouchaltii' is a cultivar with pinkish leaves margined with yellow. 'Kesselringii' has shiny purple-black stems that give a striking winter effect when grown with other *C. alba* cultivars. 'Sibirica' (Siberian or Westonbirt dogwood) is perhaps the most outstanding cultivar, with vivid red stems that are particularly effective beside water. The clusters of blue-gray berries, which stand out against the autumnal tints of the foliage, are an added bonus. Plate 78.

C. canadensis. Creeping dogwood, bunchberry. A North American native, this beautiful little woodland plant grows 3–9 in (8–23 cm) high and forms shrubby carpets of light green leaves studded all over with silver white flowers in summer and small scarlet berries in autumn.

C. mas. Cornelian cherry. A good species for background planting, it grows 10–20 ft (3–6 m) high with a spreading habit. Its chief attraction is the mass of yellow flowers produced on naked wood in February and March. In autumn it provides bright red oval fruits and bronzy red leaves.

C. sanguinea **'Winter Flame'**. An exciting discovery found in a Dutch nursery in 1982, this remarkable shrub grows 3–4 ft (1–1.2 m) when cut to 2 in (5 cm) each April and provides the best color when grown in a sunny position. The vividly colored stems, which intensify at the onset of frosts, are its main attraction. The stems, which are yellow at the base, deepen to fiery orange and red at the tips. During the summer the plant is clothed in soft green foliage, which turns orange and yellow as autumn approaches. Altogether it is a very desirable plant.

C. stolonifera **'Flaviramea'**. A yellow-stemmed cultivar, it grows 3–4 ft (1–1.2 m) high and needs regular hard pruning in April to produce the brightest yellowish green stems. If left unpruned, terminal clusters of whitish cream berries are produced in autumn.

CROCOSMIA. Iridaceae. The name is derived from the Greek *krokos*, meaning saffron, and *osme*, meaning smell. When immersed in warm water, the dried flowers smell of saffron. The seven species in this genus are native to South Africa and thrive in all soil types except bog or excessive clay, giving their best in moisture-retentive soil in sun or partial shade.

C. aurea. Growing to about 3 ft (1 m), this tender species is probably not in cultivation in temperate zones, but its wide nodding flowers and light coloring have been passed on to many fine hybrids.

C. ×crocosmiiflora. Montbretia. A hybrid resulting from a cross between *C. aurea* and *C. pottsii*, it is a common hardy plant having arching grassy leaves and elegant branching flower stems that carry pendulous lilylike flowers, orange on the outside and yellow with reddish brown markings inside. Several improved forms have been produced, including 'Emily McKenzie', a large, long-lasting hybrid growing to 2 ft (0.6 m) high with widely expanded dark orange flowers; 'George Davidson', growing 18–24 in (45–60 cm) tall and producing pale orange flowers on slightly arched stems; and 'Solfatare', which, though not quite as hardy as other cultivars, repays amply with warm apricot-yellow flowers and bronze-green swordlike leaves, growing 18–24 in (45–60 cm) tall, if protected over winter with a mulch of straw or leaves.

C. × Curtonus. Alan Bloom of Bressingham Gardens, England, has raised some excellent hybrids between *Crocosmia* and *Curtonus*, including 'Lucifer', a dramatic plant growing 4 ft (1.2 m) tall with broad handsome swordlike leaves topped by wiry purple stems supporting brilliant flame-red trumpet-shaped flowers, and 'Spitfire', growing to about 2.5 ft (0.8 m) tall with abundant sprays of fiery orange flowers whose color seems intensified by the yellow stamens produced from a yellow throat.

C. masonorum. Reaching a height of 2.5–3 ft (0.8–1 m), this species differs from the others that are mentioned because its arching stem holds vermilion-orange flowers upright instead of facing forward under the stem. The seed heads are much sought after by flower arrangers. Sword-shaped dark green leaves turn a warm beige as they fade. 'Firebird' is a marked improvement, with larger, more richly colored flame-orange flowers on arching spikes.

C. paniculata. Growing 3–4 ft (1–1.2 m) high, this South African native is highly valued for its imposing clumps of broad, stiff, grooved swordlike leaves that take on beautiful coppery tints in the autumn. Small orange-red trumpet-shaped flowers are carried in large branching sprays and are followed by attractive seed heads.

C. pottsii. This species grows to 3 ft (1 m) and is the hardy parent of *C. ×crocosmiiflora* with small flowers of vermilion-red carried on erect stems.

CYPRIPEDIUM. Lady's slipper, Venus's slipper, moccasin flower. Orchidaceae. The name is derived from the Greek *Kypris*, one of the names of Venus, and *podion*, a little foot or slipper. It is a genus of 35 species, mostly native to the Northern Hemisphere, containing some very attractive hardy slipper orchids. They prove a challenge to grow, demanding cool, peaty, moist but well-drained soil in partial shade.

C. acaule. Moccasin flower, stemless lady's slipper. A native of North America, this hardy species grows 12–16 in (30–40 cm) high with yellow-green or purplish solitary flowers, each with a pouched warm rose or white lip. The leaves are pleated and lance-shaped. It thrives in partial shade.

C. calceolus. Lady's slipper. A native of North America, Europe, and Japan, this species thrives in limestone areas in well-drained moisture-retentive soil in partial shade. It bears paired or solitary purplish flowers with a yellow-pouched lip. Lance-shaped leaves are arranged in a spiral up the stem. The variety *pubescens*, a native of North America and Japan, grows 18–24 in (45–60 cm) high and bears flowers with spirally twisted yellowish green sepals and purple-striped petals with a large, light yellow pouch that has purplish veins inside. The root is used as a nerve stimulant in the United States.

C. japonicum. A native of Japan requiring moist sandy loam, this Oriental species has a solitary flower, greenish or silvery white, flushed and splashed with crimson.

C. reginae. Showy orchid. From the tamarack and cedar swamps of North America, this beautiful large plant grows 12–24 in (30–60 cm) high and prefers partial shade. Its one to three flowers per stem have white or rose-flushed sepals and petals and a white-pouched lip that is heavily variegated with rose-pink stripes. The deeply pleated light green leaves bear short white downy hairs.

CYSTOPTERIS. Bladder fern. Dryopteridaceae. The name is derived from the Greek *kystos*, meaning a bladder, and *pteris*, meaning a fern. It is a genus of about 18 species of small attractive hardy ferns.

C. bulbifera. Berry bladder fern. A native of North America, this dainty fern grows to 18 in (45 cm) high with delicate pale green fronds with stems and midribs in a striking chestnut-brown color. This species has the unusual habit of producing tiny dark green bulbils under the fronds that sow themselves and soon produce new plants.

C. fragilis. Brittle bladder fern. From temperate regions, this extremely attractive dainty fern grows about 9 in (23 cm) high. It has broadly lance-shaped delicate sprays of tiny lacy fronds that are very light green in spring. The fronds rise from a prostrate rootstock that is handsome in its own right, being covered in broad golden brown scales. The plant must be given a shady position.

C. montana. Mountain bladder fern. From northern Europe, North America, and Australia, this hardy little fern has triangular vivid green fronds, 4–12 in (10–30 cm) high, and prefers a moist, shady situation.

DACTYLORHIZA. Orchidaceae. The name is derived from the Greek *daktylos*, meaning finger, and *rhiza*, a root. It is a genus of 30 species of deciduous terrestrial orchids from Europe, Asia, North America, and North Africa. Another *Dactylorhiza* species is discussed in Chapter 7.

D. elata. Growing to 30 in (75 cm) tall, this vigorous and striking terrestrial orchid from France, Spain, and Algeria prefers a deep, well-drained soil with plenty of humus that does not dry out and a partially shaded location. Dense clustered spikes of rich rosy purple flowers rise from a base of strap-shaped fresh green leaves.

D. foliosa. Madeira orchid. This species is sometimes confused with *D. elata* but is more pyramidal in shape and grows to only about 18 in (45 cm) with grooved shining leaves. The flower spikes are somewhat variable in color, less startling than those of *D. elata* but still of a purplish hue.

DARMERA. Saxifragaceae. It is a single-species genus of rhizomatous moisture-loving herbs from North America.

D. peltata [*Peltiphyllum peltatum*]. Umbrella plant, Indian rhubarb. The rounded leaves grow about 3 ft (1 m) high and 1 ft (0.3 m) across on single stems that appear when the flowers are finished. The starry pink flowers are borne on red-tinted stalks about 1–2 ft (0.3–0.6 m) high on rounded heads. The large thick rhizomes grow on the surface of moist or muddy soil. 'Nana' is a smaller cultivar that grows to no more than 12 in (30 cm) high and brings the same dramatic impact to the sides of a smaller pool.

DENNSTAEDTIA. Dennstaedtiaceae. Named after the German botanist August Wilhelm Dennstaedt, it is a genus of about 70 species of temperate ferns related to *Dicksonia*.

D. punctiloba. Hay-scented fern. A North American species, this delightful fern grows 2–2.5 ft (0.6–0.8 m) high and makes an excellent ground cover for damp soil in partial shade. Wiry curving carpet-forming rhizomes produce elegant arching pale green fronds fragrant of new-mown hay. The plant can become very weedy.

DESCHAMPSIA. Hair grass. Gramineae. Named in honor of the renowned French naturalist Louis Deschamps (1765–1842) of St. Omer in northern France, it is a genus of about 20 species of tufted grasses from the cooler parts of the Northern Hemisphere.

D. caespitosa. Tufted hair grass, tussock grass. Growing to 3 ft (1 m) tall, this beautiful perennial grass forms dense tufts of narrow rough-edged arching dark green leaves that send up numerous erect slender stems from which hang dainty open panicles of tiny greenish purple flowers that turn to brownish yellow spikelets lasting well into winter.

DIANTHUS. Caryophyllaceae. The name is derived from the Greek *dios*, meaning a god, and *anthos*, meaning a flower. It is a genus of about 300 species native to Europe, the Mediterranean region, Asia, and the mountains of southern and tropical Africa.

D. superbus. Perhaps the only species that thrives in a damp situation, this mat-forming plant grows 12–24 in (30–60 cm) high. It has pale greenish gray leaves from which grow slender stems bearing large very fragrant five-petaled deeply and irregularly slit pink flowers with darker purplish rose centers.

DIPHYLLEIA. Berberidaceae. The name is derived from the Greek *dis*, meaning double, and *phyllon*, a leaf, a reference to the plant's two-lobed leaves. It is a genus of three species of temperate perennials.

D. cymosa. Umbrella leaf. From the mountains of Virginia, Georgia, and Tennessee, this unusual plant produces on very long petioles enormous rounded two-lobed bright green leaves that may reach 12 in (30 cm) across. Clustered heads of inconspicuous white flowers are succeeded by deep indigo-blue berries that are further enhanced by the stalks' taking on a reddish hue. It thrives in moist, cool shade.

DODECATHEON. Shooting star. Primulaceae. The name is derived from the Greek *dodeka*, meaning twelve, and *theos*, meaning god, signifying "flower of the 12 gods." It is a genus of 14 species from North America, ranging from damp valleys in the prairies to the Rocky Mountains. The species closely resemble one another except that some are taller. All produce distinctive cyclamenlike flowers with reflexed petals and prominent stamens. After fertilization, the flowers turn skyward, hence the name shooting star. Smooth broad-bladed leaves are in the form of a basal rosette.

D. frigidum. Originating in western North America, this smaller species grows 2–10 in (5–25 cm) tall with violet flowers.

D. hendersonii. Sailor caps, mosquito-bills. A California species, it grows about 12 in (30 cm) high with small kidney-shaped leaves and pinkish purple flowers with yellow-margined anthers.

D. meadia. Shooting star, American cowslip. A larger species from North America, it grows up to 24 in (60 cm) high with rose-magenta flowers and long green leaves that are often spotted with purple.

DRYOPTERIS. Dryopteridaceae. The name is derived from the Greek *dryas*, oak, and *pteris*, meaning a

fern. It is a large genus of over 150 species distributed worldwide. Many of the species form shuttlecocklike crowns and give of their best in cool, moist conditions with some light shade.

D. affinis. Golden shield fern, golden-scaled male fern. Often known as *D. borreri* or *D. pseudomas*, it is distributed throughout Europe and most of Britain and Ireland. This extremely handsome fern produces yellowy green fronds 24–32 in (60–80 cm) in length with spectacular stalks covered with golden to orange-brown scales. For optimum growth, moisture and some shade are required.

D. dilatata. Broad prickly-toothed buckler fern. An easily grown attractive plant with dark green broadly triangular fronds, it grows 2–3 ft (0.6–1 m) high from stout scaly rootstocks. 'Cristata' is a very fine handsome cultivar with pale green divided arching fronds that are especially attractive when unfurling in the spring.

D. erythrosora. Japanese shield fern, copper shield fern. From Japan and China, this most beautiful fern produces young foliage of glossy copper and pink that matures gradually to a rich glossy green. Scarlet-colored spore capsules are produced on the undersides of fronds that grow to 24 in (60 cm) high.

D. filix-mas. Male fern. A widely distributed temperate fern, it is undemanding in cultivation, thriving in moist soils and even in quite dry conditions. Freely divided light green deepening to dark green fronds grow to 3 ft (1 m) high, making elegant sheaves that remain long into winter.

D. goldiana. Goldie's shield fern, Goldie's wood fern. From the northeastern and central United States and northeastern Canada, the fronds of this fern grow 3–4 ft (1–1.2 m) high and have a distinctly yellowish tinge when they first uncurl in the spring.

EOMECON. Snow poppy. Papaveraceae. The name is derived from the Greek *heoros*, meaning eastern, and *mekon*, meaning a poppy. A single-species genus from eastern China, this moisture-loving perennial spreads rapidly by its rhizome.

E. chionantha. Snow poppy, dawn poppy. This beautiful glabrous plant, 12 in (30 cm) in height, has rounded, slightly crinkle-edged leaves borne on caramel-colored stems. Nodding poppylike flowers filled with golden stamens are carried on erect stems in long panicles. This species is best grown in moist soil in shady positions where the running rootstock can be controlled.

EPILOBIUM. Fireweed. Onagraceae. The name is derived from the Greek *epi*, meaning upon, and *lobos*, meaning a pod, a reference to the flowers that appear to be growing on the seed pod. It is a genus of about 200 species of temperate perennial herbs, many of which are extremely attractive but can be invasive through self-seeding over vast areas. Certain less-invasive species are worthy of planting in ornamental moisture-rich beds.

E. angustifolium. Rosebay willow herb, fireweed. A well-known plant from the Northern Hemisphere, it is much too invasive for garden use but has given rise to the noninvasive white cultivar 'Album'. An attractive addition to the wild garden, it produces spires of white flowers 4 ft (1.2 m) tall.

E. glabellum. Originating in New Zealand, it makes a useful ground cover plant, growing to no more than 12 in (30 cm) and forming clumps of small mid-green shiny leaves above which are masses of cream-colored outward-facing cup-shaped flowers borne singly on slender stems.

EPIMEDIUM. Bishop's hat, bishop's mitre. Berberidaceae. A genus of about 25 species from the North Temperate regions of the Old World, it is an extremely useful group of hardy plants for ground cover that are at their best in moist soil in partial shade.

E. grandiflorum. A species that originated in Japan and Manchuria, it grows 8–12 in (20–30 cm) tall with fawny brown spring foliage and sprays of mauvey pink flowers. 'Rose Queen' has extra large rose-pink flowers with long white-tipped spurs. 'White Queen' is an attractive white cultivar, while 'Violaceum' is rather dwarfer with dark lilac flowers.

E. ×*perralchicum*. A very attractive evergreen hybrid between *E. perralderanum* and *E. pinnatum* subsp. *colchicum*, it was raised at the Royal Horticultural Society's gardens at Wisley, England, and has large yellow spurless flowers.

E. perralderanum. From Algeria and growing 12–15 in (30–38 cm) tall, this handsome evergreen species has an array of large glossy leaves and bright yellow flowers.

E. pinnatum subsp. *colchicum*. A nearly evergreen plant originating in Transcaucasia and Georgia, it grows 12 in (30 cm) tall, produces wide yellow flowers, and has the added foliage bonus of turning to bright tints in the autumn and winter.

E. pubigerum. Originating in Asia Minor and southeastern Europe, this plant grows 18 in (45 cm) tall and is made all the more attractive by tiny creamy white or pink flowers held in tall elegant sprays above pale green rounded leaves.

E. ×*rubrum*. This extremely attractive hybrid between *E. grandiflorum* and *E. alpinum* grows to 9 in (23 cm) tall with small crimson white-spurred flowers and beautifully tinted foliage that passes from pale green to a brick-red color.

E. ×*versicolor*. This cross between *E. grandiflorum* and *E. pinnatum* subsp. *colchicum* has produced several attractive cultivars that have been separately named. One example is 'Sulphureum', which, with its pale yellow flowers, makes an excellent ground cover.

E. ×*warleyense*. This hybrid was raised in the garden of one of the great 19th-century English patrons of ornamental gardening, Ellen Willmott, and has unusual orange-colored flowers but does not make as dense a cluster of leaves as the other kinds.

E. ×*youngianum* **'Niveum'**. This compact, low-growing hybrid, a cross between *E. grandiflorum* and *E. diphyllum*, reaches 6–10 in (15–25 cm) high. In spring showy tiny white flowers stand out above small brownish green leaves that gradually become light green as the flowers fade.

EPIPACTIS. Helleborine. Orchidaceae. The name originates from the Greek *epipegnuo*, meaning to coagulate, a reference to the plant's supposed effects on milk. It is a genus of about 24 species of terrestrial orchids from Europe, Mexico, and North America that thrive best just above the waterline in partial shade.

E. gigantea. Stream orchid, brook orchid, giant orchid, giant helleborine, chatterbox. Found on the banks of streams in North America and Mexico, this robust plant grows 12–24 in (30–60 cm) tall with ornate leaves at the base that become narrower as they ascend the stem. The flowers are carried in spikes and are greenish brown with purple veining. The open lower lip is orangey red on the inside, changing to a dark purplish crimson at the heart.

E. palustris. Marsh helleborine. Originating in Europe, this sturdy plant grows 12–18 in (30–45 cm) high with lanceolate stem-clasping leaves and slightly drooping flowers that are whitish, tinged with crimson, and carried in a loose ovate spike.

ERANTHIS. Winter aconite. Ranunculaceae. The name is derived from the Greek *ar*, meaning spring, and *anthos*, meaning a flower, a reference to the plant's early-flowering habit. It is a genus of about seven species of clump-forming dwarf herbaceous perennials.

E. hyemalis. Winter aconite. Originating in shady woods of southeastern Europe, this species has naturalized widely. A delightful, hardy little plant, it carries buttercup-yellow cup-shaped flowers surrounded by leaflike ruffs of green bracts that appear very early in the year. Growing 4–5 in (10–13 cm) high but varying in size with the locality, it becomes much larger in moist, shady places.

ERICA. Heath. Ericaceae. The name is derived from the Greek *ereika*, meaning heath or heather. It is a genus of over 700 species of evergreen shrubs and trees native to Africa and Europe. As background plants to water, they may be used very effectively, but care and consideration must be given to the choice of species. Many of those species from southern Africa cannot be considered for outdoor cultivation in the Northern Hemisphere, but there are ample hardy forms from which to choose.

E. carnea. Winter heath, spring heath, snow heather. From central and southern Europe, this very popular species grows about 12 in (30 cm) high and is low-spreading with urn-shaped rosy red flowers about 0.25 in (0.6 cm) long growing in terminal racemes about 1–3 in (2.5–8 cm) long. A tremendous number of cultivars in a wide range of flower colors provide interest from December to April, making this species very popular. This heath is tolerant of many soil conditions, including lime. There are many varieties available, but two reliable cultivars are 'Springwood White', perhaps the best white cultivar, vigorous and rapid spreading, and 'Springwood Pink', similar but with pink flowers. There are many more compact cultivars readily available.

E. cinerea. Scotch heath, bell heather. Originating in western Europe, this summer-flowering heath grows 9–24 in (23–60 cm) high with rosy purple urn-shaped flowers, 0.25 in (0.6 cm) long, and provides many colorful variants, including 'Domino', a lovely pure snowy-white-flowered cultivar with a neat growth habit; 'C. D. Eason', flowering from June to July with bright deep pink flowers and carpetlike growth; and 'P. S. Patrick', with rich deep purple flowers carried on wiry foliage.

E. ×darleyensis. This vigorous quick-growing plant, a hybrid between *E. erigena* and *E. herbacea*, grows about 24 in (60 cm) high. Tufted bristly mounds of foliage produce pale pink flowers 0.25 in (0.6 cm) long in leafy racemes 3–6 in (8–15 cm) from November to May, making it a very desirable plant. Two cultivars are particularly outstanding: 'Silberschmelze', a pure white form with creamy pink-tipped foliage in spring, and 'Darley Dale', with pale mauvey pink flowers carried from midwinter to spring.

E. tetralix. Cross-leaved heath. Originating in northern and western Europe and flowering from June to October, this more graceful species has much softer growth. It grows 12–20 in (30–50 cm) high with rosy pink flowers about 0.25 in (0.6 cm) long in umbel-like clusters. 'Colonel Underwood' is a very good cultivar with beautiful crimson flowers and pale green leaves.

E. vagans. Cornish heath. Originating in southwestern Europe and growing 12–30 in (30–75 cm) high, this species produces masses of purplish pink flowers in erect cylindrical terminal racemes, 3–8 in (8–20 cm) long, from July to November. Many lovely cultivars are available, including 'Lyonesse', with long racemes of pure white flowers, and 'Mrs. D. F. Maxwell', with deep pinky cerise bottlebrush-like flower heads produced in profusion.

ERYTHRONIUM. Adder's-tongue, dog-tooth violet, trout lily, fawn lily. Liliaceae. The name is derived from the Greek *erythros*, meaning red, a reference to the color of the first introduced species. It is a genus of about 20 species of ornamental bulbous plants. One species is distributed from Europe to Asiatic Russia and Japan and the others in North America. These desirable spring-flowering plants thrive in cool, moist situations in light shade.

E. californicum. Fawn lily. Originating in California and growing about 12 in (30 cm) high, this clump-forming tuber has semierect basal dark green leaves mottled with brown. Above the leaves as many as three creamy white flowers with reflexed petals, which sometimes show orange-brown markings ringed around the base, are carried on each stem.

E. dens-canis. Dog-tooth violet. This widely distributed species from Europe and Asia grows about 6 in (15 cm) tall and is named after its small smooth ivory-colored corm, which is shaped like a dog's canine tooth. The pendent flowers carried on short stems vary in color from white through pinks and rose to purplish cyclamen with bands of purple, brown, and yellow near the center. The bluish green leaves are mottled with brown.

E. oregonum. Originating in Oregon, Washington, and southern British Columbia, and growing to 15 in (38 cm) high, this vigorous species bears a loose spike of up to 10 whitish cream reflex-petaled pendent flowers with yellowish centers surrounded by a deep orangey brown ring. The green basal leaves are mottled light brown and white.

E. revolutum. Originating in California and Oregon and growing 10–12 in (25–30 cm) high, this species has faint brown-and-white mottling on the green leaves with one to four large drooping rose-pink flowers with reflexed petals. There are several named cultivars available.

E. tuolumnense. Originating in California and growing about 12 in (30 cm) tall, this species has plain glossy yellow-green leaves about 8–12 in (20–30 cm) long, above which are held bright yellow pendent flowers with reflexed petals with up to 10 flowers on one stem.

EUPATORIUM. Boneset, thoroughwort. Compositae. The name is derived from Mithradates Eupator, ancient king of Pontus, who discovered in one of the species an antidote for poison. It is a genus of over 400 species, mostly from America, with some from the Old World. They are rather coarse, easily grown perennials.

E. cannabinum. Hemp agrimony. Native to Europe, where it flourishes in damp places, this tall downy plant grows 2–5 ft (0.6–1.5 m) high with reddish stems and reddish purple flowers in terminal clusters. There is a double-flowered cultivar, 'Plenum'.

E. purpureum. Joe-Pye weed. Originating in North America and growing up to 9 ft (2.7 m) high, this species resembles *E. cannabinum* but is larger and more brightly colored with large flat heads, sometimes reaching 12 in (30 cm) across, of fluffy mauve-pink upturned flowers on dark purplish stalks.

EUPHORBIA. Spurge. Euphorbiaceae. The genus is named after Euphorbus, physician to Juba II, king of Mauritania. It is a very large genus of around 2000 species, differing widely in habit, distributed throughout the world.

E. palustris. Originating in marshy places in Europe and growing about 3 ft (1 m) high, this spectacular spring-flowering plant produces many leafy stems topped with great heads of yellow bractlike flowers. The foliage turns to brilliant shades of yellow and orange in the autumn.

FILIPENDULA. Meadowsweet. Rosaceae. The botanical name is derived from the Latin *filum*, meaning a thread, and *pendulus*, meaning hanging, a reference to the many small tubers of *F. vulgaris* that hang together by threadlike roots. A small genus separated from *Spiraea*, it is found in the Himalayas, northern Asia, Europe, and North America mostly in moist places.

F. kamtschatica. A native of Kamchatka and Manchuria, this species grows 4–10 ft (1.2–3 m) tall with huge spreading dark green leaves and loose panicles of white fragrant flowers. These are ideal plants for the sides of large pools in bog gardens.

F. purpurea [*Spiraea palmata*]. A native of Japan and growing about 4 ft (1.2 m) high, this very handsome plant for the waterside forms clumps of large leaves above which are heavy cymes of carmine or deep rose-pink flowers. The plant flourishes in deep, rich soil in partial shade. The attractive white cultivar is 'Alba'.

F. rubra. Queen-of-the-prairie. A native of the eastern United States, this plant grows 6–8 ft (2–2.5 m) tall, making a magnificent sight with its large jagged leaves growing up the stems to the enormous feathery plumes about 12 in (30 cm) long of tiny fragrant rosy carmine flowers. This is a vigorous plant that will soon colonize a boggy site.

F. ulmaria. Queen-of-the-meadow, meadowsweet. Originating in Europe and temperate western Siberia in wet places, this species is rarely cultivated but has a place in the wildlife garden. Growing 3–5 ft (1–1.5 m) high, it produces creamy flowers on leafy stems. 'Aurea' is an extremely choice foliage plant that requires plenty of moisture and light to encourage the production of its rich yellow leaves—but not direct sunlight, which tends to cause the foliage to scorch. Remove the insignificant flower heads to encourage the growth of fresh foliage.

F. vulgaris [*F. hexapetala*]. Dropwort. Originating in Europe and Asia and growing to 2 ft (0.6 m) high, this species tolerates drier conditions and makes hummocks of ferny carrotlike foliage with crowded heads of white flowers that are often tinged with pink on the outside. The double cultivar 'Flore Pleno' is more attractive.

GALAX. Diapensiaceae. The name is derived from the Greek *gala*, meaning milk, probably in reference to the plant's milk-white flowers. It is a genus of one species from eastern North America.

G. urceolata [*G. aphylla*]. An attractive evergreen clump-forming perennial, it is at its best in moist soil and partial shade. The large heart-shaped leathery midgreen leaves are carried on fine wiry stems and turn bronze in autumn and winter. In midsummer slender spires of tiny white flowers are produced.

GAULTHERIA. Ericaceae. Named after Dr. Gaultier, a mid-18th-century botanist and physician of Quebec, this is a genus of about 170 species of evergreen shrubs from North America, the Himalayas, eastern Asia, Australia, Tasmania, and New Zealand.

G. nummularioides. From the Himalayas and China, this useful prostrate shrub has long, slender, somewhat bristly densely leafy twining stems that make a tough carpet of foliage. The solitary pink, white, or brownish red flowers are hidden beneath the leaves and are followed by oval blue-black fruits 0.25 in (0.6 cm) long.

G. procumbens. Wintergreen, checkerberry. A creeping shrub from eastern North America, its aromatic foliage turns reddish in winter. In summer, solitary pink-flushed white flowers appear, followed by scarlet berries. This plant likes to grow in shady situations in moist soil.

GENTIANA. Gentian. Gentianaceae. Named after Gentius, king of Illyria, who first used the plant in medicine, this is a genus of about 400 species of annual or perennial plants widely distributed in Europe, Asia, North and South America, and New Zealand. A few of these desirable plants are adapted for moist situations in the bog garden.

G. andrewsii. Bottle gentian, closed gentian, blind gentian. Originating in North America, this perennial plant grows 12–24 in (30–60 cm) high with leafy erect stems and axillary clusters of rich blue flowers with white on the lobes. This plant enjoys a sandy soil at the pool's edge. Forma *albiflora* is white and not quite so tall.

G. asclepiadea. Willow gentian. A European native, this thoroughly reliable and graceful plant grows 12–24 in (30–60 cm) tall with narrow willowlike leaves and rich blue flowers that are arranged in axillary clusters around the upper half of the stem. Plants thrive in deep, moist soil in part or full shade and improve if left undisturbed. 'Alba' is a good white cultivar whose flowers have greenish cream throats. 'Knightshayes' is a more erect cultivar producing deep blue trumpets with conspicuous white throats.

G. pneumonanthe. Marsh gentian. This charming perennial species from the Northern Hemisphere grows 6–12 in (15–30 cm) high with slender leafy stems bearing several bell-shaped purplish blue flowers that are lined with five greenish stripes.

GERANIUM. Cranesbill. Geraniaceae. The name is derived from the Greek *geranos*, meaning a crane, as the fruit resembles the head and beak of the bird, hence the common name cranesbill. This is a genus of about 300 species, some of which respond to moist conditions, making them excellent for disguising difficult pool edges.

G. endressii. Originating in the Pyrenees and growing about 18 in (45 cm) high, this attractive nearly evergreen plant quickly covers the ground with its elegantly divided apple-green leaves and cup-shaped rose-pink flowers. The cultivar 'Wargrave Pink' bears bright salmon-pink flowers.

G. ×magnificum. This handsome sterile hybrid grows to 18 in (45 cm) high with deeply cut hairy rounded leaves that are often richly tinted in autumn. A profusion of cup-shaped prominently veined violet-blue flowers are produced in small clusters in summer.

G. psilostemon. Originating in Armenia, this taller plant grows 3–4 ft (1–1.2 m) high, making a large lump of elegant broad deeply cut leaves that color well in the autumn. The many cup-shaped single flowers of an intense magenta-carmine color with black centers make a wonderful sight in midsummer.

GEUM. Avens. Rosaceae. The name was used by Pliny for a plant with black thin aromatic roots. This is a genus of about 50 species of perennial plants widely distributed, especially in temperate and cold regions.

G. rivale. Water avens, Indian chocolate. A lover of wet meadows and marshy places in the North Temperate Zone, it grows 10–12 in (25–30 cm) high with dull purplish pink flowers and strawberrylike leaves. More attractive garden forms have been developed, such as 'Leonard's Variety', which grows 12–15 in (30–38 cm) high with clumps of dark green divided leaves and somewhat bell-shaped flowers of coppery creamy pink flushed orange with yellow stamens just visible below, and 'Lionel Cox', which is similar in size and foliage to 'Leonard's Variety' but has primrose yellow flowers held in brown calyces.

GUNNERA. Gunneraceae. Named after Norwegian botanist J. E. Gunner (1718–1773), it is a genus of 40 to 50 slightly tender species of herbaceous perennials widely distributed in the Southern Hemisphere. Some of these are gigantic plants that produce the largest leaves that can be grown in temperate regions, looking like enormous green rhubarb. Plenty of moisture is needed if they are to be seen at their best. In the autumn, when frost kills the leaves, they should be cut and inverted over the crown of the plant for protection.

G. magellanica. Originating in Patagonia and the Falkland Islands, this tiny mat-forming perennial has dark green rounded reniform leaves, 2.5 in (6 cm) across, that are often bronze-tinged when young. It reaches about 3–6 in (8–15 cm) in height.

G. manicata. Giant rhubarb. From Colombia, this is the largest species with stems 6 ft (2 m) tall and vast leaves up to 6 ft (2 m) across that are harsh, bristly, and deeply lobed. The curious much-branching flower spike is like a huge green bottlebrush, 1–3 ft (0.3–1 m) tall, tinged with red. The plant grows from a thick creeping rhizome, which is thickly covered in brown papery scales that look like fur. These plants are spectacular when planted where they can be reflected in the water. Plate 79.

G. tinctoria [*G. chilensis*]. A native of Chile, this plant grows 3–6 ft (1–2 m) tall with leaves 4–5 ft (1.2–1.5 m) across. The flowers are borne on dense spikes and are reddish green in color.

HACQUETIA. Umbelliferae. Named after B. Hacquet (1740–1815), a German botanist, this is a genus of a single species of herbaceous perennials.

H. epipactis. A European native, this attractive spring-flowering plant requiring moisture and partial shade makes little clumps packed with fluffy yellowish green flower heads encircled by apple-green bracts. Radical palmate deeply lobed rich green leaves about 3–8 in (8–20 cm) high are usually taller than the inflorescence.

HELLEBORUS. Hellebore. Ranunculaceae. A classical name used by Hippocrates and other Greek writers, *Helleborus* contains about 15 species of herbaceous perennials from southern Europe and western Asia, including some very desirable plants for moist, peaty areas. In addition to their producing an abundance of sculptured flowers when once established, they also provide handsome ground cover with their large hand-shaped foliage. They are very poisonous.

H. argutifolius [*H. corsicus*]. Originating in Corsica, Sardinia, and the Balearic Islands, this excellent plant has tall canelike stems growing to 2 ft (0.6 m) high with extremely attractive tripartite grayish green prickly-edged veined leaves. The long-lasting flowers of palest green are pendent cups produced in upstanding clusters.

H. foetidus. Stinking hellebore. A native of southern Europe growing about 18 in (45 cm) high, this handsome plant makes clumps of finely divided fan-shaped blackish green leaves with drooping clusters of bell-shaped palest green flowers delicately edged with maroon that last from four to five months. 'Wester Flisk' is a distinctive cultivar with purplish red stems and deeply cut evergreen leaves.

H. lividus. A native of Majorca and growing about 18 in (45 cm) high, this species requires warmer conditions than *H. foetidus*. The beautiful tripartite dark glossy evergreen leaves are conspicuously veined in cream, giving an overall marbling effect, while the undersides of the young leaves and the stems are plum-colored. The flowers are pinkish green and delicately scented.

H. niger. Christmas rose. A native of Europe and western Asia and growing about 12 in (30 cm) high, this plant has dark green leathery leaves with beautiful white nodding flowers faintly tinged with pink on the outside and containing a crown of outstanding golden stamens.

H. orientalis. Lenten rose. Originating in Greece and Asia Minor, this species contains many beautiful late-winter to early-spring flowers about 18 in (45 cm) high with basin-shaped creamy green flowers fading to pale brownish yellow-green. The expansive and attractive palmate evergreen foliage makes a good ground cover. Two subspecies worthy of growing are *abchasicus* and *guttatus*. Originating in the Caucasus along the Black Sea coast, subspecies *abchasicus* grows about 12 in (30 cm) high with delicate pendent flowers of a deep purplish red, which even tints the nectaries and leaves nearer the stems. Subspecies *guttatus*, native of Russian Georgia, grows about 12–15 in (30–38 cm) high. It produces both white and deep pink flowers with dark red spots inside.

H. viridis. Originating in central and southern Europe, this species grows about 12 in (30 cm) high. The attractive olive-green foliage dies back in the winter to appear again in early spring together with pendent clusters of small saucer-shaped flowers of a distinctive bluish green.

HELONIAS. Liliaceae. The name is derived from the Greek *helos*, meaning a marsh. This is a single-species genus of moisture-loving perennials.

H. bullata. Swamp pink. A North American native flowering in April and May, this handsome plant reaches 12–24 in (30–60 cm) in height with close rosettes of dark green shiny strap-shaped leaves and hollow stems bearing a tightly packed head of small purplish pink flowers.

HEMEROCALLIS. Daylily. Liliaceae. The name is derived from the Greek *hemeres*, meaning a day, and *kallos*, a reference to the individual flower's fleeting beauty. This genus of about 15 species of herbaceous perennials from eastern Asia provides a most useful and colorful addition to the moist garden, reveling in full sun in really wet soil. The individual flowers last only one day but are produced in long succession. In addition to the various species, many of which have considerable merit, there are countless cultivars.

H. aurantiaca. Native to Japan, this species grows about 3 ft (1 m) tall with more or less evergreen foliage. The trumpet-shaped flowers are brilliant orange with a purplish tinge in the middle of the segments. The variety *major*, also from Japan, has larger open flowers of pure rich orange.

H. citrina. Of uncertain origin, this species grows to about 3 ft (1 m) with dark green leaves and citron-yellow funnel-shaped fragrant flowers that open in the late afternoon.

H. fulva. Orange daylily. Found from southern Europe to eastern Asia, this plant grows about 4 ft (1.2 m) tall. The flowers have broad and blunt petals with a zone of brown around the throat and an apricot central line on each segment.

'Flore Pleno' (syn. 'Kwanso Flore Pleno'), originating in Japan and growing 3–4 ft (1–1.2 m) high in vigorous clumps, has rich orange-buff double flowers with a central V-shape of reddish copper on the petals. They are longer lasting than most other cultivars. 'Maculata', growing about 4 ft (1.2 m) high, has graceful stems bearing elegant flowers with re-flexed top segments, soft coppery buff in color with a dark area in the center. 'Rosea', growing to 3 ft (1 m), is a natural variant from China and a forerunner of pink cultivars. Its flowers are a delightful soft glowing rose color with attractive graceful grassy foliage.

H. lilioasphodelus [*H. flava*]. Lemon lily, yellow daylily. An important early species from temperate Europe and Asia, it grows about 2.5 ft (0.8 m) high. The graceful arching bright green leaves make neat tufts from which arise beautiful lily-shaped clear yellow sweetly scented flowers with recurving petals.

H. multiflora. A native of China and growing to 4 ft (1.2 m) high, this is one of the last species to flower and has a much-branched scape of small, scented, soft orange to yellow flowers. It is possibly a parent of such well-known cultivars as 'Golden Chimes', with reddish brown buds opening to rich yellow flowers, and 'Corky', a dainty form about 2 ft (0.6 m) high with pale yellow flowers with a bronze reverse. Attention is being given, particularly in the United States, to breeding dwarf species.

HEPATICA. Liverleaf. Ranunculaceae. The name is derived from the Greek *hepar*, meaning liver, which the lobed leaves are said to resemble. It is a genus of 10 species of variable perennials distributed throughout the North Temperate Zone.

H. nobilis [*Anemone hepatica*]. Native to Europe and Asia and growing 4–6 in (10–15 cm) tall, this species has semievergreen rounded three-lobed fleshy leaves and shallowly cup-shaped dainty flowers borne in profusion in shades of blue, white, or pink. There are many cultivars, including 'Alba' (white), 'Caerulea' (blue), 'Rosea' (pink), and 'Lilacina' (mauve).

HERACLEUM. Cow parsnip. Umbelliferae. The name is derived from the ancient Greek name for Hercules. This is a genus of about 60 species of large biennial or perennial plants from the North Temperate Zone and tropical mountain regions.

H. mantegazzianum. Giant hogweed, cartwheel flower. An outstanding subject for the waterside, it grows 8–10 ft (2.5–3 m) tall with enormous basal divided leaves 3 ft (1 m) wide and huge wheel-like heads of white flowers borne on stout hollow cylindrical polished copper-colored stems. Some people may be allergic to this plant, so introduce with care.

HOSTA [*FUNKIA*]. Plantain lily. Liliaceae. Named after Nicolous Thomas Host (1761–1834), physician to the emperor in Vienna, these 40 species of hand-some herbaceous perennials are natives of eastern Asia, especially Japan. The nomenclature is in a rather confused state. The group as a whole is invaluable in any waterside or woodland setting with its strikingly bold, prominently veined foliage and many variegated cultivars. In summer, hostas produce long-stalked racemes of lilylike flowers.

H. crispula [*H. fortunei* var. *marginato-alba*]. From Japan and growing about 2.5 ft (0.8 m) high, this excellent foliage plant has broadly white-edged sage-green heavily corrugated leaves that are gray on the underside and tubular lavender flowers.

H. decorata. A fairly low-growing species about 24 in (60 cm) high, it has dull entirely dark green leaves, but the variety *decorata* (syn. var. *marginata*) has a broad white margin that goes right down the deeply cleft wide stalk. Rich deep lilac flowers are borne on more or less leafless stems.

H. fortunei. A native of Japan and about 2.5 ft (0.8 m) high, the cordate glaucous wavy-edged leaves are about 8 in (20 cm) long and 7 in (18 cm) wide. The pale lilac flowers are carried well above the foliage. The variety *albopicta*, growing nearly 2.5 ft (0.8 m) high, is perhaps one of the most spectacular hostas and certainly a great favorite. If left undisturbed in shade with plenty of moisture, the leaves grow about 9 in (23 cm) long, not including the stalk, and about 6 in (15 cm) across with a slight puckering between the veins. The delicate textured leaf blades are bright yellow edged with pale green. As time passes, the yellow fades to a primrose color and the green darkens slightly so that by midsummer the leaf is the same green color all over. Trumpet-shaped light lavender-colored flowers are held on graceful stalks. 'Aurea', rather less vigorous than the type, grows about 24 in (60 cm) high. The delicate leaves are completely bright yellow at first, gradually fading to light green.

H. lancifolia. A native of Japan and growing to about 2.5 ft (0.8 m) tall, this plant is an excellent ground cover because its small long-pointed shining dark green leaves make overlapping mounds from which arise in profusion large deep lilac trumpet-shaped flowers on tall slender stalks.

H. plantaginea. Originating in China and growing to 24 in (60 cm) high, this is one of the choicest plain-foliaged species with its beautiful glossy bright green arching heart-shaped leaves. The trumpetlike marble-white flowers are produced late in the season and have a delicate lilylike fragrance. 'Honey-bells' is an attractive cultivar from Bristol Nurseries, Connecticut, with fragrant pale lilac flowers and blunt-pointed wavy-edged olive-green leaves.

H. rectifolia. Originating in Japan and growing 24–30 in (60–75 cm) high, this species has rather erect plain green leaves and widely opened dark lilac flowers. 'Tall Boy' is a notable cultivar with improved long-pointed heart-shaped fresh green foliage. The rich lilac-colored bell-like flowers, carried on stalks 4 ft (1.2 m) high, are spectacular.

H. sieboldiana [*H. glauca*]. Originating in Japan and growing about 2.5 ft (0.8 m) high, this species produces the most dramatic leaves of all the hostas. The enormous distinctly pointed cordate leaves may vary in depth of coloring, being deep gray-green, bluish, or glaucous, and reach up to 14 in (35 cm) in length and width. The rather disappointing pale lilac flowers are carried in dumpy flower heads that are not much higher than the leaves. One tremendous bonus is the warm glowing honey color the leaves take on when the first frost arrives.

H. undulata. A Japanese native growing up to 18 in (45 cm), this species bears almost spirally twisted pointed leaves up to 3.5 in (9 cm) wide with bold lengthwise creamy white variegations and dark green undulating margins. The flower stem bears several leaves and narrowly funnel-shaped lilac flowers.

H. ventricosa. From eastern Asia and 4 ft (1.2 m) tall, this species makes large clumps of broad heart-shaped dark green shiny leaves with wavy edges. The beautiful large dark lilac flowers are internally veined and somewhat rounded in shape.

INULA. Compositae. A genus of about 90 species of herbaceous perennials from Europe, Asia, and Africa, it occurs mostly in temperate regions.

I. helenium. Elecampne, horseheel. Originating in northern Asia and naturalized in Europe, North America, and Japan, this showy plant, growing 3–5 ft (1–1.5 m) high, thrives in a wet, sunny situation. The large ovate toothed wrinkled leaves are downy on the underside. The bright yellow flowers, borne in terminal heads, are about 3 in (8 cm) across. It was formerly much used in medicine.

I. magnifica. This 6-ft (2-m) giant from the Caucasus requires plenty of space in which to grow and be appreciated. The enormous broad docklike leaves have a rough matte texture and make a great mound at the base of the plant, diminishing in size as they ascend the brownish stems. At the heads of the stems, brown buds open to large vivid deep yellow fine-rayed daisies 5–6 in (13–15 cm) across.

IRIS. Iris, flag, fleur-de-lis. Iridaceae. The name is derived from the Greek messenger Iris, who came to earth via a rainbow. A genus of about 300 species of herbaceous perennials, it provides us with plants that, by careful selection and positioning, can sustain a lengthy flowering period. A special mention should be made regarding the Louisiana iris group. Although the five species—*I. brevicaulis*, *I. fulva*, *I. giganticaerulea*, *I. hexagona*, and *I. nelsonii*—have been found growing in many areas of Louisiana, some are native to other south central states. Hybridizers have crossed and recrossed these species, and the results have been a wide range of beautiful and unbelievable colors, including glorious reds, purples, oranges, blues, violets, lavenders, mauves, pinks, yellows, and white. These cultivars perform quite well over nearly all the United States unless a late spring frost arrives. They can be grown and will bloom in moist soil in up to 12 in (30 cm) of water. Unfortunately, Louisiana irises do not seem to do well in Great Britain and much of Europe, especially northern Europe, where apparently it is too cold for them. They grow well, however, in Japan, Australia, and South Africa. Other *Iris* species are discussed in Chapter 7. Plate 80.

I. brevicaulis. Louisiana iris. Medium blue standards and falls with a small patch of white near the base of the falls characterize this species. It has been used extensively in hybridizing with many beautiful cultivars resulting.

I. bulleyana. Siberian iris. Originating in China, this beautiful species grows 18–30 in (45–75 cm) high and has attractive grassy foliage and rich purple-blue flowers.

I. chrysographes. Siberian iris. A native of western China and growing about 24 in (60 cm) high with grassy foliage, this species has flowers that are rich velvety purple with golden-yellow-etched veins. There are several selected and named cultivars including 'Black Knight', a velvety indigo-violet that is almost black; 'Margaret Holmes', with claret-crimson flowers exquisitely marked with lemon stripes toward the throat; and 'Rubella', which is wine red.

I. ensata [*I. kaempferi*]. Japanese water iris. The clematis-flowered irises from Japan grow about 3 ft (1 m) high and provide an exotic group of plants for the water garden, ranging in color through shades of white, pink, lavender, blue, violet, crimson, and yellow, some plain, others with bold and elaborate markings. They flourish in a sunny position by the waterside in rich soil with abundant moisture during the growing season or in shallow water not over 1 in (2.5 cm) in depth. Of all the irises they are perhaps the most sumptuous, with their butterflylike flowers with horizontally held petals giving an unequalled show of color and beauty. There are so many varieties from which to choose that it is best to select them when in flower.

I. fulva. Louisiana iris. Originating in the southern United States and about 24 in (60 cm) high, this beautiful, unusually colored species flowers in July. The arching leaves are bright green, and the horizontally spread petals are a bright rich velvety coppery brown with purple veining. A hybrid involving this species crossed with *I. brevicaulis*, also from the south central United States, has produced *I. ×fulvala*, which is perhaps a more reliable garden plant. The unique coloring of the parents has been lost, although the rich crimson-purple flower with a bright yellow center is handsome in its own right.

I. giganticaerulea. Louisiana iris. In this species the flower color ranges from pale blue, as found in the variety *alba*, to medium and dark blue to purple. There is a creamy white patch near the base of the falls.

I. hexagona. Louisiana iris. The flowers in this species are medium to dark blue with a yellowish patch near the base of the falls.

I. lacustris. Lake iris. From the shores of Lakes Huron, Michigan, and Superior in North America and growing 6–12 in (15–30 cm) high, this delightful little iris with sky-blue flowers appears in spring and again in autumn.

I. nelsonii. Louisiana iris. The flowers in this species come in a wide variety of colors: yellow, copper, red, lavender, and purple.

I. setosa. Originating in Siberia, Japan, and North America and growing to 24 in (60 cm) high, this species flourishes in damp soil in sun and makes arching clumps of gray-green leaves. From the leaves arise many-branched stems carrying flowers particularly rich in their depth of purple coloring with white-centered falls delicately veined with yellow.

I. sibirica. Siberian iris. Native to Europe and northern Asia and growing about 3 ft (1 m) high, this beautiful summer-flowering iris species is a must for the water garden and flourishes best in moist soil in sunny places. The attractive narrow green leaves grow in upright sheaths from which slender branching heads of violet-blue flowers are produced. Like *I. ensata*, there are so many good cultivars covering such a wide range of colors that personal selection is the best way to choose these beautiful plants. All the cultivars, regardless of color, bear falls marked in the center with an area of yellow or white veining. The narrow, shining chestnut-brown seed heads are an added attraction. Plate 88.

ITEA. Grossulariaceae. The name is derived from the Greek name for the willow. It is a genus of trees and shrubs with 10 species from northeastern Asia and one from North America.

I. virginica. Virginia willow, sweetspire. A native of North America and growing 2–4 ft (0.6–1.2 m) high, this dwarf shrub thrives in moist soil by the waterside. The leaves are smooth and bright green on top but paler and slightly downy beneath with the added attraction of becoming brilliantly colored in the autumn. In July, small fragrant creamy white flowers are borne on erect spikes 2–6 in (5–15 cm) long at the ends of leafy twigs.

JEFFERSONIA. Twin leaf. Berberidaceae. Named in honor of Thomas Jefferson (1743–1826), third president of the United States, it is a genus of two species of perennial herbs from North America and eastern Asia.

J. diphylla. Rheumatism root, twin leaf. From eastern North America, it grows 6–8 in (15–20 cm) high with each leaf deeply divided into two halves, hence the common name. The single flowers are pure white and poppylike, measuring about 1 in (2.5 cm) across. It thrives in damp, shady places.

KIRENGESHOMA. Hydrangeaceae. This genus of one or two species from Japan and Korea is at its best in deep, moist soil in partial shade, sheltered from damaging winds.

K. palmata. A unique and beautiful perennial plant from Japan, it grows 2–4 ft (0.6–1.2 m) high with large green papery leaves, hairy on both sides and with irregularly cut edges. The unusual pale yellow shuttlecocklike flowers, waxen in texture, are about 2 in (5 cm) long and hang in loose sprays on purplish stems. A similar species, *K. koreana*, a Korean native, has more erect flowers.

LATHYRUS. Vetchling, wild pea. Leguminosae. This is a genus of about 100 species of mostly tendril-climbing herbs, usually from temperate regions or tropical mountain ranges.

L. palustris. Marsh pea. Originating in North America, Europe, and Asia and growing 1–3 ft (0.3–1 m) high, this moisture-loving perennial has narrow leaves growing in pairs and a profusion of purplish pealike flowers about 0.5 in (1.3 cm) long. The variety *myrtifolius*, myrtle-leaved marsh pea, native to the river banks of North America, has attractive tendrils, slightly broader leaves, and lilac-colored flowers.

LEUCOJUM. Snowflake. Amaryllidaceae. The name is derived from the Greek *leukos*, meaning white, and *ion*, a violet, a reference to the color and maybe the fragrance of the flowers. It is a genus of about nine species of bulbous plants from central Europe and the Mediterranean region that grow 6–24 in (15–60 cm) high.

L. aestivum. Summer snowflake. From central and

southern Europe and growing 12–24 in (30–60 cm) high, this species looks spectacular in large clumps by the waterside, producing glossy daffodil-like leaves of richest green from which arise sturdy stems of the same color bearing white bell-shaped flowers with each turned-out petal tipped in green. The best cultivar, 'Gravetye', was selected by the great English gardener and writer William Robinson.

L. vernum. Spring snowflake. Native to central Europe and growing about 6 in (15 cm) high, this delightful little spring-flowering species has strap-shaped semierect green basal leaves. Leafless stems bear one or two pendent bell-shaped fragrant flowers with six green-tipped white petals.

LIGULARIA. Compositae. The name is derived from the Greek *ligula*, meaning a strap, a reference to the plant's strap-shaped ray florets. It is a genus of about 180 species of herbaceous moisture-loving perennials, natives of the Old World north of the tropics.

L. dentata [*L. clivorum*]. Originating in China, this magnificent plant grows about 4 ft (1.2 m) high with large leathery shining green leaves and strong stems supporting crowded heads of rich orange-colored flowers. Two improved cultivars are 'Desdemona', a more compact cultivar with striking leaves, rich brownish to purply green on the upper sides, fading to metallic green, with rich mahogany underneath, and 'Othello', similar to 'Desdemona' but with purplish leaves.

L. 'Gregynog Gold'. A cross between *L. dentata* and *L. veitchiana*, this is a superb choice for the smaller garden, growing 3–4 ft (1–1.2 m) high with handsome richly veined heart-shaped leaves and huge conical spires of large vivid orange-yellow flowers.

L. macrophylla. Originating in the Orient, this species grows about 5 ft (1.5 m) high with grayish green horseradishlike leaves and spires of yellow daisy-like flowers.

L. przewalskii. From northern China and growing 5–6 ft (1.5–2 m) high, this decorative species has very finely cut dark green leaves resembling many fingers on nearly black stems that carry a spire of small yellow daisylike flowers. A good cultivar is 'The Rocket', which grows about 6 ft (2 m) tall with large neatly cut-edged rounded leaves and narrow spires of lemon-yellow flowers.

L. veitchiana. This native of China grows about 5 ft (1.5 m) tall with almost circular basal leaves nearly 12 in (30 cm) across and slender spikes of golden flowers 1–2 in (2.5–5 cm) in diameter.

L. wilsoniana. Giant groundsel. Originating in China and growing about 4 ft (1.2 m) high, this species' rounded to heart-shaped deeply toothed leaves about 10 in (25 cm) across form a mound from which arise slender flower stems carrying rich golden flowers.

LILIUM. Lily. Liliaceae. A genus of about 100 species of bulbous plants from temperate regions of the Northern Hemisphere, it has a few members that thrive in or near the damp garden, with the North American species being very suitable for moist, shady situations so long as they are not water-logged.

L. canadense. Canadian lily, meadow lily. A summer-flowering bulb, it grows 3–5 ft (1–1.5 m) high with stem roots and thrives in a half-shady situation. The lanceolate leaves are borne in whorls, and the pendulous bell-shaped orange-yellow flowers with recurved petals with dark red or purple spots in the lower part occur in graceful clusters of about 10. The anthers are red.

L. martagon. Turk's-cap lily. Originating in Europe and Asia and growing 3–4 ft (1–1.2 m) high, it seems to thrive in either full sun or partial shade as long as the soil is deep and moist. The soft pinkish purple flowers have purple-spotted strongly recurved segments.

L. pardalinum. Leopard lily, panther lily. This Californian species grows 5–6 ft (1.5–2 m) high and is one of the hardiest lilies to grow in rich, moist soil. Up to 30 bright orange-scarlet recurved flowers with large purple spots on the lower half are carried on stout stems in July, making it a very striking feature near the waterside.

L. superbum. Swamp lily, Turk's-cap lily. From North America and growing 6–8 ft (2–2.5 m) high, this very handsome plant has purplish stems that carry recurved flowers 3–4 in (8–10 cm) across of a brilliant scarlet-orange color with maroon spotting.

LOBELIA. Campanulaceae. Named for Dutch botanist and author Matthias de L'Obel (1538–1616), it is a genus of over 350 species of annual and perennial plants from the tropical and temperate regions of the world, especially the Americas. It is the perennial species of this genus that provide us with elegant waterside plants that are at their most stunning when planted in masses. Abundant moisture is required during the growing season, but the roots should not be too wet in winter. *Lobelia* is also discussed in Chapter 6.

L. cardinalis. Cardinal flower. From North America and growing to 3 ft (1 m) high, this clump-forming perennial should be planted at the waterside to achieve the full impact of its magnificent color. Lance-shaped leaves make a basal rosette and may vary in color from fresh green to red-bronze. Leafy stems support great spikes of intensely vivid scarlet-lipped flowers from mid-August until late September. Plate 81.

L. ×gerardii **'Vedrariensis'**. A vigorous, reliable perennial growing to 3 ft (1 m) high, it has lance-shaped green leaves and racemes of long-lasting rich violet-purple flowers.

L. siphilitica. Great lobelia, blue cardinal flower. From the eastern United States and about 24 in (60 cm) high, this clump-forming hardy perennial thrives in damp, heavy soil where there is shade. Erect stems with whorls of crinkly light green leaves on the lower part carry bright blue two-lipped flowers on the top of the spire. There is a white-flowered form that is excellent for brightening shadier spots.

L. ×speciosa. This hybrid, resulting from crosses between *L. cardinalis*, *L. fulgens*, and *L. siphilitica*, closely resembles *L. cardinalis* but is not so hardy. It has deeper and showier flowers and deep maroon leaves. Many beautiful cultivars are available, including 'Queen Victoria' and 'Bees' Flame', both of which have dazzling large velvety scarlet flowers and attractive crimson-maroon foliage.

LYSIMACHIA. Loosestrife. Primulaceae. The name is derived from the Greek *lysis*, meaning loosening, and *mache*, meaning strife, hence loosestrife. Some authorities attribute its name to Lysimachus, king of Thrace, who is reputed to have discovered the plant's soothing properties. A genus of 150 species, mostly herbaceous perennials, it is found throughout the world in temperate and subtropical regions. Another species of *Lysimachia* is discussed in Chapter 6.

L. ciliata. Native to North America and growing to 3 ft (1 m) high, this attractive species is a very desirable plant for the sides of pools and streams. Brownish green rosettes that later become pale green are produced in spring with many upright stems bearing a plentiful supply from July to September of clear light yellow nodding flowers with deep orange centers.

L. clethroides. Gooseneck loosestrife. Originating in China and Japan and growing 2–3 ft (0.6–1 m) high, this species has large broadly lanceolate leaves 3–6 in (8–15 cm) long that often become tinted reddish bronze in the autumn. The long flower spikes are densely packed with small white flowers that look very effective when planted in groups.

L. nummularia. Creeping Jenny, creeping Charlie. Originating in central Europe, this prostrate plant is very useful and effective for carpeting watersides. The small rounded green leaves are in opposite pairs along creeping stems that are about 12 in (30 cm) long and which in early summer bear bright yellow cup-shaped flowers. It can be invasive in small areas. 'Aurea', an attractive cultivar with golden yellow leaves, is slightly less vigorous than the type.

L. punctata. Garden loosestrife. From Asia Minor and growing to 3 ft (1 m) high, it has flower spikes that are densely packed with bright yellow blooms.

LYTHRUM. Loosestrife. Lythraceae. The name is derived from the Greek *lythron*, meaning blood, a reference to the color of the flowers. It is a genus of 38 species of herbaceous plants or small shrubs from damp places throughout the temperate regions of the world. Ideal in appearance for mass planting in wild garden settings with plenty of moisture, it is unfortunately extremely invasive and is now prohibited in many areas of the United States, where all *Lythrum* species and cultivars are considered environmental threats. Check with the relevant state authority before including *Lythrum* in your garden plan.

L. salicaria. Purple loosestrife. From Europe and Asia and now naturalized in North America, this tall leafy plant grows about 4 ft (1.2 m) high and produces slender spires of bright magenta-pink flowers. Thirteen states in the U.S. have declared purple loosestrife a noxious weed; it has had a tremendous negative impact on wetlands across the continent.

L. virgatum. From Asia Minor and growing 2–2.5 ft (0.6–0.8 m) tall, making it an altogether smaller and daintier plant than *L. salicaria*, it is ideal for the smaller water garden. The slender spikes of flowers are violety pink in color.

MACLEAYA. Papaveraceae. Named in honor of Alexander Macleay (1767–1848), colonial secretary for New South Wales, Australia, it is a genus of three species of large herbaceous plants from China and Japan that thrive in moist but well-drained soil.

M. cordata. Originating in China and Japan, it grows 5–7 ft (1.5–2.2 m) high with deeply lobed heart-shaped leaves that are silver beneath. The creamy white to buff flowers are borne in large panicles.

M. microcarpa. Plume poppy. A native of China and for a long time known erroneously as *Bocconia cordata*, the plume poppy grows to 7 ft (2.2 m) and is most imposing with large rounded beautifully lobed leaves that are gray-green above and gray-white beneath. The numerous small bronzy-colored fluffy flowers are carried in slender panicles. 'Kelway's Coral Plume', growing 5–6 ft (1.5–2 m) tall, is a very attractive selected cultivar with coral-pink flowers and bronzed upper leaf surfaces.

MATTEUCCIA. Ostrich plume fern. Dryopteridaceae. Named in honor of C. Matteucci (1800–1868), an Italian physicist, this is a genus of four species of ferns with two forms of fronds: fertile fronds growing from the center of the erect rootstock and sterile fronds surrounding them. They require damp conditions year-round.

M. struthiopteris [*Struthiopteris germanica*]. Ostrich plume fern, shuttlecock fern. From temperate North America, Europe, and eastern Asia, this very attractive, graceful plant has lance-shaped erect divided fronds, 3–4 ft (1–1.2 m) long, that droop and spread outward like a gigantic shuttlecock. The dark brown fertile fronds stand stiffly erect throughout the winter.

MECONOPSIS. Asiatic poppy. Papaveraceae. The name is derived from the Greek *mekon*, meaning a poppy, and *opsis*, meaning like, a reference to the poppylike appearance of this genus of about 45 species of herbaceous plants from northern India, upper Burma, and northern China. One species, *M. cambrica*, Welsh poppy, occurs in western Europe. These alluring blue poppies require moist but not waterlogged lime-free soil in a partly shaded position sheltered from wind. They are a hallmark of a good gardener's collection as it is notoriously difficult to keep them blooming year after year.

M. betonicifolia. Blue poppy. One of the most attractive species from China, it grows to 4 ft (1.2 m) with rosettes of bristly betony-shaped leaves that become smaller as they ascend the erect stems. In June these stems bear the most delightful nodding saucer-shaped blue flowers. The deepest shades of blue, which highlight the contrast in the petals with the central boss of golden stamens, are achieved in moist, acid soils.

M. grandis. Tibetan poppy. From the Himalayas, this blue poppy is larger than *M. betonicifolia*, growing to 5 ft (1.5 m) under good conditions, with coarser lance-shaped leaves with reddish bristles. The flowers are deep blue to purple with creamy stamens. If grown in association with *M. betonicifolia*, it hybridizes freely, and true-to-type progeny is difficult to produce. Plate 82.

M. ×sheldonii. The result of the 1937 crossing of *M. betonicifolia* and *M. grandis* in Surrey, England, and named after the raiser, this hybrid reaches 3–4 ft (1–1.2 m) in height and has foliage similar to that of *M. betonicifolia* but produces delightful large clear blue flowers. Several cultivars with enormous long-lasting flowers are now being offered.

METASEQUOIA. Dawn redwood, water larch. Cupressaceae. This is a single-species genus discovered in the 1940s, first as a fossil and subsequently as a living population in China. It is now grown widely in parks, gardens, and arboreta throughout the world.

M. glyptostroboides. The name is derived from the Greek *glyptos*, meaning engraved, and *strobus*, meaning pine cone, alluding to the slit on the edge of each cone scale. It is a moisture-loving fast-growing deciduous conifer with a most attractive reddish fibrous bark that becomes distinctly fluted with age. Growing in a conical habit 100–115 ft (30–35 m) high, it assumes brief but attractive autumn colors when its small soft blue-green leaves turn yellow and orange before falling. It is distinguished from *Taxodium distichum* (bald cypress) by having a narrower habit, opposite instead of alternately ranked leaves, and the following year's buds underneath the branchlets. As a specimen conifer near water where space is at a premium, its narrower habit of growth has made it a more popular choice than the bald cypress.

MISCANTHUS. Gramineae. The name is derived from the Greek *miskos*, meaning a stem, and *anthos*, a flower, a reference to the plant's tall flowering stems. It is a genus of 17 species of tall perennial ornamental grasses.

M. sacchariflorus. Amur silver grass, silver banner grass, hardy sugar cane. From eastern Asia and growing about 9 ft (2.7 m) high, this vigorous species, like a bamboo, is an imposing plant with its reedy stems carrying long arching leaves that rustle in the wind. The terminal panicles of silky, silvery mauvish brown spikelets appear only in warmer climates. It makes a very good screen plant. There is a fine variegated cultivar, 'Variegata'.

M. sinensis. Eulalia. From Japan and China, this vigorous clump-forming grass grows to 6 ft (2 m) with tough erect stems and provides a good foil for plants with broader, lusher architectural foliage at the waterside. There are several interesting cultivars, including 'Gracillimus', growing to 5 ft (1.5 m) with narrower leaves than most other *Miscanthus* species and making a more subtle effect in smaller plant groupings; 'Silver Feather', one of the better-flowering cultivars, more reliable in producing pale brownish to pink almost fluffy panicles with a silvery hue, making it a fine specimen plant; 'Variegatus', not quite so tall at about 4–5 ft (1.2–1.5 m), very attractively striped with white for the whole length of the leaf with a pinkish blush on while the green-and-white stems; and 'Zebrinus' (tiger grass), growing about 6 ft (2 m) tall, a very desirable cultivar with green leaves until the end of July, then developing golden yellow bands across the leaf blades, and in October producing silky, feathery pinky white spikelets in fan-shaped panicles. Plate 83.

MONARDA. Wild bergamot, horsemint. Labiatae. Named after Spanish physician and botanist Nicolas Monardes (1493–1588), it is a genus of about 16 species of annual and perennial aromatic plants.

M. didyma. Bee balm, Oswego tea. From North America and growing 2–3 ft (0.6–1 m) high, this plant is seen at its best when planted in large groups on the banks of streams and pools. Dense, spreading clumps of nettlelike leaves on branching stems are topped with scarlet-hooded salvialike flowers. A refreshing drink can be made by infusing the aromatic leaves in boiling water. There are some excellent cultivars, including 'Beauty of Cobham', about 2.5 ft (0.8 m) high with pale pink flowers and purple calyces; 'Cambridge Scarlet', about 4–5 ft (1.2–1.5 m) high with whorls of rich scarlet flowers in crimson calyces; and 'Croftway Pink', attaining 3 ft (1 m) in height with whorls of hooded soft pink blooms.

NIEREMBERGIA. Cup flower. Solanaceae. Named after Juan E. Nieremberg (1595–1658), a Spanish Jesuit writer on natural history, it is a genus of about 20 species of creeping or spreading perennial herbs that thrive in damp, sunny positions and are native to the more temperate parts of the Americas, particularly Argentina, Chile, and Mexico.

N. repens [*N. rivularis*]. White cup. Native to Argentina, this mat-forming plant grows to no more than 2–3 in (5–8 cm) high and is good for covering moist banks. The dense underground stems produce blunt oblong leaves that vary in size and above them delightful creamy white cup-shaped flowers with yellow centers about 2 in (5 cm) across.

OLSYNIUM. Iridaceae. The name is derived from the Greek meaning hardly united, a reference to the plant's stamens. It is a genus of 12 species of perennial herbs from North and South America, closely related to *Sisyrinchium*.

O. douglasii. A North American species, it grows to 12 in (30 cm) high with bright purple drooping bell-shaped flowers about 0.75 in (2 cm) across.

ONOCLEA. Sensitive fern. Dryopteridaceae. The name is derived from the Greek *onos*, meaning a vessel, and *kleios*, to close, a reference to the plant's closely rolled fertile fronds. It is a single-species genus of ferns originating in North America and northern Asia.

O. sensibilis. Growing to 18 in (45 cm), this is an accommodating fern that can quickly clothe large areas, from dry to aquatic conditions, covering soil or water with dense carpets of arching light green segmented fronds.

OSMUNDA. Osmundaceae. The majority of species in this genus of approximately 12 moisture-loving ferns are from the warmer temperate regions.

O. cinnamonea. Cinnamon fern. Originating in North America, Mexico, the West Indies, and eastern Asia, this attractive, deciduous fern grows 3–5 ft (1–1.5 m) high in moist, shaded positions. Its young unfurling fronds, which are one of its most appealing attributes, are clothed in a soft woolly coppery-colored growth and open out into rich green fronds 6–10 in (15–25 cm) wide. During the summer, occasional erect and stout fertile fronds, covered with a cluster of cinnamon-colored spore-bearing bodies, appear among the soft greenery.

O. claytoniana. Interrupted fern. This North American species grows about 3 ft (1 m) high with vivid green fonds. The common name is derived from the appearance of the erect sterile fronds, which have a central section heavily endowed with brown spores but lacking the leaflets that occur below and above this section.

O. regalis. Royal fern. One of the finest ferns for the waterside, this species has a wide cosmopolitan temperate distribution. The sterile fronds grow 4–5 ft (1.2–1.5 m) long, starting out a delicate pale green tinted with a coppery brown. These are particularly beautiful when they unfurl, and they provide a double bonus in the autumn when they assume a deep russety color before the severe frosts. The erect pale brown fertile fronds are conspicuous. This fern prefers its roots to be near enough to reach the water and like *Gunnera* benefits from the winter protection of straw or dried leaves over its crown. Plate 84.

There are four interesting dwarfer cultivars: 'Crispa', growing to 18 in (45 cm) with wavy margins to the fronds; 'Cristata', having conspicuously crested fronds growing to 2.5 ft (0.8 m); 'Gracilis', with distinctive coppery-colored young fronds, seldom achieving a height greater than 3 ft (1 m); and 'Purpurascens', a very beautiful cultivar with purplish stems growing to 3 ft (1 m).

PARNASSIA. Grass-of-Parnassus, bog star. Saxifragaceae. Named after Mount Parnassus, the sacred mountain of the ancient Greeks from which these moisture-loving plants were supposed to have sprung, it is a genus of about 12 species of temperate, moisture-loving perennial herbs originating in the wilder regions of the Northern Hemisphere and mountains of India.

P. palustris. Grass-of-Parnassus. A native of Europe, Asia, and North America and growing about 6–12 in (15–30 cm) tall, this little gem has shining heart-shaped leaves and solitary white starlike flowers with green veining to the petals. Although this species thrives naturally near open streams, it is not the easiest of species to establish in cultivated conditions.

PENNISETUM. Gramineae. The name is derived from the Latin *penna*, meaning a feather, and *seta*, a brush, a reference to the featherlike hairs attached to the flower plumes in some species. It is a genus of about 80 species of annual and perennial grasses, mainly of tropical origin, with one or two species hardy in temperate regions.

P. alopecuroides. Chinese pennisetum. A native of eastern Asia to western Australia, this grasslike plant grows 3 ft (1 m) high and produces delightful indigo bottlebrushlike flowers in late summer among the arching foliage.

P. villosum. Feathertap. A native of northeastern tropical Africa, this is not a reliably hardy species in temperate zones and would be better with some form of winter protection or treated as a half-hardy annual. Growing to 18 in (45 cm) high and looking very much like a clump of vigorous grass, it attains its full beauty through its silvery furry tassels that are magnificent when carrying droplets of moisture or dew in the sunshine.

PETASITES. Butterbur, sweet coltsfoot. Compositae. The name is derived from the Greek *petasos*, meaning a broad-brimmed hat, a reference to the plant's large leaves. It is a genus of about 14 species of moisture-loving perennial herbs with thick rhizomes and stems native to Europe, Asia, and North America. Their large foliage is very effective by the waterside, particularly in the wild garden, but the plants are difficult to eradicate and can become a nuisance once established. A species preferring wetter conditions is discussed in Chapter 7.

P. fragrans. Winter heliotrope. A European native, this is one of the earliest-flowering plants, blooming from late winter to early spring with almond-scented clusters of white starry flowers dotted with purple and with purple calyces. Growing to 6 in (15 cm) high, the flowers are surrounded by large rounded light green leaves 6–8 in (15–20 cm) across. Plants must be introduced with great caution because of their weedy tendency.

P. japonicus. A Japanese native, this awe-inspiring species when planted en masse almost equals the grandeur of *Gunnera* with its huge leaves 3–4 ft (1–1.2 m) across and 3–4 ft (1–1.2 m) in height. The greenish white flowers occur in crowded compositelike heads and appear before the leaves in spring. 'Giganteus' grows to 6 ft (2 m) high and is also clearly suitable only for large-scale planting in wild areas.

PHALARIS. Canary grass. Gramineae. This is a genus of about 15 species of temperate perennial and annual grasses from southern Europe and temperate America.

P. arundinacea **var.** *picta*. Gardener's garters, ribbon grass. A widely distributed species from Europe, northern Asia, the northern United States, and southern Canada, it is a fairly common brightly variegated grass that grows in dry or moist soils, performing at its best in the latter. Rhizomatous roots make it invasive, but when checked, its cheerful light almost striped leaves make a bold grouping and a marked contrast to any surrounding dark foliage, particularly purple. Growing 2–3 ft (0.6–1 m) tall, it produces flowers in July in panicles that are about 4 in (10 cm) long with several short-stemmed green or purplish spikelets. The winter foliage assumes a pale biscuit color.

PHORMIUM. Flax lily. Agavaceae. The name is derived from the Greek *phormos*, meaning a basket, a reference to the use made of the plant's fibrous leaves. A genus of two species from New Zealand, these exceptionally striking plants provide strong architectural features and are seen at their best when planted in damp soil by the waterside in full sun or partial shade. As they are not totally reliable in their hardiness, they should be protected in winter as their greatest enemy is prolonged freezing conditions.

P. colensoi [*P. cookianum*]. Mountain flax. Smaller than *P. tenax* and more suitable for the smaller garden, this species has slender pointed leaves, 2–3 ft (0.6–1 m) long, with flower scapes bearing yellowish brown flowers, 3–6 ft (1–2 m) high. These in turn become decorative almost black twisted seed heads. There is a variegated form with yellowish white stripes.

P. tenax. New Zealand flax, New Zealand hemp. An extremely impressive plant, it grows about 9 ft (2.7 m) high with gigantic rigid smooth gray-green swordlike leaves edged with bright red or brown. The stout plummish purple flower stems grow 10–12 ft (3–3.5 m) long and carry dullish red tubular flowers that produce more or less erect bunches of black curved seed pods. There are several variations in size and color of the purple-leaved cultivar 'Purpureum', the best having leaves whose reddish purple sheen gives a rich dark maroony copper color. There are also several exciting variegated cultivars available; the best are beautifully striped with creamy yellow for their entire length, contrasting with the purply red flower stems.

PHYLLOSTACHYS. Bamboo. Gramineae. The name is derived from the Greek *phyllon*, meaning a leaf, and *stachys*, a spike, a reference to the plant's leafy flower spikes. It is a genus of 80 species of evergreen temperate and subtropical bamboo originating in China, Japan, and the Himalayas.

P. aurea. Fishpole bamboo, golden bamboo. A native of China and Japan and growing 10–15 ft (3–4.5 m) tall, the tough erect stems produce enlarged leaf joints bearing attractive yellow leaves, 2–4 in (5–10 cm) long, making it a good clump-forming plant for the large garden that requires a warmer texture than that provided by most bamboo foliage.

P. nigra. Black bamboo, whangee, whangee cane. Originating in China and Japan, this vigorous species grows normally 8–12 ft (2.5–3.5 m) tall but can grow to 20 ft (6 m) in warm climates. The hollow stems can become 1.25 in (3 cm) thick and turn almost black with age.

P. viridiglaucescens. A native of China, this lovely bamboo has graceful, slender canes growing to 20 ft (6 m) with a spreading habit. The hollow canes bear bright green slenderly pointed leaves 2–5 in (5–13 cm) long.

PHYSOSTEGIA. False dragonhead, lion's heart, obedience, obedient plant. Labiatae. The name is derived from the Greek *physa*, meaning a bladder, and *stege*, a covering, a reference to the plant's inflated calyx. It is a genus of about seven North American species of herbaceous plants that do well when naturalized along streambanks.

P. virginiana. Obedience, obedient plant. Native to the eastern United States and growing to 3 ft (1 m) tall, it thrives in moist, sunny situations. The creeping shoots hold neat pairs of narrow green leaves and showy spikes of pink or purple flowers. The flowers have hinged stalks allowing them to be moved around the stem in any direction, hence the common name. The outstanding cultivar 'Vivid' makes a compact, dense plant with dark lilac-pink flowers in late summer. There is a variegated cultivar, 'Variegata'.

PLEIOBLASTUS. Gramineae. The name is derived from the Greek, *pleios*, meaning many, and *blastos*, meaning buds. It is a genus of 20 species of dwarf to medium-sized bamboos from China and Japan.

P. auricoma. Golden-leaved bamboo. A beautiful species with dark green purple-splashed stems, it grows 3–6 ft (1–2 m) high and bears long slender pointed light green leaves 5 in (13 cm) long that are irregularly striped and splashed with a warm yellow color. This handsome species benefits from having the old canes cut down in spring to encourage the growth of new foliage. Plate 85.

P. humilis var. pumilus. A dwarf species from Japan, it grows only 12–24 in (30–60 cm) high and produces very slender purplish stems and bright green narrow leaves.

P. simonii. A very hardy tall species from Japan, it grows 10–20 ft (3–6 m) high with vivid green finely pointed leaves. The juvenile stems bear an attractive bloom.

PODOPHYLLUM. Berberidaceae. The name is derived from the Greek *podos*, meaning a foot, and *phyllon*, a leaf, a reference to the resemblance of the plant's leaf to a webbed foot. A genus of five or six North American or Asiatic species of perennial herbs with thick fibrous roots and creeping rootstocks, it bears some resemblance to *Trillium*, thriving in moist, peaty soils in shady places.

P. hexandrum. Himalayan May apple. A native of southwestern China and India, this rather intriguing shade-loving species grows to 18 in (45 cm) with deeply lobed rounded blotched green leaves that resemble pleated umbrellas unfolding in a mottled brown to bronzy red color as they emerge. The individual creamy white cup-shaped flowers are followed by shining red fruit like a small tree tomato in late summer.

P. peltatum. May apple, mandrake. A North American species, it produces a single large-lobed green leaf that turns orange-bronze with maturity, very similar in appearance to *P. hexandrum*. The plant has a solitary nodding creamy flower that produces a yellow fruit.

POLYGONUM. Knotweed, smartweed, fleece flower. Polygonaceae. The name is derived from the Greek *polys*, meaning many, and *gonu*, meaning a leaf joint, a reference to the swollen nodes often seen on certain species. It is a genus of about 150 cosmopolitan annual and perennial herbs, mainly from the temperate regions, that are at home in the moist soils by streams and pools. They range in size from large thicket-forming canes to low-spreading ground covers. *Polygonum* is also discussed in Chapter 7.

P. affine. A native of the Himalayas, this ground cover species, if not allowed to dry out, will clothe moist banks with carpets of pink flower spikes. Growing to 9 in (23 cm), it has deep green oval-pointed leaves that become bronzy in winter. Well established on rocky banks at the annex of Kew Gardens at Wakehurst Place in Sussex, England, it provides a memorable sight.

P. *amplexicaule*. Mountain-fleece. Another polygonum from the Himalayas, this species makes lush leafy growth to 4 ft (1.2 m) high in moist soils, culminating in thin spikes of vivid crimson flowers lasting from July well into the autumn. This species is ideal for a mixed-group planting because its foliage blends easily with other plants and the form of its flower produces delightful long-lasting highlights.

P. *bistorta*. Snakeweed, bistort. Originating in Europe and Asia, this vigorous, rather variable plant grows to 2.5 ft (0.8 m) with numerous basal leaves 3–6 in (8–15 cm) long. The flowers form erect broad pink spikes over a long period in moist soils. 'Superbum' produces lovely thick pink flower spikes and adores a waterside position. Plate 86.

P. *campanulatum*. A native of the Himalayas, this is one of the most decorative of the polygonums for moist soil in partial shade where it grows to 3 ft (1 m). The attractive crinkled foliage is distinctively veined, dark green above, and silvery or buff beneath. From midsummer onward, it produces a continuous display of delightful elegant pale pink branching heatherlike flowers.

P. *millettii*. From western China, this rather stiff, compact species grows 2 ft (0.6 m) high and produces spikes of rich crimson flowers above narrow leaves from midsummer to early autumn.

POLYPODIUM. Polypody. Polypodiaceae. The name is derived from the Greek *polys*, meaning many, and *pous*, meaning a foot, a reference to the soft footlike formation of the plant's creeping stems. This is a large genus of over 1100 species of cosmopolitan hardy and half-hardy ferns, mostly evergreen, with leathery fronds and rhizomes close to ground level. Certain species make good subjects for the shady sides of rocks near pools or waterfalls where the humidity is high but the rhizomes will not become waterlogged.

P. *vulgare*. Common polypody, wall polypody, wall fern. An evergreen fern from widespread temperate regions, this species is a superb colonizer of dry and damp places with adequate drainage. If left undisturbed, it forms attractive clumps of long midgreen deeply cut fronds, 3 in (8 cm) wide, that look excellent in a wild garden setting. The rhizomes are thickly matted with hairy brown scales. There are many variants of the type, producing fringed, crested, and other interesting frond formations.

POLYSTICHUM. Christmas fern, holly fern, shield fern. Dryopteridaceae. The name is derived from the Greek *polys*, meaning many, and *stichos*, a row, a reference to the plant's fruiting bodies' being in several ranked rows. This is a genus of 175 species of hardy and half-hardy ferns from a wide cosmopolitan distribution that enjoy moist, well-drained, shaded conditions.

P. *aculeatum*. Hard shield fern, prickly shield fern. This European evergreen fern grows to 3 ft (1 m) high with long narrow fronds, yellow-green at first and changing to deep green, that are firm and neat. The fronds carry clear rows of brown spores on the undersides.

P. *lonchitis*. Holly fern, mountain holly fern. A native of Arctic and temperate regions, it grows to 18 in (45 cm) with long spear-shaped divided fronds with toothed leaflets.

P. *munitum*. Christmas fern, western sword fern, giant holly fern. A native of western North America and growing to 3 ft (1 m), this is one of the finest evergreen shade-loving ferns, making large dramatic clumps that are particularly valuable in the winter. The long dark green fronds are often curved with many regular undivided leaflets.

P. *setiferum*. Soft shield fern, hedge fern, English hedge fern. A European native and growing to 4 ft (1.2 m), this is one of the most tolerant evergreen ferns, surviving in sun or shade and under moist or dry conditions. When grown in moist, sheltered spots, it has an elegance all its own with soft dull green fronds persisting well throughout the winter. The stems are partly encased in soft brown scales that creep up the frond, giving the origin of the common name.

POPULUS. Poplar, aspen, cottonwood. Salicaceae. The name is thought to be derived from the Latin name for "tree of the people," the Italian or Lombardy poplar being common in Roman cities. This is a genus of 30 to 35 species of deciduous trees widely spread over the temperate Northern Hemisphere. They are particularly useful trees for wet soils where they can provide a good background and shelter. The leaves are simple, alternate, usually toothed, and fairly long-stalked. The flowers are typically catkins with sexes on separate trees. They prefer full sun and tolerate exposure reasonably well. They dislike shallow, chalky soils.

P. ×*canadensis* [*P.* ×*euroamericana*] **'Aurea'**. Quivering golden leaf poplar. A hybrid between *P. nigra* from Europe and *P. deltoides* from North America, this is a most effective, vigorous tree with heart-shaped leaves of bright yellow in spring and early summer, becoming yellow-green later in summer, and brightening to golden yellow in the autumn.

P. ×*jackii* [*P. candicans*] **'Aurora'**. Balsam poplar. Growing to 100 ft (30 m), this is a striking tree, producing broad heart-shaped leaves that are strongly balsam-scented when young. The new leaves are boldly variegated in cream and white with a pink tinge, gradually turning green as they mature.

P. tremula **'Pendula'**. Weeping aspen. This smaller poplar forms a mushroom-shaped head of graceful weeping branches, making it an attractive specimen for grassy banks alongside water. Mowing the grass will keep down any suckers. The aspens are known for their rounded gray-green leaves that, because of their flattened leaf stalks, tremble in the slightest breeze.

P. trichocarpa. Western balsam poplar. Native to western North America and growing to 100 ft (30 m), it is often cultivated in European gardens but is a little prone to canker of the trunk and branches.

PRIMULA. Primrose. Primulaceae. The name is derived from the Latin *primus*, meaning first, a reference to the early-flowering habit of many primroses. This is a large genus of 400 species, mostly native to the North Temperate Zone. Many species are ideally suited to waterside planting, providing vivid displays of color in early summer, particularly when planted in large groups. They must not be waterlogged but must have a constantly moist soil that is rich in organic content.

P. alpicola. A native of Tibet and a valuable primula for semishade growing 6–20 in (15–50 cm) tall, this species has large pale yellow drooping flowers and long-petioled leaves. The names *luna*, *violacea*, and *alba* have been given to the yellow, violet, and white varieties, respectively.

P. beesiana. A Chinese native, it has rosy carmine flowers with a yellow eye, reaching to 2 ft (0.6 m).

P. bulleyana. Collected in western China by George Forrest, who was on an expedition financed by the English seedsman A. K. Bulley, this is one of the easiest of waterside primulas, reaching 1.5–2 ft (0.5–0.6 m) with buff-orange flowers. Several cultivars have been produced from it, particularly when crossed with *P. beesiana*.

P. denticulata. Drumstick primula, Himalayan primrose. From the Himalayas, it is one of the earliest of waterside primulas, producing its round flower buds at ground level in early March and eventually stretching to 9–12 in (23–30 cm) on sturdy short stems. The globular flowers open in various colors from lilac to rich carmine-red and purple. There is a white cultivar, 'Alba'. Plate 28; Figure 42.

P. florindae. Giant Himalayan cowslip. From Tibet, this is one of the most vigorous of waterside primulas, growing to 2.5 ft (0.8 m) or more when it has adequate supplies of water. Flowering later than many other primulas, established plants produce

FIGURE 42. *Primula denticulata*.

several stems with large drooping heads of scented sulfur-yellow bells, powdered with farina. The heart-shaped clump-forming leaves can reach as long as 8 in (20 cm). Plate 87.

P. japonica. This Japanese species, growing to 2 ft (0.6 m) high, is one of the more reliable and showy early-flowering candelabra forms, producing several tiers of white, pink, or crimson flowers. There are two excellent cultivars with yellow eyes: 'Miller's Crimson' (a dark red) and 'Postford White'. Plate 88.

P. polyneura. Native to Yunnan and southeastern Tibet and growing 10 in (25 cm) tall, this species has soft undulating leaves and rose-pink flowers in late May.

P. prolifera [*P. helodoxa*]. This is a vigorous Chinese species growing to 3 ft (1 m) with buttercup-yellow candelabra flowers without farina.

P. pulverulenta. Native to China, this is one of the most elegant of the candelabra primulas, growing to 2 ft (0.6 m) with rich crimson flowers with purple eyes. The leaves are slightly smaller and more wrinkled than many of the other candelabra primulas, and the flower color is enhanced by the white floury farina on the flower stem. An excellent cultivar is 'Bartley Strain', which comes true to type from seed and displays some charming shades, ranging from apricot to palest pink.

P. rosea. From the Himalayas, this early-flowering species grows to a height of only 6–9 in (15–23 cm) with polyanthuslike umbels of bright rose flowers held above pale green leaves. Plate 28.

P. secundiflora. From Yunnan and Sichuan, this species grows to 12 in (30 cm) high with the most charming pendent reddish purple flower clusters and calyces with black markings. It has narrow leaves 8–10 in (20–25 cm) long.

P. sikkimensis. Originating in the Himalayas from Nepal to China and growing at fairly high altitudes, this beautiful cowsliplike primula has soft yellow flowers reaching 18 in (45 cm) high, rather similar to those of *P. florindae* but smaller and without farina.

P. vialii. This Chinese species resembles miniature red-hot pokers with bicolor spikes of bluish violet and pink. This unusual plant grows to 12 in (30 cm) with lanceolate leaves, 8–12 in (20–30 cm) long, that appear late in the spring. It is a difficult species to grow; sometimes whole drifts unaccountably die out.

PRUNELLA. Selfheal. Labiatae. The name is derived from *Brunella*, from the German *Die Braune*, or quinsy, which the plant is supposed to cure. This is a genus of seven creeping or semierect perennial herbs dispersed widely over temperate regions.

P. grandiflora. Large selfheal. An unassuming species from southern Europe, it makes an excellent plant near the very edges of a pool where it scrambles and produces nettlelike, purple flowers surmounting small rough toothed leaves. 'Loveliness' has a pale lilac flower and 'Pink Loveliness' a pink flower.

PSEUDOSASA. Bamboo. Gramineae. The name is derived from the Greek *pseudos*, meaning false, and *Sasa*, which is itself derived from the Japanese name for smaller bamboos (*zasa*). This is a genus of six species of tall and short bamboos from China, Japan, and Korea.

P. japonica. Arrow bamboo, hardy bamboo. A temperate species from southern Japan and South Korea, this large bamboo can reach 12–15 ft (3.5–4.5 m) with olive-green canes bearing many large glossy ribbon-shaped leaves that are rough and whitened on the underside, about 8–10 in (20–25 cm) long and 1–2 in (2.5–5 cm) wide. The stems are almost permanently encased by brownish sheaths.

RANUNCULUS. Buttercup, crowfoot. Ranunculaceae. The name is derived from the Latin *rana*, meaning a frog, a reference to the preference of certain species to ground inhabited by frogs. This is a genus of 400 species of annual or perennial herbs with a cosmopolitan distribution, mainly in the temperate regions of the Northern Hemisphere. The hardy species have a distinct liking for moist or marshy places, and many are suited to planting in wild gardens. Other *Ranunculus* species are described in Chapters 6 and 7.

R. aconitifolius. A native of Europe, this tough perennial grows to 3 ft (1 m) with deeply divided dark green leaves and myriad single white buttercups in April and May. 'Flore-pleno', commonly known as

fair maids of France or white bachelor's buttons, is more decorative, slightly smaller and with double white flowers with greenish tints in the center on a branching mass of stalks.

R. platanifolius. A native of Scandinavia and central and southern Europe, this species grows 3–4 ft (1–1.2 m) tall and has larger palmate leaves and showy white cuplike flowers resembling a white *Caltha*.

RHEUM. Rhubarb. Polygonaceae. The name is derived from the Greek *rha*, meaning rhubarb. It is a genus of about 50 species of strong perennial herbs with thick woody rhizomes originating in Siberia, the Himalayas, and eastern Asia. Their stature makes them superb specimen plants by the waterside, particularly when their spires of pink or white flowers contrast wonderfully with the more spreading leaf form.

R. alexandrae. From western China, this species is much smaller than most other rheums, growing to about 3 ft (1 m) with flower spikes reaching 4–5 ft (1.2–1.5 m). It is, however, a very decorative and architectural species with attractively veined dark green glossy leaves. The individual flowers are obscured on the flower spike by cream-colored bracts that have the effect of highlighting the spike. It is not the easiest of rheums to cultivate. Plate 89.

R. palmatum. From China and Tibet, this more common species grows 6–8 ft (2–2.5 m) tall with huge apple-green deeply cut leaves and handsome tall spikes of creamy white flowers. 'Atrosanguineum' (syn. 'Atropurpureum') is a much more decorative cultivar than the ordinary *R. palmatum*, growing to the same height but having very deeply cut leaves that are vivid red as they emerge and that retain the red coloring, particularly on the reverse side of the leaf, until flowering. The flowers are striking vivid crimson fluffy spikes that ripen to attractive brown seed cases. 'Bowles' Crimson' is another cultivar with deep red foliage. The variety *tanguticum* has deeply cut leaves with crimson flowers.

RODGERSIA. Saxifragaceae. Named after John Rodgers (1812–1882), the American admiral who commanded the expedition during which *Rodgersia podophylla* was discovered in Japan, it is a genus of six temperate species of handsome erect herbaceous perennials from China and Japan that thrive in moist, peaty soils sheltered from wind.

R. aesculifolia. From China and growing 3–4 ft (1–1.2 m) high, this species has leaves that resemble a horse chestnut leaf, 12–18 in (30–45 cm) wide and divided into six or seven leaflets. The spikes of small white flowers resemble astilbes. Plate 90.

R. pinnata. From China and growing to 3 ft (1 m) high,

this is a more free-flowering species than other rodgersias, with white or pale pink astilbelike flower spikes above leaves that grow in pairs on a central stem. 'Superba' has brilliant pink flowers and beautiful coppery leaves.

R. podophylla. From Japan and growing to 4 ft (1.2 m) high, this handsome species has bronzy palmately divided young leaves that, after turning green in midsummer, become tinted with copper in the autumn. The leaflets have large jagged lobes at the edges.

ROSCOEA. Zingiberaceae. Named in honor of William Roscoe (1753–1831), the founder of the Liverpool Botanic Garden, it is a genus of about 17 Himalayan or Chinese exotic-looking perennial herbs that thrive in moist, peaty soil. Despite belonging to a family associated with tropical herbs, many species within the genus are surprisingly hardy and should become more popular in temperate gardens as they become more available.

R. cautleoides. This Chinese species grows to 12 in (30 cm) high with swordlike light green leaves sheathing a stem that carries a light cluster of exotic-looking orchidlike hooded yellow flowers.

R. humeana. Native to China, this species is similar in hardiness and habit to *R. cautleoides* but has a rich rosy purple flower.

RUBUS. Bramble. Rosaceae. The name is thought to be derived from the Latin *ruber*, meaning red, a reference to the fruit color of the majority of the species. It is a large genus of about 250 species of creeping and usually spiny herbaceous and shrubby plants abundant in the Northern Hemisphere but also found in certain tropical locations. The species of most interest to the water gardener is hardy and used for creeping over moist pool edges.

R. chamaemorus. Cloudberry, yellow berry. Originating in peat bogs of Europe, Asia, and North America, this attractive little creeping shrub grows 3–10 in (8–25 cm) high with rounded leaves 2–3 in (5–8 cm) across and solitary white flowers 1.5 in (4 cm) wide that develop into pale orange or yellow fruit.

RUMEX. Dock, sorrel. Polygonaceae. This is a genus of about 200 mainly herbaceous species widely distributed in the North Temperate Zone. Few have any horticultural or ornamental value, but one species is sometimes used for its ability to thrive in moist and waterlogged soils and establish cover for expansive wildlife pools.

R. hydrolapathum. Great water dock. Originating in Europe and Asia, this robust perennial plant grows 4–6 ft (1.2–2 m) high with dark green narrow dock-like leaves that take on crimson shades in autumn. The brownish pink flower spike, although an attraction, should be removed to prevent the plant from seeding itself. Plants can grow in shallow water, sometimes exhibiting aerating roots like a mangrove.

SALIX. Willow. Salicaceae. This is a genus of around 300 species of trees and shrubs from the cooler parts of the temperate Northern Hemisphere. Several species that thrive in wet or moist soil have considerable ornamental value, either as imposing specimen plants when provided ample space for development or as group plantings for bark color when hard pruned.

S. alba '**Chermesina**'. Scarlet willow. A white willow cultivar that grows 60–80 ft (18–24 m) tall and is originally from Europe, northern Asia, and North Africa, it provides a blaze of color in the winter landscape with its brilliant display of scarlet-orange branches. It is particularly effective when prevented from growing into a tree and severely pruned each spring to ensure a regular supply of colorful bushy stems near the ground. 'Vitellina' produces golden shoots and should be pruned in the same way.

S. babylonica. Babylon weeping willow. Despite its specific name, this is a Chinese species that grows to 40 ft (12 m) and represents one of the more commonly planted weeping willows. The leaves are lance-shaped, deciduous, dark green above, and paler beneath. It is commonly confused with *S. ×sepulcralis*, another weeping, dome-headed tree that is a hybrid between *S. babylonica* and *S. alba* 'Tristis'. The true *S. babylonica* has brown twigs, however, and the hybrid has yellow ones. It must be given ample space to be effective, and if the water area is small and out of proportion with the size of the tree, it loses its full magnificence. The falling leaves can quickly cause problems of decomposition and choke small ponds, so it should be planted near moving water or extensive expanses of water.

S. caprea. Goat willow, pussy willow. From Europe and Asia, this very common spreading deciduous tree grows 20–30 ft (6–9 m) high and is recognized by its golden catkins in spring. The broad leaves are oblong, downy at first, woolly beneath, and gray-green in color. It would only be suitable for large-scale planting in extensive natural areas. 'Pendula' is a smaller weeping tree only 5–6 ft (1.5–2 m) high and much more suited to planting near small pools.

S. daphnoides. Violet willow. Native to Europe, this handsome species reaches 30–40 ft (9–12 m) in height with shoots that at first are downy, later becoming purple with a waxy bloom. The leaves are oval to lance-shaped, smooth and shiny.

S. lanata. Woolly willow. Native to northern Europe, this is a shrubby species growing no more than 5 ft (1.5 m) high with buds and young branches that are covered with soft, gray hairs. The leaves are silky above and hairy beneath. This species is very beautiful when in flower and can form pleasant gray mounds at the waterside. Like other willows it does not mind being cut back.

S. matsudana '**Tortuosa**'. Corkscrew willow, contorted willow. A cultivar of a species native to northern China and Korea, it grows 40–50 ft (12–15 m) high and is one of the most striking and easily recognized willows by the remarkable corkscrew twisting of the branches. It is particularly striking in winter when the branches can be seen to full effect.

SANGUISORBA. Burnet. Rosaceae. The name is derived from the Latin *sanguis*, meaning blood, and *sorbeo*, to drink up or absorb, a reference to the reputed styptic properties of the plant. It is a genus of more than 12 species of large perennial herbs distributed over the entire North Temperate Zone. They are valuable in moist soils for their attractive long fluffy flowers and pinnate foliage.

S. canadensis [*Poterium canadense*]. Canadian burnet. Native to eastern North America, this species grows 5–6 ft (1.5–2 m) high with green pinnate leaves like a rose's and cylindrical fluffy whitish flower heads 2–6 in (5–15 cm) long.

SARRACENIA. Pitcher plant. Sarraceniaceae. The eight species in this genus of insectivorous herbs inhabit eastern North America. Their erect, tubular or trumpet-shaped leaves are clustered in rosettes. A wing or keel on one side of the leaf terminates in a lid. These erect pitcherlike leaves collect water and trap insects, which cannot escape due to the downward-growing hairs on the inside of the tube. Part of the plant's nutrients are derived from these trapped and decaying insects. They are native to moist or swampy areas and prefer acid muck or live sphagnum in about 1 in (2.5 cm) of water. The four species listed below are the most satisfactory for establishing around a natural-type pond.

S. flava. Yellow pitcher plant, trumpets, umbrella-trumpet. The leaves in this species are erect, trumpet-shaped, up to 4 ft (1.2 m) long, yellowish green with a crimson throat. The lid is erect, sometimes red underneath, with reflexed margins. The nodding yellow flowers are up to 4 in (10 cm) across. It is found in the southeastern United States from Virginia to Florida and west to Alabama.

S. minor. Hooded pitcher plant, rainhat-trumpet. The leaves grow erect to 2 ft (0.6 m) with an expanded upper part and an overarching lid covered with purple veins and white blotches. The nodding yellow flowers are 2.5 in (6 cm) across. It is found from North Carolina to Florida.

S. psittacina. Parrot-head pitcher plant. The evergreen, narrowly tubular, upward curving leaves form a low basal rosette and are green variegated with red and pale white blotches on the upper part. The pitchers are 8 in (20 cm) long with lateral openings. The red-purple flowers are 2 in (5 cm) across. The species is found in Georgia and Florida west to Louisiana.

S. purpurea. Common pitcher plant, sweet pitcher plant, Indian cup. The evergreen leaves to 12 in (30 cm) long are slender at the base and widen in the middle. They are green, variegated, or suffused with reddish purple and have an erect lid. The flowers are purple or greenish purple and up to 2.5 in (6 cm) across. The species is found throughout most of eastern North America.

SASA. Bamboo. Gramineae. The name is derived from *zasa*, the Japanese name for smaller bamboos.

S. veitchii. Kuma bamboo grass. A species from southern Japan, it has purplish waxy stems and bright green leaves 4–8 in (10–20 cm) long and 1–2 in (2.5–5 cm) wide that wither at the edges in the autumn, creating a slightly serrated effect. This species grows into thickets 2–3 ft (0.6–1 m) high.

SCHIZOSTYLIS. Crimson flag, Kaffir lily. Iridaceae. The name is derived from the Greek *schizo*, meaning to cut, and *stylis*, a style, a reference to the plant's deeply divided style. It is a genus of two species of temperate bulbouslike herbs from South Africa, similar to gladioli, that deserve more attention for use in moist soil near the water where their form and delightful late-summer flowers extend the interest of the waterside planting.

S. coccinea. From South Africa and growing to 3 ft (1 m) high, this species has long sheathing sword-shaped pale green leaves with a flower spike containing 10 to 14 beautifully ranked crimson flowers about 2 in (5 cm) across with rounded petals. There are several excellent cultivars in shades of pink and cherry-red.

SENECIO. Groundsel. Compositae. The name is derived from the Latin *senex*, meaning an old man, a reference to the plant's gray or white hairlike pappus. It is a huge genus containing approximately 1000 cosmopolitan species, mainly from temperate or mountain regions. One species is of interest to the water gardener for use in the moist marginal soils of pools and streams.

S. smithii. From southern Chile and the Falkland Islands, this attractive herbaceous perennial grows 4–5 ft (1.2–1.5 m) high with spear-shaped, coarsely serrated dark green leathery leaves about 18 in (45 cm) long and 9 in (23 cm) across. The densely clustered flower head is composed of several yellow-eyed white daisies, each 1 in (2.5 cm) across. Plate 91.

SINARUNDINARIA. Gramineae. The name is derived from *sino*, meaning Chinese, and *Arundinaria*, the former name for bamboos. It is a genus of 12 or more species of clumping bamboos from China.

S. nitida. Fountain bamboo. This species is an extremely elegant and graceful bamboo. It grows 6–10 ft (2–3 m) high with very slender dark purple stems that are leafless and erect in the first year but arching and graceful in the second year with very narrow leaves, bright green above and grayish beneath. It is best grown in some shade as the leaves are prone to scorching.

SISYRINCHIUM. Blue-eyed grass. Iridaceae. This is a genus of about 90 species of annual or perennial herbs from North and South America. Some species readily naturalize themselves in moist conditions where their irislike foliage and interesting flower clusters add variety and form.

S. californicum [*S. boreale*]. Golden-eyed grass. Native to California and growing to about 24 in (60 cm), this species has yellow bell-shaped flowers. It is slightly tender and needs winter protection in temperate climates. It will grow in up to 1 in (2.5 cm) of water.

STIPA. Needle grass, feather grass, spear grass. Gramineae. The name is derived from the Latin *stipa*, meaning tow, or coarse broken flax, a reference to the tufted appearance of certain species. This genus of about 300 species is widely distributed over warmer temperate regions. One or two species make excellent subjects for specimen planting. While not moisture-lovers, their grace makes them worthy of inclusion at the water's edge.

S. calamagrostis [*S. lasiagrostis*]. From southern Europe and growing to 3 ft (1 m) high, this species has fine bristly leaves and a flower spike about 12 in (30 cm) long.

SYMPLOCARPUS. Skunk cabbage. Araceae. The name is derived from the Greek *symploke*, meaning connected, and *karpos*, a fruit, a reference to the plant's seeds' being united in a mass. It is a single-species genus from North America, northeastern Asia, and Japan.

S. foetidus. Skunk cabbage. This species grows to 12 in (30 cm) tall with pale green leaves, 12–24 in (30–60 cm) long, after producing strange hooded purple spathes that give off an unpleasant odor if bruised. It makes a striking plant for the poolside.

TAXODIUM. Cupressaceae. The name is derived from the Latin *taxus*, meaning yew, and *eidos*, meaning like, a reference to the similarity of the plant's foliage to yew. It is a small genus of three species of ornamental pyramid-shaped deciduous conifers native to the southeastern United States and Mexico. They are semiaquatic in their native habitat but capable of thriving in ordinary soils.

T. distichum. Swamp cypress, bald cypress. Native to the southern United States, this species grows 100–120 ft (30–37 m) tall as a narrow pyramidal tree. The soft deciduous leaves are short and yellowish green, flat or awl shaped, turning brown in the autumn, in two ranks. Buttressed roots can appear in shallow water, producing woody bumps known as Cypress knees. It makes an imposing specimen tree that has been largely superseded for smaller situations by the dawn redwood (*Metasequoia glyptostroboides*).

TELEKIA. Compositae. Named after Telek de Szek, who founded the Great Library in Hungary in the 19th century, it is a genus of two species of tall coarse perennial herbs found in central Europe and Caucasia.

T. speciosa [*Buphthalmum speciosum*]. A robust plant from southeastern Europe to the Caucasus, it grows 3–5 ft (1–1.5 m) high. It forms great masses of huge heart-shaped coarsely serrated aromatic leaves with large showy deep yellow drooping daisylike flowers. It is ideally suited to planting by large ponds.

THALICTRUM. Meadow rue. Ranunculaceae. The name is derived from the Greek *thaliktron*, meaning a plant with corianderlike leaves. This is a genus of about 130 species of perennial herbs, mainly from the North Temperate Zone. They form a useful group of decorative background subjects with dainty light foliage framing the heavier lush foliage of many aquatic marginals.

T. delavayi [*T. dipterocarpum*]. From western China this popular species grows to 5 ft (1.5 m) with small, finely segmented very dark green leaves on slender stems that in most cases need careful staking. The exquisite flower sprays, which can measure 2 ft (0.6 m) long and 1 ft (0.3 m) wide, consist of tiny lilac flowers that have tufts of cream stamens hanging from the rich lilac sepals. 'Hewitt's Double' produces myriad tiny, long-lasting globular double flowers of a deep lilac color.

T. flavum subsp. *glaucum* [*T. speciosissimum*]. Originating in Spain, western Portugal, and North Africa, this subspecies grows to 5 ft (1.5 m) with the most delightful glaucous blue foliage that remains attractive long after the clustered fluffy heads of small greenish yellow flowers have finished. It is a particularly useful plant when the finely cut bluish foliage can be used as a contrast.

THAMNOCALAMUS. Gramineae. The name is derived from the Greek *thamnos*, meaning bush, and *kalamos*, a reed. This is a genus of six clumping species of bamboos from the Himalayas and South Africa.

T. spathaceus. A temperate species from China, this is a medium-sized bamboo that grows 6–9 ft (2–2.7 m) tall. Closely resembling *Sinarundinaria nitida* in size, it has lighter green leaves that persist longer in winter. Bright green young canes age to a dull yellowish green. This species is very neat and compact in growth.

TRADESCANTIA. Spiderwort. Commelinaceae. Named after John Tradescant the elder (1608–1662), plant explorer and gardener to Charles I, it is a genus of about 70 species of perennial herbs native to North and tropical America. They flourish in moist, shady places at the waterside.

T. virginiana. Common spiderwort, widow's tears. From eastern North America and growing to 2 ft (0.6 m) high, this species and its cultivars make large clumps of long narrow leaves, 6–15 in (15–38 cm) in length, with violet flowers. The flowers of the many cultivars come in several shades, such as 'Purewell Giant', a reddish purple, and 'Iris Pritchard', a white stained with blue.

TRICYRTIS. Toad lily. Liliaceae. The name is derived from the Greek *treis*, meaning three, and *kyrtos*, meaning convex, a reference to the plant's three outer sepals' having swollen bases. It is a genus of 10 to 16 perennial herbs from Taiwan, Japan, and the Himalayas. They are often called toad lilies for their beautiful spotted flowers, which make interesting clumps in moist, humus-rich soil.

T. formosana. A native of Taiwan and growing 2–3 ft (0.6–1 m) tall, this species has shining oval-pointed dark leaves, 4–5 in (10–13 cm) long, which clothe the arching stems alternately. Brown buds open into a loose sheaf of spotted mauve cup-shaped flowers with yellow throats.

T. macropoda. A native of Japan growing to 2 ft (0.6 m), this species' greenish yellow flowers sometimes appear creamy white with heavy mauve or purple spotting. The pale green stem-clasping leaves curl at the tips.

TRILLIUM. Wake robin. Liliaceae. The name is derived from the Greek, *tris*, meaning triple, a reference to the three-part flowers. It is an interesting genus of about 30 species of perennial herbs from North America, Asia, the Himalayas, and Japan that thrive in partly shaded, moist soil. They are often called wood lilies and are recognized by their distinctive three-lobed leaves that carry a single white or purple three-petaled flower.

T. erectum. Purple trillium, stinking Benjamin. This North American species grows to 15 in (38 cm) with large, deep green leaves and handsome maroon flowers with recurving segments and brown sepals.

T. grandiflorum. White wake robin. From eastern North America and growing to 15 in (38 cm), this is the most commonly grown species and one of the most beautiful. The pure white broad-segmented flowers, 2–3 in (5–8 cm) across, change to pink with age and dominate the broad green foliage. There is a pale pink cultivar, 'Roseum', and a quite rare double white, 'Flore Pleno'.

TROLLIUS. Globeflower. Ranunculaceae. The name is derived from the German *Trollblume*, meaning a globe-shaped flower. It is a genus of about 31 herbaceous perennials from Europe, Asia, and North America. Compact in growth, they love moist and heavy soils and bloom profusely, with the flowers of many species resembling large double buttercups. They are more easily contained than many waterside species as they lack a spreading habit.

T. chinensis [*T. ledebourii*]. A garden form growing to 3 ft (1 m) with origins in northern Asia, it differs from *T. ×cultorum* by having the inside of the globe-shaped flowers filled with narrow petaloid stamens.

T. ×cultorum. This hybrid grows to 3 ft (1 m) high and carries the parentage of *T. europaeus*, *T. asiaticus*, and *T. chinensis*, from which most of the modern *Trollius* hybrids are derived. Although the varieties may vary slightly in size and color—shades of orange and yellow—they all make clumps of glabrous heavily divided green leaves that form a basal clump from a fibrous root system. Plate 92.

T. europaeus. Globeflower. Native to Europe, this species grows to 2 ft (0.6 m) and is a lover of marshy, wet places. The deeply divided buttercuplike foliage has a lovely mass of cool lemon to yellow incurved blooms.

T. pumilus. From China, this species grows about 9 in (23 cm) high, making it a good choice for tucking into very small pool margins. Only upon close examination will the small buttercuplike flowers, surrounded by crinkled, spotted leaves, be appreciated.

VACCINIUM. Blueberry, huckleberry, cranberry, bilberry. Ericaceae. This is a genus of about 450 species of deciduous and evergreen shrubs and sometimes small trees. Some species are grown extensively for their edible fruits, and some of the more ornamental species are suitable for planting in moist, acid soil along the shady waterside.

V. angustifolium. Lowbush blueberry. A native of the eastern United States, this species grows 12 in (30 cm) tall with twiggy, wiry shoots carrying narrow lanceolate leaves, 0.5–1.25 in (1.3–3 cm) long, that turn a vivid red in the autumn. The short, compact racemes of small white flowers have reddish streaks. The fruits are edible, and considerable commercial acreage is grown in the United States and Canada.

V. corymbosum. Highbush blueberry. A variable species, probably of hybrid origin, it grows from 4–10 ft (1.2–3 m) tall with deciduous pointed oval leaves, 1–3 in (2.5–8 cm) long, that become a beautiful red in the autumn. The flowers, which resemble small lily of the valley flowers, are in short white or pink racemes, producing blue-black edible fruit.

VERATRUM. False hellebore. Liliaceae. The name is derived from the Latin *vere*, meaning truly, and *ater*, meaning black, a reference to the color of the plant's root. This is a genus of about 20 species of hardy perennial herbs from Europe, Siberia, and North America. They thrive in moist, rich soils and are outstanding in partly shaded, moist conditions with ample organic matter.

V. album. European white hellebore. From Europe, this species grows 4–6 ft (1.2–2 m) tall with beautiful clear green large leaves up to 12 in (30 cm) high with deep pleats. The imposing flower spikes are in large dense heads of pale green to almost white on tall bare stems.

V. nigrum. From southern Europe to Siberia and growing 2–4 ft (0.6–1.2 m) tall, this forms one of the most striking of plants with its beautiful arching deeply ribbed leaves emerging from the soil like a fan and forming an impressive clump with time.

The plume of dark maroon starlike flowers is borne on a tall bare spike.

VERONICA. Speedwell, brooklime. Scrophulariaceae. This is a genus of about 250 species of small trees, shrubs, and annual and perennial herbs, the herbs mainly from the Northern Hemisphere and the trees and shrubs from New Zealand, Australia, Tasmania, New Guinea, and South America. The species described below makes a good ground cover plant for moist soils; other *Veronica* species are discussed in Chapter 7.

V. gentianoides. From the Caucasus, this mat-forming species grows 6–24 in (15–60 cm) high with the lower rosette-forming broad dark green leaves 1–3 in (2.5–8 cm) long. The flowers appear in May in the form of pale blue spikes 18–24 in (45–60 cm) high. 'Variegata' is an extremely pretty variegated cultivar with lavender-white flowers.

VIOLA. Violet. Violaceae. This is a genus of about 500 species of mostly perennial herbs distributed widely over the North and South Temperate Zones. A few species favor the moist conditions that surround a pool, spreading naturally to form a delightful carpet.

V. cornuta. Horned violet, viola. A native of the Pyrenees, this species grows to 12 in (30 cm) high, forming a complete cover of clumps of small rich green leaves. The leaves are covered with large long-lasting violet-shaped flowers in white, lilac-blue, and deep blue.

V. labradorica. Labrador violet. From the northern United States, Canada, and Greenland, this species grows 1.5–3 in (4–8 cm) high. The small violet flowers with a white, violet-veined base make long-flowering carpets of bloom. A most attractive cultivar is 'Purpurea', which forms carpets of dark green to purple leaves with light purple flowers, making a useful color background for setting off many other plants.

Chapter 9

Fish and Other Creatures in Water and Bog Gardens

Under a microscope, thousands of tiny plants and animals can be seen in a single drop of pond water, some darting erratically in all directions while others move more gracefully and purposefully from point to point. These tiny planktonic microorganisms are the basis of a clean, healthy, and well-balanced pond. A diverse population of these organisms, which are constantly preying upon one another, helps to prevent explosions of troublesome algae or mosquitoes. The correct composition of a microorganism community not only achieves crystal clear water but also provides the basis of an incredibly complex food web that supports many larger animals and brings an extra dimension to the appreciation of water by young and old alike.

Hidden beneath the surface of a pool is a never-ending struggle for life. Bacteria, fungi, worms, nematodes, snails, and clams all feed on organic debris. These organisms in their turn are preyed upon by dragonfly larvae, water beetles and their larvae, and crayfish, which themselves fall prey to fish, turtles, frogs, and salamanders. Finally, often unwelcome guests, such as herons, kingfishers (Plate 93), raccoons, and alligators, complete this intriguing web. This "who eats whom" situation is not a simple one, and the more it is examined, the more fascinating and complex it becomes. Bacteria feed the worms, which are eaten by beetles, which in turn feed the fish, to be later devoured by an alligator or heron. Such a chain, however, depends on size. Small alligators can be eaten by large fish or herons, and small fish fry provide protein for large beetles. When the alligators, fish, and beetles die, they are eaten by worms, which on their demise ultimately feed the fungi and bacteria. This cycle works in a natural wetland habitat and should be the goal in the management of an ornamental garden pool.

Many aquatic animals are hard to see, hidden in the mud or among the stems of plants. Some insects spend their lives as submerged larvae, or nymphs, and catching these creatures in a small net for observation in a jar before returning them to the pool can be an interesting exercise. The secret world of many of the amphibians, which are more active at night, can be revealed by the careful placement of lights.

MAYFLIES, DRAGONFLIES, AND OTHER FLYING INSECTS

There are several species of mayflies, some of them quite small, with two or three long tails that trail elegantly behind them as they fly. Most mayflies live only for a few hours as adults, their sole purpose being to breed. Groups of airborne males perform their characteristic courtship dance in an up-and-down yo-yo flight over the water. Females are attracted to the group and quickly mate with one of the males while in flight. In most species, as soon as mating is over, the female falls to the water and, if not immediately snapped up by a hungry fish, lays her eggs. In her last moments her frantic body movements release a shower of eggs that slowly sink to the bottom. Enough manage to avoid being eaten to produce another generation. ·

Of all the aquatic insects, there is none to compare with the dragonfly. Among the largest insects in the world, their fast precision flight and dazzling colors endow them with qualities to enhance the most colorful of gardens. Beautiful as they are, they are little understood and even frightening to many. Some of their old names, such as horse stingers and devil's darning needles, bear testimony to these fears. They are, however, harmless and none possess a sting.

While identification of the many individual species is beyond the scope of this book, they can be summarized into three main groups. The true dragonflies are divided into the hawkers and the darters. Darters have relatively short, fat abdomens and fly erratically, hovering and then darting in all directions to snap up prey or chase off a rival. Hawkers, on the other hand, have graceful long, thin abdomens and fly with a much more positive attitude, cruising more leisurely over the water garden. The third group are the damselflies (Plate 94), not true dragonflies but very closely related. These are much smaller, more delicate creatures. Their flight is slow and fluttering, and those with colored wings are often mistaken for butterflies.

The eggs of darters are laid in the water, the female making graceful dipping motions with her body while flying low over the surface. Each time her abdomen touches the water, several eggs are released. Often the male accompanies her, chasing away any other potential suitors. Female hawkers lay their eggs inside emergent vegetation. A specially modified ovipositor (egg-tube) cuts a hole in the leaf or stem and deposits the eggs individually. Hawkers lay fewer eggs than the other groups because protected inside the plant, the eggs' chances of survival are much greater. Male hawkers never accompany their mates, and the female deters any persistent male by curving her abdomen back underneath herself. Damselflies also lay their eggs inside plant tissue, but in their case, the vegetation chosen is usually just below the water surface. In nearly all species the male remains attached to his mate throughout the egg-laying process. He holds her with a pair of claspers at the tip of his abdomen firmly fixed to her thorax.

The eggs eventually hatch into larvae that develop underwater for one to three years, depending on the species. In the more northerly latitudes, some species may take much longer; one species studied in Moscow is said to take 10 or more years to reach maturity. They feed avidly on anything that moves and is smaller than themselves. Beautifully camouflaged, they ambush their prey by extending hydraulically operated jaws and snatching up a victim. They seldom miss and they never let go. When young, they feed on mosquito larvae and other small creatures, but as they approach maturity, some of the larger species can easily tackle fish up to two inches long.

When fully mature, the sight of one of these ugly larvae as it metamorphoses into one of the world's most beautiful and effective flying machines is unforgettable. Using the stem of a reed or rush as a stairway to a completely new world, the larva breaks the surface during the hours of darkness or early in the morning and crawls up clear of the water. Depending upon the species, the transition to complete adulthood may take two to five hours. The emergence begins with the head appearing from a small slit in the now redundant larval skin. The crumpled wings and abdomen follow until completely free, and the creature hangs by its new legs onto the old, cast-off skin. Slowly the body inflates and the wings expand, and if observed in the morning sun, it glistens like a jewel before its maiden flight.

Dragonflies hunt on the wing for insects, and their aerobatic chases for mosquitoes are always a source of amazement. Even more dramatic is their territorial behavior. Males constantly enter combat over possession of a pool, and dogfights can be spectacular. But while feeding and defending his territory, he also has to find a mate. It is not, therefore, surprising that after a few days the male is exhausted and in defeat is killed or vanquished from the pool by a new, fitter male.

Dragonflies and other flying insects quickly find and colonize any new, suitable pool, some traveling a long distance to do so. They form, however, only one part of the life of a pool. In order to achieve a well-balanced community, the less conspicuous microorganisms have to be deliberately introduced in a newly constructed pond. This is achieved by simply collecting a sample of mud and a few pints of water from a healthy, unpolluted pool and adding them as soon after collection as possible to the new pond. These ingredients contain millions of planktonic plants and animals and the larvae of many larger creatures. Once in their new environment, they will quickly multiply, providing the basis for a well-balanced wildlife community.

AMPHIBIANS

Amphibians, such as frogs (Plate 95), toads, newts, and salamanders, are semiterrestrial animals that must return to the water each year to breed. The larvae (tadpoles) of amphibians are an important part of the wildlife in a pool. Since much of their diet consists of algae, they help to keep the water clear. In turn, they provide an important source of food for other larger creatures. Fish eat large numbers of developing tadpoles while birds and mammals prey upon the adults.

For much of the year, adult amphibians are found on land, preferring to live in the damp, shady vegetation at the pool's edge. Resting by day, they emerge to hunt at night, repaying their hospitality in the garden by consuming huge quantities of slugs and other troublesome garden pests. Amphibians can be introduced to the water garden, but if there is another pool in the neighborhood, they will probably arrive of their own accord. Their introduction can be speeded up by using spawn from a neighbor's pond. The adults resulting from this introduction will then return each year, provided the pool is suitable. It should be remembered that all amphibians require shelter during the day, and areas of dense vegetation at the pool's edge and in the bog garden are ideal for them. In cooler climates they need a place to hibernate: shallow chambers with a small entrance hole under paving stones or rocks make ideal amphibian shelters.

FISH

Fish are perhaps the most obvious creatures associated with the water garden, but what kind and how many must be considered very carefully. There are many species, both exotic and native, from which to choose. Some will adapt wonderfully to the management regime without disturbing the planting, while others will be a constant nuisance. It is very important to have fish that are in proportion to the size of the pool. In a small pool, large fish will root about, disturbing the bottom and releasing nutrients that may cloud the water. Fish that are too large will also eat many of the other animals and, as a consequence, destroy the balance that has been so carefully achieved. It is more sensible to have many smaller fish than a few large ones. Whether the fish are large or small, the guidelines for maximum stocking levels are based on the area of clear surface free of vegetation. Volume of water is not used as the criterion for stocking, as a very deep pool with only a tiny surface area does not absorb atmospheric oxygen as well as an extensive shallow pond. Depth is important in providing winter protection and stability of temperature, but it is a secondary factor in assessing stocking rates. A good formula is this: aim not to exceed 2 in (5 cm) of fish for every square foot (0.09 sq m) of surface. Ideally, a mixed community is desirable, particularly one that includes a percentage of surface-feeding species. If the fish are happy, they should soon breed and fit in well with the balance of the pond. They should always be the last introduction to a newly constructed pool. Wait until it is clear and full of natural food, preferably several weeks after construction. After such a lapse of time, they should find their particular niche and require very little artificial feeding. Excess feeding of fish often causes a rise in nitrogen levels, leading to rapid algal growth and green, murky water.

The ornamental pond justifies the inclusion of more colorful fish than the wildlife pond, where bright, exotic colorings may look out of place. With a guideline as to the number of fish to be introduced, it is a worthwhile exercise to visit a fish supplier to assess the quality of the stock and the conditions in which they are kept. As many ornamental fish are imported, particularly the very exotic species, their accommodations should be first class in order to reduce stress and help them over the trying acclimatization period. Look for lively specimens with strong dorsal and wide ventral fins, bright eyes, and no excessive scale damage. If a purchase is made, ensure that further stress is reduced to a minimum. The supplier should carefully capture the fish, put it in a bag with shallow water, inflate the bag with pure oxygen, and place it in a darkened box. In conveying the fish, avoid leaving the box in strong sunshine, particularly inside a vehicle window.

Once home acclimatize the fish by floating the bag on the surface of the pond for 30 to 40 minutes, and gradually introduce a small amount of pond water at a time. Once the water temperatures appear close, the fish may be released. Most ornamental species sold for outdoor pools are reasonably tolerant of a range of pH levels in the water, the optimum being 7.5 to 8.5 for most fish.

The beauty of goldfish (*Carassius auratus*) was recognized centuries ago in China when they were kept as pets in the Sung dynasty. Breeding began in earnest in Japan around the beginning of the 18th century, and since then several variants of the common goldfish have become available. This member of the carp family is often undervalued in its capacity to acclimatize quickly to pool conditions and live in perfect harmony with the other occupants, particularly the plants. They can live about 20 years and achieve a maximum length of 14 in (35 cm) and weigh up to 2.5 lb (1.1 kg). They are omnivorous and can tolerate a very wide pH range, from as low as 5.5 to as high as 9. Compared with many of their sporting cousins, they can tolerate much lower oxygen levels and a wider band of temperatures, their optimum temperature for growth being about

72–77°F (22–25°C). They do not need pampering, almost thriving on neglect, and a well-balanced pool should afford enough eggs and larvae to provide them a comfortable existence. As a guideline, stocking levels for goldfish should not exceed 2 in (5 cm) of body length to 1 sq ft (0.09 sq m) of pool surface area. Should the temptation to feed them prove irresistible, feed sparingly; the food should be eaten within about five minutes. Uneaten food simply fouls the water and encourages greening.

One of the most attractive and popular of the many goldfish variants is the comet goldfish with its long body and extensive, graceful fins and tail. They breed easily, are very hardy, and are among the loveliest swimmers with their delightful flowing tails. Their growth rate is usually about 2–5 in (5–13 cm) in one season. The comet is hardier than many of the fancier goldfish descendants and sometimes carries markings of white or black. Supplementary feeding with high-protein flake or pelleted food brings out the red coloring. Although similar in form, the other hardy goldfish breed, the shubunkin, differs from the comet in its coloring. It appears in a variety of colors, predominantly red, then blue, brown, black, and white. The fish has been extensively bred in Japan since the beginning of the century, particularly for the blue coloration that is especially prized when it forms the base color under the almost transparent scales.

Less hardy but beautiful additions to pools in warmer climates are the Japanese fantail and the calico fantail. Although they have long tails like the comet, their bodies are much more rounded and their tails are double and longer. Swimming in a sedate and graceful manner, they are distinguished by their colorings: the Japanese fantail is a golden orange with black-and-white splashes, and the calico a multicolored form with patches of black, blue, red, white, and gold.

The oranda (Plate 96) is a fish similar to the Japanese fantail but with a more compact body, an even longer tail and fins, and an interesting caplike addition to the head. This is a delicate fish that should not be kept out of doors in temperate climates.

Black Chinese moors are fish with incredibly extended gogglelike eyes that fascinate some fancy fish keepers. It has a velvety black color, compact body, and long fins and tail. They belong to a large group of exotic-sounding varieties such as lionheads, celestials, and red telescopes that are better kept in large indoor or tropical pools as a part of a specialist collection rather than left to fight the vagaries of life in an outdoor temperate pool, particularly since their slow movements hinder their escape from predators.

One of the most successful surface-swimming fish to add sparkle and flash to the ornamental pond is the golden orfe (*Leuciscus idus*; Plate 97), native to southern Germany. Being fast swimmers, they need more room than goldfish and are less tolerant of low oxygen levels and of chemical treatments in the water. Seen from above, they are a very sleek-looking fish, not unlike a trout in shape. They are golden yellow on top with silvery white undersides, delightful when seen in shoals in large pools where they have room to race around. They are extremely effective in controlling mosquito larvae, often leaping out of the water at high speed in the chase. For this reason, do not introduce a large orfe into a raised pool where it may accidentally leap over the side. They are prohibited in some areas; California, for instance, does not permit them.

Koi carp (*Cyprinus carpia*; Plate 98) have enjoyed a great deal of popularity in recent years, particularly because of their size and superb colorations. It is little wonder that many pond owners' appetites are whetted at the sight of these giants feeding from the hand in crystal clear water in aquatic centers. They are, however, a fish to be introduced with great caution. Being carp, they are typically bottom feeders and frequently damage the roots and leaves of water lilies and other submerged aquatics. As they grow larger, their antics on the pool bottom not only damage plants but cloud the water as they suck and blow like inefficient vacuum cleaners. Being easily tamed to enjoy hand feeding and stroking, they are hard to resist by the pond owner who enjoys a poolside greeting. Ideally, they should be kept in a pool that is designed for their requirements: deep, filtered, crystal clear water in a pool with vertical sidewalls. They should follow a carefully monitored feeding regime of high-protein pelleted food.

Such criteria do not fit the average ornamental water garden, and a compromise has to be found if koi are paramount in the fish collection. First, give the plants as much protection as possible, particularly over the roots of the water lilies. This can sometimes be achieved by placing large cobbles or stones a minimum of 2–3 in (5–8 cm) in diameter over the planting crates. Another system is to plant the water lilies or other submerged plants in containers raised on blocks well above the bottom of the pond. The growing points of the plants can be as high as 3 in (8 cm) below the water surface. The koi's natural distaste of being so close to the surface and of having their backs exposed above the waterline deters them from damaging the plants. Second, allow the koi to grow up from small fish in association with the water lilies, making particularly sure that the koi are adequately fed throughout the year.

Koi can be found in many different colors, including blue, although the majority are bicolors of red and white. They grow extremely rapidly and reach 3 ft (1 m) in length. In Japan there are authentic records of koi achieving an age of 200 years or older. In the southern United States they are capable of a growth rate of 1 in (2.5 cm) per month in their first year. Unlike goldfish, their ultimate length is less regulated by the size of the pond, and a minimum surface area of 60 sq ft (5.6 sq m) is recommended to allow adequate room for one or two fish to grow.

Koi are considered a symbol of masculinity in Japan, and on Boy's Day, 5 May, a koi banner is hung for every male in the house. In Japan the breeding and keeping of koi is something of a cult, and for many years the Japanese had the monopoly on the best koi in the world. A good example of plants growing in harmony with koi can be seen in the large ornamental water garden surrounding the administration building of the U.S. National Arboretum in Washington, D.C.

PREDATORS

Once exotic or hybrid species of fish or plants are introduced to the water garden, some degree of management becomes necessary to protect the often costly introductions. Certain species of pond life, therefore, must be discouraged or controlled, and the natural web of predatory relationships be regulated. Predators on fish are particularly unwelcome, none more so than the great diving beetle, predacious diving beetle, or water tiger (*Dytiscus marginalis*), which can achieve a length of 1.5 in (4 cm) and a width of 0.75 in (2 cm). Most water beetles do not achieve this size and can safely be left to their own devices, but the gruesome ferocity of this particular beetle and its larvae justify its removal if precious young fish are in the pond. The adult beetle is black with a narrow edge of brownish gold. The larva grows to 2 in (5 cm) with a light brown tapering body. Both attack soft-bodied prey from which they extract the body juices. The appearance of seemingly undamaged floating small dead fish signals their presence. Closer investigation reveals a small incision where an attack has been made with clinical efficiency. As they have to surface periodically to breathe, they can be spotted and netted out as soon as possible.

Water boatman (*Arctocorixa interrupta*), so called because its back legs resemble working oars, similarly preys on small fish. Like many water bugs, it has forewings modified into hard protective covers for the thin, delicate hind wings and mouthparts that are extended into a piercing beak. It hangs motionless upside down just below the surface of the water. Quickly attracted to any disturbance, it propels itself with its powerful back legs in a series of jerks. It attacks insects, small fish, and tadpoles, injecting its victim with digestive chemicals and sucking out the juices. Nearly as large as the great diving beetle, it grows to a maximum of 1 in (2.5 cm).

Fish fry and very small fish also fall prey to dragonfly larvae, dobsonfly (*Corydalis cornutus*) larvae, and the giant water bug (*Lethocerus americanus*; Plate 99). While frogs reward the gardener by devouring insects and other small animals, the giant bullfrog may stretch hospitality to the limit by devouring small fish. Similarly, many birds that are protected or admired by the ornithologist, such as kingfishers, egrets, and herons, are the bane of the water gardener. The many species of heron, particularly the great blue heron (*Ardea herodias*) and the green-backed heron (*Butorides virescens*), are renowned predators of fish. Unfortunately, prevention is extremely difficult without spoiling the appearance of the water garden.

The climax of the food chain around the water garden incorporates many small mammals and reptiles that are attracted to the fish. These include cats, muskrats, water rats, minks, nutria, raccoons, snapping turtles, alligators, snakes, and very occasionally river otters. Control measures vary with the specific situation and are too complex to be covered here.

OTHER MEMBERS OF THE POND COMMUNITY

Lower on the food chain and not nearly so glamorous, certain members of the pond community are regarded as such efficient cleaners that they are commercially available from aquatic centers. The most popular of these are snails, particularly the ramshorn snail (*Planorbis corneus*) and the Japanese livebearing trapdoor snail (*Viviparus malleatus*). Generally they leave the plants alone, preferring to crawl over the pool bottom and sides eating algae. They are not to be confused with the giant pond snail or freshwater whelk (*Limnaea stagnalis*), the apple snail (*Pomacea paludas*), or the Colombian striped ramshorn snail (*Marisa rotula*). These snails may consume plant tissue and should not be introduced.

Many commercial aquatic centers list freshwater mussels (clams), particularly the swan mussel (*Anadonta cygnaea*), describing them as consumers of algae and maintainers of crystal clear water. The swan mussel normally reaches a length of 4–5 in (10–13 cm) with a brownish green shell that changes shape and color according to the depth of water or the amount of shade. This variance leads to the assumption that there are several different species of clams in the same pond. It should only be introduced when the pond has a natural accumulation on the bottom. They bury themselves in the silt and draw water in through one siphon, filtering out the nutrients in the process, and pump the rest through another valve, producing in effect a miniature circulation system that helps to oxygenate the creature's immediate surroundings. They can live for up to a dozen years, and their age can be calculated from the concentric rings on their shells like the annual rings of a tree stem. They have an interesting life cycle that requires that the tiny hatchlings, called glochidia, hitch a ride on a passing fish, where they remain for quite a time as parasites. Their preference for congregating near any slight current increases their chances of finding a host moving by.

Although not strictly pond dwellers, a variety of nonpredatory, attractive, and often shy birds, such as hermit thrush, yellow-throated vireo, and gray wagtail, can be encouraged to visit a garden by the addition of a pool. Even a formal pool built without the slightest thought for wildlife may attract a few birds to drink, if not to dine. On the other hand, a pool with some very shallow water and a balanced community of natural plants and animals will attract many more.

An area of water only a few inches deep attracts birds for their daily wash, and several species may bathe together. Such areas should be open with a good sightline all around. Too much vegetation and the birds cannot be seen. More important, if the birds' vision is blocked, they feel insecure because cats can then sneak up on them, and they will not risk such danger. Birds also come to feed, some gathering snails, mosquito larvae, and other aquatic creatures, while others chase flying insects over the pool. Once attracted into the garden, an increased bird population may help to reduce troublesome pests. Large waterfowl should be discouraged from an ornamental pool, as they foul the water and do considerable damage to the aquatic plants. Moving water seems particularly attractive to birds, and even a slow drip from a pipe attracts them to bathe. Waterfalls and fountains can be especially attractive, providing them with a ready-made cold shower.

ENCOURAGING WILDLIFE

In order to encourage and maintain a water garden full of wildlife interest, there are just a few design tips to remember. First, there should be variation in the depth of the water. In at least one place, the depth should shelve from a few inches to nothing at the very edge. The pool should be deep enough that it will not freeze solid during a normal winter in temperate climates. (Automatic pool de-icers are now available.)

Second, native species should be incorporated into the planting as much as possible. Careful plant selection can attract many species of butterflies to breed and further enhance the garden. Dense and varied marginal plants extending right into the water afford cover so that creatures can enter and leave the pool in complete security. Plenty of upright emergent vegetation is essential to provide sites for dragonfly and other aquatic larvae to climb out of the water. Submerged plants should be plentiful and as varied as possible, providing shelter and food for many animals and maintaining a rich supply of oxygen.

A water garden that has been constructed with care and consideration for its potential wildlife provides an extra dimension of enjoyment to the gardener. Animals attracted to its richness provide constant interest. The darting, rapid flight of a dragonfly sparkling in the sunshine or the splashing of birds bathing in the shallows are exhilarating moments to experience. They help to make the garden not only beautiful but a subtle extension of nature as well: wildlife habitat, the way you want it, in your own backyard.

PLATE 1. The Taj Mahal at Agra, India, remains an outstanding example of the Persian influence in garden design.
SIMA ELIOVSON

PLATE 2. Geometrical pools, scented roses, and pots of flowers are part of the 14th-century Moorish tradition at the Generalife in Granada, Spain, among the most beautiful gardens in the world. SIMA ELIOVSON

PLATE 3. The classical Chinese style is evident in the lakes and pavilions of South Garden, Nan Yuan, near Taipei, Taiwan.
SIMA ELIOVSON

PLATE 4. At Heian Shrine, Kyoto, the tops of old stone columns are arranged in an exquisitely balanced stepping stone path.
SIMA ELIOVSON

PLATE 5. The Fountain of the Organ at the 16th-century Villa d'Este gardens in Tivoli, Italy, a masterpiece of sight and sound, resembles a huge pipe organ.
SIMA ELIOVSON

PLATE 6. The gardens at Vaux-le-Vicomte demonstrate André Le Nôtre's use of still pools on a flat site with a long symmetrical layout to provide a vista. The elaborate scrolled design (*broderie*) is of clipped box and terra-cotta chips.
SIMA ELIOVSON

PLATE 7. A stream courses through a dell at Bodnant in Gwynedd, Wales, one of the loveliest gardens in the world.
PETER ROBINSON

PLATE 8. Longwood Gardens at Kennett Square, Pennsylvania, was inspired by Italian Renaissance gardens. This great fountain garden is lit during summer evenings. SIMA ELIOVSON

PLATE 9. Violas and flowering cherries border a formal pool with a gargoyle wall fountain at the Johannesburg Botanic Garden in South Africa. SIMA ELIOVSON

PLATE 10. Situated close to the living area, this informal pool affords its owners the pleasure of viewing the water from close quarters. PETER ROBINSON

PLATE 11. This pool, created by compaction, or puddling, is densely planted with native plants, making it a haven for wildlife. PETER ROBINSON

PLATE 12. Overhanging paving stones make a pleasing effect. The shadows under the stones create the illusion of greater depth. PETER ROBINSON

PLATE 13. Logs stood vertically on the verges of this pool make an informal division between the water and the lawn. The logs, which should ideally be at the same height as the lawn, help prevent the erosion of the grass edge into the water. PETER ROBINSON

PLATE 14. Cobbles create a naturalistic edge and help to camouflage the liner. PETER ROBINSON

PLATE 15. Bricks are attractive at the edge of this pool, which features an underwater safety grid. The tumble of boulders resembles a realistic rock outcropping and creates a planting area for alpines. PETER ROBINSON

PLATE 16. A slow-moving stream meanders through a lush landscape of moisture-loving plants. PETER ROBINSON

PLATE 17. On a sloping site a lively stream enhances the garden. PETER ROBINSON

PLATE 18. A formal pool and simple fountain at Burford House in Tenbury Wells, Hereford and Worcester, England. The Georgian house dates from 1728. PETER ROBINSON

PLATE 19. An informal pool enlivened by a fountain jet at the Slocum Water Gardens in Winter Haven, Florida.
PERRY D. SLOCUM

PLATE 20. A gargoyle wall fountain spouts a refreshing stream of water. PETER ROBINSON

PLATE 21. A gushing cobble fountain makes a dramatic complement to a Japanese lantern. PETER ROBINSON

PLATE 22. This beautiful, well-planted water garden with its magnificent weeping conifer is in the historic Hortus Botanicus at Leyden in The Netherlands. SIMA ELIOVSON

PLATE 23. A garden statue is the focal point of a small formal water garden at Knightshayes Court in Devon, England, an English National Trust garden. A clipped, crenelated hedge forms the background and *Pyrus salicifolia* 'Pendula' (willow-leaved pear) guards the circular pool. PETER ROBINSON

PLATE 24. On a larger
scale a rich background
of trees and shrubs
frames the water at
Sheffield Park in
Sussex, England.
PETER ROBINSON

PLATE 25. Weeping trees should be permitted to overhang the water only when there is a large area of water to diffuse the excess
nutrients from fallen leaves. PETER ROBINSON

PLATE 26. Trees growing out of the water, such as this cypress, evoke exotic locales. PETER ROBINSON

PLATE 27. Moisture-loving plants provide opportunities to combine dramatic foliage shapes and textures with garden architecture at Cholmondely Castle in Cheshire, England. PETER ROBINSON

PLATE 29. An intimate Japanese-style water garden at Tatton Park in Cheshire, England, demonstrates the juxtaposition of fine, soft textures, such as the moss beneath the trees, with the coarser foliage of ornamental grasses. PETER ROBINSON

PLATE 28. Moisture-loving herbaceous perennials such as these primulas (*P. rosea* and *P. denticulata*) provide a display of vivid color. PETER ROBINSON

PLATE 30. *Ceratopteris pteridoides* (floating fern).
PERRY D. SLOCUM

PLATE 31.
Eichhornia crassipes
(water hyacinth).
PERRY D. SLOCUM

PLATE 32. *Lemna minor* (lesser duckweed). PERRY D. SLOCUM

PLATE 33. *Pistia stratiotes* (water lettuce).
PERRY D. SLOCUM

PLATE 34. *Salvinia auriculata* (butterfly fern). PERRY D. SLOCUM

PLATE 35. *Stratiotes aloides* (water soldier, water aloe). PERRY D. SLOCUM

PLATE 36. *Trapa natans* (water chestnut). PERRY D. SLOCUM

PLATE 37. *Aponogeton distachyos* (water hawthorn). PETER ROBINSON

PLATE 38. *Cabomba caroliniana*. PERRY D. SLOCUM

PLATE 39. *Myriophyllum aquaticum* (parrot feather).
PETER ROBINSON

PLATE 40. *Nymphoides peltata* (yellow floating heart, water
fringe, yellow fringe). PERRY D. SLOCUM

PLATE 41. *Ranunculus aquatilis* (water crowfoot, water
buttercup). PETER ROBINSON

PLATE 42. *Victoria amazonica* (giant water lily, Amazon water lily). SIMA ELIOVSON

PLATE 43. *Acorus calamus* 'Variegatus' (variegated sweet flag). PERRY D. SLOCUM

PLATE 44. *Butomus umbellatus* (flowering rush). PERRY D. SLOCUM

PLATE 45. *Calla palustris* (bog arum). PERRY D. SLOCUM

PLATE 46. *Caltha palustris* (marsh marigold, kingcup, cowslip). PETER ROBINSON

PLATE 48. *Carex elata* 'Aurea' (Bowles' golden sedge). PERRY D. SLOCUM

PLATE 47. *Caltha palustris* var. *alba* (white marsh marigold). PETER ROBINSON

PLATE 49. *Carex riparia* (great pond sedge). PETER ROBINSON

PLATE 50.
Colocasia esculenta
(green taro).
PERRY D. SLOCUM

PLATE 51. *Cotula coronopifolia* (water buttons, golden buttons, brass buttons). ANGLO AQUARIUM PLANT CO. LTD.

PLATE 52. *Cyperus papyrus* (Egyptian paper reed, giant papyrus). PERRY D. SLOCUM

PLATE 53. *Eriophorum angustifolium* (cotton grass).
PETER ROBINSON

PLATE 54. *Glyceria maxima* var. *variegata* (variegated water grass). PETER ROBINSON

PLATE 55. *Houttuynia cordata* 'Variegata'. PETER ROBINSON

PLATE 56.
Hydrocleys nymphoides (water poppy).
PERRY D. SLOCUM

PLATE 57. *Iris laevigata*. PETER ROBINSON

PLATE 58. *Lysichiton camtschatcense*. PETER ROBINSON

PLATE 59. *Mentha aquatica* (water mint). PERRY D. SLOCUM

PLATE 60. *Mimulus guttatus* (monkey musk, monkey flower). PERRY D. SLOCUM

PLATE 61. *Myosotis scorpioides* 'Mermaid' (water forget-me-not). ANGLO AQUARIUM PLANT CO. LTD.

PLATE 62.
Orontium aquaticum
(golden club).
PERRY D. SLOCUM

PLATE 63. *Peltandra sagittifolia* (white arrow arum).
PERRY D. SLOCUM

PLATE 64. *Polygonum amphibium* (amphibious bistort).
PETER ROBINSON

PLATE 65.
Pontederia cordata
(pickerel weed).
PERRY D. SLOCUM

PLATE 66. *Ranunculus lingua* 'Grandiflorus' (greater spearwort).
PERRY D. SLOCUM

PLATE 67. *Sagittaria sagittifolia* 'Flore Pleno' (double arrowhead). PERRY D. SLOCUM

PLATE 68. *Saururus cernuus* (American swamp lily, lizard's tail). PERRY D. SLOCUM

PLATE 69. *Thalia dealbata*. PERRY D. SLOCUM

PLATE 70. *Typha laxmannii* (graceful cattail). PERRY D. SLOCUM

PLATE 71. *Zantedeschia aethiopica* 'Green Goddess' (arum lily, calla lily). PERRY D. SLOCUM

PLATE 72. *Adiantum pedatum* (American maidenhair fern, hardy maidenhair fern). PETER ROBINSON

PLATE 73. *Ajuga reptans* (carpet bugle). PETER ROBINSON

PLATE 74. *Aruncus dioicus* (goatsbeard). PETER ROBINSON

PLATE 75. *Astilbe ×arendsii*. PERRY D. SLOCUM

PLATE 76. *Cardamine pratensis* (lady's smock, cuckoo flower, mayflower, meadow cress). PETER ROBINSON

PLATE 77.
Cimicifuga ramosa
'Atropurpurea'.
PETER ROBINSON

PLATE 78. *Cornus alba* 'Sibirica' (Siberian or Westonbirt dogwood). PETER ROBINSON

PLATE 79. *Gunnera manicata* (giant rhubarb). PETER ROBINSON

PLATE 80. *Iris* 'Claire Matin' (Louisiana iris). PERRY D. SLOCUM

PLATE 82. *Meconopsis grandis* (Tibetan poppy). PETER ROBINSON

PLATE 83. *Miscanthus sinensis* 'Zebrinus' (tiger grass). PETER ROBINSON

PLATE 84. *Osmunda regalis* (royal fern). PETER ROBINSON

PLATE 85. *Pleioblastus auricoma* (golden-leaved bamboo). PETER ROBINSON

PLATE 86. *Polygonum bistorta* 'Superbum' (snakeweed, bistort). PETER ROBINSON

PLATE 87. *Primula florindae* (giant Himalayan cowslip). PETER ROBINSON

PLATE 88. *Primula japonica* (right) and *Iris sibirica*, Siberian iris (left). PERRY D. SLOCUM

PLATE 89. *Rheum alexandrae*. PETER ROBINSON

PLATE 90. *Rodgersia aesculifolia*. PETER ROBINSON

PLATE 91. *Senecio smithii*. PETER ROBINSON

PLATE 92.
Trollius ×*cultorum.*
PETER ROBINSON

PLATE 93. Predators such as kingfishers are a link in the complex chain of interrelationships among the inhabitants of a water garden. PETER ROBINSON

PLATE 94. Damselflies are commonly seen in water gardens. The male damselfly remains attached to his mate during the egg-laying process. PERRY D. SLOCUM

PLATE 95. Tree frogs find a refuge among the petals of a tropical water lily. PERRY D. SLOCUM

PLATE 96. The oranda is a delicate ornamental fish similar to the Japanese fantail except that it has a longer tail and fins and an unusual head growth, which in this young red-cap oranda is just starting to develop. PERRY D. SLOCUM

PLATE 97. The dashing golden orfe brings glittering excitement to an outdoor pond. PERRY D. SLOCUM

PLATE 98. Although koi carp are potentially destructive of water lilies, they can peacefully coexist. PERRY D. SLOCUM

PLATE 99. The giant water bug (*Lethocerus americanus*) preys on fish fry. This male specimen carries eggs on its back.
PERRY D. SLOCUM

PLATE 100. Crown rot (*Phytophthora* spp.) afflicts hardy water lilies. The yellow leaves and stems break off from the rotted crown with just a touch. The green leaves are attached to a healthy side shoot and should survive.
PERRY D. SLOCUM

PLATE 101. The black aphid (*Rhopalosiphum nymphaeae*) is a common pest of lotuses and water lilies. One remedy is to dislodge the aphids with a jet of water so that fish can eat them. PERRY D. SLOCUM

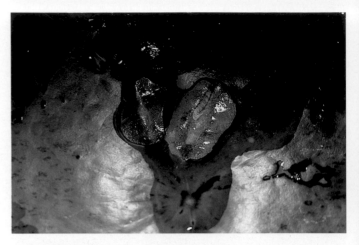

PLATE 102. The larval case of a china mark moth (*Nymphula nymphaeae*) has been torn apart to reveal the caterpillar inside, which is known as a bagman caterpillar, sandwich man, or bonnet worm. PERRY D. SLOCUM

PLATE 103. This skeletonized lotus leaf represents but a day's work for a yellow woolly bear caterpillar (*Spilosoma virginica*). PERRY D. SLOCUM

PLATE 104. The tropical apple snail (*Pomacea paludas*) eats water lilies and most other plants. Egg masses are deposited at night on plant stems just above the water's surface and must be removed with extreme care so that none of the eggs falls into the water. PERRY D. SLOCUM

PLATE 105. Plant-eating turtles such as the pond slider (*Pseudemys scripta*) can do considerable damage to water lilies. PERRY D. SLOCUM

Chapter 10

Looking After the Water Garden

Having undertaken each stage of planning, construction, planting, and stocking, one might wish to lapse into a more passive form of water gardening for some considerable time. There should be at least a few rewarding months of inactivity after the many hours of digging and some soothing relaxation after the worry of levels—water levels, pH levels, stocking levels—and possible leaks.

Reward there undoubtedly is, and a most enjoyable honeymoon period can follow, during which one can admire the new pool from every angle and scrutinize every corner and depth with enormous satisfaction. The honeymoon can take an alarming turn, however, when the attraction of the crystal clear water seems to deteriorate by the very day, and almost over a weekend the bottom of the pool disappears. Despite all the counseling that this is a natural process, one must remember that one's relationship with the water garden requires patient waiting for that sometimes elusive long-term balance of life that brings back water clarity.

WATER CLARITY

Water clouding is a perfectly natural process in a new pool caused by a surge in the growth of algae. The algae feed on the rich concentration of mineral salts present in the tap water used to fill the pool, excess fertilizer that has leached from the potting soil in the freshly planted containers, fish excretions, and decaying plant material. Once the submerged oxygenating plants and surface-leaved plants gain a foothold, they reduce the amount of available light to the algae and compete for the mineral salts and free-floating nutrients until the algae are eventually shaded and starved out, thus clearing the water. In warm water and in small pools, *Pistia* (water lettuce) and *Eichhornia* (water hyacinth) are good floaters that reduce mineral salts. Their long, hungry, filamentous roots are excellent in the surface water, but as they grow out of control so quickly, they should not be introduced into large expanses of tropical water. Water lettuce noticeably diminishes in size as it uses up the diluted food supply. In temperate or colder water, *Azolla caroliniana* is a useful surface blanket, but it must be watched closely as its rapid propagation can make it a terrible pest. About 60 percent of the water surface should be covered to be effective. The planting, therefore, must be given time to grow, and one should not resort to algicides or refill the pond in an attempt to clear the water. If long-term cloudiness persists, there may be not enough plants in the water or there may be extremes of water acidity or alkalinity. A simple pH test can diagnose the latter problem. Should an extreme reading be present, gradually make the appropriate adjustment. Various acidifying chemicals are available from an aquarium shop or water garden center if the pool is too alkaline. If too acid, add small quantities of lime subject to the volume of the pond. Seek advice before adding any chemical for this purpose.

If fish are introduced too quickly and in too large numbers, the water may stay cloudy almost indefinitely, particularly if the fish are large and receiving overgenerous quantities of supplementary food. Their movements may disturb any bottom sediments and create water currents that mix the natural layers of warm to cool water. Similarly, when the garden includes water circulating around a watercourse, one should site the submerged pump as close as possible to the point where the water returns to the pool under the bottom waterfall. This positioning avoids creating currents and mixing temperature layers, which can hinder the natural process of pool settlement and water clarification.

Microscopic single-celled algae are the cause of the most common type of green-water cloudiness, but some ponds are susceptible to a green filamentous algae commonly referred to as blanketweed. It too loves light and mineral salts and free-floating nutrients and is likely to gain a foothold in warm, shallow water in spring when even the well-planted pool is devoid of leaves. It can be a particular nuisance in badly designed ponds that are too shallow in relation to their surface area. The total elimination of blanketweed is difficult to achieve unless one resorts to strong dilutions of algicide, which may be damaging to other desirable plants and lethal to certain animal life. Blanketweed can be reduced to tolerable levels by physically removing it using a strong net or twining the strands onto a broom handle or a strong forked stick. Long periods of heavy rain can sometimes cause a dramatic reduction in blanketweed, particularly in areas where the rainfall is acid. If one's patience has run out, the use of algicides within the recommended rates may be justified, but the problem in most cases returns after their effect has worn off.

FERTILIZING THE WATER GARDEN

During the first year of a new water garden, it is unlikely that the plants will become starved of nutrients, but certain less-vigorous varieties of water lily normally benefit from summer fertilizing. In successive summers give water lilies a general feeding with proprietary feeding tablets or granules pushed into the soil close to the roots. These tablets have been specially formulated to slowly release the correct balance of plant foods, particularly phosphates, over a long period. Applying normal plant fertilizer risks clouding the water through the fast release of nutrients that will feed the algae. Marginals can be fed at half the rate recommended for water lilies. Most water garden nurseries recommend adding a prescribed number of fertilizer tablets each month during the growth season. This can be accomplished by pressing tablets into the soil around the plants, usually about 2 in (5 cm) away from rhizomes or corms.

WEEDS

Weeds must not be allowed to gain a foothold in moisture-loving or boggy beds in and around the pool margins. The available moisture makes weed growth lush, and perennial creeping weeds, such as buttercup (*Ranunculus repens*) or couch grass (*Agropyron repens*), can become a nightmare. As the cultivated plants become more established, they quickly cover the soil surface, and weeds should become less of a problem. Similarly, pests and diseases should not be allowed to establish themselves, particularly when the plants are young and vulnerable.

PLANT DISEASES

Water plants grow relatively free of disease, and serious problems are only likely to be encountered on intensively grown water lilies or lotuses. Most marginals and submerged plants remain free of disease unless badly damaged initially. If a fungus or bacterial disease should strike, check with your aquatic plant supplier for recommendations. If a chemical treatment is pursued, follow the manufacturer's instructions on the product label exactly. Exercise extreme caution using any chemical if fish are present.

A fungus disease that is mainly a problem for the hardy varieties of water lily, particularly in intensively grown commercial stocks, is crown rot (*Phytophthora* spp.; Plate 100). Certain cultivars, such as 'Gloriosa', 'Attraction', *Nymphaea* ×*marliacea* 'Chromatella', 'Comanche', 'Chrysantha', 'Paul Hariot', 'Maurice Laydeker', and *Nymphaea* ×*laydekeri* 'Alba', are thought to be more prone to infection. The increase in incidence of the disease over the last two decades has been linked to plants imported from Japan, where they are grown in semiaquatic conditions. When grown under submerged conditions, these plants showed symptoms of yellowing leaf edges and leaves becoming detached from the putrid, decomposing rootstock, indicating that the disease had become more established. Careful water lily growers are taking preventive action by keeping varieties in separate propagation tanks to avoid cross infection and by dipping plants in a fungicide as a matter of practice. The chemical 5-ethoxy-3-trichloromethyl-1,2,4-thiadiazole is the active ingredient of the fungicide Truban, which has proved effective either as a dip before planting or as an ingredient in the planting soil. Even if the infection has gained a foothold in the crown, the treatment can result in the survival of one or two of the side shoots. On a smaller scale, or where it may prove difficult to obtain these fungicides, a heaping tablespoon of alternative formulations such as Manzate can be sprinkled over susceptible varieties two or three times in the season. If the disease has gained a firm foothold, it is better to remove the infected rootstock rather than risk infecting any other varieties in the pool.

A leaf-spotting disease known as brown spot (*Ramularia nymphaearum*) often appears in wet summers as dark patches on the leaves of water lilies and lotuses. In a bad infection the leaves become so decomposed that they disintegrate. Control involves removing of the infected leaves as soon as the spots appear and spraying with a fungicide.

Dry brown spot (*Cercospora*) is another leaf-spotting disease of the water lily and lotus. It is controlled in the same way as brown spot but is usually restricted to the leaf edges, which later curl up and rot. The same fungus, *Cercospora*, is responsible for brown sepal fungus, which can cause one or more of the sepals to become brown or twisted without infecting the petals. It is not normally serious enough to require a fungicidal spray.

A bacterial wilt or fungus disease can attack lotus leaves, causing them to turn light green and die. Spread of the wilt can be restricted by sprinkling Manzate in powder form over the entire bed as soon as it appears.

Sometimes a water lily may appear completely distorted in flower and leaf without an apparent infection of fungus or pest. This condition is known as fasciation, and certain older cultivars, such as 'Ellisiana', *Nymphaea* ×*marliacea* 'Chromatella', and 'Gloriosa', are more susceptible. The malformed appearance is so unsightly that the plant has to be removed, and even its roots will be twisted. Occasionally, a shoot on the root will be unaffected and can be used for propagation purposes.

INSECT PESTS

Aquatics are more prone to pest attack than to disease, and one of the most common pests is the black aphid (*Rhopalosiphum nymphaeae*; Plate 101). Any foliage held just above the waterline is prone to infestation, and it is particularly disfiguring on water lilies. When fish are present, biological or physical control measures are advised. The introduction of ladybugs and their larvae, which devour large numbers of black aphids, is helpful, or the foliage can be sprayed vigorously with a narrow jet of water to dislodge the aphids so that the fish can eat them as they land on the pond. Knowledge of the pest's life cycle helps to determine if it has a possible weak point, and in this case, the aphids, which overwinter on plum and cherry trees, can be killed by dormant sprays. If it becomes necessary to resort to chemical controls, use extreme caution and follow the manufacturer's instructions exactly.

The brown or gray china mark moth (*Nymphula nymphaeae*; Plate 102) can be particularly disfiguring to water lilies because the larvae shred the foliage, which later crumbles away, leaving whole leaves stripped bare. The adult moth, which is seen mainly in the latter part of the summer, is about 1 in (2.5 cm) long with irregular white patches on brownish orange wings. The creamy-colored caterpillars, which hatch from clusters of eggs laid beneath or near the edge of a leaf, protect themselves from predators such as dragonfly larvae and fish by forming cocoonlike cases between two pieces of water lily leaf. It is then able to crawl about and feed with only its head and forelegs protruding, giving it the common names bagman caterpillar, casebearer, sandwich man, and bonnet worm. Encouraging moorhens and red-winged blackbirds, which are able to extract the larvae from the cases, helps to control them. Affected leaves should be removed by hand, and if fish are not present, chemical control with malathion is recommended.

Another insect pest that resorts to protection inside a case for part of its life cycle is the caddis fly. This huge group of insects, which belongs to the order Trichoptera, includes 975 species in the United States and 4450 species worldwide. About 180 species feed on water plants. The adults resemble small dull-colored moths with grayish or brown wings. They struggle in flight around early evening, when they lay up to 100 eggs in one batch in or near the water. These eggs swell up as soon as they become hydrated, and after about 10 days, the larvae hatch out and immediately start to spin protective cases that they cover with bits of leaves, small stones, or pebbles to form shelters about 0.3–0.5 in (0.8–1.3 cm) long. They then float or swim around in their structures, feeding greedily on any vegetation present, often desiccating water lily leaves. They later pupate in foliage at the water's edge. Carp, golden orfe, and goldfish are their natural enemies, and control is further effected by using electric insect traps at the water's edge in the evenings.

There are four other moths whose larvae are known to damage water lilies: *Munroessa gyralis*, *Poraponyx obscuralis*, *Eoparargyractis irroratalis*, and *Murvessa gyralis*. All the adult moths are grayish in color, and their numbers can be considerably reduced by the use of insect traps at the poolside. Otherwise, their control is limited to removal of damaged leaves. In Europe trials of a broad spectrum control material, Dipel HG, which contains the bacterium *Bacillus thuringiensis*, have been reasonably successful in control of these moths as well as of many other lawn and garden pests.

The leaf roller or stem borer, known also as the European corn borer (*Ostrinia nubilalis*) is another moth that is particularly destructive to lotus plants. The damage is done by a green worm up to 1 in (2.5 cm) long that causes the top edge of the lotus leaf to roll up. Larger larvae may bore down the leaf stalks, gaining access to the petiole and boring down the middle, completely removing the central tissue. The infected leaves soon die, and in severe infestations even the clean tissue wilts and dies. It is particularly prevalent near corn fields. Control requires removing leaves with rolled edges as soon as they appear and cutting off infected stems, taking care to destroy the tissue. Where safe to use, malathion mixed with an emulsifying oil to give better adhesion to the leaves may help.

The yellow woolly bear caterpillar (*Diacrisia virginica*; Plate 103) is a pest of raised water lily and lotus leaves in late summer. The caterpillars, which are usually yellow but may be white, brown, or red, are 1–1.5 in (2.5–4 cm) long and skeletonize leaves very quickly. They are capable of consuming an entire leaf in a day. They are mainly found on the underside of leaves, and control requires removing the individual caterpillars or spraying with a safe domestic insecticide where there are no fish or other creatures in the water. The moths are white.

A common sight when crowded water lily leaves thrust above the water in hot weather is large numbers of leafhoppers (*Megamelus davisi*). Unlike the moth larvae, which are biting insects, leafhoppers cause damage by sucking, and the vast numbers of leafhoppers present in some seasons can soon cause the leaves to turn brown. As they tend to infest only above the waterline, leaves should be prevented from building up above the surface by regularly dividing the stock as a measure of good cultivation. Localized spraying with an aerosol insecticide helps, but use caution if fish are present. On large areas where there are no fish, malathion may be used, following carefully the recommended rates.

One of the most notorious leaf-sucking insects is the red spider mite (*Tetranychus* spp.). The mites are particularly damaging in hot, dry summers when they appear on the underside of raised water lily leaves and many other aerial aquatic leaves. The symptoms begin with a yellowing of the foliage, which on closer inspection reveals a network of silky threads protecting the tiny orange-red mites. When the infection can be caught early enough, hand removal of infected leaves reduces the damage. Chemical control is not easy because the protective webbing blocks the effect of sprays. Systemic insecticides such as malathion are the remedy but can be used only when there are no fish present.

One of the most destructive of all water lily enemies is the water lily beetle (*Galerucella nymphaeae*). The small dark brown beetles are 0.25 in (0.6 cm) long and lay their eggs in June in clusters on the surface of water lily leaves. The eggs hatch in about seven days into shiny black larvae with distinctive yellow bellies. The larvae feed on most vegetation, particularly water lily leaves, stripping away the surface tissue and gradually reducing the leaves to a skeletal framework that later rots away. The larvae pupate on any aerial foliage, and the resulting beetles overwinter on any of the brown foliage at the water's edge. Removing this foliage in autumn is an important control measure. During the summer, early removal of infected foliage and rinsing the leaves with jets of water help check their spread. Fish devour all stages of the pest's life cycle, so great caution is advised in using an insecticide near fish. Although it is one of the most destructive pests, it is nevertheless fairly rare, and its attacks, when they do occur, are rather localized.

Another beetle that damages water lilies is the water lily leaf beetle (*Donacia* spp.). This beetle is 0.5–0.75 in (1.3–2 cm) long and metallic purple, green, or brown in color. The adult female bites open a hole in the leaf 0.25 in (0.6 cm) in diameter in order to lay her eggs on the underside in a semicircular cluster. Some *Donacia* species lay their eggs under the water surface to allow the larvae to sink to the bottom to eat the roots of the plants. The larvae of most species also eat leaf tissue, are white, 0.5 in (1.3 cm) long, and develop into brown, beige, or red pupae. Beetle traps by the side of the pool give some measure of control, but serious infestations may require a systemic insecticide such as malathion if there are no fish present.

The false leaf-mining midge (*Cricotopus ornatus*) is a quite common pest that can be disfiguring when numbers of them take hold. Tiny larvae eat serpentine channels through the surface of floating leaves, leaving a most unsightly result. When hand removal of affected leaves is no longer adequate, it may be necessary to remove the plant and immerse it for an hour or two in a bucket containing a dilution of the insecticide normally used for spraying aphids in the garden. After immersion, thoroughly rinse the plant before returning it to the pool.

Similar damage is done by the larvae of another fly in the midge family, *Chironomus modestus*. The tiny offending larvae, which grow up to 0.3 in (0.8 cm) long, are colorless or sometimes red. They eat tortuous, unsightly channels through water lily and floating lotus leaves. Control is exactly the same as for false leaf-mining midge, in addition to which, insect traps by the poolside will help.

SNAILS

Snails, although frequently sold in aquatic centers, should generally be regarded as pests rather than as beneficial residents, with the exception of the ramshorn snail and the Japanese livebearing trapdoor snail, which are good algae-eaters. The most common snail is the freshwater whelk, or giant pond snail (*Limnaea stagnalis*), which can act as an intermediate host for several fish parasites. It is difficult to prevent its introduction as its eggs may arrive unnoticed on aquatic plants purchased for the pool. The snails are identified by their tall, spiralled, and pointed shell about 1 in (2.5 cm) high. They are fond of soft tissue and devour young water lily leaves with relish. They are easily lured to floating lettuce leaves placed on the water as bait, which can be removed after 24 hours.

The apple snail (*Pomacea paludas*; Plate 104) is mainly a problem in the southern states where it can devour whole plants. The adults can be removed only by draining the pond to find them, so it is extremely important to look for their whitish egg masses, which are laid at night just above the water's surface on typhas, sagittarias, and various other marginal reeds. The eggs are sticky at first, later becoming dry and brittle. If the eggs are found, exercise great care in removing them from the foliage, not letting even one fall into the water.

The Colombian striped ramshorn snail, *Marisa rotula*, is of South American origin with a large ivory and reddish brown striped shell with a trapdoor. Its occurrence and eating habits are only a problem to a few aquatic plant importers who may find it necessary to drain their tanks to remove it.

WATERFOWL, TURTLES, AND MAMMAL PESTS

Most of the larger waterfowl such as ducks, geese, coots, and swans should be discouraged from the ornamental water garden, particularly one that features a valuable collection of water lilies. Such large creatures not only eat the plants but also do considerable physical damage, as well as cloud the water with their disturbance and excreta. Large clumps of sagittarias are a great attraction to ducks in the spring, and there is little one can do other than covering them with netting or clear plastic for a few weeks while other food is scarce. Moorhens do the least damage, eating mainly the algae and only occasionally pecking at blooms or eating the seeds of tropical lilies.

Turtles also can become pests, particularly the cooter (*Pseudemys floridana*), the pond slider (*Pseudemys scripta*; Plate 105), and the snapping turtle (*Chelydra serpentina*). These species can do considerable damage to water lilies. Their control leaves a lot to the ingenuity of the gardener, who must trap or net them out or where nothing else seems likely to succeed, drain the pond to find them.

Of the mammal population, muskrats, beavers, and water rats can be problems for the water gardener. The muskrat is probably the main mammal enemy, eating both lotuses and water lilies, particularly in the eastern United States and Canada in wintertime, when it chews up the rhizomes under the ice. It is not easy to control, especially if its entrance holes are hidden by snow and ice. If one must resort to trapping, use humane traps that cause the animal to drown immediately upon being caught. Beavers cause similar damage by their underwater feeding habits. Beavers have reportedly wiped out a 15-acre pond of lotus in Pennsylvania. Any trapping measures are subject to the relevant state wildlife conservation authority.

PREPARING FOR WINTER

As winter begins to make its impact on the new or established pool, it is advisable to cut back vegetation both in and surrounding the water. Yellowing water lily foliage should be removed by cutting the leafstalks as close to the crown as possible. The oxygenating plants, whose value is mainly in the summertime, should be cut back hard in autumn, even though they still appear to be thriving and making new growth. In severe winter climates, the soft tissue dies and in the process of decomposition gives off methane, which can be very harmful to fish in their torpid state. Leaves from surrounding trees should be prevented from landing and later decomposing in the pond by covering the pond with netting. Removing the dead foliage from the marginals and moisture-loving plants around the pool is a matter of personal choice and style of water garden. There is much winter beauty in the brown and dead stems and protection for both tiny creatures and young growth in the spring. The older growth can be cut back as the young spring growth emerges. If pests such as the water lily beetle are known to be prevalent, the more hygienic practice of autumn trimming back may be necessary to destroy them in the overwintering stage of their life cycle.

If any containers of hardy water lilies have been elevated in the water with stones or bricks, these supports should be removed for the winter to allow the protection of the deeper water in frosty weather. Hardy water lilies are remarkably tolerant of very cold water in winter, provided their roots are not actually frozen in the ice. In northern latitudes it may be necessary to cover small pools with planks or boards to give extra protection during hard frost. Forms of winter protection such as this are fine as long as the pool is not totally sealed with sheeting that prevents air movement. Hardy water lilies can also be removed from their planters in the fall and buried below the frost level in the garden.

In warm areas the tropical lilies can be left outside, particularly when they are growing in a muddy bottom. In cooler areas the tropicals should be taken inside and stored at a temperature of 40–45°F (5–7°C). The tubers should be placed in a moist medium or sealed with a small amount of water in Ziploc bags, well protected from rodents, and kept damp and free from frost. Room temperature is adequate in a dark area such as a closet. Cultivars such as 'Daubeniana' and 'Margaret Mary' continue to flower well into the winter if kept in greenhouses in good light and at a temperature of 60–65°F (16–18°C). In areas prone to severe winters, any pygmy form of water lily kept in a raised container such as a half barrel should be protected or moved to a warmer place.

With the approach of winter, certain aquatic plants such as frogs-bit (*Hydrocharis*) produce overwintering resting buds, or turions, that store food material and become detached from the parent plant to pass the winter in the mud at the bottom of the pond. As a precaution, turions may be collected before the severe weather and stored in wet soil in a frost-free place for the winter. In spring as they produce new shoots they can be returned to the pond.

Supplementary fish feeding should be reduced as the days shorten, allowing the fish to take small quantities on milder bright days in order to build up body tissue for the winter. Autumn is a notoriously popular time for hungry herons to visit garden pools at first light before activity begins around the house or yard. A persistent heron that has once tasted fish from a pool is one of the most difficult visitors to deter. If herons are in the area, it would be wise to cover the pool with strong netting that is well secured at the sides. They are cunning birds capable of overcoming all but the strongest preventive measures. Unfortunately, such measures can be unsightly but, during times the fish are particularly vulnerable, are much better than shutting the stable door after the horse has bolted.

As winter progresses, take precautions to prevent bubbles of methane from being trapped under the ice. This gas, if reabsorbed into the water, is detrimental to fish. A submersible electric pump can be positioned to move a small volume of water immediately above it on the surface with sufficient turbulence to prevent ice from forming at that point. Similarly, if a waterfall unit or geyser fountain has been incorporated into the design, it should be kept running to give enough movement to prevent ice from forming. An alternative method is to use an electric pond heater, frequently called a de-icer, that floats on the surface, keeping open a small hole in the ice. Where there is no electricity, a pan of boiling water placed on the ice will melt out a hole eventually, and if this is kept up as long as the freezing weather lasts, the same ventilating effect is achieved. Never break the ice forcibly, because the resultant shock waves in a small pond will give considerable distress to the fish. In addition to allowing a degree of air movement around a small portion of unfrozen water, keeping open a hole in the ice also reduces expansion pressure on the pool sides. In pools whose concrete walls have been inadequately reinforced, the concrete can crack. Some of this pressure can be absorbed by floating tennis balls or pieces of wood on the surface before the ice forms. When they become locked in the ice, they relieve extremes of lateral pressure.

PROPAGATION

As the pool becomes more established, thinning, pruning, and dividing overgrown plants becomes increasingly necessary. These operations allow plants to be propagated and at the same time improve the appearance of the water garden and reinvigorate starved and overcrowded plants. It is best not to tackle such a program all in one season, which results in a bare, immature effect for a while. Dividing plants is best undertaken over a rotation of three years so that none of the occupants, including the water lilies, loses its vigor and comfortable proportions in the overall scheme. The need for division in water lilies is often indicated by a reduction in the size of the center leaves. In Europe, certain of the weaker and dwarfer varieties of water lily require division only every five or six years. In the United States more frequent division is necessary, usually every other year in March or April. In some areas in the southern states, division may be necessary every year.

Division, in its broadest context, is the most common technique for propagating the majority of aquatic plants, particularly the marginals. As part of the cultivation program of a water garden, plants should be regularly divided even if there is no need for an increase in the quantity of stock. During spring, lift established plants from the pool and if containerized, prize them out of their planting baskets. In some cases, vigorous rootstocks will have become so entwined in the basket that the container has to be forfeited in an attempt to disentangle and wash the roots. For plants that have been grown in the natural pool bottom, one may have to sever pieces from the edge of the plant as the rootstock and plant are often too heavy to lift out. Cut away manageable pieces until old tissue, which is often better discarded, is reached. Such an operation is very difficult by hand when vigorous genera such as *Typha* have become established over a number of years in large pools. Strong hydraulic machinery is then the only way of physically reducing and dividing such stock, emphasizing the importance of care in the initial selection and of regular cutting back.

In the smaller pool with containerized plants, once the container has been removed and the roots cleaned, the mode of division will be influenced by the type of rootstock. The easiest plants to divide are those with a fibrous root system. Simply pull the clumps of root apart, use the outer and younger portions for replanting, and discard the older tissue in the center. Garden forks can be used by inserting the spikes back-to-back vertically in the clump and drawing the handles together, the forks then separating individual pieces. This system is appropriate for many of the clump-forming genera such as marsh marigold (*Caltha*).

Plants with creeping root systems such as bogbean (*Menyanthes*) require their scrambling rhizomes to be cut into individual pieces, but ensure that each piece contains a bud or in the case of the flowering rush (*Butomus*), bulbils in the axils of the leaves. The younger pieces are then replanted into containers of aquatic planting soil and returned to the pool as described in Chapter 4.

A slightly more sophisticated form of division, often referred to as bud cuttings, is used for propagating water lilies. This popular method is quick and simple and requires the removal of buds, or eyes, from the parent rootstock. These eyes form side shoots along the cylindrical rhizomes of the tuberosa and odorata types and along the thicker rhizomes of the Marliac forms. The best time for the removal of the eyes is March or April, leaving the remainder of the growing season for the new plants to become established. After taking the plant from its container, wash it and carefully examine the rather clustered rootstock, removing the tender young growths with a sharp knife. The eyes of the odorata and tuberosa rootstocks can be simply broken off by hand. Leave the parent plant with several inches of tuber, removing at the same time any thin roots and surplus leaves.

If increasing the stock of young plants is not a concern, then cut the tuber into two or three pieces, each with at least one good growing point. Only a few inches of tuber are necessary to each eye or growing point, and much of the older rootstock can be thrown away. Then pot the young plants into containers as described in Chapter 4.

The propagation of tropical water lilies is quite different from the hardy lilies in that the tropicals form walnut-sized tubers as the water temperature drops with the approach of winter. When these tubers have formed at the base of the parent plant, lift the plant, remove and wash the tubers, and cut off pieces of the older root system. Store the tubers and pieces of older root in moist sand or Ziploc bags at 40–50°F (4–10°C). Provided they are prevented from drying out, enough of them should survive the winter to provide next summer's stock. The following spring remove the tubers from the moist sand and plant them in soil under shallow water at a temperature of 70–80°F (21–27°C) in a greenhouse. If warm water temperatures are not achieved, the tubers will not produce growth. After about three to six weeks, they should produce baby plants. As soon as the plantlets have two tiny floating leaves, carefully remove them and plant them in small pots submerged in warm water. The tubers will then continue to produce baby plants until they are exhausted. As the young plants become stronger, increase the water depth. When the outdoor water temperature starts to climb, the plants can be planted into their permanent summer quarters. Any remaining baby plants attached to the tuber can be allowed to remain on the parent tuber and planted out.

Certain day-blooming tropical water lilies such as *Nymphaea* 'Daubeniana' exhibit an interesting method of viviparous vegetative reproduction. A young plant emerges from a swelling in the center of the leaf at the junction of the leaf blade to the leaf stem, with young roots emerging from the embryonic plant. Sometimes there are several growing points, forming a multiheaded plant. The leaves carrying the young plants can be removed and pinned to a compacted soil in a shallow container under approximately 1 in (2.5 cm) of water. The old leaf eventually rots away, and the young plant can be planted into a larger pot. In the case of the multiheaded plant, as soon as the small crowns have developed, tease them apart and plant them individually. Some cultivars exhibit this viviparous condition, including 'Mrs. Martin E. Randig', 'Panama Pacific', 'Charles Thomas', 'Margaret Mary', and 'Pink Platter'. Hardy water lilies are not known to be viviparous with the exceptions 'Colonel A. J. Welch', 'Perry's Viviparous Pink', 'Perry's Red Star', 'Perry's Pink Delight', and occasionally in the Deep South, 'Cherokee', all of which can be viviparous from the flower pod. Viviparity is most common in the tropical water lilies.

Many aquatics throw out obliging runners for use in propagation, one of the most common being the luxuriant and often threatening runners of water hyacinth (*Eichhornia*). It sends out adventitious shoots that support young plants at their tips and that develop roots and ultimately send out more runners. With such a method of spread, floating and submerged species can quickly become nuisances, particularly in the tropics, where introduction of certain of these types is forbidden. Only one water lily produces runners, the yellow-flowered *Nymphaea mexicana*, which can also spread excessively and require a watchful eye not to become a nuisance.

Most of the submerged aquatics, particularly those used as oxygenators, are easily propagated by cuttings taken during the growing season. Nip 2–4 in (5–10 cm) lengths of stem off the parent plant and insert them into shallow pans or trays of loamy soil and then firm and cover them with 4–6 in (10–15 cm) of water. As soon as they have developed roots, which takes no longer than two to three weeks, they can be individually potted into small containers and planted out. When sold from aquatic centers, unrooted cuttings of this soft material are gathered in bunches of six to eight stems and clasped together at the base with a piece of lead. If the pool has a muddy bottom, they can simply be dropped into the water to take root where they sink, or they can be planted as described in Chapter 4.

A form of root cutting quite different from the type performed on the eyes of hardy water lilies is practiced on one of the more common moisture-loving plants, *Primula denticulata*. During the dormant season, lift established plants and cut thin pieces of root into 1-in (2.5-cm) sections and lay them flat on multipurpose potting soil that has been firmed and levelled in a seed tray or seed pan. Once the cuttings are laid out horizontally, cover them with a fine layer of sand no deeper than 0.1 in (0.3 cm). If kept moist and placed in a greenhouse when the growing season starts, young shoots will soon appear from the roots, and as these young plants develop, they can be carefully teased from the soil and potted into small pots.

Certain woody trees and shrubs growing at the waterside such as dogwood (*Cornus*) and willow (*Salix*) can be propagated by hardwood cuttings taken during the dormant season. Remove 7–9 in (18–23 cm) lengths of young wood about pencil thickness with the base of the shoot cut to just below a bud and the top of the shoot cut to just above a bud. Insert these vertically into the soil to about two thirds of their length. During the following growing season, they should develop roots and be possible to lift the following autumn.

Sowing the seed of many hardy aquatics, particularly the hardy water lilies, is often a slow and rather unreliable process, more suited to the very keen specialist collector or hybridizer than to the average water gardener wishing to have a modest increase in stock. Most hardy water lilies are shy in setting seed with the exception of *Nymphaea tetragona* and *N. odorata*. It is appropriate to attempt to propagate *N.* ×*pygmaea* 'Alba' by seed as unlike the other hardy forms, it does not produce eyes for propagation. The tropical water lily species and all night bloomers set large quantities of seed that is likely to germinate and make seed sowing a more rewarding practice.

Successful germination depends on simulating as closely as possible conditions that would be found naturally. Seed containers should be shallow enough to be submerged in another container and covered with 1–2 in (2.5–5 cm) of water. This can achieved by submerging a seed tray or seed pan in a washtub or aquarium.

Enclose the seed pods of ripening hardy water lilies in muslin bags in order to prevent the ripe seeds, which are encased in tiny white bladders of protoplasm, from floating away if ruptured. One now has two choices: 1) Place the seeds with a little water in a Ziploc bag and hold in the refrigerator door until spring, or 2) sow the seeds immediately, spreading the jellylike mixture containing the fine seeds as evenly as possible over soil that is made up of garden loam passed through a 0.25-in (0.6-cm) sieve. The loamy soil should not have any fertilizer mixed into it to prevent algae from developing in the shallow water over the long period that some seeds take to germinate. Sieve a fine covering of soil over the mixture and water it in with a fine mist before submerging the seed pan to a depth of about 1 in (2.5 cm). The container should be placed in a greenhouse or on a sunny windowsill at a minimum temperature of 65°F (18°C). The first seed leaves are fragile, long, pointed, and extremely prone to attracting algae onto their surfaces. Once they have developed sufficiently to handle, remove and gently wash them before inserting them into larger trays and submerging them in 3 in (8 cm) of water. After further growth they can be individually potted into 3-in (8-cm) pots and submerged in 3–4 in (8–10 cm) of water. After a further period of growth under good light conditions, they can be planted into their permanent quarters.

The technique for sowing tropical water lilies is the same except that the minimum temperature is 75–80°F (23–27°C). (The seed of tropicals can be allowed to dry out before sowing and can be stored in a dry warm place.) Light levels should be as high as possible in the early growth period, and if by autumn sufficiently large tubers have not had time to form and be harvested, the young plants should be kept in warm water for the winter.

Some marginal plants can be propagated by seed, especially *Alisma* and *Pontederia*. The technique and temperature requirements are the same as for hardy water lilies, and the seed should be sown as soon as possible after harvesting.

Many of the moisture-loving species are best propagated by seed. Unlike marginals and water lilies, they are not submerged on sowing but are sown in a traditional seed-starting mix when freshly harvested and germinated in full light in cold frames or greenhouses. The soil must be well drained but never allowed to dry out, keeping the young seedlings in a more moist regime than common annuals and other seed-sown plants.

PESTS AND DISEASES OF FISH

Ornamental fish may also succumb from time to time to pests and diseases. In a well-managed pool whose stocking levels of fish and plants have been carefully thought out, the fish look after themselves, requiring little else but supplementary feeding. Any major change, however, in the water chemistry may cause problems, particularly large additions of chlorine from tap water or the chemical leachate of insecticides, herbicides, fertilizers, or metal ions from metal fountain ornaments. Fish are more prone to infection when weakened by long, severe winters, spawning, or oxygen starvation. Even with adequate oxygenating plants, the fish in a heavily stocked pool may experience oxygen starvation during hot summer nights, particularly where there is no fountain to create water turbulence. In such conditions, make every effort to disturb the water surface, preferably with a circulating pump or by spraying it vigorously with a hose. If the fish have been gulping for some hours, air diffusers such as those used in aquaria can ease the depleted oxygen supply. Since more oxygen can be absorbed by the water's surface in cooler weather, oxygen starvation is mainly a problem of pools in warm climates with stocking levels that are on the high side.

Physical injury by a predator may leave a fish with an infected wound that requires treatment. Such predators include herons, diving beetles and their larvae, and larvae of dragon- and damselflies. It is vital to keep any form of stress to a minimum, and unless the fish is seriously infected or sick, the inevitable stress of clumsy catching and handling or squeezing can end up doing much more harm than good. Be sure that the net used for catching is large enough and is made of a soft woven nylon that will not rasp scales or disturb the fish's protective mucus coating. If the fish requires spot treatment, hold it in the net and perform the operation as quickly as possible. Frequent treatments that make the fish hypochondriacs should be avoided; the old adage of prevention being better than cure is particularly appropriate in a pool full of fish.

If you suspect that the water chemistry is a contributory factor and can identify and eliminate the source, a slow water change will do much to revive the vigor of the fish and help fight infection. Whenever possible, water changes should be made with rain water, but as it is more likely that tap water will be used, a complete water change should be made over a period of a few days and the water treated with a dechlorinator. As water direct from the tap is nearly devoid of oxygen, be sure in filling the pool to raise the hose high over the water surface. This allows the stream of water to take on oxygen before it enters the pool. A hose laid in a small pool may suffocate the fish. The application of good common sense should keep a fish population in a healthy state, but unforeseen climatic extremes or attacks by predators can devastate any pool. The following summary represents the most common ailments.

Fungus disease is by far the most common fish affliction. The spores of this fungus, *Saprolegnia ferox*, are present in most water, particularly when decaying animal matter is present. The infected fish produces cottonlike growths on the body and fins. It is most commonly seen in late winter or just after spawning, but there are a variety of causes such as travel stress, water pollution, rapid temperature change, or bites from predators. Fortunately, an infected fish does not mean a greater risk to the others, and such infections are frequently overcome without treatment. If treatment becomes necessary, however, it is important to diagnose the possible cause before resorting to fungicide. Fish are easily bruised, and when alarmed they can injure themselves in small or enclosed spaces, leaving them more prone to fungus infections. If injuries to fish become common occurrences, keep debris on the pool bottom to an absolute minimum. Treatment involves removing the fish and immersing it in one of the many proprietary products based on malachite green or methylene blue.

Whitespot, or ich, another common disease, is caused by a small protozoan parasite, *Ichthyophthirius multifiliis*, that frequently accompanies new additions to the pool. If new fish are kept in a quarantine pool or tank for a period of seven or more days, infections should be prevented in the existing stock. The parasite causes considerable irritation, and infected fish can often be seen rubbing themselves against hard surfaces. In the early stages of infection, it may be diagnosed as fungus, but closer examination reveals small pure white spots with sharply defined edges spread liberally over the body and fins. It is more common in warm water and is frequently an infection of aquarium fish. After gaining a foothold and feeding on the fish, the adult parasites leave their host and become waterborne cysts. These rupture within a day or two, and the young parasites must find a host fish quickly in order to survive. In warm water they perish within 48 hours. Such a life cycle provides an opportunity to rid the infected pool of parasites: remove the fish to a tank of constantly running water that will wash away the adults as they leave their hosts. The remaining youngsters, left in the main pool and bereft of hosts, will die within three or four days. Do not reintroduce fish until sufficient time has elapsed for all the adults to have evacuated from the hosts, which is normally about seven days. The treatment tank for the infected fish should contain quinine sulfate, quinine hydrochloride, or mercurochrome.

Gill flukes, *Dactylogyrus*, are tiny worms that are almost invisible to the naked eye and that infect the gills of fish. Affected fish become very agitated, swimming erratically and regularly twitching their fins. The flukes cause breathing difficulties, and treatment with proprietary chemical remedies is not always very effective. The condition causes so much distress that it is kinder to destroy the fish humanely.

Parasites such as the fish louse, *Argulus*, can also cause similar erratic movement or jumping. One of the most commonly seen is a circular, flattish light green louse, about 0.25 in (0.6 cm) long with two feelers at the back. As they are more easily seen than gill flukes, they can be spot treated with a drop of paraffin on a small artist's brush when the fish is held in a soft net.

Another distressing crustacean is the anchor worm, *Lernaea*, which buries its barbed head into the tissue of the fish, leaving a slender thread about 0.75 in (2 cm) long protruding from a small swelling. Treatment involves removing the worms with tweezers and applying iodine or potassium permanganate at the point of origin.

Although fairly rare in lined ponds, leeches can attack fish in natural ponds with extensive vegetation. The three most common species are *Helobdella stagnalis*, *Macrobdellas decora*, and *Erpobdella punctata*. They are wormlike and usually brown, green, gray, or black in color and attach themselves to the body of the fish. Applying salt to the leech will cause it to release its hold.

Dropsy is a bloated condition in which the scales stand out. It often appears after long periods of low temperatures. Although it does not appear to be contagious, the condition is incurable, and the fish should be destroyed.

CLEANING THE POOL

It may be necessary every few years to give a lined or concrete pool a complete cleaning, particularly to remove the ever-increasing depth of mulm, or siltlike black slime, at the bottom. Such an operation requires careful planning and should not be undertaken on impulse, particularly when fish are present. Avoid the operation when the pool is teeming with desirable young tadpoles or other small creatures: the latter part of the summer is usually a good time or in early spring before plant growth starts.

Temporary quarters for the fish must resemble as closely as possible their permanent conditions, and as the job is best undertaken in the growing season, adequate oxygen must be available. In order to achieve this, provide a temporary pool with a large surface area in a shady position. Incorporate an air diffuser if possible. A child's large wading pool makes a good stopgap, or fill a sheet of polyethylene supported by boards and timbers around the edges to a depth of 9–12 in (23–30 cm).

Ideally, the temporary pool should be filled with the water from the original pool, and a submersible pump will quickly achieve the transfer. Any remaining water may be drained by opening the pool's drain plug if present or pumping out with a submersible pump and hose to a nearby drain. The fact that the pool needs cleaning means that the pump may clog as it attempts to suck out the silty material at the bottom, so keep a watchful eye while the pump is running in order to clear the pump intake as necessary. The fish should be removed when the water level has dropped to the point that it becomes easier to catch them. Be aware that in the emptying process, any disturbance of sediments may cloud the water, making it much more difficult to catch the fish. Keep the stress and flapping about of fish removal to a minimum, and avoid using a pump so powerful that small fish or fry will be sucked into its impellers. Once the fish are safely ensconced in their temporary quarters, float a large plank on the surface to provide a place for them to hide from inquisitive cats. As a precaution the water can be treated with proprietary fish treatments that act as a fungicide or antiseptic against possible ailments or accidental wounding while under stress.

The submerged plants should be given the next priority, particularly the soft foliage of the oxygenating plants, which quickly shrivels when exposed to air. These can be either put into the temporary fish pool or contained in plastic garbage cans. If there is nothing large enough to accommodate the water lilies and the operation is to last no longer than a day or two, the plants can be safely left out of water as long as they are covered with wet sacking over the foliage and roots. Finally, the marginals can be removed, and they too can be left for a short period out of water as long as they are kept moist.

The cleaning out proper can now begin. Use a plastic dust pan, which will not damage the liner, to scoop the silt into a bucket. The silt, or mulm, is full of water life, both harmful and beneficial, and after saving any amphibians found after sifting through, it should be disposed of. It is of little value to the garden, but small amounts can be spread over the soil on established shrub borders. Once clean, check a concrete pond for any signs of cracking or weakening and either grout with a quick-drying mix or treat with a waterproofing sealant. If a major leak is apparent in an old concrete pond, it might be a good idea to line the pool with a flexible liner while it is empty. If you undertake any major concreting, the water will need to be neutralized and changed before replanting as described in Chapter 3.

When you are ready to refill the pool, use as much of the original water from the temporary pond as possible to reintroduce the many invisible, beneficial microorganisms and save a large influx of tap water. Plant the submerged plants first, particularly the oxygenators. Use the opportunity to clean and cut back or divide plants that have become overgrown. If much tap water is to be used, treat it with a dechlorinator before returning the fish. As with the submerged plants, divide or cut back the marginals before returning them to their positions in the water.

In natural ponds in which plants are growing in the bottom soil, this cleaning out operation will be necessary only if a problem seems to be occurring. Such ponds are best left with a minimum of disturbance, and only after years of considerable neglect, during which leaves and other debris have been allowed to accumulate, would there be a need to empty the system to remove the decomposed organic matter and silt.

PART TWO

An Encyclopedia of
Water Lilies and Lotuses

by

PERRY D. SLOCUM

Acknowledgments

My work would not have been possible without the invaluable help of the following friends and associates whose contribution I gratefully acknowledge. Of course, any errors in the text are solely my own and do not reflect the timely assistance of the following people: Norman Bennett for his help with plant descriptions; Ray Butler, Jr., Dallas, Texas, for the loan of photographs; Ray Davies and his company, Stapeley Water Gardens, Nantwich, Cheshire, England, for the loan of photographs and assistance with descriptions; Bill Heritage, Richmansworth, Hertfordshire, England, for reviewing the manuscript, for assistance in verifying the names of hardy water lilies in illustrations, and for openly sharing his knowledge and photographs of water lily and bog plants; Kenneth C. Landon, San Angelo, Texas, water lily species expert, for the many hours spent helping sort out *Nymphaea gigantea* species and cultivars and for his advice on other matters and photographs; Jim Lawrie, manager of Waterford Gardens, for his photographs of formal and informal landscaped pools; Edith Metelik, Austral Watergardens, New South Wales, Australia, for her help with the description of *Nymphaea* 'Seignoureti' No. 2 and for giving me permission to photograph her gardens; Mary and John Mirgon for the loan of the photograph of the beautiful new lily, 'Mary Mirgon'; Patrick Nutt and Longwood Gardens, Kennett Square, Pennsylvania, for the loan of photographs and for the hours of advice; Walter Pagels for his helpful advice on the manuscript and for the loan of photographs; Jane Reader, San Angelo, Texas, for the loan of photographs; Wilfred (Bill) Schmidlin for sharing his expertise, reviewing this manuscript, and for help in verifying the names of both hardy and tropical water lily illustrations; Dr. Edward L. Schneider, executive director of the Santa Barbara Botanic Garden, Santa Barbara, California, for his indispensable help on *Barclaya* and *Ondinea* and also for his photographs of the latter; Peter Slocum, my son, for advice and the loan of photographs; Paul Stetson, Sr., for manuscript review, helpful advice, name verification on hardy water lily illustrations, and the loan of photographs; Dr. Kirk Strawn, who helped to verify the names of hardy water lily illustrations; Philip Swindells for supplying the names of European aquatic nurseries; Charles Thomas for his helpful suggestions after reviewing my manuscript and help in verifying the names of hardy water lily illustrations; George Thomas III and Lilypons Water Gardens, Buckeystown, Maryland, and Brookshire, Texas, for the loan of photographs; Joe Tomocik for assistance with plant descriptions and the loan of photographs; William (Bill) Uber and his company, Van Ness Water Gardens, Inc., Upland, California, for loaning water lily photographs; A. C. Whiteley, assistant botanist, Royal Horticultural Garden, Wisley, Woking, Surrey, England, for his help with descriptions of *Nymphaea* ×*marliacea* 'Rosea' and *N.* 'Seignoureti'; Dr. John H. Wiersema of the Systemic Botany and Mycology Laboratory, USDA-ARS, Beltsville, Maryland, for use of material excerpted from his *A Monograph of Nymphaea Subgenus Hydrocallis (Nymphaeaceae)*, volume 16 of *Systematic Botany Monographs*, published in 1987 by the American Society of Plant Taxonomists; Dr. Paula Williamson of Southwest Texas State University for help on *Barclaya* and *Ondinea*; Jack Wood, former owner of El Rancho Tropical, Thermal, California, for help with some of the water lily descriptions.

The American Society of Plant Taxonomists, University of Michigan Herbarium, Ann Arbor, Michigan; the Carnegie Institution, Washington, D.C.; and Systemic Botany Monographs, also of the University of Michigan Herbarium, generously contributed visual materials for this book.

And special thanks to Spectrum Graphics and Lisa Pierce for their help in illustrating.

Perry D. Slocum

Chapter 11

Taxonomy of the Water Lily Family

This chapter is devoted to a descriptive taxonomy of the Nymphaeaceae, or water lily family, and includes the genera *Nymphaea, Nelumbo, Nuphar, Victoria, Euryale, Barclaya* (syn. *Hydrostemma*), and *Ondinea* (Figure 43). The plants themselves, ordered according to the currently accepted taxonomy, are described in Chapters 12–18.

The classification of these plants has been considerably confused, and the present ordering represents a painstaking attempt to sort out the identification and nomenclature of the various species and cultivars. For some plant groups further study is needed before the taxonomy can be considered authoritative.

In recent years some important changes have been made in established classifications: the genera *Barclaya* and *Ondinea* have been added to the Nymphaeaceae, and the former water lily genera *Brasenia* and *Cabomba* are now in the Cabombaceae.

Anatomical, morphological, phytochemical, and other studies demonstrate that *Nelumbo* (lotus) should not be considered a member of the water lily family. Molecular studies of the Nymphaeaceae, reported in the Winter 1993 *Water Garden Journal*, show that *Nelumbo* does not have the same *rbc*L gene sequence in the chloroplast that *Nymphaea, Nuphar, Victoria, Euryale,* and *Barclaya* possess. (*Ondinea* had not been studied for this report.) Yet, because of the ecological convergence shown in flower parts, leaves, rhizomes, and aquatic preferences with the other genera of the family, I treat *Nelumbo* here as a member of the water lily family.

THE GENUS *NYMPHAEA*

A most basic distinction can be made between tropical water lilies, those native to tropical or semitropical climates, and hardy water lilies, native to cooler climates. Hardy water lily blooms open during the daytime while tropical species and cultivars can be distinguished as day blooming or night blooming. The tropical flowers of night bloomers in subgenus *Hydrocallis* bloom in the middle of the night for a short time (only two hours in some species). Flowers of the night bloomers in subgenus *Lotos* open about dusk, staying open to nearly noon on the following day. On cloudy or cool days these blooms may stay open all day. Typically *Lotos* flowers are large and showy.

Tropical water lily blooms are usually raised several inches above the water. Last-day flowers usually float. "Star" lilies, whose parentage includes *Nymphaea flavovirens* (syn. *N. gracilis*) or *N. capensis* var. *zanzibariensis*, are day bloomers that may raise their flowers 12 in (30 cm) or more above water. Hardy water lilies generally raise their blooms only slightly above the water or allow them to float. The hardy exceptions include the cultivars 'Pink Starlet' (1970) and 'Texas Dawn' (1985) with blooms held 9 and 10 in (23 and 25 cm) above the water, respectively.

An interesting and unusual method of viviparous reproduction (bearing young plants) occurs in a few tropical species and cultivars. *Nymphaea micrantha* and many of its hybrids form new baby plants or "plantlets" on their leaves at the junction to the petiole. These plantlets may bloom while still attached to the

Family Nymphaeaceae

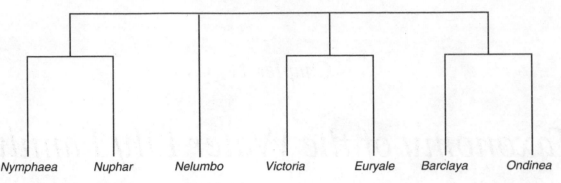

| Nymphaea | Nuphar | Nelumbo | Victoria | Euryale | Barclaya | Ondinea |

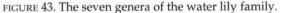

FIGURE 43. The seven genera of the water lily family.

mother plant. Still another type of viviparous reproduction occurs in two species of the *Hydrocallis* group: *N. lasiophylla* and *N. prolifera* form new plants from tubers developing in the flowers.

No species of hardy water lily is considered viviparous, at least by the botanic world as a whole. A possible exception is 'Colonel A. J. Welch'. This is a Marliac introduction and little is known about when it was introduced or its parentage. Hybridizer Reginald Henley of Odiham in Hampshire, England, considers this plant a species since it produces young plants with rhizomes from many of its flowers. Henley has presented programs on his hybridizing efforts to the International Water Lily Society and is widely acclaimed for his work.

Hardy water lily cultivars which occasionally develop plantlets from flower or bud are 'Cherokee' (syn. 'Orange Hybrid'), 'Perry's Pink Delight', 'Perry's Red Star', and 'Perry's Viviparous Pink'.

The water lily species, not necessarily the cultivars, may be broadly described as follows: Petals number 12 to 40; there are usually four sepals, rarely three or five; stamens can be numerous, 20 to 700 in number; carpels number 8 to 35; the stigma is broad, concave, and radiate; fruit is spongy and ripens underwater; seeds mature with floating sacks.

Reproduction by seed involves ripe seeds bursting to the top of the water by means of a buoyant aril (the floating sack), a spongy, gelatinous mass of tissue covering each seed. This tissue stays intact for two to three days while wind or waves move seeds to new areas. The sacks dissolve and the seeds sink to the bottom to initiate germination.

Dr. Henry S. Conard, who published his authoritative *The Waterlilies: A Monograph of the Genus Nymphaea* in 1905, describes these plants as "aquatic herbs" with perennial elongated or tuberous rhizomes that root in mud at the bottom of streams, ponds, lakes, and other bodies of water. The lovely blossoms are colored white or various shades of blue, red, or yellow. The colors orange (in hardies) and green, violet, and purple (in tropicals) also occur in cultivars.

THE "NEW" SPECIES

After several talks with Kenneth Landon, an expert on water lily species, I believe that Conard's taxonomy of water lilies provides a good working basis. Yet it is necessary to add a few species discovered since Conard's studies to bring the taxonomy up to date. In brief, the history of these additions is as follows:

In 1929 B. D. Burtt, botanist for the Tse Tse Research Bureau, Kondoa, Tanganyika Territory, Africa, discovered *Nymphaea burtii* Pring & Woodson. In 1951, Dr. George Pring determined that *N. burtii* and *N. stuhlmannii* were actually the same species—a judgment I accept.

In 1939 the Royal Botanic Gardens, Kew, England, received seeds of a new water lily from Africa. These seeds were forwarded to the Missouri Botanical Garden by R. S. Trickett. The name *Nymphaea colorata* Peter was assigned as A. Peter had originally described this plant in 1928.

In 1986 Kenneth Landon discovered a white day-blooming tropical with features that set it apart from similar species in the rain pools, rivers, and streams of the Togo region of Africa. He assigned it the name *Nymphaea togoensis* Landon.

One night-blooming tropical, *Nymphaea spontanea* Landon, has recently been elevated to species status.

Dr. John H. Wiersema of the USDA-ARS's Systemic Botany and Mycology Lab, Beltsville, Maryland, has done extensive research on the subgenus *Hydrocallis*. His studies have resulted in dropping three species, *Nymphaea blanda* Meyer, *N. stenaspidota* Caspary, and *N. gibertii* Morong, from Conard's listing and adding seven new species: *N. belophylla* Trickett, *N. conardii* Wiersema, *N. glandulifera* Rodschied, *N. lingulata* Wiersema, *N. novogranatensis* Wiersema, *N. potamophila* Wiersema, and *N. prolifera* Wiersema.

Still other species have been proposed during the years since Conard's comprehensive studies in the *Anecphya* and *Nymphaea gigantea* complex. Further research must be done on the subgenus *Anecphya* in order to properly interpret its variants.

The following is a list of seven published species closely related to *Nymphaea gigantea* that may or may not attain species rank upon further study. The first five were briefly described in the March 1989 *Water Garden Journal* by Dr. Surrey Jacobs, Royal Botanic Gardens, Sydney, Australia.

1. *Nymphaea dictyophlebia* Merrill & Perry. Blue or white flowers. Native to the Northern Territory and Queensland, Australia, and Papuasia.

2. *N. hastifolia* Domin. Small white flowers. Native to north Australia.

3. *N. macrosperma* Merrill & Perry. Blue flowers. Native to the north of the Northern Territory, Australia, and Papuasia.

4. *N. minima* Jacobs. Small blue flowers. Native to northeast Queensland, Australia.

5. *N. violacea* Lehman. Blue, white, or pink flowers, usually deep blue. Most widespread of the five species described by Dr. Jacobs. Native to the north and parts of central Australia and Papuasia.

6. *N. brownii* F. M. Bailey. Pale bluish white flowers. Plant is being grown at Longwood Gardens, Pennsylvania. According to Patrick Nutt, foreman of plant propagation at Longwood Gardens, *N. brownii* has no commercial value but could be used in hybridizing. Native to Australia.

7. *N. casparyi* (Rehnelt & Henkel) Carrière. Light to medium blue flowers. Similar to the *N. gigantea* type but with divergent sinus margins. Native to Australia.

Kenneth Landon, who has researched the group extensively for many years, considers that these seven "species" are varieties or forms of the *Nymphaea gigantea* complex. This is the view to which I subscribe.

TAXONOMY OF THE GENUS *NYMPHAEA*

The genus *Nymphaea* divides into two main groups, which in turn divide into five subgenera, according to Dr. Henry Conard. Group *Apocarpiae* includes the subgenera *Anecphya* and *Brachyceras*, while group *Syncarpiae* consists of the subgenera *Hydrocallis*, *Lotos*, and *Castalia*.

Group *Apocarpiae* consists entirely of *Nymphaea gigantea* and other tropical day-blooming water lilies. Conard has placed the hardy water lilies of subgenus *Castalia* in group *Syncarpiae* with the night-blooming tropicals (*Hydrocallis* and *Lotos*) because his studies show a closer botanical relationship between hardy water lilies and night-blooming tropicals than with day-blooming tropicals.

The *Nymphaea* subgenera are enumerated below. Plants of all but the subgenus *Castalia* are described in Chapter 12. Chapter 15 describes plants of the subgenus *Castalia*.

> Group *Apocarpiae*
>   Subgenus *Anecphya* (1)
>   *Nymphaea gigantea* Hooker
>   *N. gigantea* var. *alba* Landon comb. nov.
>   *N. gigantea* var. *neorosea* Landon comb. nov.
>   *N. gigantea* var. *violacea* (Lehman) Conard
>   Subgenus *Brachyceras* (14)
>   *N. ampla* (Salisbury) de Candolle
>   *N. ampla* var. *pulchella* (de Candolle) Caspary

N. ampla var. *speciosa* (Martius & Zuccarini) Caspary
N. caerulea Savigny
N. calliantha Conard
   N. calliantha var. *tenuis* Conard
N. capensis Thunberg
   N. capensis var. *alba* Landon
   N. capensis var. *madagascariensis* de Candolle
   N. capensis var. *zanzibariensis* Caspary
N. colorata Peter
N. elegans Hooker
N. flavovirens Lehmann [*N. gracillis* Zuccarini]
N. heudelotii Planchon
   N. heudelotii var. *nana*
N. micrantha Guillemin & Perrottet
N. nouchali Burman f. [*N. stellata* Willdenow]
   N. nouchali var. *cyanea* (Roxburgh) Hooker & Thomson
   N. nouchali var. *versicolor* (Roxburgh) Hooker & Thomson
N. ovalifolia Conard
N. stuhlmannii (Schweinfurth) Gilg
N. sulfurea Gilg
N. togoensis Landon

Group *Syncarpiae*
  Subgenus *Castalia*
    Section *Chamaenymphaea* (1)
      N. tetragona Georgi
         N. tetragona var. *angusta* Caspary
         N. tetragona var. *lata* Caspary
         N. tetragona var. *leibergii* (Morong) Porsild
    Section *Eucastalia* (4)
      N. alba (Linnaeus) J. Presl
         N. alba var. *rubra* Lonnroth
      N. candida J. Presl
      N. odorata Aiton
         N. odorata var. *gigantea* Tricker
         N. odorata var. *minor* Sims
         N. odorata var. *rosea* Pursh
      N. tuberosa Paine
    Section *Xanthantha* (1)
      N. mexicana Zuccarini [*N. mexicana* No. 1]
         N. mexicana f. *canaveralensis* Frase [*N. mexicana* No. 2]
  Subgenus *Hydrocallis* (14)
      N. amazonum subsp. *amazonum* Martius & Zuccarini
         N. amazonum subsp. *pedersenii* Wiersema
      N. belophylla Trickett
      N. conardii Wiersema
      N. gardneriana Planchon
      N. glandulifera Rodschied
      N. jamesoniana Planchon
      N. lasiophylla Martius & Zuccarini
      N. lingulata Wiersema
      N. novogranatensis Wiersema
      N. oxypetala Planchon
      N. potamophila Wiersema
      N. prolifera Wiersema

      N. rudgeana G. Meyer
      N. tenerinervia Caspary
   Subgenus *Lotos* (5)
      N. lotus (Linnaeus) Willdenow
      N. pubescens Willdenow
      N. rubra Roxburgh
      N. spontanea Landon
      N. zenkeri Gilg

TAXONOMY OF THE GENUS *NELUMBO*

For plant descriptions of *Nelumbo* see Chapter 17.

   Species (2)
   Nelumbo lutea (Willdenow) Persoon [*N. pentapetala* (Walter) Fernald]
   N. nucifera Gaertner [*N. speciosa* Willdenow]
      N. nucifera var. *caspicum* Fischer
      N. nucifera var. *rosea*

TAXONOMY OF THE GENUS *NUPHAR*

Nuphars are aquatic herbs distributed primarily in the Northern Hemisphere. Some of the species and varieties have beautiful submerged leaves, a feature highly desirable for aquaria. One species (*Nuphar japonica* de Candolle) develops orange-red flowers and reddish leaves, which makes it a good choice for the tub garden, small pool, or aquarium. For plant descriptions of *Nuphar* see Chapter 18.

Three different sources give three accounts of *Nuphar*. According to *Hortus Third* (1976) the genus includes about 25 species. *Das Buch der Nymphaeaceen oder Seerosengewächse* (1907) by Henkel, Rehnelt, and Dittman describes *Nuphar* as containing 26 species, 1 subspecies, and 17 varieties. Ernest O. Beal, in his doctoral work, "Taxonomic Revision of the Genus *Nuphar* of North America and Europe," published in the *Journal of the Elisha Mitchell Society* (1956), recognizes two species, *Nuphar japonica* and *N. lutea* with nine subspecies. Since Dr. Beal's study is more recent and since he used a vast number of specimens (4000), I am using it as the authoritative guide to nuphars in my treatment of the genus.

   Species (2)
   Nuphar japonica de Candolle
   N. lutea (Linnaeus) Sibthorp & Smith
      N. lutea subsp. *lutea* Beal
      N. lutea subsp. *macrophylla* (Small) Beal [*N. advena* (Aiton) Aiton f.]
      N. lutea subsp. *orbiculata* (Small) Beal
      N. lutea subsp. *ozarkana* (Miller & Standley) Beal
      N. lutea subsp. *polysepala* (Engelmann) Beal
      N. lutea subsp. *pumila* (Timm) Beal [*N. microphylla* Beal]
      N. lutea subsp. *sagittifolia* (Walter) Beal
      N. lutea subsp. *ulvacea* (Miller & Standley) Beal
      N. lutea subsp. *variegata* (Engelmann) Beal

I do not consider this taxonomic review of *Nuphar* definitive, as it principally covers the American and European nuphars and passes over the Japanese species in brief. Much more study is needed on this plant group before the earlier classifications are discarded.

TAXONOMY OF THE GENUS *VICTORIA*

For plant descriptions of *Victoria* see Chapter 18.

Species (2)
Victoria amazonica (Poeppig) Sowerby [*V. regia* Lindley]
V. cruziana d'Orbigny

TAXONOMY OF THE GENUS *EURYALE*

For plant descriptions of *Euryale* see Chapter 18.

Species (1)
Euryale ferox Salisbury

TAXONOMY OF THE GENUS *BARCLAYA*

For plant descriptions of *Barclaya* see Chapter 18.

Species (4)
Barclaya kunstleri (King) Ridley [*B. motleyi* var. *kunstleri* King]
B. longifolia Wallich [*Hydrostemma longifolium* (Wallich) Mabberley]
B. motleyi Hooker f. [*Hydrostemma motleyi* (Hooker f.) Mabberley]
B. rotundifolia Hotta

TAXONOMY OF THE GENUS *ONDINEA*

For plant descriptions of *Ondinea* see Chapter 18.

Species (1)
Ondinea purpurea Hartog
    O. purpurea subsp. *petaloidea* Kenneally & Schneider
    O. purpurea subsp. *purpurea* Hartog

Chapter 12

Tropical Water Lily Species

Five tropical water lily species that make very satisfactory water garden additions are commonly listed in aquatic nursery catalogs (see Appendix B for a list of these sources). These species are *Nymphaea capensis*, *N. colorata*, *N. gigantea*, *N. lotus*, and *N. rubra*.

Nymphaea capensis (cape water lily) from the Cape of Good Hope region in Africa, is often listed as "blue capensis." There are many commonly available cultivars of *N. capensis* from Zanzibar, off the coast of East Africa, many of them selections of variety *zanzibariensis*.

Nymphaea colorata is a very choice and desirable lily for the small or medium pool. It is comparable to its hybrids 'Director George T. Moore' and 'Midnight'.

Nymphaea gigantea, listed as 'Blue Gigantea' in William Tricker's catalog, is quite large, very beautiful, and very impressive. It does demand warm water of 80°F (27°C) to grow and bloom; otherwise, it enters dormancy. Two night bloomers, *N. lotus* (*N.* 'Juno' is usually considered to be *N. lotus*, and *N.* 'Trudy Slocum' was selected from a group of *N.* 'Juno') and *N. rubra*, are also being grown and sold in nurseries.

Most of the other species have similar counterparts in cultivars that are superior in performance. I would like to mention that most of the species currently not in cultivation are generally considered inferior to hybrids and are therefore not marketed.

This chapter contains a complete listing of tropical day-blooming and night-blooming water lily species, varieties, forms, and named selections. The arrangement follows the taxonomy of the genus *Nymphaea* as discussed in Chapter 11. A brief summary of the group characteristics precedes plant descriptions.

The species are arranged alphabetically by specific epithet with descriptions of related plants (varieties, forms, and named selections) immediately following; author and date of discovery are given when known. Synonyms are given after the botanical name, followed by common names, if any. Standardized color names and numbers refer to the Royal Horticultural Society's (R.H.S.) Color Chart. In descriptions of several rare species, when I could not compare live specimens (or sharp photos) with the R.H.S. chart, standard color references are omitted.

In species descriptions the stamen consists of the anther (bearing pollen), a typically slender filament holding the anther, and frequently an appendage or tip just above the anther (Figure 44). This appendage is referred to as the tip. "Stamen color" refers to the color found on the filament portion of the stamen, and "Anther color" to the various colors of the anther and its tip.

"Leaf size," given for each water lily, refers either to the diameter of the leaf of a mature plant or to the measurements of its length and width, in that order. "Leaf spread" refers to the diameter of the area on the water's surface covered by a mature plant. See Figure 45 for the variety of forms and characteristics *Nymphaea* leaves may have.

"Comments" on each plant include reference to suitable pool size. Although there are no hard rules differentiating pool sizes, general guidelines follow:

tub garden: up to 3 ft (1 m) in diameter
small: 4–6 ft (1.2–2 m) in diameter
medium: 7–9 ft (2.2–2.7 m) in diameter
large: 10 ft (3 m) in diameter or larger
natural pond: dirt or mud bottom pond of any size

Note that copper and redwood are toxic to plants and fish and should be used only in conjunction with a plastic or other fish-safe liner.

Plant tropical water lilies only when the water temperature averages 75°F (24°C) or above. Planting too early may induce dormancy. Refer to the hardiness zone maps in Appendix A and follow this general planting timetable:

IN NORTH AMERICA
Zone 10   March through early April
Zone 9   early April
Zone 8   mid April
Zone 7   mid/late May
Zone 6   late May/early June
Zone 5   early/mid June
Zone 4   mid/late June

IN EUROPE
Zone 10   mid/late May
Zone 9   June
Zones 8–4   conservatory planting, where water can be heated to 75°F (24°C) or higher

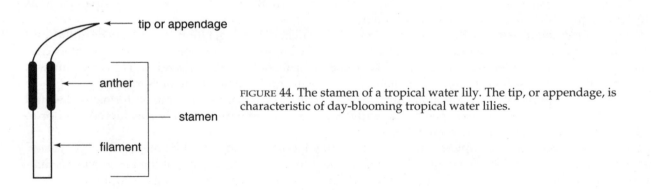

FIGURE 44. The stamen of a tropical water lily. The tip, or appendage, is characteristic of day-blooming tropical water lilies.

GROUP *NYMPHAEA APOCARPIAE* [*LYTOPLEURA* CASPARY 1865, 1878, 1888]

In general, species in the group *Apocarpiae* display carpels that are free from one another at the sides, fused along part of the suture with the axis of the flower, and fused dorsally with the perigynous torus. These are tropical species with diurnal flowers ranging in color from blue through pink to white. Blooms are raised 3–12 in (8–30 cm) above the water. Peduncles are stiff. Rhizomes are upright, tuberous, and round (or nearly so). Tubers are dormant during the dry season in their native habitat; growth initiates with the rainy season. Cold weather will also induce dormancy.

Subgenus *Anecphya* Caspary 1865, 1888

Subgenus *Anecphya* consists of a single species, *Nymphaea gigantea*, native to Australia and New Guinea. The species includes three varieties. Carpellary styles are generally absent. Stamens are plentiful with narrow filaments and short, curved anthers without appendages.

Nymphaea gigantea Hooker. Native to north Australia, New Guinea. Characteristics: Day blooming, nonviviparous, free flowering; flowers held 12 in (30 cm) above water. Plate 109.

PETAL COLOR: Inner petals, pale blue-violet; outer, deeper. *R.H.S. Chart*: Inner petals, Fan 2, Violet-Blue Group, No. 92C; outer, Nos. 92A–B. Sepal color: Medium violet-purple. *R.H.S. Chart*: Fan 2, Violet-Blue Group, No. 92A. Anther color: Deep yellow. *R.H.S. Chart*: Fan 1, Yellow Group, No. 5B. Stamen color: Yellow. Flower shape: Large, globular star. Flower size: 10–12 in (25–30 cm). Fragrance: Slight. Number of petals: 24. Number of sepals: 4.

LEAF COLOR: Top, green; underside, purplish. Leaf and sinus: Leaf egg-shaped; sinus, a half-open V. Leaf size: 15 × 13 in (38 × 33 cm). Leaf spread: 7–8 ft (2.2–2.5 m). Stem color: Peduncle, bright green; petiole, green, many tiny purple specks and dots. Pubescence on peduncle or petiole: None.

COMMENTS: *N. gigantea* is a magnificent species. The large, unique flowers are stunning. Blooms are held high above the water and the abundance of yellow stamens is very striking. This is a fine plant for the collector with a large pool in a warm climate or with a heated conservatory. Both white and pink variants exist. At least one nursery (William Tricker, Inc.) offers *N. gigantea* under the name 'Blue Gigantea'.

N. gigantea var. *alba* Landon comb. nov. 1978 [*N. gigantea* f. *alba* Bentham & Müller]. Flowers average 3.5–4 in (9–10 cm) in diameter. Petals (about 20) are a dazzling white within and without. Its four sepals are white inside. The 350 to 500 stamens have bright yellow anthers. Leaves on mature plants are nearly round, averaging 14 in (35 cm) in diameter, green above and below. Leaf margin is dentate with short, acute teeth. Variety *alba* is self-sustaining from seed yet is sometimes variable. Plates 110 and 115.

N. gigantea var. *neorosea* Landon comb. nov. 1978 [*N. gigantea* f. *neorosea*]. Flower is 3–5 in (8–13 cm) in diameter. Petals, averaging 25 in number, are long, narrow at base, longer than sepals, and, unlike most water lily blooms, not entirely covered by sepals after first-day closing. Color is deep rose, darkest at apex and lighter toward base. Outer petals are deepest rose, innermost petals lightest. The four sepals are rose-colored and colored slightly darker rose at margins. Stamens (about 412) have bright yellow anthers. Leaf shape is nearly obicular, averaging 14 × 13 in (35 × 33 cm). Leaves are dentate, green above with maroon spots, and green on underside with maroon perimeter. Sinus is open. Variety *neorosea* is self-sustaining from seed. Plate 111.

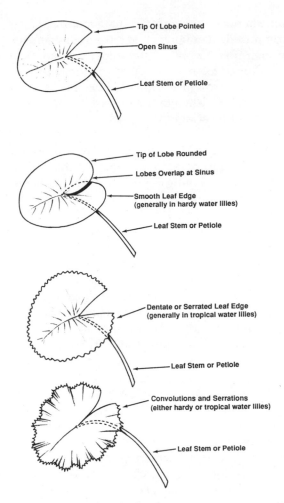

FIGURE 45. *Nymphaea* leaf traits.

N. gigantea var. *violacea* (Lehman) Conard 1905. Flowers average over 5 in (13 cm) in diameter. Petals average 27, with outermost dark violet or purple and innermost paler in color. The four sepals are dark violet on the interior side, green (as with most water lilies) on the exterior. Flowers contain 500 stamens on average. Leaf is ovate, 15 in (38 cm) average diameter, green above, and deep purple below. Margin is dentate. This variety is self-sustaining from seed yet produces some variant progeny. Seedlings sometimes develop a lighter colored bloom. Plate 112.

N. gigantea 'Albert de Lestang' Pring 1946. Flowers average 6 in (15 cm) in diameter. Petals average 33 in number and are predominantly white streaked with purplish blue, becoming darker at base. Outer petals are streaked a deeper purplish blue; inner petals are white except for purple coloring at point of attachment. Overall appearance is bluish white. Purplish blue coloring fades in later days, becoming deep rose after spent flower submerges into the water. Stamens average 500. Leaf of mature plant is nearly round, averaging 20 in (50 cm) in diameter. Leaf margin is wavy with dentate yellow- or brown-tipped teeth. Leaf is green on top and green tinged with brownish violet below. The 8–10 in (20–25 cm) bluish white flowers are the largest of the *N. gigantea* variants. Plate 113.

N. gigantea 'Hudsoniana' Hudson 1893. The blue flowers of 'Hudsoniana' are larger than those of variety *violacea*, averaging 6–8 in (15–20 cm) in diameter. Original accounts describe dark to medium blue flowers. Plate 114.

N. gigantea intermediate forms 1 and 2 Landon. Forms 1 and 2 are unnamed forms indigenous to Australia. The distinguishing characteristics of form 1 are the large flowers colored a rich royal purplish blue. The distinguishing characteristics of form 2 are its medium- to large-sized flowers, which at a distance appear totally white but upon

closer examination are white lightly streaked purplish blue. Plate 115.

In *Phytologia*, September 1978, Kenneth Landon, plant explorer and hybridizer, describes other *N. gigantea* variants as follows: "In a given colony of *N. gigantea* where various varieties and forms exist, crosses between plants are sure to eventuate with the resulting progeny giving rise to natural hybrids some of which may be individualized enough to warrant separate distinction. The vast majority of such hybrids, however, are seldom self-sustaining seed-producers, and after a short time their identity is often lost. The typical blue *N. gigantea*, along with several other variants (such as variety *violacea*), produce self-fertile seedlings, some of which evolve as botanical mutants (sports), creating other distinct variants. Generally, however, such progenal differences are so slight as to be subordinate to botanical varieties or even forms with regard to classification."

Subgenus *Brachyceras* Caspary 1865, 1878, 1888

Subgenus *Brachyceras* includes 14 species distributed throughout the tropics. In general, carpellary styles are present; styles are short, stiff, and fleshy. Stamens are numerous. Anthers are long and usually have sturdy appendages. Filaments are flat.

The day-blooming tropical cultivars commonly seen today derive from this group through hybridizing. Two of the species, *Nymphaea capensis* and *N. colorata*, are used extensively in water gardens around the world.

Nymphaea ampla (Salisbury) de Candolle. Native to south Texas, Mexico, Central America, south to central Brazil, Antilles, and the Bahamas. Characteristics: Day blooming, nonviviparous, very free flowering. Plate 116.

PETAL COLOR: White; outermost petals flushed yellowish green. *R.H.S. Chart*: Fan 4, White Group, No. 155D; flush, Fan 3, Yellow-Green Group, No. 149D. Sepal color: White, flushed green. *R.H.S. Chart*: Fan 4, White Group, No. 155A; flush, Fan 3, Yellow-Green Group, No. 145D. Anther color: Yellow, white tips. *R.H.S. Chart*: Fan 1, Yellow Group, No. 4A; tips, Fan 4, White Group, No. 155D. Stamen color: Yellow. Flower shape: Stellate. Flower size: 4–5.5 in (10–14 cm). Fragrance: Pronounced. Number of petals: 7–21. Number of sepals: 4.

LEAF COLOR: Top, new leaves bronzy red, soon bronzy green, then green; underside, reddish purple, prominent veins and numerous small black specks. Leaf and sinus: Leaf usually slightly longer than wide, dentate, many long teeth and serrations, wavy perimeter; sinus usually open. Leaf size: 15–20 in (38–50 cm). Leaf spread: 8 ft (2.5 m). Stem

color: Greenish brown. Pubescence on peduncle or petiole: None.

COMMENTS: *N. ampla*, if available, is suitable only for the collector with a medium or large pool.

N. ampla var. pulchella (de Candolle) Caspary. Native to tropical and subtropical America. Flowers have fewer stamens and are smaller than average for the species. Leaf edges are less wavy.

N. ampla var. speciosa (Martius & Zuccarini) Caspary. Native to Mexico, West Indies, and Brazil. Blooms are white but smaller than type. Leaves sharply dentate and have a relatively soft texture.

Nymphaea caerulea Savigny. Native to north and central Africa. Characteristics: Day blooming, nonviviparous, free flowering. Plate 117.

PETAL COLOR: Base, nearly white; tip, light violet blue. *R.H.S. Chart*: Tip, Fan 2, Violet-Blue Group, No. 91C; base paler than 91C. Sepal color: White. *R.H.S. Chart*: Fan 4, White Group, No. 155A. Anther color: Yellow, light blue tips. *R.H.S. Chart*: Fan 4,

Yellow-White Group, No. 158A; tips, Fan 2, Violet-Blue Group, No. 91C. Stamen color: Yellow. Flower shape: Stellate. Flower size: 3–6 in (8–15 cm). Fragrance: Very faint. Number of petals: 14–20. Number of sepals: 4.

LEAF COLOR: Top, green; underside, green, small purple spots. Leaf and sinus: Leaf egg-shaped; lobes usually overlap at sinus. Leaf size: 12–16 in (30–40 cm). Leaf spread: 8–10 ft (2.5–3 m). Stem color: Brownish green. Pubescence on peduncle or petiole: None.

COMMENTS: *N. caerulea* is known in literature as the "blue lotus of the Nile," though actually there is no such thing as a blue lotus. *N. caerulea* produces seeds easily and is a parent of 'Blue Beauty'. Due to the big leaves, the large coverage, and the small flowers, I can recommend this species only for the collector with a large pool.

Nymphaea calliantha Conard. Native to central and southwest Africa. Characteristics: Day blooming, nonviviparous, free flowering. Figure 46.

PETAL COLOR: Pink, violet-blue, or light blue. Sepal color: Base, white; apex, rose-pink for 0.6–0.75 in (1.5–2 cm). Anther color: Yellow. Stamen color: Yellow. Flower shape: Stellate. Flower size: 4–6 in (10–15 cm). Fragrance: Pleasant. Number of petals: 17. Number of sepals: 4.

LEAF COLOR: Top, green; underside, purplish margin shading to green. Leaf and sinus: Leaf nearly egg-shaped; wide-open lobes give a pronounced V. Leaf size: 5–11 × 3.5–9 in (13–28 × 9–23 cm). Leaf spread: 6–8 ft (2–2.5 m). Stem color: Greenish. Pubescence on peduncle or petiole: None.

COMMENTS: This species is not currently listed in nursery catalogs and is quite rare. Charles Masters, who has done extensive research on water lilies, believes *N. calliantha* would probably become popular once introduced.

N. calliantha var. **tenuis** Conard. Native to central and southwest Africa. Flowers white or light blue, 3.5–5.5 in (9–14 cm) in diameter; leaves green above, dark purple on underside, 3–4 × 3–3.5 in (8–10 × 8–9 cm). Conard states in his *The Waterlilies: A Monograph of the Genus Nymphaea* (1905) that *N. calliantha* var. *tenuis* should prove a valuable acquisition for the water garden. Nearly a century later, this has yet to happen.

Nymphaea capensis Thunberg. Cape water lily, blue capensis. Native to the Cape of Good Hope region, Africa. Characteristics: Day blooming, nonviviparous, very free flowering; flower usually held 8–10 in (20–25 cm) above water. Plate 118.

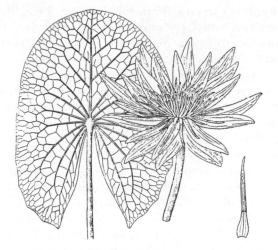

FIGURE 46. *Nymphaea calliantha*, flower and underside of leaf reduced; outer stamen enlarged. From *The Waterlilies: A Monograph of the Genus Nymphaea* by Henry S. Conard (1905).

PETAL COLOR: Light blue. *R.H.S. Chart*: Fan 2, Violet-Blue Group, No. 92C. Sepal color: Pale blue or light green. *R.H.S. Chart*: Fan 2, Violet-Blue Group, No. 92D; green, Fan 3, Green Group, No. 128D. Anther color: Violet-blue. *R.H.S. Chart*: Fan 2, Violet-Blue Group, No. 92C. Stamen color: Deep yellow. Flower shape: Stellate. Flower size: 6–8 in (15–20 cm). Fragrance: Delightful. Number of petals: 21–38. Number of sepals: 4.

LEAF COLOR: Top, green; underside, green. Leaf and sinus: Leaf nearly round, dentate, serrated; sinus usually closed, may be partly open. Leaf size: 10–16 in (25–40 cm). Leaf spread: 5–8 ft (1.5–2.5 m). Stem color: Green. Pubescence on peduncle or petiole: None.

COMMENTS: Because this plant will adapt to a limited growing area, it could be planted in pools of nearly any size. Although this is a fine lily for the collector, much more colorful cultivars are now available for water gardeners.

N. capensis var. **alba** Landon 1982. Recently discovered variety native to the Okavango River Delta, Kalahari Desert, Botswana, Africa. Differs from the type by having white flowers, 5 in (13 cm) in diameter. Leaf coloration differences include young leaves displaying maroon blotches, and leaf undersides are violet or dark purple. As there are several better (larger-flowered) white cultivars available, I would recommend this lily for the collector only.

N. capensis var. **madagascariensis** de Candolle. Native to Madagascar. This is a small variety of *N. capensis* with leaves about 2.5 in (6 cm) in diameter.

N. capensis var. *zanzibariensis* Caspary 1876. Blue Zanzibar. Native to Zanzibar. Differs from the type principally in its larger flowers, 7–10 in (18–25 cm), and fewer petals on average. Like *N. capensis*, it is very free flowering and hybridizes readily with other species of the *Brachyceras* group. Seedlings show much variation in flower size and color. Many shades of blue, pink, and even red will frequently develop. The seedlings from a single pod can even display a range of flower color. A choice seedling with light to medium blue flowers is marketed as *N. capensis* var. *zanzibariensis* 'Azurea'; a pink-flowered seedling is *N. capensis* var. *zanzibariensis* 'Rosea' (pink capensis). Other selections—including 'King of Blues', with deep violet-blue flowers, and the red-flowered 'Red Beauty'—are described in Chapter 13. Plates 119 and 120.

Nymphaea colorata Peter. Colorata. Native to Africa. Characteristics: Day blooming, nonviviparous, very free flowering. Plate 121.

PETAL COLOR: Rich, violet-blue, paling. *R.H.S. Chart*: Fan 2, Violet-Blue Group, No. 91A then 92C. Sepal color: Violet-blue, veins deeper. *R.H.S. Chart*: Fan 2, Violet-Blue Group, No. 92B; veins, No. 92A. Anther color: Deep reddish blue; tips lighter, purplish. *R.H.S. Chart*: Fan 2, Violet Group, No. 83B; tips, Violet-Blue Group, No. 94C. Stamen color: Purple-black. Flower shape: Cuplike. Flower size: 4.5–5.5 in (11–14 cm). Fragrance: Barely noticeable, if any. Number of petals: 13–15. Number of sepals: 4–5.

LEAF COLOR: Top, green; underside, bluish violet, prominent green veins. Leaf and sinus: Leaf nearly round, fairly smooth, wavy edges; sinus usually open, may be ⅓ to ½ covered by lobes. Leaf size: 8–9 in (20–23 cm). Leaf spread: 3–6 ft (1–2 m). Stem color: Green. Pubescence on peduncle or petiole: None.

COMMENTS: This species continues to flower when water temperatures drop to 65°F (18°C). I have seen it bloom all winter in central Florida in a small tub. This lily is excellent for a tub garden or a small or medium pool. Two fine cultivars derived from *N. colorata* by Dr. George Pring are 'Director George T. Moore' and 'Midnight'.

Nymphaea elegans Hooker. Native to south Florida, south Texas, Mexico, Guatemala. Characteristics: Day blooming, nonviviparous, fairly free flowering. Plate 122.

PETAL COLOR: Pale, delicate blue. *R.H.S. Chart*: Fan 2, Violet-Blue Group, No. 91D or lighter. Sepal color: Greenish. *R.H.S. Chart*: Fan 3, Green Group, No. 130D. Anther color: Yellow; tips, pale blue.

R.H.S. Chart: Fan 1, Yellow-Orange Group, No. 19A; tips, Fan 2, Violet-Blue Group, No. 91D. Stamen color: Deep yellow. Flower shape: Stellate. Flower size: 3–5 in (8–13 cm). Fragrance: Slight. Number of petals: 12–24. Number of sepals: 4–5.

LEAF COLOR: Top, green, freckled purple; underside, red or purple (on same plant), green veins, many small purple blotches. Leaf and sinus: Leaf longer than wide; sinus usually an open V. Leaf size: 6–8 in (15–20 cm). Leaf spread: 4 ft (1.2 m). Stem color: Red and reddish brown. Pubescence on peduncle or petiole: None.

COMMENTS: This species is occasionally found growing in south Florida yet is quite scarce. I have collected this species from two south Florida swamps about 100 miles (160 km) apart. When cold weather arrives, this is one of the first tropicals to go to sleep in central Florida. For this reason *N. elegans* is not a practical water lily for the average water garden.

Nymphaea flavovirens Lehmann [*N. gracilis* Zuccarini]. Conard considers this species "uncertain." Landon found it growing wild at Toluca, Mexico; Masters believes it to be endemic to Brazil and Peru as well. Characteristics: Day blooming, nonviviparous, very free flowering; flowers held 8–12 in (20–30 cm) above water. Plate 123.

PETAL COLOR: White. *R.H.S. Chart*: Fan 4, White Group, No. 155C. Sepal color: White. *R.H.S. Chart*: Fan 4, White Group, No. 155C. Anther color: Yellow; tips white. *R.H.S. Chart*: Fan 1, Yellow Group, No. 7A; tips, Fan 4, White Group, No. 155C. Stamen color: Yellow. Flower shape: Stellate. Flower size: 4–6 in (10–15 cm). Fragrance: Sweet. Number of petals: 18–19. Number of sepals: 4.

LEAF COLOR: Top, green; underside, green. Leaf and sinus: Leaves nearly round, lobe tips rounded; sinus open. Leaf size: 12–18 in (30–45 cm). Leaf spread: 6–10 ft (2–3 m). Stem color: Olive green. Pubescence on peduncle or petiole: None.

COMMENTS: This species propagates easily from seeds or tubers and also hybridizes readily with other water lilies, including *N. capensis* var. *zanzibariensis*. Such hybrids are typically colorful and free blooming. Some cultivars of *N. flavovirens* are 'Red Star' (syn. 'Mrs. C. W. Ward'), 'Pink Star' (syn. 'Stella Gurney'), and 'Blue Star' (syn. 'William Stone'). (Most of the "star" lilies include *N. flavovirens* as a parent.) If this species is available, I would recommend it for the medium or large pool.

Nymphaea gracilis. See **N. flavovirens**.

Nymphaea heudelotii Planchon. Native to West Africa (rare). Characteristics: Day blooming, nonviviparous, free flowering. Anthers are 5–6 times as long as the filaments. Figure 47.

PETAL COLOR: Bluish white. Sepal color: White or bluish white. Anther color: Yellow. Stamen color: Yellow. Flower shape: Stellate. Flower size: 1.25–2 in (3–5 cm). Fragrance: Slight. Number of petals: 5–8. Number of sepals: 4.

LEAF COLOR: Top, green; underside, purplish, spotted violet. Leaf and sinus: Leaf egg-shaped or nearly round; sinus narrow, sometimes nearly closed. Leaf size: 1–3 in (2.5–8 cm). Leaf spread: 12–16 in (30–40 cm). Stem color: Greenish. Pubescence on peduncle or petiole: None.

COMMENTS: This species is scarce even in its native habitat. It probably has no future commercially due to its rarity, poor flower color, and market competition from the similar *N.* 'Daubeniana' (syn. 'Dauben').

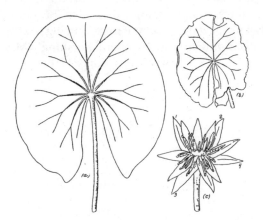

FIGURE 47. *Nymphaea heudelotii*, leaves (a, b); flower (c); sepals (1–4). From *The Waterlilies: A Monograph of the Genus Nymphaea* by Henry S. Conard (1905).

N. heudelotii **var.** *nana.* Native to West Africa. This variety has very small white flowers, 1–1.25 in (2.5–3 cm). Leaves are round, green, reddish on the underside, 0.75–1.5 in (2–4 cm) in diameter. This variety failed to attract a market in the United States, and I do not see any commercial future for this plant.

Nymphaea micrantha Guillemin & Perrottet. Native to the west coast of Africa. Characteristics: Day blooming, viviparous, free flowering. Young plants develop at top of petiole and may bloom while still on mother plant; petiole decay allows young plants to float to another location. Anthers twice as long as filaments. Rhizomes display soft wool at petiole base. Figure 48.

PETAL COLOR: Pale blue to white. Sepal color: Mostly white. Anther color: Outer anthers, creamy white, tipped blue; inner anthers creamy white. Stamen color: Creamy white. Flower shape: Cuplike, then stellate. Flower size: 1–4 in (2.5–10 cm). Fragrance: Faint. Number of petals: 10. Number of sepals: 5.

LEAF COLOR: Top, pale green; underside, reddish, violet-black dots. Leaf and sinus: Leaves nearly round; sinus wide open. Leaf size: 3 × 2 in (8 × 5 cm). Leaf spread: 2–2.5 ft (0.6–0.8 m). Stem color: Greenish. Pubescence on peduncle or petiole: Yes, at petiole and peduncle where attached to rhizome.

COMMENTS: This species is parent to several wonderful hybrids—'August Koch', 'Charles Thomas' (not to be confused with the lotus 'Charles Thomas'), 'Daubeniana' (syn. 'Dauben'), 'Margaret Mary', 'Mrs. Martin E. Randig', 'Panama Pacific', 'Patricia', 'Paul Stetson', and 'Royal Purple'. According to species expert Kenneth Landon of San Angelo, Texas, it is doubtful that any true plants of *N. micrantha* are in cultivation in North or South America. Plants grown as such are probably the very similar 'Daubeniana', and further, the species is thought to be intermixed with 'Daubeniana'. True *N. micrantha* is most likely limited to the west coast of Africa.

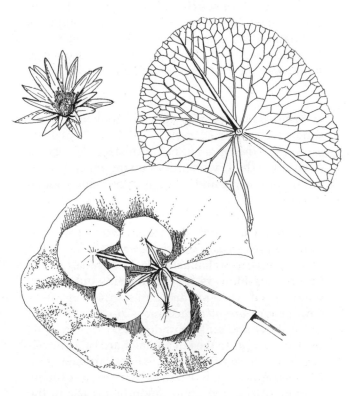

FIGURE 48. *Nymphaea micrantha*, flower (upper left); leaf underside (upper right); plantlet on top of leaf (bottom). After a plate from *The Waterlilies: A Monograph of the Genus Nymphaea* by Henry S. Conard (1905).

Nymphaea nouchali Burman f. [*N. stellata* Willdenow]. Native to southern and eastern Asia, Borneo, Philippines, Sri Lanka. Characteristics: Day blooming, nonviviparous, free flowering; blooms held about 12 in (30 cm) above water. Plate 124.

PETAL COLOR: Usually pale blue; can vary to pink or white. *R.H.S. Chart*: Fan 2, Violet-Blue Group, No. 92C. Sepal color: Bluish white, usually. *R.H.S. Chart*: Fan 2, Violet-Blue Group, No. 92D. Anther color: Pale yellow, tips blue or same as petals. *R.H.S. Chart*: Fan 1, Yellow Group, No. 4D; tips, Fan 2, Violet-Blue Group, No. 92C. Stamen color: Pale yellow. Flower shape: Stellate. Flower size: 2–5 in (5–13 cm). Fragrance: Nearly absent. Number of petals: 10–16. Number of sepals: 4.

LEAF COLOR: Top, green, faint brownish blotches; underside, pink or blue-violet. Leaf and sinus: Leaf oval to round, sinuate margin; sinus usually open. Leaf size: 5–6 in (13–15 cm). Leaf spread: 4.5–5 ft (1.4–1.5 m). Stem color: Greenish. Pubescence on peduncle or petiole: None.

COMMENTS: This water lily is often referred to in literature as the blue lotus of India, but of course it is not a lotus at all. For centuries it has been cultivated in Southeast Asia, especially around temples. It has also been cultivated for food in Sri Lanka as the rhizomes are full of starch and reputedly quite tasty when boiled. In 1899 the plant flowered outdoors in England and received considerable publicity. This species does well in tubs, small pools, or large pools, though it is rarely available in the United States.

N. nouchali **var.** *cyanea* (Roxburgh) Hooker & Thomson [*N. stellata* var. *cyanea*]. The native habitat is the same as for the type. The medium-sized flowers are deep or pale blue, with little or no fragrance. Leaves are slightly wavy and margins may or may not be dentate.

N. nouchali **var.** *versicolor* (Roxburgh) Hooker & Thomson [*N. stellata* var. *versicolor*]. Variety *versicolor* is native to Sri Lanka, India, Indochina, and the Philippines. Flowers are usually pink but may be white or red. They are medium size, 4–5 in (10–13 cm). Leaves are also medium size, 8 in (20 cm), green above and pink on underside with some purplish markings. In the fall a small hard tuber develops at the base of each leaf stem. Particularly in USDA zones 3–8, it will be necessary to store tubers indoors during the winter months for use in the spring.

Many thousands of tubers are exported annually from Sri Lanka to the aquarium trade in America and Europe. When placed in warm water for a few weeks, tubers become very attractive "instant" aquarium plants.

Nymphaea ovalifolia Conard. Native to East Africa. Characteristics: Day blooming, nonviviparous, free flowering. Figure 49.

PETAL COLOR: White, tipped blue. Sepal color: White or delicate blue. Anther color: Yellow. Stamen color: Yellow. Flower shape: Stellate. Flower size: 5–8 in (13–20 cm). Fragrance: Very sweet. Number of petals: 16–18. Number of sepals: 4.

LEAF COLOR: Top, light green, brown blotches; underside, green. Leaf and sinus: Leaf oval to elliptical; sinus 4 in (10 cm) long, sides nearly parallel. Leaf size: 10 × 6 in (25 × 15 cm). Leaf spread: 5–7 ft (1.5–2.2 m). Stem color: Greenish. Pubescence on peduncle or petiole: None.

COMMENTS: *N. ovalifolia*, even if generally available, would not be a very desirable plant for cultivation due to its poor off-white flower color. George Pring of the Missouri Botanical Garden, St. Louis, nonetheless used it as a parent in producing several very outstanding hybrids: 'General Pershing', 'Mrs. Edwards Whitaker', and 'Mrs. George H. Pring'.

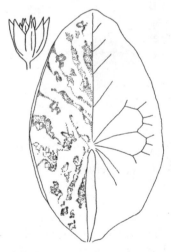

FIGURE 49. *Nymphaea ovalifolia*, leaf and flower. Upper side of leaf displaying mottling (left; note leaf edge fold at margin); underside of leaf showing veins (right). After an illustration from *The Waterlilies: A Monograph of the Genus Nymphaea* by Henry S. Conard (1905).

Nymphaea stellata. See *N. nouchali*.

Nymphaea stellata **var.** *cyanea*. See *N. nouchali* **var.** *cyanea*.

Nymphaea stellata **var.** *versicolor*. See *N. nouchali* **var.** *versicolor*.

Nymphaea stuhlmannii (Schweinfurth) Gilg 1890 [*N. burtii* Pring & Woodson]. Native to Tanzania, Dodoma District, Mgunda Mkali, Bibisande, Africa. Characteristics: Day blooming, nonviviparous, free flowering. Figure 50.

PETAL COLOR: Bright sulfur-yellow. Sepal color: Yellowish green. Anther color: Sulfur-yellow. Stamen color: Orange-yellow. Flower shape: Full, stellate. Flower size: 4–6 in (10–15 cm). Fragrance: Sweet. Number of petals: 22. Number of sepals: 4.

LEAF COLOR: Top, green; underside, green, prominent veins. Leaf and sinus: Leaves oval to round, rounded tips on lobes; sinus open. Leaf size: 10 × 8 in (25 × 20 cm). Leaf spread: 5–6 ft (1.5–2 m). Stem color: Green. Pubescence on peduncle or petiole: None.

COMMENTS: Dr. George P⸱ ⸱ng used this species in his hybridizing to produce some magnificent yellow tropical water lilies. One example is 'St. Louis'. He was working with a species from eastern Africa known as *Nymphaea burtii* Pring & Woodson. In February 1951, after carefully comparing specimens, Dr. Pring determined that *N. burtii* and *N. stuhlmannii* were the same species. As *N. stuhlmannii* was discovered in 1890, this name took precedence over *N. burtii*, discovered in 1929.

Nymphaea sulfurea Gilg. Native to south central Africa. Characteristics: Day blooming, nonviviparous, free flowering. Plate 108.

PETAL COLOR: Rich sulfur-yellow. Sepal color: Purplish. Anther color: Bright yellow. Stamen color: Yellow. Flower shape: Stellate. Flower size: 2–3 in (5–8 cm). Fragrance: Sweet. Number of petals: 13. Number of sepals: 4.

LEAF COLOR: Top, reddish; underside, red. Leaf and sinus: Leaves nearly round; sinus open. Leaf size: 1.75–2.25 in (4.5–5.5 cm). Leaf spread: 15–20 in (38–50 cm). Stem color: Reddish or bronzy. Pubescence on peduncle or petiole: None.

COMMENTS: *N. sulfurea* is a pygmy type. Dr. George Pring used it in producing 'St. Louis Gold' and 'Aviator Pring'.

Nymphaea togoensis Landon 1986. Native to the Togo region of Africa. Characteristics: Day blooming,

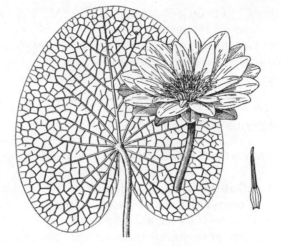

FIGURE 50. *Nymphaea stuhlmannii*, flower, underside of leaf, and outer stamen. From *The Waterlilies: A Monograph of the Genus Nymphaea* by Henry S. Conard (1905).

nonviviparous, very free flowering until onset of fruiting. Plate 125.

PETAL COLOR: White. *R.H.S. Chart*: Fan 4, White Group, No. 155D. Sepal color: White. *R.H.S. Chart*: Fan 4, White Group, No. 155D. Anther color: Yellow, white tips. *R.H.S. Chart*: Fan 1, Yellow Group, No. 5A; tips, Fan 4, White Group, No. 155D. Stamen color: Yellow. Flower shape: Stellate. Flower size: 4–6 in (10–15 cm). Fragrance: Faint. Number of petals: 16–18. Number of sepals: 4.

LEAF COLOR: Top, green, few purple flecks; underside, grayish green, suffused purple. Leaf and sinus: Leaves slightly sinuate toward base; sinus varies. Leaf size: 5–10 in (13–25 cm). Leaf spread: 8 ft (2.5 m). Stem color: Maroon. Pubescence on peduncle or petiole: None.

COMMENTS: This is a species recently discovered in coastal swamps, rivers, streams, and rain pools throughout Togo, Africa. Kenneth Landon first described this species and supplied the above information.

GROUP *NYMPHAEA SYNCARPIAE* [*SYMPHYTOPLEURA* CASPARY 1865]

In Group *Syncarpiae* carpels are completely fused with one another at the sides and are attached also to the axis of the flower and to the torus as in Group *Apocarpiae*. Flowers are white, pink, purple, or yellow, never blue. Plants are either day or night flowering.

Subgenus *Hydrocallis* Planchon

The *Hydrocallis* water lilies share the following characteristics:

1. All are night-blooming tropicals (artificial light has little effect on blooming).
2. Blooms either float or remain close to the water surface.
3. Flowers open for a short period (about two hours in the case of some varieties) in the middle of the night or very early morning. (See subgenus *Lotos* for blooms open from dusk to about 11 a.m.)
4. None of the 14 species is suited for the average water garden as blooms are short-lived and open in the middle of the night. These lilies are for the collector with a medium or large pool.
5. All species are native to the tropics of the Western Hemisphere.
6. Petals are usually in whorls of four.
7. Pollination is frequently accomplished by the scarab beetle (*Cyclocephala* spp.).
8. Styles are slender and cylindrical with enlarged club-shaped tips.

In *A Monograph of Nymphaea Subgenus Hydrocallis (Nymphaeaceae)* (1987), Dr. John H. Wiersema lists the 14 species described here. This is four more species than Dr. Henry S. Conard lists in his *The Waterlilies: A Monograph of the Genus Nymphaea*, written almost a century earlier. Dr. Wiersema dropped *N. blanda*, *N. gibertii*, and *N. stenaspidota* and added *N. belophylla*, *N. conardii*, *N. glandulifera*, *N. lingulata*, *N. novogranatensis*, *N. potamophila*, and *N. prolifera*.

Note that "Sepal color" in the following *Hydrocallis* descriptions refers to the outside of the sepals not the inside as with other *Nymphaea* species and cultivars. The inside of the sepals usually matches the petals—creamy white, in most cases.

Nymphaea amazonum* subsp. *amazonum Martius & Zuccarini. Native to tropical South America, Caribbean Islands, particularly in lowlands near coastal areas; rare in Central America and Mexico. Mostly found growing in still water, sometimes in slightly brackish water. Characteristics: Night blooming, nonviviparous, flowers floating, sepals and petals in whorls of four. Propagates by short sprouts, by stolons from rhizomes, and by seeds. Stamens usually number less than 200. Plate 126; Figure 51.

PETAL COLOR: Creamy white. Sepal color: Green, short black streaks. Anther color: Creamy white. Stamen color: Creamy white. Flower shape: Stellate. Flower size: 4–5 in (10–13 cm). Fragrance: Strong odor resembling turpentine, xylol, gasoline, or acetone. Number of petals: 16, 20, or 24. Number of sepals: 4.

LEAF COLOR: Top, green, purple spots; underside, purple, small dark flecks. Leaf and sinus: Leaf oval, 1–1.35 times as long as wide; lobes slightly tapered to rounded. Sinus open. Leaf size: 13 × 11 in (33 × 28 cm). Leaf spread: 5–6 ft (1.5–2 m). Stem color: Green. Pubescence on peduncle or petiole: Peduncle usually bare, occasionally pubescent at apex;

petioles display ring of pubescence at apex, the remaining bare or occasionally pubescent.

COMMENTS: This species is mostly for the collector as its nocturnal blooming habit would limit its use in the average water garden: first-day flower opens partially two to three hours before dawn and closes by dawn; second-day flower opens at dusk and closes by an hour after dawn.

Nymphaea amazonum* subsp. *pedersenii Wiersema [*N. amazonum* Martius & Zuccarini]. Native to subtropical portions of Argentina and southern Brazil; probably also in adjacent Paraguay and Uruguay. Characteristics: Night blooming, nonviviparous, flowers floating, sepals and petals in whorls of four. Appears to propagate mostly by stolons. Stamens usually number more than 225.

PETAL COLOR: Creamy white. Sepal color: Green, short black streaks. Anther color: Creamy white. Stamen color: Creamy white. Flower shape: Stellate. Flower size: 4–5 in (10–13 cm). Fragrance: Strong aromatic odor. Number of petals: 16, 20, or 24. Number of sepals: 4.

LEAF COLOR: Top, green, usually variegated red;

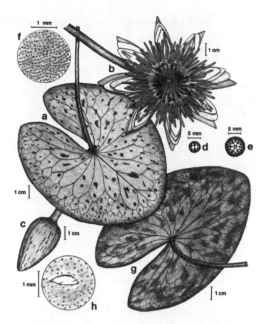

FIGURE 51. *Nymphaea amazonum* subsp. *amazonum* (a–f) and *N. amazonum* subsp. *pedersenii* (g, h). Underside of leaf (a); opened flower (b); unopened flower bud (c); cross section of petiole (d); cross section of peduncle (e); upper side of leaf (f); underside of leaf (g); upper side of leaf (h). From *A Monograph of Nymphaea Subgenus Hydrocallis (Nymphaeaceae)* by John H. Wiersema (1987).

underside, green or somewhat reddened, often splotched deeper red, prominent central veins. Leaf and sinus: Leaf 1.25–1.5 times as long as wide, egg-shaped; lobes end in dull point at apex. Sinus open. Leaf size: 13 × 9 in (33 × 23 cm). Leaf spread: 5–6 ft (1.5–2 m). Stem color: Greenish. Pubescence on peduncle or petiole: Peduncle, bare; petiole apex usually displays ring of pubescence.

COMMENTS: I recommend *N. amazonum* subsp. *pedersenii* only for the collector because of its nocturnal blooming habit, similar to that of *N. amazonum* subsp. *amazonum*. Requires a medium or large pool.

Nymphaea belophylla Trickett. Native to the Amazon and Orinoco Basins, South America. Characteristics: Night blooming, nonviviparous, flowers floating, sepals and petals in whorls of four. Seldom produces seeds. Figure 52.

PETAL COLOR: Creamy white or light yellow; tips greenish changing to creamy white or light yellow. Sepal color: Green. Anther color: Creamy white to light yellow. Stamen color: Creamy white to light yellow. Flower shape: Somewhat stellate. Flower size: 3.5–6 in (9–15 cm). Fragrance: Almondlike. Number of petals: 16 or 20. Number of sepals: 4.

LEAF COLOR: Top, green; underside, green. Leaf

and sinus: Leaf more than twice as long as wide, acute lobes at apex; arrow-shaped; sinus long and wide open. Leaf size: 12 × 4.5 in (30 × 11 cm). Leaf spread: 3–4 ft (1–1.2 m). Stem color: Green. Pubescence on peduncle or petiole: None.

COMMENTS: *Belophylla* is Greek for arrow-shaped leaves. Like the other *Hydrocallis* water lilies, *N. belophylla* blooms for a short period in the middle of the night. As such, its use is limited in the average water garden. This species is rare and most studies are done on museum specimens.

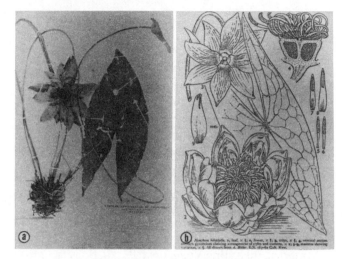

FIGURE 52. *Nymphaea belophylla*. Photo of *Trujillo 11430* (MY) from Barinas, Venezuela (a); illustration from the original publication reproduced in Kew Bulletin, vol. 26 (b). From *A Monograph of Nymphaea Subgenus Hydrocallis (Nymphaeaceae)* by John H. Wiersema (1987).

Nymphaea blanda. See *N. glandulifera*.

Nymphaea conardii Wiersema. Native to southern Mexico through Central America to northern South America, including Colombia, Venezuela, northern Brazil; also found in Cuba, Hispaniola, and Puerto Rico. Characteristics: Night blooming, nonviviparous, flowers floating, sepals and petals in whorls of four. Propagates by seed. Figure 53.

PETAL COLOR: Creamy white. Sepal color: Green. Anther color: Creamy white. Stamen color: Creamy white. Flower shape: Stellate. Flower size: 5 in (13 cm). Fragrance: Strong but pleasant. Number of petals: 12, 16, or 20. Number of sepals: 3–6.

LEAF COLOR: Top, green; underside, green. Leaf and sinus: Leaf 1–1.5 times as long as wide, pronounced weblike venation; lobes acute to rounded at apex with slight protuberance. Sinus open. Leaf size: 7 × 5.5 in (18 × 14 cm). Leaf spread: 2–4 ft (0.6–1.2 m). Stem color: Green. Pubescence on peduncle or petiole: None.

COMMENTS: This species, as with other *Hydrocallis* water lilies, has a limited commercial future due to its short, nocturnal bloom period. Flowers begin opening at dusk and start closing around midnight, being fully closed by 1:00 a.m. Blooms open for two successive nights.

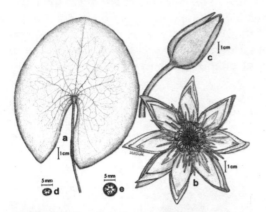

FIGURE 53. *Nymphaea conardii*, underside of leaf (a); opened flower (b); unopened flower bud (c); cross section of petiole (d); cross section of peduncle (e). From *A Monograph of Nymphaea Subgenus Hydrocallis (Nymphaeaceae)* by John H. Wiersema (1987).

Nymphaea gardneriana Planchon. Native to South America, including Venezuela, Brazil, Bolivia, Paraguay, Argentina. Characteristics: Night blooming, nonviviparous, flowers floating, sepals and petals in whorls of four. Propagates by stolons from rhizome. Figure 54.

PETAL COLOR: Creamy white; tips greenish. Sepal color: Green. Anther color: Creamy white. Stamen color: Creamy white. Flower shape: Stellate. Flower size: 3.5–5 in (9–13 cm). Fragrance: Strong, somewhat sweet. Number of petals: 16–28. Number of sepals: 4.

LEAF COLOR: Top, green; underside, green, often suffused or mottled rusty brown. Leaf and sinus: Leaf 1–1.5 times as long as wide, pronounced web-like venation; lobes acute to rounded at apex. Sinus wide open. Leaf size: 9 × 6 in (23 × 15 cm). Leaf spread: 2–4 ft (0.6–1.2 m). Stem color: Green. Pubescence on peduncle or petiole: Occasional few hairs on petiole.

COMMENTS: *N. gardneriana* is limited for water garden use as flowers open about dusk and close about midnight. Blooms for two consecutive nights.

Nymphaea glandulifera Rodschied [*N. blanda* G. Meyer]. Native to northern South America and Central America from Amazonas, Brazil, west to northern Peru and Ecuador and north to Guatemala, Belize, Trinidad, and French Guiana. Charac-

teristics: Night blooming, nonviviparous, flowers floating, sepals and petals in whorls of four. Propagates by seed. Figure 55.

PETAL COLOR: Creamy white. Sepal color: Green. Anther color: Creamy white. Stamen color: Creamy white. Flower shape: Stellate. Flower size: 6 in (15 cm). Fragrance: Not mentioned in report studied. Number of petals: 12–20. Number of sepals: 4.

LEAF COLOR: Top, green; underside, pale green. Leaf and sinus: Leaf nearly round, lobes obtuse to rounded at apex. Sinus open. Leaf size: 8 × 7.5 in (20 × 19 cm). Leaf spread: 2–4 ft (0.6–1.2 m). Stem color: Green. Pubescence on peduncle or petiole: Sometimes slightly pubescent.

COMMENTS: Due to its short nightly blooming period (from dusk to midnight), it is not suited for the average water garden.

Nymphaea jamesoniana Planchon. Native to tropical and subtropical America, including Florida, Mexico, Central America, Argentina, Brazil, Colombia, Ecuador, and Paraguay. Found growing in freshwater ditches, ponds, or slow-moving streams. Characteristics: Night blooming, nonviviparous, flowers floating, sepals and petals in whorls of four. Propagates by seed. Figure 56.

PETAL COLOR: Mostly creamy white, greenish tip edges. Sepal color: Green, slender rusty brown lines. Anther color: Creamy white. Stamen color: Creamy white. Flower shape: Stellate. Flower size: 3–5 in (8–13 cm). Fragrance: Disagreeable odor re-

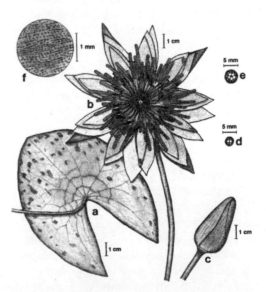

FIGURE 54. *Nymphaea gardneriana*, underside of leaf (a); opened flower (b); unopened flower bud (c); cross section of petiole (d); cross section of peduncle (e); upper side of leaf (f). From *A Monograph of Nymphaea Subgenus Hydrocallis (Nymphaeaceae)* by John H. Wiersema (1987).

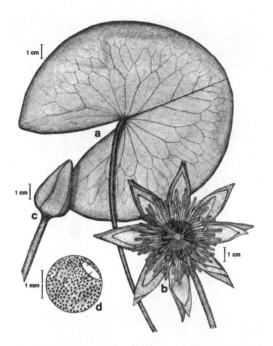

FIGURE 55. *Nymphaea glandulifera*, underside of leaf (a); opened flower (b); unopened flower bud (c); upper side of leaf (d). From *A Monograph of Nymphaea Subgenus Hydrocallis (Nymphaeaceae)* by John H. Wiersema (1987).

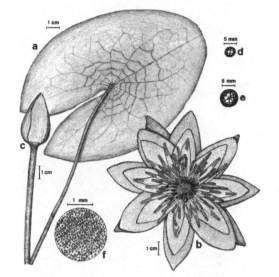

FIGURE 56. *Nymphaea jamesoniana*, underside of leaf (a); opened flower (b); unopened flower bud (c); cross section of petiole (d); cross section of peduncle (e); upper side of leaf (f). From *A Monograph of Nymphaea Subgenus Hydrocallis (Nymphaeaceae)* by John H. Wiersema (1987).

sembling used motor oil or acetone. Number of petals: 12, 16, or 20. Number of sepals: 4.

LEAF COLOR: Top, green, sometimes with dark flecks; underside, green, sometimes flecked purple. Leaf and sinus: Leaf egg-shaped, prominent venation webbing, lobes usually ending in fairly sharp point. Sinus long and open. Leaf size: 9 × 7 (23 × 18 cm). Leaf spread: 4–5 ft (1.2–1.5 m). Stem color: Green. Pubescence on peduncle or petiole: None.

COMMENTS: I recommend this species for the collector with a medium or large pool. This plant is not suited to the average water garden as flowers begin opening about dusk and close about midnight.

Nymphaea lasiophylla Martius & Zuccarini. Native to the coastal regions of eastern Brazil, Rio de Janeiro north to Piauí, with a separate population (probably introduced) on Isla de Margarita, Venezuela. Usually found growing in stagnant water, frequently in artificial ponds. Characteristics: Night blooming, viviparous, new growth from submerged tuberiferous flowers. Flowers floating, sepals and petals in whorls of four. Propagation from stolons, seed, and submerged flowers, which later detach. Figure 57.

PETAL COLOR: Creamy white. Sepal color: Green or yellow-green. Anther color: Creamy white. Stamen color: Creamy white. Flower shape: Full, stellate. Flower size: 4 in (10 cm). Fragrance: Strongly

aromatic. Number of petals: 20–26. Number of sepals: 4.

LEAF COLOR: Top, green, often with darker flecks; underside, green, slight reddish tint. Leaf and sinus: Leaf nearly round; prominent, slightly raised veins radiate from center. Lobes rounded or with small obtuse protuberance. Sinus open. Leaf size: 13 × 12 in (33 × 30 cm). Leaf spread: 6 ft (2 m). Stem color: Green. Pubescence on peduncle or petiole: None.

COMMENTS: I recommend *N. lasiophylla* for the collector with a medium or large pool. Tubers develop from the abortive submerged flowers and later detach, remain floating briefly, eventually developing into adult plants. Collectors may find this an interesting process, though with its short bloom period (from midnight to before 4 a.m.), it would not be suitable for most gardeners.

Nymphaea lingulata Wiersema. Native to northeastern Brazil. Characteristics: Night blooming, nonviviparous, flowers floating, sepals and outer petals in whorls of four. Propagation mainly by seed, also by stolon production from rhizome. Figure 58.

PETAL COLOR: Creamy white. Sepal color: Yellowish green, sometimes flecked black. Anther color: Creamy white. Stamen color: Creamy white, dark purple base. Flower shape: Stellate, long, narrow petals. Flower size: 5 in (13 cm). Fragrance: Faint. Number of petals: 8–14. Number of sepals: 4.

LEAF COLOR: Top, green; underside, red to reddish purple. Leaf and sinus: Leaf a little longer than

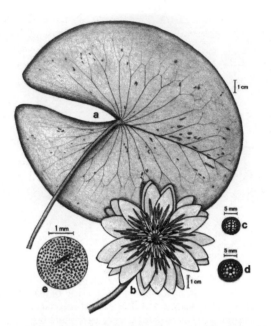

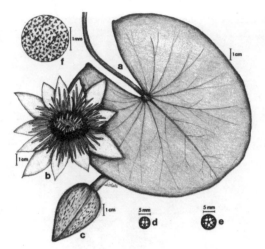

FIGURE 57. *Nymphaea lasiophylla*, underside of leaf (a); opened flower (b); cross section of = petiole (c); cross section of peduncle (d); upper side of leaf (e). From *A Monograph of Nymphaea Subgenus Hydrocallis (Nymphaeaceae)* by John H. Wiersema (1987).

FIGURE 58. *Nymphaea lingulata*, underside of leaf (a); opened flower (b); unopened flower bud (c); cross section of petiole (d); cross section of peduncle (e); upper side of leaf (f). From *A Monograph of Nymphaea Subgenus Hydrocallis (Nymphaeaceae)* by John H. Wiersema (1987).

wide, lobes rounded or with small obtuse protuberance. Sinus open. Leaf size: 10 × 8 in (25 × 20 cm). Leaf spread: 3–5 ft (1–1.5 m). Stem color: Green. Pubescence on peduncle or petiole: None.

COMMENTS: *N. lingulata* begins to open approximately two hours after dark and closes around 2 to 3 a.m. For this reason I do not recommend it for most water gardens.

Nymphaea novogranatensis Wiersema. Native to Venezuela and Colombia. Characteristics: Night blooming, nonviviparous, flowers floating or slightly emergent, sepals and petals in whorls of four. Propagation by seed. Figure 59.

PETAL COLOR: White. Sepal color: Green or somewhat brownish purple. Anther color: Cream. Stamen color: Cream, inner filaments purplish at base. Flower shape: Stellate. Flower size: 3–5 in (8–13 cm). Fragrance: Faint. Number of petals: 16 or 20. Number of sepals: 4.

LEAF COLOR: Top, glossy green, new leaves flecked purple; underside, brownish purple, darker flecks evident, especially on younger leaves. Leaf and sinus: Leaf nearly round; quite prominent veins radiate from center. Lobes obtuse to rounded with slight protuberance. Sinus open. Leaf size: 9.5 × 8 in (24 × 20 cm). Leaf spread: 3–5 ft (1–1.5 m). Stem color: Green. Pubescence on peduncle or petiole: None.

COMMENTS: Flowers start opening one to two hours after dark and close by midnight the first night. Second-day flowers begin opening at dusk and close at dawn. I do not recommend it for the water garden.

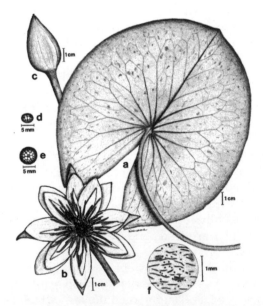

FIGURE 59. *Nymphaea novogranatensis*, underside of leaf (a); opened flower (b); unopened flower bud (c); cross section of petiole (d); cross section of peduncle (e); upper side of leaf (f). From *A Monograph of Nymphaea Subgenus Hydrocallis (Nymphaeaceae)* by John H. Wiersema (1987).

Nymphaea oxypetala Planchon. Native to southern Brazil, Ecuador, Venezuela. Characteristics: Night blooming, nonviviparous, flowers floating, sepals and outermost petals in whorls of four, leaves mostly submerged. Reproduction by seed. Figure 60.

PETAL COLOR: Creamy white; tips greenish. Sepal color: Green. Anther color: Creamy white, suffused purple. Stamen color: Creamy white, suffused purple. Flower shape: Very stellate. Flower size: 5–7 in (13–18 cm). Fragrance: Strong etherlike aroma. Number of petals: 16–34. Number of sepals: 4.

LEAF COLOR: Top, green; underside, purplish. Leaf and sinus: Floating leaves very small, 1.9–2.5 times as long as wide, acute to rounded at the apex, lobes acute and tapering; sinus open. Submerged leaves large, 1–1.8 times as long as wide, lobes acute to rounded; sinus open. Leaf size: Floating leaves, 2.5 × 1 in (6 × 2.5 cm); submerged leaves, 16 × 13 in (40 × 33 cm). Leaf spread: 2–3 ft (0.6–1 m). Stem color: Green. Pubescence on peduncle or petiole: None.

COMMENTS: This species has beautiful underwater foliage. Dr. Wiersema believes *N. oxypetala* might be suitable as an aquarium plant. He advises that it prefers gently flowing fresh water, yet there is a possibility that it would adapt to a clean, well-filtered tank.

Nymphaea potamophila Wiersema. Native to the states of Amazonas and Pará, northern Brazil. Characteristics: Night blooming, nonviviparous, flowers floating, sepals and petals in whorls of four. Reproduction by seed. Figure 61.

PETAL COLOR: Creamy white, greenish tips and edges. Sepal color: Green. Anther color: Creamy white. Stamen color: Creamy white. Flower shape: Stellate. Flower size: 6 in (15 cm). Fragrance: Unknown. Number of petals: 16. Number of sepals: 4.

LEAF COLOR: Top, green, often variegated red; underside, greenish, variegated dark red. Leaf and sinus: Leaf 1.8–2.5 times as long as wide, acute-tapering to somewhat rounded at apex; lobes long and pointed. Sinus open. Leaf size: About 8 × 4 in (20 × 10 cm). Leaf spread: 2–4 ft (0.6–1.2 m). Stem color: Green. Pubescence on peduncle or petiole: None.

COMMENTS: This is a rare water lily and not much is known about the flowering except that it blooms for a short period in the middle of the night. I do not recommend it for the water garden.

Nymphaea prolifera Wiersema. Native to northern Argentina, southern Brazil, western Ecuador, Paraguay, Costa Rica, and El Salvador. Mostly found growing in lowland savannas. Characteristics: Night blooming, viviparous, producing tiny tubers

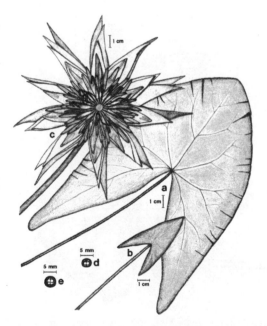

FIGURE 60. *Nymphaea oxypetala*, underside of submerged leaf (a); upper side of floating leaf (b); opened flower (c); cross section of petiole (d); cross section of peduncle (e). From *A Monograph of Nymphaea Subgenus Hydrocallis (Nymphaeaceae)* by John H. Wiersema (1987).

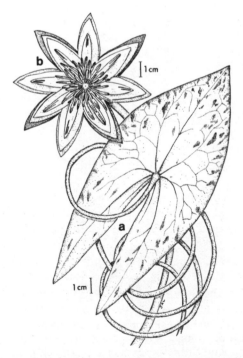

FIGURE 61. *Nymphaea potamophila*, underside of leaf (a); opened flower (b). From *A Monograph of Nymphaea Subgenus Hydrocallis (Nymphaeaceae)* by John H. Wiersema (1987).

from flowers. Flowers floating, sepals and outer petals in whorls of four. Asexual reproduction from tuber-bearing flowers. Figure 62.

PETAL COLOR: Creamy white. Sepal color: Green, sometimes suffused purple, usually short black streaks. Anther color: Cream; inner anthers tinged indigo or purple toward flower center. Stamen color: Cream; inner stamens tinged indigo or purple. Flower shape: Full star. Flower size: 5 in (13 cm). Fragrance: Etherlike. Number of petals: 19–35. Number of sepals: 4.

LEAF COLOR: Top, green, often flecked purple; underside, green or purple-tinged with dark flecks. Leaf and sinus: Leaf nearly round, lobes slightly tapering to broadly rounded. Sinus open. Leaf size: 9–12 × 8.5–11.5 in (23–30 × 22–29 cm). Leaf spread: 4–5 ft (1.2–1.5 m). Stem color: Green. Pubescence on peduncle or petiole: None.

COMMENTS: Flowers of *N. prolifera* open for two successive days as follows: initial opening, from one hour after dusk to around 3 or 4 a.m.; second opening, at dusk, closing one to two hours before dawn. Although watching the tuber-bearing flowers form new plants would be interesting, most gardeners would find that the timing of the flower opening leaves much to be desired. I cannot recommend it for the water garden except for the collector.

Nymphaea rudgeana G. Meyer. Native to eastern and northern South America, north of the state of Paraná, Brazil, and east of northern Colombia; also in Cuba, Guadeloupe, Jamaica, Martinique, Trinidad, and Nicaragua. Mostly found growing in lowland coastal areas in stagnant, sometimes brackish, or flowing water. Characteristics: Night blooming, nonviviparous, flowers floating, sepals and petals in whorls of four. Reproduction by seed. Figure 63.

PETAL COLOR: Creamy white to light yellow, developing pinkish tinge. Sepal color: Greenish, base yellowish; underside, yellowish, tinged red. Anther color: Creamy white to light yellow. Stamen color: Creamy white to light yellow. Flower shape: Stellate. Flower size: 3–6 in (8–15 cm). Fragrance: Variously described as fruity, aniselike, and "reminiscent of acetone." Number of petals: 12–29. Number of sepals: 4.

LEAF COLOR: Top, green, sometimes purplish, occasionally flecked purple; underside, greenish or brownish purple, sometimes darker flecks. Leaf and sinus: Leaf nearly round, irregularly dentate, teeth obtuse, dentate apex on lobes, margins often slightly upturned in larger leaves. Sinus open. Leaf size: 14–18 in (35–45 cm). Leaf spread: 6–7 ft (2–2.2 m). Stem color: Bronzy green. Pubescence on peduncle or petiole: None.

COMMENTS: *N. rudgeana* blooms for two or three successive nights. Flowers open at dusk and close between midnight and dawn. This opening period alone makes this lily potentially undesirable for the water garden. Commercial aquarium-plant grower

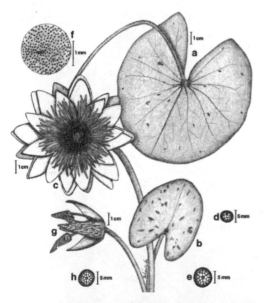

FIGURE 62. *Nymphaea prolifera*, underside of leaf (a); upper side of young leaf (b); opened flower (c); cross section of petiole (d); cross section of peduncle (e); upper side of leaf (f); tuberiferous flower (g); cross section of peduncle of tuberiferous flower (h). From *A Monograph of Nymphaea Subgenus Hydrocallis (Nymphaeaceae)* by John H. Wiersema (1987).

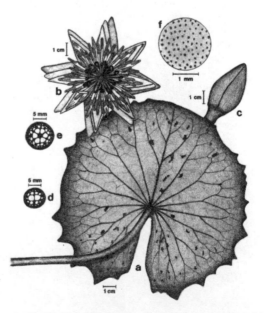

FIGURE 63. *Nymphaea rudgeana*, underside of leaf (a); opened flower (b); unopened flower bud (c); cross section of petiole (d); cross section of peduncle (e); upper side of leaf (f). From *A Monograph of Nymphaea Subgenus Hydrocallis (Nymphaeaceae)* by John H. Wiersema (1987).

Don Bryne of Suwannee Laboratories, Lake City, Florida, discovered that under ideal conditions, *N. rudgeana* produces beautiful reddish submerged leaves. Plants would lose the red coloring after a while, however, and die during cooler times of the year.

Nymphaea tenerinervia Caspary. Native to northern Brazil, mostly north Bahia and northern Goiás and east of the Amazon Basin, although also collected in Roraima. Common to natural swamps and marshes in northern Piauí and Ceará. Characteristics: Night blooming, nonviviparous, flowers floating, sepals and petals in whorls of four. Propagation mostly by stolons from rhizome. Figure 64.

PETAL COLOR: Creamy white to light yellow. Sepal color: Green, short purple streaks. Anther color: Creamy white to light yellow. Stamen color: Creamy white to light yellow. Flower shape: Somewhat stellate. Flower size: 3–4 in (8–10 cm). Fragrance: Faint. Number of petals: 16 or 20. Number of sepals: 4.

LEAF COLOR: Top, green or occasionally reddish, often flecked purple; underside, purple or red-purple, often short, darker purple flecks. Leaf and sinus: Leaf nearly round; lobes rounded, little or no protuberance. Sinus open. Leaf size: Up to 8.5 × 7.5 in (22 × 19 cm). Leaf spread: 3–5 ft (1–1.5 m). Stem color: Green. Pubescence on peduncle or petiole: Both bare or slightly pubescent.

COMMENTS: Flowers open two consecutive

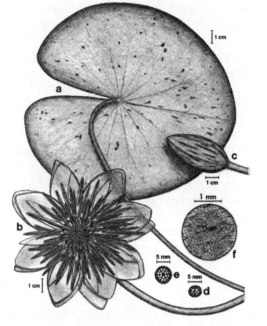

FIGURE 64. *Nymphaea tenerinervia*, underside of leaf (a); opened flower (b); unopened flower bud (c); cross section of petiole (d); cross section of peduncle (e); upper side of leaf (f). From *A Monograph of Nymphaea Subgenus Hydrocallis (Nymphaeaceae)* by John H. Wiersema (1987).

nights. Initial opening one hour after dusk, closing by midnight, followed by second opening at dusk, remaining until dawn. Such opening periods makes this species undesirable for water gardens.

Subgenus *Lotos* de Candolle 1821

The *Lotos* water lilies include the night-blooming tropicals that have been variously hybridized to create the night-blooming cultivars popular in the trade today. Conard includes only four species in the subgenus *Lotos*, but Kenneth Landon has identified one more (*N. spontanea*, closely related to *N. pubescens*), bringing the current total to five.

Plants are native to the tropics of the Old World, the Philippine Islands, Madagascar, and to two isolated warm-water areas of Hungary. In their native habitats many of the *Lotos* group experience a wet season alternating with a dry season. During the end of the wet season, tubers form under the plants, leaves die down, and plants survive the dry season as dormant tubers. In cultivation the roundish tubers usually go dormant when cold weather arrives.

Flowers of *Lotos* open about dusk. On warm days blooms close between 11 a.m. and noon, opening and closing for three or four successive days. Plants hold their blooms 6–12 in (15–30 cm) above the water yet the last-day flowers may float. In the fall, when cool days arrive, the blooms stay open day and night continuously for a few days. Flower scent is generally considered more pungent than pleasing.

Nymphaea lotus (Linnaeus) Willdenow. Native to Egypt, central and West Africa, Madagascar, and Grosswardein, Hungary. Characteristics: Night blooming, occasionally viviparous from flower, flowers freely for four successive days (each flower lasts four days). Plate 127.

PETAL COLOR: White. *R.H.S. Chart*: Fan 4, White Group, No. 155D. Sepal color: White, 10–16 prominent, creamy white veins. *R.H.S. Chart*: Fan 4, White Group, No. 155D; veins, No. 155A. Anther color: Yellow. *R.H.S. Chart*: Fan 1, Yellow Group, No. 11B. Stamen color: Yellow. Flower shape: Flat when fully open. Flower size: 6–10 in (15–25 cm). Fragrance: Slight. Number of petals: 19–20. Number of sepals: 4.

LEAF COLOR: Top, green, new leaves reddish; underside, greenish or dull purplish brown. Leaf and sinus: Mature leaf round, dentate, small waves at perimeter. Sinus usually open yet lobes may overlap. Leaf size: 8–20 in (20–50 cm). Leaf spread: 5–10 ft (1.5–3 m). Stem color: Brownish green. Pubescence on peduncle or petiole: Peduncle pubescent; petiole usually pubescent.

COMMENTS: *N. lotus* confuses many people because of its name. Remember that this "lotus" is in *Nymphaea*, not in the lotus genus, *Nelumbo*. Most of the white night-blooming water lily cultivars in use today come from *Nymphaea lotus*. If you can find it, this species makes a fine plant for medium and large pools.

Nymphaea pubescens Willdenow. Hairy water lily. Native to India, Philippine Islands, Java, Australia. Characteristics: Night blooming, nonviviparous. Rhizomes covered with thick hairs. Figure 65.

PETAL COLOR: White. Sepal color: White. Anther color: Yellow. Stamen color: Yellow. Flower shape: Stellate, opening out flat. Flower size: 6–10 in (15–25 cm). Fragrance: Moderately sweet. Number of petals: 18–20. Number of sepals: 4

LEAF COLOR: Top, dark green; underside, dull purplish green. Leaf and sinus: Leaf egg-shaped, irregularly dentate, lobe may display small protuberance, whole leaf frequently hairy underneath. Sinus either open or closed, margin usually curved. Leaf size: Up to 10 × 8 in (25 × 20 cm). Leaf spread: 4–5 ft (1.2–1.5 m). Stem color: Greenish. Pubescence on peduncle or petiole: Yes.

COMMENTS: This species is commonly known as the hairy water lily because its rhizome, stems, and leaf undersides are usually tomentose. There are now new hybrids with flowers 10–13 in (25–33 cm) better suited to the water garden.

Nymphaea rubra Roxburgh. Native to central and southern India. Characteristics: Night blooming, nonviviparous, very free flowering. Plate 128.

PETAL COLOR: Deep purplish red in warm weather, then pink as weather cools. *R.H.S. Chart*: Fan 2, Red-Purple Group, No. 63A then 63C. Sepal color: Dull purplish red. *R.H.S. Chart*: Fan 2, Red-Purple Group, No. 64B. Anther color: Orange-red. *R.H.S. Chart*: Fan 4, Greyed-Orange Group, No. 168B. Stamen color: Orange-red. Flower shape: Flat, starlike when fully open. Flower size: 6–10 in (15–25 cm). Fragrance: Slight. Number of petals: 12–20. Number of sepals: 5–7.

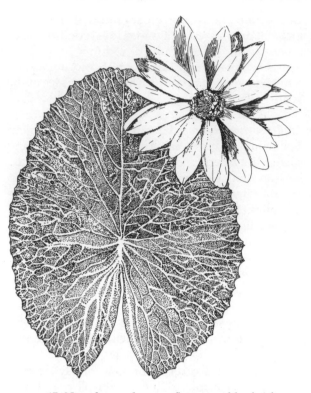

FIGURE 65. *Nymphaea pubescens*, flower and leaf. After a plate from *The Waterlilies: A Monograph of the Genus Nymphaea* by Henry S. Conard (1905).

LEAF COLOR: Top, reddish brown, very old leaves greenish; underside, dark reddish brown. Leaf and sinus: Leaf nearly round, dentate, underside pubescent, lobes usually pointed; sinus usually open, may be partly closed. Leaf size: 10–18 in (25–45 cm). Leaf spread: 6–10 ft (2–3 m). Stem color: Reddish brown. Pubescence on peduncle or petiole: Some on petiole; occasionally some on peduncle.

COMMENTS: This species is a very good bloomer in small, medium, or large pools and has been used in hybridizing several cultivars with larger and more attractive blooms.

Nymphaea spontanea Landon. Native to Southeast Asia. Characteristics: Night blooming, nonviviparous, very free flowering, and producing much less fruit than *N. pubescens*. Plate 129.

PETAL COLOR: Cerise. *R.H.S. Chart*: Fan 2, Red-Purple Group, No. 63B. Sepal color: Purplish red. *R.H.S. Chart*: Fan 2, Red-Purple Group, No. 70C. Anther color: Cerise. *R.H.S. Chart*: Fan 2, Red-Purple Group, No. 63B. Stamen color: Reddish. Flower shape: Broad, stellate. Flower size: 5–7 in (13–18 cm). Fragrance: Slight but pungent. Number of petals: 15–17. Number of sepals: 4.

LEAF COLOR: Top, maroon to olive green; underside, maroon to purple. Leaf and sinus: Leaf dentate; sinus open. Leaf size: 8–12 in (20–30 cm). Leaf spread: 5–7 ft (1.5–2.2 m). Stem color: Maroon. Pubescence on peduncle or petiole: Occasionally on both.

COMMENTS: In regard to Southeast Asian *Nymphaea*, subgenus *Lotos*, Kenneth Landon states: "The basic white-flowered plants are generally classed as *Nymphaea pubescens* in the wild, while those plants possessing cerise or reddish colored flowers are referred to as *N. spontanea*. Those with pink petals are considered natural hybrids. It should be noted that all are closely interrelated. The color forms are most likely natural hybrids of *N. pubescens* and *N. rubra*. These forms are often self-perpetuating—sometimes producing numerous intermediates."

As there are many new cultivars that possess larger and more striking flowers than *N. spontanea*, I do not recommend this species for the water garden.

Nymphaea zenkeri Gilg. Native to the former Cameroons, West Africa. Characteristics: Night blooming, nonviviparous, very small, free flowering. Figure 66.

PETAL COLOR: White. Sepal color: White. Anther color: Yellow. Stamen color: Yellow. Flower shape: Stellate. Flower size: 2–3 in (5–8 cm). Fragrance: Slight. Number of petals: 7–8. Number of sepals: 4.

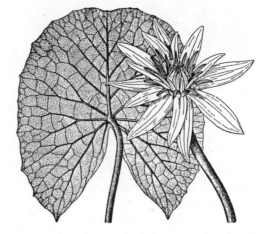

FIGURE 66. *Nymphaea zenkeri*, flower and underside of leaf. From *The Waterlilies: A Monograph of the Genus Nymphaea* by Henry S. Conard (1905).

LEAF COLOR: Top, green; underside, greenish. Leaf and sinus: Leaf nearly round, prominent veins, short hairs underneath on adult leaves; lobes far apart, protuberance on tips. Sinus wide open. Leaf size: 4–6 × 3.5–5 in (10–15 × 9–13 cm). Leaf spread: 20–24 in (50–60 cm). Stem color: Greenish. Pubescence on peduncle or petiole: Short hairs on both.

COMMENTS: *N. zenkeri* is very rare and so I cannot recommend it for the water garden.

Chapter 13

Tropical Water Lilies: Day-Blooming Cultivars

Flowers of the tropical water lily cultivars are generally considered the largest and showiest of all water lilies and are available in just about every color of the rainbow, including green ('Green Smoke'). Flowers of day bloomers open in midmorning and close in late afternoon. Cool fall days may allow them to remain open for longer periods. Blooms generally open for three to four consecutive days. This chapter includes complete descriptions of tropical water lily day-blooming cultivars; night-blooming cultivars are discussed in the next chapter.

Two hybridizers in particular deserve thanks for the beautiful tropical water lily cultivars available today: Dr. George H. Pring, hybridizer at the Missouri Botanical Garden in St. Louis, and Martin E. Randig of San Bernardino, California, who gave his hybrids to Van Ness Water Gardens of Upland, California, for introduction to the public.

The following plant descriptions are arranged alphabetically by cultivar name. This name is followed by any synonyms; next is the name of the hybridizer or originator, followed by the date, if known. Standardized color references are to the Royal Horticultural Society (R.H.S.) Color Chart.

Note that "Stamen color" refers to the basal portion of the stamen or filament. "Leaf size" is either the diameter of the leaf of a mature plant or the measurements of its length and width, in that order. "Leaf spread" refers to the diameter of the area on the water's surface covered by the leaves of the mature plant.

Some cultivars hold a U.S. plant patent; these are noted under "Comments," along with their patent number. Such patents expire 17 years from issue and are not renewable. "Comments" also include reference to what size pool is suitable. Although there are no hard rules differentiating pool sizes, general guidelines follow:

> tub garden: up to 3 ft (1 m) in diameter
> small: 4–6 ft (1.2–2 m) in diameter
> medium: 7–9 ft (2.2–2.7 m) in diameter
> large: 10 ft (3 m) in diameter or larger
> natural pond: dirt or mud bottom pond of any size

Note that copper and redwood are toxic to plants and fish and should be used only in conjunction with a plastic or other fish-safe liner.

To plant a tropical water lily, separate the plant from the sprouted tuber and spread the roots out in a depression in the middle of the planter. Firm the soil down and top with 1 in (2.5 cm) of fine gravel or coarse sand. Place the planting immediately under 6–12 in (15–30 cm) of water (Plates 130–132). Plant tropical water lilies only when the water temperature averages 75°F (24°C) or above. Planting too early may cause plants to go dormant. See the hardiness zone maps in Appendix A and follow this general planting timetable:

IN NORTH AMERICA

Zone 10	March/early April
Zone 9	early April
Zone 8	mid April
Zone 7	mid/late May
Zone 6	late May/early June
Zone 5	early/mid June
Zone 4	mid/late June

IN EUROPE

Zone 10	mid/late May
Zone 9	June
Zones 8–4	conservatory planting, where water can be heated to 75°F (24°C) or higher

Nymphaea **'Afterglow'** Martin E. Randig 1946. Parentage: Unknown. Characteristics: Nonviviparous, very free flowering. Plate 133.

PETAL COLOR: Yellow, orange tips. *R.H.S. Chart*: Fan 1, Yellow Group, No. 11A; tips, Orange Group, No. 29B. Sepal color: Deep, pinkish orange. *R.H.S. Chart*: Fan 1, Orange-Red Group, No. 31B. Anther color: Yellow, outer anthers tipped deep pinkish orange. *R.H.S. Chart*: Fan 1, Yellow Group, No. 11C; tips, Orange-Red Group, No. 31B. Stamen color: Golden orange. Flower shape: Like a big sunflower after first day. Flower size: 6–10 in (15–25 cm). Fragrance: Delightful. Number of petals: 21. Number of sepals: 4.

LEAF COLOR: Top, green; underside, red, prominent green veins. Leaf and sinus: Leaf nearly round, smooth, wavy edges; sinus an open V. Leaf size: 11.5 × 11 in (29 × 28 cm). Leaf spread: 6–8 ft (2–2.5 m). Stem color: Brownish red. Pubescence on peduncle or petiole: None.

COMMENTS: One of the most colorful of the "sunset" tropicals. Worthy of a place in any medium or large pool. Flowers open out flatter than those of 'Albert Greenberg', yet the color is quite similar.

Nymphaea **'Albert Greenberg'** Monroe Birdsey 1969. Parentage: Chance seedling. Characteristics: Nonviviparous, very free flowering. Plate 134.

PETAL COLOR: Yellow, orange-pink tips. *R.H.S. Chart*: Fan 1, Yellow Group, No. 11B; tips, Orange Group, No. 29B. Sepal color: Outer ⅔ deep pinkish orange, yellowish green base. *R.H.S. Chart*: Outer ⅔, Fan 1, Orange-Red Group, No. 32D; base, Fan 3, Yellow-Green Group, No. 144B. Anther color: Yellow, pink tips. *R.H.S. Chart*: Fan 1, Yellow Group, No. 4B; tips, Red Group, No. 38C. Stamen color: Deep yellow. Flower shape: Cuplike. Flower size: 6–7 in (15–18 cm). Fragrance: Very lovely. Number of petals: 20. Number of sepals: 4.

LEAF COLOR: Top, green, heavily blotched purple; underside, green center, pinkish red perimeter, all heavily blotched deep red. Leaf and sinus: Leaf large, nearly round, rounded notches and wavy convolutions along edge. Lobes usually overlap completely at sinus. On mature leaves one lobe frequently raised. Leaf size: Up to 19 × 18 in (48 × 45 cm). Leaf spread: 5–8 ft (1.5–2.5 m). Stem color: Peduncle bright yellowish green; petiole mostly brown. Pubescence on peduncle or petiole: None.

COMMENTS: One of the most popular "sunset" tropicals. Flowers are distinctly cup-shaped. Freedom of bloom, rich color, and beautifully mottled leaves make this lily very desirable for the medium and large pool.

Nymphaea **'Alice Tricker'** Charles Tricker 1937. Parentage: Possibly a seedling, hybrid, or mutation of *N.* 'Mrs. George H. Pring'. Characteristics: Nonviviparous, very free flowering. Plate 135.

PETAL COLOR: White. *R.H.S. Chart*: Fan 4, White Group, No. 155B. Sepal color: White, greenish gray stripes. *R.H.S. Chart*: Fan 4, White Group, No. 155B; stripes, Greyed-Green Group, No. 193D. Anther color: Yellow, white tips. *R.H.S. Chart*: Fan 1, Yellow Group, No. 7A; tips, Fan 4, White Group, No. 155B. Stamen color: Deep, golden yellow. Flower shape: Stellate with broad petals. Flower size: 7–9 in (18–23 cm). Fragrance: Delightful. Number of petals: 21. Number of sepals: 4.

LEAF COLOR: Top, green, new leaves mottled purple; underside, green, purplish blue mottles. Leaf and sinus: Leaves egg-shaped; lobes overlap about halfway down sinus. Leaf size: 15 × 12 in (38 × 30 cm). Leaf spread: 6–8 ft (2–2.5 m). Stem color: Bronzy green underwater; bright green above water. Pubescence on peduncle or petiole: None.

COMMENTS: An excellent lily for the medium and large water garden due to its long blooming period and reliability for good performance.

Nymphaea **'American Beauty'** George H. Pring 1941. Parentage: *N. colorata* × *N.* 'William Stone'. Characteristics: Nonviviparous, free flowering. Plate 136.

PETAL COLOR: Rich raspberry pink. *R.H.S. Chart*: Fan 2, Red-Purple Group, No. 70C. Sepal color: Deep pink. *R.H.S. Chart*: Fan 2, Red-Purple Group, No. 70B. Anther color: Orange-pink, rich raspberry-pink tips. *R.H.S. Chart*: Fan 4, Greyed-Orange Group, No. 171D; tips, Fan 2, Red-Purple Group, No. 70C. Stamen color: Yellow. Flower shape: Cuplike then flat. Flower size: 5–6 in (13–15 cm). Fragrance: Very sweet. Number of petals: 25. Number of sepals: 4.

LEAF COLOR: Top, green, a few purple blotches on new leaves; underside, red, prominent green veins. Leaf and sinus: Leaf large, nearly round, many serrations and convolutions along edge. Sinus occasionally open, generally ⅔ to completely closed due to overlap of lobes. Leaf size: 12 × 10.5 in (30 × 27 cm). Leaf spread: 6 ft (2 m). Stem color: Bright green. Pubescence on peduncle or petiole: None.

COMMENTS: A fine lily for medium and large pools.

Nymphaea '**Aquarius**' Patrick Nutt 1972. Parentage: *N.* 'Judge Hitchcock' × *N. colorata*. Characteristics: Nonviviparous, very free flowering, petals somewhat crumpled.

PETAL COLOR: Deep violet-blue. *R.H.S. Chart*: Fan 2, Violet Group, No. 88C. Sepal color: Slightly deeper than petals. *R.H.S. Chart*: Fan 2, Violet Group, No. 88B. Anther color: Brown, almost chocolate, deep violet-blue tips. *R.H.S. Chart*: Fan 4, Greyed-Orange Group, No. 176C; tips, Fan 2, Violet Group, No. 88C. Stamen color: Deep yellow. Flower shape: Very full star. Flower size: About 8–10 in (20–25 cm). Fragrance: Slight. Number of petals: 28–29. Number of sepals: 4.

LEAF COLOR: Top, dark green, some purple mottling; underside, green, suffused purple, very prominent veins. Leaf and sinus: Leaves oval-shaped, somewhat dentate. Sinus usually closed, may be partly open. Leaf size: Up to 18 × 16 in (45 × 40 cm). Leaf spread: 6–7 ft (2–2.2 m). Stem color: Bronzy green. Pubescence on peduncle or petiole: None.

COMMENTS: 'Aquarius' is a fine water lily for the medium and large pool. It is somewhat similar to 'Director George T. Moore', but blooms are larger and more double.

Nymphaea '**August Koch**' August Koch and George H. Pring 1922. Parentage: Probably *N.* 'Blue Beauty' × *N.* 'Mrs. Woodrow Wilson'. Characteristics: Viviparous, extremely free flowering. Plate 137.

PETAL COLOR: Rich blue. *R.H.S. Chart*: Fan 2, Vio-let-Blue Group, No. 92C or lighter. Sepal color: Lilac-purple. *R.H.S. Chart*: Fan 2, Purple-Violet Group, No. 90D. Anther color: Inner anthers brownish orange, tipped rich blue; outer lilac-purple, tipped rich blue. *R.H.S. Chart*: Inner anthers, Fan 4, Greyed-Orange Group, No. 166D; outer anthers, Fan 2, Purple-Violet Group, No. 90D; tips, Violet-Blue Group, No. 92C or lighter. Stamen color: Inner, orange-brown; outer, lilac-purple. Flower shape: Cuplike. Flower size: 4.5–5.5 in (11–14 cm). Fragrance: Very pleasant. Number of petals: 22–25. Number of sepals: 4.

LEAF COLOR: Top, olive green; underside, mostly green, pink on lobes; lobes display prominent green veins. Leaf and sinus: Leaf nearly round, unevenly serrated, some convolutions along edges. Sinus usually, yet not always, closed due to overlap of lobes. Leaf size: 12.5 × 12 in (32 × 30 cm). Leaf spread: 4–6 ft (1.2–2 m). Stem color: Bronzy green; portions of peduncle above water bright green. Pubescence on peduncle or petiole: None.

COMMENTS: The cross that resulted in 'August Koch' was made at Garfield Park, Chicago, Illinois. Since all leaves are viviparous, this lily will reproduce well from plantlets that form on leaves if insects are kept from devouring new starts. Aphids love to congregate around tender new growth. 'August Koch' is excellent for small or medium pools and will also bloom well in tub gardens. It can withstand crowding.

Nymphaea '**Aviator Pring**' George H. Pring 1956. Parentage: *N. sulfurea* × *N.* 'St. Louis'. Characteristics: Nonviviparous, very free flowering. Plate 138.

PETAL COLOR: Yellow. *R.H.S. Chart*: Fan 1, Yellow Group, No. 3B. Sepal color: Yellow. *R.H.S. Chart*: Fan 1, Yellow Group, No. 3B. Anther color: Yellow. *R.H.S. Chart*: Fan 1, Yellow Group, No. 3B. Stamen color: Yellow. Flower shape: Large, full star. Flower size: 8–10 in (20–25 cm). Fragrance: Delightful. Number of petals: 25–26. Number of sepals: 4.

LEAF COLOR: Top, green; underside, green. Leaf and sinus: Leaf somewhat egg-shaped; sinus usually half open. Leaf size: 12 × 10.5 in (30 × 27 cm). Leaf spread: 6–8 ft (2–2.5 cm). Stem color: Bronzy green. Pubescence on peduncle or petiole: None.

COMMENTS: One of the very best yellow tropicals for the medium and large pool. I highly recommend it.

Nymphaea '**Bagdad**' George H. Pring 1941. Parentage: *N.* 'Pink Platter' × unnamed hybrid. Characteristics: Viviparous, very free flowering. Plate 139.

PETAL COLOR: Light blue (wisteria blue). *R.H.S. Chart*: Fan 2, Blue Group, No. 106D. Sepal color:

Lavender. *R.H.S. Chart*: Fan 2, Purple Group, No. 76C. Anther color: Butterscotch-yellow, wisteria-blue tips. *R.H.S. Chart*: Fan 4, Greyed-Orange Group, No. 165D; tips, Fan 2, Blue Group, No. 106D. Stamen color: Yellow. Flower shape: Full, stellate. Flower size: 8 in (20 cm). Fragrance: Sweet. Number of petals: 30–32. Number of sepals: 4.

LEAF COLOR: Top, green, heavily mottled and blotched purple and red; underside, dark green, heavily blotched purple. Leaf and sinus: Leaf nearly round; sinus usually partly open. Leaf size: 10–12 in (25–30 cm). Leaf spread: 6–7 ft (2–2.2 m). Stem color: Bright green. Pubescence on peduncle or petiole: None.

COMMENTS: I consider 'Bagdad' a very choice tropical. Since it is viviparous, it can withstand more cold and is not so apt to go to sleep in early spring. It has beautiful leaves, a distinct plus. In addition, the light blue color of the flower is very lovely. I highly recommend 'Bagdad' for medium and large pools.

Nymphaea **'Bill Yohn'** William Frase 1989. Parentage: *N. ampla* × *N.* 'Director George T. Moore'. Characteristics: Nonviviparous, very free flowering. Plate 140.

PETAL COLOR: Deep blue then medium blue. *R.H.S. Chart*: Fan 2, Violet-Blue Group, No. 94C; last day, No. 94D. Sepal color: Deep blue. *R.H.S. Chart*: Fan 2, Violet-Blue Group, No. 94C. Anther color: Deep yellow; inner rows (about 3) also have yellow tips. *R.H.S. Chart*: Fan 1, Yellow Group, No. 11A; inner tips, Fan 1, Yellow Group, No. 11A; outer tips, blue, Fan 2, Violet-Blue Group, No. 94C. Stamen color: Yellowish brown. Flower shape: Stellate. Flower size: 6–9 in (15–23 cm). Fragrance: Very pleasant. Number of petals: 19–20. Number of sepals: 5–6.

LEAF COLOR: Top, green, few purple blotches, perimeter of new leaves purple, especially around sinus; underside, red, green veins. Leaf and sinus: Leaf almost round, serrated edges; sinus usually an open V. Leaf size: 12–15 in (30–38 cm). Leaf spread: 5–8 ft (1.5–2.5 m). Stem color: Brownish turning purplish. Pubescence on peduncle or petiole: Heavy short fuzz on all stems.

COMMENTS: A very striking blue that is bound to make a name for itself among the blue water lilies. I recommend it for the medium or large pool.

Nymphaea **'Black Prince'** Charles Winch 1987. Parentage: Unknown. Characteristics: Nonviviparous, free flowering. Plate 141.

PETAL COLOR: Deep blue. *R.H.S. Chart*: Fan 2, Violet-Blue Group, Nos. 94B–C. Sepal color: Deep vi-

olet. *R.H.S. Chart*: Fan 2, Violet-Blue Group, No. 90D. Anther color: Deep golden yellow, deep blue tips. *R.H.S. Chart*: Fan 1, Yellow Group, No. 12B; tips, Fan 2, Violet-Blue Group, No. 90D. Stamen color: Deep yellow. Flower shape: Stellate. Flower size: 6 in (15 cm). Fragrance: Pronounced. Number of petals: 21. Number of sepals: 4.

LEAF COLOR: Top, green; underside, green, portion under lobes purple. Leaf and sinus: Leaf nearly round, deeply serrated, sharp teeth around edges. Sinus usually half open, sometimes fully open or fully closed on same plant. Leaf size: 15 × 14 in (38 × 35 cm). Leaf spread: 10 ft (3 m). Stem color: Green. Pubescence on peduncle or petiole: None.

COMMENTS: 'Black Prince' is a "star" lily. Flowers, which are rather small in comparison to the large leaves, are held very high above the water. Like most of the star lilies, it performs best when given plenty of room. I recommend 'Black Prince' for medium and large pools.

Nymphaea **'Blue Ampla'** Kenneth Landon 1978. Parentage: *N. ampla* × *N. capensis* var. *zanzibariensis* 'Rosea'. Characteristics: Nonviviparous, flowers freely.

PETAL COLOR: Blue. *R.H.S. Chart*: Fan 2, Blue Group, No. 100C. Sepal color: Medium blue then pale blue. *R.H.S. Chart*: Fan 2, Blue Group, No. 106C then 108D. Anther color: Butterscotch-yellow, blue tips. *R.H.S. Chart*: Fan 4, Greyed-Orange Group, No. 165D; tips, Fan 2, Blue Group, No. 100C. Stamen color: Deep, golden yellow. Flower shape: Stellate after first day. Flower size: 8–10 in (20–25 cm). Fragrance: Very pleasant. Number of petals: 18–22. Number of sepals: 4.

LEAF COLOR: Top, green; underside, red-purple. Leaf and sinus: Leaf longer than wide, very dentate; sinus frequently half open. Leaf size: 12–14 in (30–35 cm). Leaf spread: 7–8 ft (2.2–2.5 m). Stem color: Bronzy green. Pubescence on peduncle or petiole: None.

COMMENTS: 'Blue Ampla', with its very striking deep sky-blue blooms, is a fine water lily for the medium or large water garden.

Nymphaea **'Blue Beauty'** (syn. 'Pennsylvania') Henry Conard and William Tricker 1897. Parentage: *N. caerulea* × *N. capensis* var. *zanzibariensis*. Characteristics: Nonviviparous, very free flowering. Plate 142.

PETAL COLOR: Deep, rich blue. *R.H.S. Chart*: Fan 2, Violet-Blue Group, No. 92B. Sepal color: Pale blue background, heavily streaked greenish blue near base. *R.H.S. Chart*: Fan 2, Violet-Blue Group, No. 92C; streaks near base, Fan 3, Green Group, No.

139D. Anther color: Brownish yellow beginning second day. *R.H.S. Chart*: Fan 4, Greyed-Orange Group, No. 164C. Stamen color: Deep yellow. Flower shape: Stellate. Flower size: 8–11 in (20–28 cm). Fragrance: Very sweet. Number of petals: 21–23. Number of sepals: 4.

LEAF COLOR: Top, green, few purple specks and small blotches prominent on newest leaves; underside, purplish brown, numerous small, dark purple mottles. Leaf and sinus: Leaf longer than wide, numerous serrations and waves around edges and 0.5 in (1.3 cm) projection at each lobe tip. Lobes overlap about halfway down sinus. Leaf size: 14 × 13 in (35 × 33 cm). Leaf spread: 4–7 ft (1.2–2.2 m). Stem color: Brown. Pubescence on peduncle or petiole: Fuzz and fine hairs on petiole.

COMMENTS: Due to its abundance of flowers and excellent color, I rate 'Blue Beauty' as one of the greatest water lilies of all time. If it is planted too early, however, and cold weather arrives, the plant may go dormant and not recover. I recommend this lily for medium and large pools.

Nymphaea **'Blue Bird'** William Tricker, Inc. 1946. Parentage: Unknown. Characteristics: Viviparous, very free flowering. Plate 143.

PETAL COLOR: Very brilliant blue. *R.H.S. Chart*: Fan 2, Violet-Blue Group, No. 94D. Sepal color: Light blue. *R.H.S. Chart*: Fan 2, Violet-Blue Group, No. 92C. Anther color: Rich butterscotch-brown, blue tips. *R.H.S. Chart*: Fan 4, Greyed-Orange Group, No. 165C; tips, Fan 2, Violet-Blue Group, No. 94D. Stamen color: Deep yellow. Flower shape: Cuplike then flat. Flower size: 5–6 in (13–15 cm). Fragrance: Sweet. Number of petals: 28–30. Number of sepals 4.

LEAF COLOR: Top, bright olive green; underside, purple, green veins. Leaf and sinus: Leaf nearly round, fairly smooth edges; sinus either closed or partly open. Leaf size: 8–10 in (20–25 cm). Leaf spread: 5 ft (1.5 m). Stem color: Stems purplish, short green portion on peduncle just below flower. Pubescence on peduncle or petiole: None.

COMMENTS: Though this lily is currently in scarce supply, it is a fine choice for the small, medium, or large pool.

Nymphaea **'Blue Star'** (syn. 'William Stone') William Tricker 1899. Parentage: *N. flavovirens* × unknown (probably *N. capensis* var. *zanzibariensis*). Characteristics: Nonviviparous, very free flowering. Peduncles hold flowers 12–15 in (30–38 cm) above the water.

PETAL COLOR: Blue. *R.H.S. Chart*: Fan 2, Violet-Blue Group, No. 91A. Sepal color: Deeper blue than petals. *R.H.S. Chart*: Fan 2, Violet-Blue Group, No. 92A. Anther color: Orange-brown, blue tips. *R.H.S. Chart*: Fan 4, Greyed-Orange Group, No. 171C; tips, Fan 2, Violet-Blue Group, No. 91A. Stamen color: Deep yellow. Flower shape: Stellate. Flower size: 5–6 in (13–15 cm). Fragrance: Delightful. Number of petals: 13–14. Number of sepals: 4.

LEAF COLOR: Top, green; underside, violet. Leaf and sinus: Leaf a little longer than wide, slightly dentate edges, lobes have pointed tips. Sinus open. Leaf size: 12 × 10.5 in (30 × 27 cm). Leaf spread: 8 ft (2.5 m). Stem color: Bronzy green or green. Pubescence on peduncle or petiole: None.

COMMENTS: Like most of the star lilies, 'Blue Star' adapts somewhat to the given area. If allowed, however, this plant can fill an 8-ft (2.5-m) or larger surface area with leaves. For this reason I recommend it for the medium or large pool only.

Nymphaea **'Bob Trickett'** George H. Pring 1949. Parentage: *N. stellata* var. *caerulea* × *N.* 'Mrs. Edwards Whitaker'. Characteristics: Nonviviparous, very free flowering. Plate 144.

PETAL COLOR: Sky blue. *R.H.S. Chart*: Fan 2, Violet-Blue Group, No. 92C. Sepal color: Light blue, prominent greenish veins. *R.H.S. Chart*: Fan 2, Violet-Blue Group, No. 97D; veins, Fan 3, Green Group, No. 138D. Anther color: Butterscotch, sky-blue tips. *R.H.S. Chart*: Fan 4, Greyed-Orange Group, No. 165D; tips, Fan 2, Violet-Blue Group, No. 92C. Stamen color: Deep yellow. Flower shape: Cuplike then stellate. Flower size: 10–14 in (25–35 cm). Fragrance: Very pleasing. Number of petals: 36–37. Number of sepals: 4.

LEAF COLOR: Top, green; underside, red, green veins. Leaf and sinus: Leaves round; sinus usually open. Leaf size: 12 in (30 cm). Leaf spread: 6 ft (2 m). Stem color: Green. Pubescence on peduncle or petiole: None.

COMMENTS: 'Bob Trickett' is a very choice lily. It was named by George H. Pring to honor a friend who devoted most of his life studying, working with, and promoting water lilies. Truly a giant in the field, Bob Trickett became one of the world's experts and richly merits the tribute. I recommend 'Bob Trickett' for the medium and large pool.

Nymphaea **'Charles Thomas'** John Wood 1985. Parentage: Unknown. Characteristics: Viviparous, very free flowering. Plate 145.

PETAL COLOR: Sky blue. *R.H.S. Chart*: Fan 2, Blue Group, No. 100C. Sepal color: Light blue, darker blue veins. *R.H.S. Chart*: Fan 2, Blue Group, No. 106D; veins, No. 106B. Anther color: Yellow, sky-blue tips. *R.H.S. Chart*: Fan 1, Yellow Group, No.

11A; tips, Fan 2, Blue Group, No. 100C. Stamen color: Yellow. Flower shape: Stellate. Flower size: 5–6 in (13–15 cm). Fragrance: Very pleasant. Number of petals: 24–25. Number of sepals: 4.

LEAF COLOR: Top, green, heavily mottled and blotched purple; underside, green, purple blotches. Leaf and sinus: Leaf nearly round; sinus usually open. Leaf size: 10–11 in (25–28 cm). Leaf spread 4–6 ft (1.2–2 m). Stem color: Green. Pubescence on peduncle or petiole: None.

COMMENTS: With its magnificently mottled leaves, 'Charles Thomas' is one of the finest blue tropicals. I recommend it for any size pool, including tub gardens. Being viviparous, it will take more cold in early spring than many of the blue tropicals.

Nymphaea **'Charles Winch'** Charles Winch 1986. Parentage: Unknown. Characteristics: Nonviviparous, very free flowering. Plate 146.

PETAL COLOR: White. *R.H.S. Chart*: Fan 4, White Group, No. 155C. Sepal color: White, greenish tips and veins. *R.H.S. Chart*: Fan 4, White Group, No. 155C; tips and veins, Fan 3, Yellow-Green Group, No. 145D. Anther color: Butterscotch, white tips. *R.H.S. Chart*: Fan 4, Greyed-Yellow Group, No. 160C; tips, White Group, No. 155C. Stamen color: Deep yellow. Flower shape: Large, cuplike. Flower size: 8–10 in (20–25 cm). Fragrance: Very sweet. Number of petals: 32–34. Number of sepals: 4.

LEAF COLOR: Top, green; underside, bronzy green. Leaf and sinus: Leaf a little longer than wide, lobes usually overlap about halfway. Sinus varies, usually partly open. Leaf size: 10–12 in (25–30 cm). Leaf spread: 6 ft (2 m). Stem color: Green or bronzy. Pubescence on peduncle or petiole: None.

COMMENTS: Probably the very best white day-blooming tropical. Many of the petals (especially the inner ones) are beautifully rolled, creating a unique and very pleasing effect. Since this plant adapts to available space, I recommend it for any size pool.

Nymphaea **'Christine Lingg'** Joseph Lingg. Parentage: Unknown. Characteristics: Nonviviparous, very free flowering. Plate 147.

PETAL COLOR: Lavender-blue. *R.H.S. Chart*: Fan 2, Violet-Blue Group, No. 92B. Sepal color: Pale lavender. *R.H.S. Chart*: Fan 2, Violet Group, No. 84C. Anther color: Rich butterscotch-yellow, lavender-blue tips. *R.H.S. Chart*: Fan 1, Yellow Group, No. 11A and Fan 4, Greyed-Orange Group, No. 165C; tips, Fan 2, Violet-Blue Group, No. 92B. Stamen color: Deep yellow. Flower shape: Large, cuplike. Flower size: 6–8 in (15–20 cm). Fragrance: De-

lightful. Number of petals: 54–56. Number of sepals: 4.

LEAF COLOR: Top, green, heavily mottled purple; underside, red, maroon blotches. Leaf and sinus: Leaves nearly round, somewhat dentate; sinus usually closed. Leaf size: 10–12 in (25–30 cm). Leaf spread: 5–6 ft (1.5–2 m). Stem color: Pinkish red. Pubescence on peduncle or petiole: None.

COMMENTS: One of the choicest of all the tropical lilies for any size pool except the tub garden. The magnificent leaves alone make it well worthwhile. The very double lavender-blue blooms add to its charm.

Nymphaea **'Clint Bryant'** John Wood 1980. Parentage: Unknown. Characteristics: Nonviviparous, free flowering, long flower stem.

PETAL COLOR: Violet-blue. *R.H.S. Chart*: Fan 2, Violet-Blue Group, No. 98D. Sepal color: Bluish purple. *R.H.S. Chart*: Fan 2, Violet-Blue Group, No. 96D. Anther color: Purplish brown, violet-blue tips. *R.H.S. Chart*: Fan 4, Greyed-Purple Group, No. 185C; tips, Fan 2, Violet-Blue Group, No. 98D. Stamen color: Yellow. Flower shape: Cuplike. Flower size: 7–8 in (18–20 cm). Fragrance: Lovely. Number of petals: 28. Number of sepals: 4.

LEAF COLOR: Top, green; underside, blushed pink. Leaf and sinus: Leaves nearly round, highly dentate; sinus usually open. Leaf size: 10–12 in (25–30 cm). Leaf spread: 6–7 ft (2–2.2 m). Stem color: Greenish. Pubescence on peduncle or petiole: None.

COMMENTS: An excellent free-blooming lily for the medium and large pool. The plant does quite well in shaded or partly shaded areas.

Nymphaea **'Daubeniana'** (syn. 'Dauben' in the United States) Daubeny 1863. Parentage: Probably *N. micrantha* and *N. caerulea*. Characteristics: Highly viviparous, very free flowering. Plates 148 and 149.

PETAL COLOR: Light blue, slightly darker tips. *R.H.S. Chart*: Fan 2, Violet-Blue Group, No. 92D; tips, No. 92C. Sepal color: Light blue, striped green. *R.H.S. Chart*: Fan 2, Blue Group, No. 108D (or lighter); stripes, Fan 3, Green Group, No. 138D. Anther color: Yellow, blue tips. *R.H.S. Chart*: Fan 1, Yellow Group, No. 13B; tips, Fan 2, Violet-Blue Group, No. 92C. Stamen color: Golden yellow. Flower shape: Cuplike. Flower size: 4–6 in (10–15 cm). Fragrance: Very highly scented. Number of petals: 21. Number of sepals: 4.

LEAF COLOR: Top, green; underside, green, many small purple specks. Leaf and sinus: Leaf egg-shaped, edges wavy, convoluted; almost all leaves produce a fast-growing plantlet. Sinus a wide-open

V. Leaf size: Up to 12 × 10 in (30 × 25 cm). Leaf spread: 3–7 ft (1–2.2 m). Stem color: Peduncle, reddish brown; petiole, brownish. Pubescence on peduncle or petiole: None.

COMMENTS: Nearly every leaf develops a plantlet that frequently blooms while still attached to the mother plant. This water lily is ideal for the tub garden or small pool as it adapts readily to a small planting area. Like other viviparous tropicals, it withstands more cold than most tropical lilies without going dormant.

Nymphaea **'Director George T. Moore'** George H. Pring 1941. Parentage: *N.* 'Judge Hitchcock' × *N. colorata*. Characteristics: Nonviviparous, very free flowering. Plate 150.

PETAL COLOR: Deep violet-blue. *R.H.S. Chart*: Fan 2, Violet-Blue Group, No. 94B. Sepal color: Deep violet. *R.H.S. Chart*: Fan 2, Violet-Blue Group, No. 90A. Anther color: Purple, deep violet-blue tips. *R.H.S. Chart*: Fan 2, Violet-Blue Group, No. 89D; tips, No. 94B. Stamen color: Deep violet-blue. Flower shape: Wide-open star after first day. Flower size: 7–10 in (18–25 cm). Fragrance: Delightful. Number of petals: 13–26. Number of sepals: 4–5.

LEAF COLOR: Top, green, a few purple blotches and mottles; underside, rich royal purple, green veins. Leaf and sinus: Leaf almost round; lobes overlap broadly at sinus. Leaf size: 10–12 in (25–30 cm). Leaf spread 5–8 ft (1.5–2.5 m). Stem color: Varies from green to purple. Pubescence on peduncle or petiole: A few short hairs on both, bare on above-water portion of peduncle.

COMMENTS: 'Director George T. Moore' is one of my two favorite tropicals (the other is 'Pamela'). The blooms are of the richest violet imaginable and are borne very freely. It is somewhat similar to 'Aquarius' but much deeper in color. I highly recommend it for the medium or large pool.

Nymphaea **'Edward D. Uber'** Van Ness Water Gardens 1985. Parentage: Unknown. Characteristics: Viviparous, very free flowering. Plate 151.

PETAL COLOR: Pinkish purple. *R.H.S. Chart*: Fan 2, Red-Purple Group, No. 63C. Sepal color: Pinkish purple. *R.H.S. Chart*: Fan 2, Red-Purple Group, No. 63C. Anther color: Butterscotch, pinkish purple tips. *R.H.S. Chart*: Fan 1, Orange Group, No. 26C; tips, Fan 2, Red-Purple Group, No. 63C. Stamen color: Deep yellow. Flower shape: Starlike, long sepals. Flower size: 8 in (20 cm). Fragrance: Delightful. Number of petals: 18–22. Number of sepals: 4.

LEAF COLOR: Top, deep green; underside, pinkish, small maroon flecks. Leaf and sinus: Leaves a little longer than wide; sinus open. Leaf size: 10 in (25 cm). Leaf spread: 5–6 ft (1.5–2 m). Stem color: Pinkish red. Pubescence on peduncle or petiole: None.

COMMENTS: Being a viviparous variety, 'Edward D. Uber' can take more cold and shade than most tropicals and still bloom well. Also, it can be planted a little earlier in the spring than nonviviparous varieties. I highly recommend it for any size pool.

Nymphaea **'Eldorado'** Martin E. Randig 1963. Parentage: Unknown. Characteristics: Nonviviparous, very free flowering. Plate 152.

PETAL COLOR: Medium lemon yellow. *R.H.S. Chart*: Fan 1, Yellow Group, No. 13B. Sepal color: Lemon yellow, edges frequently touched pinkish orange. *R.H.S. Chart*: Fan 1, Yellow Group, No. 12C; edges, Orange-Red Group, No. 31D or lighter. Anther color: Yellow, medium lemon-yellow tips. *R.H.S. Chart*: Fan 1, Yellow-Orange Group, No. 14B; tips, Yellow Group, No. 13B. Stamen color: Deep golden orange. Flower shape: Large, stellate. Flower size: 9–11 in (23–28 cm). Fragrance: Very lovely. Number of petals: 20–22. Number of sepals: 4.

LEAF COLOR: Top, green, numerous purple blotches, new leaves bronzy; underside, green, heavily blotched deep violet-purple. Leaf and sinus: Leaf large, egg-shaped, smooth edges; sinus usually an open V. Leaf size: Up to 12 × 10 in (30 × 25 cm). Leaf spread: 6 ft (2 m). Stem color: Reddish brown. Pubescence on peduncle or petiole: None.

COMMENTS: Among the best of the yellow tropicals. With its heavily mottled leaves it can be among the prettiest of any yellow tropical; its rich yellow flowers are nearly as large as the leaves, and it performs well even in a small pool. Its only drawback is that leaves often disintegrate around the center of pads. I recommend it for any size pool.

Nymphaea **'Enchantment'** Martin E. Randig 1963. Parentage: Unknown. Characteristics: Nonviviparous, free flowering. Plate 153.

PETAL COLOR: Rich medium pink. *R.H.S. Chart*: Fan 2, Purple Group, Nos. 75B–C. Sepal color: Same as petals. Anther color: Pinkish orange, rich medium pink tips. *R.H.S. Chart*: Fan 1, Orange-Red Group, No. 31C; tips, Fan 2, Purple Group, Nos. 75B–C. Stamen color: Yellow. Flower shape: Huge, round, flat. Flower size: 7–10 in (18–25 cm). Fragrance: Delightful. Number of petals: 24–25. Number of sepals: 4.

LEAF COLOR: Top, bright green; underside, yellow-green. Leaf and sinus: Leaf large, oval, some serrations and many convolutions along edges.

Lobes overlap completely along sinus; on older leaves one lobe raised 1 in (2.5 cm). Leaf size: Up to 15 × 13.5 in (38 × 34 cm). Leaf spread: 5–9 ft (1.5–2.7 m). Stem color: Green. Pubescence on peduncle or petiole: None.

COMMENTS: To my mind, 'Enchantment' is tops for a medium pink tropical. The color is terrific, flowers are large, and blooms are plentiful. I highly recommend it for the medium or large pool.

Nymphaea 'Evelyn Randig' Martin E. Randig 1931. Parentage: Unknown. Characteristics: Nonviviparous, excellent bloomer. Plate 154.

PETAL COLOR: Deep raspberry pink. *R.H.S. Chart*: Fan 2, Red-Purple Group, No. 72C. Sepal color: Outer ⅔, same as petals; base, greenish, with many tiny purple lines or veins. *R.H.S. Chart*: Base, Fan 3, Yellow-Green Group, No. 144C; veins, Fan 2, Red-Purple Group, No. 72B. Anther color: Inner anthers yellow, outer anthers purple; tips, deep raspberry pink. *R.H.S. Chart*: Fan 1, Yellow Group, No. 2B; outer, Fan 2, Red-Purple Group, No. 72B; tips, No. 72C. Stamen color: Deep yellow. Flower shape: Cuplike then full star. Flower size: 7–9 in (18–23 cm). Fragrance: Slight. Number of petals: 25. Number of sepals: 4.

LEAF COLOR: Top, deep green, large purple blotches cover more than half the leaf; underside, greenish yellow, numerous red blotches. Leaf and sinus: Leaf almost round, smooth or nearly smooth edges. Sinus usually closed due to overlapping lobes; some young leaves have partly open sinuses. Leaf size: 14–15 in (35–38 cm). Leaf spread: 5–7 ft (1.5–2.2 m). Stem color: Brown, short green portion on peduncle just below flower. Pubescence on peduncle or petiole: None.

COMMENTS: With its rich raspberry-pink blooms and magnificent mottled leaves, this lily has to be considered one of the most beautiful and desirable lilies. Suitable for medium and large pools.

Nymphaea 'General Pershing' George H. Pring 1920. Parentage: *N.* 'Mrs. Edwards Whitaker', from which it received its large size, and *N.* 'Castaliflora', its rich pink color. Characteristics: Nonviviparous, very free flowering. Plate 155.

PETAL COLOR: Lavender-pink. *R.H.S. Chart*: Fan 2, Purple Group, No. 75C. Sepal color: Lavender-pink, green base. *R.H.S. Chart*: Fan 2, Red-Purple Group, No. 73D; base, Fan 3, Green Group, No. 138D. Anther color: Deep yellow, lavender-pink tips. *R.H.S. Chart*: Fan 1, Yellow Group, No. 12B; tips, Fan 2, Purple Group, No. 75C. Stamen color: Deep yellow. Flower shape: Cuplike then flat. Flower size: 8–11 in (20–28 cm). Fragrance: Won-

derfully sweet. Number of petals: 25–27. Number of sepals: 4.

LEAF COLOR: Top, olive green, many small purple blotches; underside, bronzy pink, many small red flecks and mottles. Leaf and sinus: Leaf almost round, smooth, wavy edges; sinus usually closed or barely open. Leaf size: 9.5–10.5 in (24–27 cm). Leaf spread: 5–6 ft (1.5–2 m). Stem color: Brown. Pubescence on peduncle or petiole: None.

COMMENTS: 'General Pershing' has always been one of my favorite water lilies. The orchid-pink color and mottled leaves are especially lovely, and the blooms are pleasantly large in relation to the medium-sized leaves. I recommend this lily for any size pool except the tub garden.

Nymphaea 'Golden Fascinator' Martin E. Randig 1946. Parentage: Unknown. Characteristics: Nonviviparous, very free flowering. Plate 156.

PETAL COLOR: Yellow, orange-pink outer petals and tips. *R.H.S. Chart*: Fan 1, Yellow Group, No. 13B; outer petals and tips, Red Group, No. 37A. Sepal color: Pinkish orange, reddish tips. *R.H.S. Chart*: Fan 1, Yellow Group, No. 13B, flushed by Orange Group, No. 29A; tips, Red Group, No. 37A. Anther color: Yellow, pink tips. *R.H.S. Chart*: Fan 1, Yellow Group, No. 13C; tips, Red Group, No. 37A. Stamen color: Deep yellow. Flower shape: Both cuplike and stellate. Flower size: 6.5–9 in (16–23 cm). Fragrance: Wonderful. Number of petals: 18–22. Number of sepals: 4.

LEAF COLOR: Top, green; underside, deep red, prominent green veins. Leaf and sinus: Leaf a little longer than wide, a few jagged points and waves around edges. Sinus mostly closed due to overlap of lobes. Leaf size: 11–12 in (28–30 cm). Leaf spread: 6–7 ft (2–2.2 m). Stem color: Peduncle mostly brown; petiole red. Pubescence on peduncle or petiole: None.

COMMENTS: This is a beautiful lily for the medium or large pool. Blooms are striking and quite large in relation to the leaves.

Nymphaea 'Golden West' Martin E. Randig 1936. Parentage: Seedling of *N.* 'St. Louis'. Characteristics: Nonviviparous, extremely free flowering. Plate 157.

PETAL COLOR: Peach. *R.H.S. Chart*: Fan 1, Red Group, No. 38C. Sepal color: Peach, prominent greenish gray lengthwise veins. *R.H.S. Chart*: Fan 1, Red Group, No. 36C; veins, Fan 4, Greyed-Green Group, No. 193C. Anther color: Yellow-orange, peach tips. *R.H.S. Chart*: Fan 1, Yellow-Orange Group, No. 22B; tips, Red Group, No. 38C. Stamen color: Deep, golden yellow. Flower shape: Flat after first day. Flower size: 8–10 in (20–25 cm). Fragrance: Very sweet. Number of petals: 21. Number of sepals: 4.

LEAF COLOR: Top, green, new leaves heavily mottled purple; underside, pink or greenish, heavily mottled red. Leaf and sinus: Leaf a little longer than wide; sinus usually open, sometimes halfway open. Leaf size: 10–11 in (25–28 cm). Leaf spread: 5–6 ft (1.5–2 m). Stem color: Bright green. Pubescence on peduncle or petiole: None.

COMMENTS: A beautiful lily for medium and large pools.

Nymphaea **'Green Smoke'** Martin E. Randig 1965. Parentage: Unknown. Characteristics: Nonviviparous, flowers quite freely. Plate 158.

PETAL COLOR: Inner petals, greenish yellow, tipped blue; outer petals blue. *R.H.S. Chart*: Inner petals, Fan 3, Green Group, No. 142D; tips and outer petals, Fan 2, Violet-Blue Group, No. 92B. Sepal color: Outer ⅔ light blue, greenish yellow base. *R.H.S. Chart*: Outer ⅔, Fan 2, Violet-Blue Group, No. 92C; base, Fan 3, Green Group, No. 142D. Anther color: Golden yellow, greenish yellow tips. *R.H.S. Chart*: Fan 1, Yellow Group, No. 11A; tips, Fan 3, Green Group, No. 142D. Stamen color: Yellow. Flower shape: Cuplike. Flower size: 5–6 in (13–15 cm). Fragrance: Pleasant. Number of petals: 21–22. Number of sepals: 5.

LEAF COLOR: Top, greenish, faint purple blotches, new leaves bronzy, faintly blotched purple; underside, green, prominent violet mottling, new leaves pinkish, many violet flecks and mottles. Leaf and sinus: Leaves egg-shaped, a little longer than wide, wavy edges, rounded teeth. Sinus wide-open V; on new leaves lobes usually overlap. Leaf size: Up to 12 × 10.5 (30 × 27 cm). Leaf spread: 5–6 ft (1.5–2 m). Stem color: Peduncle, mostly yellow-green; petiole green, base brown. Pubescence on peduncle or petiole: None.

COMMENTS: 'Green Smoke' has a most unusual color, making it very desirable for medium and large pools. Nurseries currently have a hard time keeping up with the demand for this lily.

Nymphaea **'Henry Shaw'** George H. Pring 1917. Parentage: Seedling of *N.* 'Castaliflora', which is itself a seedling of *N. capensis* var. *zanzibariensis* 'Rosea'. Characteristics: Nonviviparous, free flowering. Plate 159.

PETAL COLOR: Campanula blue. *R.H.S. Chart*: Fan 2, Violet Group, Nos. 84C–D. Sepal color: Lighter blue than petals. *R.H.S. Chart*: Fan 2, Violet Group, No. 84D. Anther color: Inner anthers, lemon-chrome; outer anthers brownish purple; all tipped

campanula blue. *R.H.S. Chart*: Inner anthers, Fan 1, Yellow Group, No. 12C; outer anthers, Fan 4, Greyed-Purple Group, No. 186D; tips, Fan 2, Violet Group, Nos. 84C–D. Stamen color: Deep yellow. Flower shape: Cuplike then flat. Flower size: 8–10 in (20–25 cm). Fragrance: Very sweet. Number of petals: 28–30. Number of sepals: 4.

LEAF COLOR: Top, green, new leaves sparsely spotted light brown; underside, light green, suffused pink. Leaf and sinus: Leaf oval, indented wavy margin; sinus ⅓ open. Leaf size: Up to 15 × 13.5 in (38 × 34 cm). Leaf spread: 6–8 ft (2–2.5 m). Stem color: Brown. Pubescence on peduncle or petiole: None.

COMMENTS: This plant honors the founder of the Missouri Botanical Garden, Henry Shaw. A very charming plant, worthy of a place in any medium or large pool.

Nymphaea **'Ineta Ruth'** (syn. 'Yellow Star') Kenneth Landon 1990. Parentage: *N. flavovirens* × *N.* 'St. Louis Gold'. Characteristics: Nonviviparous, free flowering. Plate 160.

PETAL COLOR: Yellow. *R.H.S. Chart*: Fan 1, Yellow Group, No. 8C. Sepal color: Yellowish green, greenish veins. *R.H.S. Chart*: Fan 1, Green-Yellow Group, No. 1C; veins, Fan 3, Yellow-Green Group, No. 145C. Anther color: Dark yellow, lighter yellow tips. *R.H.S. Chart*: Fan 1, Yellow Group, No. 12A; tips, No. 8C. Stamen color: Deep yellow. Flower shape: Stellate. Flower size: 7–8 in (18–20 cm). Fragrance: Delightful. Number of petals: 15–20, average 18. Number of sepals: 4.

LEAF COLOR: Top, green; underside, green, suffused purple or violet, prominent green veins. Leaf and sinus: Leaf a little longer than wide; sinus usually open. Leaf size: 13 in (33 cm), much smaller than most star lilies. Leaf spread: 4–8 ft (1.2–2.5 m), average 6 ft (2 m). Stem color: Pale olive green. Pubescence on peduncle or petiole: None.

COMMENTS: Kenneth Landon selected 'Ineta Ruth' as the very best of 85 seedlings. Blooms open early and stay open until late afternoon—an average of 14 hours per day. This is the first true yellow star lily. Flowers are produced in profusion. I highly recommend it for the medium and large pool.

Nymphaea **'Isabella Pring'** George H. Pring 1941. Parentage: Unknown. Characteristics: Viviparous, very free flowering. Plate 161.

PETAL COLOR: Creamy white. *R.H.S. Chart*: Fan 4, White Group, No. 155C. Sepal color: Creamy white. *R.H.S. Chart*: Fan 4, White Group, No. 155C. Anther color: Yellow, creamy white tips. *R.H.S. Chart*: Fan 1, Yellow Group, No. 4B; tips, Fan 4, White Group,

No. 155C. Stamen color: Yellow. Flower shape: Large star. Flower size: 7–10 in (18–25 cm). Fragrance: Delightful. Number of petals: 23–24. Number of sepals: 4.

LEAF COLOR: Top, green, scattering of purple flecks; underside, green, flecked reddish brown. Leaf and sinus: Leaves nearly round, quite dentate; lobes usually overlap considerably at sinus. Leaf size: 12–14 in (30–35 cm). Leaf spread: 5–7 ft (1.5–2.2 m). Stem color: Peduncle, bronzy green; petiole brownish. Pubescence on peduncle or petiole: None.

COMMENTS: A fine white tropical for the medium and large pool. Being viviparous, it can withstand more cold and more shade than most other white day-blooming tropicals.

Nymphaea 'Jack Wood' John Wood 1972. Parentage: Unknown. Characteristics: Nonviviparous, very free flowering. Plate 162.

PETAL COLOR: Raspberry red. *R.H.S. Chart*: Fan 2, Red-Purple Group, No. 66C. Sepal color: Deep red. *R.H.S. Chart*: Fan 1, Red Group, No. 53C. Anther color: Brownish orange, raspberry-red tips. *R.H.S. Chart*: Fan 4, Greyed-Orange Group, No. 172C; tips, Fan 2, Red-Purple Group, No. 66C. Stamen color: Bright yellow. Flower shape: Stellate, long sepals. Flower size: 8–10 in (20–25 cm). Fragrance: Lovely. Number of petals: 25–26. Number of sepals: 4.

LEAF COLOR: Top, green, some purple blotches on new leaves; underside, reddish, dark purple blotches. Leaf and sinus: Leaves nearly round, dentate edges; lobes overlap at sinus. Leaf size: 10–12 in (25–30 cm). Leaf spread: 6–7 ft (2–2.2 m). Stem color: Bronzy green. Pubescence on peduncle or petiole: None.

COMMENTS: This is one of the most striking water lilies ever developed. I highly recommend 'Jack Wood' for medium and large pools. It can even be used in small pools if planted in a 10-in (25-cm) pot to restrict growth. In most pools I would recommend building a pedestal out of blocks or bricks so that there is 8–10 in (20–25 cm) of water over the pot. Blooms will be produced freely if fertilizer tablets are added once a month.

Nymphaea 'Janice C. Wood' John Wood 1982. Parentage: Unknown. Characteristics: Nonviviparous, flowers freely. Plate 163.

PETAL COLOR: White. *R.H.S. Chart*: Fan 4, White Group, No. 155D. Sepal color: White. *R.H.S. Chart*: Fan 4, White Group, No. 155D. Anther color: Yellow, white tips. *R.H.S. Chart*: Fan 1, Yellow Group, No. 5C; tips, Fan 4, White Group, No. 155D. Stamen color: Yellow. Flower shape: Stellate, full. Flower

size: 7–8 in (18–20 cm). Fragrance: Very nice, sweet. Number of petals: 25–26. Number of sepals: 4.

LEAF COLOR: Top, very heavily blotched and mottled purple, smaller areas of green or yellow; underside, greenish, very heavily blotched purple. Leaf and sinus: Leaf nearly round, slightly serrated; sinus usually closed yet about 1 in (2.5 cm) may be open. Leaf size: 12 in (30 cm). Leaf spread: 6 ft (2 m). Stem color: Greenish bronze. Pubescence on peduncle or petiole: None.

COMMENTS: 'Janice C. Wood' has magnificent leaves—among the most beautiful of any day-blooming tropical. I recommend it for any medium or large pool.

Nymphaea 'Jo Ann' Van Ness Water Gardens 1981. Parentage: Unknown. Characteristics: Nonviviparous, very free flowering. Plate 164.

PETAL COLOR: Raspberry red. *R.H.S. Chart*: Fan 2, Red-Purple Group, No. 64D. Sepal color: Deeper red than petals. *R.H.S. Chart*: Fan 2, Red-Purple Group, No. 60B. Anther color: Orange, raspberry-red tips. *R.H.S. Chart*: Fan 1, Orange Group, No. 26A; tips, Fan 2, Red-Purple Group, No. 64D. Stamen color: Glowing yellow. Flower shape: Cuplike. Flower size: 7–8 in (18–20 cm). Fragrance: Very pleasant. Number of petals: 32–33. Number of sepals: 4.

LEAF COLOR: Top, deep green; underside, pinkish red. Leaf and sinus: Leaf large, nearly round; sinus usually open. Leaf size: 10–13 in (25–33 cm). Leaf spread: 5–6 ft (1.5–2 m). Stem color: Pink. Pubescence on peduncle or petiole: A few hairs on petiole and on underwater portion of peduncle.

COMMENTS: A fine lily for medium and large pools. It will do well in semishaded pools.

Nymphaea 'Judge Hitchcock' George H. Pring 1941. Parentage: *N. stuhlmannii* is probably one parent according to Charles Masters. Characteristics: Nonviviparous, very free flowering. Plate 165.

PETAL COLOR: Blue, nearly purple. *R.H.S. Chart*: Fan 2, Violet-Blue Group, No. 91A. Sepal color: More purplish than petals, 12–14 prominent gray or greenish lengthwise veins. *R.H.S. Chart*: Fan 2, Violet Group, No. 95A; veins, Fan 4, Greyed-Green Group, No. 190C. Anther color: Butterscotch, purplish blue tips. *R.H.S. Chart*: Fan 1, Orange Group, No. 26C; tips, Violet-Blue Group, No. 91A. Stamen color: Yellow. Flower shape: Cuplike, full. Flower size: 6–8 in (15–20 cm). Fragrance: Very highly scented. Number of petals: 24. Number of sepals: 4.

LEAF COLOR: Top, green, many purple blotches radiating from center; underside, pinkish, many purple mottles. Leaf and sinus: Leaf nearly round, slightly longer than wide, slight indentation at apex opposite main vein. Lobes overlap about halfway down sinus. Leaf size: 10 in (25 cm). Leaf spread: 5 ft (1.5 m). Stem color: Brown. Pubescence on peduncle or petiole: None.

COMMENTS: A medium-sized tropical that can be used in pools of any size, including small pools. In central Florida (USDA zone 9a) this water lily has performed well in half-shade.

Nymphaea **'King of Blues'** Perry D. Slocum 1955. Parentage: Seedling of *N. capensis* var. *zanzibariensis*. Characteristics: Nonviviparous, very free flowering. Plate 166.

PETAL COLOR: Very deep violet-blue. *R.H.S. Chart*: Fan 2, Violet-Blue Group, No. 90D. Sepal color: Deep violet-blue. *R.H.S. Chart*: Fan 2, Violet Group, No. 87C. Anther color: Butterscotch, deep violet-blue tips. *R.H.S. Chart*: Fan 1, Orange Group, No. 26C; tips, No. 90D. Stamen color: Deep yellow. Flower shape: Stellate, full. Flower size: 7–9 in (18–23 cm). Fragrance: Very delightful. Number of petals: 26–28. Number of sepals: 4.

LEAF COLOR: Top, yellowish green, some purple blotches; underside, purple, prominent green veins. Leaf and sinus: Leaf egg-shaped, longer than wide, edges convoluted, dully serrated; sinus either open or fully closed. Leaf size: Up to 13 × 11 in (33 × 28 cm). Leaf spread: 6–8 ft (2–2.5 m). Stem color: Yellowish green. Pubescence on peduncle or petiole: None.

COMMENTS: I selected this magnificent seedling for propagation and feel it is truly one of the most beautiful blues for a medium or large pool. It readily produces seeds; some seedlings may develop pink flowers as well as various shades of blue.

Nymphaea **'Laura Frase'** Bill Frase 1960. Parentage: *N.* 'Blue Beauty' × *N.* 'Panama Pacific'. Characteristics: Nonviviparous, free flowering. Plate 167.

PETAL COLOR: Medium dark blue. *R.H.S. Chart*: Fan 2, Blue Group, No. 100C. Sepal color: Lighter blue than petals. *R.H.S. Chart*: Fan 2, Violet-Blue Group, No. 97B. Anther color: Yellow, medium dark blue tips. *R.H.S. Chart*: Fan 1, Yellow Group, No. 8C; tips, Fan 2, Blue Group, No. 100C. Stamen color: Yellow. Flower shape: Somewhat cuplike. Flower size: 8–11 in (20–28 cm). Fragrance: Delightful. Number of petals: 36. Number of sepals: 4.

LEAF COLOR: Top, green, blotched purple, new leaves bronzy; underside, red, purple blotches, prominent green veins. Leaf and sinus: Leaf nearly round; sinus open on new leaves, overlapped by lobe on older leaves. Leaf size: 12–14 in (30–35 cm). Leaf spread: 6–8 ft (2–2.5 m). Stem color: Olive

green. Pubescence on peduncle or petiole: None.

COMMENTS: 'Laura Frase' is a beautiful shade of forget-me-not blue that strongly impresses most viewers. Bill named this cultivar after his wife. I recommend it for medium and large pools.

Nymphaea **'Leopardess'** Martin E. Randig 1931. Parentage: Unknown. Characteristics: Nonviviparous, free flowering; noted for its remarkably beautiful leaves. Plate 168.

PETAL COLOR: Clear blue, purple tips. *R.H.S. Chart*: Fan 2, Violet-Blue Group, No. 97C; tips, Purple Group, No. 78B. Sepal color: Clear blue. *R.H.S. Chart*: Fan 2, Violet-Blue Group, No. 97C. Anther color: Yellowish. *R.H.S. Chart*: Fan 1, Yellow Group, No. 8D. Stamen color: Yellow. Flower shape: Cuplike. Flower size: 4–5 in (10–13 cm). Fragrance: Slight. Number of petals: 30. Number of sepals 4.

LEAF COLOR: Top, purple, green blotches; underside, green, heavily speckled purple. Leaf and sinus: Leaf nearly round; lobes usually overlap at sinus. Leaf size: 10–12 in (25–30 cm). Leaf spread: 4–5 ft (1.2–1.5 m). Stem color: Gray-brown. Pubescence on peduncle or petiole: None.

COMMENTS: With its magnificent purple mottled leaves and clear blue flowers, 'Leopardess' commands instant attention. I highly recommend it for any size pool.

Nymphaea **'Louella G. Uber'** Van Ness Water Gardens 1970. Parentage: Unknown. Characteristics: Nonviviparous, very free flowering; blooms stay open later than most tropicals. Plate 169.

PETAL COLOR: White. *R.H.S. Chart*: Fan 4, White Group, No. 155D. Sepal color: White, prominent grayish green veins. *R.H.S. Chart*: Fan 4, White Group, No. 155D; veins, Fan 4, Greyed-Green Group, No. 195C. Anther color: Yellow, white tips. *R.H.S. Chart*: Fan 1, Yellow Group, No. 13A; tips, Fan 4, White Group, No. 155D. Stamen color: Yellow. Flower shape: Stellate. Flower size: 8–10 in (20–25 cm). Fragrance: Very pleasant. Number of petals: 16–18. Number of sepals: 4.

LEAF COLOR: Top, green; underside, pink, flecked maroon. Leaf and sinus: Leaves nearly round, quite dentate; sinus either open or closed. Leaf size: 10–12 in (25–30 cm). Leaf spread: 6 ft (2 m). Stem color: Pink. Pubescence on peduncle or petiole: None.

COMMENTS: A fine water lily for the medium and large water garden.

Nymphaea **'Margaret Mary'** George L. Thomas, Jr., 1964. Parentage: Unknown. Characteristics: Moderately viviparous, extremely free flowering. Plate 170.

PETAL COLOR: Deep, rich blue. *R.H.S. Chart*: Fan

2, Violet-Blue Group, No. 94C. Sepal color: Lighter blue than petals. *R.H.S. Chart*: Fan 2, Violet-Blue Group, No. 92C. Anther color: Deep, rich yellow. *R.H.S. Chart*: Fan 1, Yellow Group, No. 13B. Stamen color: Yellow. Flower shape: Cuplike then stellate. Flower size: 5–6.5 in (13–16 cm). Fragrance: Delightful. Number of petals: 24. Number of sepals: 4.

LEAF COLOR: Top, green, new leaves lightly mottled purple; underside, purple, green veins. Leaf and sinus: Leaf longer than wide; lobes usually overlap sinus halfway to completely, occasionally an open V. Leaf size: 10 × 9 in (25 × 23 cm). Leaf spread: 4–5 ft (1.2–1.5 m). Stem color: Brown to purplish brown. Pubescence on peduncle or petiole: Tiny hairs on underwater portions.

COMMENTS: The beautiful blue color is similar to that of 'Blue Beauty.' This is one of my favorites for a small pool or a tub garden. For many years I have chosen this lily for a bathtub pool in a North Carolina display garden in a spot that receives shade for over half the day. Once it starts to bloom it is practically always with flower—frequently more than one at a time. This lily held plant patent No. 2453 (now expired) by George L. Thomas, Jr.

Nymphaea **'Margaret Randig'** Martin E. Randig 1939. Parentage: Unknown. Characteristics: Nonviviparous, very free flowering. Plate 171.

PETAL COLOR: Blue. *R.H.S. Chart*: Fan 2, Violet-Blue Group, No. 91C. Sepal color: Blue. *R.H.S. Chart*: Fan 2, Violet-Blue Group, No. 91C. Anther color: Inner anthers yellowish orange, tips blue; outer anthers deeper blue-purple. *R.H.S. Chart*: Fan 1, Orange Group, No. 26C; tips, Fan 2, Violet-Blue Group, No. 91C; outer, No. 90D. Stamen color: Golden yellow. Flower shape: Very large, round, flat. Flower size: 8–11 in (20–28 cm). Fragrance: Delightful. Number of petals: 22. Number of sepals: 4.

LEAF COLOR: Top, deep green; underside, purplish, darker in lobes, prominent green veins. Leaf and sinus: Leaves nearly round, large round serrations; younger leaves may not show serrations. Sinus varies, usually about ⅔ open. Leaf size: Up to 13 × 12 in (33 × 30 cm). Leaf spread: 8–9 ft (2.5–2.7 m). Stem color: Peduncle, reddish brown, green closest to flower; petiole, brown. Pubescence on peduncle or petiole: None.

COMMENTS: Flower color is the same even shade throughout each flower. 'Margaret Randig' is a great lily for medium and large pools.

Nymphaea **'Marian Strawn'** Kirk Strawn 1969. Parentage: *N.* 'Mrs. George H. Pring' × unknown. Characteristics: Nonviviparous, very free flowering. Plate 172.

PETAL COLOR: White. *R.H.S. Chart*: Fan 4, White Group, No. 155D. Sepal color: White. *R.H.S. Chart*: Fan 4, White Group, No. 155D. Anther color: Yellow, white tips. *R.H.S. Chart*: Fan 1, Yellow Group, No. 4C; tips, Fan 4, White Group, No. 155D. Stamen color: Yellow. Flower shape: Stellate, full. Flower size: 8–10 in (20–25 cm). Fragrance: Lovely. Number of petals: 22. Number of sepals: 6.

LEAF COLOR: Top, green, many irregular purple blotches radiate from center; underside, light green, mottled reddish purple. Leaf and sinus: Leaf longer than wide, convoluted, serrated, lightly dentate; lobes overlap at sinus. Leaf size: Up to 13 × 11 in (33 × 28 cm). Leaf spread: 7–8 ft (2.2–2.5 m). Stem color: Green or bronzy green. Pubescence on peduncle or petiole: None.

COMMENTS: A very fine tropical for the medium and large pool.

Nymphaea **'Mark Pullen'** Charles Winch 1987. Parentage: Unknown. Characteristics: Nonviviparous, flowers freely. Plate 173.

PETAL COLOR: Rich violet-blue. *R.H.S. Chart*: Fan 2, Violet-Blue Group, No. 91A. Sepal color: Pale bluish green. *R.H.S. Chart*: Fan 3, Blue-Green Group, No. 123C. Anther color: Inner anthers yellow, violet-blue tips; outer anthers violet-blue. *R.H.S. Chart*: Fan 1, Yellow Group, No. 13B; tips and outer anthers, Fan 2, Violet-Blue Group, No. 91A. Stamen color: Yellow. Flower shape: Cuplike then stellate, full. Flower size: 7–8 in (18–20 cm). Fragrance: Lightly scented. Number of petals: 37–44. Number of sepals: 4–5.

LEAF COLOR: Top, green; underside, purplish red, small red freckles, prominent green veins. Leaf and sinus: Leaf nearly round, edges wavy; lobes overlap at sinus, one lobe usually raised slightly. Leaf size: Up to 12 × 11.5 in (30 × 29 cm). Leaf spread: 5–6 ft (1.5–2 m). Stem color: Peduncle brown, green above water; petiole mostly brown, greenish near leaf. Pubescence on peduncle or petiole: None.

COMMENTS: 'Mark Pullen' is a new introduction from Charles Winch of Sydney, Australia, and is named after his grandson. The color is terrific, one of my favorite blues, and the flower is very double. I highly recommend this lily for medium and large pools.

Nymphaea **'Mary Mirgon'** Charles Winch 1988. Parentage: *N.* 'Cup Pink' × unknown. Characteristics: Nonviviparous, very free flowering. Plate 174.

PETAL COLOR: Lavender-purple. *R.H.S. Chart*: Fan 2, Red-Purple Group, Nos. 70B–C. Sepal color: Slightly deeper lavender-purple than petals. *R.H.S. Chart*: Fan 2, Red-Purple Group, No. 70B. Anther color: Butterscotch, lavender-purple tips. *R.H.S. Chart*: Fan 4, Greyed-Orange Group, No. 167B; tips, Fan 2, Red-Purple Group, Nos. 70B–C. Stamen color: Deep yellow. Flower shape: Cuplike, full. Flower size: 6–8 in (15–20 cm). Fragrance: Sweet, reminiscent of raspberries. Number of petals: 32. Number of sepals: 4.

LEAF COLOR: Top, medium green, slightly mottled near sinus; underside, blushed red. Leaf and sinus: Leaves heart-shaped, undulating edges; lobes open at sinus. Leaf size: Up to 10 in (25 cm). Leaf spread: 3–4 ft (1–1.2 m). Stem color: Deep green. Pubescence on peduncle or petiole: None.

COMMENTS: 'Mary Mirgon', a beautifully colored tropical, is a magnificent introduction from Australia. It will do well in any size pool. It is named in honor of the wife of John Mirgon, founder and first president of the Colorado Water Lily Society, the first such society in the United States.

Nymphaea **'Midnight'** George H. Pring 1941. Parentage: *N. colorata* × *N. capensis* var. *zanzibariensis*. Characteristics: Nonviviparous, very free flowering. Anthers develop as small petals. Plate 175.

PETAL COLOR: Deep violet-blue. *R.H.S. Chart*: Fan 2, Violet-Blue Group, No. 94B. Sepal color: Deep violet-blue. *R.H.S. Chart*: Fan 2, Violet-Blue Group, No. 94B. Anther color: Deep violet-blue. *R.H.S. Chart*: Fan 2, Violet-Blue Group, No. 94B. (No true anthers.) Stamen color: Yellow. Flower shape: Starlike, full. Flower size: 6–8 in (15–20 cm). Fragrance: Slight. Number of petals: 95–123. Number of sepals: 4.

LEAF COLOR: Top, bright green; underside, violet. Leaf and sinus: Leaf nearly round, quite dentate; lobes overlap at sinus. Leaf size: 9–10 in (23–25 cm). Leaf spread: 4–6 ft (1.2–2 m). Stem color: Bronzy to purple. Pubescence on peduncle or petiole: A few hairs on underwater portions of peduncle and on petiole.

COMMENTS: 'Midnight' is unique among tropical cultivars in that the stamen tops have become small petals. These displace the anthers and create a delicate fringe in the center of the blooms. A good choice for any size pool.

Nymphaea **'Mr. Martin E. Randig'** Martin E. Randig 1967. Parentage: Unknown. Characteristics: Nonviviparous, free flowering. Plate 176.

PETAL COLOR: Deep pink. *R.H.S. Chart*: Fan 2, Red-Purple Group, No. 68B. Sepal color: Slightly deeper pink than petals. *R.H.S. Chart*: Fan 2, Red-Purple Group, No. 70B. Anther color: Yellowish orange, deep pink tips. *R.H.S. Chart*: Fan 1, Yellow-Orange Group, No. 23B; tips, Fan 2, Red-Purple

Group, No. 68B. Stamen color: Deep yellow. Flower shape: Cuplike then almost flat. Flower size: 6–8 in (15–20 cm). Fragrance: Pleasant. Number of petals: 20–21. Number of sepals: 4.

LEAF COLOR: Top, olive green, heavily mottled deep purple; underside, red, heavily mottled deep red-purple. Leaf and sinus: Leaf nearly round, rounded projections at perimeter; lobes usually overlap completely at sinus. Leaf size: Up to 12 × 10.5 in (30 × 27 cm). Leaf spread: 5–6 ft (1.5–2 m). Stem color: Bronzy green. Pubescence on peduncle or petiole: None.

COMMENTS: Wonderful flower color and marvelous leaves with particularly beautiful markings make this a fine choice for medium and large pools.

Nymphaea **'Mrs. C. W. Ward'**. See *N.* **'Red Star'**.

Nymphaea **'Mrs. Charles Winch'** Charles Winch 1986. Parentage: Unknown. Characteristics: Nonviviparous, free flowering. Plate 177.

PETAL COLOR: Bright yellow. *R.H.S. Chart*: Fan 1, Yellow Group, No. 4A. Sepal color: Greenish yellow. *R.H.S. Chart*: Fan 1, Green-Yellow Group, No. 1B. Anther color: Greenish yellow. *R.H.S. Chart*: Fan 1, Green-Yellow Group, No. 1B. Stamen color: Yellow. Flower shape: Starlike. Flower size: 6 in (15 cm). Fragrance: Very pleasant. Number of petals: 16. Number of sepals: 6.

LEAF COLOR: Top, green, variegated blue and red; underside, green, mottled blue. Leaf and sinus: Leaf, oval-shaped; sinus, closed. Leaf size: 6–8 in (15–20 cm). Leaf spread: 6 ft (2 m). Stem color: Bronze. Pubescence on peduncle or petiole: None.

COMMENTS: 'Mrs. Charles Winch' needs heat to get established. It should not be placed outdoors until temperatures reach 75°F (24°C). Like most yellow tropicals, it opens late and closes late. I recommend it for the medium or large pool.

Nymphaea **'Mrs. Edwards Whitaker'** George H. Pring 1917. Parentage: *N. ovalifolia* × *N.* **'Castaliflora'**. Characteristics: Nonviviparous, extremely free flowering. Plate 178.

PETAL COLOR: Light blue. *R.H.S. Chart*: Fan 2, Violet-Blue Group, No. 92D. Sepal color: Light blue, green tips. *R.H.S. Chart*: Fan 2, Violet-Blue Group, No. 92D; tips, Fan 3, Green Group, No. 143D. Anther color: Yellow, light blue tips. *R.H.S. Chart*: Fan 1, Yellow Group, No. 13B; tips, Fan 2, Violet-Blue Group, No. 92D. Stamen color: Deep yellow. Flower shape: Stellate, large. Flower size: 9–12 in (23–30 cm). Fragrance: Pronounced. Number of petals: 21. Number of sepals: 4.

LEAF COLOR: Top, green, some small purple mottles; underside, green, purple blotches. Leaf and sinus: Leaf a little longer than wide; lobes usually overlap at sinus. Leaf size: Up to 13 × 12 in (33 × 30 cm). Leaf spread: 6–7 ft (2–2.2 m). Stem color: Green. Pubescence on peduncle or petiole: None.

COMMENTS: One of the older tropical water lilies and still one of the best for the medium and large pool. The huge flowers are very impressive.

Nymphaea '**Mrs. George H. Pring**' George H. Pring 1922. Parentage: *N. ovalifolia* × *N.* 'Mrs. Edwards Whitaker'. Characteristics: Nonviviparous, very free flowering. Plate 179.

PETAL COLOR: Creamy white, greenish gray stripes in outer petals. *R.H.S. Chart*: Fan 4, White Group, No. 155B; stripes, Greyed-Green Group, No. 190C. Sepal color: Creamy white, greenish gray stripes. *R.H.S. Chart*: Fan 4, White Group, No. 155B; stripes, Greyed-Green Group, No. 190C. Anther color: Yellow, creamy white tips. *R.H.S. Chart*: Fan 1, Yellow Group, No. 7A; tips, Fan 4, White Group, No. 155B. Stamen color: Deep golden yellow. Flower shape: Stellate. Flower size: 7–8 in (18–20 cm). Fragrance: Pleasant, delicate. Number of petals: 21. Number of sepals: 4.

LEAF COLOR: Top, green, new leaves blotched purple; underside, green, purple blotches on old leaves fade somewhat. Leaf and sinus: Leaf egg-shaped, longer than wide, smooth edges. Extra-long lobes sometimes overlap completely at sinus, sometimes leave sinus partly open. Leaf size: Up to 16.5 × 13 in (42 × 33 cm). Leaf spread: 6–9 ft (2–2.7 m). Stem color: Peduncle, above water bright green, below water bronzy green; petiole, bronzy green. Pubescence on peduncle or petiole: None. Fuzzy algae frequently accumulate on stems and can easily be mistaken for pubescence.

COMMENTS: This water lily is the "old reliable" of white day-blooming tropicals. It is still hard to beat for all-around performance. Often an established plant will have five or six blooms at a time. I recommend it for medium or large pools.

Nymphaea '**Mrs. Martin E. Randig**' Martin E. Randig 1938. Parentage: Includes *N.* 'Panama Pacific', *N.* 'Daubeniana', *N.* 'Lilac Queen', *N.* 'Royal Zanzibar', *N.* 'Indigo Zanzibar', and *N.* 'Amethyst', according to Charles Masters, author of *Encyclopedia of the Water-lily*. Characteristics: Viviparous, very free flowering. Plate 180.

PETAL COLOR: Deep violet-blue. *R.H.S. Chart*: Fan 2, Violet-Blue Group, No. 91A. Sepal color: Purple. *R.H.S. Chart*: Fan 2, Purple Group, No. 75A. Anther color: Deep yellow. *R.H.S. Chart*: Fan 1, Yellow

Group, No. 13B. Stamen color: Yellow. Flower shape: Somewhat cuplike. Flower size: 4.5–6 in (11–15 cm). Fragrance: Very lovely. Number of petals: 23–24. Number of sepals: 4.

LEAF COLOR: Top, green; underside, deep red, prominent bright green veins on new pads. Leaf and sinus: Leaf nearly round; sinus usually an open V. Leaf size: 10 × 8 in (25 × 20 cm). Leaf spread: 3–5 ft (1–1.5 m). Stem color: Brown. Pubescence on peduncle or petiole: Fine fuzz and hair on underwater portions.

COMMENTS: U.S. plant patent No. 294 (now expired), the second ever issued for a water lily, was given to Martin E. Randig in November 1938 for *N.* 'Mrs. Martin E. Randig'. This is one of the finest water lilies. Like other viviparous varieties, it will withstand more cold weather than most blue tropicals. I recommend it for any size pool, including tub gardens.

Nymphaea '**Noelene**' Charles Winch 1972. Parentage: Unknown. Characteristics: Nonviviparous, free flowering.

PETAL COLOR: Lavender-pink. *R.H.S. Chart*: Fan 2, Purple Group, Nos. 75B–C. Sepal color: Lavender-pink. *R.H.S. Chart*: Fan 2, Purple Group, No. 75B. Anther color: Deep yellow. *R.H.S. Chart*: Fan 1, Yellow Group, No. 13B. Stamen color: Yellow. Flower shape: Stellate. Flower size: 6–9 in (15–23 cm). Fragrance: Very sweet. Number of petals: 16. Number of sepals: 4.

LEAF COLOR: Top, bright green, maroon mottles; underside, yellow-green, maroon mottles. Leaf and sinus: Leaf nearly round, convoluted along perimeter; lobes overlap at sinus. Leaf size: 8–10 in (20–25 cm). Leaf spread: 5–7 ft (1.5–2.2 m). Stem color: Bright green. Pubescence on peduncle or petiole: None.

COMMENTS: 'Noelene' is an Australian introduction in a new color class (lavender). It is a very worthwhile lily. I recommend it for medium and large pools. Like all tropicals in northern states, it should not be planted outside until all danger of cold is past.

Nymphaea '**Pamela**' August Koch 1931. Parentage: Unknown. Characteristics: Nonviviparous, very free flowering. Plate 181.

PETAL COLOR: Rich sky blue. *R.H.S. Chart*: Fan 2, Violet-Blue Group, No. 97B. Sepal color: Rich sky blue. *R.H.S. Chart*: Fan 2, Violet-Blue Group, No. 97B. Anther color: Yellow. *R.H.S. Chart*: Fan 1, Yellow Group, No. 12B. Stamen color: Outer stamens blue, base yellow; inner stamens yellow. Flower shape: Stellate, round, flat. Flower size: 8–13 in (20–33 cm). Fragrance: Very sweet. Number of petals: 21–27. Number of sepals: 4.

LEAF COLOR: Top, green, new leaves heavily blotched purple; underside, reddish, new leaves green, display many red blotches, prominent green veins on older leaves. Leaf and sinus: Leaf longer than wide; both lobes frequently rise up 1 in (2.5 cm) at junction or overlap. Leaf size: Up to 15 × 13.5 in (38 × 34 cm). Leaf spread: 5–8 ft (1.5–2.5 m). Stem color: Mostly brown; peduncle green above water. Pubescence on peduncle or petiole: Fine fuzz and hairs on older petioles and peduncles below water; none on peduncles above water.

COMMENTS: 'Pamela' is one of my favorite blues. The color of the flower is terrific, the leaves are magnificent, and the plant is a profuse bloomer. This lily is ideal for the medium or large pool.

Nymphaea **'Panama Pacific'** William Tricker 1914. Parentage: Unknown. Characteristics: Viviparous, very free flowering. Plate 182.

PETAL COLOR: Deep violet-purple. *R.H.S. Chart*: Fan 2, Purple Group, No. 82C. Sepal color: Purple. *R.H.S. Chart*: Fan 2, Violet Group, No. 87D. Anther color: Yellow, violet tips. *R.H.S. Chart*: Fan 1, Yellow Group, No. 11A; tips, Fan 2, Purple Group, No. 77C. Stamen color: Yellow. Flower shape: Cuplike then stellate. Flower size: 4.5–6 in (11–15 cm). Fragrance: Very sweet. Number of petals: 21–22. Number of sepals: 4.

LEAF COLOR: Top, green; underside, purple, new leaves green then red, all heavily mottled purple. Leaf and sinus: Leaves nearly round; sinus an open V or lobes may overlap up to halfway down sinus. Leaf size: 9–11 in (23–28 cm). Leaf spread: 4–6 ft (1.2–2 m). Stem color: Brown. Pubescence on peduncle or petiole: Fine fuzz and tiny hairs on both.

COMMENTS: One of the viviparous varieties and among the hardiest of the tropicals. Produces young plants freely in the middle of its pads. I recommend it for any size pool, including a tub garden.

Nymphaea **'Patricia'** William Tricker pre-1940. Parentage: *N. colorata* is one of its parents. Characteristics: Viviparous, free flowering, small leaf spread. Plate 183.

PETAL COLOR: Pinkish red. *R.H.S. Chart*: Fan 2, Red-Purple Group, No. 70C. Sepal color: Slightly darker than petals. *R.H.S. Chart*: Fan 2, Red-Purple Group, Nos. 70B–C. Anther color: Yellowish orange, pinkish red tips. *R.H.S. Chart*: Fan 1, Orange Group, No. 26B; tips, Fan 2, Red-Purple Group, No. 70C. Stamen color: Yellow. Flower shape: Cuplike

then stellate. Flower size: 3–5 in (8–13 cm). Fragrance: Faint yet noticeably sweet. Number of petals: 19–20. Number of sepals: 4.

LEAF COLOR: Top, yellowish green; underside, red, many purplish red specks and blotches, prominent green veins. Leaf and sinus: Leaf a little longer than wide, moderately dentate, many small convolutions; usually an open V at sinus. Leaf size: 9–10 in (23–25 cm). Leaf spread: 3–5 ft (1–1.5 m). Stem color: Reddish brown. Pubescence on peduncle or petiole: Tiny hairs scattered on petiole and underwater portion of peduncle.

COMMENTS: More viviparous than most viviparous lilies as every leaf develops a plantlet. An excellent lily for the tub garden or small pool. Performs well in medium and large pools too.

Nymphaea **'Paul Stetson'** John Wood 1984. Parentage: Unknown. Characteristics: Viviparous, very free flowering. Plate 184.

PETAL COLOR: Sky blue. *R.H.S. Chart*: Fan 2, Violet-Blue Group, Nos. 92D–C. Sepal color: Light blue, darker blue veins. *R.H.S. Chart*: Fan 2, Violet-Blue Group, No. 92D; veins, No. 92C. Anther color: Yellowish orange. *R.H.S. Chart*: Fan 1, Orange Group, No. 26C. Stamen color: Yellow. Flower shape: Stellate. Flower size: 4–6 in (10–15 cm). Fragrance: Lovely. Number of petals: 18. Number of sepals: 4.

LEAF COLOR: Top, bright green, spotted maroon; underside, yellowish green, maroon mottles. Leaf and sinus: Leaf nearly round, lobe tips pointed; lobes overlap at sinus. Leaf size: 6–9 in (15–23 cm). Leaf spread: 3–4 ft (1–1.2 m). Stem color: Brownish red. Pubescence on peduncle or petiole: None.

COMMENTS: A wonderful cultivar for the tub garden or small or medium pool. It can be kept small by planting it in an 8–10 in (20–25 cm) pot or plastic dishpan. This lily frequently produces two or more blooms at a time.

Nymphaea **'Peach Blow'** George H. Pring 1941. Parentage: Unknown. Characteristics: Viviparous, very free flowering. Plate 185.

PETAL COLOR: Inner petals, light pink; outer petals medium pink. *R.H.S. Chart*: Inner petals, Fan 2, Red-Purple Group, No. 65C; outer, No. 65A. Sepal color: Greenish yellow. *R.H.S. Chart*: Fan 3, Yellow-Green Group, No. 150D. Anther color: Yellow, light pink tips. *R.H.S. Chart*: Fan 1, Yellow Group, No. 4C; tips, Fan 2, Red-Purple Group, No. 65C. Stamen color: Yellow. Flower shape: Full, peony-style. Flower size: 8–10 in (20–25 cm). Fragrance: Lovely. Number of petals: 34–36. Number of sepals: 4–5.

LEAF COLOR: Top, light green, new leaves sparsely flecked purple; underside, light green, flushed red. Leaf and sinus: Leaves nearly round, somewhat dentate; lobes overlap at sinus. Leaf size: Up to 12 in (30 cm). Leaf spread: 7–8 ft (2.2–2.5 m). Stem color: Green. Pubescence on peduncle or petiole: None.

COMMENTS: A two-toned pink lily displaying a large yellow center when the flower opens after the first day. The lovely pink-and-yellow combination makes one think of the peace rose or the 'Mrs. Perry D. Slocum' lotus. I highly recommend it for the medium and large pool.

Nymphaea **'Pennsylvania'**. See *N.* **'Blue Beauty'**.

Nymphaea **'Persian Lilac'** George H. Pring 1941. Parentage: Unknown. Characteristics: Nonviviparous, very free flowering. Plate 186.

PETAL COLOR: Pinkish lilac. *R.H.S. Chart*: Fan 2, Red-Purple Group, Nos. 69A–B. Sepal color: Paler than petals. *R.H.S. Chart*: Fan 2, Red-Purple Group, Nos. 69C–D. Anther color: Butterscotch, pinkish lilac tips. *R.H.S. Chart*: Fan 4, Greyed-Orange Group, No. 164B; tips, Fan 2, Purple Group, No. 75B. Stamen color: Deep yellow. Flower shape: Very full, peony-style. Flower size: 8–10 in (20–25 cm). Fragrance: Delightful. Number of petals: 41–42. Number of sepals: 4.

LEAF COLOR: Top, light green, new leaves sparsely flecked brownish red; underside, red. Leaf and sinus: Leaf a little longer than wide, dentate; sinus usually closed, lobes overlapping. Leaf size: Up to 10 in (25 cm). Leaf spread: 5–6 ft (1.5–2 m). Stem color: Bronzy green. Pubescence on peduncle or petiole: None.

COMMENTS: The flower is very full and the color is wonderful. I recommend 'Persian Lilac' for the small, medium, or large pool.

Nymphaea **'Pink Pearl'** August Koch. Parentage: *N.* 'Mrs. George H. Pring' is included in parentage. Characteristics: Nonviviparous, very free flowering; blooms held up to 12 in (30 cm) above water. Plate 187.

PETAL COLOR: Pinkish lavender. *R.H.S. Chart*: Fan 2, Purple Group, Nos. 75B–C. Sepal color: Pale lavender with grayish green veins. *R.H.S. Chart*: Fan 2, Red-Purple Group, No. 73D; veins, Fan 4, Greyed-Green Group, No. 193B. Anther color: Butterscotch, pinkish lavender tips. *R.H.S. Chart*: Fan 4, Greyed-Orange Group, No. 163A; tips, Fan 2, Purple Group, Nos. 75B–C. Stamen color: Deep yellow-orange. Flower shape: Cuplike. Flower size: 7–8 in

(18–20 cm). Fragrance: Very pleasant. Number of petals: 40–42. Number of sepals: 4.

LEAF COLOR: Top, deep green; underside, reddish brown. Leaf and sinus: Leaf nearly round, undulating perimeter; sinus either open or partly open. Leaf size: Up to 10 in (25 cm). Leaf spread: 4–5 ft (1.2–1.5 m). Stem color: Deep green. Pubescence on peduncle or petiole: None.

COMMENTS: Flowers are quite double and the color is excellent. 'Pink Pearl' is a fine lily for the small, medium, or large pool.

Nymphaea **'Pink Perfection'** Joseph Lingg 1951. Parentage: Unknown. Characteristics: Nonviviparous, very free flowering. Plate 188.

PETAL COLOR: Lavender-pink. *R.H.S. Chart*: Fan 2, Purple Group, No. 75B. Sepal color: Pale lavender-pink. *R.H.S. Chart*: Fan 2, Purple Group, No. 75D. Anther color: Yellow, lavender-pink tips. *R.H.S. Chart*: Fan 1, Yellow Group, No. 11A; tips, Fan 2, Purple Group, No. 75B. Stamen color: Yellow. Flower shape: Stellate, long, pointed sepals. Flower size: 8–10 in (20–25 cm). Fragrance: Very sweet. Number of petals: 24–26. Number of sepals: 4.

LEAF COLOR: Top, heavily variegated reddish purple and green; underside, green, purple blotches. Leaf and sinus: Leaf nearly round, somewhat dentate; sinus usually open, sometimes closed. Leaf size: 10–12 in (25–30 cm). Leaf spread: 5–7 ft (1.5–2.2 m). Stem color: Greenish. Pubescence on peduncle or petiole: None.

COMMENTS: Its magnificent leaves and gorgeous lavender-pink blooms with prominent yellow centers make 'Pink Perfection' a beautiful addition to any medium or large pool.

Nymphaea **'Pink Platter'** George H. Pring 1941. Parentage: Unknown. Characteristics: Slightly to moderately viviparous, very free flowering. Plate 189.

PETAL COLOR: Medium pink. *R.H.S. Chart*: Fan 1, Red Group, Nos. 37C–D. Sepal color: Deeper pink than petals. *R.H.S. Chart*: Fan 1, Red Group, No. 37C. Anther color: Inner anthers yellow, pink tips; outer anthers orange-pink. *R.H.S. Chart*: Inner anthers, Fan 1, Yellow Group, No. 12B, tips, Red Group, Nos. 37C–D; outer, Orange-Red Group, No. 31C. Stamen color: Deep yellow. Flower shape: Large, round, flat. Flower size: 7–10 in (18–25 cm). Fragrance: Some. Number of petals: 26–30. Number of sepals: 4.

LEAF COLOR: Top, olive green, lightly mottled purple (mottles more prominent on new leaves); underside, green, perimeter pink, new leaves pinkish, prominent green veins. Leaf and sinus: Leaves nearly round, wavy, somewhat serrated; sinus usually an open V on young plants, lobes overlap on older plants. Leaf size: 9–10 in (23–25 cm). Leaf spread: 5–6 ft (1.5–2 m). Stem color: Peduncle green above water, mostly brown below water; petiole brown, green near leaf. Pubescence on peduncle or petiole: None.

COMMENTS: 'Pink Platter' is moderately viviparous when conditions are right. On one plant I once found four leaves with small plants starting. Like other viviparous lilies, this plant will take more cold, especially in spring, than most day-blooming varieties. It is an excellent choice for medium and large pools.

Nymphaea **'Pink Star'** (syn. 'Stella Gurney') James Gurney 1900–1905(?). Parentage: Chance seedling of *N.* 'Mrs. C. W. Ward' according to George H. Pring. Characteristics: Nonviviparous, very free flowering.

PETAL COLOR: Pink. *R.H.S. Chart*: Fan 2, Red-Purple Group, No. 73C. Sepal color: Slightly deeper pink than petals. *R.H.S. Chart*: Fan 2, Red-Purple Group, No. 73B. Anther color: Yellowish brown, pink tips. *R.H.S. Chart*: Fan 4, Greyed-Orange Group, No. 167B; tips, Fan 2, Red-Purple Group, No. 73C. Stamen color: Orange-yellow. Flower shape: Stellate. Flower size: 7–8 in (18–20 cm). Fragrance: Pleasant. Number of petals: 17–18. Number of sepals: 4.

LEAF COLOR: Top, green; underside, green, usually flushed pinkish. Leaf and sinus: Leaf longer than wide, dentate; sinus usually open. Leaf size: 17 × 15.5 in (43 × 39 cm). Leaf spread: Up to 10–12 ft (3–3.5 m). Stem color: Green. Pubescence on peduncle or petiole: None.

COMMENTS: Like other star lilies, 'Pink Star' withstands more cold than many of the other tropicals. Prolific leaf production. It is an excellent plant, but only for the large water garden.

Nymphaea **'Red Beauty'** Perry D. Slocum 1966. Parentage: Seedling of *N. capensis* var. *zanzibariensis*. Characteristics: Nonviviparous, free flowering. Plate 190.

PETAL COLOR: Deep pinkish red. *R.H.S. Chart*: Fan 2, Purple Group, No. 77B. Sepal color: Dark red-purple. *R.H.S. Chart*: Fan 2, Red-Purple Group, No. 70A. Anther color: Inner anthers, yellow, red-purple tips; outer anthers, red-purple. *R.H.S. Chart*: Inner anthers, Fan 1, Yellow Group, No. 13C, tips, Fan 2, Purple Group, No. 77B; outer anthers, Red-Purple Group, Nos. 64B–C. Stamen color: Yellow.

Flower shape: Cuplike. Flower size: 5–6 in (13–15 cm). Fragrance: Delightful. Number of petals: 34. Number of sepals: 4.

LEAF COLOR: Top, green, few faint purple blotches; new leaves on young plants bronzy, purple mottles. Underside color varies widely; some mostly green, some red or pinkish at perimeter with green center and prominent green veins. Leaf and sinus: Leaf longer than wide, convoluted, serrated; sinus either an open V or up to × closed. Leaf size: 12.5–14 in (32–35 cm). Leaf spread: 5–6 ft (1.5–2 m). Stem color: Top several inches green, lower portions light brown. Pubescence on peduncle or petiole: None.

COMMENTS: 'Red Beauty' has excellent color and is a good choice for medium or large pools. It does have a rather small flower relative to its large leaves, however.

Nymphaea **'Red Star'** (syn. 'Mrs. C. W. Ward') William Tricker 1899(?). Parentage: *N. flavovirens* × unknown. Characteristics: Nonviviparous, very free flowering; blooms held 12 in (30 cm) above water. Plate 191.

PETAL COLOR: Reddish pink. *R.H.S. Chart*: Fan 2, Red-Purple Group, No. 64D. Sepal color: Slightly deeper reddish pink than petals. *R.H.S. Chart*: Fan 2, Red-Purple Group, No. 64B. Anther color: Orange, reddish pink tips. *R.H.S. Chart*: Fan 1, Orange-Red Group, No. 31B; tips, Fan 2, Red-Purple Group, No. 64D. Stamen color: Yellow. Flower shape: Stellate. Flower size: 6–8 in (15–20 cm). Fragrance: Sweet and lovely. Number of petals: 15–16. Number of sepals: 4.

LEAF COLOR: Top, green; underside, red, maroon spots. Leaf and sinus: Leaves large, egg-shaped, somewhat convoluted; sinus generally open. Leaf size: 12–15 in (30–38 cm). Leaf spread: 8 ft (2.5 m). Stem color: Bronzy red. Pubescence on peduncle or petiole: None.

COMMENTS: Where space allows, 'Red Star' is a fine addition to the medium or large pool.

Nymphaea **'Rhonda Kay'** Kenneth Landon 1984. Parentage: *N. capensis* var. *zanzibariensis* 'Purpurea' × *N. flavovirens*. Characteristics: Nonviviparous, very free flowering; blooms held 12 in (30 cm) above water. Plate 192.

PETAL COLOR: Violet-blue. *R.H.S. Chart*: Fan 2, Violet-Blue Group, No. 96B. Sepal color: Deeper violet than petals. *R.H.S. Chart*: Fan 2, Violet-Blue Group, No. 96A. Anther color: Butterscotch. *R.H.S. Chart*: Fan 4, Greyed-Orange Group, No. 167B. Stamen color: Deep yellow. Flower shape: Stellate.

Flower size: 6 in (15 cm). Fragrance: Sweet. Number of petals: 23. Number of sepals: 4.

LEAF COLOR: Top, green; underside, green. Leaf and sinus: Leaf a little longer than wide; lobes overlap at sinus. Leaf size: 11–12 in (28–30 cm), very small for a star lily. Leaf spread: 6–9 ft (2–2.7 m). Stem color: Green or bronzy green. Pubescence on peduncle or petiole: None.

COMMENTS: Blooms, held very high above the water, have a most striking color. This is an excellent new tropical and a terrific bloomer as well. I highly recommend it for the medium or large pool.

Nymphaea **'Robert Strawn'** Kirk Strawn 1969. Parentage: *N. elegans* × unknown. Characteristics: Nonviviparous, free flowering; blooms held 12 in (30 cm) above water. Plate 193.

PETAL COLOR: Deep lavender-blue. *R.H.S. Chart*: Fan 2, Violet Group, No. 85A. Sepal color: Outer ⅔ deep lavender-blue, light green base. *R.H.S. Chart*: Outer ⅔, Fan 2, Violet Group, No. 85A; base, Fan 4, Greyed-Green Group, No. 192D. Anther color: Orange, lavender-blue tips. *R.H.S. Chart*: Fan 4, Greyed-Red Group, No. 179D; tips, Fan 2, Violet Group, No. 85A. Stamen color: Yellow. Flower shape: Starlike. Flower size: 5–6 in (13–15 cm). Fragrance: Slight. Number of petals: 19–21. Number of sepals: 4–6.

LEAF COLOR: Top, green, small purple blotches; underside, purple, deep purple blotches, prominent green veins. Leaf and sinus: Leaf longer than wide; lobes usually overlap about halfway down sinus. Leaf size: Up to 15 × 13 in (38 × 33 cm). Leaf spread: 6–8 ft (2–2.5 m). Stem color: Purplish red. Pubescence on peduncle or petiole: A few tiny hairs on underwater stems.

COMMENTS: Dr. Kirk Strawn named this lily after his father. Flower stems are very long, holding flowers high above the water. I consider this only a fair plant for medium and large pools as its leaf spread is huge compared with its medium-sized flowers.

Nymphaea **'Rose Pearl'** John Wood 1976. Parentage: Unknown. Characteristics: Nonviviparous, very free flowering. Plate 194.

PETAL COLOR: Raspberry red. *R.H.S. Chart*: Fan 2, Red-Purple Group, No. 63B. Sepal color: Deeper raspberry red than petals. *R.H.S. Chart*: Fan 2, Red-Purple Group, No. 63A. Anther color: Orange-red, pink tips. *R.H.S. Chart*: Fan 1, Red Group, No. 37A; tips, Fan 2, Red-Purple Group, No. 63C. Stamen color: Yellow. Flower shape: Broad stellate. Flower size: 8–10 in (20–25 cm). Fragrance: Very pleasant. Number of petals: 28. Number of sepals: 4.

LEAF COLOR: Top, green; underside, green. Leaf and sinus: Leaves large, dentate, prominent light green veins on top; sinus usually open, sometimes partly closed. Leaf size: Up to 15 in (38 cm). Leaf spread: 6–8 ft (2–2.5 m). Stem color: Greenish. Pubescence on peduncle or petiole: None.

COMMENTS: 'Rose Pearl', with its magnificent raspberry-red blossoms, is a fine lily for the medium and large pool.

Nymphaea **'Rose Star'** Edmund D. Sturtevant pre-1905. Parentage: Probably one parent is *N. flavovirens*, common to most star lilies. Characteristics: Nonviviparous, very free flowering; blooms held 12–15 in (30–38 cm) above water. Plate 195.

PETAL COLOR: Rosy pink, sometimes purplish near tips. *R.H.S. Chart*: Fan 2, Red-Purple Group, No. 65B; tips, No. 67B. Sepal color: Same as petals. Anther color: Orange, purple-pink tips. *R.H.S. Chart*: Fan 1, Orange Group, No. 26B; tips, Fan 2, Red-Purple Group, No. 67C. Stamen color: Inner stamens, burnt orange; outer, purplish. Flower shape: Stellate. Flower size: 7–8 in (18–20 cm). Fragrance: Very nice. Number of petals: 19–21. Number of sepals: 4.

LEAF COLOR: Top, green, a few purple mottles; underside, pinkish, a few purple blotches, prominent green veins. New leaves are red. Leaf and sinus: Leaves large, oval, convoluted, dentate; sinus varies from half open to fully closed. Leaf size: Up to 17 × 15.5 in (43 × 39 cm). Leaf spread 10–12 ft (3–3.5 m). Stem color: Bright yellowish green, bronzy underwater. Pubescence on peduncle or petiole: None.

COMMENTS: Plants can be very impressive, especially well-established plants that produce a great many flowers. The huge leaf spread limits 'Rose Star' to very large pools.

Nymphaea **'Royal Purple'** Buskirk. Parentage: Unknown. Characteristics: Viviparous, free flowering. Plate 196.

PETAL COLOR: Rich violet-purple. Late season flower color pales in the southern United States, according to water lily expert Kenneth Landon of San Angelo, Texas. *R.H.S. Chart*: Fan 2, Violet-Blue Group, No. 92A. Sepal color: Purple. *R.H.S. Chart*: Fan 2, Violet-Blue Group, No. 90C. Anther color: Inner anthers, yellow; outer anthers, orange, violet-purple tips. *R.H.S. Chart*: Fan 1, Yellow Group, No. 11A; outer, Orange Group, No. 24B; tips, Fan 2, Violet-Blue Group, No. 92A. Stamen color: Yellowish. Flower shape: Cuplike then stellate. Flower size: 4–5 in (10–13 cm). Fragrance: Pleasant. Number of petals: 20–22. Number of sepals: 4.

LEAF COLOR: Top, green; underside, greenish purple, few mottles. Leaf and sinus: Leaf nearly round, irregularly dentate. Sinus usually open; lobes sometimes overlap, especially on new leaves. Leaf size: 9–11 in (23–28 cm). Leaf spread: 3.5–5 ft (1.1–1.5 m). Stem color: Brown. Pubescence on peduncle or petiole: Fine hairs on underwater portions.

COMMENTS: 'Royal Purple' is a slightly smaller and has more richly colored flowers than 'Panama Pacific' (which see). The flower almost appears to have a glow to it. I recommend it for the tub garden and small pool.

Nymphaea **'St. Louis'** George H. Pring 1932. Parentage: *N. stuhlmannii* × *N.* 'Mrs. George H. Pring'. Characteristics: Nonviviparous, very free flowering. Plate 197.

PETAL COLOR: Lemon yellow. *R.H.S. Chart*: Fan 1, Yellow Group, No. 2D. Sepal color: Lemon yellow, lengthwise green stripes. *R.H.S. Chart*: Fan 1, Yellow Group, No. 2D; stripes, Fan 3, Green Group, No. 130D. Anther color: Dark yellow, lemon-yellow tips. *R.H.S. Chart*: Fan 1, Yellow Group, No. 11A; tips, No. 2C. Stamen color: Deep golden yellow. Flower shape: Stellate. Flower size: 8–11 in (20–28 cm). Fragrance: Very pleasant. Number of petals: 29–31. Number of sepals: 4.

LEAF COLOR: Top, green, new leaves delicately blotched purple; underside, green. Leaf and sinus: Leaves very large, nearly round, smooth, edges somewhat wavy; sinus usually an open V. Leaf size: Up to 20 × 19 in (50 × 48 cm). Leaf spread: 8–10 ft (2.5–3 m). Stem color: Underwater stems bronzy brown; peduncle yellowish green above water. Pubescence on peduncle or petiole: None.

COMMENTS: Plant patent No. 55 (now expired) was issued in February 1933 to George H. Pring for 'St. Louis', making it the first water lily in the United States to be patented. This lily is one of the best performers of all the tropicals and very striking for the medium or large pool.

Nymphaea **'St. Louis Gold'** George H. Pring 1956. Parentage: *N. sulfurea* × *N.* 'African Gold'. Characteristics: Nonviviparous, free flowering. Plate 198.

PETAL COLOR: Deep yellow. *R.H.S. Chart*: Fan 1, Yellow-Orange Group, No. 20A. Sepal color: Deep yellow. *R.H.S. Chart*: Fan 1, Yellow-Orange Group, No. 20A. Anther color: Yellow-orange, deep yellow tips. *R.H.S. Chart*: Fan 1, Yellow-Orange Group, No. 14B; tips, No. 20A. Stamen color: Deep yellowish orange. Flower shape: Stellate. Flower size: 5–6 in (13–15 cm). Fragrance: Slightly sweet. Number of petals: 20–22. Number of sepals: 4.

LEAF COLOR: Top, olive green, new leaves bronzy, covered with small purple blotches, prominent light green veins; underside, green, new leaves light purple. Leaf and sinus: Leaf oval-shaped; sinus slightly open. Leaf size: 8–10 in (20–25 cm). Leaf spread 4–5 ft (1.2–1.5 m). Stem color: Purplish brown. Pubescence on peduncle or petiole: None.

COMMENTS: Flowers of 'St. Louis Gold' open late and close late. A magnificent lily for any size pool and an especially good choice for the small pool due to its restricted leaf spread.

Nymphaea **'Stella Gurney'**. See *N.* **'Pink Star'**.

Nymphaea **'Tammie Sue Uber'** Van Ness Water Gardens 1970. Parentage: Unknown. Characteristics: Nonviviparous, extremely free flowering.

PETAL COLOR: Fuchsia pink. *R.H.S. Chart*: Fan 2, Red-Purple Group, No. 73B. Sepal color: Lighter than petals. *R.H.S. Chart*: Fan 2, Red-Purple Group, No. 73D. Anther color: Yellow, fuchsia pink tips. *R.H.S. Chart*: Fan 1, Yellow Group, No. 2B; tips, Fan 2, Red-Purple Group, No. 73B. Stamen color: Yellow. Flower shape: Cuplike. Flower size: 7–8 in (18–20 cm). Fragrance: Pronounced. Number of petals: 18. Number of sepals: 4.

LEAF COLOR: Top, green, new leaves heavily mottled purple; underside, green. Leaf and sinus: Leaf nearly round, fairly smooth edges; sinus open. Leaf size: 10 in (25 cm). Leaf spread: 5–6 ft (1.5–2 m). Stem color: Brown or bronze. Pubescence on peduncle or petiole: None.

COMMENTS: Due to its restricted leaf spread, 'Tammie Sue Uber' can be used in any size pool.

Nymphaea **'Ted Uber'** Martin E. Randig 1965. Parentage: Unknown. Characteristics: Nonviviparous, very free flowering. Plate 199.

PETAL COLOR: White. *R.H.S. Chart*: Fan 4, White Group, No. 155D. Sepal color: White. *R.H.S. Chart*: Fan 4, White Group, No. 155A. Anther color: Yellow, white tips. *R.H.S. Chart*: Fan 1, Yellow Group, No. 13B; tips, Fan 4, White Group, No. 155D. Stamen color: Yellow. Flower shape: Large, cuplike then round, flat. Flower size: 8–10 in (20–25 cm). Fragrance: Very pronounced, pleasant. Number of petals: 24. Number of sepals: 4.

LEAF COLOR: Top, green; underside, green, new leaves red, turning to pink under lobes. Leaf and sinus: Leaf a little longer than wide, slightly serrated; lobes usually overlap at sinus, one lobe frequently raised. Leaf size: 11.5–12.5 in (29–32 cm). Leaf spread: 6–8 ft (2–2.5 m). Stem color: Peduncle, purplish brown above water, green below water; petiole green. Pubescence on peduncle or petiole: None.

COMMENTS: 'Ted Uber' is a wonderful lily when it grows properly, yet some growers complain that grotesque leaves develop. For the most part, this is an excellent choice for the medium or large pool.

Nymphaea **'Tina'** Van Ness Water Gardens 1974. Parentage: Unknown. Characteristics: Viviparous, very free flowering. Plate 200.

PETAL COLOR: Deep violet-purple. *R.H.S. Chart*: Fan 2, Violet-Blue Group, No. 91A. Sepal color: Outer ⅔ purple, base greenish. *R.H.S. Chart*: Outer ⅔, Fan 2, Purple Group, No. 76B; base, Fan 3, Yellow-Green Group, No. 144D. Anther color: Yellow, purple tips. *R.H.S. Chart*: Fan 1, Yellow Group, No. 13C; tips, Fan 2, Violet-Blue Group, No. 90C. Stamen color: Yellow. Flower shape: Cuplike. Flower size: 4.5–6 in (11–15 cm). Fragrance: Very nice. Number of petals: 15–16. Number of sepals: 4.

LEAF COLOR: Top, green, new leaves bronzy; underside, light red or pink, new leaves red, prominent green veins. Leaf and sinus: Leaf slightly longer than wide, smooth, wavy edges; sinus usually wide open. Leaf size: 10.5 × 9.5 in (27 × 24 cm). Leaf spread: 3–5 ft (1–1.5 m). Stem color: Reddish purple. Pubescence on peduncle or petiole: None.

COMMENTS: Although this lily has relatively few petals, it is one of the most satisfactory water lilies for the small pool or tub garden. It is a great favorite at some water gardens in Australia where it outsells all other water lilies, both hardies and tropicals. 'Tina' is a good performer in medium and large pools too.

Nymphaea **'White Delight'** Charles Winch 1984. Parentage: Unknown. Characteristics: Nonviviparous, extremely free flowering. Plate 201.

PETAL COLOR: Light yellow, center petals slightly deeper yellow; occasionally older flowers tipped pink. *R.H.S. Chart*: Inner petals, Fan 1, Yellow Group, No. 2C; outer petals, No. 4D or paler; pink tips (occasional), Fan 2, Red-Purple Group, Nos. 65B–C. Sepal color: Whitish yellow, pink-tipped on older blooms, prominent greenish gray veins. *R.H.S. Chart*: Fan 4, White Group, No. 155A; tips, Fan 2, Red-Purple Group, Nos. 65B–C; veins, Fan 4, Greyed-Green Group, No. 193C. Anther color: Deep yellow. *R.H.S. Chart*: Fan 1, Yellow Group, No. 6A. Stamen color: Deep yellow. Flower shape: Stellate. Flower size: 10–12 in (25–30 cm). Fragrance: Pronounced. Number of petals: 26–29. Number of sepals: 4.

LEAF COLOR: Top, green, new leaves heavily mottled purple; underside, greenish, pink under lobes, heavily mottled. Leaf and sinus: Leaves large, egg-shaped; lobes overlap sinus, one lobe frequently

raised. Leaf size: Up to 13 × 12 in (33 × 30 cm). Leaf spread: 6–7 ft (2–2.2 m). Stem color: Greenish bronze. Pubescence on peduncle or petiole: None.

COMMENTS: 'White Delight', with its huge and numerous blooms, is one of the finest recent introductions. I highly recommend it for medium and large pools.

Nymphaea **'William C. Uber'** Van Ness Water Gardens 1970. Parentage: Unknown. Characteristics: Nonviviparous, very free flowering. Plate 202.

PETAL COLOR: Fuchsia red. *R.H.S. Chart*: Fan 2, Red-Purple Group, No. 58C. Sepal color: Fuchsia red. *R.H.S. Chart*: Fan 2, Red-Purple Group, No. 58C. Anther color: Reddish orange, pink tips. *R.H.S. Chart*: Fan 1, Orange-Red Group, No. 31B; tips, Fan 2, Red-Purple Group, No. 73C. Stamen color: Deep yellow. Flower shape: Cuplike, full. Flower size: 8–9 in (20–23 cm). Fragrance: Pleasant. Number of petals: 18–19. Number of sepals: 4.

LEAF COLOR: Top, green; underside, green. Leaf and sinus: Leaf nearly round, fairly smooth edge; sinus open. Leaf size: 10–12 in (25–30 cm). Leaf spread: 5–6 ft (1.5–2 m). Stem color: Bronzy green. Pubescence on peduncle or petiole: None.

COMMENTS: A beautiful, splendidly colored cultivar. This is one I can recommend for pools of every size, especially medium and large pools.

Nymphaea **'William Stone'**. See *N.* **'Blue Star'**.

Nymphaea **'Wood's Blue Goddess'** John Wood 1989. Parentage: *N. ampla* is one of the parents. Characteristics: Nonviviparous, free flowering. Forms bulblets around main tuber, similar to *N. colorata*. Plate 203.

PETAL COLOR: Deep sky blue then lighter blue in bright sunny weather. *R.H.S. Chart*: Fan 2, Blue Group, Nos. 104B–D. Sepal color: Generally lighter blue than petals. *R.H.S. Chart*: Fan 2, Blue Group, No. 104D. Anther color: Very deep violet, sky-blue tips. *R.H.S. Chart*: Fan 2, Violet-Blue Group, No. 94A; tips, Blue Group, Nos. 104B–D. Stamen color: Deep violet. Flower shape: Stellate. Flower size: 10–12 in (25–30 cm). Fragrance: Faint. Number of petals: 20. Number of sepals: 4.

LEAF COLOR: Top, olive green; underside, purple-blue. Leaf and sinus: Leaf nearly round, sharply serrated; sinus usually closed. Leaf size: 12–13 in (30–33 cm). Leaf spread: 8 ft (2.5 m). Stem color: Reddish brown. Pubescence on peduncle or petiole: None.

COMMENTS: This is a unique water lily—its large medium blue flowers with very dark, almost black, violet stamens give a very striking effect. 'Wood's

Blue Goddess' was voted most outstanding tropical water lily introduction at the 1987 International Water Lily Society Symposium, where it was on display as 'Blue Ampla'. I recommend it for medium or large pools.

Nymphaea **'Yellow Dazzler'** Martin E. Randig 1938. Parentage: Unknown. Characteristics: Nonviviparous, free flowering. Plate 204.

PETAL COLOR: Lemon yellow. *R.H.S. Chart*: Fan 1, Yellow Group, No. 2C. Sepal color: Yellowish green, prominent darker yellowish green veins. *R.H.S. Chart*: Fan 3, Yellow-Green Group, No. 150D; veins, No. 148D. Anther color: Golden yellow, lemon-yellow tips. *R.H.S. Chart*: Fan 1, Yellow Group, No. 7B; tips, No. 2C. Stamen color: Deep golden yellow. Flower shape: Stellate, large. Flower size: 8–10 in (20–25 cm). Fragrance: Very pleasant. Number of petals: 23. Number of sepals: 4.

LEAF COLOR: Top, green, a few purple blotches; underside, green, faint purplish or bluish tinge. Leaf and sinus: Leaves large, egg-shaped, edges quite smooth, some convolutions; sinus usually closed. Leaf size: Up to 17 × 14.5 in (43 × 37 cm). Leaf spread: 6–8 ft (2–2.5 m). Stem color: Brownish red. Pubescence on peduncle or petiole: None.

COMMENTS: 'Yellow Dazzler' is an excellent lily for the medium and large pool. Flowers can seem rather small relative to the leaves.

Nymphaea **'Yellow Star'**. See *N.* **'Ineta Ruth'**.

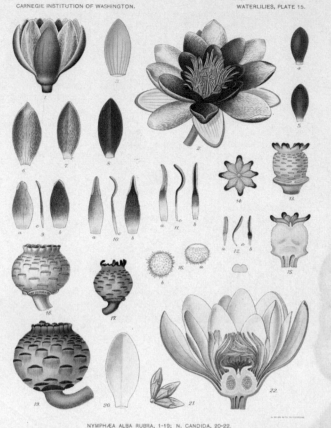

NYMPHÆA ALBA RUBRA, 1–19; N. CANDIDA, 20–22.

Nymphæa alba rubra. 1, Partly opened flower. 2, Fully opened flower on its last day. 3, Sepal. 4–8, Petals. 9–12, Stamens of successive whorls from outside inward, viewed from front side and back. 13, Ovary stripped of sepals, petals and stamens, from the side. 14, Stigma and styles from above. 15, Section of ovary. 16, Pollen, from pole and from side. 17–19, Fruits. 20, Petal. 21, Stigmas and styles. 22, Flower cut in half.

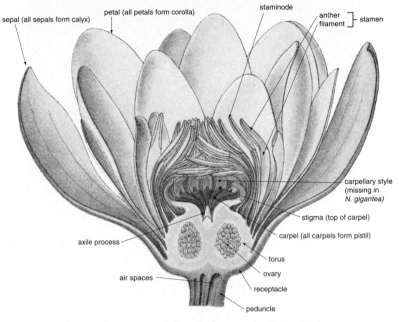

PLATE 107. Cross section of a hardy water lily flower. After a plate from *The Waterlilies: A Monograph of the Genus Nymphaea* by Henry S. Conard (1905).

PLATE 106. *Nymphaea alba* var. *rubra* (1–19) and *N. candida* (20–22). Partly opened flower (1); fully opened flower on its last day (2); sepal (3); petals (4–8); stamens of successive whorls from outside inward, viewed from front and back (9–12); ovary stripped of sepals, petals, and stamens, from the side (13); stigma and styles, from above (14); section of ovary (15); pollen, from pole and from side (16); fruits (17–19); petal (20); stigma and styles (21); cross section of flower (22). From *The Waterlilies: A Monograph of the Genus Nymphaea* by Henry S. Conard (1905).

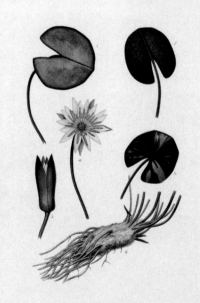

PLATE 108. *Nymphaea sulfurea*. From *The Waterlilies: A Monograph of the Genus Nymphaea* by Henry S. Conard (1905).

PLATE 109. *Nymphaea gigantea*. PERRY D. SLOCUM

PLATE 111. *Nymphaea gigantea* var. *neorosea*. PERRY D. SLOCUM

PLATE 112. *Nymphaea gigantea* var. *violacea*. PERRY D. SLOCUM

PLATE 113. *Nymphaea gigantea* 'Albert de Lestang'.
KENNETH C. LANDON

PLATE 114. *Nymphaea gigantea* 'Hudsoniana'.
KENNETH C. LANDON

PLATE 115. *Nymphaea gigantea* intermediate form 1, foreground; *Nymphaea gigantea* var. *alba*, background. KENNETH C. LANDON

PLATE 116. *Nymphaea ampla*. KENNETH C. LANDON

PLATE 117. *Nymphaea caerulea*. KENNETH C. LANDON

PLATE 118. *Nymphaea capensis* (cape water lily, blue capensis).
KENNETH C. LANDON

PLATE 119. *Nymphaea capensis* var. *zanzibariensis*
(blue Zanzibar), blue variation. PERRY D. SLOCUM

PLATE 120. *Nymphaea capensis* var. *zanzibariensis* 'Rosea'
(pink capensis). PERRY D. SLOCUM

PLATE 122. *Nymphaea elegans.* KENNETH C. LANDON

PLATE 123. *Nymphaea flavovirens.* KENNETH C. LANDON

PLATE 124. *Nymphaea nouchali,* white variation.
KENNETH C. LANDON

PLATE 125. *Nymphaea togoensis*. KENNETH C. LANDON

PLATE 126. *Nymphaea amazonum* subsp. *amazonum*. JANE READER

PLATE 127. *Nymphaea lotus*. KENNETH C. LANDON

PLATE 128. *Nymphaea rubra*. KENNETH C. LANDON

PLATE 129. *Nymphaea spontanea*. KENNETH C. LANDON

PLATE 130. Sprouted tropical water lily tuber. PERRY D. SLOCUM

PLATE 131. Tropical water lily plants showing tuber attached (left) and with tuber removed (right). PERRY D. SLOCUM

PLATE 132. Planting a tropical water lily. PERRY D. SLOCUM

PLATE 133. *Nymphaea* 'Afterglow'. PERRY D. SLOCUM

PLATE 134. *Nymphaea* 'Albert Greenberg'. PERRY D. SLOCUM

PLATE 135. *Nymphaea* 'Alice Tricker'. PERRY D. SLOCUM

PLATE 136.
Nymphaea
'American
Beauty'.
PERRY D. SLOCUM

PLATE 137. *Nymphaea* 'August Koch'. PERRY D. SLOCUM

PLATE 138.
Nymphaea
'Aviator Pring'.
PERRY D. SLOCUM

PLATE 139. *Nymphaea* 'Bagdad'. PERRY D. SLOCUM

PLATE 140. *Nymphaea* 'Bill Yohn'. PERRY D. SLOCUM

PLATE 141.
Nymphaea
'Black Prince'.
PERRY D. SLOCUM

PLATE 142.
Nymphaea
'Blue Beauty'.
PERRY D. SLOCUM

PLATE 143. *Nymphaea* 'Blue Bird', third-day flower.
PERRY D. SLOCUM

PLATE 144. *Nymphaea* 'Bob Trickett'. PERRY D. SLOCUM

PLATE 145. *Nymphaea* 'Charles Thomas'. PERRY D. SLOCUM

PLATE 146. *Nymphaea* 'Charles Winch'. PERRY D. SLOCUM

PLATE 147. *Nymphaea* 'Christine Lingg'. VAN NESS WATER GARDENS

PLATE 148. *Nymphaea* 'Daubeniana'. PERRY D. SLOCUM

PLATE 149. *Nymphaea* 'Daubeniana' showing plantlet in center of leaf. PERRY D. SLOCUM

PLATE 150. *Nymphaea* 'Director George T. Moore'.
PERRY D. SLOCUM

PLATE 151. *Nymphaea* 'Edward D. Uber'.
VAN NESS WATER GARDENS

PLATE 152. *Nymphaea* 'Eldorado'. PERRY D. SLOCUM

PLATE 153.
Nymphaea
'Enchantment'.
PERRY D. SLOCUM

PLATE 154.
Nymphaea
'Evelyn Randig'.
PERRY D. SLOCUM

PLATE 155.
Nymphaea
'General
Pershing', second-
day flower.
PERRY D. SLOCUM

PLATE 156.
Nymphaea 'Golden
Fascinator'.
PERRY D. SLOCUM

PLATE 157. *Nymphaea* 'Golden West'. PERRY D. SLOCUM

PLATE 158. *Nymphaea*
'Green Smoke'.
VAN NESS WATER GARDENS

PLATE 159. *Nymphaea* 'Henry Shaw'. LONGWOOD GARDENS

PLATE 160. *Nymphaea* 'Ineta Ruth'. PERRY D. SLOCUM

PLATE 161. *Nymphaea* 'Isabella Pring'. PERRY D. SLOCUM

PLATE 162. *Nymphaea*
'Jack Wood'.
VAN NESS WATER GARDENS

PLATE 164. *Nymphaea* 'Jo Ann'. VAN NESS WATER GARDENS

PLATE 163. *Nymphaea* 'Janice C. Wood'. PERRY D. SLOCUM

PLATE 165.
Nymphaea
'Judge Hitchcock'.
PERRY D. SLOCUM

PLATE 166.
Nymphaea
'King of Blues'.
PERRY D. SLOCUM

PLATE 167. *Nymphaea* 'Laura Frase'. PERRY D. SLOCUM

PLATE 168. *Nymphaea* 'Leopardess'. PERRY D. SLOCUM

PLATE 169. *Nymphaea* 'Louella G. Uber'.
VAN NESS WATER GARDENS

PLATE 170.
Nymphaea
'Margaret Mary'.
PERRY D. SLOCUM

PLATE 171.
Nymphaea
'Margaret
Randig'.
PERRY D. SLOCUM

PLATE 172. *Nymphaea* 'Marian Strawn'. PERRY D. SLOCUM

PLATE 173.
Nymphaea
'Mark Pullen'.
PERRY D. SLOCUM

PLATE 174. *Nymphaea* 'Mary Mirgon'. JOHN MIRGON

PLATE 175. *Nymphaea* 'Midnight'. PERRY D. SLOCUM

PLATE 176. *Nymphaea* 'Mr. Martin E. Randig'. PERRY D. SLOCUM

PLATE 178. *Nymphaea* 'Mrs. Edwards Whitaker'.
PERRY D. SLOCUM

PLATE 177. *Nymphaea* 'Mrs. Charles Winch'.
VAN NESS WATER GARDENS

PLATE 179. *Nymphaea* 'Mrs. George H. Pring'. PERRY D. SLOCUM

PLATE 180. *Nymphaea* 'Mrs. Martin E. Randig'. PERRY D. SLOCUM

PLATE 181. *Nymphaea* 'Pamela'. PERRY D. SLOCUM

PLATE 182. *Nymphaea* 'Panama Pacific'. PERRY D. SLOCUM

PLATE 183. *Nymphaea* 'Patricia'. PERRY D. SLOCUM

PLATE 184. *Nymphaea* 'Paul Stetson'. PERRY D. SLOCUM

PLATE 185. *Nymphaea* 'Peach Blow'. LONGWOOD GARDENS

PLATE 187. *Nymphaea* 'Pink Pearl'. PERRY D. SLOCUM

PLATE 186. *Nymphaea* 'Persian Lilac'. LONGWOOD GARDENS

PLATE 188. *Nymphaea* 'Pink Perfection'.
VAN NESS WATER GARDENS

PLATE 189. *Nymphaea* 'Pink Platter'. PERRY D. SLOCUM

PLATE 190. *Nymphaea* 'Red Beauty'. PERRY D. SLOCUM

PLATE 191. *Nymphaea* 'Red Star'. VAN NESS WATER GARDENS

PLATE 192. *Nymphaea* 'Rhonda Kay'. PERRY D. SLOCUM

PLATE 193.
Nymphaea
'Robert Strawn'.
PERRY D. SLOCUM

PLATE 194. *Nymphaea* 'Rose Pearl'. VAN NESS WATER GARDENS

PLATE 195. *Nymphaea* 'Rose Star'. PERRY D. SLOCUM

PLATE 197.
Nymphaea
'St. Louis'.
PERRY D. SLOCUM

PLATE 196. *Nymphaea* 'Royal Purple'. KENNETH C. LANDON

PLATE 199.
Nymphaea
'Ted Uber'.
PERRY D. SLOCUM

PLATE 198. *Nymphaea* 'St. Louis Gold'. PERRY D. SLOCUM

PLATE 200.
Nymphaea 'Tina'.
PERRY D. SLOCUM

PLATE 201.
Nymphaea
'White Delight'.
PERRY D. SLOCUM

PLATE 202. *Nymphaea* 'William C. Uber'. VAN NESS WATER GARDENS

PLATE 203. *Nymphaea* 'Wood's Blue Goddess'. PERRY D. SLOCUM

PLATE 204. *Nymphaea* 'Yellow Dazzler'. PERRY D. SLOCUM

PLATE 205. *Nymphaea* 'Antares'. PERRY D. SLOCUM

PLATE 206. *Nymphaea* 'Catherine Marie'. PERRY D. SLOCUM

PLATE 207. *Nymphaea* 'Emily Grant Hutchings'. LONGWOOD GARDENS

PLATE 208. *Nymphaea* 'H. C. Haarstick'. PERRY D. SLOCUM

PLATE 210.
Nymphaea 'Juno'.
PERRY D. SLOCUM

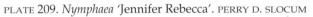

PLATE 209. *Nymphaea* 'Jennifer Rebecca'. PERRY D. SLOCUM

PLATE 211. *Nymphaea* 'Maroon Beauty'.
PERRY D. SLOCUM

PLATE 212. *Nymphaea* 'Missouri'.
PERRY D. SLOCUM

PLATE 213. *Nymphaea* 'Mrs. George C.
Hitchcock'. PERRY D. SLOCUM

PLATE 214. *Nymphaea* 'Red Cup'.
PERRY D. SLOCUM

PLATE 215. *Nymphaea* 'Red Flare'.
PERRY D. SLOCUM

PLATE 216. *Nymphaea* 'Sir Galahad'.
PERRY D. SLOCUM

PLATE 217. *Nymphaea* 'Texas Shell Pink'. GEORGE THOMAS III

PLATE 218.
Nymphaea
'Trudy Slocum'.
PERRY D. SLOCUM

PLATE 219. *Nymphaea* 'Wood's White Knight'.
VAN NESS WATER GARDENS

PLATE 220. Hardy water lily rhizomes. From top to bottom: upright, or pineapple; Marliac; odorata; tuberosa; and finger, or thumb.

PLATE 221.
Nymphaea
tetragona.
PERRY D. SLOCUM

PLATE 222. *Nymphaea alba*. KENNETH C. LANDON

PLATE 223. *Nymphaea alba*, Australian variation.
PERRY D. SLOCUM

PLATE 224. *Nymphaea candida*. BILL HERITAGE

PLATE 225. *Nymphaea odorata* (fragrant water lily) growing
naturally in a lake in south Georgia. PERRY D. SLOCUM

PLATE 226. *Nymphaea odorata*. PERRY D. SLOCUM

PLATE 227. *Nymphaea odorata* var. *gigantea*. PERRY D. SLOCUM

PLATE 228. *Nymphaea odorata* var. *rosea*. KENNETH C. LANDON

PLATE 229. *Nymphaea tuberosa*. PERRY D. SLOCUM

PLATE 230. *Nymphaea tuberosa*. PERRY D. SLOCUM

PLATE 231. *Nymphaea mexicana* (banana water lily). PERRY D. SLOCUM

PLATE 232. *Nymphaea mexicana* f. *canaveralensis*. PERRY D. SLOCUM

PLATE 233. *Nymphaea* 'Albatross'. PERRY D. SLOCUM

PLATE 234. *Nymphaea* 'Amabilis'.
PERRY D. SLOCUM

PLATE 235. *Nymphaea* 'American Star'.
PERRY D. SLOCUM

PLATE 236. *Nymphaea* 'Andreana'.
PERRY D. SLOCUM

PLATE 237. *Nymphaea* 'Apple Blossom
Pink'. PERRY D. SLOCUM

PLATE 238. *Nymphaea* 'Arc-en-Ciel'. PERRY D. SLOCUM

PLATE 239. *Nymphaea* 'Arethusa'.
PERRY D. SLOCUM

PLATE 240. *Nymphaea* 'Atropurpurea'.
PERRY D. SLOCUM

PLATE 241. *Nymphaea* 'Attraction'.
PERRY D. SLOCUM

PLATE 242.
Nymphaea
'Aurora', first-day
flower (left),
second-day flower
(bottom right),
third-day flower
(top).
PERRY D. SLOCUM

PLATE 243. *Nymphaea* 'Bory de Saint-Vincent'. PERRY D. SLOCUM

PLATE 245.
Nymphaea
'Carolina Sunset'.
PERRY D. SLOCUM

PLATE 244. *Nymphaea* 'Brackleyi Rosea'. PERRY D. SLOCUM

PLATE 247.
Nymphaea
'Charlene Strawn'.
PERRY D. SLOCUM

PLATE 246. *Nymphaea* 'Caroliniana Nivea'.
STAPELEY WATER GARDENS

PLATE 248.
Nymphaea 'Charles de Meurville'.
PERRY D. SLOCUM

PLATE 249.
Nymphaea 'Cherokee'.
PERRY D. SLOCUM

PLATE 250. *Nymphaea* 'Cherokee' showing new growth from blossom. JANE READER

PLATE 252. *Nymphaea* 'Colonel A. J. Welch'. PERRY D. SLOCUM

PLATE 251. *Nymphaea* 'Chrysantha', first-day flower (upper left), third-day flower (bottom). PERRY D. SLOCUM

PLATE 253. *Nymphaea* 'Colonel A. J. Welch' showing new growth from old blossom. PERRY D. SLOCUM

PLATE 254. *Nymphaea* 'Colossea'. PERRY D. SLOCUM

PLATE 255. *Nymphaea* 'Comanche', first- , second- , and third-day flowers (clockwise from top). PERRY D. SLOCUM

PLATE 256. *Nymphaea* 'Conqueror', first-day flower. PERRY D. SLOCUM

PLATE 257. *Nymphaea* 'Ellisiana', first-day flower (right), second-day flower (left). PERRY D. SLOCUM

PLATE 258. *Nymphaea* 'Escarboucle'. PERRY D. SLOCUM

PLATE 259. *Nymphaea* 'Eugene de Land'. PERRY D. SLOCUM

PLATE 260. *Nymphaea* 'Fabiola'. PERRY D. SLOCUM

PLATE 261.
Nymphaea
'Fantastic Pink'.
PERRY D. SLOCUM

PLATE 262. *Nymphaea* 'Firecrest'.
PERRY D. SLOCUM

PLATE 263. *Nymphaea* 'Formosa'.
PERRY D. SLOCUM

PLATE 264. *Nymphaea* 'Froebeli', first-day
flower and bud. PERRY D. SLOCUM

PLATE 265. *Nymphaea* 'Fulva'.
PERRY D. SLOCUM

PLATE 266. *Nymphaea* 'Gladstoniana'.
PERRY D. SLOCUM

PLATE 267. *Nymphaea* 'Gloire du Temple-sur-Lot'. PERRY D. SLOCUM

PLATE 268. *Nymphaea* 'Gloriosa'. PERRY D. SLOCUM

PLATE 269. *Nymphaea* 'Gold Medal'.
PERRY D. SLOCUM

PLATE 270. *Nymphaea* 'Gonnère'.
PERRY D. SLOCUM

PLATE 271. *Nymphaea* 'Hal Miller'
No. 2. PERRY D. SLOCUM

PLATE 272. *Nymphaea* 'Helen Fowler'. BILL HERITAGE

PLATE 273. *Nymphaea* 'Helvola'.
PERRY D. SLOCUM

PLATE 274. *Nymphaea* 'Hermine'.
PERRY D. SLOCUM

PLATE 275. Formerly 'Hermine' No. 2,
Nymphaea 'Alba Plenissima'.
PERRY D. SLOCUM

PLATE 276. Formerly 'Hollandia',
Nymphaea 'Darwin'. PERRY D. SLOCUM

PLATE 277. *Nymphaea* 'Indiana'.
PERRY D. SLOCUM

PLATE 278. *Nymphaea* 'Irene Heritage'.
PERRY D. SLOCUM

PLATE 279. *Nymphaea* 'James Brydon'.
PERRY D. SLOCUM

PLATE 280. *Nymphaea* 'Japanese Pygmy
Red', first-day flower (right), third-day
flower (left). PERRY D. SLOCUM

PLATE 281. *Nymphaea* 'Joanne Pring'.
PERRY D. SLOCUM

PLATE 282. *Nymphaea ×laydekeri* 'Alba'.
PERRY D. SLOCUM

PLATE 283. *Nymphaea ×laydekeri* 'Fulgens'.
PERRY D. SLOCUM

PLATE 284. *Nymphaea ×laydekeri* 'Fulgens' showing bacterial infection of the roots; note the profusion of blooms and foliage.
PERRY D. SLOCUM

PLATE 285. *Nymphaea ×laydekeri* 'Lilacea'. BILL HERITAGE

PLATE 286.
*Nymphaea
×laydekeri*
'Purpurata'.
PERRY D. SLOCUM

PLATE 287.
*Nymphaea
×laydekeri* 'Rosea'.
PERRY D. SLOCUM

PLATE 288. *Nymphaea* 'Louise'. HAL HOROWITZ

PLATE 289.
Nymphaea
'Luciana'.
PERRY D. SLOCUM

PLATE 290. *Nymphaea* 'Lucida'. PERRY D. SLOCUM

PLATE 291. *Nymphaea* 'Lustrous'.
PERRY D. SLOCUM

PLATE 292. *Nymphaea* 'M. Evelyn Stetson'.
PERRY D. SLOCUM

PLATE 293. *Nymphaea* 'Madame Wilfron Gonnère'. PERRY D. SLOCUM

PLATE 294. *Nymphaea* 'Marguerite Laplace', first-day flower (bottom), second-day flower (top). BILL HERITAGE

PLATE 295.
Nymphaea ×*marliacea* 'Albida'.
PERRY D. SLOCUM

PLATE 296.
Nymphaea ×*marliacea* 'Carnea'.
PERRY D. SLOCUM

PLATE 297. *Nymphaea ×marliacea* 'Chromatella'. PERRY D. SLOCUM

PLATE 298. *Nymphaea ×marliacea* 'Rosea' No. 2. PERRY D. SLOCUM

PLATE 299. *Nymphaea ×marliacea* 'Rubra Punctata'. PERRY D. SLOCUM

PLATE 301. *Nymphaea* 'Maurice Laydeker'. PERRY D. SLOCUM

PLATE 300. *Nymphaea* 'Masaniello'. PERRY D. SLOCUM

PLATE 302. *Nymphaea* 'Meteor'. PERRY D. SLOCUM

PLATE 303.
Nymphaea
'Moorei'.
PERRY D. SLOCUM

PLATE 304. *Nymphaea* 'Mrs. C. W. Thomas'.
LILYPONS WATER GARDENS

PLATE 305. *Nymphaea* 'Newton'. PERRY D. SLOCUM

PLATE 306. *Nymphaea* 'Norma Gedye'. PERRY D. SLOCUM

PLATE 307. *Nymphaea* 'Odalisque'. BILL HERITAGE

PLATE 308.
Nymphaea odorata
'Sulphurea'.
PERRY D. SLOCUM

PLATE 309. *Nymphaea odorata* 'Turicensis'.
STAPELEY WATER GARDENS

PLATE 310. *Nymphaea* 'Paul Hariot', first-day flower (top), third-day flower (bottom). PERRY D. SLOCUM

PLATE 311. *Nymphaea* 'Paul Hoffman'. PERRY D. SLOCUM

PLATE 312.
Nymphaea
'Pearl of the Pool'.
PERRY D. SLOCUM

PLATE 313.
Nymphaea 'Perry's
Baby Red'.
PERRY D. SLOCUM

PLATE 314. *Nymphaea* 'Perry's Black Opal', first-day flower (top), third-day flower (bottom). PERRY D. SLOCUM

PLATE 315. *Nymphaea* 'Perry's Cactus Pink'. PERRY D. SLOCUM

PLATE 316. *Nymphaea* 'Perry's Crinkled Pink'. PERRY D. SLOCUM

PLATE 317. *Nymphaea* 'Perry's Deepest Red'. PERRY D. SLOCUM

PLATE 318. *Nymphaea* 'Perry's Double White'. PERRY D. SLOCUM

PLATE 319. *Nymphaea* 'Perry's Dwarf Red'. PERRY D. SLOCUM

PLATE 320. *Nymphaea* 'Perry's Fire Opal'. PERRY D. SLOCUM

PLATE 321. *Nymphaea* 'Perry's Magnificent'. PERRY D. SLOCUM

PLATE 322. *Nymphaea* 'Perry's Pink'. PERRY D. SLOCUM

PLATE 323. *Nymphaea* 'Perry's Pink Beauty'. PERRY D. SLOCUM

PLATE 324. *Nymphaea* 'Perry's Pink Bicolor'. PERRY D. SLOCUM

PLATE 325. *Nymphaea* 'Perry's Pink Delight'. PERRY D. SLOCUM

PLATE 326. *Nymphaea* 'Perry's Pink Heaven'. PERRY D. SLOCUM

PLATE 327. *Nymphaea* 'Perry's Red Beauty'. PERRY D. SLOCUM

PLATE 328. *Nymphaea* 'Perry's Red Bicolor'. PERRY D. SLOCUM

PLATE 329. *Nymphaea* 'Perry's Red Blaze'. PERRY D. SLOCUM

PLATE 330. *Nymphaea* 'Perry's Red Glow'. PERRY D. SLOCUM

PLATE 331. *Nymphaea* 'Perry's Red Star'. PERRY D. SLOCUM

PLATE 332. *Nymphaea* 'Perry's Red Wonder'. PERRY D. SLOCUM

PLATE 333. *Nymphaea* 'Perry's Rich Rose'. PERRY D. SLOCUM

PLATE 334. *Nymphaea* 'Perry's Stellar Red'. PERRY D. SLOCUM

PLATE 335. *Nymphaea* 'Perry's Strawberry Pink'. PERRY D. SLOCUM

PLATE 336.
Nymphaea 'Perry's
Super Red'.
PERRY D. SLOCUM

PLATE 337.
Nymphaea 'Perry's
Super Rose'.
PERRY D. SLOCUM

PLATE 338. *Nymphaea* 'Perry's Vivid Rose'. PERRY D. SLOCUM

PLATE 339. *Nymphaea* 'Perry's Viviparous Pink', first-day flower in bloom, faded flower in hand showing new plantlet. PERRY D. SLOCUM

PLATE 340. *Nymphaea* 'Perry's White Star'. PERRY D. SLOCUM

PLATE 341. *Nymphaea* 'Perry's White Wonder'. PERRY D. SLOCUM

PLATE 342. *Nymphaea* 'Perry's Wildfire'. PERRY D. SLOCUM

PLATE 343.
Nymphaea
'Peter Slocum'.
PERRY D. SLOCUM

PLATE 344. *Nymphaea* 'Picciola'. PERRY D. SLOCUM

PLATE 345. *Nymphaea* 'Pink Opal'. PERRY D. SLOCUM

PLATE 346. *Nymphaea* 'Pink Sensation'. PERRY D. SLOCUM

PLATE 347. *Nymphaea* 'Pink Starlet'. PERRY D. SLOCUM

PLATE 348. *Nymphaea* 'Pöstlingberg'. PERRY D. SLOCUM

PLATE 349. *Nymphaea* ×*pygmaea* 'Rubra'. PERRY D. SLOCUM

PLATE 350. *Nymphaea* 'Queen of Whites'. PERRY D. SLOCUM

PLATE 351. *Nymphaea* 'Radiant Red'.
PERRY D. SLOCUM

PLATE 352. *Nymphaea* 'Ray Davies'.
PERRY D. SLOCUM

PLATE 353. *Nymphaea* 'Red Joanne Pring'.
PERRY D. SLOCUM

PLATE 354. *Nymphaea* 'Red Sensation'. PERRY D. SLOCUM

PLATE 355. *Nymphaea* 'René Gérard'. PERRY D. SLOCUM

PLATE 356.
Nymphaea
'Robinsoniana'.
PERRY D. SLOCUM

PLATE 357. *Nymphaea* 'Rosanna'. PERRY D. SLOCUM

PLATE 358. *Nymphaea* 'Rosanna Supreme'. PERRY D. SLOCUM

PLATE 359. *Nymphaea* 'Rose Arey'. PERRY D. SLOCUM

PLATE 360. *Nymphaea* 'Rose Magnolia'. PERRY D. SLOCUM

PLATE 361. *Nymphaea* 'Rosennymphe' No. 2. PERRY D. SLOCUM

PLATE 362. The true *Nymphaea* 'Rosénnymphe'. KIRK STRAWN

PLATE 364. *Nymphaea* 'Sanguinea'. BILL HERITAGE

PLATE 365. *Nymphaea* 'Seignoureti' No. 1. BILL HERITAGE

PLATE 366. *Nymphaea* 'Seignoureti' No. 2. PERRY D. SLOCUM

PLATE 367. *Nymphaea* 'Sioux', first-day flower (bottom), second-day flower (right), third-day flower (top left). PERRY D. SLOCUM

PLATE 368. *Nymphaea* 'Sirius', first-day flower. PERRY D. SLOCUM

PLATE 369. *Nymphaea* 'Solfatare'. PERRY D. SLOCUM

PLATE 370. *Nymphaea* 'Somptuosa', first-day flower. PERRY D. SLOCUM

PLATE 371. *Nymphaea* 'Splendida'. PERRY D. SLOCUM

PLATE 372. *Nymphaea* 'Sultan'. PERRY D. SLOCUM

PLATE 373. Formerly *N.* 'Sunrise', *Nymphaea odorata* 'Sulphurea Grandiflora'. PERRY D. SLOCUM

PLATE 374. *Nymphaea* 'Superba'.
PERRY D. SLOCUM

PLATE 375. *Nymphaea* 'Texas Dawn'.
PERRY D. SLOCUM

PLATE 376. *Nymphaea tuberosa* 'Maxima'.
PERRY D. SLOCUM

PLATE 377. *Nymphaea tuberosa* 'Richardsonii'. PERRY D. SLOCUM

PLATE 378. *Nymphaea* 'Venus'.
PERRY D. SLOCUM

PLATE 379. *Nymphaea* 'Vesuve'.
PERRY D. SLOCUM

PLATE 380. *Nymphaea* 'Virginalis'.
PERRY D. SLOCUM

PLATE 381. *Nymphaea* 'Virginia', third-day flower. PERRY D. SLOCUM

PLATE 382. *Nymphaea* 'White Cup'. PERRY D. SLOCUM

PLATE 383. *Nymphaea* 'William Falconer'. PERRY D. SLOCUM

PLATE 384. *Nymphaea* 'Wow'. PERRY D. SLOCUM

PLATE 385. *Nymphaea* 'Yellow Comanche'. PERRY D. SLOCUM

PLATE 386. *Nymphaea* 'Yellow Princess'.
PERRY D. SLOCUM

PLATE 387. *Nymphaea* 'Yellow Queen'.
PERRY D. SLOCUM

PLATE 388. *Nymphaea* 'Yellow Sensation'.
PERRY D. SLOCUM

PLATE 389. *Nelumbo nucifera*, rhizomes of the "edible lotus" variant. PERRY D. SLOCUM

PLATE 390. *Nelumbo lutea* (American yellow lotus, water chinquapin). PERRY D. SLOCUM

PLATE 391. *Nelumbo lutea* 'Yellow Bird'. PERRY D. SLOCUM

PLATE 392. *Nelumbo nucifera* (Hindu lotus, Egyptian lotus, sacred lotus, speciosa). PERRY D. SLOCUM

PLATE 393. *Nelumbo nucifera* var. *caspicum* (Russian lotus, red Russian lotus). PERRY D. SLOCUM

PLATE 394.
Nelumbo nucifera
var. *rosea* (rose
lotus), first-day
flower.
PERRY D. SLOCUM

PLATE 395.
Nelumbo nucifera
var. *rosea*, second-
day flower.
PERRY D. SLOCUM

PLATE 396. *Nelumbo nucifera* 'Alba Plena' (Shiroman lotus).
PERRY D. SLOCUM

PLATE 397. *Nelumbo nucifera* 'Japanese Double White'.
PERRY D. SLOCUM

PLATE 398.
Nelumbo nucifera
'Shirokunshi'
(tulip lotus).
PERRY D. SLOCUM

PLATE 399.
Nelumbo nucifera
'Waltzing
Matilda'.
PERRY D. SLOCUM

PLATE 400. *Nelumbo nucifera* 'Waltzing Matilda', leaves. PERRY D. SLOCUM

PLATE 401. *Nelumbo* 'Alba Grandiflora' (Asiatic lotus).
PERRY D. SLOCUM

PLATE 402. *Nelumbo* 'Alba Striata' (empress lotus), first-day flower. PERRY D. SLOCUM

PLATE 403. *Nelumbo* 'Alba Striata', second-day flower.
PERRY D. SLOCUM

PLATE 404. *Nelumbo* 'Angel Wings', foreground.
PERRY D. SLOCUM

PLATE 405. *Nelumbo* 'Angel Wings'.
PERRY D. SLOCUM

PLATE 406. *Nelumbo* 'Baby Doll' growing
in a plastic bushel planter.
PERRY D. SLOCUM

PLATE 407. *Nelumbo* 'Ben Gibson'.
PERRY D. SLOCUM

PLATE 408. *Nelumbo* 'Charles Thomas'. PERRY D. SLOCUM

PLATE 409.
Nelumbo
'Chawan Basu'.
PERRY D. SLOCUM

PLATE 410.
Nelumbo
'Debbie Gibson'.
PERRY D. SLOCUM

PLATE 412. *Nelumbo* 'Gregg Gibson'. PERRY D. SLOCUM

PLATE 411. *Nelumbo* 'Glen Gibson'. PERRY D. SLOCUM

PLATE 413. *Nelumbo* 'Linda'. PERRY D. SLOCUM

PLATE 414. *Nelumbo* 'Maggie Belle Slocum', the lotus and the lady. PERRY D. SLOCUM

PLATE 415. *Nelumbo* 'Momo Botan'. PERRY D. SLOCUM

PLATE 416. *Nelumbo* 'Mrs. Perry D. Slocum'. PERRY D. SLOCUM

PLATE 417. *Nelumbo* 'Nikki Gibson', first-day flower. PERRY D. SLOCUM

PLATE 418. *Nelumbo* 'Patricia Garrett'. PERRY D. SLOCUM

PLATE 419. Co-owner Ben Gibson and a display bed of *Nelumbo* 'Pekinensis Rubra' (red lotus) at Perry's Water Gardens, Franklin, North Carolina. PERRY D. SLOCUM

PLATE 420. *Nelumbo* 'Pekinensis Rubra', first-day flower. PERRY D. SLOCUM

PLATE 421. *Nelumbo* 'Pekinensis Rubra', second-day flower. PERRY D. SLOCUM

PLATE 422. *Nelumbo* 'Pekinensis Rubra', third-day flower. PERRY D. SLOCUM

PLATE 423. *Nelumbo* 'Perry's Giant Sunburst'. PERRY D. SLOCUM

PLATE 424. *Nelumbo* 'Perry's Super Star', first-day flower. PERRY D. SLOCUM

PLATE 426. *Nelumbo* 'Perry's Super Star', third-day flower. PERRY D. SLOCUM

PLATE 425. *Nelumbo* 'Perry's Super Star', second-day flower. PERRY D. SLOCUM

PLATE 427. *Nelumbo* 'Rosea Plena' (double rose lotus). PERRY D. SLOCUM

PLATE 428. *Nelumbo* 'Sharon'. PERRY D. SLOCUM

PLATE 429.
Nelumbo
'Suzanne'.
PERRY D. SLOCUM

PLATE 430.
Nelumbo
'The Queen'.
PERRY D. SLOCUM

PLATE 431. *Nuphar japonica* (Japanese pond lily), third-day flower and new floating leaf. PERRY D. SLOCUM

PLATE 432. *Nuphar lutea* subsp. *macrophylla* (American spatterdock), Lake Pierce, Florida. PERRY D. SLOCUM

PLATE 433. *Victoria amazonica* (giant water lily, Amazon water lily), first-day flower. PERRY D. SLOCUM

PLATE 434. *Victoria amazonica*, second-day flower. PERRY D. SLOCUM

PLATE 435.
Victoria amazonica,
leaf coverage.
PERRY D. SLOCUM

PLATE 436.
Victoria amazonica,
underside of leaf.
PERRY D. SLOCUM

PLATE 437. *Victoria cruziana* (Santa Cruz water lily), second-day flower. PERRY D. SLOCUM

PLATE 438. *Victoria* 'Longwood Hybrid', first-day flower. PERRY D. SLOCUM

PLATE 439. *Victoria* 'Longwood Hybrid', second-day flower. PERRY D. SLOCUM

PLATE 440. *Victoria* 'Longwood Hybrid', spines on underside of leaf. KENNETH C. LANDON

PLATE 441. *Euryale ferox* (prickly water lily, Gorgon plant), leaf coverage. PERRY D. SLOCUM

PLATE 442. *Euryale ferox*. PERRY D. SLOCUM

PLATE 443. *Euryale ferox*, underside of leaf. PERRY D. SLOCUM

PLATE 444. *Barclaya longifolia*. PERRY D. SLOCUM

PLATE 445. *Ondinea* tubers. ED SCHNEIDER

PLATE 446. *Ondinea purpurea* subsp. *petaloidea*. ED SCHNEIDER

Chapter 14

Tropical Water Lilies: Night-Blooming Cultivars

The cultivars of night-blooming tropical water lilies usually open about dusk and close between 11 a.m. and noon the following day. Cold fall days can cause them to remain open for longer periods. Like the day bloomers, these cultivars usually open and close for three or four successive days.

The following plant descriptions are an alphabetical listing of the night-blooming cultivars currently listed in nursery catalogs (see Appendix B for a list of these sources). The cultivar name is followed by any synonyms; next is the name of the hybridizer or originator, followed by the date, if known. Standardized color references are to the Royal Horticultural Society (R.H.S.) Color Chart.

Note that "Stamen color" refers to the color of the filament, the basal portion of the stamen. "Leaf size" is either the diameter of the leaf of a mature plant or the measurements of its length and width, in that order. "Leaf spread" refers to the diameter of the area on the water's surface covered by the leaves of a mature plant.

"Comments" on each plant include reference to what size pool is suitable. Although there are no hard rules differentiating pool sizes, general guidelines follow:

> tub garden: up to 3 ft (1 m) in diameter
> small: 4–6 ft (1.2–2 m) in diameter
> medium: 7–9 ft (2.2–2.7 m) in diameter
> large: 10 ft (3 m) in diameter or larger
> natural pond: dirt or mud bottom pond of any size

Note that copper and redwood are toxic to plants and fish and should be used only in conjunction with a plastic or other fish-safe liner.

Plant tropical water lilies only when the water temperature averages 75°F (24°C) or above. Planting too early may induce dormancy. See the hardiness zone maps in Appendix A and follow this general planting timetable:

> IN NORTH AMERICA
> Zone 10   March/early April
> Zone 9   early April
> Zone 8   mid April
> Zone 7   mid/late May
> Zone 6   late May/early June
> Zone 5   early/mid June
> Zone 4   mid/late June

In Europe
Zone 10   mid/late May
Zone 9   June
Zones 8–4   conservatory planting, where water can be heated to 75°F (24°C) or higher

Nymphaea '**Antares**' Longwood Gardens 1962. Parentage: *N.* 'H. C. Haarstick' × *N.* 'Emily Grant Hutchings'. Characteristics: Nonviviparous, free flowering. Plate 205.

PETAL COLOR: Dark rosy red. *R.H.S. Chart*: Fan 1, Red Group, No. 50A. Sepal color: Dark rosy red. *R.H.S. Chart*: Fan 1, Red Group, No. 50A. Anther color: Deep red. *R.H.S. Chart*: Fan 1, Orange-Red Group, No. 31C. Stamen color: Orange. Flower shape: Cuplike. Flower size: 6–10 in (15–25 cm). Fragrance: Pungent. Number of petals: 30–36. Number of sepals: 4.

LEAF COLOR: Top, green, newest leaves bronzy with green veins; underside, brown. Leaf and sinus: Leaf round, perimeter undulating, pointed projections; sinus open. Leaf size: 10–12 in (25–30 cm). Leaf spread: 5–7 ft (1.5–2.2 m). Stem color: Reddish brown. Pubescence on peduncle or petiole: Very short hairs on both.

COMMENTS: This is an exceptional night-blooming tropical with excellent color. 'Antares' was developed at Longwood Gardens by Patrick Nutt. I recommend this lily for medium and large pools.

Nymphaea '**Catherine Marie**' Kenneth Landon 1990. Parentage: *N.* 'Wood's White Knight' × *N.* 'Red Flare'. Characteristics: Nonviviparous, free flowering. Plate 206.

PETAL COLOR: Rich pink. *R.H.S. Chart*: Fan 2, Red-Purple Group, No. 68A. Sepal color: Maroon. *R.H.S. Chart*: Fan 1, Red Group, No. 47C. Anther color: Orange-red. *R.H.S. Chart*: Fan 1, Red Group, No. 42B. Stamen color: Pale yellow. Flower shape: Round, full, somewhat flat across top when fully open. Flower size: 8–10 in (20–25 cm). Fragrance: Very pungent. Number of petals: 30. Number of sepals: 4.

LEAF COLOR: Top, olive green; underside, olive green. Leaf and sinus: Leaf nearly round, lobes slightly divergent or overlap at sinus. Leaf size: 12–14 in (30–35 cm). Leaf spread: 6–8 ft (2–2.5 m). Stem color: Maroon. Pubescence on peduncle or petiole: Occasionally faint on both.

COMMENTS: Kenneth Landon selected this cultivar out of many seedlings due to its outstanding beauty and performance. I consider it a raving beauty that will go far in the water garden world. I recommend it for medium and large pools.

Nymphaea '**Emily Grant Hutchings**' George H. Pring 1922. Parentage: *N.* 'C. E. Hutchings' × unknown.

Characteristics: Nonviviparous, very free flowering. Plate 207.

PETAL COLOR: Dark pink. *R.H.S. Chart*: Fan 2, Red-Purple Group, No. 66D. Sepal color: Dark pink. *R.H.S. Chart*: Fan 2, Red-Purple Group, No. 67B. Anther color: Dark orange-pink. *R.H.S. Chart*: Fan 1, Red Group, No. 39B. Stamen color: Red. Flower shape: Large, cuplike. Flower size: 6–8 in (15–20 cm). Fragrance: Slight. Number of petals: 20. Number of sepals: 4.

LEAF COLOR: Top, bronzy green; underside, olive green. Leaf and sinus: Leaves round, undulating; lobes overlap at sinus. Leaf size: 10–12 in (25–30 cm). Leaf spread: 6–7 ft (2–2.2 m). Stem color: Bronze. Pubescence on peduncle or petiole: Short hairs on both.

COMMENTS: 'Emily Grant Hutchings' is an excellent night bloomer that propagates very freely. Tubers send out short runners, developing new plants at the tips. This cultivar blooms earlier in the season than most other night-blooming varieties. I highly recommend it for medium and large pools; alternatively, by using an 8–10 in (20–25 cm) pot, its growth can be restricted and yet it will still produce plenty of blooms for the small pool.

Nymphaea '**H. C. Haarstick**' James Gurney 1922. Parentage: *N.* 'Mrs. D. R. Francis' × unknown. Characteristics: Nonviviparous, very free flowering. Plate 208.

PETAL COLOR: Red. *R.H.S. Chart*: Fan 2, Red-Purple Group, No. 61C. Sepal color: Red. *R.H.S. Chart*: Fan 2, Red-Purple Group, No. 61C. Anther color: Orange-red. *R.H.S. Chart*: Fan 1, Red Group, No. 47B. Stamen color: Orange-red. Flower shape: Large, round, flat. Flower size: 10–12 in (25–30 cm). Fragrance: Pungent. Number of petals: 22–24. Number of sepals: 4.

LEAF COLOR: Top, reddish brown; underside, purple. Leaf and sinus: Leaf round, dentate, small convolutions at perimeter; sinus usually open or partly open. Leaf size: Up to 16 in (40 cm). Leaf spread: 6–12 ft (2–3.5 m). Stem color: Purple. Pubescence on peduncle or petiole: Tiny hairs on underwater stems.

COMMENTS: This cultivar was produced at the Missouri Botanical Garden in St. Louis and is one of the first night bloomers developed. It remains an excellent choice for the medium or large pool.

Nymphaea 'Jennifer Rebecca' Kenneth Landon 1990. Parentage: *N.* 'Wood's White Knight' × *N.* 'Red Flare'. Characteristics: Nonviviparous, free flowering. Plate 209.

PETAL COLOR: Dark red. *R.H.S. Chart*: Fan 2, Red-Purple Group, Nos. 67B–C. Sepal color: Dark maroon. *R.H.S. Chart*: Fan 1, Red Group, No. 47A. Anther color: Dark maroon. *R.H.S. Chart*: Fan 1, Red Group, No. 46B. Stamen color: Deep pink. Flower shape: Sunflowerlike. Flower size: 8–10 in (20–25 cm). Fragrance: Quite pungent. Number of petals: 32. Number of sepals: 4.

LEAF COLOR: Top, reddish brown; underside, reddish brown. Leaf and sinus: Leaves nearly round, sharply dentate, perimeter wavy on older leaves; sinus closed. Leaf size: 15 in (38 cm). Leaf spread: 7–9 ft (2.2–2.7 m). Stem color: Dark maroon. Pubescence on peduncle or petiole: Slight on both.

COMMENTS: One of the most striking red night bloomers I have ever seen. With its amazing color and plentiful blooms it is sure to stand out in a water garden. I recommend it for the medium and large pool.

Nymphaea 'Juno' 1906. Parentage: *N. lotus* is one of the parents. Characteristics: Nonviviparous, free flowering. Plate 210.

PETAL COLOR: White. *R.H.S. Chart*: Fan 4, White Group, No. 155B. Sepal color: White. *R.H.S. Chart*: Fan 4, White Group, No. 155A. Anther color: Yellow. *R.H.S. Chart*: Fan 1, Yellow Group, No. 12B. Stamen color: Yellow. Flower shape: Cuplike then flat. Flower size: 6–10 in (15–25 cm). Fragrance: Pungent. Number of petals: 19–20. Number of sepals: 4.

LEAF COLOR: Top, green, new leaves green or bronzy, a few purple blotches; underside, brown or purplish, prominent greenish yellow veins. Leaf and sinus: Leaf nearly round, dentate; sinus usually open, lobes may overlap partially or completely. Leaf size: 13 × 12 in (33 × 30 cm). Leaf spread: 5–6 ft (1.5–2 m). Stem color: Mostly brown; peduncle above water usually greenish. Pubescence on peduncle or petiole: Short fuzz on both.

COMMENTS: Although its hybridizer is unknown, 'Juno' was first offered for sale in 1906, according to water lily researcher and author Charles Masters. It performs well in any size pool.

Nymphaea 'Maroon Beauty' Perry D. Slocum 1950. Parentage: Seedling of *N.* 'H. C. Haarstick'. Characteristics: Nonviviparous, free flowering. Plate 211.

PETAL COLOR: Deep red. *R.H.S. Chart*: Fan 2, Red-Purple Group, No. 64B. Sepal color: Deep red. *R.H.S. Chart*: Fan 2, Red-Purple Group, No. 63A. Anther color: Chocolate, tipped red. *R.H.S. Chart*: Fan 4, Greyed-Red Group, No. 178B; tips, Fan 2, Red-Purple Group, No. 64B. Stamen color: Inner stamens reddish brown, outer red. Flower shape: Huge, round, flat. Flower size: 10–12 in (25–30 cm). Fragrance: Pungent. Number of petals: 24–26. Number of sepals: 4.

LEAF COLOR: Top, reddish brown; underside, purple. Leaf and sinus: Leaf round, dentate, perimeter convoluted; sinus an open V. Leaf size: Up to 16 in (40 cm). Leaf spread: 6–12 ft (2–3.5 m). Stem color: Purple. Pubescence on peduncle or petiole: Tiny hairs on underwater stems.

COMMENTS: 'Maroon Beauty', a magnificent, striking water lily, is best suited to the medium and larger pools because of its large leaf spread.

Nymphaea 'Missouri' George H. Pring 1932. Parentage: Probably *N.* 'Mrs. George C. Hitchcock' × *N.* 'Sturtevantii', according to Charles Masters. Characteristics: Nonviviparous, fairly free flowering. Plate 212.

PETAL COLOR: White. *R.H.S. Chart*: Fan 4, White Group, No. 155B. Sepal color: White. *R.H.S. Chart*: Fan 4, White Group, No. 155B. Anther color: Deep yellow. *R.H.S. Chart*: Fan 1, Yellow Group, No. 13C. Stamen color: Yellow. Flower shape: Flat, platelike. Flower size: 10–14 in (25–35 cm). Fragrance: Pungent. Number of petals: 31. Number of sepals: 4.

LEAF COLOR: Top, green, new leaves bronze; underside, green, flecked purple. Leaf and sinus: Leaves large, a little longer than wide, very dentate, margins wavy. Lobes usually overlap at sinus or sinus may be partly open. Leaf size: Up to 14 × 12 in (35 × 30 cm). Leaf spread: 6–10 ft (2–3 m). Stem color: Bronzy. Pubescence on peduncle or petiole: Tiny short hairs on both.

COMMENTS: 'Missouri' can produce blooms larger than those of any other night bloomer if planted in a large container with at least 2 cu ft (0.05 cu m) of soil and given plenty of fertilizer. I recommend it only for the large pool due to its extensive leaf spread.

Nymphaea 'Mrs. George C. Hitchcock' George H. Pring 1926. Parentage: Seedling of *N.* 'Omarana'. Characteristics: Nonviviparous, very free flowering, seed production profuse. Plate 213.

PETAL COLOR: Light to medium pink. *R.H.S. Chart*: Fan 2, Red-Purple Group, No. 65A. Sepal color: Darker pink than petals. *R.H.S. Chart*: Fan 2, Red-Purple Group, No. 66D. Anther color: Burnt orange. *R.H.S. Chart*: Fan 1, Orange-Red Group, No. 34D. Stamen color: Burnt orange, same as anthers. Flower shape: Large, flat. Flower size: 10–11 in (25–

28 cm). Fragrance: Pungent. Number of petals: 20. Number of sepals: 4.

LEAF COLOR: Top, bronzy, newer pads darker bronze, some purple blotches; underside, purple. Leaf and sinus: Leaves longer than wide, serrated, perimeter convoluted; sinus closed on newer leaves, open on older leaves. Leaf size: Up to 15 × 13.5 in (38 × 34 cm). Leaf spread: 7–8 ft (2.2–2.5 m). Stem color: Peduncle, orange-brown; petiole brownish. Pubescence on peduncle or petiole: Very short fuzz on both.

COMMENTS: A true show lily. Blooms usually open about dark and close toward midday, yet will stay open all day on cool, overcast days. This is a fine choice for a medium or large pool.

Nymphaea **'Red Cup'** Kirk Strawn 1986. Parentage: *N.* 'Red Flare' × unknown. Characteristics: Nonviviparous, free flowering. Plate 214.

PETAL COLOR: Dark red then deep pink late summer and fall. *R.H.S. Chart*: Fan 2, Red-Purple Group, No. 67A then 67B. Sepal color: Dark red then deep pink late summer and fall. *R.H.S. Chart*: Fan 2, Red-Purple Group, No. 67A then 67B. Anther color: Red. *R.H.S. Chart*: Fan 1, Red Group, No. 50A. Stamen color: Red. Flower shape: Cuplike. Flower size: 5–8 in (13–20 cm). Fragrance: Slightly pungent. Number of petals: 18–20. Number of sepals: 4.

LEAF COLOR: Top, bronzy brown; underside, purple. Leaf and sinus: Leaves longer than wide, heavily serrated, wavy edges; sinus open. Leaf size: 13–18 in (33–45 cm). Leaf spread: 5–12 ft (1.5–3.5 m). Stem color: Peduncle purple; petiole purple, browning. Pubescence on peduncle or petiole: Very short fuzz on both.

COMMENTS: This cultivar has a unique vaselike bloom and excellent petal color and foliage. I recommend it for medium or large pools.

Nymphaea **'Red Flare'** Martin E. Randig 1938. Parentage: Unknown. Characteristics: Nonviviparous, very free flowering; blooms held 12 in (30 cm) above water. Plate 215.

PETAL COLOR: Deep red. *R.H.S. Chart*: Fan 2, Red-Purple Group, No. 67A. Sepal color: Deep red. *R.H.S. Chart*: Fan 2, Red-Purple Group, No. 67A. Anther color: Reddish brown. *R.H.S. Chart*: Fan 4, Greyed-Orange Group, No. 175B. Stamen color: Light pink or yellowish. Flower shape: Large, round, flat. Flower size: 7–10 in (18–25 cm). Fragrance: Faint but pungent. Number of petals: 19–20. Number of sepals: 4.

LEAF COLOR: Top, reddish bronze, fading only slightly, few small purple blotches; underside, pur-

ple. Leaf and sinus: Young leaves much longer than wide; older leaves nearly round, heavily serrated, wavy edges. Sinus usually a wide-open V. Leaf size: 10–12 in (25–30 cm). Leaf spread: 5–6 ft (1.5–2 m). Stem color: Peduncle, reddish brown; petiole brown. Pubescence on peduncle or petiole: Tiny short hairs on both.

Comment: This is one of the very best red night bloomers for small, medium, or large pools.

Nymphaea **'Sir Galahad'** Martin E. Randig 1965. Parentage: Unknown. Characteristics: Nonviviparous, free flowering; flowers held 10–11 in (25–28 cm) above water. Plate 216.

PETAL COLOR: White. *R.H.S. Chart*: Fan 4, White Group, No. 155D. Sepal color: White. *R.H.S. Chart*: Fan 4, White Group, No. 155D. Anther color: Rich yellow. *R.H.S. Chart*: Fan 1, Yellow-Orange Group, No. 14A. Stamen color: Rich yellow. Flower shape: Round, flat. Flower size: 9–12 in (23–30 cm). Fragrance: Pungent. Number of petals: 28. Number of sepals: 4.

LEAF COLOR: Top, green; underside, green, touched purple. Leaf and sinus: Leaf nearly round, sharply serrated. Lobes usually overlap at sinus except for outer 1–2 in (2.5–5 cm). Leaf size: 13–15 in (33–38 cm). Leaf spread: 6–9 ft (2–2.7 m). Stem color: Peduncle, green; petiole, purplish green. Pubescence on peduncle or petiole: Very short fuzz on all underwater stems.

COMMENTS: 'Sir Galahad' is a wonderful plant. Its stout peduncles hold massive flowers high above the water. This water lily is dramatic and beautiful, producing several blooms at a time once it is established. I recommend it for large pools.

Nymphaea **'Texas Shell Pink'** Rolf Nelson 1979. Parentage: Unknown. Characteristics: Nonviviparous, free flowering. Plate 217.

PETAL COLOR: Creamy white, tips reddish purple. *R.H.S. Chart*: Fan 4, White Group, No. 155D; tips, Fan 2, Red-Purple Group, No. 65A. Sepal color: Base 1/3 white; tips (outer 2/3) red-purple. *R.H.S. Chart*: Base, Fan 4, White Group, No. 155D; tips, Fan 2, Red-Purple Group, No. 65B. Anther color: Grayish orange. *R.H.S. Chart*: Fan 4, Greyed-Orange Group, No. 166A. Stamen color: Yellowish green. Flower shape: Platelike. Flower size: Up to 8 in (20 cm). Fragrance: Cinnamonlike. Number of petals: 16–20. Number of sepals: 4.

LEAF COLOR: Top, dark yellow-green, grayish brown cast; underside, greenish. Leaf and sinus: Leaf a little longer than wide; sinus open. Leaf size: 13–15 in (33–38 cm). Leaf spread: 5–6 ft (1.5–2 m).

Stem color: Dark gray-green at base, gray-brown near flower and leaf. Pubescence on peduncle or petiole: Very fine hairs on both.

COMMENTS: The blending of white to a soft red-purple gives this flower a glowing effect. I recommend it for medium and large pools.

Nymphaea **'Trudy Slocum'** Perry D. Slocum 1948. Parentage: Seedling of *N.* 'Juno'. Characteristics: Nonviviparous, very free flowering. Plate 218.

PETAL COLOR: White. *R.H.S. Chart*: Fan 4, White Group, No. 155B. Sepal color: White. *R.H.S. Chart*: Fan 4, White Group, No. 155A. Anther color: Yellow, brown vertical stripes. *R.H.S. Chart*: Fan 1, Yellow Group, No. 11A; stripes, Fan 4, Greyed-Orange Group, No. 176C. Stamen color: Deep yellow. Flower shape: Round, nearly flat. Flower size: 6–8 in (15–20 cm). Fragrance: Pungent. Number of petals: 19–29. Number of sepals: 4.

LEAF COLOR: Top, green, new leaves green or brownish, lightly blotched purple; underside, brown or purplish, prominent greenish veins. Leaf and sinus: Leaf nearly round; sinus usually open, lobes may overlap partially or completely. Leaf size: 13.5 × 12.5 in (34 × 32 cm). Leaf spread: 5–6 ft (1.5–2 m). Stem color: Mostly brown, peduncle greenish above water. Pubescence on peduncle or petiole: Short fuzz on both.

COMMENTS: 'Trudy Slocum' is outstanding in beauty and performance. It readily produces seed and the variable seedlings grow easily. One plant may develop into a clump containing several plants by the end of the season. This lily is suited for any size pool.

Nymphaea **'Wood's White Knight'** John Wood 1977. Parentage: *N.* 'Sir Galahad' and *N.* 'Missouri' are included in parentage. Characteristics: Nonviviparous, very free flowering. Plate 219.

PETAL COLOR: White. *R.H.S. Chart*: Fan 4, White Group, No. 155A. Sepal color: White, flushed green. *R.H.S. Chart*: Fan 4, White Group, No. 155A; flush, Fan 3, Green Group, No. 142D and lighter. Anther color: Yellow. *R.H.S. Chart*: Fan 4, Greyed-Yellow Group, No. 162A. Stamen color: Yellow. Flower shape: Full, peony-style. Flower size: 10–12 in (25–30 cm). Fragrance: Pungent. Number of petals: 28–30. Number of sepals: 4.

LEAF COLOR: Top, green; underside, greenish, variegated. Leaf and sinus: Leaves nearly round, scalloped, edges somewhat wavy; sinus usually open. Leaf size: 12–15 in (30–38 cm). Leaf spread: 8–10 ft (2.5–3 m). Stem color: Greenish brown. Pubescence on peduncle or petiole: Tiny hairs on all underwater stems.

COMMENTS: Blooms are quite double. 'Wood's White Knight' is an excellent lily for medium and large pools.

Chapter 15

Hardy Water Lily Species

All hardy water lily species described in this chapter are listed in one or more aquatic nursery catalogs (see Appendix B for a list of these sources). Most hardy water lily species now have counterparts in cultivars that are superior in garden performance; the collector will find the species worthwhile, however. *Nymphaea odorata* and *N. mexicana* flowers, and hybrids from these species, are pleasantly fragrant. Flowers of the other hardy species are not at all or are only slightly scented. Plate 107 shows a representative cross section of a hardy water lily flower; Figure 67 illustrates the variety of its parts.

The arrangement of this chapter follows the taxonomy of the genus *Nymphaea* as outlined in Chapter 11. Following each taxonomic section are the plant descriptions arranged alphabetically by specific epithet with descriptions of related plants (varieties, forms, and named selections) immediately following. All plant names are given with their author and year of discovery when known. Common names, if any, appear after the botanical name. Standardized color names and numbers refer to the Royal Horticultural Society (R.H.S.) Color Chart.

"Characteristics" includes the type of rhizome, as described below. "Stamen color" refers to the color found on the basal portion of the stamen (the filament) and the base of the staminodes. "Flower size" is bloom diameter. "Leaf size" refers either to the diameter of the leaf of a mature plant or to the measurements of its length and width, in that order. "Leaf spread" refers to the diameter of the area on the water's surface covered by the mature plant.

"Comments" on each plant include reference to what size pool is suitable. Although there are no hard rules differentiating pool sizes, general guidelines follow:

> tub garden: up to 3 ft (1 m) in diameter
> small: 4–6 ft (1.2–2 m) in diameter
> medium: 7–9 ft (2.2–2.7 m) in diameter
> large: 10 ft (3 m) in diameter or larger
> natural pond: dirt or mud bottom pond of any size

Note that copper and redwood are toxic to plants and fish and should be used only in conjunction with a plastic or other fish-safe liner.

Plant hardy water lilies only when the water temperature reaches 60°F (16°C) or above. Refer to the hardiness zone maps in Appendix A and follow this general planting timetable:

> In North America and Europe
> Zone 10   any time of year
> Zone 9   March through September
> Zone 8   April through September
> Zone 7   April through August

Zone 6   mid-April through August
Zone 5   late April / early May through mid August
Zone 4   mid May through 1 August

GROUP *NYMPHAEA SYNCARPIAE* [*SYMPHYTOPLEURA* CASPARY 1865]

In general, species in the group *Syncarpiae* display carpels that are completely fused with one another at the sides; they are also attached to the axis of the flower and to the torus, as in day-blooming tropicals. Flowers are diurnal, colored white, rose, or yellow, but not blue.

Subgenus *Castalia* de Candolle 1821

Subgenus *Castalia* comprises the hardy water lily species. This subgenus consists of six species divided into three sections, *Chamaenymphaea*, *Eucastalia*, and *Xanthantha*, according to variations. All plants in subgenus *Castalia* bloom during the daytime. Sepals frequently have prominent veins. Leaves usually have smooth edges, lacking the dentation of many tropical water lilies. Rhizomes vary considerably and may be separated into five types: upright, or pineapple; Marliac; odorata; tuberosa; and finger, or thumb (also grows upright). Plate 220 shows all five sorts.

The upright, or pineapple, rhizome is tuberous and may be 4 in (10 cm) thick. As its name implies, it grows upright and is the approximate shape of a pineapple. In general, water lilies with upright rhizomes are very vigorous growers and very free flowering. At least a bushel (35 l) of soil is recommended for water lilies of this group, which includes *Nymphaea mexicana*. Some growers recommend planting these rhizomes upright. I have had good success planting them horizontally (the same as most water lily rhizomes are planted) with the crown just peeking through the soil. *Nymphaea tetragona* also forms upright tubers, but these are tiny and of the finger, or thumb, type.

The Marliac rhizome grows a thick, horizontally traveling main root. Frequently this rhizome is 2 in (5 cm) thick. Water lilies with Marliac rhizomes are among the freest blooming hardies. Plants are also heavy feeders and do best in a bushel (35 l) or more of soil. *Nymphaea alba* and *N. candida* are in this group. Both are very easy to grow.

The odorata-type rhizome is long and more slender than the upright or Marliac types. The thickness varies from 1–1.5 in (2.5–4 cm). Usually several small, new, firmly attached rhizomes ("eyes") form along the main rhizome. It is called a "crawling root" in England because it spreads so rapidly. New plants develop from the eyes. Odorata rhizomes need room to spread out and develop a colony of several plants in order to become free bloomers. This may take two or more months. I recommend planting in a container 24 × 24 × 12 in (60 × 60 × 30 cm). *Nymphaea odorata* is the species represented.

The tuberosa-type rhizome is usually 0.75–1 in (2–2.5 cm) thick, more slender than the odorata type, which it closely resembles. A very noticeable difference is that the side rhizomes are joined by a very slender attachment and nearly all detach when the main rhizome is pulled. Like odorata rhizomes, tuberosa rhizomes need room to spread out and develop colonies in order to become free-bloomers. *Nymphaea tuberosa* is in this group.

The last of the five types, the finger or thumb rhizome, is small—finger size in poor soil, thumb size in rich loamy soil with regular fertilization. The rhizome grows upright and very seldom divides. A half bushel (17.5 l) is enough soil for this miniature. *Nymphaea tetragona* is in this group.

• Section *Chamaenymphaea* Planchon 1853

Flowers of species in section *Chamaenymphaea* are white or rosy, opening near noon and closing in the late afternoon. Leaves are egg-shaped to oval and leaf edges are smooth. Rhizomes are upright and short. It includes one species native to the North Temperate regions of North America, China, Japan, Siberia, Finland, and eastern Europe.

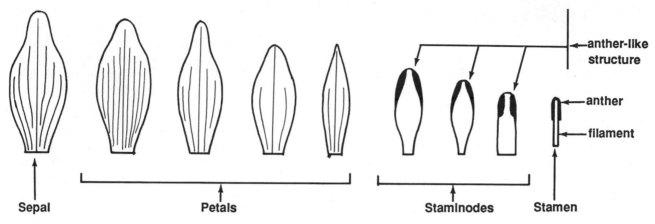

FIGURE 67. Size and shape transition in hardy *Nymphaea* floral parts.

Nymphaea fennica Mela. See *N. tetragona*.

Nymphaea tetragona Georgi. Native to circumboreal regions mostly: in North America from Maine, along the Canadian border to the West Coast, from Quebec to Lake Superior, and western Canada. Also Finland, Japan, China, much of Asia, eastern Europe, and Australia. Characteristics: Day blooming, finger rhizome, free flowering when conditions are suitable. Plate 221; see also Figure 4 in Chapter 1.

PETAL COLOR: White. *R.H.S. Chart*: Fan 4, White Group, No. 155C. Sepal color: White. *R.H.S. Chart*: Fan 4, White Group, No. 155C. Anther color: Yellow. *R.H.S. Chart*: Fan 1, Yellow Group, No. 6A. Stamen color: Yellow. Flower shape: Cuplike. Flower size: 1–2 in (2.5–5 cm). Fragrance: Slight. Number of petals: 8–13. Number of sepals: 4.

LEAF COLOR: Top, green, blotched purple, new leaves purplish; underside, purple. Leaf and sinus: Leaf longer than wide; sinus an open V. Leaf size: 2.75×2 in (7×5 cm). Leaves 1–2 in (2.5–5 cm) larger in rich soil. Leaf spread: 10–15 in (25–38 cm). Up to 30 in (75 cm) in rich soil. Stem color: Green. Pubescence on peduncle or petiole: Tiny hairs on petiole.

COMMENTS: *N. tetragona* is the tiniest of all water lilies and well suited to a small tub garden. Flowers do not open until early afternoon yet they do stay open late.

For many years *N. fennica* was believed to be a separate species, but Pertti Uotila, professor of botany at the University of Helsinki, Finland, advises that *N. fennica* Mela is really *N. tetragona* Georgi. *N. tetragona* is parent of 'Helvola' (syn. 'Yellow Pygmy') and probable parent to several cultivars of the *N. ×laydekeri* hybrid group. Because of their need for cold water temperatures, *N. tetragona* varieties *lata* and *leibergii* are best suited for northern climates. *N. tetragona* var. *angusta* does well in warm climates.

N. tetragona var. *angusta* Caspary 1865. Native to China and Japan. Sepals and petals are larger and narrower than the type. Sinus is equal to or exceeds half the length of the leaf. Leaves are bright olive green on plants that I grew in North Carolina from seeds sent by Kenneth Landon. (Landon's original stock came from France, though Walter Pagels believes the French stock is actually from China.) After being stored in the refrigerator for a few months, the seeds were sown outside in April 1991. Germination and growth was fast. Blooms appeared in August without any transplanting. The young plants flowered in profusion in September and October. My conclusion is that this variety has an excellent commercial future. It also bloomed freely for Landon in San Angelo, Texas, where summer temperatures reach 100°F (38°C) or higher.

N. tetragona var. *lata* Caspary 1865. Found growing in Siberia, Manchuria, and the Ural Mountains. Sepals and petals are shorter and broader than the type. Sinus is less than half the length of the leaf. I have never grown this variety.

N. tetragona var. *leibergii* (Morong) Porsild. Native to southeast and east central Alaska and northwestern North America. Leaves are quite wavy around the perimeter; sinus is usually wide open; a few purple blotches are prominent in new leaves. I tried growing two Alaskan specimens sent to me by Walter Pagels in 1990. Plants arrived in beautiful shape with flowers and seed pods ready to burst. I collected some seeds and let some seeds drop. Seeds were stored in a refrigerator. In 1991 only a few seeds germinated and they, along with the two tubers, produced only a rosette of underwater leaves close to the rhizome. No surface leaves or blooms developed. My conclusion is that the commercial future of variety *leibergii* is nil.

• Section *Eucastalia* Planchon 1853

The four species included in section *Eucastalia* represent the majority of hardy water lilies of subgenus *Castalia*. Flowers are white, pink, or red, opening in early morning and closing from noon to midafternoon. Some species have fragrant flowers. Leaves are nearly round with solid color on top. Rhizomes grow horizontally and are long and branching. These water lilies are native to the North Temperate regions of North America and Europe, south to North Africa and Guyana.

Nymphaea alba (Linnaeus) J. Presl. Native to Europe and northern Africa. Characteristics: Day blooming, Marliac rhizome, very free flowering; usually produces two to four flowers at a time. Plate 222.

PETAL COLOR: White. *R.H.S. Chart*: Fan 4, White Group, No. 155C. Sepal color: Green, white tips. *R.H.S. Chart*: Fan 3, Green Group, Nos. 136D–135D; tips, Fan 4, White Group, No. 155C. Anther color: Light yellow. *R.H.S. Chart*: Fan 1, Yellow Group, No. 6B. Stamen color: Yellow. Flower shape: Cuplike then stellate. Flower size: 4–5 in (10–13 cm). Fragrance: Slight, on first day only. Number of petals: 12–28. Number of sepals: 4.

LEAF COLOR: Top, green; underside, yellowish green, margins tinged red. Leaf and sinus: Leaf orbicular; sinus usually an open V. Leaf size: 8–10 in (20–25 cm). Leaf spread: 5.5 ft (1.7 m). Stem color: Green. Pubescence on peduncle or petiole: None.

COMMENTS: This species was used extensively by Joseph Bory Latour-Marliac in hybridizing. As a result many fine cultivars have *N. alba* parentage. Suitable for small, medium, or large pools.

N. alba var. *rubra* Lonnroth. Swedish red water lily. This variety is native to two very cold lakes (Lakes Fayer and Fagertarn) near Nerike, Hammar Parish, Sweden. Flowers are pale pink on opening, changing to rose-pink or red, often with a bluish flush. Third-day flowers have the richest color. Blooms are deepest pink in the center, becoming progressively lighter toward the outer petals. Flowers are 3–6 in (8–15 cm) in diameter. Leaves and rhizomes resemble those of the species. Reputedly this variety was used by Marliac to develop his red, pink, and changeable hardy water lilies. Plate 106.

N. alba Australian variation. This distinct variant of *N. alba* from Australia produces rather small blooms, 3–3.5 in (8–9 cm) in diameter. Leaves are medium size, and the sinus is an open V. The plant produces seeds profusely, an indication of a species. Rhizome is Marliac. Plate 223.

N. alba New Zealand variation. This distinct variant from New Zealand produces large blooms, 5–6 in (13–15 cm) in diameter. Leaves are also large, with lobes that overlap at sinus. The plant produces

seeds in quantity, an indication of a species. Rhizome is a thick Marliac. The New Zealand variation has been a parent of many fine commercially available hybrids, such as *N*. 'Perry's Pink Beauty', 'Perry's Pink Bicolor', 'Perry's Strawberry Pink', 'Perry's White Wonder', and 'Yellow Sensation'.

Nymphaea candida J. Presl. Native to northern and central Europe, northern Asia. Characteristics: Day blooming, Marliac rhizome, very free flowering; stigmas yellow, red, or violet. Plates 106 and 224.

PETAL COLOR: White. *R.H.S. Chart*: Fan 4, White Group, No. 155D. Sepal color: White, blushed pink, green borders and tips. *R.H.S. Chart*: Fan 4, White Group, No. 155D; blush, Fan 2, Red-Purple Group, No. 65D or paler; borders and tips, Fan 4, Greyed-Green Group, No. 193B. Anther color: Yellow. *R.H.S. Chart*: Fan 1, Yellow Group, No. 3A. Stamen color: Yellow. Flower shape: Cuplike. Flower size: 3 in (8 cm). Fragrance: None or very slight. Number of petals: 12–20. Number of sepals: 4–5.

LEAF COLOR: Top, green; underside, reddish purple, prominent green veins. Leaf and sinus: Leaves a little longer than wide; lobes may overlap halfway down sinus or sinus open. Leaf size: 7 × 6 in (18 × 15 cm). Leaf spread: 30–36 in (75–90 cm). Stem color: Mostly purple-bronze, peduncle a little paler than petiole. Pubescence on peduncle or petiole: Many fine hairs on both.

COMMENTS: *N. candida* can be grown successfully in a tub garden or a small pool. Blooms are relatively small compared to its leaves. Fertilizing seems to enhance this relative difference, yielding 10-in (25-cm) leaves and 4-in (10-cm) blooms. I think there are better whites (such as *N.* ×*marliacea* 'Albida', 'Perry's Double White', 'Perry's White Star', 'Perry's White Wonder', 'Queen of Whites', 'Venus', 'Virginalis') for medium and large pools.

Nymphaea odorata Aiton. Fragrant water lily. Native to eastern North America from Newfoundland south to and including Florida, west to northeastern Texas, Kansas, Michigan, and Indiana; also Mexico, West Indies, and the Guianas. Characteristics: Day blooming, odorata rhizome, fairly free flowering when established. Plates 225 and 226.

PETAL COLOR: White, outer petals occasionally

develop pink blush. *R.H.S. Chart*: Fan 4, White Group, No. 155C; blush, Fan 2, Red-Purple Group, No. 65D or lighter. Sepal color: White or pale pink. *R.H.S. Chart*: Fan 4, White Group, No. 155C; pink, Fan 2, Red-Purple Group, No. 65D or lighter. Anther color: Yellow. *R.H.S. Chart*: Fan 1, Yellow Group, No. 3A. Stamen color: Yellow. Flower shape: Stellate. Flower size: 2–4.5 in (5–11 cm). Fragrance: Delightful. Number of petals: 24–32. Number of sepals: 4–5.

LEAF COLOR: Top, green; underside, varies widely from bronze to pink, purple, red. Leaf and sinus: Some leaves wider than long, some round; sinus usually wide open. Leaf size: 6–8 in (15–20 cm). Leaf spread: 3–4 ft (1–1.2 m). Stem color: Usually green or greenish purple. Pubescence on peduncle or petiole: None.

COMMENTS: This species has considerable variation. In some ponds in south Georgia flower petals are narrow; in Maine, petals may be very broad. Likewise, in some ponds in Georgia sepals are quite pink, while in Maine some flowers have pink at the base of all the petals. Leaves also vary considerably. Some south Georgia specimens have brilliant red undersides, while bronze is the predominant color elsewhere. Some tiny plants growing naturally in Georgia develop flowers only 2–3 in (5–8 cm) in diameter, yet flowers develop twice that size when planted in rich soil at a nursery. *N. odorata* is suitable for any size pool but must form a colony of rhizomes before blooming freely.

N. odorata var. gigantea Tricker 1897, Conard 1901. Native to Florida, Oklahoma, Missouri, Texas, Louisiana, Cuba, Mexico, and the Guianas. It has been reported in eastern states as far north as Delaware. Flowers, which are 6–8 in (15–20 cm) across, are much larger than the type. Blooms are also more double, with 36–38 petals. Leaves average much larger, 11–12 in (28–30 cm) across, with leaf sinus ⅔ to ¾ closed, and leaf spread is likewise much larger at 5–7 ft (1.5–2.2 m). This variety is especially suited to natural ponds. It can be used in a large pool if planted in a large container. This water lily varies considerably; occasionally a plant develops blooms similar to many tropicals, with long, lanceolate petals, sepals that fold down, and blooms held 6–8 in (15–20 cm) above the water. "Hopatcong" is the Native American name for this plant. Plate 227.

N. odorata var. minor Sims. The native habitat of this small water lily is limited to certain shallow ponds in New Jersey. Flowers are pure white, only 2–3 in

(5–8 cm) in diameter, and very fragrant. Leaves are 2–5 in (5–13 cm) across, green on top and dark red on underside. Peduncles are deep reddish brown. This is an interesting plant for small pools or for the collector.

N. odorata var. rosea Pursh. Native to the northeastern and north central United States. Flowers are 5–6 in (13–15 cm) in diameter and very fragrant. Petals and sepals are a beautiful clear pink. Leaves are round with an open sinus. Leaf color is initially reddish purple on top, turning to green with age. Leaf undersides are a very brilliant red. Leaves are 8–9 in (20–23 cm) in diameter with a leaf spread of 4–5 ft (1.2–1.5 m). Stems are green with light fuzz on petiole but none on peduncle. This variety makes a fine plant for medium and large pools when planted in a large container, but many cultivars now available would give more blooms. Plate 228.

Nymphaea tuberosa Paine. Native to Ontario and Quebec, and west of the Appalachian Mountains from Lake Champlain west through the Great Lakes to Minnesota and south to Arkansas; also found growing in New Jersey and Maryland. Characteristics: Day blooming, tuberosa rhizome, fairly free flowering, very fast propagator. Plates 229 and 230.

PETAL COLOR: Pure white. *R.H.S. Chart*: Fan 4, White Group, No. 155D. Sepal color: Pure white. *R.H.S. Chart*: Fan 4, White Group, No. 155D. Anther color: Yellow. *R.H.S. Chart*: Fan 1, Yellow Group, No. 3A. Stamen color: Yellow. Flower shape: Cup-like. Flower size: 4–9 in (10–23 cm). Fragrance: Slight. Number of petals: 27–31. Number of sepals: 4.

LEAF COLOR: Top, green, new leaves purplish; underside, green. Leaf and sinus: Leaf round or wider than long; sinus usually a wide-open V; lobes may overlap along the first 0.75 in (2 cm). Leaf size: 7–10 in (18–25 cm). Leaf spread: 4–6 ft (1.2–2 m). Stem color: Petiole green, striped brownish purple; peduncle green. Pubescence on peduncle or petiole: Fine fuzz on petiole.

COMMENTS: *N. tuberosa* is an interesting species for the collector. A unique feature is a pink spot about the size of a pinhead right in the middle of the stigma. This is most prominent in the first-day flower. 'Perry's Pink', a chance seedling with probable *N. tuberosa* genes, has a similar red dot in the same place. If planted in a large container it could be used in a large pool. Many freer-blooming white cultivars are now available for the water garden.

• Section *Xanthantha* Caspary 1888

Section *Xanthantha* includes only one species, *Nymphaea mexicana*. Flowers are yellow, opening about noon and closing in late afternoon. Floating new leaves have blotches of reddish brown. The upright rhizomes are usually short; long white stolons develop laterally all summer and send up new plants like a strawberry plant. In autumn tiny white runners are sent straight downward from these stolons, and tiny clusters of "bananas," about 1–2 in (2.5–5 cm) in length, form about 6 in (15 cm) under the main plant. In the spring, these bananalike structures form new plants. This species tends to be invasive when grown in a natural pond. A variant, which produces larger flowers than the type, has been identified in the Cape Canaveral area of Florida.

Nymphaea mexicana Zuccarini [*N. mexicana* No. 1]. Banana water lily. Native to Mexico, South Carolina, Georgia, Florida, along the Gulf of Mexico to Texas. Characteristics: Semihardy, day blooming, upright rhizome produces runners (stolons), fairly free flowering. Plate 231.

PETAL COLOR: Deep yellow. *R.H.S. Chart*: Fan 1, Yellow Group, No. 2B. Sepal color: Greenish yellow. *R.H.S. Chart*: Fan 1, Yellow Group, No. 9A. Anther color: Deep yellow. *R.H.S. Chart*: Fan 1, Yellow Group, No. 9A. Stamen color: Deep yellow. Flower shape: Cuplike then stellate. Flower size: 3–4.5 in (8–11 cm). Fragrance: Very sweet. Number of petals: 20–23. Number of sepals: 4.

LEAF COLOR: Top, green, new leaves olive green, heavily splashed purple or reddish brown; underside, bronzy red, small purple specks. Leaf and sinus: Leaf egg-shaped, slightly serrated; sinus usually open. Leaf size: 7.5–9 in (19–23 cm). Leaf spread: 3.5–4 ft (1.1–1.2 m). Stem color: Greenish yellow. Pubescence on peduncle or petiole: None.

COMMENTS: Flowers do not open until midday. *N. mexicana* No. 1 is hardy in USDA zones 6–10, semihardy in zones 3–5. It is parent to many yellow and orange changeable hardies and a desirable water lily although very difficult to eradicate once planted in a natural pond, however. Its invasive qualities can be checked by planting in a container in a concrete or liner pond.

N. mexicana* f. *canaveralensis Frase 1958 [*N. mexicana* No. 2]. This large-flowered form grows in the Cape Canaveral area of Florida. Its hardiness is the same as that of *N. mexicana* No. 1. The principal difference between this and the type is the larger flower, 6–8 in (15–20 cm) across with 23 or 24 petals. Blooms are a very deep yellow, opening at midday and lasting three days. A novelty for the collector or hybridizer, this water lily is beautiful when grown in a large container and properly fertilized. In a small planter, with less space and nourishment, blooms are smaller and flower color weaker. This plant is a parent of 'Yellow Sensation'. I recommend this plant for the collector or hybridizer with a medium or large pool, but *N. mexicana* f. *canaveralensis* is unsuitable for the natural pond as it can take over and become a pest. Plate 232.

Chapter 16

Hardy Water Lily Cultivars

One hybridizer of hardy water lilies in particular deserves recognition for many of the fine cultivars available today—Joseph Bory Latour-Marliac. He was born 6 March 1830, at Granges, Lot-et-Garonne, France, and did most of his hybridizing work between 1880 and 1910 at Temple-sur-Lot, about 80 miles (130 km) east of Bordeaux. After his death (26 January 1911) his son-in-law, Maurice Laydeker, continued operating the Latour-Marliac Nursery. Two generations of Laydekers succeeded Maurice until the Latour-Marliac Nursery was finally sold to Stapeley Water Gardens of Nantwich, Cheshire, England, in 1991.

More than 100 Marliac varieties resulted from Joseph Bory Latour-Marliac's work. Many of these are still grown and sold by aquatic nurseries worldwide, and they still rank among the best varieties currently available. (See Chapter 2 for information on other water lily hybridizers.)

The term "hardy," when used to describe water lily cultivars, generally means that the plant will survive winter temperatures as long as the rhizome itself does not actually freeze. Many of the finest descend from *Nymphaea alba* var. *rubra*, the Swedish red water lily, which species is native to ponds and two cold lakes (Lakes Fayer and Fagertarn) in Nerike, Hammar Parish, Sweden.

Descendants include red, pink, white, yellow, and orange flowering cultivars. These can be generally referred to as "hardies," a term which also applies to hardy water lily species. The term "changeable" indicates that flower color changes after the bloom opens, usually from light to darker shades of the same hue. The following schedule details the development of flowers from opening to closing.

FIRST DAY: Opening time varies depending mainly on air temperatures. Warm days initiate flower opening earlier than cooler ones. The flowers of some cultivars, however, such as *Nymphaea* 'Helvola', and the species *N. tetragona* and *N. mexicana* Nos. 1 and 2, never open until midday. The first-day flower contains a pool of nectar (slightly sweet to the taste), topping the pistil in the flower center. This nectar serves to catch pollen from visiting insects. Small insects such as "sweat bees" (*Halictus* spp.) or even honeybees (*Apis mellifera*) sometimes drown in this pool of nectar. The carpellary appendages (lacking in *N. gigantea*) encircling the nectar pool are erect. Frequently, first-day flowers do not open completely and remain somewhat cup-shaped.

SECOND DAY: The pool of nectar disappears. Any nectar not drunk by visiting insects has evaporated. Carpellary appendages turn inward, as do the stamens and inner rows of staminodes. Pollen on the anthers is now ripe, and pollen on the outer rows of staminodes may or may not be ripe. Bees can pick up this ripe pollen and carry it to a first-day flower. Fertilization will occur on species flowers or the rare seed-producing cultivar. Although bees consume most of this protein-laden pollen, enough is carried on their bodies to serve fertilization.

THIRD DAY: The stamens and staminodes circling the flower center now bend into the center as much as possible. In the case of changeable lilies, this is the day when petals reach their deepest color. Only a slight darkening can be noticed in sepal color. Third-day flowers usually float or are held slightly above the water.

FOURTH DAY: With few exceptions the fourth-day flower does not open and sinks down into the water. In species flowers and seed-producing cultivars, the seeds start development inside the ovaries if the flower was fertilized. In other situations, the fourth-day flower becomes a jellylike mass, disintegrating in a few days.

Some cultivars will not bloom freely, or blooming will be interrupted, when air temperatures remain in the 80–90°F (27–32°C) range for prolonged periods. For example, *Nymphaea* 'William Falconer' is a free bloomer in USDA zones 3–5. When grown in USDA zones 6 and 7, however, it will stop blooming completely in mid-summer and resume blooming in the fall when cooler weather arrives.

When grown in USDA zones 8–10 'William Falconer' will produce few blooms to no blooms at all. Other cultivars unsuitable for zones 8–10 include 'Atropurpurea', 'Chrysantha', 'Conqueror', 'Ellisiana', 'Gloire du Temple-sur-Lot', 'Gonnère', 'Helvola', *Nymphaea* ×*laydekeri* 'Purpurata', 'Maurice Laydeker', and 'Norma Gedye'.

Another climatic effect resulting from high summer temperatures is an effect known as petal "burning" or "melting." During hot days when summer temperatures reach the upper 80s to 90s (29–32°C or more), flower petals may blacken. Blooming is not necessarily interrupted and the burning of the petals stops with cooler weather.

Some of the cultivars most susceptible to petal burning are 'Atropurpurea', 'Conqueror', 'Perry's Red Beauty' (somewhat susceptible), 'Perry's Wildfire', and 'William Falconer'. 'Atropurpurea' (when grown in USDA zones 8–10) and 'William Falconer' (in zones 6–10) can be expected to have their bloom interrupted along with petal burning.

In the southern United States some of the hardy water lilies, particularly the red- and pink-flowered, do not thrive, probably because of their Swedish ancestry.

This chapter includes a full description of current hardy water lily cultivars as noted in water lily catalogs from around the world (see Appendix B for a list of these sources). Plants are listed alphabetically by published name, followed by any synonyms. Next, the author and year of introduction are given, when known. Common names, if any, follow. Some of these cultivars are my own introductions, developing largely from work carried out in North Carolina (USDA zone 6b). I have been told that the summer climate there is very similar to that of the area in southern France where Marliac did much of his work. Although many of my introductions resulted from hand-pollination, many others are the result of natural (bee) crosses; it is thought that many of Marliac's originations developed from bee crosses too.

"Characteristics" includes type of rhizome. The five rhizome types are described in Chapter 15. Standardized color names and numbers, as given for petals, anthers, and sepals, refer to the Royal Horticultural Society (R.H.S.) Color Chart.

Note that "Stamen color" refers to the color found on the basal portion of the stamen, also known as the filament. As hardy water lilies also have staminodes, located just outside the stamens, my reference to stamens also includes the base portion of the staminodes. "Leaf size" refers either to the diameter of the leaf of a mature plant or to the measurements of its length and width, in that order. "Leaf spread" refers to the diameter of the area on the water's surface covered by the leaves of the mature plant.

"Comments" on each plant include reference to what size pool is suitable. Although there are no hard rules differentiating pool sizes, general guidelines follow:

> tub garden: up to 3 ft (1 m) in diameter
> small: 4–6 ft (1.2–2 m) in diameter
> medium: 7–9 ft (2.2–2.7 m) in diameter
> large: 10 ft (3 m) in diameter or larger
> natural pond: dirt or mud bottom pond of any size

Note that copper and redwood are toxic to plants and fish and should be used only in conjunction with a plastic or other fish-safe liner.

Plant hardy water lily cultivars only when the water temperature reaches 60°F (16°C) or above. Refer to the hardiness zone maps in Appendix A and follow this general planting timetable:

> IN NORTH AMERICA AND EUROPE
> Zone 10   any time of year
> Zone 9   March through September
> Zone 8   April through September
> Zone 7   April through August
> Zone 6   mid April through August
> Zone 5   late April/early May through mid August
> Zone 4   mid May through 1 August

Nymphaea 'Aflame'. See *N.* 'Escarboucle'.

Nymphaea 'Alba Plenissima' (formerly 'Hermine' No. 2). Parentage: Unknown. Characteristics: Day blooming, tuberosa rhizome, moderately free flowering. Plate 275.

PETAL COLOR: White. *R.H.S. Chart*: Fan 4, White Group, No. 155C. Sepal color: Greenish white. *R.H.S. Chart*: Fan 3, Yellow-Green Group, No. 145D. Anther color: Yellow. *R.H.S. Chart*: Fan 1, Yellow Group, No. 10A. Stamen color: Yellow. Flower shape: Cuplike then stellate. Flower size: 4.5–5 in (11–13 cm). Fragrance: Pleasant. Number of petals: 28–29. Number of sepals: 4.

LEAF COLOR: Top, green, newest leaves bronzy; underside, bronzy purple. Leaf and sinus: Leaves nearly round; lobes usually overlap sinus or sinus may be open 1 in (2.5 cm) or wide open. Generally there is a tip at the end of each leaf lobe. Leaf size: 6–7 in (15–18 cm). Leaf spread: 4 ft (1.2 m). Stem color: Reddish brown. Pubescence on peduncle or petiole: Thick fuzz on both.

COMMENTS: This is a small- to medium-growing tuberosa best suited to the small or medium pool. Blooms are not plentiful until a colony of several plants has formed in a large planter. 'Alba Plenissima' has a tendency to develop an abundance of leaves.

Nymphaea 'Albatross' Joseph B. L. Marliac 1910. Parentage: Unknown. Characteristics: Day blooming, Marliac rhizome, very free flowering. Plate 233.

PETAL COLOR: White. *R.H.S. Chart*: Fan 4, White Group, No. 155C. Sepal color: White. *R.H.S. Chart*: Fan 4, White Group, No. 155C. Anther color: Yellow. *R.H.S. Chart*: Fan 1, Yellow Group, No. 6B. Stamen color: Yellow. Flower shape: Stellate. Flower size: 6–8 in (15–20 cm). Fragrance: None. Number of petals: 29–30. Number of sepals: 5.

LEAF COLOR: Top, olive green with a few purple blotches; underside, red. Leaf and sinus: Leaf round; sinus ½ to ⅔ open. Leaf size: 8–10 in (20–25 cm). Leaf spread: 3–5 ft (1–1.5 m). Stem color: Yellowish. Pubescence on peduncle or petiole: A few very fine hairs on both.

COMMENTS: Pointed petal tips distinguish this lily from the "Albatross" with rounded petal tips that is sometimes mislabeled in European nurseries. The true 'Albatross' is a fine plant for any size pool.

Nymphaea 'Amabilis' (syn. 'Pink Marvel') Latour-Marliac Nursery 1921. Parentage: Unknown. Characteristics: Day blooming, Marliac rhizome, fairly free flowering. Plate 234.

PETAL COLOR: Medium pink, tips light pink. *R.H.S. Chart*: Fan 2, Red-Purple Group, No. 63D; tips, No. 65D. Sepal color: Silvery pink. *R.H.S. Chart*: Fan 2, Red-Purple Group, Nos. 65C–D. Anther color: Deep yellow. *R.H.S. Chart*: Fan 1, Yellow Group, No. 13A. Stamen color: Deep yellow. Flower shape: Stellate. Flower size: 6–7.5 in (15–19 cm). Fragrance: Slight to medium. Number of petals: 20–23. Number of sepals: 4.

LEAF COLOR: Top, green, young leaves reddish purple; underside, light green, reddish perimeter. Leaf and sinus: Leaf nearly round; sinus wide open. Leaf size: 9.5 in (24 cm). Leaf spread: 5–7.5 ft (1.5–2.3 m). Stem color: Bronze to red. Pubescence on peduncle or petiole: Fine hairs on both.

COMMENTS: 'Amabilis', with its very large flowers, is a fine lily for the medium or large pool.

Nymphaea 'American Star' Perry D. Slocum 1985. Parentage: Chance seedling of *N.* 'Rose Arey'. Characteristics: Day blooming, odorata rhizome, fairly free flowering. Plate 235.

PETAL COLOR: Rich salmon-pink, tips lighter pink. *R.H.S. Chart*: Fan 2, Red-Purple Group, No. 62B; tips, No. 62C. Sepal color: Rich salmon-pink, border greenish. *R.H.S. Chart*: Fan 2, Red-Purple Group, No. 62C; border, Fan 3, Green Group, No. 143C. Anther color: Yellow. *R.H.S. Chart*: Fan 1, Yellow-Orange Group, No. 20B. Stamen color: Inner rows yellow; outer rows pinkish orange. Flower shape: Starlike. Flower size: 6–7 in (15–18 cm). Fragrance: Pleasant. Number of petals: 30–31. Number of sepals: 4.

LEAF COLOR: Top, green, new leaves purple-green; underside, red, prominent green V along midvein on new leaves. Leaf and sinus: Leaves round; lobes cover ¾ of sinus. Leaf size: 10–11 in (25–28 cm). Leaf spread: 4–5 ft (1.2–1.5 m). Stem color: Purple. Pubescence on peduncle or petiole: Both stems very fuzzy.

COMMENTS: This lily, which has very long, narrow petals, was named by Ray Davies of Stapeley Water Gardens, England, while visiting the seedling beds at Perry's Water Gardens, Franklin, North Carolina (USDA zone 6b). It was introduced by Stapeley Water Gardens. For best results plant 'American Star' in a large planter and allow a colony of several rhizomes to develop. It will then bloom fairly well. I recommend this plant for medium or large pools and natural ponds.

Nymphaea 'Andreana' Joseph B. L. Marliac 1895. Parentage: *N. alba* var. *rubra* × *N. mexicana*. Characteristics: Day blooming, upright rhizome, very free flowering. Plate 236.

PETAL COLOR: Inner petals reddish orange then

rusty orange; outer petals medium pale yellow then peach-yellow. *R.H.S. Chart*: Inner petals, first day, Fan 1, Orange-Red Group, No. 34B; third day, Red Group, No. 42B. Outer petals, first day, Fan 1, Yellow-Orange Group, No. 19B; third day, Red Group, No. 41D. Sepal color: Yellowish. *R.H.S. Chart*: Fan 1, Yellow-Orange Group, No. 19B. Anther color: Golden yellow. *R.H.S. Chart*: Fan 1, Yellow-Orange Group, No. 19A. Stamen color: Deep yellow. Flower shape: Cuplike then peony-style. Flower size: 5–7 in (13–18 cm). Fragrance: Very slight, if any. Number of petals: 20–22. Number of sepals: 4.

LEAF COLOR: Top, green, dark reddish brown blotches; underside, green, numerous dark reddish brown spots and blotches. Leaf and sinus: Leaf nearly round; sinus wide open. Leaf size: 7–8 in (18–20 cm). Leaf spread: 3–4 ft (1–1.2 m). Stem color: Green; brown when young. Pubescence on peduncle or petiole: None.

COMMENTS: 'Andreana' is frequently confused with 'Aurora', which it resembles very closely. The main difference is 'Andreana' has larger blooms, larger leaves, and larger leaf spread. 'Andreana' is one of the choicest of the changeable hardies and I would recommend it for any size pool.

Nymphaea **'Apple Blossom Pink'** Perry D. Slocum 1988. Parentage: Chance seedling of *N*. 'Perry's Pink'. Characteristics: Day blooming, odorata rhizome, fairly free flowering. Plate 237.

PETAL COLOR: Shell pink. *R.H.S. Chart*: Fan 1, Red Group, No. 56D or paler. Sepal color: Shell pink. *R.H.S. Chart*: Fan 1, Red Group, No. 56D or paler. Anther color: Deep yellow. *R.H.S. Chart*: Fan 1, Yellow Group, No. 13B. Stamen color: Deep yellow. Flower shape: Peony-style. Flower size: 7–9 in (18–23 cm). Fragrance: Delightful. Number of petals: 38–40. Number of sepals: 4.

LEAF COLOR: Top, green; underside, pinkish brown. Leaf and sinus: Leaf round; sinus an open V. Leaf size: 10–11 in (25–28 cm). Leaf spread: 6–7 ft (2–2.2 m). Stem color: Brown. Pubescence on peduncle or petiole: None.

COMMENTS: Blooms are quite double. 'Apple Blossom Pink' is a volunteer seedling from one of the clay-bottom propagating ponds at Perry's Water Gardens. Due to its remarkable beauty and huge size, I recommend it for the medium or large pool or even the natural pond. One caution: in the natural pond it may travel 2 ft (0.6 m) or more per year. I recommend planting in a container at least 24 × 24 × 12 in (60 × 60 × 30 cm) for optimum performance.

Nymphaea **'Arc-en-Ciel'** Joseph B. L. Marliac 1901. Parentage: Unknown. Characteristics: Day bloom-

ing, odorata rhizome, fairly free flowering, beautiful leaves. Plate 238.

PETAL COLOR: Usually shell pink on first day, white or nearly white by second day. *R.H.S. Chart*: First day, Fan 1, Red Group, No. 36D; second day, Fan 4, White Group, No. 155B. Sepal color: Medium pink then off-white. *R.H.S. Chart*: First day, Fan 1, Red Group, No. 36C; second day, No. 56D. Anther color: Deep yellow. *R.H.S. Chart*: Fan 1, Yellow Group, No. 12A. Stamen color: Deep yellow. Flower shape: Stellate, long narrow petals and sepals. Flower size: 5–6 in (13–15 cm). Fragrance: Pronounced sweet scent on larger blooms. Number of petals: 18–24. Number of sepals: 4.

LEAF COLOR: Top, olive green, frequently splashed yellow, cream, pink, and even red radiating from center or large pink or reddish areas; underside, reddish brown. Leaf and sinus: Leaf round; sinus wide open. Leaf size: 9.5 in (24 cm). Leaf spread: 4–5 ft (1.2–1.5 m). Stem color: Green; some peduncles display prominent, light yellow stripes. Pubescence on peduncle or petiole: None.

COMMENTS: 'Arc-en-Ciel' has magnificent leaves and is a wonderful plant for the collector. Some leaf colorations are truly beautiful and no two leaves are exactly alike. I recommend this cultivar for medium and large pools.

Nymphaea **'Arethusa'** (syn. 'Bateau') Joseph B. L. Marliac. Parentage: *N. alba* var. *rubra* × *N. mexicana*. Characteristics: Day blooming, Marliac rhizome, free flowering. Plate 239.

PETAL COLOR: Dark red center then deep purplish red; outer petals lighter then deepening. *R.H.S. Chart*: Fan 2, Red-Purple Group, No. 59B; third day, No. 59A. Outer petals, No. 64D; third day, No. 59D. Sepal color: Nearly white then rosy pink. *R.H.S. Chart*: Fan 4, White Group, No. 155A; rosy pink, Fan 2, Red-Purple Group, No. 65C. Anther color: Burnt orange. *R.H.S. Chart*: Fan 1, Orange-Red Group, No. 32C. Stamen color: Orange-red. Flower shape: Globular. Flower size: 5–5.5 in (13–14 cm). Fragrance: Slight. Number of petals: 27. Number of sepals: 4.

LEAF COLOR: Top, green, blotched purple, newest leaves purplish; underside, red. Leaf and sinus: Leaves round; sinus a wide-open V. Leaf size: 8 in (20 cm). Leaf spread: 3–4 ft (1–1.2 m). Stem color: Red to reddish brown. Pubescence on peduncle or petiole: Some fuzz on both.

COMMENTS: Flowers are more globular than cuplike, in a shape similar to that of the cultivar *N.* ×*marliacea* 'Rubra Punctata'. Magnificent leaves and beautiful flowers make this water lily an excellent choice for any size pool.

Nymphaea **'Atropurpurea'** Joseph B. L. Marliac 1901. Parentage: Unknown. Characteristics: Day blooming, Marliac rhizome, free flowering except in very hot climates. Plate 240.

PETAL COLOR: Deep red, deepening each day, occasional flecking in tips. *R.H.S. Chart*: Fan 2, Red-Purple Group, No. 61A and darker. Sepal color: Deep pink then pinkish red; veins darker. *R.H.S. Chart*: Fan 2, Red-Purple Group, No. 63 then 64A; veins, No. 61A. Anther color: Very deep yellow. *R.H.S. Chart*: Fan 1, Yellow Group, No. 13A. Stamen color: Burnt orange. Flower shape: Round, flat, then stellate. Flower size: 7–8 in (18–20 cm). Fragrance: Very slight. Number of petals: 30–33. Number of sepals: 4.

LEAF COLOR: Top, green, new leaves purple; underside, purple, green V along midvein. Leaf and sinus: Leaf round; sinus a very large V. Leaf size: 9–10 in (23–25 cm). Leaf spread: 4 ft (1.2 m). Stem color: Peduncle, purple; petiole green. Pubescence on peduncle or petiole: None.

COMMENTS: With its deep, rich red petals and sepals, 'Atropurpurea' is extremely striking. Center petals on second-day flowers sometimes "burn," however, when this plant is grown in hot summer climates (comparable to USDA zones 7–10). Also, when grown in USDA zone 7 this cultivar blooms all summer; in zone 9 blooming slows in the summer. I recommend this lily for medium and large pools.

Nymphaea **'Attraction'** Joseph B. L. Marliac 1910. Parentage: Unknown. Characteristics: Day blooming, Marliac rhizome, free flowering. Plate 241.

PETAL COLOR: Inner petals deep garnet red; outer petals lighter. *R.H.S. Chart*: Inner petals, Fan 2, Red-Purple Group, No. 64A; outer petals, No. 64B. Sepal color: White, striped pink; pink base developing on older flowers. *R.H.S. Chart*: Fan 4, White Group, No. 155C; stripes, Fan 2, Red-Purple Group, No. 64D; base, No. 65A. Anther color: Golden yellow. *R.H.S. Chart*: Fan 1, Yellow-Orange Group, No. 19A. Stamen color: Glowing orange. Flower shape: Cuplike then stellate. Flower size: 6–8 in (15–20 cm). Fragrance: Very slight. Number of petals: 26–28. Number of sepals: 4–5, usually 5.

LEAF COLOR: Top, green, new leaves light bronze; underside, green, light bronze perimeter. Leaf and sinus: Leaf oval; lobes overlap at sinus, one lobe usually raised. Leaf size: 10–12 in (25–30 cm). Leaf spread: 4–5 ft (1.2–1.5 m). Stem color: Purplish. Pubescence on peduncle or petiole: None.

COMMENTS: This cultivar is among the largest of the red hardy water lilies and the very best red hardy to use for cut flowers. Inner petals are subject

to "burn" and blackening on hot days, however. This lily is also subject to crown rot.

Nymphaea **'Aurora'** Joseph B. L. Marliac 1895. Parentage: Probably *N. alba* var. *rubra* × *N. mexicana*. Characteristics: Day blooming, upright rhizome, very free flowering. Plate 242.

PETAL COLOR: First day, yellow-apricot, darker center; second day, orange-red, slightly flecked; third day, deep burgundy-red, slightly flecked. *R.H.S. Chart*: First day, Fan 1, Orange Group, Nos. 24D and 29A; second day, Orange-Red Group, No. 35B; third day, Red Group, No. 47A. Sepal color: Creamy white, flushing pink and white. *R.H.S. Chart*: Fan 4, White Group, No. 155A; second and third days, flush, Fan 1, Red Group, No. 55C. Anther color: Yellow then orange. *R.H.S. Chart*: Fan 1, Yellow Group, No. 13A; then Yellow-Orange Group, No. 23A. Stamen color: Glowing, golden orange, especially on second and third days. Flower shape: Cuplike, later flattening. Flower size: 4–4.5 in (10–11 cm). Fragrance: Very slight. Number of petals: 24–25. Number of sepals: 4–5.

LEAF COLOR: Top, green, new leaves blotched purple; underside, light purple, many small red-purple mottles. Leaf and sinus: Leaf slightly longer than wide; sinus a wide-open V. Leaf size: 6–6.5 in (15–16 cm). Leaf spread: 3 ft (1 m). Stem color: Bright green. Pubescence on peduncle or petiole: None.

COMMENTS: I think 'Aurora' is one of the most beautiful water lilies ever created. It has the widest color range of any changeable, and flowers stay open very late in the day. This lily is ideal for the tub garden or small to medium pool.

Nymphaea **'Bateau'**. See *N.* **'Arethusa'**.

Nymphaea **'Bory de Saint-Vincent'** Latour-Marliac Nursery 1937. Parentage: Unknown. Characteristics: Day blooming, Marliac rhizome, very free flowering. Plate 243.

PETAL COLOR: Inner petals red; outer petals pink, lighter tips. *R.H.S. Chart*: Inner petals, Fan 1, Red Group, No. 48A; outer petals, No. 48D, tips, No. 49C. Sepal color: White, greenish veins and border. *R.H.S. Chart*: Fan 4, White Group, No. 155B; veins and border, Greyed-Green Group, No. 193C. Anther color: Burnt orange. *R.H.S. Chart*: Fan 1, Orange Group, No. 29B. Stamen color: Orange. Flower shape: A full star. Flower size: 5.5–6 in (14–15 cm). Fragrance: Very slight. Number of petals: 24. Number of sepals: 4.

LEAF COLOR: Top, green, new leaves mottled purple; underside, brownish green. Leaf and sinus:

Leaf nearly round; sinus open. Leaf size: 9–10 in (23–25 cm). Leaf spread: 4–5 ft (1.2–1.5 m). Stem color: Greenish bronze. Pubescence on peduncle or petiole: None.

COMMENTS: 'Bory de Saint-Vincent', with its four-colored blooms (red-and-pink petals, orange centers, and white sepals), is certainly among the most striking of the hardy water lilies. I highly recommend it for any size pool.

Nymphaea **'Brackleyi Rosea'**. Parentage: Unknown. Characteristics: Day blooming, odorata rhizome, fairly free flowering. Plate 244.

PETAL COLOR: Shell pink. *R.H.S. Chart*: Fan 1, Red Group, No. 36D. Sepal color: Slightly darker than petals, one prominent central pink vein. *R.H.S. Chart*: Fan 1, Red Group, No. 36C; vein, No. 36B. Anther color: Deep yellow. *R.H.S. Chart*: Fan 1, Yellow Group, No. 11A. Stamen color: Deep yellow. Flower shape: Stellate. Flower size: 5 in (13 cm). Fragrance: Very sweet. Number of petals: 21. Number of sepals: 4.

LEAF COLOR: Top, green, new leaves purple; underside, bronzy green, new leaves purple. Leaf and sinus: Leaf nearly round; sinus open. Leaf size: 9–10 in (23–25 cm). Leaf spread: 4–5 ft (1.2–1.5 m). Stem color: Bronzy green. Pubescence on peduncle or petiole: None.

COMMENTS: 'Brackleyi Rosea', available since 1909, is one of the older pink water lilies. Today many other pink hardy lilies are freer blooming with more striking shades of pink. For best results 'Brackleyi Rosea' should be planted in a large container and allowed to form a colony of several plants. Suitable for medium or large pools or natural ponds where it can be expected to spread about 1 ft (0.3 m) or more per year.

Nymphaea **'Carolina Sunset'** Perry D. Slocum 1991. Parentage: Seedling of *N.* 'Texas Dawn'. Characteristics: Day blooming, Marliac rhizome, free flowering. Plate 245.

PETAL COLOR: Inner petals deep yellow; middle petals light yellow, blushed peach. *R.H.S. Chart*: Inner petals, Fan 1, Yellow-Orange Group, Nos. 18C–D; middle petals, Yellow Group, No. 7A; blush, lighter than Fan 2, Red-Purple Group, No. 62D. Sepal color: Pale green, tips darker green. *R.H.S. Chart*: Fan 1, Green-Yellow Group, No. 1D; tips, Fan 3, Green Group, No. 139D and lighter. Anther color: Deep yellow. *R.H.S. Chart*: Fan 1, Yellow Group, No. 11A. Stamen color: Deep yellow. Flower shape: Cuplike; sepals turn down, touch petiole. Flower size: 7–8 in (18–20 cm). Fragrance: Very pleasant. Number of petals: 29–33. Number of sepals: 4.

LEAF COLOR: Top, green, new leaves chartreuse, heavily mottled purple and/or green; underside, pinkish, heavily blotched purple. Leaf and sinus: Leaf nearly round; sinus a wide-open V. Leaf size: 11 × 11.5 in (28 × 29 cm). Leaf spread: 4–5 ft (1.2–1.5 m). Stem color: Peduncle purplish brown, petiole purple. Pubescence on peduncle or petiole: Heavy fuzz on both.

COMMENTS: Flowers of 'Carolina Sunset' display a beautiful pastel color by the third day. The yellow petals are suffused with a blush of peach—a new flower color for hardy water lilies. Flower color and the unique chartreuse of new leaves set this cultivar apart. With its large blooms, unusual flower color, and magnificent leaves, this cultivar should become a favorite. I recommend it for medium or large pools.

Nymphaea **'Caroliniana Nivea'** Joseph B. L. Marliac 1893. Parentage: *N. odorata* is one parent. Characteristics: Day blooming, odorata rhizome, fairly free flowering. Plate 246.

PETAL COLOR: Ivory white. *R.H.S. Chart*: Fan 4, White Group, No. 155A. Sepal color: Greenish yellow. *R.H.S. Chart*: Fan 3, Yellow-Green Group, No. 145D. Anther color: Yellow. *R.H.S. Chart*: Fan 1, Yellow Group, No. 3C. Stamen color: Yellow. Flower shape: Stellate. Flower size: 5–6 in (13–15 cm). Fragrance: Lovely. Number of petals: 27–28. Number of sepals: 4.

LEAF COLOR: Top, green; underside, green. Leaf and sinus: Leaf nearly round; sinus slightly open. Leaf size: 8–10 in (20–25 cm). Leaf spread: 4–5 ft (1.2–1.5 m). Stem color: Green. Pubescence on peduncle or petiole: Some fuzz on both.

COMMENTS: As 'Caroliniana Nivea' is a hybrid involving *N. odorata*, it needs a large planter in order to form a colony of rhizomes and produce more blooms. This is a very old cultivar. Freer-blooming cultivars with more striking flowers in the same color class are available today. It has been dropped from catalog listings in the United States but some nurseries in Europe and Australia still carry stock. I would recommend 'Caroliniana Nivea' for the large pool or the collector.

Nymphaea **'Caroliniana Perfecta'** Joseph B. L. Marliac 1893. Parentage: Unknown. Characteristics: Day blooming, odorata rhizome, fairly free flowering.

PETAL COLOR: Salmon-pink. *R.H.S. Chart*: Fan 1, Red Group, No. 36A. Sepal color: Light salmon-pink. *R.H.S. Chart*: Fan 1, Red Group, No. 36D. Anther color: Yellow. *R.H.S. Chart*: Fan 1, Yellow Group, No. 11A. Stamen color: Yellow. Flower shape: Cuplike. Flower size: 5–6 in (13–15 cm). Fragrance: Very sweet. Number of petals: 30. Number of sepals: 4.

LEAF COLOR: Top, dark green, new leaves bronzy; underside, reddish brown. Leaf and sinus: Leaf nearly round; sinus open. Leaf size: 9–10 in (23–25 cm). Leaf spread: 4–5 ft (1.2–1.5 m). Stem color: Peduncle, brownish green; petiole green. Pubescence on peduncle or petiole: None.

COMMENTS: This is one of the first pink cultivars. There are many better pink hardies among the newer creations. I recommend planting 'Caroliniana Perfecta' in a planter at least 24 × 24 × 12 in (60 × 60 × 30 cm) where it can form a colony of several plants. It is suitable for medium and large pools.

Nymphaea **'Charlene Strawn'** Kirk Strawn 1969. Parentage: Unknown. Characteristics: Day blooming, Marliac rhizome, quite free flowering. Plate 247.

PETAL COLOR: Inner petals, rich yellow; outer petals lighter yellow. *R.H.S. Chart*: Inner petals, Fan 1, Yellow Group, Nos. 2B–C; outer petals, No. 2D. Sepal color: Greenish yellow, tips green, edges often blushed pink. *R.H.S. Chart*: Fan 1, Green-Yellow Group, No. 1D; tips, Fan 3, Yellow-Green Group, No. 145C; edges, Fan 2, Red-Purple Group, No. 73D. Anther color: Deep yellow. *R.H.S. Chart*: Fan 1, Yellow Group, No. 12A. Stamen color: Yellow. Flower shape: Stellate. Flower size: 6–8 in (15–20 cm). Fragrance: Very sweet. Number of petals: 27–29. Number of sepals: 4.

LEAF COLOR: Top, green, new leaves display small purple specks and mottles; underside, light purple and green, mottled purple, newest leaves red, mottled purple. Leaf and sinus: Leaf nearly round; lobes sometimes overlap at sinus, more often sinus an open V. Leaf size: 8–9 in (20–23 cm). Leaf spread: 3–5 ft (1–1.5 m). Stem color: Brown. Pubescence on peduncle or petiole: Thick fuzz on both.

COMMENTS: This is the most fragrant hardy water lily I know and makes an excellent cut flower. The plant develops an abundance of leaves, however, which sometimes hide the flowers. Dr. Strawn named this water lily after his wife. I recommend it for medium and large pools.

Nymphaea **'Charles de Meurville'** Latour-Marliac Nursery 1931. Parentage: Unknown. Characteristics: Day blooming, Marliac rhizome, very free flowering. Plate 248.

PETAL COLOR: Inner petals, dark pinkish red; outer petals, pink. *R.H.S. Chart*: Inner petals, Fan 2, Red-Purple Group, No. 64B; outer petals, No. 65A. Sepal color: Very pale pink. *R.H.S. Chart*: Fan 2, Red-Purple Group, No. 65D. Anther color: Golden orange. *R.H.S. Chart*: Fan 1, Yellow-Orange Group,

No. 19A. Stamen color: Brilliant orange. Flower shape: Stellate. Flower size: 6–7 in (15–18 cm). Fragrance: Slight. Number of petals: 22. Number of sepals: 4.

LEAF COLOR: Top, dark green; underside, dark green, light green veins. Leaf and sinus: Leaf very long; sinus a long V. Leaf size: 10 × 8 in (25 × 20 cm). Leaf spread: 4–5 ft (1.2–1.5 m). Stem color: Purple. Pubescence on peduncle or petiole: Very short fuzz on both.

COMMENTS: Subject to crown rot. Many petals are raised rather than flat. This lily is a very good choice for a medium or large pool.

Nymphaea **'Château le Rouge'**. See *N.* **'William Falconer'**.

Nymphaea **'Cherokee'** (syn. 'Orange Hybrid') Perry's Water Gardens 1989. Parentage: *N.* 'Colonel A. J. Welch' × *N.* 'Aurora'. Characteristics: Day blooming, upright rhizome, occasionally viviparous, free flowering. New plants and rhizomes develop from about 5 percent of flowers or less. Plates 249 and 250.

PETAL COLOR: Rich red; outer petals cream, flushed pink, becoming deep red by third day. *R.H.S. Chart*: Fan 1, Red Group, No. 53D; outer petals, Yellow Group, No. 11D; flush, Red Group, No. 36D; third day, Red Group No. 44A. Sepal color: Creamy white. *R.H.S. Chart*: Fan 1, Yellow Group, No. 11D. Anther color: Bright orange. *R.H.S. Chart*: Fan 1, Orange Group, No. 24A. Stamen color: Orange-red. Flower shape: Cuplike. Flower size: 3–4 in (8–10 cm). Fragrance: Slight, lemony. Number of petals: 21. Number of sepals: 4.

LEAF COLOR: Top, green, newest leaves richly mottled maroon; underside, purple. Leaf and sinus: Leaves round; sinus a wide-open V. Leaf size: 4–6 in (10–15 cm). Leaf spread: 3–4 ft (1–1.2 m). Stem color: Maroon. Pubescence on peduncle or petiole: None.

COMMENTS: The second- and third-day flower color of 'Cherokee' is quite similar to the flower color of 'Aurora'. 'Cherokee' is also similar to 'Perry's Red Star' and 'Colonel A. J. Welch' in that some of the flowers are viviparous, developing new plants from blooms. The new plants produced in this manner have yellow flowers that soon turn to normal color. Subject to crown rot. I recommend this lily for any size pool and even the tub garden.

Nymphaea **'Chromatella'**. See *N.* ×*marliacea* **'Chromatella'**.

Nymphaea **'Chrysantha'** (formerly 'Graziella') Joseph B. L. Marliac 1905. Parentage: Unknown. Characteristics: Day blooming, changeable, upright rhizome, very free flowering. Plate 251.

PETAL COLOR: Outer petals cream-yellow, large green patch on outside; inner petals deeper cream-yellow. All petals flushed orange, deepening. *R.H.S. Chart*: Outer petals, first day, Fan 1, Yellow Group, No. 10D; third day, Orange Group, Nos. 29C–D; green patch, Fan 3, Yellow-Green Group, No. 152B. Inner petals, first day, Fan 1, Orange Group, Nos. 24C–D; third day, Orange-Red Group, Nos. 31B–C; flush, No. 29D. Sepal color: Creamy, deepening, usually a few short red stripes on one or more sepals; slight red blush and flecks by third day. *R.H.S. Chart*: First day, Fan 1, Yellow Group, No. 11D; third day, No. 12D; stripes, Fan 2, Red-Purple Group, No. 64C; blush and flecks, Fan 1, Red Group, No. 54D. Anther color: Golden yellow. *R.H.S. Chart*: Fan 1, Yellow-Orange Group, No. 23B. Stamen color: Inner rows, golden yellow; outer rows orange-pink. Flower shape: Cuplike. Flower size: 3–4 in (8–10 cm). Fragrance: None. Number of petals: 16–19. Number of sepals: 4 or 5.

LEAF COLOR: Top, green, new leaves blotched purple; underside, reddish, freckled purple, new leaves bronzy. Leaf and sinus: Leaf almost round; sinus a wide-open V. Leaf size: 6.5 × 5.5 in (16 × 14 cm). Leaf spread: 2–3 ft (0.6–1 m). Stem color: Green to purple. Pubescence on peduncle or petiole: Short fuzz and tiny hairs on both.

COMMENTS: 'Chrysantha' is frequently mislabeled and sold in some nurseries in the United States as 'Paul Hariot' or 'Graziella'. Flower color is quite similar among the three, though the 'Paul Hariot' flower is larger. The rhizome of 'Paul Hariot' is subject to crown rot, however, while that of 'Chrysantha' is fairly free from such problems. 'Chrysantha' is an ideal plant for a tub garden or a small pool except in very hot regions, where it does not bloom well.

Nymphaea '**Colonel A. J. Welch**' Joseph B. L. Marliac. Parentage: Unknown. Characteristics: Day blooming, viviparous from the blossom, Marliac rhizome, not free flowering. Plates 252 and 253.

PETAL COLOR: Lemon yellow, inner row slightly deeper yellow. *R.H.S. Chart*: Fan 1, Yellow Group, No. 12C; inner row, No. 12B. Sepal color: Lemon yellow, tips and borders touched green. *R.H.S. Chart*: Fan 1, Yellow Group, No. 12D; tips and borders, Fan 3, Yellow-Green Group, No. 151D. Anther color: Bright yellow. *R.H.S. Chart*: Fan 1, Yellow Group, No. 13C. Stamen color: Bright yellow. Flower shape: Stellate. Flower size: 5.5–6 in (14–15 cm). Fragrance: Pleasant in new blooms. Number of petals: 22–23. Number of sepals: 4.

LEAF COLOR: Top, olive green, perimeter of newest leaves flecked purple; underside, green, newest leaves display small purple blotches and specks. Leaf and sinus: Leaves round; lobes may overlap ⅓ to ½ of sinus or sinus may be an open V. Leaf size: 9 in (23 cm). Leaf spread: 6 ft (2 m). Stem color: Peduncles usually purple; petioles yellow-green, striped purple, or solid purple. Pubescence on peduncle or petiole: None.

COMMENTS: This cultivar is a viviparous hardy that frequently develops new plants with rhizomes directly from the old blossom head. It is sometimes mistakenly sold as 'Sunrise' (syn. *N. odorata* 'Sulphurea Grandiflora'), which it closely resembles. 'Colonel A. J. Welch' is a poor substitute, however, since it produces very few blooms and its abundant foliage crowds together above the water. It is best used in a pond that is very deep, 4–7 ft (1.2–2.2 m) or so, or as a novelty plant for its viviparous trait.

Nymphaea '**Colossea**' Joseph B. L. Marliac 1901. Parentage: Unknown. Characteristics: Day blooming, Marliac rhizome, very free flowering. Plate 254.

PETAL COLOR: Light pink, paling. *R.H.S. Chart*: Fan 1, Red-Purple Group, No. 65D, paling to Fan 4, White Group, No. 155D. Sepal color: Medium pink, paling. *R.H.S. Chart*: Fan 1, Red-Purple Group, No. 65D then 49D. Anther color: Yellow. *R.H.S. Chart*: Fan 1, Yellow Group, No. 11A. Stamen color: Yellow. Flower shape: Cuplike then stellate. Flower size: 6–8 in (15–20 cm). Fragrance: Slight. Number of petals: 23–25. Number of sepals: 4.

LEAF COLOR: Top, green, new leaves bronzy; underside, green. Leaf and sinus: Leaf a little longer than wide; sinus wide open. Leaf size: 10–12 in (25–30 cm). Leaf spread: 5–6 ft (1.5–2 m). Stem color: Greenish. Pubescence on peduncle or petiole: A few tiny hairs on both.

COMMENTS: Flower color of 'Colossea' is quite similar to that of *N.* ×*marliacea* 'Rosea', but 'Colossea' flowers are larger and petals are more rounded on tips. According to Paul Stetson, owner of Paradise Water Gardens, Whitman, Massachusetts, this water lily produces more flowers over a longer period than any other Marliac. I recommend it for medium or large pools.

Nymphaea '**Comanche**' (formerly 'J. C. N. Forestier') Joseph B. L. Marliac 1908. Parentage: Unknown. Characteristics: Day blooming, pineapple rhizome, very free flowering. Plate 255.

PETAL COLOR: First day, yellow-apricot, deeper toward center; second day, gold-orange flushed pink; third day, deep orange, center petals flushed red, pale yellow tips. *R.H.S. Chart*: First day, Fan 1,

Yellow Group, No. 11B, 1B by second day; Red Group, No. 43D, 54C by second day; third day, Red Group, No. 54B; tips, Yellow Group, No. 12D. Sepal color: Creamy, more orange with age, pink base. *R.H.S. Chart*: Fan 1, Green-Yellow Group, No. 1D; third day, Yellow Group, No. 13B; base, Red Group, No. 54C. Anther color: Deep golden yellow, more orange with age. *R.H.S. Chart*: First day, Fan 1, Yellow Group, No. 13B; third day, Yellow-Orange Group, No. 21D. Stamen color: Golden yellow, orange outer row. Flower shape: Cuplike then stellate. Flower size: 5–6 in (13–15 cm). Fragrance: Very pleasant. Number of petals: 22–26. Number of sepals: 4.

LEAF COLOR: Top, green, newest leaves bronzy green, few purple flecks; underside, red, flecked purple, flecks prominent on new leaves. Leaf and sinus: Leaves nearly round. Sinus usually a wide-open V, some lobes may overlap partially even on same plant. Leaf size: Up to 12 × 11 in (30 × 28 cm). Leaf spread: 4–5 ft (1.2–1.5 m). Stem color: Brown. Pubescence on peduncle or petiole: Fine fuzz and small hairs on both.

COMMENTS: 'Comanche' is the largest and showiest of the orange changeables, but it is also more subject to crown rot than most of the others. This water lily does well in both southern and northern areas and is an excellent choice for medium and large pools.

Nymphaea **'Conqueror'** Joseph B. L. Marliac 1910. Parentage: Unknown. Characteristics: Day blooming, Marliac rhizome, very free flowering. Plate 256.

PETAL COLOR: Inner petals deep red then deeper; outer petals white then light pink. *R.H.S. Chart*: Inner petals, Fan 2, Red-Purple Group, No. 64C; third day, No. 61B. Outer petals, Fan 4, White Group, No. 155C; then Fan 2, Red-Purple Group, No. 68D. Sepal color: White, pink veins. *R.H.S. Chart*: Fan 4, White Group, No. 155C; veins, Fan 2, Red-Purple Group, No. 68D. Anther color: Bright yellow. *R.H.S. Chart*: Fan 1, Yellow Group, No. 13B. Stamen color: Brilliant orange. Flower shape: Star-like. Flower size: 7–8 in (18–20 cm). Fragrance: Slight. Number of petals: 28. Number of sepals: 4–5.

LEAF COLOR: Top, deep green, new leaves slightly bronzed; underside, green, perimeter bronze, new leaves purple, green V in center. Leaf and sinus: Leaf almost round; sinus usually a wide-open V. Leaf size: Up to 10–11 in (25–28 cm). Leaf spread: 5 ft (1.5 m). Stem color: Purple. Pubescence on peduncle or petiole: None.

COMMENTS: 'Conqueror' is really a tricolored water lily (red, pink, and white) and a very satisfactory plant on the whole. In hot weather, however,

the inner deep red petals nearly always "burn" and blacken. I recommend it for medium and large pools.

Nymphaea **'Crystal White'**. See *N*. **'Gonnère'**.

Nymphaea **'Darwin'** (formerly 'Hollandia') Joseph B. L. Marliac 1909. Parentage: Probably a mutation of *N*. 'Madame Wilfron Gonnère'. Characteristics: Day blooming, Marliac rhizome, free flowering. Plate 276.

PETAL COLOR: Inner petals light pink then deeper; outer petals white, pinkish by third day. *R.H.S. Chart*: Inner petals, Fan 2, Red-Purple Group, No. 65A then 73B. Outer petals, Fan 4, White Group, No. 155B; third day, Fan 2, Red-Purple Group, No. 73D. Sepal color: Pinkish white, pink flush by third day, green border. *R.H.S. Chart*: Closest to Fan 4, White Group, No. 155B; flush, Red-Purple Group, No. 73D; border, Fan 3, Yellow-Green Group, No. 144A. Anther color: Golden yellow. *R.H.S. Chart*: Fan 1, Yellow Group, No. 13B. Stamen color: Pinkish yellow. Flower shape: Double, peony-style. Flower size: 6–7.5 in (15–19 cm). Fragrance: Slight. Number of petals: 36–37. Number of sepals: 4.

LEAF COLOR: Top, green; underside, green, new leaves brownish. Leaf and sinus: Leaf round. Sinus varies considerably, even on same plant; some lobes overlap, some separated by an open V. Leaf size: 10–11 in (25–28 cm). Leaf spread: 4–5 ft (1.2–1.5 m). Stem color: Purple underwater, green above water. Pubescence on peduncle or petiole: Short fuzz on underwater stems.

COMMENTS: 'Darwin' is a great favorite and makes a terrific cut flower. A well-grown plant is a joy to behold. I highly recommend this lily for medium and large pools.

Nymphaea **'Ellisiana'** Joseph B. L. Marliac 1896. Parentage: Unknown. Characteristics: Day blooming, Marliac rhizome, very free flowering. Plate 257.

PETAL COLOR: Very brilliant red. *R.H.S. Chart*: Fan 2, Red-Purple Group, No. 61B. Sepal color: Greenish white, pink veins, pink toward base. *R.H.S. Chart*: Fan 4, Greyed-Green Group, No. 193D; veins, Fan 2, Red-Purple Group, No. 62B; base, No. 62C. Anther color: Rich golden yellow. *R.H.S. Chart*: Fan 1, Yellow-Orange Group, No. 22A. Stamen color: Orange-red. Flower shape: Full, stellate. Flower size: 4–5 in (10–13 cm). Fragrance: Quite noticeable. Number of petals: 21–22. Number of sepals: 4.

LEAF COLOR: Top, green, new leaves dark green, blotched purple; underside, green, new leaves purple-bronze. Leaf and sinus: Leaf a little longer than wide. Lobes overlap slightly on new leaves; sinus wide open on older leaves. Leaf size: 7–8 in (18–20 cm). Leaf spread: 3 ft (1 m). Stem color: Bronze. Pubescence on peduncle or petiole: A few short hairs on both.

COMMENTS: This is a first-rate plant for a tub garden or small pool. Note, however, that it performs best in northern regions. As it tends to stop blooming in very hot weather, I do not recommend it for USDA zones 8–10; it does bloom freely all summer in North Carolina (zone 6b), however.

Nymphaea **'Escarboucle'** (syn. 'Aflame') Joseph B. L. Marliac 1909. Parentage: Unknown. Characteristics: Day blooming, Marliac rhizome, very free flowering. Plate 258.

PETAL COLOR: Very bright vermilion-red, outer petal row tipped white. *R.H.S. Chart*: Fan 2, Red-Purple Group, No. 64B; tips, Fan 4, White Group, No. 155A. Sepal color: Pink, deepening; white tips. *R.H.S. Chart*: Fan 2, Red-Purple Group, No. 62D; last day, No. 66D. Tips, Fan 4, White Group, No. 155A. Anther color: Golden yellow. *R.H.S. Chart*: Fan 1, Orange Group, No. 26B. Stamen color: Burnt orange. Flower shape: Cuplike then stellate. Flower size: 6–7 in (15–18 cm). Fragrance: Some, even in older flowers. Number of petals: 25. Number of sepals: 4.

LEAF COLOR: Top, green, newer leaves brownish; underside, green, perimeter brownish near sinus, newer leaves brownish. Leaf and sinus: Leaf almost round; lobes overlap about 1 in (2.5 cm) at sinus. Leaf size: 10–11 in (25–28 cm). Leaf spread: 4–5 ft (1.2–1.5 m). Stem color: Bronzy green, sometimes fine red lengthwise stripes. Pubescence on peduncle or petiole: None.

COMMENTS: This is undoubtedly one of the very best red hardies for medium and large pools. Blooms stay open very late in the afternoon—long after most other red hardies have closed.

Nymphaea **'Eugene de Land'** Latour-Marliac Nursery. Parentage: Unknown. Characteristics: Day blooming, odorata rhizome, fairly free flowering. Plate 259.

PETAL COLOR: Light to medium pink. *R.H.S. Chart*: Fan 1, Red Group, No. 36A. Sepal color: Light to medium pink. *R.H.S. Chart*: Fan 1, Red Group, No. 36A. Anther color: Deep yellow. *R.H.S. Chart*: Fan 1, Yellow-Orange Group, No. 15B. Stamen color: Deep yellow. Flower shape: Full, cuplike, then star effect from very long outer petals. Flower size: 7–8 in (18–20 cm). Fragrance: Very pleasant. Number of petals: 21–22. Number of sepals: 4.

LEAF COLOR: Top, green; underside, salmon-pink. Leaf and sinus: Leaf nearly round; sinus usually open. Leaf size: Up to 10–11 in (25–28 cm). Leaf spread: 4–5.5 ft (1.2–1.7 m). Stem color: Bronzy green. Pubescence on peduncle or petiole: None.

COMMENTS: 'Eugene de Land' is a very attractive lily. For optimal blooming, it should be planted in a large planter where it can form a colony of several plants. I recommend it for the medium and large pool.

Nymphaea **'Fabiola'** (formerly 'Mrs. Richmond') Latour-Marliac Nursery 1913. Parentage: Unknown. Characteristics: Day blooming, Marliac rhizome, very free flowering. Plate 260.

PETAL COLOR: Inner petals pinkish red, highly flecked; outer petals lighter, highly flecked, white tips. *R.H.S. Chart*: Inner petals, Fan 2, Red-Purple Group, No. 64B; outer petals, Nos. 62C–D; tips, Fan 4, White Group, No. 155C. Sepal color: Whitish; pink developing at base. *R.H.S. Chart*: Closest to Fan 4, White Group, No. 155B; third day, base, Fan 2, Red-Purple Group, No. 62C. Anther color: Yellow. *R.H.S. Chart*: Fan 1, Yellow-Orange Group, No. 22B. Stamen color: Orange, pink outer row. Flower shape: Peony-style. Flower size: 6–7 in (15–18 cm). Fragrance: Pleasant and noticeable in new flowers. Number of petals: 24–25. Number of sepals: 4.

LEAF COLOR: Top, green, new leaves bronzy purple; underside, brownish purple. Leaf and sinus: Leaf longer than wide; lobes overlap almost entirely. Leaf size: 12 × 11 in (30 × 28 cm). Leaf spread: 5 ft (1.5 m). Stem color: Purple. Pubescence on peduncle or petiole: Thick fuzz on both.

COMMENTS: Due to its profusion of beautiful large bicolored flowers, 'Fabiola' is a wonderful plant for medium and large pools.

Nymphaea **'Fantastic Pink'** Perry D. Slocum 1987. Parentage: Seedling or mutation of *N.* 'Pink Sensation'. Characteristics: Day blooming, Marliac rhizome, quite free flowering yet somewhat slow in starting. Plate 261.

PETAL COLOR: Shell pink. *R.H.S. Chart*: Fan 2, Red-Purple Group, No. 65D. Sepal color: Shell pink; 11–12 bluish pink lengthwise veins. *R.H.S. Chart*: Fan 2, Red-Purple Group, No. 65D; veins, No. 65A. Anther color: Deep golden yellow. *R.H.S. Chart*: Fan 1, Yellow Group, No. 5B. Stamen color: Deep golden yellow, same as anthers. Flower shape: Full, stellate. Flower size: 6–8 in (15–20 cm). Fragrance: Slight. Number of petals: 24–30. Number of sepals: 4.

LEAF COLOR: Top, olive green, new leaves deep purple; underside, red or reddish purple. Leaf and sinus: Leaf quite large, nearly round. Lobes usually raised at sinus, overlap partially; sinus open or open 1 in (2.5 cm). Leaf size: 10–12 in (25–30 cm). Leaf spread: 5–6 ft (1.5–2 m). Stem color: Peduncle, yellow-green, slight purple flecking; petiole green. Pubescence on peduncle or petiole: On both, heavier on peduncle.

COMMENTS: This selection developed in the 'Pink Sensation' bed at Perry's Water Gardens in North Carolina (USDA zone 6b). It is rare for a seedling or mutation to suddenly appear with a thick Marliac rhizome. This particular water lily is especially striking with its very broad petals and sepals. I recommend 'Fantastic Pink' for the medium or large pool.

Nymphaea **'Firecrest'**. Parentage: Unknown. Characteristics: Day blooming, odorata rhizome, moderately free flowering. Plate 262.

PETAL COLOR: Lavender-pink. *R.H.S. Chart*: Fan 2, Red-Purple Group, Nos. 65B–C. Sepal color: Lavender-pink, greenish margin. *R.H.S. Chart*: Fan 2, Red-Purple Group, No. 65B; margin, Fan 4, Greyed-Green Group, No. 194D. Anther color: Burnt orange. *R.H.S. Chart*: Fan 1, Orange-Red Group, No. 31B. Stamen color: Inner rows, orange; outer rows pink. Flower shape: Stellate. Flower size: 5.5–6 in (14–15 cm). Fragrance: Slight. Number of petals: 29. Number of sepals: 4.

LEAF COLOR: Top, green, new leaves very deep purple; underside, deep purple. Leaf and sinus: Leaf round; sinus usually an open V. Leaf size: 9 in (23 cm). Leaf spread: 4 ft (1.2 m). Stem color: Green. Pubescence on peduncle or petiole: Considerable fuzz on both.

COMMENTS: Flowers are held above the water with sepals and outer petals hanging down. For most frequent blooming, plant in a large container at least 2 ft (0.6 m) in diameter and 1 ft (0.3 m) deep so that a colony of several roots can form. This lily will spread 12 in (30 cm) or more per year. If space is plentiful, it is a fine lily for medium or large pools or natural ponds.

Nymphaea **'Formosa'** Joseph B. L. Marliac 1909. Parentage: Unknown. Characteristics: Day blooming, Marliac rhizome, very free flowering. Plate 263.

PETAL COLOR: Outer petals medium pink, deepening toward flower center, highly flecked throughout. *R.H.S. Chart*: Outer petals, Fan 2, Red-Purple Group, No. 62D; inner petals, No. 62B. Sepal color: Nearly white, blushed pink. *R.H.S. Chart*: Fan 4, White Group, No. 155A; blush, Fan 2, Red-Purple Group, No. 65D or lighter. Anther color: Deep yellow. *R.H.S. Chart*: Fan 1, Yellow Group, No. 13A. Stamen color: Yellow. Flower shape: Full, cuplike. Flower size: 5–6 in (13–15 cm). Fragrance: Very slight. Number of petals: 26. Number of sepals: 4.

LEAF COLOR: Top, olive green, some new leaves purple, others bronzy; underside, red. Leaf and sinus: Leaf nearly round; sinus usually open except for 0.5 in (1.3 cm) near leaf center. Leaf size: 8 in (20 cm). Leaf spread: 4–5 ft (1.2–1.5 m). Stem color: Peduncle, bright green; petiole bronzy yellow. Pubescence on peduncle or petiole: None.

COMMENTS: An excellent plant for small, medium, and large pools. One possibly disappointing feature is the large amount of unevenly distributed flecking on the petals.

Nymphaea **'Froebeli'** Otto Froebel 1898. Parentage: Seedling of *N. alba* var. *rubra*. Characteristics: Day blooming, Marliac rhizome, free flowering. Plate 264.

PETAL COLOR: Deep burgundy-red. *R.H.S. Chart*: Fan 2, Red-Purple Group, No. 64B. Sepal color: Light pink, deepening; deeper pink lengthwise veins; white tips. *R.H.S. Chart*: Fan 2, Red-Purple Group, No. 62D then 63C; veins, No. 64D; tips, Fan 4, White Group, No. 155B. Anther color: Yellow. *R.H.S. Chart*: Fan 1, Yellow Group, No. 10B. Stamen color: Orange-red. Flower shape: Cuplike then stellate. Flower size: 4.5–5 in (11–13 cm). Fragrance: Slight. Number of petals: 18. Number of sepals: 4.

LEAF COLOR: Top, green, new leaves bronzy; underside, purplish. Leaf and sinus: Leaf almost round; sinus a wide-open V. Leaf size: 6 in (15 cm). Leaf spread: 3 ft (1 m). Stem color: Purple. Pubescence on peduncle or petiole: A few fine hairs on both.

COMMENTS: Otto Froebel of Zurich, Switzerland, developed this water lily by selective breeding over a 40-year period. 'Froebeli' performs best in cooler regions. It is a fine choice for tub gardens or small pools.

Nymphaea **'Fulva'** Joseph B. L. Marliac 1894. Parentage: Unknown. Characteristics: Day blooming, upright rhizome, free flowering. Plate 265.

PETAL COLOR: First day, orange, turning to red by third day. *R.H.S. Chart*: First day, Fan 1, Orange Group, Nos. 24B–C; third day, Fan 1, Red Group, Nos. 54A (base) and 50C (tip). Sepal color: White turning to light pink at base. *R.H.S. Chart*: First day, Fan 4, White Group, No. 155A; third day, white tip, same; base, Fan 1, Red Group, Nos. 56B–C. Anther color: Yellow-orange turning to orange-red. *R.H.S. Chart*: First day, Fan 1, Yellow-Orange Group, Nos. 14B–C; third day, Fan 1, Orange-Red Group, No. 30D or 32C. Stamen color: Orange. Flower shape: Cuplike. Flower size: 3–4 in (8–10 cm). Fragrance: None or slight. Number of petals: 22 or 23. Number of sepals: 4.

LEAF COLOR: Top, green mottled purple; underside, pink with reddish purple flecks. Leaf and sinus: Leaf nearly round but a little longer than wide; sinus wide open. Leaf size: 3.5–4 in (9–10 cm). Leaf spread: 1.5–4 ft (0.5–1.2 m). Stem color: Yellowish green. Pubescence on peduncle or petiole: Both are glabrous.

COMMENTS: This richly colored changeable water lily is suitable for any size pool but is especially suited for the tub garden or small pool.

Nymphaea **'Gladstone'**. See *N.* **'Gladstoniana'**.

Nymphaea **'Gladstoniana'** (syn. 'Gladstone') George Richardson 1897. Parentage: *N. tuberosa* × unknown. Characteristics: Day blooming, Marliac rhizome, fairly free flowering. Plate 266.

PETAL COLOR: White. *R.H.S. Chart*: Fan 4, White Group, No. 155C. Sepal color: White; purple veins, green tips. *R.H.S. Chart*: Fan 4, White Group, No. 155C; veins, Fan 2, Red-Purple Group, No. 70B; tips, Fan 3, Yellow-Green Group, No. 144C. Anther color: Yellow. *R.H.S. Chart*: Fan 1, Yellow Group, No. 9B. Stamen color: Yellow. Flower shape: Stellate, full. Flower size: 5.5–7 in (14–18 cm). Fragrance: Very slight. Number of petals: 22–25. Number of sepals: 4.

LEAF COLOR: Top, green, new leaves bronzy; underside, bronzy brown. Leaf and sinus: Leaf nearly round, perimeter usually quite wavy; sinus occasionally a wide-open V. Both lobes generally raised, usually overlapping, frequently crimped along sinus. Leaf size: 11–12 in (28–30 cm). Leaf spread: 5–8 ft (1.5–2.5 m). Stem color: Usually green, striped purple. Pubescence on peduncle or petiole: Fine fuzz and numerous hairs on both.

COMMENTS: George Richardson developed this water lily while working at Lordstown, Ohio. 'Gladstoniana' is an ideal plant for a large water garden or natural pond.

Nymphaea **'Gloire du Temple-sur-Lot'** Latour-Marliac Nursery 1913. Parentage: Unknown. Characteristics: Day blooming, odorata rhizome, not free flowering. Plate 267.

PETAL COLOR: Shell pink then white. *R.H.S. Chart*: Fan 2, Red-Purple Group, No. 62D; paling to Fan 4, White Group, No. 155B. Sepal color: Greenish, blushed shell pink, white by second day. *R.H.S. Chart*: Fan 3, Yellow-Green Group, No. 147D; blush, Fan 2, Red-Purple Group, No. 62D; second day, Fan 4, White Group, No. 155B. Anther color: Yellow. *R.H.S. Chart*: Fan 1, Yellow Group, No. 4A. Stamen color: Yellow. Flower shape: Like a double chrysanthemum. Flower size: 5–6 in (13–15 cm). Fragrance:

Very slight. Number of petals: 128–129. Number of sepals: 4–6.

LEAF COLOR: Top, green, new leaves brown, orange spot in center; underside, red. Leaf and sinus: Leaf round; lobes overlap completely at sinus. Leaf size: 10 in (25 cm). Leaf spread: 4–5 ft (1.2–1.5 m). Stem color: Green. Pubescence on peduncle or petiole: A little fuzz on both.

COMMENTS: Many people consider this the most beautiful hardy water lily. For the greatest number of blooms, plant in a large container at least 2 ft (0.6 m) in diameter and place under 1 ft (0.3 m) of water to allow a colony of several rhizomes to develop. This plant is suitable for natural ponds or very large pools.

Nymphaea **'Gloriosa'** Joseph B. L. Marliac 1896. Parentage: Unknown. Characteristics: Day blooming, Marliac rhizome, very free flowering. Plate 268.

PETAL COLOR: Bright red, some flecking. *R.H.S. Chart*: Fan 2, Red-Purple Group, No. 66C. Sepal color: White, flushed pink, deeper pink veins. *R.H.S. Chart*: Fan 4, White Group, No. 155B; flush, Fan 2, Red-Purple Group, No. 65D; veins, No. 66C. Anther color: Bright yellow. *R.H.S. Chart*: Fan 1, Yellow-Orange Group, No. 16A. Stamen color: Orange-red. Flower shape: Cuplike, somewhat stellate. Flower size: 5 in (13 cm). Fragrance: Slight. Number of petals: 27–30. Number of sepals: 4–5, usually 5.

LEAF COLOR: Top, green, new leaves light purple, dark purple blotches; underside, purple-brown, prominent green veins. Leaf and sinus: Leaf longer than wide. Lobes on new leaves usually overlap at sinus; overlap may be absent on older leaves. Leaf size: 8–9 in (20–23 cm). Leaf spread: 5 ft (1.5 m). Stem color: Purplish brown. Pubescence on peduncle or petiole: None.

COMMENTS: 'Gloriosa' used to be considered the very best red hardy. In recent years crown rot has decimated this cultivar in many parts of the world. Nurseries are learning how to combat crown rot and chances are good that this water lily will become plentiful again. When grown under the right conditions, 'Gloriosa' is hard to beat in any size pool.

Nymphaea **'Gold Medal'** Perry D. Slocum 1991. Parentage: Seedling of *N.* 'Texas Dawn'. Characteristics: Day blooming, Marliac rhizome, free flowering. Plate 269.

PETAL COLOR: Inner petals, rich yellow; outer petals, light yellow. *R.H.S. Chart*: Inner petals, Fan 1, Green-Yellow Group, No. 1C; outer petals, Yellow Group, No. 4D. Sepal color: Greenish yellow. *R.H.S. Chart*: Fan 1, Green-Yellow Group, No. 1D. Anther color: Deep yellow. *R.H.S. Chart*: Fan 1, Yellow Group, No. 6A. Stamen color: Deep yellow. Flower shape: Round then chrysanthemumlike. Flower size: 6–8 in (15–20 cm). Fragrance: Pronounced and delightful. Number of petals: 27–31. Number of sepals: 4.

LEAF COLOR: Top, olive green, mottled purple, yellow blotches prominent on new leaves, yellow pattern sometimes retained; underside, pinkish, many reddish purple blotches. Leaf and sinus: Leaf nearly round; sinus usually wide open, lobes may overlap sinus halfway. Leaf size: 10 in (25 cm). Leaf spread: 4–5 ft (1.2–1.5 m). Stem color: Brownish purple. Pubescence on peduncle or petiole: Both covered with thick fuzz.

COMMENTS: 'Gold Medal' has a more double flower (up to 31 petals) than many of the yellow hardy water lilies currently available. Although the color is paler than 'Texas Dawn', its many petals and freedom of bloom make it highly desirable. I recommend it for medium or large pools.

Nymphaea 'Golden Cup'. See *N.* ×*marliacea* 'Chromatella'.

Nymphaea 'Gonnère' (syn. 'Snowball', 'Crystal White') Latour-Marliac Nursery 1914. Parentage: *N. tuberosa* 'Richardsonii' seedling × unknown. Characteristics: Day blooming, Marliac rhizome, fairly free flowering. Plate 270.

PETAL COLOR: White. *R.H.S. Chart*: Fan 4, White Group, No. 155C. Sepal color: White, flushed pink, usually bordered and striped green. *R.H.S. Chart*: Fan 4, White, Group, No. 155C; flush, Fan 2, Red-Purple Group, No. 62D; border and stripes, Fan 3, Yellow-Green Group, No. 146D. Anther color: Yellow. *R.H.S. Chart*: Fan 1, Yellow Group, No. 7A. Stamen color: Yellow. Flower shape: Ball-shaped. Flower size: 4–6 in (10–15 cm). Fragrance: Pleasant, noticeable in new blooms. Number of petals: 57–62. Number of sepals: 4.

LEAF COLOR: Top, green, newest leaves slightly bronzed; underside, green, newest leaves deep bronze. Leaf and sinus: Leaf round; sinus usually a wide-open V. Leaf size: Usually 6–8 in (15–20 cm), up to 10 in (25 cm). Leaf spread: 3–4 ft (1–1.2 m). Stem color: Mostly green. Pubescence on peduncle or petiole: Fairly thick fuzz and hairs on both.

COMMENTS: Except in very hot regions, such as USDA zones 7–10 (particularly zones 8–10), this is a fine choice for a beautiful white water lily. 'Gonnère' is ideal for small, medium, or large pools. One excellent feature is that blooms stay open late in the day. Though many hardy water lily flowers close in early afternoon, 'Gonnère' matches the benefits of

'Pink Sensation', 'Escarboucle', 'Yellow Sensation,' and all the orange changeables in that its flowers stay open until 3:30 to 5:30 p.m. or so.

Nymphaea 'Graziella'. See *N.* 'Chrysantha'.

Nymphaea 'Grésille'. See *N.* 'Sultan'.

Nymphaea 'Hal Miller' No. 1. Parentage: *N.* 'Virginalis' × *N. odorata* 'Sulphurea Grandiflora'. Characteristics: Day blooming, Marliac rhizome, free flowering.

PETAL COLOR: Inner petals, yellow; outer petals creamy white. *R.H.S. Chart*: Inner petals, Fan 1, Yellow Group, No. 4C; outer petals, Fan 4, White Group, No. 155B. Sepal color: Creamy white. *R.H.S. Chart*: Fan 1, Yellow Group, No. 4D. Anther color: Yellow. *R.H.S. Chart*: Fan 1, Yellow Group, No. 7A. Stamen color: Yellow. Flower shape: Stellate. Flower size: 7–10 in (18–25 cm). Fragrance: Very slight, if any. Number of petals: 23–24. Number of sepals: 4.

LEAF COLOR: Top, green, new leaves reddish, small purple blotches; underside, green, blotched purple, new leaves red. Leaf and sinus: Leaf a little longer than wide; sinus an open V. Leaf size: 9–12 in (23–30 cm). Leaf spread: 4–6 ft (1.2–2 m). Stem color: Green. Pubescence on peduncle or petiole: Fine fuzz on both.

COMMENTS: A similar 'Hal Miller' with more petals and smaller flower ('Hal Miller' No. 2, which see) is being sold by some nurseries. Both are highly desirable water lilies. Although the flowers of 'Hal Miller' No. 1 have fewer petals, they are huge. Subject to crown rot, and some petal-browning may occur in midsummer when this plant is grown in warm, humid regions. I consider this an excellent choice for medium and large pools.

Nymphaea 'Hal Miller' No. 2. Parentage: Possibly *N.* 'Virginalis' × *N. odorata* 'Sulphurea Grandiflora'. Characteristics: Day blooming, Marliac rhizome, quite free flowering. Plate 271.

PETAL COLOR: Creamy white, yellow innermost petals. *R.H.S. Chart*: Fan 4, White Group, No. 155B; inner petals, Fan 1, Yellow Group, No. 2D. Sepal color: Creamy green, occasional light pink blush. *R.H.S. Chart*: Fan 1, Green-Yellow Group, No. 1D; blush, Fan 1, Red Group, No. 49D. Anther color: Yellow. *R.H.S. Chart*: Fan 1, Yellow Group, No. 5A. Stamen color: Yellow. Flower shape: Stellate. Flower size: 7–9 in (18–23 cm). Fragrance: Slight but noticeable. Number of petals: 28–30. Number of sepals: 4.

LEAF COLOR: Top, olive green; underside, deep

red, new leaves red, flecked and mottled red-purple. Leaf and sinus: Leaf egg-shaped; lobes overlap sinus somewhat, occasionally sinus an open V. Leaf size: 10.5 × 8.5 in (27 × 22 cm). Leaf spread: 5–6 ft (1.5–2 m). Stem color: Green. Pubescence on peduncle or petiole: Most stems fuzzy, diminishing on older petioles.

COMMENTS: Flowers are generally held a few inches above the water. Subject to crown rot. Widespread brown flecking may occur on older blooms, especially in early and midsummer, when this cultivar is grown in warm and humid regions. I have observed brown flecking on plants grown in North Carolina (USDA zone 6b); however, flecking is absent on some plants grown in Texas and California. This water lily is suited for medium or large pools.

Nymphaea **'Helen Fowler'** Walter B. Shaw. Parentage: Unknown. Characteristics: Day blooming, odorata rhizome, fairly free flowering. Plate 272.

PETAL COLOR: Medium pink. *R.H.S. Chart*: Fan 2, Red-Purple Group, No. 65B. Sepal color: Deeper pink than petals. *R.H.S. Chart*: Fan 2, Red Group, No. 49A. Anther color: Deep golden yellow. *R.H.S. Chart*: Fan 1, Yellow-Orange Group, No. 20A. Stamen color: Deep yellow. Flower shape: Stellate. Flower size: 6–8 in (15–20 cm). Fragrance: Very sweet. Number of petals: 19–20. Number of sepals: 4.

LEAF COLOR: Top, green, new leaves bronzy; underside, brownish, new leaves purple. Leaf and sinus: Leaves round; sinus narrow, usually open. Leaf size: 9 in (23 cm). Leaf spread: 4–5 ft (1.2–1.5 m). Stem color: Brownish. Pubescence on peduncle or petiole: Fine fuzz on both.

COMMENTS: 'Helen Fowler' is named for W. B. Shaw's daughter. Mr. Shaw operated the Shaw Water Gardens (later known as the Kenilworth Aquatic Gardens) in Washington, D.C. This lily has a particularly beautiful color. For best performance, plant it in a large planter so that it can form a colony of plants. I recommend it for the medium or large pool.

Nymphaea **'Helvola'** (syn. 'Yellow Pygmy') Joseph B. L. Marliac 1879. Parentage: Probably *N. tetragona* × *N. mexicana*. Characteristics: Day blooming, finger-type rhizome, very free flowering. Plate 273.

PETAL COLOR: Medium yellow. *R.H.S. Chart*: Fan 1, Yellow Group, No. 3C. Sepal color: Pale yellow. *R.H.S. Chart*: Fan 1, Green-Yellow Group, No. 1D. Anther color: Yellow. *R.H.S. Chart*: Fan 1, Yellow Group, No. 8A. Stamen color: Yellow. Flower shape: Cuplike then stellate. Flower size: 2–3 in (5–8 cm). Fragrance: Very slight. Number of petals: 16–17. Number of sepals: 4.

LEAF COLOR: Top, green, heavily mottled and blotched deep purple; underside, red, small deep purple mottles. Leaf and sinus: Leaf egg-shaped; sinus an open V. Both lobes have an extra projection at the tips. Leaf size: 5 × 3.5 in (13 × 9 cm). Leaf spread: 2–3 ft (0.6–1 m). Stem color: Green and/or brown; both colors sometimes appear on same plant. Pubescence on peduncle or petiole: None.

COMMENTS: Flowers do not open until early afternoon, but they do stay open until quite late in the afternoon. 'Helvola' is ideal for a tub or a small pool.

Nymphaea **'Hermine'** Joseph B. L. Marliac 1910. Parentage: Unknown. Characteristics: Day blooming, Marliac rhizome, very free flowering. Plate 274.

PETAL COLOR: White. *R.H.S. Chart*: Fan 4, White Group, No. 155D. Sepal color: White. *R.H.S. Chart*: Fan 4, White Group, No. 155D. Anther color: Bright yellow. *R.H.S. Chart*: Fan 1, Yellow Group, No. 9B. Stamen color: Yellow. Flower shape: Starlike. Flower size: 5–5.5 in (13–14 cm). Fragrance: Very slight. Number of petals: 17–20. Number of sepals: 4.

LEAF COLOR: Top, olive green, new leaves slightly bronzed; underside, bronzy or purplish, new leaves red. Leaf and sinus: Leaf heart-shaped; sinus wide open. Leaf size: 7 × 6 in (18 × 15 cm). Leaf spread: 30 in (75 cm). Stem color: Peduncle green, some tinged bronze; petiole bronzy purple. Pubescence on peduncle or petiole: None.

COMMENTS: Flowers are quite single and very lovely. I recommend this plant very highly for the small pool or tub garden.

Nymphaea **'Hermine'** No. 2. See *N.* **'Alba Plenissima'**.

Nymphaea **'Hollandia'**. See *N.* **'Darwin'**.

Nymphaea **'Indiana'** Latour-Marliac Nursery 1912. Parentage: Unknown. Characteristics: Day blooming, upright rhizome, very free flowering. Plate 277.

PETAL COLOR: Apricot then apricot-orange then deep orange-red. *R.H.S. Chart*: Fan 1, Orange Group, No. 39A; second day, No. 41B; third day, Red Group, No. 51A. Sepal color: Pale yellow, pinkish veins. *R.H.S. Chart*: Fan 4, Orange-White Group, No. 159D; veins, Fan 1, Red Group, Nos. 37C–D. Anther color: Golden orange. *R.H.S. Chart*: Fan 1, Yellow-Orange Group, No. 23B. Stamen color: Glowing orange. Flower shape: Cuplike then wide open. Flower size: 3.5–4 in (9–10 cm). Fragrance: Very slight. Number of petals: 15–19. Number of sepals: 4.

LEAF COLOR: Top, green, purple blotches, new

leaves bronzy green, quite heavily mottled deeper purple; underside, bronzy pink, many red speckles and small blotches. Leaf and sinus: Leaf small, nearly round; sinus wide open. Leaf size: 5 × 4.5 in (13 × 11 cm). Leaf spread: 30 in (75 cm). Stem color: Peduncle, yellow-green; petiole, darker green. Pubescence on peduncle or petiole: Many fine hairs on both.

COMMENTS: Subject to crown rot. 'Indiana', with its freedom of bloom, wide color variation, and small leaf spread, is one of the best of the changeables. It is very similar to 'Aurora' in flower color and shape and leaf color, shape, and spread, yet 'Indiana' flowers have about six fewer petals. 'Indiana' is an excellent plant for the tub garden and small pool.

Nymphaea **'Irene Heritage'** Perry D. Slocum 1988. Parentage: Chance seedling; *N.* 'Atropurpurea' is a probable parent. Characteristics: Day blooming, Marliac-odorata rhizome, fairly free flowering. Plate 278.

PETAL COLOR: Brilliant glowing red, deepening; outer petals somewhat flecked. *R.H.S. Chart*: Fan 2, Red-Purple Group, No. 63A then 64A. Sepal color: Pale pink, about 8 lengthwise deep pink stripes, much flecking. *R.H.S. Chart*: Fan 2, Red-Purple Group, No. 70C; stripes, No. 64A. Anther color: Golden yellow. *R.H.S. Chart*: Fan 1, Yellow Group, No. 10B. Stamen color: Inner rows, mostly orange; outer rows, red. Flower shape: Stellate. Flower size: 5–6 in (13–15 cm). Fragrance: Slight. Number of petals: 29–34. Number of sepals: 4.

LEAF COLOR: Top, green, new leaves bronzy purple; underside, green, new leaves purplish bronze. Leaf and sinus: Leaves a little longer than wide; lobes usually overlap sinus, a few sinuses wide open. Leaf size: 9 × 8 in (23 × 20 cm). Leaf spread: 4–5 ft (1.2–1.5 m). Stem color: Dark brown. Pubescence on peduncle or petiole: Thick fuzz on all stems.

COMMENTS: 'Irene Heritage' is a water lily of exceptionally good color. It honors Bill and Irene Heritage, who have spent a lifetime with water lilies. Bill managed two water lily companies in England and authored two excellent books on water gardens (see Recommended Reading). He also received one of the two 1989 Water Lily Hall of Fame awards, presented by the International Water Lily Society. 'Irene Heritage' has moderate-sized leaves and restricted leaf coverage. This makes it especially well suited to small and medium pools, though it is an excellent choice for pools of any size. For maximum success, plant it in a large container and allow it to form a colony of plants.

Nymphaea **'James Brydon'** Dreer Nurseries 1900. Parentage: Possibly includes *N. alba* var. *rubra, N. candida,* and at least one from the *N.* ×*laydekeri* hybrid group, according to Charles Masters. Characteristics: Day blooming, Marliac rhizome, very free flowering. Plate 279.

PETAL COLOR: Brilliant rose-red. *R.H.S. Chart*: Fan 2, Red-Purple Group, No. 66C. Sepal color: Brilliant rose-red. *R.H.S. Chart*: Fan 2, Red-Purple Group, No. 66C. Anther color: Bright orange-yellow. *R.H.S. Chart*: Fan 1, Orange Group, No. 24B. Stamen color: Orange-red. Flower shape: Cuplike. Flower size: 4–5 in (10–13 cm). Fragrance: Reminiscent of ripe apples. Number of petals: 27. Number of sepals: 4.

LEAF COLOR: Top, green, new leaves purplish brown, dark purple blotches; underside, purple-red, prominent green V from apex to sinus. Leaf and sinus: Leaf round; lobes overlap at sinus. Leaf size: 7 in (18 cm). Leaf spread: 3–4 ft (1–1.2 m). Stem color: Purple. Pubescence on peduncle or petiole: Some fuzz on lower portion of petiole.

COMMENTS: Unlike 'Gloriosa', for many years the finest red water lily available, 'James Brydon' is not at all subject to crown rot. It is a first choice for tub garden or small pool and is also excellent for medium and large pools.

Nymphaea **'Japanese Pygmy Red'**. Parentage: Unknown. Characteristics: Day blooming, Marliac rhizome, free flowering. Plate 280.

PETAL COLOR: Pale pink then deep red, flecked. *R.H.S. Chart*: Fan 2, Red-Purple Group, No. 62D; third day, Fan 1, Red Group, No. 53B. Sepal color: White then pink; veins prominent, greenish then red. *R.H.S. Chart*: Fan 4, Greyed-Green Group, No. 195D, then Fan 2, Red Group, No. 55D; veins, Fan 3, Green Group, No. 138C, then Fan 1, Red Group, No. 53B. Anther color: Deep yellow-orange. *R.H.S. Chart*: Fan 1, Yellow-Orange Group, No. 20A. Stamen color: Deep yellow. Flower shape: Cuplike then stellate. Flower size: 3–4 in (8–10 cm). Fragrance: None. Number of petals: 14. Number of sepals: 4.

LEAF COLOR: Top, dark green, new leaves purplish; underside, bronzy brown. Leaf and sinus: Leaf nearly round; sinus open. Leaf size: 7–8 in (18–20 cm). Leaf spread: 3–3.5 ft (1–1.1 m). Stem color: Brownish. Pubescence on peduncle or petiole: None.

COMMENTS: This water lily grows successfully in England but does not do well in warm regions of the middle and southern United States. In the United States, 'Japanese Pygmy Red' does well in zones 3–5, is doubtful in zone 6, and does poorly and usually dies in zones 7–10. I recommend it for northern regions, and then only for the collector. My experience in growing it in Florida (zone 9) and North Carolina (zone 6b) is that it starts to grow and bloom and then dies out.

Nymphaea '**J. C. N. Forestier**'. See *N.* '**Comanche**'.

Nymphaea '**Joanne Pring**' George H. Pring 1942. Parentage: Mutation of *N. tetragona*. Characteristics: Day blooming, Marliac rhizome, free flowering. Plate 281.

PETAL COLOR: Inner petals light to medium pink, outer petals pale pink; all deepening. *R.H.S. Chart*: Inner petals, Fan 2, Red-Purple Group, No. 73C; third day, No. 72C. Outer petals, Fan 2, Red-Purple Group, No. 62D; third day, No. 73C. Sepal color: White, pink flush, green border. *R.H.S. Chart*: Fan 4, White Group, No. 155B; flush, Fan 2, Red-Purple Group, No. 73D; border, Fan 3, Green Group, No. 138D. Anther color: Golden yellow. *R.H.S. Chart*: Fan 1, Yellow-Orange Group, No. 15A. Stamen color: Orange. Flower shape: Cuplike. Flower size: 3–4 in (8–10 cm). Fragrance: Slight. Number of petals: 15–16. Number of sepals: 4.

LEAF COLOR: Top, green, new leaves bronzy light purple, deep purple blotches; underside, reddish brown, new leaves reddish purple. Leaf and sinus: Leaf a little longer than wide; sinus a wide-open V. Leaf size: 5.5 in (14 cm). Leaf spread: 3 ft (1 m). Stem color: Purplish brown. Pubescence on peduncle or petiole: None.

COMMENTS: This cultivar is somewhat subject to crown rot; otherwise, it is an excellent performer and an ideal choice for a tub garden or small pool.

Nymphaea '**La Beaugère**'. See *N.* '**René Gérard**'.

Nymphaea ×*laydekeri* '**Alba**' (syn. 'White Laydeker') Latour-Marliac Nursery. Parentage: Unknown. Characteristics: Day blooming, upright rhizome, very free flowering. Plate 282.

PETAL COLOR: Waxy white. *R.H.S. Chart*: Fan 4, White Group, No. 155A. Sepal color: Greenish cream, green lengthwise stripes. *R.H.S. Chart*: Fan 4, Greyed-Yellow Group, No. 160D; stripes, Greyed-Green Group, No. 193C. Anther color: Yellow. *R.H.S. Chart*: Fan 1, Yellow Group, No. 12A. Stamen color: Yellow. Flower shape: Cuplike. Flower size: 3–4 in (8–10 cm). Fragrance: Noticeable in first-day flowers. Number of petals: 17–19. Number of sepals: 4.

LEAF COLOR: Top, deep green, prominent yellow veins, new leaves quite purplish, a few deep purple blotches; underside, red, usually green V along midvein. Leaf and sinus: Leaf round; lobes usually

overlap ⅔ down sinus. Leaf size: 8 in (20 cm). Leaf spread: 3–4 ft (1–1.2 m). Stem color: Green. Pubescence on peduncle or petiole: None.

COMMENTS: I have seen first-year plants with 8 to 10 blooms at a time. This beautiful water lily, which is in very short supply, is in most respects ideal for a tub garden or a small pool. It occasionally dies back, especially in very hot weather.

Nymphaea '**Laydekeri Carmine**'. See *N.* ×*laydekeri* '**Purpurata**'.

Nymphaea ×*laydekeri* '**Fulgens**' (syn. 'Red Laydeker') Joseph B. L. Marliac 1895. Parentage: Unknown. Characteristics: Day blooming, Marliac rhizome, extremely free flowering. Plates 283 and 284.

PETAL COLOR: Vivid burgundy-red, deepening, flecked. *R.H.S. Chart*: Fan 2, Red-Purple Group, No. 64B; last day, No. 64A. Sepal color: Pale pink, deepening; white tips. *R.H.S. Chart*: Fan 2, Red-Purple Group, No. 64D; last day, No. 60C; tips, Fan 4, White Group, No. 155A. Anther color: Golden yellow. *R.H.S. Chart*: Fan 1, Yellow-Orange Group, No. 20A. Stamen color: Deep orange-red. Flower shape: Cuplike. Flower size: 5–6 in (13–15 cm). Fragrance: Slight. Number of petals: 20. Number of sepals: 4.

LEAF COLOR: Top, green, new leaves purplish green, dark purple blotches; underside, purple, prominent V on new leaves. Leaf and sinus: Leaf almost round; lobes overlap, covering ⅔ of sinus. Leaf size: 8.5 × 7.5 in (22 × 19 cm). Leaf spread: 4–5 ft (1.2–1.5 m). Stem color: Purple-brown. Pubescence on peduncle or petiole: None.

COMMENTS: This is one of the most magnificent water lilies of all time. It is one of the very best bloomers and also has the largest flowers and largest leaf spread of any of the *N.* ×*laydekeri* water lilies. A bed of these commands instant attention. 'Fulgens' is one of the first to bloom in spring and keeps on flowering through summer and far into the fall. I highly recommend it for any size pool.

Nymphaea ×*laydekeri* '**Lilacea**' (syn. 'Pink Laydeker') Latour-Marliac Nursery. Parentage: Unknown. Characteristics: Day blooming, Marliac rhizome, very free flowering. Plate 285.

PETAL COLOR: Lilac-pink, paling toward outer petals. *R.H.S. Chart*: Inner petals, Fan 2, Red-Purple Group, No. 73C; outer petals, No. 73D. Sepal color: Pale pink, deepening; prominent greenish veins. *R.H.S. Chart*: Fan 2, Red-Purple Group, No. 69B or lighter; third day, No. 73D; veins, Fan 4, Greyed-Green Group, No. 192C. Anther color: Deep yellow. *R.H.S. Chart*: Fan 1, Yellow-Orange Group, No. 19A. Stamen color: Deep yellow. Flower shape: Cuplike.

Flower size: 2.5–3.5 in (6–9 cm). Fragrance: Slight. Number of petals: 16. Number of sepals: 4.

LEAF COLOR: Top, olive green, a few purple mottles; underside, green, newer leaves purplish. Leaf and sinus: Leaf nearly round; sinus open. Leaf size: 7–8 in (18–20 cm). Leaf spread: 3–4 ft (1–1.2 m). Stem color: Brownish. Pubescence on peduncle or petiole: None.

COMMENTS: 'Lilacea' is a fine lily for the tub garden or small pool. The blooms are an unusual lilac-pink, very close to the flower color of the common lilac (*Syringa vulgaris*). It is in short supply and may be hard to find. Caution: An inferior substitute is being sold.

Nymphaea ×laydekeri **'Purpurata'** (syn. 'Laydekeri Carmine') Joseph B. L. Marliac 1895. Parentage: Unknown. Characteristics: Day blooming, upright rhizome, extremely free flowering. Plate 286.

PETAL COLOR: Tips white; inner rows pinkish red, deepening; outer rows slightly paler, deepening, flecked. *R.H.S. Chart*: Tips, Fan 4, White Group, No. 155A; inner petals, Fan 2, Red-Purple Group, No. 62B then 63A–B; outer petals, No. 62C then 63D. Sepal color: White, prominent green veins; last day, pink, flecked, prominent gray-green veins. *R.H.S. Chart*: Fan 4, White Group, No. 155A; veins, Fan 3, Green Group, No. 138B. Last day, Fan 2, Red-Purple Group, No. 62C; veins, Fan 3, Green Group, No. 138B. Anther color: Brilliant yellow. *R.H.S. Chart*: Fan 1, Yellow-Orange Group, No. 21B. Stamen color: Orange-red. Flower shape: Starlike. Flower size: 5 in (13 cm). Fragrance: None. Number of petals: 22–23. Number of sepals: 4.

LEAF COLOR: Top, green, newest leaves purplish green, dark purple blotches; underside, purple, prominent green lengthwise V on new leaves. Leaf and sinus: Leaves nearly round; sinus a wide-open V. Leaf size: 8–9 in (20–23 cm). Leaf spread: 4–5 ft (1.2–1.5 m). Stem color: Purple. Pubescence on peduncle or petiole: None.

COMMENTS: This cultivar is a very reliable water lily which I highly recommend for any size pool. Despite the high degree of flecking in the petals, which some consider a detraction, its very free-blooming habit makes it a great water lily.

Nymphaea ×laydekeri **'Rosea'** Joseph B. L. Marliac 1893. Parentage: Probably *N. tetragona* × *N. alba* var. *rubra*, according to Charles Masters. Characteristics: Day blooming, upright rhizome, free flowering. Plate 287.

PETAL COLOR: Pink, inner petals deeper. *R.H.S. Chart*: Outer petals, Fan 2, Red-Purple Group, No. 65C; inner petals, No. 64D. Sepal color: Light pink,

slightly deeper pink veins and borders. *R.H.S. Chart*: Fan 2, Red-Purple Group, No. 73D; veins and borders, No. 65B. Anther color: Deep yellow. *R.H.S. Chart*: Fan 1, Orange Group, No. 24B. Stamen color: Orange. Flower shape: Cuplike. Flower size: 4–5 in (10–13 cm). Fragrance: None. Number of petals: 25–26. Number of sepals: 4.

LEAF COLOR: Top, green, newest leaves purple, mottled deeper purple; underside, purple-brown. Leaf and sinus: Leaf a little longer than wide; lobes overlap about 1.5 in (4 cm). Leaf size: 9 × 7.5 in (23 × 19 cm). Leaf spread: 4–5 ft (1.2–1.5 m). Stem color: Brown. Pubescence on peduncle or petiole: A few hairs on both.

COMMENTS: Of all the *N. ×laydekeri* pinks, and those close to pink, this is perhaps the finest with its rich pink color, abundance of blooms, and adaptability to small pools and tub gardens. I recommend it for medium-sized pools as well.

Nymphaea **'Louise'** Charles Thomas 1962. Parentage: *N.* 'Escarboucle' × *N.* 'Mrs. C. W. Thomas'. Characteristics: Day blooming, odorata rhizome, fairly free flowering. Plate 288.

PETAL COLOR: Red. *R.H.S. Chart*: Fan 1, Red Group, No. 42A. Sepal color: Light pink, white tips. *R.H.S. Chart*: Fan 1, Red Group, No. 50C; tips, Fan 4, White Group, No. 155B. Anther color: Deep yellow. *R.H.S. Chart*: Fan 1, Yellow-Orange Group, No. 20A. Stamen color: Deep yellow. Flower shape: Cuplike, full. Flower size: 6 in (15 cm). Fragrance: Very sweet. Number of petals: 20. Number of sepals: 4.

LEAF COLOR: Top, green, new leaves slightly bronzy; underside, brown, new leaves purplish. Leaf and sinus: Leaf nearly round; sinus wide open. Leaf size: 9–10 in (23–25 cm). Leaf spread: 4–5 ft (1.2–1.5 m). Stem color: Brownish. Pubescence on peduncle or petiole: None.

COMMENTS: Charles Thomas was issued U.S. plant patent No. 2161 (now expired) in August 1962 for 'Louise'. Plant in a large container so that it can form a colony. It will then produce more blooms. I recommend 'Louise' for any size pool and especially medium and large pools.

Nymphaea **'Luciana'** (formerly 'Fabiola'; syn. 'Pink Beauty') Henry A. Dreer 1899. Parentage: Unknown. Characteristics: Day blooming, Marliac rhizome, extremely free flowering. Plate 289.

PETAL COLOR: Medium pink. *R.H.S. Chart*: Fan 2, Red-Purple Group, Nos. 62B or 65A. Sepal color: Medium pink. *R.H.S. Chart*: Fan 2, Red-Purple Group, Nos. 62B or 65A. Anther color: Golden yellow. *R.H.S. Chart*: Fan 1, Yellow Group, No. 11A. Stamen color: Inner rows, yellow; outer rows pink.

Flower shape: Cuplike. Flower size: 6–7 in (15–18 cm). Fragrance: Very slight. Number of petals: 24–25. Number of sepals: 4–5.

LEAF COLOR: Top, green, new leaves slightly bronzed; underside, green, new leaves purple. Leaf and sinus: Leaf round; sinus an open V. Leaf size: 8–9 in (20–23 cm). Leaf spread: 3–4 ft (1–1.2 m). Stem color: Green, striped purple. Pubescence on peduncle or petiole: None.

COMMENTS: 'Luciana' is an excellent lily for any size pool. It has become one of the most popular pink hardies in the United States, where it is sold by some nurseries as 'Pink Beauty'.

Nymphaea 'Lucida' Joseph B. L. Marliac 1894. Parentage: Unknown. Characteristics: Day blooming, Marliac rhizome, free flowering. Plate 290.

PETAL COLOR: Inner petals, red; outer petals whitish pink, pink veins. *R.H.S. Chart*: Inner petals, Fan 1, Red Group, No. 51A; outer petals, closest to No. 36D; veins, No. 51D. Sepal color: White, pink base. *R.H.S. Chart*: Fan 4, White Group, No. 155A; base, Fan 1, Red Group, No. 36D. Anther color: Yellow-orange. *R.H.S. Chart*: Fan 1, Yellow-Orange Group, No. 14A. Stamen color: Deep yellow. Flower shape: Stellate. Flower size: 5–6 in (13–15 cm). Fragrance: Slight, if any. Number of petals: 18–20. Number of sepals: 4.

LEAF COLOR: Top, green, scattering of large purple mottles and blotches; underside, purple-brown. Leaf and sinus: Leaf a little longer than wide; sinus open. Leaf size: Up to 10 × 9 in (25 × 23 cm). Leaf spread: 4–5 ft (1.2–1.5 m). Stem color: Greenish bronze, striped purple. Pubescence on peduncle or petiole: None.

COMMENTS: 'Lucida' has attractive leaves, beautiful flower color, and a very free-flowering habit. Subject to crown rot. It is a fine choice for any size pool.

Nymphaea 'Lustrous'. Parentage: Unknown. Characteristics: Day blooming, Marliac rhizome, very free flowering. Plate 291.

PETAL COLOR: Light salmon-pink. *R.H.S. Chart*: Fan 1, Red Group, No. 36C. Sepal color: Medium salmon-pink. *R.H.S. Chart*: Fan 1, Red Group, No. 37C. Anther color: Yellow. *R.H.S. Chart*: Fan 1, Yellow Group, No. 9C. Stamen color: Yellow. Flower shape: Cuplike. Flower size: 5–6 in (13–15 cm). Fragrance: Slight. Number of petals: 28–30. Number of sepals: 4.

LEAF COLOR: Top, green, new leaves bronzy; underside, brownish purple, new leaves red. Leaf and sinus: Leaf a little longer than wide, wavy edges; sinus usually open. Leaf size: 9 × 8 in (23 × 20 cm).

Leaf spread: 3–5 ft (1–1.5 m). Stem color: Brownish green. Pubescence on peduncle or petiole: Some fuzz on both.

COMMENTS: This North American hybrid makes an excellent water lily for any size pool. Unlike most hardy water lily cultivars, 'Lustrous' develops viable seeds. It is believed to be a parent of 'Pink Sensation'.

Nymphaea 'M. Evelyn Stetson' Paul Stetson, Sr., 1986. Parentage: Unknown. Characteristics: Day blooming, odorata rhizome, free flowering. Plate 292.

PETAL COLOR: Inner petals (10 or 12), yellow; outer petals (30), white. *R.H.S. Chart*: Inner petals, Fan 1, Yellow Group, No. 6A; outer petals, Fan 4, White Group, No. 155B. Sepal color: Greenish yellow. *R.H.S. Chart*: Fan 3, Green Group, No. 142C. Anther color: Deep yellow. *R.H.S. Chart*: Fan 1, Yellow Group, No. 6A. Stamen color: Yellow. Flower shape: Stellate. Flower size: 6–8 in (15–20 cm). Fragrance: Very sweet. Number of petals: 40–42. Number of sepals: 5.

LEAF COLOR: Top, deep green; underside, yellow to pink. Leaf and sinus: Leaves nearly round; lobes have pointed tips, overlap at sinus. Leaf size: 8–9 in (20–23 cm). Leaf spread: 6 ft (2 m). Stem color: Brown and red. Pubescence on peduncle or petiole: Some fuzz on both.

COMMENTS: 'M. Evelyn Stetson', with its very double flowers and distinctive long petals, grows quite large if given room. I recommend this plant for the medium or large pool.

Nymphaea 'Madame Wilfron Gonnère' (syn. 'Pink Gonnère') Latour-Marliac Nursery after 1912. Parentage: Unknown. Characteristics: Day blooming, Marliac rhizome, very free flowering. Plate 293.

PETAL COLOR: Inner petals rich pink; outer petals lighter. *R.H.S. Chart*: Inner petals, Fan 2, Red-Purple Group, No. 62C; outer petals, No. 62D. Sepal color: Greenish white, veins slightly darker; older flowers blushed pink. *R.H.S. Chart*: Fan 4, Greyed-Green Group, No. 193D; veins, No. 193A; blush, Fan 2, Red-Purple Group, No. 62D or paler. Anther color: Golden yellow. *R.H.S. Chart*: Fan 1, Yellow Group, No. 12A. Stamen color: Gold, pink outer row. Flower shape: Peony-style. Flower size: 5 in (13 cm). Fragrance: None. Number of petals: 33. Number of sepals: 4.

LEAF COLOR: Top, green, new leaves slightly bronzed; underside, same as top. Early spring leaves display an attractive broad yellow lengthwise stripe on top that disappears completely when warm weather arrives. Leaf and sinus: Leaf round; lobes overlap considerably at sinus. Leaf size:

9.5–10 in (24–25 cm). Leaf spread: 4 ft (1.2 m). Stem color: Greenish brown, faint purple stripes; oldest stems brown. Pubescence on peduncle or petiole: Short fuzz and hairs on both.

COMMENTS: 'Madame Wilfron Gonnère', with its very double blooms, is a beautiful water lily for small, medium, or large pools.

Nymphaea **'Marguerite Laplace'** Latour-Marliac Nursery 1913. Parentage: Unknown. Characteristics: Day blooming, Marliac rhizome, free flowering. Plate 294.

PETAL COLOR: Medium pink. *R.H.S. Chart*: Fan 2, Red-Purple Group, No. 68C. Sepal color: White, flushed pink, pink veins near base. *R.H.S. Chart*: Fan 4, White Group, No. 155C; flush, Fan 2, Red-Purple Group, No. 62D; veins, No. 62C. Anther color: Yellow. *R.H.S. Chart*: Fan 1, Yellow Group, No. 13A. Stamen color: Yellow-orange. Flower shape: Cuplike, full. Flower size: 6.5–7 in (16–18 cm). Fragrance: Slight. Number of petals: 30. Number of sepals: 4.

LEAF COLOR: Top, deep green; underside, bronzy green. Leaf and sinus: Leaves round; sinus usually about ⅓ open. Leaf size: 9 in (23 cm). Leaf spread: 5 ft (1.5 m). Stem color: Green. Pubescence on peduncle or petiole: A few hairs on both.

COMMENTS: 'Marguerite Laplace' is a very beautiful pink lily developed in France. I recommend it for medium and large water gardens.

Nymphaea **'Marliac Flesh'**. See *N. ×marliacea* **'Carnea'**.

Nymphaea **'Marliac Rose'**. See *N. ×marliacea* **'Rosea'** Nos. 1 and 2.

Nymphaea **'Marliac White'**. See *N. ×marliacea* **'Albida'**.

Nymphaea **'Marliac Yellow'**. See *N. ×marliacea* **'Chromatella'**.

Nymphaea ×marliacea **'Albida'** (syn. 'Marliac White') Joseph B. L. Marliac 1880. Parentage: Unknown. Characteristics: Day blooming, Marliac rhizome, very free flowering. Plate 295.

PETAL COLOR: White. *R.H.S. Chart*: Fan 4, White Group, No. 155C. Sepal color: Pale green, pink tint and veins evident in older blooms. *R.H.S. Chart*: Fan 1, Green-Yellow Group, No. 1D; tint and veins, Red Group, No. 55B. Anther color: Yellow. *R.H.S. Chart*: Fan 1, Yellow Group, No. 9A. Stamen color: Yellow. Flower shape: Cuplike. Flower size: 5–6 in (13–15 cm). Fragrance: Very slight. Number of petals: 23–26. Number of sepals: 4.

LEAF COLOR: Top, green; underside, green, new leaves slightly bronzed. Leaf and sinus: Leaf round; sinus on older leaves generally an open V, lobes on younger leaves overlap to cover ⅓ to ¾ of sinus. Lobes sometimes raised. Leaf size: 9 in (23 cm). Leaf spread: 3–4 ft (1–1.2 m). Stem color: Greenish brown. Pubescence on peduncle or petiole: Fine fuzz and numerous hairs on both.

COMMENTS: Due to its moderate leaf spread and abundance of blooms, 'Albida' is a great lily for any size pool.

Nymphaea ×marliacea **'Carnea'** (syn. 'Marliac Flesh', 'Morning Glory') Joseph B. L. Marliac 1887. Parentage: Unknown. Characteristics: Day blooming, Marliac rhizome, very free flowering. Plate 296.

PETAL COLOR: Light pink. *R.H.S. Chart*: Fan 2, Red-Purple Group, No. 62D or lighter. Sepal color: Slightly deeper pink than petals, still deeper pink veins. *R.H.S. Chart*: Fan 2, Red-Purple Group, No. 62D; veins, No. 62C. Anther color: Deep yellow. *R.H.S. Chart*: Fan 1, Yellow Group, No. 12A. Stamen color: Deep yellow. Flower shape: Cuplike. Flower size: 4.5–5 in (11–13 cm). Fragrance: Slight. Number of petals: 23. Number of sepals: 4.

LEAF COLOR: Top, green, new leaves purplish; underside, red. Leaf and sinus: Leaf a little longer than wide; lobes may overlap sinus completely, halfway, or not at all. Leaf size: 7.5–8 in (19–20 cm). Leaf spread: 4–5 ft (1.2–1.5 m). Stem color: Yellowish green. Pubescence on peduncle or petiole: None.

COMMENTS: 'Carnea' is one of Marliac's finest creations. Some people confuse this lily with his *N. ×marliacea* 'Rosea' No. 2, which is very similar but whose flowers are one or two shades deeper. Also, differences are found in stem color, sinuses, and pubescence on stems (lacking in 'Carnea'). I recommend 'Carnea' for any size pool and especially for medium and large ones.

Nymphaea ×marliacea **'Chromatella'** (syn. 'Golden Cup', 'Marliac Yellow') Joseph B. L. Marliac 1887. Parentage: *N. alba* × *N. mexicana*. Characteristics: Day blooming, pineapple rhizome, very free flowering. Plate 297.

PETAL COLOR: Light yellow. *R.H.S. Chart*: Fan 1, Yellow Group, No. 2D. Sepal color: Pale greenish yellow, faint pink blush, pinkish veins at base. *R.H.S. Chart*: Fan 1, Green-Yellow Group, No. 1D; blush, Fan 2, Red-Purple Group, No. 62D or lighter; veins, No. 62D. Anther color: Deep yellow. *R.H.S. Chart*: Fan 1, Yellow Group, No. 10A. Stamen color: Yellow. Flower shape: Cuplike. Flower size: 4–5.5 in (10–14 cm). Fragrance: Quite noticeable in new blooms. Number of petals: 22–25. Number of sepals: 4–5.

LEAF COLOR: Top, green, young leaves blotched and mottled purple; underside, reddish purple, new leaves green, small purple blotches. Leaf and sinus: Leaf round; sinus an open V. Leaf size: 8–9 in (20–23 cm). Leaf spread: 3 ft (1 m). Stem color: Green. Pubescence on peduncle or petiole: Short fuzz and hairs on both.

COMMENTS: For beauty and performance, 'Chromatella' rates among the very best of the hardy water lilies. It is very satisfactory for any size pool, including the tub garden. Note: rhizome of a mature plant does actually resemble a pineapple.

Nymphaea ×*marliacea* **'Rosea'** No. 1 (syn. 'Marliac Rose') Joseph B. L. Marliac 1879. Parentage: Unknown. Characteristics: Day blooming, Marliac rhizome, very free flowering.

PETAL COLOR: Light pink, paling. *R.H.S. Chart*: Fan 2, Red-Purple Group, No. 65C paling to 65D. Sepal color: Very deep pink. *R.H.S. Chart*: Fan 1, Red Group, Nos. 54C–D. Anther color: Deep golden yellow. *R.H.S. Chart*: Fan 1, Yellow Group, No. 6A. Stamen color: Deep yellow. Flower shape: Cuplike. Flower size: 4–5 in (10–13 cm). Fragrance: Slight. Number of petals: 22. Number of sepals: 4.

LEAF COLOR: Top, deep olive green; underside, brownish red, deep olive green center. Leaf and sinus: Leaf nearly round; sinus usually open. Leaf size: 8–9 in (20–23 cm). Leaf spread: 4–5 ft (1.2–1.5 m). Stem color: Green, tinged red. Pubescence on peduncle or petiole: None.

COMMENTS: According to the 1912 catalog of the Latour-Marliac Nursery, sepals of 'Rosea' are deep pink. Thus I consider 'Rosea' No. 1 the true 'Rosea', although many nurseries sell a pale-sepal variation by the same name. I would recommend this lily for any size pool.

Nymphaea ×*marliacea* **'Rosea'** No. 2 (syn. 'Marliac Rose') Joseph B. L. Marliac(?) 1879(?). Parentage: Unknown. Characteristics: Day blooming, Marliac rhizome, very free flowering. Plate 298.

PETAL COLOR: Pale pink near base, lighter toward tip. *R.H.S. Chart*: Fan 2, Red-Purple Group, No. 65D or lighter. Sepal color: Shell pink, darker pink veins. *R.H.S. Chart*: Fan 2, Red-Purple Group, No. 69A; veins, No. 63A. Anther color: Golden yellow. *R.H.S. Chart*: Fan 1, Yellow Group, No. 12A. Stamen color: Same as anthers or very close. Flower shape: Cuplike then stellate. Flower size: 5–6 in (13–15 cm). Fragrance: Very slight. Number of petals: 17–23. Number of sepals: 4–5.

LEAF COLOR: Top, green, new leaves bronzy pur-

ple; underside, red. Leaf and sinus: Leaf nearly round; sinus wide open. Leaf size: 8–9 in (20–23 cm). Leaf spread: 4–6 ft (1.2–2 m). Stem color: Peduncle, bronzy; petiole, bronzy green. Pubescence on peduncle or petiole: Many fine hairs on both.

COMMENTS: 'Rosea' No. 2 is one of the choicest water lilies for any size pool. It is quite similar to *N.* ×*marliacea* 'Carnea'.

Nymphaea ×*marliacea* **'Rubra Punctata'** Joseph B. L. Marliac 1889. Parentage: Unknown. Characteristics: Day blooming, Marliac rhizome, moderately free flowering. Plate 299.

PETAL COLOR: Deep purple-red, some flecking. *R.H.S. Chart*: Fan 2, Red-Purple Group, No. 64B. Sepal color: Pinkish. *R.H.S. Chart*: Fan 2, Red-Purple Group, No. 62C. Anther color: Golden yellow. *R.H.S. Chart*: Fan 1, Yellow-Orange Group, No. 20B. Stamen color: Bright orange. Flower shape: Globular or cuplike. Flower size: 4 in (10 cm). Fragrance: Pleasant, noticeable even in older flowers. Number of petals: 20–22. Number of sepals: 4.

LEAF COLOR: Top, green; underside, bronzy purple. Leaf and sinus: Leaf round; lobes overlap 1 in (2.5 cm) at sinus. Leaf size: 9 in (23 cm). Leaf spread: 3 ft (1 m). Stem color: Purplish brown. Pubescence on peduncle or petiole: Thick fuzz on both.

COMMENTS: Petals and sepals alike are short and rounded. The very unusual flower shape makes this a collector's lily for a small or medium pool.

Nymphaea **'Masaniello'** Joseph B. L. Marliac 1908. Parentage: Unknown. Characteristics: Day blooming, Marliac rhizome, very free flowering. Plate 300.

PETAL COLOR: Inner petals, strawberry pink; outer petals, lighter. *R.H.S. Chart*: Inner petals, Fan 2, Red-Purple Group, No. 65A; outer petals, No. 65C. Sepal color: White; pink flush at base, deepening. *R.H.S. Chart*: Fan 4, White Group, No. 155A; flush, Fan 2, Red-Purple Group, No. 65D then 65C. Anther color: Golden yellow. *R.H.S. Chart*: Fan 1, Yellow-Orange Group, No. 19A. Stamen color: Golden orange. Flower shape: Cuplike. Flower size: 5–6 in (13–15 cm). Fragrance: Slight but noticeable. Number of petals: 25. Number of sepals: 4.

LEAF COLOR: Top, green; underside, green, new leaves slightly bronzed. Leaf and sinus: Leaf nearly round; sinus usually open; lobes may overlap 1 in (2.5 cm) at petiole. Leaf size: Up to 10 × 9 in (25 × 23 cm). Leaf spread: 4 ft (1.2 m). Stem color: Brown, occasional faint purple stripes; petiole green near leaf base. Pubescence on peduncle or petiole: None.

COMMENTS: Slightly subject to crown rot. 'Masaniello', with its bicolor flowers, is an excellent plant for any size pool.

Nymphaea **'Maurice Laydeker'** Latour-Marliac Nursery. Parentage: Unknown. Characteristics: Day blooming, Marliac rhizome, free flowering. Plate 301.

PETAL COLOR: Inner petals strawberry red; outer petals paler. *R.H.S. Chart*: Inner petals, Fan 2, Red-Purple Group, No. 62B; outer petals, No. 62D. Sepal color: White, base develops pink blush. *R.H.S. Chart*: Fan 4, White Group, No. 155D; blush, Fan 2, Red-Purple Group, No. 62D. Anther color: Yellow-Orange. *R.H.S. Chart*: Fan 1, Orange Group, No. 26C. Stamen color: Burnt orange. Flower shape: Cuplike. Flower size: 4 in (10 cm). Fragrance: Slight. Number of petals: 20–21. Number of sepals: 4.

LEAF COLOR: Top, green; underside, purple-brown. Leaf and sinus: Leaf almost round; sinus usually a wide-open V yet lobes sometimes overlap at sinus. Leaf size: 6–7 in (15–18 cm). Leaf spread: 2–3 ft (0.6–1 m). Stem color: Green. Pubescence on peduncle or petiole: None.

COMMENTS: With its red-and-white bicolor combination, small leaves, and small leaf spread, 'Maurice Laydeker' makes a fine choice for the tub garden, small, or medium pool. In North Carolina, however, it is frequently afflicted with crown rot.

Nymphaea **'Meteor'** Joseph B. L. Marliac 1909. Parentage: Unknown. Characteristics: Day blooming, Marliac rhizome, free flowering. Plate 302.

PETAL COLOR: Inner petals red; outer petals pink, white tips. *R.H.S. Chart*: Inner petals, Fan 2, Red-Purple Group, No. 63A; outer petals, No. 63C; tips, Fan 4, White Group, No. 155D. Sepal color: Light pink, light green border. *R.H.S. Chart*: Fan 2, Red-Purple Group, No. 62D or lighter; border, Fan 3, Green Group, No. 142D. Anther color: Yellow. *R.H.S. Chart*: Fan 1, Yellow Group, No. 13B. Stamen color: Orange. Flower shape: Stellate. Flower size: 6–7 in (15–18 cm). Fragrance: Slight. Number of petals: 26–27. Number of sepals: 4.

LEAF COLOR: Top, medium green; underside, medium green, young leaves bronzy. Leaf and sinus: Leaf round; sinus closed. Leaf size: 9 in (23 cm). Leaf spread: 4–6 ft (1.2–2 m). Stem color: Rhubarb red, some purple stripes. Pubescence on peduncle or petiole: Fuzz on both stems, especially on peduncle.

COMMENTS: This cultivar's flowers are a brilliant, glowing color. 'Meteor' is a fine lily for medium and large pools.

Nymphaea **'Moorei'** Adelaide Botanic Gardens 1900. Parentage: *N. alba* × *N. mexicana*. Characteristics: Day blooming, upright rhizome, fairly free flowering. Plate 303.

PETAL COLOR: Medium yellow. *R.H.S. Chart*: Fan 1, Green-Yellow Group, No. 1C. Sepal color: Greenish white, tips greenish yellow; veins and edges pinkish, especially in older flowers. *R.H.S. Chart*: Fan 4, Green-White Group, No. 157B; tips, Fan 3, Yellow-Green Group, No. 145C; veins and edges, Fan 1, Red Group, No. 38C. Anther color: Deep yellow. *R.H.S. Chart*: Fan 1, Yellow Group, No. 10A. Stamen color: Yellow. Flower shape: Cuplike then stellate. Flower size: 4–5 in (10–13 cm). Fragrance: Very slight, if any. Number of petals: 25–26. Number of sepals: 4 or 5.

LEAF COLOR: Top, green, numerous purple specks and small mottles around perimeter of new leaves; underside, red, newest leaves brown, all leaves covered with numerous purple specks and small purple mottles. Leaf and sinus: Leaf a little longer than wide; sinus an open V. Leaf size: 9 in (23 cm). Leaf spread: 3–4 ft (1–1.2 m). Stem color: Green. Pubescence on peduncle or petiole: None.

COMMENTS: Flowers are a lovely shade of yellow, a shade deeper than those of *N.* ×*marliacea* 'Chromatella'; however, this plant does not match 'Chromatella' in the number of blooms produced. 'Moorei' could be used in any size pool. I have found it subject to crown rot in North Carolina.

Nymphaea **'Morning Glory'**. See *N.* ×*marliacea* **'Carnea'**.

Nymphaea **'Mrs. C. W. Thomas'** George L. Thomas 1931. Parentage: Unknown. Characteristics: Day blooming, odorata rhizome, fairly free flowering. Plate 304.

PETAL COLOR: Inner petals pale pink; outer petals shell pink. *R.H.S. Chart*: Inner petals, Fan 1, Red Group, No. 36D; outer petals, Fan 2, Red-Purple Group, No. 62D. Sepal color: Shell pink. *R.H.S. Chart*: Fan 2, Red-Purple Group, No. 62D. Anther color: Deep yellow. *R.H.S. Chart*: Fan 1, Yellow Group, No. 13A. Stamen color: Deep yellow. Flower shape: Peony-style. Flower size: 6–7 in (15–18 cm). Fragrance: Delightful. Number of petals: 36. Number of sepals: 4.

LEAF COLOR: Top, green, new leaves bronzy; underside, brown, new leaves purplish. Leaf and sinus: Leaf nearly round, edges smooth; sinus open. Leaf size: 9–10 in (23–25 cm). Leaf spread: 4–6 ft (1.2–2 m). Stem color: Brownish. Pubescence on peduncle or petiole: Fine fuzz and hair on both.

COMMENTS: 'Mrs. C. W. Thomas', originally a chance seedling from Lilypons Water Gardens, is a beautiful cultivar. If planted in a large container so that it can form a colony of rhizomes, it will bloom quite freely. I recommend it for the medium and large pool.

Nymphaea '**Mrs. Richmond**'. See *N.* '**Fabiola**'.

Nymphaea '**Newton**' Joseph B. L. Marliac 1910. Parentage: Unknown. Characteristics: Day blooming, Marliac rhizome, very free flowering. New flowers held several inches above the water, last-day flowers float. Plate 305.

PETAL COLOR: Red. *R.H.S. Chart*: Fan 1, Red Group, No. 51A. Sepal color: Pink, white tips. *R.H.S. Chart*: Fan 1, Red Group, No. 55D; tips, Fan 4, White Group, No. 155A. Anther color: Orange. *R.H.S. Chart*: Fan 1, Yellow-Orange Group, No. 21A. Stamen color: Deep yellow. Flower shape: Stellate, long narrow petals. Flower size: 6–8 in (15–20 cm). Fragrance: Slight. Number of petals: 19. Number of sepals: 4.

LEAF COLOR: Top, green, purple blotches; underside, brownish red. Leaf and sinus: Leaf nearly round; sinus open. Leaf size: 9 in (23 cm). Leaf spread: 3.5–5 ft (1.1–1.5 m). Stem color: Reddish brown. Pubescence on peduncle or petiole: Some short fuzz on both.

COMMENTS: Long narrow petals and sepals are found in only two red hardy water lilies. These traits are unique to 'Newton' and 'Perry's Red Beauty'. New flowers closely resemble many tropical water lilies. 'Newton' is an exquisite lily and I recommend it for any size pool.

Nymphaea '**Norma Gedye**' Laurence Gedye 1973. Parentage: Unknown. Characteristics: Day blooming, Marliac rhizome, fairly free flowering. Plate 306.

PETAL COLOR: Medium pink, deepening toward base. *R.H.S. Chart*: Fan 2, Red-Purple Group, No. 65A; base, No. 68B or lighter. Sepal color: Pink, same as petal base. *R.H.S. Chart*: Fan 2, Red-Purple Group, No. 68B or lighter. Anther color: Yellow. *R.H.S. Chart*: Fan 1, Yellow Group, No. 12A. Stamen color: Inner rows golden yellow; outer rows pink. Flower shape: Stellate, open. Flower size: 6.5–7.5 in (16–19 cm). Fragrance: Slight. Number of petals: 19–20. Number of sepals: 4.

LEAF COLOR: Top, green, new leaves purple-red; underside, red. Leaf and sinus: Leaf a little longer than wide; sinus usually a wide-open V. Leaf size: Up to 11 in (28 cm). Leaf spread: 4–5 ft (1.2–1.5 m). Stem color: Green, striped purple. Pubescence on peduncle or petiole: Fine hairs on both, more on petiole.

COMMENTS: This beautiful water lily, developed at Gedye's Water Gardens in Doncaster East, Australia, is named for the wife of nursery owner Laurence Gedye. Truly, a large 'Norma Gedye' is one of the most beautiful of all water lilies. I highly recommend it for medium and large pools.

Nymphaea '**Odalisque**' Joseph B. L. Marliac 1908. Parentage: Unknown. May include *N. tuberosa* according to Charles Masters. Characteristics: Day blooming, tuberosa rhizome, fairly free flowering; flowers held 5–6 in (13–15 cm) above water. Plate 307.

PETAL COLOR: Pinkish. *R.H.S. Chart*: Fan 1, Red Group, No. 36A. Sepal color: Pinkish. *R.H.S. Chart*: Fan 1, Red Group, No. 36A. Anther color: Yellowish orange. *R.H.S. Chart*: Fan 1, Yellow-Orange Group, No. 22C. Stamen color: Yellowish orange. Flower shape: Stellate; sepals and outer petals point downward when flower is open. Flower size: 5–6 in (13–15 cm). Fragrance: Some. Number of petals: 23. Number of sepals: 4–5, usually 5.

LEAF COLOR: Top, apple green; underside, dark brownish red. Leaf and sinus: Leaves nearly round, unusually a little broader than long; sinus a small V. Leaf size: 6.5 × 7 in (16 × 18 cm). Leaf spread: 4–5 ft (1.2–1.5 m). Stem color: Green. Pubescence on peduncle or petiole: None.

COMMENTS: 'Odalisque' has unusual features for a hardy: the flowers are held several inches above the water and the sepals and outer petals hang down. To become a frequent bloomer, 'Odalisque' needs to be planted in a large container and allowed to form a colony. I would recommend it for medium and large pools.

Nymphaea odorata '**Sulphurea**' Joseph B. L. Marliac 1879. Parentage: *N. odorata* × *N. mexicana*. Characteristics: Day blooming, Marliac-odorata rhizome, fairly free flowering. Plate 308.

PETAL COLOR: Rich yellow. *R.H.S. Chart*: Fan 1, Yellow Group, No. 4A. Sepal color: Pale yellowish green. *R.H.S. Chart*: Fan 1, Green-Yellow Group, No. 1D. Anther color: Yellow. *R.H.S. Chart*: Fan 1, Yellow Group, Nos. 7A–B. Stamen color: Yellow. Flower shape: Cuplike then stellate. Flower size: 6–7 in (15–18 cm). Fragrance: Quite sweet. Number of petals: 21–24. Number of sepals: 4.

LEAF COLOR: Top, green, new leaves speckled and blotched purple; underside, red or purple, deep purple mottles. Leaf and sinus: Leaves nearly round; lobes pointed at tips. Sinus usually an open V; lobes may overlap somewhat, especially on new leaves. Leaf size: Up to 10 × 9 in (25 × 23 cm). Leaf spread: 3–4 ft (1–1.2 m). Stem color: Peduncle, yellowish green, occasional purple stripe; petiole, purple or brown. Pubescence on peduncle or petiole: Fine hairs on both.

COMMENTS: *N. odorata* 'Sulphurea' flowers have a very good color and scent. The blooms are open only a short time, however, opening late in the morning and closing in midafternoon. This lily is suited for medium or large pools.

Nymphaea odorata **'Sulphurea Grandiflora'** (formerly *N.* 'Sunrise') Joseph B. L. Marliac 1888. Parentage: Probably *N. odorata* var. *gigantea* × *N. mexicana*. Characteristics: Day blooming, Marliac rhizome, free flowering in USDA zones 6–10, less so in zones 3–5. Plate 373.

PETAL COLOR: Yellow, outer petals lighter. *R.H.S. Chart*: Inner petals, Fan 1, Yellow Group, No. 4B; outer petals, Green-Yellow Group, No. 1D. Sepal color: Light green, veins greenish gray; tips greenish. *R.H.S. Chart*: Fan 4, Green-White Group, No. 157A; veins, Greyed-Green Group, Nos. 194B–C; tips, Fan 3, Yellow-Green Group, No. 145C. Anther color: Deep yellow. *R.H.S. Chart*: Fan 1, Yellow Group, No. 6B. Stamen color: Yellow. Flower shape: Stellate. Flower size: 7–9.5 in (18–24 cm). Fragrance: Very slight. Number of petals: 23–28. Number of sepals: 4–5.

LEAF COLOR: Top, green, tiny purple mottles on new leaves; underside, red, small dark purple blotches on new leaves lighten with age. Leaf and sinus: Leaf a little longer than wide; sinus usually a wide-open V. Leaf size: 11 × 10 in (28 × 25 cm). Leaf spread: 4–5 ft (1.2–1.5 m). Stem color: Yellow-green, usually striped purple. Pubescence on peduncle or petiole: Fine fuzz on both.

COMMENTS: Around 1930, this lily was renamed 'Sunrise' by Johnson Water Gardens, Hynes, California. With its huge blooms and long narrow pointed petals, *N. odorata* 'Sulphurea Grandiflora' can be a real show lily for warm or temperate regions. In cool regions expect fewer blooms. It is currently one of the four largest-flowered hardy water lilies (the others are 'Hal Miller', 'Yellow Queen', and 'Apple Blossom Pink'). New spring leaves are frequently twisted and poorly formed; however with warmer weather, leaves develop perfectly. This lily is a good choice for medium and large pools.

Nymphaea odorata **'Turicensis'**. Parentage: Seedling of *N. odorata*. Characteristics: Day blooming, odorata rhizome, fairly free flowering. Plate 309.

PETAL COLOR: Soft pink. *R.H.S. Chart*: Fan 2, Red-Purple Group, No. 62D. Sepal color: Greenish yellow. *R.H.S. Chart*: Fan 3, Yellow-Green Group, No. 145D. Anther color: Deep yellow. *R.H.S. Chart*: Fan 1, Group, No. 13A. Stamen color: Deep yellow. Flower shape: Stellate. Flower size: 5–6 in (13–15 cm). Fragrance: Lovely and pleasant. Number of petals: 25–26. Number of sepals 4.

LEAF COLOR: Top, green; underside, bronzy red. Leaf and sinus: Leaf nearly round with rounded lobes; sinus usually open. Leaf size: 5–6 in (13–15 cm). Leaf spread: 2.5 ft (0.8 m). Stem color: Greenish. Pubescence on peduncle or petiole: None.

COMMENTS: For best performance, this lily, as with other odorata types, should be planted in a large container so that it can form a colony of plants. It will then bloom fairly well. *N. odorata* 'Turicensis' is currently more widely known in England than in the United States. I recommend it for the medium or large pool.

Nymphaea **'Orange Hybrid'**. See *N.* 'Cherokee'.

Nymphaea **'Paul Hariot'** Joseph B. L. Marliac 1905. Parentage: Unknown. Characteristics: Day blooming, upright rhizome, very free flowering. Plate 310.

PETAL COLOR: Inner petals orange, deepening; outer petals apricot, by third day deep pinkish orange. *R.H.S. Chart*: Inner petals, first day, Fan 1, Red Group, No. 38B; third day, No. 38A. Outer petals, first day, Orange Group, No. 29D; third day, Red Group, No. 49C or 41D. Sepal color: Creamy apricot then light pink. *R.H.S. Chart*: Fan 1, Orange Group, No. 29D; third day, Red Group, No. 36D. Anther color: Golden yellow. *R.H.S. Chart*: Fan 1, Yellow-Orange Group, No. 21C. Stamen color: Burnt orange. Flower shape: Cuplike. Flower size: 4–5 in (10–13 cm). Fragrance: Slight. Number of petals: 22. Number of sepals: 4–5.

LEAF COLOR: Top, green, yet variable. New leaves on young plants olive green, speckled and freckled; larger leaves from main plant very deep green with covering of large and small purple blotches. Underside, smallest leaves light purple, purple specks and freckles; larger leaves green or purple, purple specks and mottles. Leaf and sinus: Leaves oval; sinus an open V or lobes overlap about halfway. Lobes rounded at tips. Leaf size: 6–7 in (15–18 cm). Leaf spread: 3–4 ft (1–1.2 m). Stem color: Brown. Pubescence on peduncle or petiole: A few fine hairs on both.

COMMENTS: This cultivar blooms very freely once it is established. I consider this water lily an ideal plant for a tub garden or a small or medium pool. Some commercial water gardens in the United States and England sell both 'Sioux' and 'Chrysantha' (which see) for this fine plant, which is not currently available from most nurseries. Propagation can be difficult due to the rhizome of 'Paul Hariot' being subject to crown rot in Europe, the United States, and Japan. Currently Australian nurseries have a good supply.

Nymphaea **'Paul Hoffman'** Leeann Connelly 1989. Parentage: Natural hybrid of *N. mexicana* No. 1 × *N. odorata*. Characteristics: Day blooming, Marliac-odorata rhizome, free flowering. Plate 311.

PETAL COLOR: Center petals deep yellow, outer

rows lighter. *R.H.S. Chart*: Center petals, Fan 1, Yellow Group, No. 8A; outer rows, No. 8C. Sepal color: Light yellowish green. *R.H.S. Chart*: Fan 1, Green-Yellow Group, No. 1D. Anther color: Very deep yellow. *R.H.S. Chart*: Fan 1, Yellow Group, No. 12A. Stamen color: Deep yellow. Flower shape: Cuplike then stellate. Flower size: 6–7 in (15–18 cm). Fragrance: Fairly sweet, first two days. Number of petals: 21–22. Number of sepals: 4.

LEAF COLOR: Top, green, new leaves flecked purple; underside, reddish, blotched dark brown and purple. Leaf and sinus: Leaves nearly round, lobe tips projecting; sinus open. Leaf size: 9 × 8.5 in (23 × 22 cm). Leaf spread: 4–5 ft (1.2–1.5 m). Stem color: Reddish purple. Pubescence on peduncle or petiole: All covered with fine hairs.

COMMENTS: Leeann Connelly discovered a large group of 'Paul Hoffman' growing between natural plantings of *Nymphaea mexicana* No. 1 and *N. odorata* in Lake Okeechobee, Florida. She named it after a close friend. The flower color is rich and flowers are freely produced. An excellent choice for the small, medium, or large pool, especially in southern states. Appears to be subject to crown rot in more northerly climes.

***Nymphaea* 'Pearl of the Pool'** Perry D. Slocum 1946. Parentage: *N.* 'Pink Opal × *N.* ×*marliacea* 'Rosea'. Characteristics: Day blooming, odorata rhizome, moderately free flowering. Plate 312.

PETAL COLOR: Medium pink. *R.H.S. Chart*: Fan 2, Red-Purple Group, No. 62C. Sepal color: Medium pink. *R.H.S. Chart*: Fan 2, Red-Purple Group, No. 62C. Anther color: Yellow. *R.H.S. Chart*: Fan 1, Yellow Group, No. 12B. Stamen color: Pinkish orange. Flower shape: Cuplike, then stellate. Flower size: 5–6 in (13–15 cm). Fragrance: Very nice. Number of petals: 40–48. Number of sepals: 4.

LEAF COLOR: Top, green, first leaves bronzy; underside, red, green V along midvein. Leaf and sinus: Leaf round; lobes may or may not overlap at sinus, one or both lobes may be raised. Leaf size: Up to 10 in (25 cm). Leaf spread: 4–5 ft (1.2–1.5 m). Stem color: Light brown, purple stripes. Pubescence on peduncle or petiole: Occasionally fine fuzz on some stems.

COMMENTS: This cultivar blooms most freely when planted in a large container where it can form a colony of several plants. A planter 24 × 24 × 12 in (60 × 60 × 30 cm) is ideal. This was the first hardy water lily ever patented in the United States—plant patent No. 666 (now expired) was issued for 'Pearl of the Pool' in January 1946. I recommend it for the medium or large pool or the natural pond.

***Nymphaea* 'Perry's Baby Red'** Perry D. Slocum 1989. Parentage: Probably *N.* 'Alba Plenissima' × *N.* 'Atropurpurea'. Characteristics: Day blooming, small Marliac rhizome, very free flowering. Plate 313.

PETAL COLOR: Deep red. *R.H.S. Chart*: Fan 2, Red-Purple Group, Nos. 61A–B. Sepal color: Pink, prominent red veins. *R.H.S. Chart*: Fan 2, Red-Purple Group, No. 69B; veins, No. 61B. Anther color: Yellow-orange. *R.H.S. Chart*: Fan 1, Yellow-Orange Group, No. 19A. Stamen color: Orange. Flower shape: Cuplike. Flower size: 3–3.5 in (8–9 cm). Fragrance: Slight yet noticeable. Number of petals: 24–31. Number of sepals: 4.

LEAF COLOR: Top, green, newest leaves purple; underside, brown, newest leaves red. Leaf and sinus: Leaves heart-shaped; sinus a wide-open V. Lobe tips usually pointed. Leaf size: 4.5–6 in (11–15 cm). Leaf spread: 30 in (75 cm). Stem color: Peduncle brown, petiole red. Pubescence on peduncle or petiole: Thick short fuzz on both.

COMMENTS: 'Perry's Baby Red' is a water lily with excellent qualities for the tub garden or small pool. Unfortunately, the high demand for this lily may exceed supply.

***Nymphaea* 'Perry's Black Opal'** Perry D. Slocum 1990. Parentage: Probably *N.* 'Vesuve' × *N.* 'Splendida'. Characteristics: Day blooming, Marliac rhizome, free flowering. Plate 314.

PETAL COLOR: Very dark red. *R.H.S. Chart*: Fan 2, Red-Purple Group, No. 71A. Sepal color: Lighter than petals. *R.H.S. Chart*: Fan 2, Red-Purple Group, No. 64A. Anther color: Orange. *R.H.S. Chart*: Fan 1, Yellow-Orange Group, No. 23C. Stamen color: Deep orange-red. Flower shape: Stellate. Flower size: 6–7 in (15–18 cm). Fragrance: None. Number of petals: 24. Number of sepals: 4.

LEAF COLOR: Top, green, new leaves bronzy red; underside, reddish, wide green midstripe. Leaf and sinus: Leaf nearly round; sinus wide open. Leaf size: 10 × 9.5 in (25 × 24 cm). Leaf spread: 3.5–5 ft (1.1–1.5 m). Stem color: Purple. Pubescence on peduncle or petiole: Thick fuzz on both.

COMMENTS: This is one of the darkest red hardy lilies I have ever seen. Furthermore, flowers do not burn or melt (at least in North Carolina, USDA zone 6b) during the very hot summer days as do many red-flowered cultivars. 'Perry's Black Opal' blooms freely in hot weather while the dark red–flowered cultivar 'William Falconer' gives up completely. A comparison of flower color with 'Atropurpurea' (another dark red lily that blooms throughout the summer) reveals these flowers to be several shades deeper. I recommend this cultivar for any size pool, especially medium and large pools.

Nymphaea **'Perry's Cactus Pink'** Perry D. Slocum 1990. Parentage: Probably *N.* 'Perry's Pink' × *N.* 'American Star'. Characteristics: Day blooming, odorata rhizome, fairly free blooming, petals uniquely rolled, narrow. Plate 315.

PETAL COLOR: Shell pink, base deeper pink. *R.H.S. Chart*: Fan 2, Red-Purple Group, No. 65D; base, No. 65A. Sepal color: Deep pink. *R.H.S. Chart*: Fan 2, Red-Purple Group, Nos. 67C–D. Anther color: Deep yellow. *R.H.S. Chart*: Fan 1, Yellow Group, No. 13A. Stamen color: Orange. Flower shape: Stellate. Flower size: 5–6 in (13–15 cm). Fragrance: Delightful. Number of petals: 28. Number of sepals: 4.

LEAF COLOR: Top, green, new leaves purplish; underside, red. Leaf and sinus: Leaf nearly round; sinus usually ⅔ open, sometimes completely open or closed. Leaf size: 7–8 in (18–20 cm). Leaf spread: About 4 ft (1.2 m). Stem color: Reddish purple. Pubescence on peduncle or petiole: Thick fuzz on both.

COMMENTS: The unique long, rolled petals of 'Perry's Cactus Pink' distinguish this lily from all others and instantly command attention. I have never seen any other water lily with these flower features. Plant this cultivar in a large container and let it form a colony of plants for best results. I recommend it for medium or large pools.

Nymphaea **'Perry's Crinkled Pink'** Perry D. Slocum 1989. Parentage: *N.* 'Gloire du Temple-sur-Lot' × *N.* 'Vesuve'. Characteristics: Day blooming, Marliac rhizome, fairly free flowering. Plate 316.

PETAL COLOR: Deep shell pink. *R.H.S. Chart*: Fan 2, Red-Purple Group, No. 62C. Sepal color: Light pink. *R.H.S. Chart*: Fan 2, Red-Purple Group, No. 62D. Anther color: Deep yellow. *R.H.S. Chart*: Fan 1, Yellow Group, No. 12A. Stamen color: Deep yellow. Flower shape: Stellate, full. Flower size: 4.5–5.5 in (11–14 cm). Fragrance: Slight. Number of petals: 27–33. Number of sepals: 4.

LEAF COLOR: Top, green, newest leaves purplish brown; underside, iridescent red, prominent green veins. Leaf and sinus: Leaves round; sinus a wide-open V. Leaf size: 8–9 in (20–23 cm). Leaf spread: 4 ft (1.2 m). Stem color: Brown; petioles darker brown than peduncles. Pubescence on peduncle or petiole: None.

COMMENTS: 'Perry's Crinkled Pink', with its crinkled pink petals, is unique among pink hardy water lilies. It has an excellent future. I recommend it for the small, medium, or large pool.

Nymphaea **'Perry's Deepest Red'** Perry D. Slocum 1990. Parentage: Seedling of *N.* 'Vesuve'. Charac-

teristics: Day blooming, Marliac rhizome, moderate bloomer. Plate 317.

PETAL COLOR: Deep burgundy-red, underside a shade deeper. *R.H.S. Chart*: Fan 4, Greyed-Purple Group, No. 187B; underside, No. 187A. Sepal color: Reddish, reddish purple veins, tips light green. *R.H.S. Chart*: Fan 2, Red-Purple Group, No. 70C; veins, No. 70B; tips, Fan 3, Yellow-Green Group, No. 145D. Anther color: Yellow. *R.H.S. Chart*: Fan 1, Yellow Group, No. 11B. Stamen color: Orange. Flower shape: Cuplike. Flower size: 3.5–4.5 in (9–11 cm). Fragrance: Slight. Number of petals: 33–36. Number of sepals: 4.

LEAF COLOR: Top, green, new leaves purple; underside, newest leaves red, green midband, red develops to bronze, mature leaves green. Leaf and sinus: Leaf nearly round; sinus closed by lobe overlap. Leaf size: 8–9 in (20–23 cm). Leaf spread: About 3–4 ft (1–1.2 m). Stem color: Light brown, striped purple, green near leaf or flower. Pubescence on peduncle or petiole: Short fuzz on both.

COMMENTS: This cultivar has the darkest red flowers I have ever seen in water lilies, comparable to the blackest tulips, particularly in the second- and third-day blooms. Flowers are quite double with excellent form. 'Perry's Deepest Red' is a moderate bloomer, however. Blooms are rather small relative to the leaves, and the leaves on an established plant rise up, sometimes covering the blooms. Leaf perimeters frequently turn downward while the center is elevated. For these reasons I recommend it only for the collector with a medium or large pool.

Nymphaea **'Perry's Double White'** Perry D. Slocum 1990. Parentage: Seedling of *N. tuberosa* 'Richardsonii' No. 2 and probably *N.* 'Perry's Super Red'. Characteristics: Day blooming, Marliac-tuberosa rhizome, free flowering. Plate 318.

PETAL COLOR: Pure white. *R.H.S. Chart*: Fan 4, White Group, No. 155D. Sepal color: White, tipped green, prominent dark gray veins. *R.H.S. Chart*: Fan 4, White Group, No. 155A; tips, Fan 3, Yellow-Green Group, No. 144A; veins, Fan 4, Grey Group, No. 201B. Anther color: Yellow. *R.H.S. Chart*: Fan 1, Yellow Group, No. 8A. Stamen color: Deep yellow. Flower shape: Stellate, open. Flower size: 6–7 in (15–18 cm). Fragrance: None. Number of petals: 39–46, usually 44. Number of sepals: 4.

LEAF COLOR: Top, deep green, new leaves slightly bronzed; underside, green. Leaf and sinus: Leaves nearly round, edges slightly ruffled; sinus an open V. Leaf size: 9–10 in (23–25 cm). Leaf spread: 4–5 ft (1.2–1.5 m). Stem color: Brown, dense red mottling. Pubescence on peduncle or petiole: None.

COMMENTS: 'Perry's Double White' has a beautiful flower form and is quite free flowering. Its bloom season is unusually long, frequently lasting through October in North Carolina (USDA zone 6b). Plant in a large container, about 24 × 24 × 12 in (60 × 60 × 30 cm), so that it can form a colony; it will then produce its maximum number of blooms. I consider it one of the best, if not *the* best, of all the large white hardies. Suitable for tub gardens and small, medium, or large pools.

Nymphaea **'Perry's Dwarf Red'** (syn. 'Perry's Red Dwarf') Perry D. Slocum 1989. Parentage: Probably *N.* 'Alba Plenissima' and *N.* 'Atropurpurea'. Characteristics: Day blooming, Marliac-tuberosa rhizome, free flowering. Plate 319.

PETAL COLOR: Brilliant red. *R.H.S. Chart*: Fan 2, Red-Purple Group, Nos. 64A–B. Sepal color: Light pink, darker pink veins. *R.H.S. Chart*: Fan 2, Red-Purple Group, No. 68D; veins, No. 68C. Anther color: Burnt orange. *R.H.S. Chart*: Fan 1, Orange-Red Group, No. 35B. Stamen color: Orange-red. Flower shape: Cuplike, peony-style. Flower size: 4–4.5 in (10–11 cm). Fragrance: Slight. Number of petals: 30. Number of sepals: 4.

LEAF COLOR: Top, green, newest leaves bronzy purple; underside, green, newest leaves bronzy. Leaf and sinus: Leaves round; sinus usually open, sometimes partly closed. Leaf size: 6 in (15 cm). Leaf spread: 3 ft (1 m). Stem color: Peduncle, brown; petiole purple. Pubescence on peduncle or petiole: Thick fuzz and fine hairs on both.

COMMENTS: 'Perry's Dwarf Red' is a very striking new red cultivar. I recommend it for the tub garden or any size pool, especially small gardens because of its limited leaf spread.

Nymphaea **'Perry's Fire Opal'** Perry D. Slocum 1987. Parentage: *N.* 'Peter Slocum' × *N.* 'Director George T. Moore' (a tropical water lily). Characteristics: Day blooming, odorata rhizome, free flowering; unusual vein pattern radiates from leaf center. Plate 320.

PETAL COLOR: Very rich pink, darker pink lengthwise stripe. *R.H.S. Chart*: Fan 2, Red-Purple Group, No. 66D; stripe, No. 66C. Sepal color: Pink. *R.H.S. Chart*: Fan 2, Red-Purple Group, No. 63D. Anther color: Golden yellow. *R.H.S. Chart*: Fan 1, Yellow Group, No. 13A. Stamen color: Orange. Flower shape: Peony-style. Flower size: 5–6 in (13–15 cm). Fragrance: Delightful. Number of petals: 40–50. Number of sepals: 4.

LEAF COLOR: Top, green, new leaves purplish red, veins light green on green leaves, purplish on new leaves; underside, red. Leaf and sinus: Leaf round; lobes usually overlap at sinus. Leaf size: 7–10 in (18–25 cm). Leaf spread: 3–4 ft (1–1.2 m). Stem color: Green. Pubescence on peduncle or petiole: Thick fuzz on both.

COMMENTS: 'Perry's Fire Opal' is one of the very best odorata water lilies for the tub garden or small pool, and it can also be used in medium and large pools. It blooms quite well in a restricted area, and its flower color is wonderful. To achieve the best possible performance, however, plant it in a large planter and allow it to form a colony of plants. Flowers are very double and often are nearly as large as the leaves. When 'Perry's Fire Opal' is more widely known, it may very well displace 'Pink Opal' as *the* pink odorata for the tub garden. Recipient of the International Water Lily Society's America Award for 1990, it is the first odorata water lily ever given such an award.

Nymphaea **'Perry's Magnificent'** Perry D. Slocum 1990. Parentage: *N.* 'Perry's Pink' × *N.* 'Director George T. Moore' (a tropical water lily). Characteristics: Day blooming, odorata rhizome, fairly free flowering. Plate 321.

PETAL COLOR: Very deep dusty rose; center petals edged yellow. *R.H.S. Chart*: Fan 2, Red-Purple Group, No. 63B; edging, Fan 1, Green-Yellow Group, No. 1D. Sepal color: Deep pink. *R.H.S. Chart*: Fan 4, Greyed-Purple Group, No. 185C. Anther color: Orange. *R.H.S. Chart*: Fan 1, Orange-Red Group, No. 32C. Stamen color: Orange. Flower shape: Stellate. Flower size: 6–7 in (15–18 cm). Fragrance: Delightful. Number of petals: 33–38. Number of sepals: 4.

LEAF COLOR: Top, green, new leaves bronzy purple; underside, red. Leaf and sinus: Leaf round; sinus frequently ⅔ open, sometimes fully open or nearly closed. Leaf size: 10 in (25 cm). Leaf spread: 4–5 ft (1.2–1.5 m). Stem color: Brown, striped purple. Pubescence on peduncle or petiole: None.

COMMENTS: 'Perry's Magnificent', with a prominent red center dot in the stigmal area and deep, evenly textured petals, is one of the most striking of the new pink hardy water lilies. Plant it in a large planter, about 24 × 24 × 12 in (60 × 60 × 30 cm), and allow it to form a colony of plants in order to maximize bloom. I recommend this cultivar for the medium or large pool as well as the natural pond.

Nymphaea **'Perry's Pink'** Perry D. Slocum 1984. Parentage: Chance seedling of *N.* 'Rose Arey'. Characteristics: Day blooming, odorata rhizome, moderately free flowering. Plate 322.

PETAL COLOR: Rich pink. *R.H.S. Chart*: Fan 2, Red-Purple Group, No. 64D. Sepal color: Rich pink.

R.H.S. Chart: Fan 2, Red-Purple Group, No. 64D. Anther color: Golden yellow. *R.H.S. Chart*: Fan 1, Orange-Red Group, Nos. 31C–D. Stamen color: Inner stamens, yellow; outer stamens orange. Flower shape: Stellate, many petals. Flower size: 6–7 in (15–18 cm). Fragrance: Delightful. Number of petals: 35–39. Number of sepals: 4.

LEAF COLOR: Top, green, new leaves purple; underside, purple, new leaves red, persistent bright green lengthwise V along midvein. Leaf and sinus: Leaves round; sinus on older leaves a wide-open V, lobes overlap on new leaves. Leaf size: Up to 11 in (28 cm). Leaf spread: 4–5 ft (1.2–1.5 m). Stem color: Greenish brown, purple stripes. Pubescence on peduncle or petiole: None.

COMMENTS: 'Perry's Pink', one of the most beautiful of all water lilies, has an unusual red dot in the center of every flower (precisely in the middle of the stigmal area). For best flowering it should be planted in a large container and allowed to form a colony of several plants. This is an excellent choice for medium or large pools as well as natural ponds.

Nymphaea **'Perry's Pink Beauty'** Perry D. Slocum 1989. Parentage: Probably *N. alba* plant received from New Zealand and *N.* 'Vesuve'. Characteristics: Day blooming, Marliac rhizome, free flowering; very wide stigmal area, especially noticeable in newly opened flowers. Plate 323.

PETAL COLOR: Medium to light pink; inner row deep golden yellow. *R.H.S. Chart*: Fan 2, Red-Purple Group, Nos. 65B–C; inner row, Fan 1, Yellow-Orange Group, Nos. 19B–C. Sepal color: Medium pink. *R.H.S. Chart*: Fan 2, Red-Purple Group, No. 65B. Anther color: Yellow. *R.H.S. Chart*: Fan 1, Yellow Group, No. 12A. Stamen color: Deep yellow. Flower shape: Cuplike. Flower size: 4–5 in (10–13 cm). Fragrance: Pleasant, quite pronounced in new blooms. Number of petals: 23. Number of sepals: 4.

LEAF COLOR: Top, green, newest leaves purplish brown; underside, red, prominent green veins. Leaf and sinus: Leaves round; lobes overlap at sinus. Leaf size: 8.5 in (22 cm). Leaf spread: 4–5 ft (1.2–1.5 m). Stem color: Olive green. Pubescence on peduncle or petiole: A few fine hairs on both.

COMMENTS: This appears to be a darker version of *N.* ×*marliacea* 'Rosea'. 'Perry's Pink Beauty' has several attractive features: a clear pink flower color with deep yellow center, a distinct and pleasant fragrance from new blooms, and a very free-flowering habit. Less attractive is that the flower color fades with age and the flowers are rather small relative to the leaves. I recommend it for medium and large pools.

Nymphaea **'Perry's Pink Bicolor'** Perry D. Slocum 1989. Parentage: *N. alba* plant received from New Zealand and *N.* 'Fabiola'. Characteristics: Day blooming, Marliac rhizome, free flowering. Plate 324.

PETAL COLOR: Center petals deep pink, outer petals whitish pink, pink veins. *R.H.S. Chart*: Center petals, Fan 2, Red-Purple Group, Nos. 64B–C; outer petals, Nos. 69B–C; veins, No. 70D. Sepal color: White, pink veins. *R.H.S. Chart*: Fan 4, White Group, No. 155A; veins, Fan 2, Red-Purple Group, No. 70D. Anther color: Golden yellow. *R.H.S. Chart*: Fan 1, Yellow Group, No. 13C. Stamen color: Orange. Flower shape: Stellate. Flower size: 5.5–6 in (14–15 cm). Fragrance: Slight. Number of petals: 20–21. Number of sepals: 4.

LEAF COLOR: Top, green, newest leaves bronzy; underside, purplish, green lengthwise stripe, 2 in (5 cm) wide. Leaf and sinus: Leaves egg-shaped; sinus a wide-open V. Leaf size: Up to 11 × 10 in (28 × 25 cm). Leaf spread: 5–6 ft (1.5–2 m). Stem color: Purplish. Pubescence on peduncle or petiole: Short fuzz on both.

COMMENTS: 'Perry's Pink Bicolor' is a very pleasing pink-and-white combination. I recommend it for medium and large pools.

Nymphaea **'Perry's Pink Delight'** Perry D. Slocum 1990. Parentage: Probably *N.* 'Colonel A. J. Welch' × *N.* 'Splendida'. Characteristics: Day blooming, Marliac rhizome, mildly viviparous, very free blooming. Plate 325.

PETAL COLOR: Evenly pink, paling. *R.H.S. Chart*: Fan 2, Red-Purple Group, No. 63B then 62D. Sepal color: Light pink, striped darker pink. *R.H.S. Chart*: Fan 2, Red-Purple Group, No. 62D; stripes, No. 62A. Anther color: Orange. *R.H.S. Chart*: Fan 1, Yellow-Orange Group, No. 15C. Stamen color: Yellow. Flower shape: Stellate. Flower size: 5.5–7 in (14–18 cm). Fragrance: Not noticeable. Number of petals: 28. Number of sepals: 4.

LEAF COLOR: Top, green, new leaves purplish red; underside, reddish. Leaf and sinus: Leaf nearly round; sinus open. Leaf size: Up to 10 in (25 cm). Leaf spread: About 4–5 ft (1.2–1.5 m). Stem color: Peduncle reddish, striped purple; petiole chartreuse, striped purple. Pubescence on peduncle or petiole: None.

COMMENTS: Flowers of 'Perry's Pink Delight' are in the same color group as flowers of 'Pink Sensation' yet average 8 to 10 more petals. Being a Marliac type and very free flowering, it should make a name for itself for use in medium and large pools. It is a delight to behold. A decided plus is its occasional ability to produce plantlets from the base of the flowers.

Nymphaea **'Perry's Pink Heaven'** Perry D. Slocum 1990. Parentage: Probably *N.* 'Perry's Fire Opal' × *N.* 'Pearl of the Pool'. Characteristics: Day blooming, odorata rhizome, fairly free flowering. Plate 326.

PETAL COLOR: Pink, darker pink base and center vein. *R.H.S. Chart*: Fan 2, Red-Purple Group, No. 62C; base and vein, No. 62B. Sepal color: Deep pink, fairly even texture. *R.H.S. Chart*: Fan 2, Red-Purple Group, No. 65A. Anther color: Very deep yellow. *R.H.S. Chart*: Fan 1, Yellow-Orange Group, No. 19A. Stamen color: Orange. Flower shape: Stellate. Flower size: 6–8 in (15–20 cm). Fragrance: Slight yet pleasant. Number of petals: 44–45. Number of sepals: 4.

LEAF COLOR: Top, green, new leaves bronzy; underside, red. Leaf and sinus: Leaf nearly round; lobes overlap sinus. Leaf size: 7.5 × 8 in (19 × 20 cm). Leaf spread: 4–5 ft (1.2–1.5 m). Stem color: Bright green. Pubescence on peduncle or petiole: Sparse short hairs on both.

COMMENTS: This cultivar develops flowers remarkably close to its leaves in size, closest of any water lily I know. The many-petaled, large, fragrant flowers delight everyone with their beauty. I recommend planting 'Perry's Pink Heaven' in a large container so that it can form a colony of plants. It is suitable for medium or large pools.

Nymphaea **'Perry's Red Beauty'** Perry D. Slocum 1989. Parentage: *N.* 'Vesuve' is one of the parents. Characteristics: Day blooming, Marliac rhizome, free flowering. Plate 327.

PETAL COLOR: Very deep red, deepening. *R.H.S. Chart*: Fan 2, Red-Purple Group, No. 61B; last day, No. 61A. Sepal color: White, splashed pale pink, green tips. *R.H.S. Chart*: Fan 4, White Group, No. 155A; splashes, Fan 2, Red-Purple Group, No. 62C; tips, Fan 3, Yellow-Green Group, Nos. 144A–B. Anther color: Yellow. *R.H.S. Chart*: Fan 1, Yellow Group, No. 11B. Stamen color: Orange-red. Flower shape: Stellate. Flower size: 6.5–7 in (16–18 cm). Fragrance: Slight. Number of petals: 24–30. Number of sepals: 4.

LEAF COLOR: Top, green, newest leaves purplish brown; underside, reddish. Leaf and sinus: Leaves oblong; lobes overlap at sinus. Leaf size: Up to 10 × 8.5 in (25 × 22 cm). Leaf spread: 4 ft (1.2 m). Stem color: Reddish brown. Pubescence on peduncle or petiole: Thick fuzz on both.

COMMENTS: 'Perry's Red Beauty' fills the need for a very deep red, stellate, hardy water lily. Many of its petals curl inward in a unique way. A fine water lily for the medium or large pool, it resembles 'Newton' in flower shape yet has a much deeper color.

Nymphaea **'Perry's Red Bicolor'** Perry D. Slocum 1989. Parentage: *N.* 'Vesuve' is a probable parent. Characteristics: Day blooming, Marliac rhizome, free flowering. Plate 328.

PETAL COLOR: Inner petals deep rich red; outer petals pinkish red. *R.H.S. Chart*: Inner petals, Fan 2, Red-Purple Group, No. 64B; outer petals, No. 66D. Sepal color: White, green tips and margins, pink base, usually pink veins. *R.H.S. Chart*: Fan 4, White Group, No. 155B; tips and margins, Fan 3, Yellow-Green Group, No. 145B; veins and base, Fan 2, Red-Purple Group, No. 70D. Anther color: Yellow-Orange. *R.H.S. Chart*: Fan 1, Yellow-Orange Group, No. 18A. Stamen color: Orange. Flower shape: Stellate. Flower size: 5.5–6 in (14–15 cm). Fragrance: Slight. Number of petals: 16–19. Number of sepals: 4–6.

LEAF COLOR: Top, green, ragged purple circle about 1 in (2.5 cm) in diameter midleaf at petiole, newest leaves purplish; underside, red. Leaf and sinus: Leaves nearly round; sinus a wide-open V. Leaf size: 7.5 × 7 in (19 × 18 cm). Leaf spread: 4 ft (1.2 m). Stem color: Peduncle, brown; petiole purplish. Pubescence on peduncle or petiole: Thick fuzz on both.

COMMENTS: 'Perry's Red Bicolor', with its contrasting red-and-white flowers, is a striking water lily for any size pool.

Nymphaea **'Perry's Red Blaze'** Perry D. Slocum 1989. Parentage: *N.* 'Pearl of the Pool' × *N.* 'Charles de Meurville'. Characteristics: Day blooming, odorata rhizome, moderately free flowering. Plate 329.

PETAL COLOR: Cherry red. *R.H.S. Chart*: Fan 2, Red-Purple Group, Nos. 61A–B. Sepal color: Light pink, some darker pink veins. *R.H.S. Chart*: Fan 2, Red-Purple Group, No. 73D; veins, No. 73B. Anther color: Bright yellow. *R.H.S. Chart*: Fan 1, Yellow Group, No. 11B. Stamen color: Deep yellow. Flower shape: Stellate, full; sepals and outer petals frequently turn downward. Flower size: 6 in (15 cm). Fragrance: Pleasant. Number of petals: 33. Number of sepals: 4.

LEAF COLOR: Top, green, newest leaves purple; underside, bronzy red. Leaf and sinus: Leaves nearly round, usually dull point at round end of each leaf opposite lobes, lobe tips pointed; sinus a wide-open V. Leaf size: 9.5 × 8.5 (24 × 22 cm). Leaf spread: 4–5 ft (1.2–1.5 m). Stem color: Red. Pubescence on peduncle or petiole: None.

COMMENTS: Flowers draw attention because of their bright red color, wide golden center, and pointed petals. For best performance plant in a large container so that it can form a colony of several plants. I recommend it for medium and large pools.

Nymphaea **'Perry's Red Dwarf'**. See *N.* **'Perry's Dwarf Red'**.

Nymphaea **'Perry's Red Glow'** Perry D. Slocum 1989. Parentage: Probably *N.* 'Alba Plenissima' × *N.* 'Atropurpurea'. Characteristics: Day blooming, small Marliac-tuberosa rhizome, fairly free flowering. Plate 330.

PETAL COLOR: Very deep red. *R.H.S. Chart*: Fan 2, Red-Purple Group, Nos. 61A–B. Sepal color: Rich green, slightly deeper at tips and margins, red veins and splashes. *R.H.S. Chart*: Fan 3, Yellow-Green Group, No. 146D; veins and splashes, Fan 2, Red-Purple Group, No. 64C. Anther color: Inner anthers, medium orange; outer anthers burnt orange. *R.H.S. Chart*: Inner anthers, Fan 1, Orange Group, No. 29B; outer anthers, Red Group, No. 42D. Stamen color: Purple-red. Flower shape: Stellate. Flower size: 3.5–4 in (9–10 cm). Fragrance: Slight. Number of petals: 23–30. Number of sepals: 4.

LEAF COLOR: Top, green, newest leaves purple; underside, red. Leaf and sinus: Leaves heart-shaped; sinus a wide-open V. Leaf size: 6–7 in (15–18 cm). Leaf spread: 3 ft (1 m). Stem color: Brownish purple. Pubescence on peduncle or petiole: Thick fuzz on both.

COMMENTS: 'Perry's Red Glow', one of the deepest red lilies I have ever seen, has excellent flower color. Its 16 carpels are especially pronounced—more so than on any other hardy I know. I recommend it for small or medium pools.

Nymphaea **'Perry's Red Star'** Perry D. Slocum 1989. Parentage: *N.* 'Vesuve' × *N.* 'Colonel A. J. Welch'. Characteristics: Day blooming, Marliac rhizome, free flowering. Partially viviparous from flower early in season. Plate 331.

PETAL COLOR: Bright red. *R.H.S. Chart*: Fan 2, Red-Purple Group, Nos. 61A–B. Sepal color: Pale pink, veins deeper. *R.H.S. Chart*: Fan 2, Red-Purple Group, No. 65C; veins, No. 64D. Anther color: Burnt orange. *R.H.S. Chart*: Fan 1, Red Group, No. 37B. Stamen color: Orange-red. Flower shape: Stellate. Flower size: 5–6 in (13–15 cm). Fragrance: Slight, noticeably sweet. Number of petals: 23. Number of sepals: 4.

LEAF COLOR: Top, green, newest leaves purple; underside, red, green band midleaf. Leaf and sinus: Leaves round; sinus a wide-open V. Leaf size: 7 in (18 cm). Leaf spread: 30–36 in (75–90 cm). Stem color: Reddish purple. Pubescence on peduncle or petiole: Very small fine hairs on both.

COMMENTS: 'Perry's Red Star' is a vivid red lily with a unique chartreuse stigmal area. It is the first red viviparous hardy water lily. A new plant with tiny reddish purple leaves develops from the full-sized flower bud. Early in the season flower buds frequently develop new plants (at least they have in North Carolina), some of which bloom while still attached to the mother plant. Plantlets do not form on later buds. I recommend this lily for any size pool.

Nymphaea **'Perry's Red Volunteer'**. See *N.* **'Perry's Red Wonder'**.

Nymphaea **'Perry's Red Wonder'** (syn. 'Perry's Red Volunteer') Perry D. Slocum 1989. Parentage: *N.* 'Splendida' is a probable parent. Characteristics: Day blooming, Marliac rhizome, free flowering. Plate 332.

PETAL COLOR: Bright red. *R.H.S. Chart*: Fan 2, Red-Purple Group, No. 67B. Sepal color: Pale pink, reddish pink center veins; green flush at edges. *R.H.S. Chart*: Fan 2, Red-Purple Group, No. 73D; veins, No. 63B; flush, Fan 3, Yellow-Green Group, No. 145D. Anther color: Orange. *R.H.S. Chart*: Fan 1, Orange Group, No. 24B. Stamen color: Orange. Flower shape: Stellate. Flower size: 5.5–6.5 in (14–16 cm). Fragrance: Slight. Number of petals: 21–22. Number of sepals: 4.

LEAF COLOR: Top, green, newest leaves purplish; underside, brown, newest leaves red. Leaf and sinus: Leaves round; sinus a wide-open V. Leaf size: 5.5–7 in (14–18 cm). Leaf spread: 30–36 in (75–90 cm). Stem color: Peduncle, reddish brown; petiole, red. Pubescence on peduncle or petiole: Thick fuzz on both.

COMMENTS: 'Perry's Red Wonder' is a brilliantly colored newcomer with two outstanding features: it is one of the freest-blooming hardy water lilies I have ever seen, and the blooms are nearly as large as the leaves. I highly recommend it for the tub garden or small or medium pool.

Nymphaea **'Perry's Rich Rose'** Perry D. Slocum 1990. Parentage: *N.* 'Perry's Pink' × *N.* 'Mrs. Martin E. Randig' (a tropical water lily). Characteristics: Day blooming, odorata rhizome, fairly free flowering. Plate 333.

PETAL COLOR: Rich old rose. *R.H.S. Chart*: Fan 2, Red-Purple Group, Nos. 64C–D. Sepal color: Red. *R.H.S. Chart*: Fan 2, Red-Purple Group, No. 64B. Anther color: Orange. *R.H.S. Chart*: Fan 1, Orange Group, No. 29B. Stamen color: Orange. Flower shape: Stellate. Flower size: 6–8 in (15–20 cm). Fragrance: Slight, pleasant. Number of petals: 29–30. Number of sepals: 4.

LEAF COLOR: Top, green, new leaves purple then bronze; underside, red, broad green midstripe lengthwise and inside lobes. Leaf and sinus: Leaves round; sinus usually ⅔ open. Leaf size: 9 in (23 cm). Leaf spread: 4–4.5 ft (1.2–1.4 m). Stem color: Peduncle, bright chartreuse; petiole, medium green; both striped purple. Pubescence on peduncle or petiole: None.

COMMENTS: The flowers of this cultivar are frequently nearly as large as the leaves, and they stay open quite late in the afternoon, long after most other odoratas have closed. Although one parent is a tropical water lily (N. 'Mrs. Martin E. Randig'), this cultivar has survived temperatures of –5°F (–21°C); from this same parent, 'Perry's Rich Rose' undoubtedly received its very rich and even flower color and bloom period. A rare identifying feature is the pink dot in the middle of the stigmal area. Plant in a large container so that it can form a colony of rhizomes, and then it will flower freely. I recommend it for any size pool.

Nymphaea 'Perry's Stellar Red' Perry D. Slocum 1989. Parentage: Probably N. tuberosa 'Richardsonii' No. 2 × N. 'Charles de Meurville'. Characteristics: Day blooming, Marliac-tuberosa rhizome, free flowering. Plate 334.

PETAL COLOR: Inner petals deep red; outer petals lighter red, pink tips. R.H.S. Chart: Inner petals, Fan 2, Red-Purple Group, Nos. 61A–B; outer petals, No. 61D or lighter; tips, No. 62D. Sepal color: Light pink, red veins. R.H.S. Chart: Fan 2, Red-Purple Group, No. 65C; veins, No. 63B. Anther color: Deep yellow. R.H.S. Chart: Fan 1, Yellow Group, No. 8A. Stamen color: Orange. Flower shape: Very stellate. Flower size: 6–8 in (15–20 cm). Fragrance: Slight. Number of petals: 24. Number of sepals: 4.

LEAF COLOR: Top, green, newest leaves brownish purple; underside, bronze. Leaf and sinus: Leaves nearly round; sinus usually an open V. Leaf size: 9 in (23 cm). Leaf spread: 4 ft (1.2 m). Stem color: Brownish purple. Pubescence on peduncle or petiole: Some short fuzz on both.

COMMENTS: 'Perry's Stellar Red' is a striking new lily. Flowers have the same general shape as 'Newton' but are a darker red. I recommend this cultivar for the medium or large pool.

Nymphaea 'Perry's Strawberry Pink' Perry D. Slocum 1989. Parentage: Probably N. alba plant received from New Zealand and N. 'Vesuve'. Characteristics: Day blooming, Marliac rhizome, free flowering. Plate 335.

PETAL COLOR: Inner petals deep strawberry pink; outer petals deeper. R.H.S. Chart: Inner petals, Fan 2, Red-Purple Group, No. 66D; outer petals, No. 65C. Sepal color: Pink, greenish white tips. R.H.S.

Chart: Fan 2, Red-Purple Group, No. 65D; tips, Fan 3, Yellow-Green Group, No. 145D. Anther color: Orange. R.H.S. Chart: Fan 1, Yellow-Orange Group, No. 19A. Stamen color: Orange. Flower shape: Cuplike, petals stellate. Flower size: 5–5.5 in (13–14 cm). Fragrance: Slight yet noticeable. Number of petals: 29–30. Number of sepals: 4.

LEAF COLOR: Top, green, newest leaves purplish; underside, bronze, newest leaves iridescent purple. Leaf and sinus: Leaves round; lobes overlap at sinus. Leaf size: 7 in (18 cm). Leaf spread: 4–5 ft (1.2–1.5 m). Stem color: Brownish purple. Pubescence on peduncle or petiole: Fine fuzz on both.

COMMENTS: Due to its small leaves, I recommend 'Perry's Strawberry Pink' for any size pool garden. The freedom of bloom and beautiful flowers make it an excellent choice.

Nymphaea 'Perry's Super Red' Perry D. Slocum 1989. Parentage: N. 'Charles de Meurville' × N. 'Gloire du Temple-sur-Lot'. Characteristics: Day blooming, Marliac rhizome, free flowering. Plate 336.

PETAL COLOR: Inner petals brilliant vermilion-red; outer petals pink. R.H.S. Chart: Inner petals, Fan 2, Red-Purple Group, No. 67A; outer petals, No. 61D. Sepal color: Greenish white, pink center veins. R.H.S. Chart: Fan 3, Yellow-Green Group, No. 147D; veins, Fan 2, Red-Purple Group, No. 61D. Anther color: Inner anthers yellow-orange; outer anthers scarlet-orange. R.H.S. Chart: Inner anthers, Fan 1, Yellow Group, No. 11A; outer, Red Group, No. 37A. Stamen color: Orange-red. Flower shape: Full, peony-style. Flower size: 5.5–7.5 in (14–19 cm). Fragrance: Slight. Number of petals: 38–43. Number of sepals: 4.

LEAF COLOR: Top, green, newest leaves brown; underside, red, green veins. Leaf and sinus: Leaves round; lobes usually overlap, cover sinus, occasionally sinus partly open. Leaf size: Up to 10 in (25 cm). Leaf spread: 5 ft (1.5 m). Stem color: Reddish purple. Pubescence on peduncle or petiole: Thick fuzz on both.

COMMENTS: 'Perry's Super Red' flowers have several outstanding features: they are very double (more double than any other red water lily I know), the color is particularly glowing and brilliant, and their size places this cultivar—along with 'Atropurpurea', 'Attraction', and 'Perry's Stellar Red'— among the largest of the red hardy water lilies. Blooms also stay open later in the day than those of most red water lilies. I recommend 'Perry's Super Red' for medium and large pools. It is especially suited to deep water pools, up to 7 ft (2.2 m) in depth.

Nymphaea **'Perry's Super Rose'** Perry D. Slocum 1990. Parentage: Probably *N.* 'Perry's Pink' × *N.* 'Sirius'. Characteristics: Day blooming, odorata rhizome, fairly free flowering. Plate 337.

PETAL COLOR: Rich deep rose-pink. *R.H.S. Chart*: Fan 2, Red-Purple Group, No. 72C. Sepal color: Rich deep rose-pink. *R.H.S. Chart*: Fan 2, Red-Purple Group, No. 72C. Anther color: Golden orange. *R.H.S. Chart*: Fan 1, Orange Group, No. 26C. Stamen color: Orange. Flower shape: Stellate. Flower size: 6.5–7.5 in (16–19 cm). Fragrance: Very pleasant. Number of petals: 37–38. Number of sepals: 4.

LEAF COLOR: Top, green, new leaves reddish brown; underside, reddish. Leaf and sinus: Leaf wider than long, distinct indentation at apex; sinus usually open in young leaves, lobes overlap in mature leaves. Leaf size: Up to 10.5 × 11 in (27 × 28 cm). Leaf spread: 4–5 ft (1.2–1.5 m). Stem color: Olive green, striped purple. Pubescence on peduncle or petiole: Heavy fuzz on both.

COMMENTS: This cultivar is somewhat similar to 'Rose Arey', but flower color is deeper and less subject to fading and spring leaves are not distorted. Inner petals are beautifully rolled. Plant 'Perry's Super Rose' in a large container, allowing it to form a colony of rhizomes, and it will produce several blooms at a time. I highly recommend it for medium and large pools.

Nymphaea **'Perry's Vivid Rose'** Perry D. Slocum 1990. Parentage: *N.* 'Perry's Pink' × *N.* 'Pamela' (a tropical water lily). Characteristics: Day blooming, odorata rhizome, fairly free flowering. Plate 338.

PETAL COLOR: Pinkish red; inner petals edged yellow. *R.H.S. Chart*: Fan 2, Red-Purple Group, No. 74C; edging, Fan 1, Yellow-Orange Group, No. 19B. Sepal color: Deep pinkish red. *R.H.S. Chart*: Fan 2, Red-Purple Group, No. 61B. Anther color: Orange. *R.H.S. Chart*: Fan 1, Orange Group, No. 29B. Stamen color: Orange. Flower shape: Cuplike, full. Flower size: 5.5–6 in (14–15 cm). Fragrance: Very pleasant. Number of petals: 38–39. Number of sepals: 4.

LEAF COLOR: Top, green, new leaves reddish; underside, light brown, new leaves pinkish. Leaf and sinus: Leaf round; sinus an open V. Leaf size: 8–8.5 in (20–22 cm). Leaf spread: 4–5 ft (1.2–1.5 m). Stem color: Peduncle, brown; petiole, greenish brown. Pubescence on peduncle or petiole: None.

COMMENTS: Flower color of 'Perry's Vivid Pink' is certainly one of the most striking deep pinks of any water lily. As it is an odorata, plant in a large container and allow it to form a colony of plants to maximize bloom. I recommend it for medium and large pools and natural ponds.

Nymphaea **'Perry's Viviparous Pink'** Perry D. Slocum 1990. Parentage: *N.* 'Perry's Pink' × *N.* 'Colonel A. J. Welch'. Characteristics: Day blooming, mildly viviparous, odorata rhizome, free flowering. Plate 339.

PETAL COLOR: Deep pink. *R.H.S. Chart*: Fan 2, Red-Purple Group, No. 68B. Sepal color: Deep pink; base lighter. *R.H.S. Chart*: Fan 2, Red-Purple Group, No. 68B; base, No. 68C. Anther color: Orange. *R.H.S. Chart*: Fan 1, Yellow-Orange Group, No. 15B. Stamen color: Orange. Flower shape: Stellate. Flower size: 6–7.5 in (15–19 cm). Fragrance: Slight to none. Number of petals: 44–47. Number of sepals: 4.

LEAF COLOR: Top, green, new leaves red, brilliant orange-red spot at petiole; underside, red. Leaf and sinus: Leaf round; sinus usually open, occasionally partly closed. Leaf size: Up to 10.5 in (27 cm). Leaf spread: About 5 ft (1.5 m). Stem color: Brownish purple. Pubescence on peduncle or petiole: A few, fine short hairs on both.

COMMENTS: 'Perry's Viviparous Pink' is much admired for its beautiful new red leaves and vivid, very double, rich pink blooms with a glowing red spot in the flower center. Bloom season is unusually long for a pink hardy, continuing well into late October in North Carolina (USDA zone 6b). Expect first-day flowers to close by midday on hot sunny days. Although it is less than 5 percent viviparous, even a 5-percent production of plantlets from its spent flowers is a definite plus. Watching the new plantlet form and develop while still attached to the mother plant can be a very gratifying experience. Another pink hardy that develops plantlets is 'Perry's Pink Delight'. I recommend 'Perry's Viviparous Pink' for medium and large pools.

Nymphaea **'Perry's White Star'** Perry D. Slocum 1990. Parentage: *N.* 'Pink Starlet' × *N.* 'Pamela' (a tropical water lily). Characteristics: Day blooming, Marliac-tuberosa rhizome, free blooming. Plate 340.

PETAL COLOR: White. *R.H.S. Chart*: Fan 4, White Group, No. 155B. Sepal color: Grayish green, grayish green prominent veins, green tips and borders. *R.H.S. Chart*: Fan 4, Greyed-Green Group, No. 195C; veins No. 194C; tips and borders, Fan 3, Yellow-Green Group, No. 145B. Anther color: Yellow. *R.H.S. Chart*: Fan 1, Yellow Group, No. 6B. Stamen color: Yellow. Flower shape: Stellate, long narrow petals. Flower size: 5.5–7 in (14–18 cm). Fragrance: Very pleasant. Number of petals: 32–34. Number of sepals: 4.

LEAF COLOR: Top, green, new leaves bronzy; underside, reddish. Leaf and sinus: Leaf slightly longer than wide; sinus usually an open V. Leaf size: 8–9.5 × 7.5–9 in (20–24 × 19–23 cm). Leaf spread: 4–5 ft (1.2–1.5 m). Stem color: Peduncle, reddish brown; petiole, red. Pubescence on peduncle or petiole: Thick fuzz on both.

COMMENTS: 'Perry's White Star' is a white variation of N. 'Pink Starlet', one of its parents. Blooms are held 2–4 in (5–10 cm) above the water. Plant it in a large container, about 24 × 24 × 12 in (60 × 60 × 30 cm), so that it can form a colony of free-flowering plants. It is very hardy and winters well. I recommend this cultivar for medium and large pools.

Nymphaea 'Perry's White Wonder' Perry D. Slocum 1990. Parentage: Probably N. tetragona and N. alba plant received from New Zealand. Characteristics: Day blooming, Marliac rhizome, very free flowering. Plate 341.

PETAL COLOR: White. R.H.S. Chart: Fan 4, White Group, No. 155A. Sepal color: White; pale pink blush. R.H.S. Chart: Fan 4, White Group, No. 155A; blush, lighter than Fan 2, Red-Purple Group, No. 73D. Anther color: Yellow. R.H.S. Chart: Fan 1, Yellow Group, No. 3A. Stamen color: Deep yellow. Flower shape: Cuplike then stellate. Flower size: 3.5–6 in (9–15 cm). Fragrance: Very slight. Number of petals: 27–31. Number of sepals: 4.

LEAF COLOR: Top, green, new leaves bronzy; underside, reddish. Leaf and sinus: Leaves nearly round, lobe tips project 0.25 in (0.5 cm); sinus generally open, occasionally up to ¾ closed. Leaf size: Up to 9 × 8 in (23 × 20 cm). Leaf spread 3.5–4.5 ft (1.1–1.4 m). Stem color: Bronzy green. Pubescence on peduncle or petiole: A few tiny hairs on both.

COMMENTS: A lovely white-flowered cultivar with very sturdy stems, 'Perry's White Wonder' is not subject to crown rot. Its restrained growth makes it ideal for tub gardens or small to large pools.

Nymphaea 'Perry's Wildfire' Perry D. Slocum 1990. Parentage: N. 'Perry's Pink' × N. 'Mrs. Martin E. Randig' (a tropical water lily). Characteristics: Day blooming, odorata rhizome, fairly free flowering. Plate 342.

PETAL COLOR: Glowing purplish red. R.H.S. Chart: Fan 2, Red-Purple Group, No. 64B. Sepal color: Glowing purplish red. R.H.S. Chart: Fan 2, Red-Purple Group, No. 64B. Anther color: Orange. R.H.S. Chart: Fan 1, Orange Group, No. 29B. Stamen color: Orange-red. Flower shape: Stellate. Flower size: 6–7 in (15–18 cm). Fragrance: Delightful. Number of petals: 28–29. Number of sepals: 4.

LEAF COLOR: Top, deep green, new leaves purplish brown; underside, pinkish red. Leaf and sinus: Heart-shaped leaves; sinus ⅔ open. Leaf size: Up to

10 × 9 in (25 × 23 cm). Leaf spread: 4–5 ft (1.2–1.5 m). Stem color: Greenish, striped purple. Pubescence on peduncle or petiole: A few fine hairs on both.

COMMENTS: The color of 'Perry's Wildfire'—similar to a brush fire—is new to hardy water lilies, and since people go wild over it, the name 'Perry's Wildfire' took shape. Flowers also stay open quite late in the afternoon. Although this cultivar has a tropical parent, undoubtedly supplying its deep purple-red color, it has survived winter lows of –5°F (–21°C) in an outdoor pond. Plant 'Perry's Wildfire' in a large container so that it can form a colony of rhizomes. I recommend this cultivar for medium and large pools.

Nymphaea 'Peter Slocum' Perry D. Slocum 1984. Parentage: Chance seedling of N. 'Pearl of the Pool'. Characteristics: Day blooming, odorata rhizome, moderately free flowering. Plate 343.

PETAL COLOR: Medium pink, fading slightly. R.H.S. Chart: Fan 2, Red-Purple Group, Nos. 62B–C. Sepal color: Medium pink, fading slightly. R.H.S. Chart: Fan 2, Red-Purple Group, Nos. 62B–C. Anther color: Yellow. R.H.S. Chart: Fan 1, Yellow-Orange Group, No. 19A. Stamen color: Yellow, orange and pinkish exterior rows. Flower shape: Peony-style. Flower size: 6–7.5 in (15–19 cm). Fragrance: Very sweet. Number of petals: 40–41. Number of sepals: 4.

LEAF COLOR: Top, green, newest leaves purple; underside, red, prominent green lengthwise V along midvein, underside green when above water. Leaf and sinus: Leaf round; lobes overlap, cover sinus. Leaf size: Up to 11 in (28 cm). Leaf spread: 5–6 ft (1.5–2 m). Stem color: Green. Pubescence on peduncle or petiole: Short fuzz on both.

COMMENTS: This cultivar is named after my son Peter, owner of Slocum Water Gardens in Winter Haven, Florida. Concave petals give this exquisitely beautiful water lily a bicolor effect and a silvery sheen. 'Peter Slocum' blooms are also superb as cut flowers. This is a lovely garden plant that will bloom plentifully if planted in a large container and allowed to form a colony of several plants. Flowers stay open later than most odorata water lilies. I highly recommend this plant for medium or large pools and natural ponds.

Nymphaea 'Picciola' Latour-Marliac Nursery 1913. Parentage: Unknown. Characteristics: Day blooming, Marliac rhizome, free flowering. Plate 344.

PETAL COLOR: Inner petals, rich clear purple-red; outer petals purple-red, flecked, pink toward tips. R.H.S. Chart: Inner petals, Fan 4, Greyed-Red Group, No. 182A; outer petals, Fan 1, Red Group,

No. 47B; tips, No. 43D. Sepal color: Pink, deep purplish lengthwise stripes, green edges, white tips. *R.H.S. Chart*: Fan 2, Red-Purple Group, No. 68D; stripes, No. 60D; edges, Fan 3, Green Group, No. 134D; tips, Fan 4, White Group, No. 155A. Anther color: Orange. *R.H.S. Chart*: Fan 1, Yellow-Orange Group, No. 20A. Stamen color: Orange-red. Flower shape: Stellate. Flower size: 5.5–6 in (14–15 cm). Fragrance: Slight. Number of petals: 29. Number of sepals: 4.

LEAF COLOR: Top, green, heavily blotched purple; underside, red, prominent green veins. Leaf and sinus: Leaf almost round, lobes sharply pointed at tips; lobes overlap 1 in (2.5 cm) at sinus. Leaf size: 8.5–9 in (22–23 cm). Leaf spread: 4–5 ft (1.2–1.5 m). Stem color: Red. Pubescence on peduncle or petiole: None.

COMMENTS: Leaf and flower colors are quite similar to those of 'Sirius', yet 'Picciola' has a smaller leaf spread and is therefore more suitable for small and medium pools. 'Picciola' is more subject to crown rot than 'Sirius'.

Nymphaea '**Pink Beauty**'. See *N.* '**Luciana**'.

Nymphaea '**Pink Gonnère**'. See *N.* '**Madame Wilfron Gonnère**'.

Nymphaea '**Pink Laydeker**'. See *N.* ×*laydekeri* '**Lilacea**'.

Nymphaea '**Pink Marvel**'. See *N.* '**Amabilis**'.

Nymphaea '**Pink Opal**' Helen Fowler 1915. Parentage: Unknown. Characteristics: Day blooming, odorata rhizome, moderately free flowering; flowers held 3–5 in (8–13 cm) above water. Plate 345.

PETAL COLOR: Coral pink. *R.H.S. Chart*: Fan 1, Red Group, No. 38A. Sepal color: Deep pink. *R.H.S. Chart*: Fan 1, Red Group, No. 39B. Anther color: Deep yellow. *R.H.S. Chart*: Fan 1, Yellow Group, No. 12B. Stamen color: Deep yellow. Flower shape: Cuplike. Flower size: 3–4 in (8–10 cm). Fragrance: Lovely, sweet. Number of petals: 26. Number of sepals: 4.

LEAF COLOR: Top, green, new leaves bronzy; underside, reddish. Leaf and sinus: Leaf nearly round; lobes usually overlap at sinus. Leaf size: 8–9 in (20–23 cm). Leaf spread: Up to 3 ft (1 m). Stem color: Brownish. Pubescence on peduncle or petiole: Some fuzz on both.

COMMENTS: 'Pink Opal' holds its blooms above the water on especially strong peduncles. Blooms make fine cut flowers, although this is a trait considered incidental when selecting hardy water lilies. For many years this lily was heavily recommended for tub gardens. It is now superseded by hardy water lilies such as 'Perry's Fire Opal', 'Masaniello', 'Perry's Baby Red', and 'Perry's Dwarf Red', which have improved all-around performance. I would generally recommend 'Pink Opal' only for collectors.

Nymphaea '**Pink Sensation**' Perry D. Slocum 1947. Parentage: Chance seedling or mutation of *N.* 'Lustrous'. Characteristics: Day blooming, Marliac rhizome, very free flowering. Plate 346.

PETAL COLOR: Smooth rich pink. *R.H.S. Chart*: Fan 2, Red-Purple Group, No. 62B. Sepal color: Slightly darker than petals. *R.H.S. Chart*: Fan 2, Red-Purple Group, Nos. 62A–B. Anther color: Golden yellow. *R.H.S. Chart*: Fan 1, Yellow Group, No. 11A. Stamen color: Yellow, orange and pink outer rows. Flower shape: Cuplike then stellate. Flower size: 5–6 in (13–15 cm). Fragrance: Slight. Number of petals: 20. Number of sepals: 4.

LEAF COLOR: Top, green, first leaves purplish green; underside, purplish brown, first leaves red. Leaf and sinus: Leaf round; sinus a narrow, open V. Leaf size: Up to 10 in (25 cm). Leaf spread: 4 ft (1.2 m). Stem color: Greenish. Pubescence on peduncle or petiole: Thick fuzz on both.

COMMENTS: For all-around performance, this is probably the very best pink hardy for any size pool. Flowers stay open very late in the afternoon, later than those of any other pink hardy. I recommend this fine lily without reservations.

Nymphaea '**Pink Starlet**' Kenneth Landon 1970. Parentage: Natural hybrid involving *N. tuberosa*. Characteristics: Day blooming, tuberosa rhizome, very free flowering early in the season, less so with onset of fruiting; flowers held 9 in (23 cm) above the water. Plate 347.

PETAL COLOR: Light pink. *R.H.S. Chart*: Fan 1, Red Group, No. 36D. Sepal color: Pinkish, slightly deeper than petals. *R.H.S. Chart*: Fan 1, Red Group, No. 36C. Anther color: Deep yellow. *R.H.S. Chart*: Fan 1, Yellow Group, No. 13B. Stamen color: Yellow. Flower shape: Stellate. Flower size: 5–7 in (13–18 cm). Fragrance: Lemony. Number of petals: 29–30. Number of sepals: 4.

LEAF COLOR: Top, olive green, new leaves bronzy; underside, green suffused with pink and maroon, new leaves bronzy. Leaf and sinus: Leaves round, smooth edges; sinus open. Leaf size: 6–10 in (15–25 cm). Leaf spread: 3–6 ft (1–2 m). Stem color: Reddish brown. Pubescence on peduncle or petiole: None.

COMMENTS: 'Pink Starlet' is an especially delicate-looking lily. I recommend it for any size pool, but especially medium and large ones.

Nymphaea 'Pöstlingberg' Wendelin Buggele. Parentage: Unknown. Characteristics: Day blooming, tuberosa rhizome, fairly free flowering, very fast, vigorous grower. Plate 348.

PETAL COLOR: White. *R.H.S. Chart*: Fan 4, White Group, No. 155C. Sepal color: White; pale pink center. *R.H.S. Chart*: Fan 4, White Group, No. 155C; center, Fan 2, Red-Purple Group, No. 65D. Anther color: Golden yellow. *R.H.S. Chart*: Fan 1, Yellow Group, No. 13C. Stamen color: Golden yellow. Flower shape: Cuplike, petals stellate. Flower size: 6–7 in (15–18 cm). Fragrance: Mild and pleasant. Number of petals: 19–20. Number of sepals: 4.

LEAF COLOR: Top, green, new leaves bronzy green; underside, green, new leaves bronzy, prominent green veins. Leaf and sinus: Leaf nearly round; lobes sharply pointed, usually overlap sinus to cover all but 1 in (2.5 cm). Leaf size: 13 × 12 in (33 × 30 cm). Leaf spread: 6 ft (2 m). Stem color: Yellowish green, purple lengthwise stripes. Pubescence on peduncle or petiole: None.

COMMENTS: 'Pöstlingberg', developed in Linz, Austria, has large leaves and a very large leaf spread if given ample growing room. It is a very pretty lily for the collector with a large pool.

Nymphaea ×pygmaea 'Rubra' (syn. 'Red Pygmy'). Parentage: Unknown. Characteristics: Day blooming, finger-type rhizome, free flowering. Plate 349.

PETAL COLOR: Inner petals red; outer petals pink. *R.H.S. Chart*: Inner petals, Fan 1, Red Group, No. 47C; outer petals, No. 55D. Sepal color: Creamy white, pinkish veins. *R.H.S. Chart*: Fan 4, White Group, No. 155D; veins, Fan 1, Red Group, No. 49B. Anther color: Yellow-orange. *R.H.S. Chart*: Fan 1, Yellow-Orange Group, No. 20A. Stamen color: Deep yellow. Flower shape: Cuplike. Flower size: 2 in (5 cm). Fragrance: Very slight, if any. Number of petals: 13. Number of sepals: 4.

LEAF COLOR: Top, green, new leaves bronzy; underside, red. Leaf and sinus: Leaf nearly round; sinus usually open. Leaf size: 6–7 in (15–18 cm). Leaf spread: 30 in (75 cm). Stem color: Brownish. Pubescence on peduncle or petiole: None.

COMMENTS: This hybrid grows well in England, but I have never seen it grown in the United States. Apparently it thrives in cool water. In North America possibly only the Pacific Northwest would be cool enough. Most of Europe, except perhaps along the Mediterranean, may also be suitable for growing this plant. I recommend it for the tub garden or small pool in cooler regions.

Nymphaea 'Queen of Whites' Laurence Gedye 1970. Parentage: Unknown. Characteristics: Day blooming, Marliac rhizome, very free flowering. Plate 350.

PETAL COLOR: White. *R.H.S. Chart*: Fan 4, White Group, No. 155C. Sepal color: White; sometimes blushed pale pink. *R.H.S. Chart*: Fan 4, White Group, No. 155C; blush, Fan 1, Red Group, Nos. 36C–D. Anther color: Yellow. *R.H.S. Chart*: Fan 1, Yellow Group, No. 12B. Stamen color: Yellow. Flower shape: Cuplike, petals stellate. Flower size: 6–7 in (15–18 cm). Fragrance: Lovely, mild. Number of petals: 27–29. Number of sepals: 4.

LEAF COLOR: Top, green; underside, red or bronzy red, green if above water. Leaf and sinus: Leaf nearly round. Sinus usually an open V; lobes overlap partially on new leaves, one lobe frequently raised. Leaf size: Up to 11.5 × 10.5 in (29 × 27 cm). Leaf spread: 4–6 ft (1.2–2 m). Stem color: Green or greenish brown. Pubescence on peduncle or petiole: Very fine fuzz and hairs on both.

COMMENTS: This lily, from Gedye's Water Gardens, Doncaster East, Australia, has one more row of petals than *N.* ×*marliacea* 'Albida' and usually produces larger and wider flowers. A first-year plant may develop five or six blooms at a time beginning in midsummer. 'Queen of Whites' is ideal for medium and large pools.

Nymphaea 'Radiant Red'. Parentage: Unknown. Characteristics: Day blooming, Marliac rhizome, free flowering. Plate 351.

PETAL COLOR: Red, somewhat flecked. *R.H.S. Chart*: Fan 2, Red-Purple Group, No. 66C. Sepal color: White, developing green tint and pink stripes. *R.H.S. Chart*: Fan 4, White Group, No. 155C; tint, Fan 3, Yellow-Green Group, No. 149D; stripes, Fan 2, Red-Purple Group, No. 66D. Anther color: Yellow-orange. *R.H.S. Chart*: Fan 1, Yellow-Orange Group, No. 21C. Stamen color: Orange. Flower shape: Full, stellate, long sepals. Flower size: 5–6 in (13–15 cm). Fragrance: Slight. Number of petals: 22. Number of sepals: 4.

LEAF COLOR: Top, green; underside, green, newer leaves touched bronze. Leaf and sinus: Leaf nearly round; sinus ⅔ to completely open. Leaf size: Up to 10 in (25 cm). Leaf spread: 3–4 ft (1–1.2 m). Stem color: Peduncle, brownish purple; petiole purple. Pubescence on peduncle or petiole: Fuzz on both, especially on peduncle.

COMMENTS: 'Radiant Red' is a fine red hardy water lily for any size pool.

Nymphaea 'Ray Davies' Perry D. Slocum 1985. Parentage: Seedling of *N.* 'Rosanna'. Characteris-

tics: Day blooming, odorata rhizome, moderately free flowering. Plate 352.

PETAL COLOR: Inner petals yellow; outer petals light pink, deeper toward base. *R.H.S. Chart*: Fan 1, Yellow Group, No. 5D; outer petals, Fan 2, Red-Purple Group, No. 62D; base, No. 62C. Sepal color: Light pink. *R.H.S. Chart*: Fan 2, Red-Purple Group, No. 62D. Anther color: Yellow. *R.H.S. Chart*: Fan 1, Yellow Group, No. 6A. Stamen color: Yellow. Flower shape: Peony-style. Flower size: 6–7 in (15–18 cm). Fragrance: Slight yet noticeable. Number of petals: 53–55. Number of sepals: 4.

LEAF COLOR: Top, deep green, new leaves slightly bronzed; underside, brownish purple, prominent V along midvein, new leaves red. Leaf and sinus: Leaf round; lobes overlap slightly along ⅔ of sinus. Leaf size: Up to 10–11 in (25–28 cm). Leaf spread: 5 ft (1.5 m). Stem color: Green, purple stripes. Pubescence on peduncle or petiole: Some fine fuzz and hairs on both.

COMMENTS: I developed this cultivar in North Carolina (USDA zone 6b) and named it in honor of the owner of Stapeley Water Gardens, Nantwich, England. 'Ray Davies', with its very double blooms, is undoubtedly one of the most beautiful lilies in the world today. It was voted Best New Hardy Water Lily for 1987 by the members of the International Water Lily Society. For best results, plant it in a large container and allow it to form a colony of rhizomes. It will then produce quite an abundance of flowers. This lily is ideal for a large pool or natural pond, yet it will also adapt to a medium-sized pool.

Nymphaea **'Red Joanne Pring'**. Parentage: Probable mutation of *N*. 'Joanne Pring'. Characteristics: Day blooming, small Marliac rhizome, very free flowering. Plate 353.

PETAL COLOR: Rich pink then rich red. *R.H.S. Chart*: Fan 2, Red-Purple Group, Nos. 62B–C; third day, Nos. 63A–B. Sepal color: White then pink, flecked lighter pink. *R.H.S. Chart*: Fan 4, White Group, No. 155A; third day, Fan 2, Red-Purple Group, No. 65B. Anther color: Yellow then burnt orange. *R.H.S. Chart*: Fan 1, Yellow Group, No. 13B; third day, Orange Group, No. 24A. Stamen color: Yellow to orange. Flower shape: Cuplike. Flower size: 3–4 in (8–10 cm). Fragrance: Slight. Number of petals: 15–16. Number of sepals: 4.

LEAF COLOR: Top, green, young leaves mottled purple; underside, red-brown, young leaves red-purple. Leaf and sinus: Leaf a little longer than wide; sinus a wide V. Leaf size: 5.5 in (14 cm). Leaf spread: 3 ft (1 m). Stem color: Purplish brown. Pubescence on peduncle or petiole: None.

COMMENTS: 'Red Joanne Pring' showed up in a bed of 'Joanne Pring' at Perry's Water Gardens in North Carolina (USDA zone 6b). Apparently it is a mutation or sport of 'Joanne Pring' and identical to it in every way (including a susceptibility to crown rot) except flower color. The deep red flowers of this chance lily are magnificent. I consider it a fine choice for a tub garden or small pool in all climates.

Nymphaea **'Red Laydeker'**. See *N*. ×*laydekeri* **'Fulgens'**.

Nymphaea **'Red Pygmy'**. See *N*. ×*pygmaea* **'Rubra'**.

Nymphaea **'Red Sensation'** Perry D. Slocum 1991. Parentage: Probably *N*. 'Alba Plenissima' × *N*. 'Atropurpurea'. Characteristics: Day blooming, Marliac rhizome, free flowering. Plate 354.

PETAL COLOR: Deep red, some flecking. *R.H.S. Chart*: Fan 2, Red-Purple Group, No. 64A. Sepal color: Tip half greenish; base reddish pink. *R.H.S. Chart*: Tip, Fan 3, Yellow-Green Group, No. 145B; base, Fan 2, Red-Purple Group, No. 63C. Anther color: Deep yellow. *R.H.S. Chart*: Fan 1, Yellow Group, No. 5B. Stamen color: Deep yellow. Flower shape: Peony-style. Flower size: 6–7.5 in (15–19 cm). Fragrance: Slight. Number of petals: 37–38. Number of sepals: 4.

LEAF COLOR: Top, green, new leaves bronzy green; underside, mostly green, new leaves pinkish, prominent green veins. Leaf and sinus: Leaf nearly round, undulating margin; sinus an open V. Leaf size: Up to 10 in (25 cm). Leaf spread: 4–5 ft (1.2–1.5 m). Stem color: Brownish. Pubescence on peduncle or petiole: None.

COMMENTS: 'Red Sensation' is one of the most striking new red hardies ever developed at Perry's Water Gardens. The slight flecking on the petals seems to add to the flower's beauty rather than detract. I highly recommend this cultivar for the medium or large pool.

Nymphaea **'René Gérard'** (syn. 'La Beaugère') Latour-Marliac Nursery 1914. Parentage: Unknown. Characteristics: Day blooming, Marliac rhizome, free flowering. Plate 355.

PETAL COLOR: Inner petals deep rosy red, paling toward outer petals. Much flecking, especially in outer petals. *R.H.S. Chart*: Inner petals, Fan 2, Red-Purple Group, No. 63B; outer petals, No. 65C. Sepal color: White. *R.H.S. Chart*: Fan 4, White Group, No. 155A. Anther color: Yellow-orange. *R.H.S. Chart*: Fan 1, Yellow-Orange Group, No. 14B. Stamen color: Yellow-orange. Flower shape: Stellate. Flower size: 6–9 in (15–23 cm). Fragrance: Slight. Number of petals: 20–24. Number of sepals: 4.

LEAF COLOR: Top, green, newest leaves bronzy green; underside, green, newest leaves bronzy. Leaf and sinus: Leaves nearly round; sinus usually an open V. Leaf size: Up to 10–11 in (25–28 cm). Leaf spread: 5 ft (1.5 m). Stem color: Usually bronzy green. Pubescence on peduncle or petiole: None, or a few hairs may appear on both.

COMMENTS: With its pleasing flowers, shading from darker center to pale outer petals, this plant is quite attractive, although some people object to the heavy flecking. I highly recommend it for medium and large pools.

Nymphaea '**Robinsoni**'. See *N.* '**Robinsoniana**'.

Nymphaea '**Robinsonii**'. See *N.* '**Robinsoniana**'.

Nymphaea '**Robinsoniana**' (syn. 'Robinsoni', 'Robinsonii') Joseph B. L. Marliac 1895. Parentage: Probably *N. alba* var. *rubra* × *N. mexicana*. Characteristics: Day blooming, upright rhizome (same size and shape as a pineapple), free flowering. Plate 356.
PETAL COLOR: Orange-red, lighter tips. *R.H.S. Chart*: Fan 1, Red Group, No. 41D; tips, No. 39D. Sepal color: Lighter orange-red than petals, greenish cream tips. *R.H.S. Chart*: Fan 1, Red Group, No. 39C; tips, Fan 3, Yellow-Green Group, No. 149D. Anther color: Yellow-orange. *R.H.S. Chart*: Fan 1, Yellow-Orange Group, No. 23B. Stamen color: Orange. Flower shape: Inner portion cuplike, outer stellate. Flower size: 4.5–5 in (11–13 cm). Fragrance: Slight. Number of petals: 24–27. Number of sepals: 4.
LEAF COLOR: Top, beautiful light purple, deep purple blotches, greener with age; underside, deep red, purple specks and mottles. Leaf and sinus: Leaf a little longer than wide; lobes overlap about halfway down sinus. Each lobe, except in some young leaves, has a distinctive notch about halfway down the sinus. Leaf size: 8 in (20 cm). Leaf spread: 4–5 ft (1.2–1.5 m). Stem color: Greenish brown, faint purple stripes. Pubescence on peduncle or petiole: None.
COMMENTS: This plant is closer to an orange-flowered hardy water lily than any I know. Leaves are especially beautiful and have a unique notch displayed halfway down each lobe along the sinus (not always present in late summer). 'Robinsoniana' is best suited for medium and large pools, but its restrained growth makes it suitable also for small pools. I have found this cultivar to be somewhat subject to crown rot.

Nymphaea '**Rosanna**' Ambassador Water Gardens (where it was sold as *N.* 'Rosanna Supreme'). Parentage: Unknown. Characteristics: Day blooming, odorata rhizome, fairly free flowering. Plate 357.
PETAL COLOR: Base, medium pink; upper portion shell pink. *R.H.S. Chart*: Base, Fan 2, Red-Purple Group, No. 62C; upper portion, No. 62D. Sepal color: Medium pink, some green patches. *R.H.S. Chart*: Fan 2, Red-Purple Group, No. 62D; patches, Fan 3, Green Group, No. 135D. Anther color: Deep golden yellow. *R.H.S. Chart*: Fan 1, Yellow Group, No. 9A. Stamen color: Deep golden yellow. Flower shape: Stellate. Flower size: 6–7 in (15–18 cm). Fragrance: Some. Number of petals: 20. Number of sepals: 4.
LEAF COLOR: Top, green, new leaves purplish; underside, red, green V lengthwise along midvein. Leaf and sinus: Leaf round; sinus a wide-open V. Leaf size: 9–9.5 in (23–24 cm). Leaf spread: 4 ft (1.2 m). Stem color: Green, purple stripes. Pubescence on peduncle or petiole: Thick fuzz on both.
COMMENTS: Unusual bicolor pink blooms make this one of the prettiest hardy water lilies. For best results, plant it in a large container so that a colony of rhizomes can develop. This lovely lily was confused with 'Rosanna Supreme' (which see) for many years. I recommend 'Rosanna' for the medium and large pool.

Nymphaea '**Rosanna Supreme**' Martin E. Randig. Parentage: Unknown. Characteristics: Day blooming, Marliac rhizome, very free flowering. Plate 358.
PETAL COLOR: Inner petals pale pink, some flecking, developing deeper pink base; outer petals lighter pink, turning to a deeper pink. *R.H.S. Chart*: Inner petals, first day, Fan 2, Red-Purple Group, No. 65D or lighter; inner petals, third day, base, No. 63C; outer petals, first day, Fan 1, Red Group, No. 63D; third day, Fan 2, Red-Purple Group, No. 65D or lighter. Sepal color: Nearly white, prominent gray-green veins. *R.H.S. Chart*: Fan 4, White Group, No. 155B; veins, Fan 4, Greyed-Green Group, No. 191C. Anther color: Yellow. *R.H.S. Chart*: Fan 1, Yellow Group, No. 12B. Stamen color: Inner stamens yellow, outer orange. Flower shape: Stellate. Flower size: 4–5 in (10–13 cm). Fragrance: None. Number of petals: 24–26. Number of sepals: 4.
LEAF COLOR: Top, green, new leaves deep green, mottled purple; underside, pale red-brown or green, green V along midvein, new leaves red-brown. Leaf and sinus: Leaf nearly round; sinus a wide-open V. Leaf size: 8–9 in (20–23 cm). Leaf spread: 4 ft (1.2 m). Stem color: Peduncles, brown; petioles purple. Pubescence on peduncle or petiole: Some hairs on both.
COMMENTS: 'Rosanna Supreme' is very free flowering and can be used in any size pool. Flowers are

highly flecked, lacking the clear smooth pink of the immensely popular 'Luciana', 'Perry's Pink', 'Peter Slocum', 'Pink Sensation', 'Rose Arey', and other evenly colored pinks.

Nymphaea **'Rose Arey'** Helen Fowler 1913. Parentage: Unknown. Characteristics: Day blooming, odorata rhizome, fairly free flowering. Plate 359.

PETAL COLOR: Very rich medium or deep pink. *R.H.S. Chart*: Fan 2, Red-Purple Group, No. 63C or 68C. Sepal color: Deep pink. *R.H.S. Chart*: Fan 2, Red-Purple Group, No. 58D. Anther color: Yellow. *R.H.S. Chart*: Fan 1, Yellow Group, No. 11A. Stamen color: Inner stamens golden yellow; outer orange-pink. Flower shape: Stellate. Flower size: 7–8 in (18–20 cm). Fragrance: Very sweet. Number of petals: 33–39. Number of sepals: 4.

LEAF COLOR: Top, green, new leaves purple; underside, brown, new leaves purple. Leaf and sinus: Leaves round; sinus narrow and open. Leaf size: 9 in (23 cm). Leaf spread: 4–5 ft (1.2–1.5 m). Stem color: Brown, purple stripes. Pubescence on peduncle or petiole: Fine fuzz and hair on both.

COMMENTS: This is one of the most beautiful lilies known. By using a large container for planting, about 24 × 24 × 12 in (60 × 60 × 30 cm), and allowing it to form a colony of several rhizomes, it will produce numerous blooms. Blooms also make fine cut flowers. 'Rose Arey' is an excellent choice for the medium or large pool or the natural pond. In natural ponds plants may develop at a rate of 1–2 ft (0.3–0.6 m) per year and may also drop very viable seeds.

Nymphaea **'Rose Magnolia'**. Parentage: Unknown. Characteristics: Day blooming, tuberosa rhizome, fairly free flowering if given room to mature. Plate 360.

PETAL COLOR: Shell pink, deeper at base. *R.H.S. Chart*: Fan 1, Red Group, No. 56D; base, Nos. 56B–C. Sepal color: Light pink. *R.H.S. Chart*: Fan 1, Red Group, No. 56C. Anther color: Deep yellow. *R.H.S. Chart*: Fan 1, Yellow-Orange Group, No. 18A. Stamen color: Deep yellow. Flower shape: Cuplike. Flower size: 4–5 in (10–13 cm). Fragrance: Slight. Number of petals: 20. Number of sepals: 4.

LEAF COLOR: Top, green, new leaves bronzy; underside, pinkish brown. Leaf and sinus: Leaf nearly round, edges frequently wavy; sinus either open or closed. Leaf size: Up to 10 in (25 cm). Leaf spread: 5–6 ft (1.5–2 m). Stem color: Brownish. Pubescence on peduncle or petiole: None.

COMMENTS: This is an older, North American hybrid. As there are much more free-blooming and more richly colored pink hardies available today, I

would recommend 'Rose Magnolia' only for the collector with a large pool.

Nymphaea **'Rosennymphe'** No. 2 Junge. Parentage: Unknown. Characteristics: Day blooming, odorata rhizome, moderately free flowering. Plate 361.

PETAL COLOR: Medium pink with one or two darker pink lengthwise stripes. *R.H.S. Chart*: Fan 2, Red-Purple Group, No. 63D; stripes, No. 68B. Sepal color: Light pink, splashed green, especially near tips. *R.H.S. Chart*: Fan 2, Red-Purple Group, No. 68D; splashes, Fan 3, Yellow-Green Group, No. 146D. Anther color: Deep yellow. *R.H.S. Chart*: Fan 1, Yellow Group, No. 11A. Stamen color: Deep yellow. Flower shape: A full star. Flower size: 5.5–6.5 in (14–16 cm). Fragrance: Slight. Number of petals: 32. Number of sepals: 4.

LEAF COLOR: Top, green, newest leaves bronzy red; underside, red, green veins. Leaf and sinus: Leaves heart-shaped; lobe tips sharply pointed. Lobes usually overlap ⅔ of sinus; sinus occasionally wide open, especially on young leaves. Leaf size: Up to 10 × 9.5 in (25 × 24 cm). Leaf spread: 3.5–5 ft (1.1–1.5 m). Stem color: Reddish brown. Pubescence on peduncle or petiole: A few very fine hairs on both.

COMMENTS: I was advised by 10 German nurserymen visiting Perry's Water Gardens in Franklin, North Carolina, that the true *N.* 'Rosennymphe' (Plate 362) opens pink and changes to white. Nursery proprietors in the United States and Australia, however, continue to promote the aforementioned variation, which came from a nursery in Australia, as 'Rosennymphe'; I am therefore identifying it as 'Rosennymphe' No. 2.

Flowers of 'Rosennymphe' No. 2 closely resemble those of 'Rose Arey'. There are many superior pinks today, however. (Those with a Marliac rhizome require less container space and do not require two to three months in order to become free blooming as do the odorata.) I would recommend 'Rosennymphe' No. 2 for the collector or the water gardener with a large pool.

Nymphaea **'Rosy Morn'** Harry Johnson 1932. Parentage: *N.* 'Rose Arey' × *N.* 'Escarboucle'. Characteristics: Day blooming, Marliac rhizome, very free flowering. Plate 363.

PETAL COLOR: Inner petals rich strawberry pink; outer petals very pale pink, fading. *R.H.S. Chart*: Inner petals, Fan 2, Red-Purple Group, No. 62B; outer petals, No. 62D or lighter, fading to Fan 1, Red Group, No. 36D or lighter. Sepal color: Pale pink, veins pink, both whitening. *R.H.S. Chart*: Fan 2, Red-Purple Group, No. 65D or lighter; veins No.

65B or C; both to Fan 4, White Group, No. 155A. Anther color: Deep golden yellow. *R.H.S. Chart*: Fan 1, Yellow Group, No. 13B. Stamen color: Yellow. Flower shape: Starlike. Flower size: 6–7 in (15–18 cm). Fragrance: Very slight. Number of petals: 24. Number of sepals: 4.

LEAF COLOR: Top, green, new leaves purplish, prominent reddish purple blotch at junction with petiole; underside, red, green V along midvein. Leaf and sinus: Leaf round; sinus usually open. Leaf size: 8–9 in (20–23 cm). Leaf spread: 3–4 ft (1–1.2 m). Stem color: Peduncle, brownish; petiole purple. Pubescence on peduncle or petiole: Thick fuzz on both.

COMMENTS: 'Rosy Morn', with its very striking, abundant, and large flowers, would be an outstanding addition to any pool.

Nymphaea **'Sanguinea'** Joseph B. L. Marliac 1894. Parentage: Unknown. Characteristics: Day blooming, Marliac rhizome, free flowering. Plate 364.

PETAL COLOR: Crimson red, deepening. *R.H.S. Chart*: Fan 2, Red-Purple Group, No. 63B; third day, No. 63A. Sepal color: White, light pink near base. *R.H.S. Chart*: Fan 4, White Group, No. 155B; base, Fan 2, Red-Purple Group, No. 73D. Anther color: Yellow. *R.H.S. Chart*: Fan 1, Yellow Group, No. 9C. Stamen color: Yellow-orange. Flower shape: Somewhat stellate. Flower size: 5–6 in (13–15 cm). Fragrance: Slight. Number of petals: 23–24. Number of sepals: 4.

LEAF COLOR: Top, green, newest leaves lightly mottled deep purple; underside, red, prominent green lengthwise vein. Leaf and sinus: Leaf nearly round; sinus 1/3 to 2/3 open. Leaf size: 9–10 in (23–25 cm). Leaf spread: Up to 5 ft (1.5 m). Stem color: Red. Pubescence on peduncle or petiole: None.

COMMENTS: The glowing blood-red blooms make this one of the most striking of all the red hardies. I recommend it for the medium or large pool.

Nymphaea **'Seignoureti'** No. 1 Joseph B. L. Marliac 1893. Parentage: Possibly *N. alba* var. *rubra* × *N. mexicana*. Characteristics: Day blooming, changeable, upright rhizome, very free flowering; flowers held 5–6 in (13–15 cm) above water. Plate 365.

PETAL COLOR: First day, inner petals apricot-orange, outer petals yellowish white; third day, all petals predominantly orange-red. *R.H.S. Chart*: First day, Fan 1, Orange Group, Nos. 33C–D; outer petals, Yellow Group, Nos. 11C–D; third day, all, Red Group, No. 37A. Sepal color: Light yellow then peach, pink base. *R.H.S. Chart*: First day, Fan 1, Yellow Group, No. 2D; third day, Orange Group, No. 29C; base, Red Group, No. 54D. Anther color: Deep

yellow. *R.H.S. Chart*: Fan 1, Yellow Group, No. 13B. Stamen color: Pale orange. Flower shape: Cuplike. Flower size: 3–4 in (8–10 cm). Fragrance: None. Number of petals: 18. Number of sepals: 4.

LEAF COLOR: Top, green, new leaves bronzy, all lightly mottled maroon; underside, purplish, many deeper maroon spots. Leaf and sinus: Leaf nearly round; sinus 1/3 to 2/3 open. Leaf size: 6–7 in (15–18 cm). Leaf spread: 4 ft (1.2 m). Stem color: Reddish. Pubescence on peduncle or petiole: None.

COMMENTS: This lovely changeable water lily is available in two entirely different variants: 'Seignoureti' No. 1 and 'Seignoureti' No. 2 (which see). The original 'Seignoureti' was described in the 1912 Latour-Marliac catalog. This description was translated by Fr. J. M. Berghs for the March 1989 *Water Garden Journal* (p. 11): "Medium-sized flowers, standing 15 cm (about 6 in) above the water, shaded with pink and carmine on a pale-yellow background; leaves marked with brown; stamens orange-yellow." Based on this description, 'Seignoureti' No. 1 appears to be the original variant. I recommend 'Seignoureti' No. 1 for any size pool.

Nymphaea **'Seignoureti'** No. 2 Joseph B. L. Marliac(?) 1893(?). Parentage: Unknown. Characteristics: Day blooming, changeable, upright rhizome, free flowering. Plate 366.

PETAL COLOR: Inner petals apricot-orange; outer petals very pale apricot-orange, deepening. *R.H.S. Chart*: Inner petals, Fan 1, Orange-Red Group, Nos. 31C–D; outer petals, Orange Group, No. 27D, deepening to No. 27B. Sepal color: Greenish white. *R.H.S. Chart*: Fan 4, White Group, No. 155A. Anther color: Yellow. *R.H.S. Chart*: Fan 1, Yellow Group, No. 10A. Stamen color: Yellow. Flower shape: Stellate, very long sepals and outer petals. Flower size: 3–5 in (8–13 cm). Fragrance: None. Number of petals: 19. Number of sepals: 4.

LEAF COLOR: Top, green, maroon splashes and spots; underside, green, maroon spots. Leaf and sinus: Leaf slightly longer than wide; sinus wide open. Leaf size: 6.5 × 5.5 in (16 × 14 cm). Leaf spread: 30–36 in (75–90 cm). Stem color: Brown. Pubescence on peduncle or petiole: None.

COMMENTS: 'Seignoureti' No. 2, a continuous bloomer, is the most stellate of any changeable. With its narrow petals and long sepals the effect truly is "starry." The delicate coloration of the freshly opened flowers makes it quite different from 'Seignoureti' No. 1. I recommend this lovely lily for any size pool.

Nymphaea **'Sioux'** Joseph B. L. Marliac 1908. Parentage: Unknown. Characteristics: Day blooming, changeable, upright rhizome, extremely free flowering. Plate 367.

PETAL COLOR: Petal coloration deepens each day; progression also from lightest center petal row to deepening outer rows. Inner petals yellowish apricot then orange-red; outer petals yellow then apricot-orange. *R.H.S. Chart*: First-day inner petals vary from Fan 1, Yellow-Orange Group, No. 16C to Orange Group, No. 25B; third-day inner petals vary from Orange Group, No. 29B to Orange-Red Group, No. 30D. First-day outer petals vary from Fan 1, Yellow Group, No. 11B to Orange Group, No. 24D; third day, Orange Group, No. 25C. Sepal color: White then pinkish orange at base. *R.H.S. Chart*: Fan 4, White Group, No. 155A; base, Fan 1, Orange-Red Group, No. 35B or 35C. Anther color: Yellow. *R.H.S. Chart*: Fan 1, Yellow-Orange Group, No. 20A. Stamen color: Inside of stamens, golden yellow; outside, orange. Flower shape: Starlike, lanceolate petals. Flower size: 5–6 in (13–15 cm). Fragrance: Quite nice, especially in new flowers. Number of petals: 19–20. Number of sepals: 4.

LEAF COLOR: Top, green, perimeter dappled purple on new leaves; underside, green, freckled purple, new leaves red, prominent green V along midvein. Leaf and sinus: Leaf almost round; sinus a wide-open V. Leaf size: 8–9 in (20–23 cm). Leaf spread: 4 ft (1.2 m). Stem color: Green. Pubescence on peduncle or petiole: Fine fuzz and hairs on both.

COMMENTS: 'Sioux' performs magnificently and flowers stay open very late in the day. It is my first choice among the larger orange changeables as an excellent water lily for the medium or large pool.

Nymphaea **'Sirius'** Latour-Marliac Nursery 1913. Parentage: Unknown. Characteristics: Day blooming, Marliac rhizome, very free flowering. Plate 368.

PETAL COLOR: Inner petals, deep purple-red, some flecking; outer petals, purplish red, some flecking, white tips. *R.H.S. Chart*: Inner petals, Fan 2, Red-Purple Group, No. 61A; outer petals, No. 70B; tips, Fan 4, White Group, No. 155B. Sepal color: Pink, shading to white at tips, flecked. *R.H.S. Chart*: Fan 2, Red-Purple Group, Nos. 63C–D; tips, Fan 4, White Group, No. 155B. Anther color: Burnt orange. *R.H.S. Chart*: Fan 1, Orange-Red Group, No. 34B. Stamen color: Deep glowing red. Flower shape: Stellate. Flower size: 6–7 in (15–18 cm). Fragrance: Very slight. Number of petals: 27. Number of sepals: 4–5.

LEAF COLOR: Top, deep green, new leaves lightly blotched purple; underside, green, prominent light green veins. Leaf and sinus: Leaf round; sinus a very wide V. Leaf size: Up to 11 in (28 cm). Leaf spread: 5–6 ft (1.5–2 m). Stem color: Brownish pur-

ple. Pubescence on peduncle or petiole: Some fuzz on all stems.

COMMENTS: 'Sirius', named for the brightest star in the heavens, is a strikingly star-shaped lily. I highly recommend it for the medium and large pool.

Nymphaea **'Snowball'**. See *N.* **'Gonnère'**.

Nymphaea **'Solfatare'** Joseph B. L. Marliac 1906. Parentage: Unknown. Characteristics: Day blooming, changeable, upright rhizome, free flowering. Plate 369.

PETAL COLOR: Inner petals, yellowish apricot, deepening; outer petals, creamy peach then peach. *R.H.S. Chart*: Inner petals, Fan 1, Orange Group, No. 27A; third day, Orange-Red Group, No. 31D; outer petals, Yellow-Orange Group, No. 20D; third day, Orange Group, No. 27C. Sepal color: Pale yellowish apricot. *R.H.S. Chart*: Fan 1, Orange Group, No. 27D. Anther color: Yellowish apricot then orange. *R.H.S. Chart*: Fan 1, Yellow-Orange Group, No. 23D; third day, Orange Group, No. 24C. Stamen color: Orange. Flower shape: Cuplike. Flower size: 3–4 in (8–10 cm). Fragrance: None. Number of petals: 29. Number of sepals: 4.

LEAF COLOR: Top, green, new leaves spotted purple; underside, bronzy green, maroon spots and blotches. Leaf and sinus: Leaf a little longer than wide; sinus wide open. Leaf size: 6 × 5 in (15 × 13 cm). Leaf spread: 30–40 in (75–100 cm). Stem color: Light green. Pubescence on peduncle or petiole: None.

COMMENTS: 'Solfatare', a continuous bloomer, is currently more widely available in Australia than in the United States. If it can be found, it is an ideal water lily for the small or medium pool. Unfortunately, my experience in importing 'Solfatare' plants from Australia is that they did well for a few months and then succumbed to crown rot.

Nymphaea **'Somptuosa'** Joseph B. L. Marliac 1909. Parentage: Unknown. Characteristics: Day blooming, Marliac rhizome, free flowering. Plate 370.

PETAL COLOR: Inner petals deep pink then glowing red, flecked except on innermost petals; outer petals white then blushed pink. *R.H.S. Chart*: Inner petals, first day, Fan 2, Red-Purple Group, No. 70C; third day, No. 63A. Outer petals, Fan 4, White Group, No. 155B; third day, blush, Fan 2, Red-Purple Group, No. 65D or lighter. Sepal color: White then blushed pink. *R.H.S. Chart*: Fan 4, White Group, No. 155B; blush, Fan 2, Red-Purple Group, No. 65D or lighter. Anther color: Golden yellow. *R.H.S. Chart*: Fan 1, Yellow-Orange Group, No. 16B. Stamen color: Golden yellow. Flower shape: Peony-style. Flower size: 5–6 in (13–15 cm). Fragrance: Slight. Number of petals: 35. Number of sepals: 4.

LEAF COLOR: Top, bright green, faint purple mottling, new leaves light purple, dark purple mottles; underside, red. Leaf and sinus: Leaf quite round; lobe tips rounded. Lobes usually overlap 0.75 in (2 cm) at beginning of sinus, rest of sinus wide open. Leaf size: 8 in (20 cm). Leaf spread: 4–5 ft (1.2–1.5 m). Stem color: Bronzy green. Pubescence on peduncle or petiole: None.

COMMENTS: This is a very fine pink-and-white bicolor suited for the medium and large pool. Flower color is somewhat flecked, yet blooms are still quite pretty. For many years nurseries in the United States confused 'Somptuosa' with 'Masaniello', but this confusion is finally being sorted out.

Nymphaea 'Splendida' Joseph B. L. Marliac 1909. Parentage: Unknown. Characteristics: Day blooming, Marliac rhizome, very free flowering. Plate 371.

PETAL COLOR: Inner petals, reddish pink, deepening; outer petals, light pink, deepening. *R.H.S. Chart*: Inner petals, Fan 2, Red-Purple Group, No. 63C then 63B; outer petals, No. 65D then Nos. 63C–D. Sepal color: White, prominent red veins. *R.H.S. Chart*: Fan 4, White Group, No. 155A; veins, Fan 2, Red-Purple Group, Nos. 63B–C. Anther color: Bright yellow. *R.H.S. Chart*: Fan 1, Yellow Group, No. 12B. Stamen color: Orange-red. Flower shape: Quite large, globular after first day. Flower size: 5–6 in (13–15 cm). Fragrance: Delightful, especially second-day blooms. Number of petals: 30. Number of sepals: 4.

LEAF COLOR: Top, green, new leaves purplish brown; underside, mostly brown, touched purple, prominent greenish yellow veins. Leaf and sinus: Leaf nearly round. Sinus usually a small V; lobes in older leaves frequently overlap. Leaf size: 9 in (23 cm). Leaf spread: 4–5 ft (1.2–1.5 m). Stem color: Brown. Pubescence on peduncle or petiole: Fuzz completely covers all stems.

COMMENTS: 'Splendida' is a magnificent lily. Established plants in rich soil develop more deeply colored blooms than young plants in ordinary soil. This cultivar is one of the best for medium or large pools.

Nymphaea 'Sultan' (syn. 'Grésille') Latour-Marliac Nursery. Parentage: Unknown. Characteristics: Day blooming, Marliac rhizome, very free flowering. Plate 372.

PETAL COLOR: Inner petals, deep pink, deep red by second day; outer petals, pale pink, rich red by second day; flecking develops from inner to outer petals. *R.H.S. Chart*: Inner petals, first day, Fan 2, Red-Purple Group, No. 68C or 66D; second day, No. 63A; outer petals No. 65D; second day, Nos. 63B–C. Sepal color: White, base flushed rose-pink, veins rose-pink. *R.H.S. Chart*: Fan 4, White Group, No. 155B; base and veins, Fan 2, Red-Purple Group, Nos. 65A–B. Anther color: Yellow. *R.H.S. Chart*: Fan 1, Yellow Group, No. 13B. Stamen color: Burnt orange. Flower shape: Cuplike then wide stellate. Flower size: 6–7 in (15–18 cm). Fragrance: Slight. Number of petals: 24–25. Number of sepals: 4.

LEAF COLOR: Top, green; underside, green, new leaves bronzy. Leaf and sinus: Leaf round; lobes overlap sinus; frequently both lobes turn upward. Leaf size: 10–11 in (25–28 cm). Leaf spread: 4–5 ft (1.2–1.5 m). Stem color: Brown; older stems striped purple. Pubescence on peduncle or petiole: Fuzz only on underwater stems.

COMMENTS: 'Sultan' is one of the very top red water lilies for USDA zones 4–10, doing well in the South, Florida, and Texas. 'Charles de Meurville', 'Escarboucle', 'Froebeli', 'James Brydon', 'Perry's Black Opal', 'Perry's Baby Red', 'Perry's Red Wonder', and 'Splendida' also perform well in southern zones. The Latour-Marliac Nursery, Temple-sur-Lot, France, recently renamed this cultivar 'Grésille'. It is ideal for medium and large pools.

Nymphaea 'Sunrise'. See *N. odorata* 'Sulphurea Grandiflora'.

Nymphaea 'Superba'. Parentage: Unknown. Characteristics: Day blooming, Marliac rhizome, free flowering. Plate 374.

PETAL COLOR: Pure white. *R.H.S. Chart*: Fan 4, White Group, No. 155D. Sepal color: Pure white; numerous grayish green veins. *R.H.S. Chart*: Fan 4, White Group, No. 155D; veins, Greyed-Green Group, No. 196D. Anther color: Yellow. *R.H.S. Chart*: Fan 1, Yellow Group, No. 12A. Stamen color: Deep yellow. Flower shape: Cuplike. Flower size: 5–7 in (13–18 cm). Fragrance: Some. Number of petals: 20. Number of sepals: 4.

LEAF COLOR: Top, green; underside, green. Leaf and sinus: Leaf nearly round; sinus usually closed. Leaf size: 10 in (25 cm). Leaf spread: 5 ft (1.5 m). Stem color: Greenish brown. Pubescence on peduncle or petiole: None.

COMMENTS: This water lily is distinguished by its very broad petals with rounded tips. I imported it from New Zealand in 1972 and find it to be a good performer. I would recommend it for the medium and large pool.

Nymphaea 'Texas Dawn' Kenneth Landon 1985. Parentage: *N.* 'Pink Starlet' × *N. mexicana* No. 1.

Characteristics: Day blooming, tuberosa-Marliac rhizome, very free flowering; flowers frequently held 10 in (25 cm) above water. Plate 375.

PETAL COLOR: Inner petals, rich yellow; outer petals blushed pink. *R.H.S. Chart*: Inner petals, Fan 1, Yellow Group, No. 4C; outer petals, No. 8D; blush, Red Group, No. 36D. Sepal color: Greenish yellow, pink border. *R.H.S. Chart*: Fan 1, Green-Yellow Group, No. 1D; border, Fan 1, Red Group, No. 36C. Anther color: Deep yellow. *R.H.S. Chart*: Fan 1, Yellow Group, No. 6A. Stamen color: Yellow. Flower shape: Stellate, long narrow petals. Flower size: 6–8 in (15–20 cm). Fragrance: Delightful, lemony. Number of petals: 26–28. Number of sepals: 4.

LEAF COLOR: Top, green, new leaves speckled purple; underside, purplish. Leaf and sinus: Leaf nearly round; sinus ⅔ to completely open. Leaf size: 8 in (20 cm). Leaf spread: 3–5 ft (1–1.5 m). Stem color: Red or purple. Pubescence on peduncle or petiole: Some fuzz on both.

COMMENTS: This lovely lily was developed by Kenneth Landon in San Angelo, Texas (USDA zone 7b). 'Texas Dawn' is probably one of the best yellow-flowered water lilies since *N. ×marliacea* 'Chromatella' made its appearance in 1887. 'Texas Dawn' received the International Water Lily Society's 1990 American Award. When grown in USDA zones 6–10, spring-planted plants can be expected to produce seven or eight blooms at a time by midsummer. In late summer and fall the flowers may take on an attractive pinkish cast. I highly recommend 'Texas Dawn' for any size pool in zones 6–10; possibly the rhizome will survive zone 5 if given winter protection.

***Nymphaea tuberosa* 'Maxima'** (formerly *N. tuberosa* 'Richardsonii' No. 2). Parentage: Seedling of *N. tuberosa*. Characteristics: Day blooming, tuberosa rhizome, not free blooming though moderate in early summer. Plate 376.

PETAL COLOR: Pure white. *R.H.S. Chart*: Fan 4, White Group, No. 155C. Sepal color: Greenish white. *R.H.S. Chart*: Fan 4, Green-Yellow Group, No. 1D. Anther color: Bright yellow. *R.H.S. Chart*: Fan 1, Yellow Group, No. 12A. Stamen color: Yellow. Flower shape: Peony-style, petals stellate. Flower size: 5 in (13 cm). Fragrance: Pleasant, quite noticeable. Number of petals: 30. Number of sepals: 4–5.

LEAF COLOR: Top, green; underside, green, prominent green veins. Leaf and sinus: Leaves round. Lobes generally overlap at sinus on large leaves; on small leaves sinus frequently open or partly open. Leaf size: 8–9 in (20–23 cm). Leaf spread: 6 ft (2 m). Stem color: Green, purple stripes. Pubescence on peduncle or petiole: Very thick fuzz on both.

COMMENTS: Although moderately free flowering early in the season, by midsummer *N. tuberosa* 'Maxima' has rampant leaf growth and fewer blooms. Leaves are produced so abundantly that they crowd above the water. I consider it most suited to the natural pond.

***Nymphaea tuberosa* 'Pöstlingberg'** Buggele. See *N.* **'Pöstlingberg'**.

***Nymphaea tuberosa* 'Richardsonii'** George Richardson 1894. Parentage: Unknown. Characteristics: Day blooming, tuberosa rhizome, moderately free flowering. Plate 377.

PETAL COLOR: White. *R.H.S. Chart*: Fan 4, White Group, No. 155D. Sepal color: Greenish cream. *R.H.S. Chart*: Fan 1, Green-Yellow Group, No. 1D. Anther color: Yellow. *R.H.S. Chart*: Fan 1, Yellow Group, No. 11A. Stamen color: Yellow. Flower shape: Full, peony-style. Flower size: 6–8 in (15–20 cm). Fragrance: Some. Number of petals: 46–50. Number of sepals: 4–5.

LEAF COLOR: Top, green; underside, green. Leaf and sinus: Leaf large, nearly round, wavy edges; sinus open. Leaf size: 10–11 in (25–28 cm). Leaf spread: 6–7 ft (2–2.2 m). Stem color: Green, purple stripes. Pubescence on peduncle or petiole: None.

COMMENTS: *N. tuberosa* 'Richardsonii', which I consider the genuine or original strain, is truly the most beautiful white hardy. It will grow in water 3 ft (1 m) deep, but it is not suitable for many water gardens due to its large leaf spread and limited number of blooms. I would recommend it only for the collector with a large pool or natural pond, where it would have plenty of room to spread.

***Nymphaea tuberosa* 'Richardsonii'** No. 2. See *N. tuberosa* **'Maxima'**.

***Nymphaea* 'Venus'** Perry D. Slocum 1991. Parentage: *N.* 'Pink Starlet' × *N.* 'Pamela' (a tropical water lily). Characteristics: Day blooming, Marliac-tuberosa rhizome, free flowering; blooms held 3–6 in (8–15 cm) above water. Plate 378.

PETAL COLOR: White, blushed very pale pink. *R.H.S. Chart*: Fan 4, White Group, No. 155D; blush too pale to show on chart. Sepal color: White, blushed very pale pink, tips green, veins deep purplish. *R.H.S. Chart*: Fan 4, White Group, No. 155D; blush too pale to show on chart; tips, Fan 3, Yellow-Green Group, No. 146D; veins, Fan 2, Purple Group, No. 77A. Anther color: Yellow. *R.H.S. Chart*:

Fan 1, Yellow Group, No. 6C. Stamen color: Yellow. Flower shape: Stellate. Flower size: 6–7 in (15–18 cm). Fragrance: Slight in new flowers. Number of petals: 29–32. Number of sepals: 4.

LEAF COLOR: Top, green, new leaves bronzy; underside, reddish, wide green midstripe. Leaf and sinus: Leaf nearly round; sinus usually open. Leaf size: 10.5 in (27 cm). Leaf spread: 4–5 ft (1.2–1.5 m). Stem color: Peduncle brown, petiole reddish; both faintly striped purple. Pubescence on peduncle or petiole: A few sparse hairs on both.

COMMENTS: Flowers on this cultivar appear totally white when viewed from a distance. The delicate pink is discovered up close. Although one of its parents is a tropical water lily (*N.* 'Pamela'), this plant has survived in North Carolina temperatures of 0°F (–18°C) without loss. As the planet Venus is frequently one of the most brilliant objects in the sky, so also *N.* 'Venus' may become the showiest object in one's pool. It attracts much attention with its large double blooms, which are held high above the water. I recommend 'Venus' for medium or large pools.

Nymphaea **'Vesuve'** Joseph B. L. Marliac 1906. Parentage: Unknown. Characteristics: Day blooming, Marliac rhizome, very free flowering. Plate 379.

PETAL COLOR: Brilliant, glowing red, deepening. *R.H.S. Chart*: Fan 2, Red-Purple Group, No. 61B; last day, No. 61A. Sepal color: Pink, white tips. *R.H.S. Chart*: Fan 2, Red-Purple Group, No. 70D; tips, Fan 4, White Group, No. 155B. Anther color: Rich yellow. *R.H.S. Chart*: Fan 1, Yellow-Orange Group, No. 14C. Stamen color: Burnt orange. Flower shape: Starlike. Flower size: 7 in (18 cm). Fragrance: Especially noticeable in first-day flowers. Number of petals: 22–23. Number of sepals: 4–5.

LEAF COLOR: Top, green; underside, bronzy brown. Leaf and sinus: Leaf nearly round; sinus a wide-open V. Leaf size: 9–10 in (23–25 cm). Leaf spread: 4 ft (1.2 m). Stem color: Purple. Pubescence on peduncle or petiole: None.

COMMENTS: 'Vesuve', with a flower color somewhat similar to 'Escarboucle', is one of the great lilies of all time. It has a very long blooming season, and flowers open early in the day and stay open late. Most petals are concave, and many have two lengthwise creases, giving the flowers a unique appearance. I recommend this lily for any size pool.

Nymphaea **'Virginalis'** Joseph B. L. Marliac 1910. Parentage: Unknown. Characteristics: Day blooming, Marliac rhizome, very free flowering. Plate 380.

PETAL COLOR: White. *R.H.S. Chart*: Fan 4, White Group, No. 155D. Sepal color: White. *R.H.S. Chart*: Fan 4, White Group, No. 155B. Anther color: Yellow. *R.H.S. Chart*: Fan 1, Yellow Group, No. 7B. Stamen color: Yellow. Flower shape: Cuplike. Flower size: 4.5–5.5 in (11–14 cm). Fragrance: Noticeable in new blooms. Number of petals: 21–22. Number of sepals: 4.

LEAF COLOR: Top, green, newest leaves purple or bronze; underside, bronzy green, newest leaves purple. Leaf and sinus: Leaves round. Lobes overlap at sinus, frequently one lobe is raised. Each lobe apex tipped up to 0.25 in (0.6 cm) long. Leaf size: 9 in (23 cm). Leaf spread: 3–4 ft (1–1.2 m). Stem color: Green to light brown. Pubescence on peduncle or petiole: Heavy fuzz on both.

COMMENTS: Because of its freedom of bloom and always dependable performance, many nursery people consider 'Virginalis' one of the best all-around white hardies. I highly recommend it for any size pool.

Nymphaea **'Virginia'** Charles Thomas 1962. Parentage: *N. odorata* 'Sulphurea Grandiflora' × *N.* 'Gladstoniana'. Characteristics: Day blooming, Marliac rhizome, free flowering. Plate 381.

PETAL COLOR: Inner petals, pale yellow, deeper toward flower center; outer petals white. *R.H.S. Chart*: Inner petals, Fan 1, Yellow Group, No. 2D to 6A; outer petals, Fan 4, White Group, No. 155B. Sepal color: White, green flush and edges. *R.H.S. Chart*: Fan 4, White Group, No. 155B; flush and edges, Fan 3, Yellow-Green Group, No. 145D. Anther color: Yellow. *R.H.S. Chart*: Fan 1, Yellow Group, No. 13A. Stamen color: Yellow. Flower shape: Quite full and stellate. Flower size: 7–8 in (18–20 cm). Fragrance: Noticeable in new blooms. Number of petals: 23–27. Number of sepals: 4.

LEAF COLOR: Top, green, perimeter blotched purple, new leaves green, heavily blotched with small purple blotches; underside, reddish, many small purple blotches. Leaf and sinus: Leaf egg-shaped; sinus usually an open V. Lobes occasionally overlap near petiole. Leaf size: 10 × 8.5 in (25 × 22 cm). Leaf spread: 5–6 ft (1.5–2 m). Stem color: Dark olive green. Pubescence on peduncle or petiole: Fuzz and fine hairs on both.

COMMENTS: 'Virginia', U.S. plant patent No. 2172 (1962, now expired), held by Charles Thomas, is similar to *N. odorata* 'Sulphurea Grandiflora' in every way except flower color. It could be considered a white version of this classic water lily. A large and showy lily, its flowers are also quite similar to 'Hal Miller' No. 2. I recommend it for medium and large pools.

Nymphaea 'White Cup' Perry D. Slocum 1986. Parentage: *N.* 'Peter Slocum' × *N.* 'Panama Pacific' (a tropical water lily). Characteristics: Day blooming, odorata rhizome, fairly free flowering. Plate 382.

PETAL COLOR: Pure white. *R.H.S. Chart*: Fan 4, White Group, No. 155D. Sepal color: White, flushed chartreuse, especially along edges. *R.H.S. Chart*: Fan 4, White Group, No. 155D; flush and edges, Fan 3, Yellow-Green Group, No. 145B. Anther color: Golden yellow. *R.H.S. Chart*: Fan 1, Yellow Group, No. 5A. Stamen color: Golden yellow. Flower shape: Cuplike. Flower size: 3–4 in (8–10 cm). Fragrance: Some. Number of petals: 19–20. Number of sepals: 4.

LEAF COLOR: Top, green, newest leaves purple; underside, red, green on perimeter above water. Leaf and sinus: Leaf round; sinus an open V. Lobe usually has a sharply pointed tip. Leaf size: 8–10 in (20–25 cm). Leaf spread: 4–5 ft (1.2–1.5 m). Stem color: Chartreuse. Pubescence on peduncle or petiole: Fine fuzz on both.

COMMENTS: This cup-shaped white lily, a cross between 'Peter Slocum' and the tropical 'Panama Pacific', is quite an amazing hybrid. For an odorata type it blooms quite freely. 'White Cup' is for the collector or the water gardener with a medium or large pool.

Nymphaea 'White Laydeker'. See *N.* ×*laydekeri* 'Alba'.

Nymphaea 'William Falconer' (syn. 'Château le Rouge') Henry A. Dreer 1899. Parentage: Unknown. Characteristics: Day blooming, Marliac rhizome, very free flowering in cool-summer areas, moderately free flowering in milder zones. Plate 383.

PETAL COLOR: Very deep red. *R.H.S. Chart*: Fan 2, Red-Purple Group, No. 64A. Sepal color: Very deep pink. *R.H.S. Chart*: Fan 2, Red-Purple Group, No. 63C. Anther color: Burnt orange. *R.H.S. Chart*: Fan 1, Orange-Red Group, No. 31B. Stamen color: Burgundy-red. Flower shape: Cuplike. Flower size: 4.5–5 in (11–13 cm). Fragrance: None. Number of petals: 25. Number of sepals: 4.

LEAF COLOR: Top, green, new leaves purple, dark purple blotches; underside, purple, bright green lengthwise V. Leaf and sinus: Leaf slightly longer than wide; sinus an open V. Leaf size: 8 × 7.5 in (20 × 19 cm). Leaf spread: 3 ft (1 m). Stem color: Purple. Pubescence on peduncle or petiole: Fine hairs on both.

COMMENTS: This lily performs magnificently where summer temperatures remain moderate, but it will stop flowering during prolonged hot periods. 'William Falconer' blooms not at all or very little in places such as Florida and the other Gulf states.

Inner petals blacken during very hot periods. I recommend this lily for any size pool in the temperate zones, but it is the wrong choice for hot-summer areas.

Nymphaea 'Wow' Perry D. Slocum 1990. Parentage: *N.* 'Perry's Pink' × *N.* 'Pamela' (a tropical water lily). Characteristics: Day blooming, odorata rhizome, moderately free flowering, very striking flower color, red dot in center of stigmal area, excellent cut flower. Plate 384.

PETAL COLOR: Reddish purple. *R.H.S. Chart*: Fan 2, Red-Purple Group, No. 58A. Sepal color: Reddish purple. *R.H.S. Chart*: Fan 2, Red-Purple Group, No. 59A. Anther color: Yellowish orange. *R.H.S. Chart*: Fan 1, Orange Group, No. 29A. Stamen color: Orange. Flower shape: Cuplike, full. Flower size: 5–6 in (13–15 cm). Fragrance: Very pleasant. Number of petals: 31–35. Number of sepals: 4.

LEAF COLOR: Top, green, new leaves reddish; underside, brown, new leaves reddish. Leaf and sinus: Leaf nearly round, pointed tips at lobe ends; sinus either fully open or ⅔ closed. Leaf size: Up to 10 in (25 cm). Leaf spread: 3–5 ft (1–1.5 m). Stem color: Peduncle brownish, petiole yellowish green, both striped purple. Pubescence on peduncle or petiole: None.

COMMENTS: The flower color of 'Wow' is somewhat similar to 'Perry's Wildfire', yet the flower form is more rigid and flowers make excellent cut flowers. When using as a cut flower, be sure the whole stem is placed in water. Flower color is so striking that many people exclaim "Wow!" when observing blooms for the first time. I recommend this cultivar for medium and large pools.

Nymphaea 'Yellow Comanche'. Parentage: Probable mutation of *N.* 'Comanche'. Characteristics: Day blooming, Marliac rhizome, free flowering. Plate 385.

PETAL COLOR: Yellow, changing each day; second day blushed pink at base; third day, strong orange-pink flush and flecks over basal ⅔. *R.H.S. Chart*: First day, Fan 1, Yellow Group, No. 4B; second day, No. 6D; third day, No. 13D. Second-day blush, Red Group, No. 37D; third day, flush and flecks, No. 38B. Sepal color: Yellow; second day blushed rose-pink; third day upper ⅓ yellow, pink base. *R.H.S. Chart*: First day, Fan 1, Yellow Group, No. 2D; third day, upper ⅓, No. 4C. Blush, lighter than Red Group, No. 49D; third day, basal ⅔, No. 49C. Anther color: Yellow. *R.H.S. Chart*: Fan 1, Yellow Group, No. 10A. Stamen color: Yellow. Flower shape: Cuplike then stellate. Flower size: 5.5–6 in (14–15 cm). Fragrance: Noticeable in first-day flower. Number of petals: 25. Number of sepals: 4.

LEAF COLOR: Top, green, new leaves bronzy green, lightly flecked purple; underside, red, flecked purple, flecks prominent on new leaves. Leaf and sinus: Leaves nearly round; sinus usually a wide-open V. Some lobes may overlap partially even on the same plant. Leaf size: Up to 11.5 × 10.5 in (29 × 27 cm). Leaf spread: 4–5 ft (1.2–1.5 m). Stem color: Brown. Pubescence on peduncle or petiole: A few fine hairs on both.

COMMENTS: 'Yellow Comanche' is very similar to 'Comanche' (which see), with virtually identical leaves and stems and the same free blooming character in all zones. It is probably a sport of 'Comanche'. Today it is most widely planted in Australia, New Zealand, and the West Coast of the United States. Should it become more widely available, it will be a fine plant for medium and large pools for warm areas. In North Carolina, however, it is very subject to crown rot.

Nymphaea **'Yellow Princess'** Perry D. Slocum 1991. Parentage: Seedling of *N.* 'Texas Dawn'. Characteristics: Day blooming, Marliac rhizome, free flowering. Plate 386.

PETAL COLOR: Inner petals, rich yellow; outer petals, light yellow. *R.H.S. Chart*: Inner petals, Fan 1, Yellow Group, No. 3A; outer petals, Green-Yellow Group, No. 1D. Sepal color: Greenish yellow, base paler. *R.H.S. Chart*: Fan 3, Yellow-Green Group, No. 145C; base, Fan 1, Green-Yellow Group, No. 1D. Anther color: Deep yellow. *R.H.S. Chart*: Fan 1, Yellow Group, No. 6B. Stamen color: Deep yellow. Flower shape: Stellate. Flower size: 6–7.5 in (15–19 cm). Fragrance: Very pleasant. Number of petals: 24–28. Number of sepals: 4.

LEAF COLOR: Top, deep olive green, perimeter flecked purple on new leaves; underside, yellowish green, heavily blotched reddish purple. Leaf and sinus: Leaf nearly round, pointed tips at lobe ends; sinus a wide-open V. Leaf size: Up to 12 in (30 cm). Leaf spread: 4–5 ft (1.2–1.5 m). Stem color: Brownish. Pubescence on peduncle or petiole: Thick fuzz on both.

COMMENTS: 'Yellow Princess', with its freedom of bloom and excellent stellate flower form, is sure to take a place among the outstanding yellow hardies. I recommend it for small, medium, and large pools.

Nymphaea **'Yellow Pygmy'**. See *N.* **'Helvola'**.

Nymphaea **'Yellow Queen'** Perry D. Slocum 1991. Parentage: Seedling of *N.* 'Texas Dawn'. Characteristics: Day blooming, Marliac rhizome, free flower-

ing; blooms open earlier than other yellow hardies. Plate 387.

PETAL COLOR: Inner petals, rich yellow; outer, lighter. *R.H.S. Chart*: Inner petals, Fan 1, Yellow Group, No. 8B; outer, No. 2D. Sepal color: Greenish yellow. *R.H.S. Chart*: Fan 3, Yellow-Green Group, No. 145D. Anther color: Deep yellow. *R.H.S. Chart*: Fan 1, Yellow Group, No. 13B. Stamen color: Deep yellow. Flower shape: Unique star-shape. Flower size: 7–10 in (18–25 cm). Fragrance: Delightful. Number of petals: 30–32. Number of sepals: 4.

LEAF COLOR: Top, deep olive green, new leaves heavily mottled purple, mottling fades slightly with age; underside, red or deep pink, heavily mottled reddish purple. Leaf and sinus: Leaf nearly round; sinus a wide-open V. Leaf size: Up to 12 in (30 cm). Leaf spread: 4–5 ft (1.2–1.5 m). Stem color: Purplish brown. Pubescence on peduncle or petiole: Thick fuzz on both.

COMMENTS: One outstanding trait of 'Yellow Queen' is the flower's resemblance to a tropical day bloomer yet with an unusual upward curl to the petal tips. Blooms open much earlier than any other yellow hardy cultivar (about 9:30 a.m.) and the beautiful, heavily mottled leaves are among the prettiest of hardies—ranking with 'Arc-en-Ciel' in their beauty. I recommend this cultivar for medium or large pools.

Nymphaea **'Yellow Sensation'** Perry D. Slocum 1991. Parentage: *N. alba* plant received from New Zealand × *N. mexicana* No. 2. Characteristics: Day blooming, upright rhizome, free flowering, very double flower for a yellow hardy; blooms held up to 6 in (15 cm) above water. Plate 388.

PETAL COLOR: Rich yellow. *R.H.S. Chart*: Fan 1, Yellow Group, No. 3C. Sepal color: Pale greenish yellow, green tips and border. *R.H.S. Chart*: Fan 3, Yellow-Green Group, No. 145D and lighter; tips and border, No. 145B. Anther color: Deep yellow. *R.H.S. Chart*: Fan 1, Yellow Group, No. 11A. Stamen color: Deep yellow. Flower shape: Cuplike. Flower size: 5–8 in (13–20 cm). Fragrance: Slight, pleasant. Number of petals: 33–36. Number of sepals: 4.

LEAF COLOR: Top, olive green, new leaves greenish, flecked purple, perimeter blotched purple; underside, yellowish green, perimeter flecked reddish purple. Leaf and sinus: Leaf nearly round. Lobes frequently overlap in new leaves, partially overlap in medium-sized leaves; sinus completely open in large leaves. Leaf size: Up to 10 in (25 cm). Leaf spread: 3–5 ft (1–1.5 m). Stem color: Peduncle brownish, petiole greenish brown, striped purple. Pubescence on peduncle or petiole: Thick fuzz on both.

COMMENTS: 'Yellow Sensation' is so striking that, if the supply ever permits, it could be the most popular contemporary yellow hardy. It shares one parent in common with *N. ×marliacea* 'Chromatella', yet flowers are larger, more richly colored, and have more petals (33 to 36 compared to the 22 to 25 of 'Chromatella'). I hybridized this cultivar using the larger form of *N. mexicana* No. 2, whereas Joseph B. L. Marliac probably did not have access to this rare plant over a century ago when he hybridized 'Chromatella'. I recommend 'Yellow Sensation' for small, medium, or large pools. It does well in water that is 3–4 ft (1–1.2 m) deep and in fact is not recommended for shallow ponds, as its leaves will crowd each other on the water surface.

Chapter 17

Lotus Species and Cultivars

There are just two recognized species of the genus *Nelumbo* (lotus): *N. lutea* (Willdenow) Persoon, the native American species, and *N. nucifera* Gaertner, native to the Orient, the Philippines, north Australia, Egypt (probably introduced from India about 500 B.C.), and the Volga River delta at the Caspian Sea. It should be noted that the "blue lotus of the Nile" and the "blue lotus of India" are not lotuses but are *Nymphaea caerulea* and *Nymphaea nouchali* (syn. *N. stellata*), respectively.

Nelumbo nucifera, the sacred lotus, is revered by Buddhists in the Orient. Over 2500 years ago, Buddha is reputed to have risen up in the heart of a lotus bud out of the murky waters. (The water was probably "murky" because tadpoles, frogs, and fish usually stir up the water around nelumbos.) Lotuses can frequently be seen growing in lagoons close to Buddhist temples.

Decorative lotus seed pods are used extensively in bouquets and wreaths. To my knowledge, all lotus tubers are edible. The tubers and seeds of *Nelumbo lutea* were commonly eaten by Native Americans, and lotus tubers and seeds are still a part of the Oriental diet and are available in the United States from Oriental markets. The leaves are also eaten or used to wrap various foods for baking.

In some areas, particularly Taiwan and China, a very compact, thick-rhizomed variant of *Nelumbo nucifera* is a dietary staple. Commonly called the edible lotus, its rhizomes are grown, cooked, and used very much like potatoes (Plate 389). In Taiwan particularly, it is planted extensively as a food crop, sometimes grown in tanks of pure rotted cow manure. The short, thick tubers are a staple in the diet of the Taiwanese. The flower is pink or white, but little else is known about this lotus. My experience has shown this plant to be difficult to flower; perhaps I have not found the right soil conditions. I do not know of anyone who has been successful in bringing it to flower in the United States.

In North America, lotuses do well over most of the United States and southern Canada as long as there is enough summer heat to bring plants into flower. Lotuses require two to three months of temperatures in the 75–85°F (24–29°C) range. Regions of the United States where lotuses do not perform at their very best are the very hot Southwest, with summer temperatures of 95–115°F (35–46°C), and the cooler mountainous regions of the Pacific Northwest with summer temperatures in the 60–70°F (16–21°C) range.

The summer weather in the British Isles and northern Europe is too cold for lotuses to bloom except in a greenhouse or conservatory. Blooms are produced, however, in the southern half of France, most of Spain, Portugal, Italy, Greece, and western and southern portions of the former Yugoslavia. In southern Australia and New Zealand there is not enough heat for lotuses to bloom except in greenhouses.

While there are many known variants of *Nelumbo nucifera*—in white, pink, red, and bicolor types and single and double blooms—only one variant of *N. lutea*, a natural hybrid, has been identified: *N. lutea* 'Yellow Bird'. It was discovered in 1975 at Lilypons Water Gardens, Buckeystown, Maryland. How all the variants of *N. nucifera* developed is not recorded and many are considered natural hybrids. Although historical details are scant, most of the original cultivars of *N. nucifera* are still being grown and sold today. Over the years aquatic nurseries have assigned trade names to these plants, but the names of decades ago are no longer commonly used in the United States. The names given in this chapter are those most widely used by Western growers.

Sometime before 1911, Joseph B. L. Marliac hybridized *Nelumbo lutea* and came up with *N.* 'Flavescens', the first recorded *Nelumbo* cultivar in the West. After a void of nearly a century, magnificent new lotus cultivars are again being developed, and some of the most widely available ones are described in this chapter.

These plants, widely acclaimed by water garden experts, perform very well in areas where summer temperatures are in the 75–85°F (24–29°C) range. They should do well in southern Europe, though they are not yet available in many regions. Lotus cultivars grow and bloom quite freely at the Palm House, a conservatory for tropical and semitropical plants at Stapeley Water Gardens, Nantwich, Cheshire, England.

More than 300 types of lotus are grown in the People's Republic of China, but little information is available on these plants. A poster from the Nanjing Botanical Garden displayed at the fourth annual Water Lily Symposium, held in Harrogate, England, in 1988, featured a list of an astonishing 125 *Nelumbo nucifera* cultivars grown in their gardens. These likely include botanical varieties and hybrids, whether naturally occurring or the result of planned crosses. The same list appears in Ni Xueming's *Lotus of China* (1987).

The cultivars are listed below. Four names include the phrase "thousand petals," and I think one can presume these are cultivars with very double blooms. Only the name 'Red Lotus' coincides with a name used in the West, as red lotus is the common name for *Nelumbo* 'Pekinensis Rubra'. One cannot presume that these are the same plants, however.

'Autumn Sky'	'Hongcha Bowl'
'Bai Wanwan'	'Hunan'
'Bamboo Joint'	'Hunanpao'
'Beijing Pink Flower'	'Hundred Petals'
'Beijing White Flower'	'Jia Yu'
'Big Green'	'Jianzuihonghua'
'Big Leaf White'	'Jiaopa'
'Big Lying Dragon'	'Jifei Lian'
'Big Magpie'	'June Early'
'Big Red Coat'	'Liberation Red'
'Big Square'	'Little Green'
'Big Versicolor'	'Long June Early'
'Big White'	'Lushan Pink'
'Big White Flower'	'Lushan White'
'Birthday's Peach'	'Lutouzhong'
'Buddha's Seat'	'Maojie'
'Changing Face'	'Nehru Lotus'
'Cherry'	'Ohga Lotus'
'Cherry Pink'	'Paozi'
'Children Lotus'	'Phoenix'
'Chinese Antique Lotus'	'Pig Tail'
'Chongchuantai'	'Pink Bowl'
'Chongshihua'	'Pink Double'
'Damaojie'	'Pink Double Palace'
'Daqingkai'	'Pink Jade'
'Early Lotus'	'Pink Lotus'
'East Lake Pink'	'Pink Rose'
'East Mountain Red Coat'	'Pink Thousand Petals'
'Falling Flowers'	'Pink Tip White Bowl'
'Fenchuantai'	'Qingmaojfe'
'Flower Lotus'	'Qinglianzi'
'Fragrant Flower Lotus'	'Quianling White'
'Fresh Flowers'	'Red Bowl'
'Gui Yang'	'Red Coat'
'Hainan'	'Red Flower Fujian'
'Han Lotus'	'Red Lotus'
'Hangxhou White Flower'	'Red Peony'
'Hong Wanwan'	'Red Thousand Petals'

'Red Tip'
'Sesame Lake'
'Shanxi White'
'Shaoxing Pink'
'Shijiazhuang White'
'Shuhong Lian'
'Single Pink'
'Sino-Japanese Friendship'
'Small Magpie'
'Snow Lake'
'Sparrow'
'Sunyatsen Lotus'
'Table Lotus'
'Taibai'
'Tardy Lotus'
'Tenghu Lian'
'Thousand Petals'
'Two White Flowers'
'Wan Er Hong'
'Wax Gourd'
'Welcoming Guests'
'West Lake Pink'
'White Bloom'
'White Bowl'
'White Cherry'

'White Flower Fujian'
'White Hunan'
'White Peony'
'White Sea'
'White Small Gentleman'
'White Stamen Hunan'
'White Swan'
'White Thousand Petals'
'Winter Lotus'
'Wufei Lian'
'Wuxi White'
'Xuanwuhu Red'
'Xiamen Bowl'
'Xiamaojie'
'Xiang Cheng'
'Xiangtan Huaye'
'Yacheng'
'Yizhangging'
'Yueyapao'
'Yushan'
'Yuxiu'
'Zhaohongoha Bowl'
'Zhouou'
'Zuifei'

All lotuses are day bloomers, usually opening quite early in the morning and closing by midafternoon for three successive days. First-day flowers close earlier. The cultivar 'Momo Botan' is an exception as older blooms frequently last for nearly a week, often without ever closing. The blooms of 'Ben Gibson', a hybrid seedling of 'Momo Botan', also last several extra days.

A "changeable" lotus means that its flower color gradually changes over a three-day period. For example, the flowers of *Nelumbo* 'Mrs. Perry D. Slocum' open dark pink and are a creamy yellow-flushed pink by the third day.

The following dwarf or semidwarf cultivars make excellent patio plants: 'Angel Wings', 'Baby Doll', 'Ben Gibson', 'Carolina Queen', 'Charles Thomas', 'Chawan Basu', 'Gregg Gibson', 'Momo Botan', and 'Momo Botan Minima'. Any of these is suitable for planting in a half barrel or comparable container. Round containers are preferable for lotuses because the tubers and runners can jam up in the corners of square planters.

If a wooden half barrel is chosen, line the barrel with black plastic and staple the plastic around the top edge of the barrel. This will prevent leaking as well as the leaching of any toxins from the barrel's former contents. The soil needs to be heavy enough so that it will not float, eliminating for use most of the potting soil mixes found at garden centers. Well-rotted and composted cow manure can be used in the bottom half if mixed one part composted manure to two or three parts topsoil. A heavy loam topsoil from the garden is excellent. Fill the container with soil to within 3–6 in (8–15 cm) of the top. Fertilizer, such as the convenient tablet forms, can also be added to the soil at this time. Look for an N–P–K ratio of 20–10–5 or 20–14–8. I generally use four to six tablets. If granular fertilizer (5–10–10) is used, keep it away from tubers and use in small amounts. Finish the container planting by adding 1 in (2.5 cm) of coarse sand or pea gravel and fill to the top with water.

A bushel planter or large plastic pan filled in the same manner can also be used. Place bricks or blocks inside the tub or barrel to elevate the planter to within 4–6 in (10–15 cm) of the water's surface. I have used this bushel planter method, incorporating a concrete block 8 × 8 × 16 in (20 × 20 × 40 cm) in a half barrel with excellent results. Two or three fertilizer tablets per month during the early summer months will provide sufficient fertilization. A sunny location is preferable yet partial shade is usually satisfactory.

For best performance of the large lotuses, plant them in large boxes, the Aqualite pool, or the Super Tub and place in the pool under 3–6 in (8–15 cm) of water. The Aqualite pool is 46 × 38 × 12 in (120 × 95 × 30 cm) and widely available in the United States (see Appendix B). The Super Tub is 36 × 24 × 8 in (90 × 60 × 20 cm) with a capacity of about 4 cu ft (0.11 cu m). A box $3 \times 3 \times 1$ ft ($90 \times 90 \times 30$ cm) will usually allow for excellent growth and many blooms.

For the bottom half of large containers I recommend mixing one part very well rotted manure to two parts heavy loam or garden soil. Composted cow manure is usually available at garden centers. Other manures, such as sheep manure, are also suitable if well rotted. Use plain garden soil and 10 to 12 fertilizer tablets in the top half. Add 1 in (2.5 cm) of pea gravel to maintain the soil surface. (If fish complement the pool, the gravel helps prevent them from disturbing the soil.)

Add four to six more fertilizer tablets per month during the early summer. Refrain from fertilizing when new plant growth is plentiful because pushing the tablets into the soil may break the new sprouts.

All lotuses are hardy and can be planted when danger of freezing is over. Plant them at the same time as hardy water lilies. In Europe, lotuses can be grown in zone 10 and warmer parts of zones 9 and 8 where daytime temperatures reach 75°F (24°C) or above for long periods during the summer. Refer to the hardiness zone maps in Appendix A and follow this general planting timetable:

In North America
Zones 10 and 9   March through May
Zones 8–5   April/May
Zone 4   May

In Europe
Zones 10 and 9   March through May
Zone 8   April/May
Zones 7–4   conservatory planting, where water can be heated to 75°F (24°C) or higher

In the descriptions of the *Nelumbo* species, varieties, and cultivars that follow, common names, if any, are given after the botanical name. Many lotus varieties and cultivars are of cloudy and unknown parentage. As a result, some listed names have no botanical standing yet have widespread use among growers and nursery people.

Some categories used in describing water lilies are inappropriate for lotuses. Throughout *Nelumbo*, flower shape (Figure 68) is quite similar, though petal count varies considerably; sepal color is quite similar as well throughout lotuses, though some sepals may have a red spot at the apex. Anthers vary only slightly from flower to flower, whether species or cultivar. The leaves too are quite standard, either green or bluish green, and the few variations that do exist are mentioned. The sinus is not present, and the stems are hispid, with small spines. Therefore, categories used in describing *Nelumbo* differ from the water lily descriptions and reflect the distinguishing characteristics of lotus.

On the other hand, two categories are added in this chapter: "Seed capsule color" and "Plant height," both of which vary considerably among lotus species and varieties. Seed capsule color can be helpful in identification. Dried capsules, all brown, are widely sought for use in bouquets and wreaths. "Plant height" reflects the measurement above water and can be used as a relative figure to determine whether the plant is dwarf, semidwarf, or full size.

I found it difficult to give a sepal count, as was done for the water lilies, since it is frequently impossible to distinguish between the sepals and outer petals. "Petal number" therefore includes the tiny outside sepals. Standardized color references are to the Royal Horticultural Society (R.H.S.) Color Chart.

"Leaf size" refers to the diameter of the mature leaf. U.S. plant patents on lotuses are mentioned in "Comments." Note that these expire after 17 years and are not renewable. "Comments" also include reference to what size pool is suitable. Although there are no hard rules differentiating pool sizes, general guidelines follow:

tub garden: up to 3 ft (1 m) in diameter
small: 4–6 ft (1.2–2 m) in diameter
medium: 7–9 ft (2.2–2.7 m) in diameter
large: 10 ft (3 m) in diameter or larger
natural pond: dirt or mud bottom pond of any size

Note that copper and redwood are toxic to plants and fish and should be used only in conjunction with a plastic or other fish-safe liner.

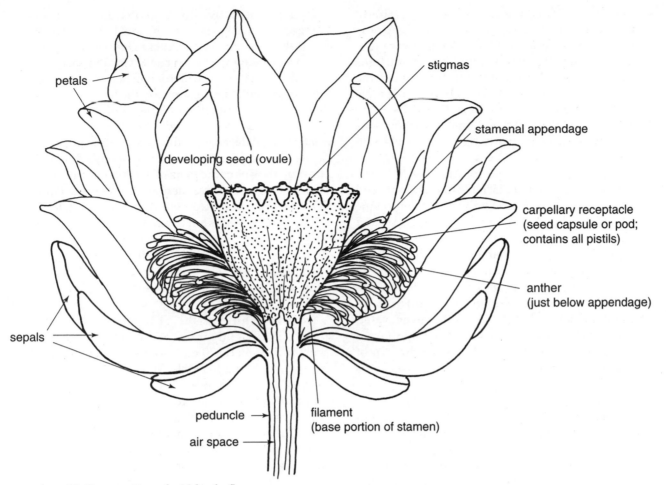

petals

stigmas

developing seed (ovule)

stamenal appendage

carpellary receptacle
(seed capsule or pod;
contains all pistils)

anther
(just below appendage)

sepals

peduncle

filament
(base portion of stamen)

air space

FIGURE 68. Cross section of a *Nelumbo* flower.

Nelumbo lutea (Willdenow) Persoon [*N. pentapetala* (Walter) Fernald]. American yellow lotus, water chinquapin. Native to eastern and central United States. Plate 390.

PETAL COLOR: Rich yellow, slightly lighter tips. *R.H.S. Chart*: Fan 1, Yellow Group, No. 3A; tips, No. 3C. Seed capsule color: Yellow then green. *R.H.S. Chart*: Fan 1, Yellow Group, No. 9A, then Fan 3, Yellow-Green Group, No. 144D. Flower size: 7–11 in (18–28 cm). Fragrance: Slight. Number of petals: 22–25. Leaf size: 13–17 in (33–43 cm); in rich soil leaves may reach 24 in (60 cm). Plant height: 2.5–5 ft (0.8–1.5 m).

COMMENTS: *N. lutea*, the lotus species native to America, is a good bloomer that usually holds its flowers 10 in (25 cm) above its leaves. This plant is suitable for any size pool. American yellow lotus, as this plant is commonly called, has been used extensively in hybridizing and is the parent of the cultivars 'Carolina Queen', 'Debbie Gibson', 'Glen Gibson', 'Mrs. Perry D. Slocum', 'Patricia Gibson', 'Perry's Giant Sunburst', and 'The Queen', among others.

N. lutea **'Yellow Bird'**. This seedling or mutation of the American yellow lotus appeared in a pond at Lilypons Water Gardens, Buckeystown, Maryland, in 1975. 'Yellow Bird' has much broader petals and more rounded tips than *N. lutea*. As it has been only a moderate bloomer for me, I recommend it only for the collector or the owner of a large pool. Plate 391.

Nelumbo nucifera Gaertner [*N. speciosa* Willdenow]. Hindu lotus, Egyptian lotus, sacred lotus, speciosa. Native to India, Egypt, China, Japan, Philippines, northern Australia, Thailand, Vietnam, and the Volga River delta at the Caspian Sea. Plate 392.

PETAL COLOR: Deep pink, paling; base ⅓ creamy yellow, paling. *R.H.S. Chart*: Fan 1, Red Group, No. 49A then 49C; base, Yellow Group, No. 8B then 8D. Seed capsule color: Yellow then chartreuse. *R.H.S. Chart*: Fan 1, Yellow Group, No. 7A; then Fan 3, Yellow-Green Group, No. 149D. Flower size: 9–12 in (23–30 cm). Fragrance: Pleasant, especially noticeable on first and second days. Number of petals: 24. Leaf size: 20–36 in (50–90 cm). Plant height: 3–5 ft (1–1.5 m).

COMMENTS: This species of lotus, the Hindu lotus, was called the Egyptian lotus for a long time as it also grows along the Nile River and was probably imported to Egypt from India. The Hindu lotus can now be found growing wild throughout the Orient. For many years it was the best-selling lotus in the United States, though the cultivar 'Mrs. Perry D. Slocum' has now achieved this distinction. This especially beautiful lotus is worthy of a place in pools of every size.

N. nucifera **var.** *caspicum* Fischer. Russian lotus, red Russian lotus. Native to the Volga River delta at the Caspian Sea. The pinkish red flowers are large and quite similar to the cultivar 'Pekinensis Rubra' (which see) except that it has a slightly larger bloom and a smaller seed capsule in the flower stage. The flowers average 22 petals and are only slightly fragrant. Leaves average 20–24 in (50–60 cm) in diameter and are held 3–5 ft (1–1.5 m) above the water. This very outstanding lotus is a recent import from southern Russia by Dr. Creech, former director of the National Arboretum in Washington, D.C. It is worthy of a place in every pool. Plate 393.

N. nucifera **var.** *rosea*. Rose lotus. Native to China and Japan. The flowers, with a rich anise fragrance, are rose-pink with a yellow center and are 8–10 in (20–25 cm) in diameter. Leaves are 18–20 in (45–50 cm) in diameter and are held 4–5 ft (1.2–1.5 m) above the water. The first-day flower somewhat resembles a full rose. This variety is similar in many ways to the cultivar 'Rosea Plena' (which see) except that *N. nucifera* var. *rosea* develops a single flower whereas 'Rosea Plena' forms a double flower. Flowers also closely resemble those of *N. nucifera*, yet those of variety *rosea* are more of a salmon-pink color. I recommend this variety for any size pool. Plates 394 and 395.

N. nucifera **'Alba Plena'**. Shiroman lotus. Native to China and Japan. The flowers are creamy white and very double, numbering 115 to 120 petals. The blooms are large, 10 in (25 cm) across, with only a slight fragrance, if any. Leaves average 25 in (63 cm) in diameter and grow 3–5 ft (1–1.5 m) in height. This lotus needs a large planter and is a fine plant for the medium or large pool. For outstanding performance, plant it in an Aqualite pool under 6–8 in (15–20 cm) of water. Plate 396.

N. nucifera **'Japanese Double White'**. Found growing in Japan. The fragrant white flowers are semidouble. With 52 petals, blooms are more double than most lotuses and have great flower form, dis-

playing an attractive flower center. Leaves are average size, 18–23 in (45–58 cm), and held 5–6 ft (1.5–2 m) above the water. 'Japanese Double White' was found growing in the Japanese Garden section of the Missouri Botanical Garden in St. Louis. Flowers are occasionally hidden among the leaves. I recommend it for the medium or large pool. Plate 397.

N. nucifera **'Paleface'**. Found growing in northern Australia. The fragrant flower is mostly white with pink on the tips of the petals. The flowers are 9–10 in (23–25 cm) in diameter and are borne quite freely. The leaves average 20 in (50 cm) and are held 5 ft (1.5 m) above the water. Its unique color pattern sets 'Paleface' apart from other lotuses. The cultivar *N.* 'Chawan Basu' (which see), with its pink veins and petal edges, is the closest in color combination. I recommend 'Paleface' for any size pool.

N. nucifera **'Shirokunshi'**. Tulip lotus. Native to Japan. This slightly fragrant dwarf white lotus develops 7–8 in (18–20 cm) flowers which are quite single, averaging 16 petals. The 12–18 in (30–45 cm) leaves are raised only 18–30 in (45–75 cm) above the water. It is a very free-blooming plant ideal for the small or medium-sized pool. By planting it in a 30–32 quart (33–35 l) container and placing it in the pool under 3–6 in (8–15 cm) of water, one can usually expect several blooms the first season. Consider it, also, for planting in a half barrel on the patio. Plate 398.

N. nucifera **'Waltzing Matilda'**. Found growing in northwestern Australia. The outer ¾ of the petal is a very deep pink turning to medium pink with age; the basal ¼ is a light yellow. The very fragrant flower is 8–10 in (20–25 cm) in diameter with 21 petals on the average. The leaves are 24 in (60 cm) in diameter and are held 4–5 ft (1.2–1.5 m) above the water. The inner petals are uniquely curled, giving the flower a very special beauty. The new leaves are unusual in that they are red or reddish purple when they first rise out of water, later turning to green. A unique feature of the leaves is the indentations that appear on opposite sides of each leaf. I have not observed these indentations in any other lotus species or cultivar. I grew this cultivar for one full season in USDA zone 7, and a negative feature showed up that may prevent it from becoming popular: the plant does not develop tubers like most lotuses but has runners—most of which do not survive the winter. Moving the plant into warm quarters such as a greenhouse in the fall in the north would help it to survive. If one can find it, I would recommend it for any size pool. Plates 399 and 400.

Nelumbo pentapetala. See *N. lutea*.

Nelumbo speciosa. See *N. nucifera*.

RECENT LOTUS CULTIVARS

Nelumbo **'Alba Grandiflora'**. Asiatic lotus. Parentage: Unknown. Plate 401.

PETAL COLOR: White. *R.H.S. Chart*: Fan 4, White Group, No. 155A. Seed capsule color: Chartreuse; rim bright green then bluish green; stigmas bright yellow. *R.H.S. Chart*: Fan 3, Yellow-Green Group, No. 149D; rim, Green Group, No. 136D then 128A; stigmas, Yellow Group, No. 6B. Flower size: 9–10 in (23–25 cm). Fragrance: Slight in new blooms. Number of petals: 22. Leaf size: 16–23 in (40–58 cm). Plant height: 4–6 ft (1.2–2 m).

COMMENTS: Asiatic lotus has been the standard white lotus for many decades. The flower is beautiful, the plant is a fairly good bloomer, and the leaves are very impressive with their bluish green color and many convolutions around the edges. The flowers are frequently hidden among the leaves, however. I recommend this plant for medium and large pools.

Nelumbo **'Alba Striata'**. Empress lotus. Parentage: Unknown. Plates 402 and 403.

PETAL COLOR: White; both sides of outer petals flushed pale green; prominent uneven red margins. *R.H.S. Chart*: Fan 4, White Group, No. 155C; flush, Fan 3, Yellow-Green Group, No. 149D; margins, Fan 1, Red-Purple Group, No. 71C. Seed capsule color: Yellow then chartreuse. *R.H.S. Chart*: Fan 1, Yellow Group, No. 8C, then Fan 3, Yellow-Green Group, No. 145D. Flower size: 10–12 in (25–30 cm). Fragrance: Pleasant in new flowers. Number of petals: 18–19. Leaf size: 19–20 in (48–50 cm); in rich soil leaves may reach 28 in (70 cm). Plant height: 4–5 ft (1.2–1.5 m).

COMMENTS: The empress lotus is very beautiful and, generally, a moderate bloomer. A distinctive flower feature is the jagged red margin on the petals. I recommend it for medium and large pools.

Nelumbo **'Angel Wings'** Perry D. Slocum 1984. Parentage: *N. nucifera* 'Shirokunshi' × *N.* 'Pekinensis Rubra'. Plates 404 and 405.

PETAL COLOR: White. *R.H.S. Chart*: Fan 4, White Group, No. 155C. Seed capsule color: Greenish yellow then green, deeper green rim, prominent yellow stigmas. *R.H.S. Chart*: Fan 1, Green-Yellow Group, No. 1C, then Fan 3, Yellow-Green Group, No. 150C; rim, Green Group, No. 142A; stigma, Fan 1, Yellow Group, No. 4A. Flower size: 8–10 in (20–25 cm). Fragrance: Slight, aniselike. Number of petals: 20–24. Leaf size: 18–23 in (45–58 cm). Plant height: 2–4 ft (0.6–1.2 m).

COMMENTS: 'Angel Wings' is my favorite of the white lotuses. It is very free flowering and ideal for any size pool, including a tub or barrel garden. The especially beautiful leaves of this plant are highly convoluted, with many waves and a deep cup in the middle of each leaf. The petals roll inward at the edges, making a very pleasing effect. 'Angel Wings' was crossed in 1984 and holds U.S. plant patent No. 5799, issued in 1986.

Nelumbo **'Baby Doll'** Perry D. Slocum 1985. Parentage: Seedling of *N.* 'Angel Wings'. Plate 406.

PETAL COLOR: White. *R.H.S. Chart*: Fan 4, White Group, No. 155C. Seed capsule color: Chartreuse then green. *R.H.S. Chart*: Fan 3, Yellow-Green Group, No. 145C, then Green Group, No. 130C. Flower size: 4–6 in (10–15 cm). Fragrance: Very slight. Number of petals: 21. Leaf size: 9–11 in (23–28 cm). Plant height: 24–30 in (60–75 cm).

COMMENTS: 'Baby Doll' is an ideal plant for a tub or barrel garden. Its tiny seed capsules are only 0.75 in (2 cm) across, and the cup-shaped flowers are lovely. This lotus is very free flowering. A single plant may produce 12 blooms at a time in an Aqualite pool. Grown in a more restricted container, 'Baby Doll' produces less growth and fewer blooms—about 20 blooms total per season when grown in a 30-qt (33-l) planter.

Nelumbo **'Ben Gibson'** Perry D. Slocum 1988. Parentage: *N. nucifera* 'Alba Plena' × *N.* 'Momo Botan'. Plate 407.

PETAL COLOR: Tip pink, paling, veins red; base, pale yellow. *R.H.S. Chart*: Tip, Fan 2, Red-Purple Group, Nos. 63B–C; veins, No. 63A; base, Fan 1, Yellow Group, No. 4C. Seed capsule color: Yellow then green; about 7 yellow pistils project part way. *R.H.S. Chart*: Fan 1, Yellow Group, No. 11A; third day, Fan 3, Green Group, No. 142A; pistils, Fan 1, Yellow Group, No. 11A. Flower size: 5.5–6 in (14–15 cm). Fragrance: Very pleasant. Number of petals: 96–115. Leaf size: 10–13 in (25–33 cm), small for a lotus. Plant height: 3–4 ft (1–1.2 m).

COMMENTS: 'Ben Gibson' is named after one of my twin stepsons, who is co-owner with wife, Debbie, of Perry's Water Gardens. This is an ideal plant for the small, medium, or large pool. A bicolor hybrid, it is very free blooming, quite double, and most pleasing. It has all the outstanding characteristics of 'Momo Botan', including the long-lasting bloom quality. Each flower lasts up to a week, and older flowers frequently stay open through the night. Blooms are usually held several inches above the leaves. The red-veined new flowers are particularly striking.

Nelumbo 'Carolina Queen' Perry D. Slocum 1984. Parentage: *N. lutea* × *N.* 'Pekinensis Rubra'. Back cover.

PETAL COLOR: Pink, creamy yellow base. *R.H.S. Chart*: Fan 2, Red-Purple Group, No. 62B; base ⅓, Fan 1, Yellow Group, No. 4A. Seed capsule color: Yellow then green. *R.H.S. Chart*: Fan 1, Yellow Group, No. 13A, then Fan 3, Yellow-Green Group, No. 145D. Flower size: 9–11 in (23–28 cm). Fragrance: Slight in new flowers. Number of petals: 21. Leaf size: 18–19 in (45–48 cm); in rich soil leaves may reach 25 in (63 cm). Plant height: 3–6 ft (1–2 m).

COMMENTS: 'Carolina Queen' has two wonderful features—it is very free flowering and it holds its flowers very high, nearly 2 ft (0.6 m) above the leaves. An excellent choice for pools of any size, it may be placed in a small container and used in small pools, where it will bloom for several years.

Nelumbo 'Charles Thomas' Perry D. Slocum 1984. Parentage: *N. nucifera* 'Shirokunshi' × *N.* 'Pekinensis Rubra'. Plate 408.

PETAL COLOR: Lavender-pink, paling. *R.H.S. Chart*: Fan 2, Red-Purple Group, No. 68B; second and third days, No. 68C. Seed capsule color: Yellow then chartreuse. *R.H.S. Chart*: Fan 1, Yellow Group, No. 13A, then Fan 3, Green Group, No. 140C. Flower size: 6–8 in (15–20 cm). Fragrance: Very pleasant anise scent in new flowers. Number of petals: 21. Leaf size: 14–22 in (35–56 cm). Plant height: 2–3 ft (0.6–1 m).

COMMENTS: The first lotus ever to receive a U.S. plant patent (1986, No. 5794), 'Charles Thomas' is named after the president of Lilypons Water Gardens, Buckeystown, Maryland. The first-day flower is more pinkish; the lavender-pink flower color that appears on the second day is rare in lotuses. This plant may be placed in a small container—preferably, bushel size (35 l) or larger—and used in pools of any size. It is ideal for a small pool.

Nelumbo 'Chawan Basu'. Parentage: Unknown. Plate 409.

PETAL COLOR: Ivory, deep pink margins and veins. *R.H.S. Chart*: Fan 1, Yellow Group, No. 11D; margins, Fan 2, Red-Purple Group, No. 63C; veins, No. 63B. Seed capsule color: Center light green then deep chartreuse, deep yellow stigma; first day rimmed deep chartreuse. *R.H.S. Chart*: Center, Fan 3, Green Group, No. 142C then 142A; stigma, Fan 1,

Yellow Group, No. 11A; rim, Fan 3, Green Group, No. 142A. Flower size: 5–9 in (13–23 cm). Fragrance: Delicate, pleasant in new flowers. Number of petals: 21–22. Leaf size: 14–17 in (35–43 cm). Plant height: 2–3 ft (0.6–1 m).

COMMENTS: 'Chawan Basu', a dwarf cultivar with small tubers, is a beautiful plant for the small or medium pool. (*Chawan basu* refers to a rice bowl.) Because of its small size, it is well suited to planting in containers. In hot summer climates flowers tend to wilt and in cool climates flowers will not develop. In temperate zones 'Chawan Basu' is generally a moderate bloomer.

Nelumbo 'Debbie Gibson' Perry D. Slocum 1988. Parentage: *N. nucifera* 'Alba Plena' × *N. lutea*. Plate 410.

PETAL COLOR: Cream, paling toward center. *R.H.S. Chart*: Fan 4, Yellow-White Group, Nos. 158D and 155A. Seed capsule color: Yellow then green. *R.H.S. Chart*: Fan 1, Yellow Group, No. 5A; third day, Fan 3, Yellow-Green Group, No. 142A. Flower size: 10 in (25 cm). Fragrance: Very pleasant. Number of petals: 23. Leaf size: 18 in (45 cm). Plant height: 5–6 ft (1.5–2 m).

COMMENTS: This is one of the finest lotus cultivars. 'Debbie Gibson' is very free flowering and the flower form is excellent. The large, lovely blooms are held high above the leaves. I especially recommend this graceful lotus for medium and large pools, though it may also be used in small water gardens. It is named for my daughter-in-law, co-owner with husband, Ben, of Perry's Water Gardens in Franklin, North Carolina.

Nelumbo 'Flavescens' Joseph B. L. Marliac. Parentage: *N. lutea* is one parent.

PETAL COLOR: Pale yellow; red spot at base. *R.H.S. Chart*: Fan 1, Yellow Group, No. 11D; spot, Red Group, No. 39B. Seed capsule color: Yellow then green. *R.H.S. Chart*: Fan 1, Yellow Group, No. 8C, then Fan 3, Yellow-Green Group, No. 144C. Flower size: 6–8 in (15–20 cm). Fragrance: Faint, aniselike. Number of petals: 22–25. Leaf size: 13–17 in (33–43 cm). Plant height: 3–5 ft (1–1.5 m).

COMMENTS: Leaves of 'Flavescens' have a conspicuous center red spot that complements the red spots on the petal bases. It produces smaller blooms than its parent, *N. lutea*. As it is only a moderate bloomer, and there are better pale yellow cultivars available now, I recommend 'Flavescens' for the collector only.

Nelumbo 'Glen Gibson' Perry D. Slocum 1986. Parentage: *N. nucifera* var. *caspicum* × *N. lutea*. Plate 411.

PETAL COLOR: Pink; base yellowish orange. *R.H.S. Chart*: Fan 2, Red-Purple Group, No. 63D; base, Fan 1, Yellow Group, No. 3A. Seed capsule color: Yellow. *R.H.S. Chart*: Fan 1, Yellow Group, No. 10A. Flower size: 8–9 in (20–23 cm). Fragrance: Slight. Number of petals: 19–20. Leaf size: 15–18 in (38–45 cm). Plant height: 3 ft (1 m).

COMMENTS: 'Glen Gibson' is named after one of my twin stepsons. It is an impressive lotus similar to 'Carolina Queen' yet of different parentage. Blooms are held very high, about 12 in (30 cm) above the leaves. I recommend this lotus for pools of any size.

Nelumbo '**Gregg Gibson**' Perry D. Slocum 1985. Parentage: Seedling of *N.* 'Charles Thomas'. Plate 412.

PETAL COLOR: Lavender-pink, paling. *R.H.S. Chart*: Fan 2, Red-Purple Group, No. 70C then 70D. Seed capsule color: Pale chartreuse then darker green. *R.H.S. Chart*: Fan 3, Yellow-Green Group, Nos. 149C–D; third day, No. 149A. Flower size: 6.5–7 in (16–18 cm). Fragrance: Pleasant. Number of petals: 22. Leaf size: 13 in (33 cm). Plant height: 24 in (60 cm).

COMMENTS: 'Gregg Gibson', a dwarf cultivar, is an excellent lotus of unusual color suitable for any size pool. A unique flower feature is the way the inner petals curve, giving a very striking effect. It is named for my grandson, son of Ben and Debbie Gibson.

Nelumbo '**Linda**' Perry D. Slocum 1988. Parentage: Seedling of *N.* 'Mrs. Perry D. Slocum'. Plate 413.

PETAL COLOR: Deep pink, outer petals flushed yellow, some middle petals flushed yellow. *R.H.S. Chart*: Fan 2, Red-Purple Group, No. 61D; flush, Fan 1, Yellow Group, No. 3C. Seed capsule color: Yellow. *R.H.S. Chart*: Fan 1, Yellow Group, No. 8B. Flower size: 7–9 in (18–23 cm). Fragrance: Very pleasant. Number of petals: 48–52. Leaf size: 18 in (45 cm). Plant height: 4–5 ft (1.2–1.5 m).

COMMENTS: 'Linda' is unique among lotuses for its pleasing combination of pink and yellow on both inner and outer petals. The blooms are quite double. I recommend this plant for pools of any size. It is a moderate bloomer.

Nelumbo '**Maggie Belle Slocum**' Perry D. Slocum 1984. Parentage: *N. nucifera* 'Shirokunshi' × *N.* 'Pekinensis Rubra'. Plate 414.

PETAL COLOR: Very rich, deep lavender-pink, paling; base pale yellow. *R.H.S. Chart*: Fan 2, Red-Purple Group, Nos. 65A and 68B then 62C; base, Fan 1, Yellow Group, No. 11C. Seed capsule color: Yellow then chartreuse; rim chartreuse then dark green. *R.H.S. Chart*: Fan 1, Yellow Group, No. 2A, then Fan 3, Yellow-Green Group, No. 149C; rim, No. 149D then 149C. Flower size: 10–12 in (25–30 cm). Fragrance: Delightful anise scent, first two days. Number of petals: 22. Leaf size: 20–25 in (50–63 cm). Plant height: 4–5 ft (1.2–1.5 m).

COMMENTS: 'Maggie Belle Slocum', a hybrid of which I am especially proud, is named after my wife. It is one of the most striking lotuses ever developed and only the second lotus ever patented in the United States (1986, No. 5798). The huge lavender-pink flowers are truly splendid. For the most impressive display, this lotus should be planted in a large container or an Aqualite pool and placed under 3–6 in (8–15 cm) of water. I highly recommend it for medium or large pools.

Nelumbo '**Momo Botan**'. Parentage: Unknown. Plate 415.

PETAL COLOR: Very deep rosy pink, yellow toward base. *R.H.S. Chart*: Fan 2, Red-Purple Group, No. 66D; base 1/3, Fan 1, Yellow Group, No. 11B. Seed capsule color: Light green then yellow; projecting pistils and stigmas remain yellow. *R.H.S. Chart*: Fan 3, Yellow-Green Group, No. 145D, then Fan 1, Yellow Group, No. 7A; pistils and stigmas, Fan 1, Yellow Group, No. 12A. Flower size: 5–6 in (13–15 cm). Fragrance: Quite noticeable, pleasant. Number of petals: 106–118. Leaf size: 12–15 in (30–38 cm). Plant height: 2–4 ft (0.6–1.2 m).

COMMENTS: 'Momo Botan' flowers, which resemble large, deep pink peonies, have some wonderful features. Flowers are open for several days longer than those of most lotuses, and they stay open quite late in the day. While first-day flowers close in midafternoon, second-day flowers stay open until after 6 p.m., and older flowers may remain open all night. Additionally, the plant has an exceptionally long bloom season. Seed capsules are very small and pretty. Though this lotus is ideal for pools of every size, I especially recommend it for small pools. 'Momo Botan' will bloom in a tub garden and makes an excellent patio plant when placed by itself in a half barrel.

Nelumbo '**Momo Botan Minima**'. Miniature 'Momo Botan'. Parentage: Unknown.

PETAL COLOR: Deep pink. *R.H.S. Chart*: Fan 2, Red-Purple Group, No. 65A. Seed capsule color: Chartreuse; projecting pistils yellow. *R.H.S. Chart*: Fan 3, Yellow-Green Group, No. 149C; pistils, Fan 1, Yellow Group, No. 12A. Flower size: 3–4 in (8–10 cm). Fragrance: Delightful. Number of petals: 90–110. Leaf size: 5–12 in (13–30 cm). Plant height: 2–3 ft (0.6–1 m).

COMMENTS: As its name indicates, this cultivar is a smaller version of 'Momo Botan'. It has all the fine features of that lotus, including long-lasting blooms that stay open late in the day and a long flowering season. It is ideal for the tub garden or the small pool. In general, it blooms quite well when planted in a 16-qt (15-l) container and submerged in a pool under 3–4 in (8–10 cm) of water.

Nelumbo 'Mrs. Perry D. Slocum' Perry D. Slocum 1964. Parentage: *N. lutea* × *N.* 'Rosea Plena'. Plate 416.

PETAL COLOR: First day pink, flushed yellow; second day pink and yellow; third day cream, flushed pink. *R.H.S. Chart*: First day, Fan 2, Red-Purple Group, No. 62A; flush, Fan 1, Yellow Group, No. 3D. Second day, Fan 1, Red Group, No. 38B, and Yellow Group, Nos. 8B and 10C. Third day, Fan 1, Yellow Group, Nos. 10B–C; flush, Red Group, No. 38D. Seed capsule color: Yellow then green. *R.H.S. Chart*: Fan 1, Yellow Group, No. 11A, then Fan 3, Green Group, No. 139D. Flower size: 9–12 in (23–30 cm). Fragrance: Strong anise scent, very pleasant. Number of petals: 86. Leaf size: 18–23 in (45–58 cm). Plant height: 4–5 ft (1.2–1.5 m).

COMMENTS: 'Mrs. Perry D. Slocum', a changeable pink-and-yellow bicolor *Nelumbo*, is reminiscent of the peace rose in flower color. It is one of the finest lotuses in the world today. This cultivar is especially free flowering, and one plant may produce three differently colored flowers at the same time. For the most striking display it should be planted in a rounded container (an Aqualite pool is ideal) about 4 × 3 × 1 ft (1.2 × 1 × 0.3 m) and placed under 3–6 in (8–15 cm) of water. This cultivar will bloom in a tub or barrel garden, but I strongly recommend it for medium or large pools.

Nelumbo 'Nikki Gibson' Perry D. Slocum 1988. Parentage: Seedling of *N.* 'Mrs. Perry D. Slocum'. Plate 417.

PETAL COLOR: Tips pink; midsection whitish yellow; base yellow. *R.H.S. Chart*: Tips, Fan 2, Red-Purple Group, No. 66D; midsection, Fan 1, Yellow Group, No. 11D; base, No. 10B. Seed capsule color: Yellow, rimmed green, then green. *R.H.S. Chart*: Fan 1, Yellow Group, No. 7C; rim, Fan 3, Yellow-Green Group, No. 144B; then all No. 144B. Flower size: 10–12 in (25–30 cm). Fragrance: Very pleasant. Number of petals: 20. Leaf size: 18–20 in (45–50 cm). Plant height: 5 ft (1.5 m).

COMMENTS: 'Nikki Gibson', a true tricolor, is one of the choicest single lotuses. Blooms are initially cup-shaped then open out flat on the second and third days. All are held high above the leaves. This cultivar is named for my granddaughter, daughter of Ben and Debbie Gibson. I recommend this plant for medium and large water gardens.

Nelumbo 'Patricia Garrett' Perry D. Slocum 1988. Parentage: *N.* 'Maggie Belle Slocum' × *N. lutea*. Plate 418.

PETAL COLOR: Pink, slightly darker tips, apricot-yellow center. *R.H.S. Chart*: Fan 1, Red Group, No. 49B; tips, No. 49A; center, Yellow-Orange Group, Nos. 18B–C. Seed capsule color: Yellow then lime green. *R.H.S. Chart*: Fan 1, Yellow Group, No. 10A, then Fan 3, Yellow-Green Group, No. 142A. Flower size: 7–10 in (18–25 cm). Fragrance: Delightful. Number of petals: 22. Leaf size: 17 in (43 cm). Plant height: 4–5 ft (1.2–1.5 m).

COMMENTS: 'Patricia Garrett', with its lovely pink-and-yellow petal combination, has one of the most beautiful blooms of all the single lotuses. The flowers are held very high, up to 30 in (75 cm) above the leaves. I highly recommend this lotus, which was named after my oldest stepdaughter, for the medium and large pool.

Nelumbo 'Pekinensis Rubra'. Red lotus. Parentage: Unknown. Plates 419–422.

PETAL COLOR: Rosy red then deep pink. *R.H.S. Chart*: Fan 2, Red-Purple Group, No. 64C then 64D. Seed capsule color: Yellow; green rim developing in older flowers. *R.H.S. Chart*: Fan 1, Yellow Group, No. 6A; rim, Fan 3, Yellow-Green Group, No. 145D. Flower size: 8–12 in (20–30 cm). Fragrance: Slight. Number of petals: 16–17. Leaf size: 20–24 in (50–60 cm). Plant height: 4–6 ft (1.2–2 m).

COMMENTS: 'Pekinensis Rubra' is a splendid plant. It is quite similar to *N. nucifera* var. *caspicum*, though flowers of 'Pekinensis Rubra' are slightly deeper in color and a bit smaller and plants develop a much larger seed capsule. It is free blooming and may be used in any size pool.

Nelumbo 'Perry's Giant Sunburst' Perry D. Slocum 1987. Parentage: *N. nucifera* 'Alba Plena' × *N. lutea*. Plate 423.

PETAL COLOR: Cream; outer petals pale green. *R.H.S. Chart*: Fan 1, Green-Yellow Group, No. 1D; outer petals, Fan 3, Yellow-Green Group, No. 149D. Seed capsule color: Yellow then lime-yellow; green rim then all-green capsule. *R.H.S. Chart*: Fan 1, Yellow Group, No. 11A, then Fan 3, Yellow-Green Group, No. 149D; rim, same No. 149D. Flower size: 10–13.5 in (25–34 cm). Fragrance: Pleasant. Number of petals: 24–25. Leaf size: 16–18 in (40–45 cm). Plant height: 4.5–5.5 ft (1.4–1.7 m).

COMMENTS: The huge flowers of 'Perry's Giant Sunburst' create a magnificent display. A rich, creamy color, they are raised high above the leaves.

This lotus is very free flowering and is an excellent choice for pools of any size.

Nelumbo **'Perry's Super Star'** Perry D. Slocum 1988. Parentage: Seedling of *N.* 'Mrs. Perry D. Slocum'. Plates 424–426.

Petal color: First day, rich pink; second day, mostly yellow; third day, mostly cream with some pink tips; 6–8 center petals (petaloids) tipped green, paling slightly. *R.H.S. Chart*: Fan 2, Red-Purple Group, No. 63D, then Fan 1, Yellow Group, No. 11C then 11D. Green tips, Fan 3, Blue-Green Group, Nos. 149C and 142A, then Green Group, No. 142C. Pink tips, Fan 2, Red-Purple Group, No. 63D then 65C. Seed capsule color: Yellow then chartreuse. *R.H.S. Chart*: Fan 1, Yellow Group, No. 11A, then Fan 3, Green Group, No. 142A. Flower size: 7–8 in (18–20 cm). Fragrance: Very sweet, aniselike. Number of petals: 75, including petaloids. Leaf size: 17–21 in (43–53 cm). Plant height: 3–4 ft (1–1.2 m).

Comments: This is a new changeable cultivar with an impressive color pattern. The color changes dramatically over three days, and the blooms are beautiful in each phase. The six to eight green-tipped petals at the flower center make this lotus unique. Known as petaloids, these smaller petals occur near the center of double flowers, always with an anther at the tip. This free-blooming cultivar is an excellent choice for pools of any size.

Nelumbo **'Rosea Plena'**. Double rose lotus. Parentage: Unknown. Plate 427.

Petal color: Very deep rose-pink, yellowing toward base. *R.H.S. Chart*: Fan 2, Red-Purple Group, No. 58D; base ⅓, Fan 1, Yellow Group, No. 11C. Seed capsule color: Yellow then green. *R.H.S. Chart*: Fan 1, Yellow Group, No. 6C, then Fan 3, Yellow-Green Group, No. 149D. Flower size: 10–13 in (25–33 cm). Fragrance: None. Number of petals: 89–102, including petaloids. Leaf size: 18–20 in (45–50 cm). Plant height: 4–5 ft (1.2–1.5 m); in rich soil plants may reach 6 ft (2 m).

Comments: The double rose lotus is a very free-flowering plant. With its huge, richly colored double blooms it is among the most striking of lotus cultivars. A distinguishing feature is the small seed capsule, only 1 in (2.5 cm) across. I highly recommend this impressive lotus for medium and large pools.

Nelumbo **'Sharon'** Perry D. Slocum 1987. Parentage: *N. nucifera* 'Alba Plena' × *N.* 'Momo Botan'. Plate 428.

Petal color: Pink, deepening; pink veins. *R.H.S. Chart*: Fan 2, Red-Purple Group, No. 64D then Nos. 65A–B; veins, No. 64C. Seed capsule color: Yellow; rim pale green. *R.H.S. Chart*: Fan 1, Yellow Group, No. 11A; rim, Green-Yellow Group, No. 1C. Flower size: 8 in (20 cm). Fragrance: Slight. Number of petals: 80, including petaloids. Leaf size: 12–14 in (30–35 cm). Plant height: 4 ft (1.2 m).

Comments: 'Sharon', with its double blossoms and the free-blooming habit of 'Momo Botan', is a lotus I recommend highly for pools of any size. It resembles 'Momo Botan' somewhat but is taller with larger flowers. It is named after my oldest daughter, who worked with lotuses and water lilies for many years at the Slocum Water Gardens.

Nelumbo **'Suzanne'** Perry D. Slocum 1988. Parentage: Seedling of *N.* 'Alba Striata'. Plate 429.

Petal color: Medium pink, darker pink stripes. *R.H.S. Chart*: Fan 1, Red Group, No. 38C; stripes, Fan 2, Red-Purple Group, No. 62A. Seed capsule color: Yellow, green rim; by third day, rim color develops throughout. *R.H.S. Chart*: Fan 1, Yellow Group, No. 5A; rim, Fan 3, Yellow-Green Group, No. 150C. Flower size: 6–8 in (15–20 cm). Fragrance: Delightful. Number of petals: 22. Leaf size: 15–20 in (38–50 cm). Plant height: 4–5 ft (1.2–1.5 m).

Comments: Flowers of 'Suzanne' are a rare combination of medium pink petals overlaid with darker stripes, and the effect is very pleasing. I recommend it for pools of any size. It is named in honor of my youngest daughter, who worked with lotuses and water lilies for many years at the Slocum Water Gardens.

Nelumbo **'The Queen'** Perry D. Slocum 1984. Parentage: *N.* 'Alba Striata' × *N. lutea*. Plate 430.

Petal color: Cream; outer petals green. *R.H.S. Chart*: Fan 1, Yellow Group, No. 4D; outer petals, Fan 3, Green Group, No. 139D. Seed capsule color: Yellow then green. *R.H.S. Chart*: Fan 1, Yellow Group, No. 11A, then Fan 3, Green Group, No. 139D. Flower size: 10 in (25 cm). Fragrance: Very pleasant in first-day flower. Number of petals: 21. Leaf size: 14–23 in (35–58 cm). Plant height: 4–5 ft (1.2–1.5 m).

Comments: 'The Queen' is a hybrid developed at Perry's Water Gardens in North Carolina. The blooms are held unusually high, 16–18 in (40–45 cm) above the leaves. Its very free-blooming habit makes this lotus a fine choice for pools of any size.

Chapter 18

Other Genera of the Water Lily Family

This chapter covers the five remaining genera of the water lily family: *Nuphar, Victoria, Euryale, Barclaya,* and *Ondinea*. Linnaeus originally classified *Nuphar* as *Nymphaea*, and indeed these two genera have many similarities. *Victoria* and *Euryale* too share many similar characteristics, while *Barclaya* and *Ondinea* have only a slight resemblance.

THE GENUS *NUPHAR*

The genus *Nuphar* (spatterdock, yellow pond lily, yellow cow lily) was at one time thought to include 26 species, as presented by Henkel, Rehnelt, and Dittman in their 1907 study, *Das Buch der Nymphaeaceen oder Seerosengewächse*. In 1956 Dr. Ernest O. Beal reduced the genus to two species, *N. japonica* and *N. lutea* (with nine subspecies). His study was intensive, covering the entire *Nuphar* field (he examined 4000 specimens), and I accept it as the primary authority. Although Dr. Beal discusses *N. japonica* only briefly, he gives extensive coverage to the American and European *N. lutea* and its subspecies. His findings are further discussed under *N. lutea*.

As nuphars are quite different in floral structure from water lilies and lotuses (Figure 69), different categories are required to describe them. *Nuphar lutea* subsp. *macrophylla* grows in central Florida, and I have been able to give it very careful study and include in its description all the categories used for hardy water lilies.

For the other *Nuphar lutea* subspecies, I am concentrating on the traits that distinguish them from each other. Flower size, number of sepals, length of anthers, number of stigmatic rays, and shape of leaf and sinus are all such distinguishing traits. Sepal color, usually green and yellow for each subspecies, is omitted as a descriptive category. Likewise, petals, anthers, and stamens are generally yellow. Flower shape; fragrance; leaf color, size, and spread; and stem color cannot be considered suitable distinguishing characteristics.

Nuphars are not generally included in a water garden planting except perhaps by the rare plant collector. Hardiness zone information is not detailed. Furthermore, as nuphars are hardy perennials, there is no specific planting period other than spring and summer. In areas comparable to USDA zones 8–10, nuphars can be planted year-round.

Nuphars develop from thick rhizomes growing in mud in pond, lake, or stream bottoms in water up to 10 ft (3 m) deep. *Nuphar japonica* and *N. lutea* subsp. *sagittifolia* are exceptions, producing small rhizomes, and are suitable for aquarium use. Nuphars are day blooming at first, occasionally becoming day and night blooming.

Leaf shape varies from nearly round to lanceolate with overlapping to widely divergent lobes, smooth above and smooth to densely hairy on the underside. Leaves may be floating, emersed, or submerged. They

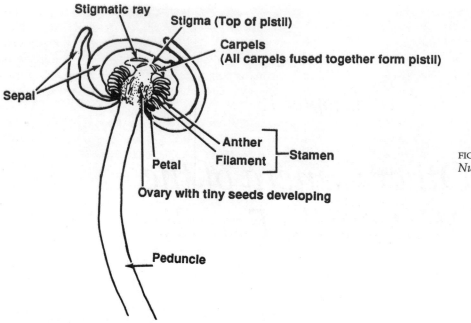

FIGURE 69. Cross section of a *Nuphar* flower.

are arranged spirally, with round, somewhat flattened or winged petioles at the base of a long sinus. Petioles and peduncles are smooth to densely pubescent.

Sepals, varying in number from 5 to 14, are greenish or yellow- or red-tinged. These are casually recognized as "petals" since they are the larger and more colorful parts of the flower. The actual petals are generally yellow, quite small, numerous, thick, and oblong or sometimes thin and spatulate. Petals are often notched, sometimes scalelike, and are located directly under the stamens. Stamens are numerous, yellow- or red-tinged, attached in spiral rows below the seed capsule, recurving, exposing anthers that are 0.05–0.4 in (0.1–1 cm) long. Carpels are fused together with few to many stigmatic rays. Flowers are borne just above water to several inches above water. Seed pods usually ripen above water.

Nuphar lutea was included by Linnaeus with white water lilies in the genus *Nymphaea*. Sibthorp & Smith designated the separate genus *Nuphar* in 1809. After examining both herbarium and living specimens, Dr. Beal says that a close morphological relationship exists among previously recognized North American and Eurasian species. He also says that plants are extremely variable and therefore advises recognizing only those forms associated with geographical or ecological features.

The subspecies of *Nuphar lutea* are separated and classified according to shape of fruit, variations in stigmatic disk, anthers, petals, number of sepals, and variations in leaves and petioles. The descriptions overlap in many instances, and there are many intermediate specimens showing a combination of features. As a result, any decision to assign an intermediate plant to a nearby subspecies is arbitrary. Plants intermediate between *N. lutea* subsp. *lutea* and *N. lutea* subsp. *pumila*, as well as between the latter and *N. lutea* subsp. *variegata*, are especially abundant in areas of overlap. Therefore they are not recognized as subspecies but as natural hybrids.

In the following descriptions common names, if any, follow the botanical name. Standardized color references are to the Royal Horticultural Society (R.H.S.) Color Chart. "Stamen color" refers to the coloring at the base of the stamen, known also as the filament. Note that "Leaf size" refers either to the diameter of the mature leaf or to the measurements of its length and width, in that order. "Leaf spread" is the amount of water surface covered by leaves.

Nuphar advena. See **N. lutea** subsp. **macrophylla.**

Nuphar japonica de Candolle. Japanese pond lily. Native to Japan. Characteristics: Day blooming, small finger-type rhizome, fairly free flowering, sepals moderately large, petals very small (hidden beneath anthers); develops both submerged and floating leaves, which become aerial in shallow water. Leaf color differs above and below water; both submerged and floating leaves smooth. Plate 431.

PETAL COLOR: Deep yellow. *R.H.S. Chart*: Fan 1, Yellow-Orange Group, No. 21C. Sepal color: On outside, deep green center surrounded with rich yellow changing to orange by second or third day and then to red. On inside, green at base with yellow above. *R.H.S. Chart*: On outside, green spot, Fan 3, Yellow-Green Group, Nos. 144D–B (darker in center); outside of green spot, Fan 1, Yellow Group, No. 11B, changing to Orange Group, No. 25A by second or third day and then to Orange-Red Group, No. 34B. *R.H.S. Chart*: Inside sepals, at base, Fan 3, Yellow-Green Group, No. 144D; yellow above green base of sepals: Fan 1, Yellow-Orange Group, No. 14B. Anther color: Yellowish orange. *R.H.S. Chart*: Fan 1, Yellow-Orange Group, No. 14C. Anther length: 0.2–0.4 in (0.5–1 cm). Stamen color: Yellowish orange. Flower shape: Cuplike. Flower size: 1–2 in (2.5–5 cm). Fragrance: None. Number of petals: 16–18. Number of sepals: 6 or 7. Number of stigmatic rays: Usually 12–13.

LEAF COLOR: Top, floating leaves reddish brown at first, turning to olive green; underside, same. Submerged leaves reddish purple on both sides. Leaf and sinus: Floating leaves heart-shaped, leathery; sinus open. Submerged leaves heart-shaped, thin, undulating. Leaf size: Floating leaves 4.5 × 3 in (11 × 8 cm); submerged leaves 3.5 × 2.5 in (9 × 6 cm). Leaf spread: 18–24 in (45–60 cm). Stem color: Peduncle bronzy green; petioles greenish, submerged petioles to submerged leaves reddish. Pubescence on peduncle or petiole: None.

COMMENTS: This species makes a very desirable aquarium plant with its yellow to orange to red blooms and red submerged leaves and small rhizome. Its small leaf spread also makes it an excellent choice for tub gardens or small pools.

Nuphar lutea **subsp.** *lutea* Beal. Native to Eurasia; throughout Europe except the far north, south to Algeria, Palestine, Iran, eastward in central Asia to southern Siberia and Manchuria. Found growing in ponds, lakes, and slow-moving streams. Characteristics: Day blooming, exposed leaves floating, petiole more or less flattened, petals thin and broadly spatulate, most longer than stamens. Fruit displays a narrowly constricted neck below the notched stigmatic disk.

PETAL COLOR: Yellow. Anther length: 0.1–0.4 in (0.3–1 cm). Flower shape: Cuplike. Flower size: 1.25–2.5 in (3–6 cm). Number of sepals: 5. Number of stigmatic rays: 5–28. Leaf and sinus: Leaf egg-shaped, lobes close or overlapping; sinus usually closed.

COMMENTS: In the average water garden I see no future for this plant. In the plant's native areas fish farmers may find this plant provides fine coverage.

Nuphar lutea **subsp.** *macrophylla* (Small) Beal [*N. advena* (Aiton) Aiton f.]. American spatterdock. Native to North and Central America, Cuba; eastern United States, southern Maine west to southern Wisconsin, south to northeastern Mexico. Found growing in ponds, lakes, sluggish streams, marshes, swamps, ditches, and canals. Characteristics: Day blooming, thick, fleshy, frequently branching, long rhizome, fairly free flowering, sepals large, many leaves carried above water. Plate 432.

PETAL COLOR: Deep yellow, underside tipped orange. *R.H.S. Chart*: Fan 1, Yellow Group, No. 13B; tips, Orange Group, No. 24B. Sepal color: Outer three, deep green; inner three mostly deep yellow, patch of deep green same color of outer sepals. *R.H.S. Chart*: Outer three, Fan 3, Yellow-Green Group, No. 144A; inner, Fan 1, Yellow Group, No. 12A. Anther color: Deep yellow. *R.H.S. Chart*: Fan 1, Yellow Group, No. 12A. Anther length: 0.2–0.4 in (0.5–1 cm). Stamen color: Yellow. Flower shape: Cuplike. Flower size: 2–2.5 in (5–6 cm). Fragrance: None. Number of petals: 20. Number of sepals: 6. Number of stigmatic rays: 5–18.

LEAF COLOR: Top, green, new leaves bronzy brown, red spot at petiole; underside, green, new leaves yellowish green. Leaf and sinus: Leaf egg-shaped; sinus usually wide open. Leaf size: 14.5 × 10 in (37 × 25 cm). Leaf spread: 5–8 ft (1.5–2.5 m). Stem color: Bright green. Pubescence on peduncle or petiole: None.

COMMENTS: *Nuphar lutea* subsp. *macrophylla*, compared to the water lily *Nymphaea odorata*, has several drawbacks for water garden use. Blooms are small relative to leaf size, flowers are not scented, leaves rise up out of the water, sometimes hiding the blooms, and a deeper water depth of 4–6 ft (1.2–2 m) is required for optimum growth. Due to its large leaf spread and small blooms, I recommend it only for collectors or for use by fish farmers for coverage.

Nuphar lutea **subsp.** *orbiculata* (Small) Beal. Native to North America, United States; south central and southwestern Georgia, north central Florida. Found growing in acidic pools and ponds. Characteristics: Day blooming, exposed leaves floating, densely pubescent underneath, petiole round. Fruit slightly constricted below a round to irregularly scalloped stigmatic disk. Stigmatic disk green, yellow, or sometimes tinged red.

PETAL COLOR: Yellow. Anther length: 0.2–0.4 in (0.5–1 cm). Flower shape: Cuplike. Flower size: 1.5–2.5 in (4–6 cm). Number of sepals: 6. Number of stigmatic rays: 12–28. LEAF COLOR: Green. Leaf and sinus: Leaves round to egg-shaped; thick, leathery, rounded lobes may or may not overlap at sinus; submerged leaves similar yet thin, flaccid. Sinus may or may not be open. Pubescence on peduncle or petiole: Yes.

COMMENTS: Probable best use is for fish farmers for coverage.

Nuphar lutea **subsp.** *ozarkana* (Miller & Standley) Beal. Native to North America, United States; Ozark region of Missouri and northwestern Arkansas. Found growing in ponds, lakes, and slow-moving streams. Characteristics: Day blooming, exposed leaves usually floating. Differs from *N. lutea* subsp. *variegata* in having round petioles. Differs from the highly variable *N. lutea* subsp. *macrophylla* in leaf shape and presence of red pigmentation in sepals and fruit.

PETAL COLOR: Yellow. Anther length: 0.2–0.4 in (0.5–1 cm). Flower shape: Cuplike. Flower size: 2–2.5 in (5–6 cm). Number of sepals: 6. Number of stigmatic rays: 5–18. Leaf and sinus: Leaves oblong to egg-shaped to roundish; lobes close or nearly parallel; sinus slightly open.

COMMENTS: This plant is not usually sought by water gardeners due to its small blooms relative to leaf size. It could conceivably provide good coverage for fish in a lake or fish farm.

Nuphar lutea **subsp.** *polysepala* (Engelmann) Beal. Native to North America; Alaska southward along the Pacific Coast and Sierra Nevada range to San Luis Obispo County, California, southeastward in the Rocky Mountains to northeastern Colorado and Utah. Found growing in ponds, lakes, streams. Characteristics: Day blooming, leaves usually floating, sometimes immersed. Petioles round. Filament often extending 0.05–0.2 in (0.1–0.5 cm) beyond the anther. Stigmatic disk round to deeply notched.

PETAL COLOR: Usually yellow, sometime tinged red. Anther color: Yellow to deep red-tinged. Anther length: 0.2–0.4 in (0.5–1 cm). Flower shape: Cuplike. Flower size: 3.5–5 in (9–13 cm). Number of sepals: 7–9. Number of stigmatic rays: 9–36, usually 20–25. Leaf and sinus: Leaves round to oblong, smooth; lobes rounded to acute, may or may not overlap. Sinus either closed or open.

COMMENTS: This plant could be used in mountain ponds too cold for water lilies to thrive.

Nuphar lutea **subsp.** *pumila* (Timm) Beal [*N. microphylla* Beal]. Native to North Temperate regions of northeastern North America, Europe, and Asia. Found growing in ponds, lakes, and streams. Characteristics: Day blooming, petals thin to thicker, broadly spatulate, sometimes thicker. Exposed leaves floating, sometimes only 1 in (2.5 cm) in diameter, underside varying from smooth to densely pubescent. Petioles vary from nearly round to angular near leaf. Fruit with narrowly constricted neck below a deeply dentate disk. Stigmatic disk yellow to red-tinged.

Anther length: 0.05–0.1 in (0.1–0.3 cm). Flower shape: Cuplike. Flower size: 0.6–1.25 in (1.5–3 cm). Number of sepals: Usually 5. Number of stigmatic rays: 5–14. Leaf and sinus: Leaves round or nearly round, lobes lined up close, sinus slightly open. Leaf size: 5.5 in (14 cm) or smaller.

COMMENTS: Though representatives of *Nuphar* from southeastern China and Japan appear to be closely related to *N. lutea* subsp. *pumila*, Dr. Beal states that a scarcity of material from southeastern China and Japan has prevented a determination of the position of those plants within the genus *Nuphar*.

Nuphar lutea **subsp.** *sagittifolia* (Walter) Beal. Cape Fear spatterdock. Native to North America, United States; Virginia, North Carolina, South Carolina. Found growing in rivers. Characteristics: Day blooming, leaves glabrous, exposed leaves floating, submerged leaves numerous, thin, translucent.

PETAL COLOR: Yellow. *R.H.S. Chart*: Fan 1, Yellow Group, No. 13A. Sepal color: Outer three, bright green; inner three, rich yellow. *R.H.S. Chart*: Outer sepals, Fan 3, Yellow-Green Group, No. 144A; inner sepals, Fan 1, Yellow Group, No. 12A. Anther color: Rich yellow. *R.H.S. Chart*: Fan 1, Yellow Group, No. 12A. Anther length: About 0.1 in (0.3 cm). Stamen color: Yellow. Flower shape: Cuplike. Flower size: 1 in (2.5 cm). Fragrance: Not noticeable. Number of petals: 16. Number of sepals: 6. Number of stigmatic rays: 12–18.

LEAF COLOR: Top, bright green; underside, yellowish green. Leaf and sinus: Leaves oblong to lanceolate; sinus not over 1.5 in (4 cm) deep. Leaf size: 6–16 × 2–4 in (15–40 × 5–10 cm); submerged leaves usually larger. Leaf spread: 24–30 in (60–75 cm). Stem color: Bright green.

COMMENTS: This subspecies has beautiful underwater leaves and is sold by the thousands to the aquarium trade. Its common name, Cape Fear spatterdock, comes from the fact that many of the plants are collected from the Cape Fear River, North Carolina. The blooms are too small to generate much interest as a pool plant, so I do not recommend it for the water garden.

Nuphar lutea **subsp.** *ulvacea* (Miller & Standley) Beal. Native to North America, United States; Blackwater River, western Florida. Found growing in freshwater rivers and streams. Characteristics: Day blooming, exposed leaves floating, smooth, submerged leaves numerous, thin, translucent. Stigmatic rays usually elliptical.

Anther length: About 0.1 in (0.3 cm). Flower shape: Cuplike. Flower size: 1–1.25 in (2.5–3 cm). Number of sepals: 6–9. Number of stigmatic rays: 9–12. Leaf and sinus: Leaves lanceolate; sinus ¼ length of leaf or less. Leaf size: 8–10 × 3–4 in (20–25 × 8–10 cm).

COMMENTS: Small flowers rule out this plant for pool use, but it should make an excellent aquarium plant due to its numerous submerged leaves. Because of its scarcity, however, it is rarely used in aquaria.

Nuphar lutea **subsp.** *variegata* (Engelmann) Beal. Native to North America; Yukon Territory and the Great Bear Lake to Newfoundland, south to western Montana, Nebraska, Iowa, northern Illinois, northern Ohio and Delaware; possibly in northwestern Arkansas and Kentucky. Found growing in ponds, lakes, and slow-moving streams. Characteristics: Day blooming, exposed leaves usually floating, smooth. Petiole flattened, winged. Fruit slightly constricted. Somewhat notched stigmatic disk, greenish, often tinged red.

Anther length: 0.2–0.4 in (0.5–1 cm). Flower shape: Cuplike. Flower size: 1.5–2.5 in (4–6 cm). Number of sepals: Usually 6. Number of stigmatic rays: 7–26. Leaf and sinus: Leaves oblong to round; lobes either close or overlapping; sinus either partly open or closed.

COMMENTS: I do not see any future for this small-bloomed plant in the water garden. Undoubtedly it provides good coverage for fish in lakes and ponds.

Nuphar microphylla. See *N. lutea* **subsp.** *pumila*.

THE GENUS *VICTORIA*

Victorias (giant water lilies, water platters), with their huge pie-plate–shaped leaves reaching 8 ft (2.5 m) in diameter and with blooms as large as 16 in (40 cm) across, are without doubt the queens of the water lily world. The gigantic pads can support the weight of a full-grown person if a thin plywood disk is placed on the leaf to distribute the weight evenly. These dramatic plants are worth going many miles to see. There are two species, both originating from South America. *Victoria amazonica* mostly grows along the Amazon River basin. This is the more tropical and tender of the two. *Victoria cruziana*, from Paraguay, Bolivia, and Argentina, is somewhat similar but hardier.

Patrick Nutt, foreman of aquatics and display greenhouses at Longwood Gardens, Kennett Square, Pennsylvania, hybridized these two species and came up with the beautiful 'Longwood Hybrid', which is far superior in terms of performance to either species.

Victorias have several distinguishing characteristics. First, nearly every part of the plant has sharp spines, including the underside of the pads, the stems, and the exterior of buds. The only exception to this general rule is that *Victoria cruziana* lacks spines on its sepals.

Second, the flowers, which change color from day to day, have a distinctive bloom pattern. First-day flowers are white, opening near nightfall and remaining open until late morning the following day. Second-day flowers are pink or reddish, or even purplish red in the case of 'Longwood Hybrid', and reopen in late afternoon. These second-day blooms fold their sepals and petals down and sink into the water during the night.

A third distinguishing trait is that the flowers (first-day blooms in particular) have a delightful, potent fragrance that can be detected from a distance of 15–20 ft (4.5–6 m).

Fourth, the leaves (pads) are unusual in that they develop heavy trusses with pronounced veining on the underside, and leaf edges are raised. The trusses, an underside support, develop 4–6 in (10–15 cm) vertically and about 0.5–1 in (1.3–2.5 cm) in thickness.

The raised leaf edges or rims give the leaves a somewhat grand pie-plate look. Rims are not present on young leaves and start forming after several increasingly large flat leaves have been produced. Such rims may be up to 8 in (20 cm) high in *Victoria cruziana*.

Two notches form on opposite sides in the tops of these verticle rims; the notch closest to the plant center is the deeper of the two. Since pads do not sink after a heavy rain, one theory is that these notches allow excess rainwater to drain out. Yet I have never observed the notches facilitating rainwater runoff. As the bottom of this notch is frequently 0.4–1.25 in (1–3 cm) above the surface level of the pad, I believe that rainwater dissipates by transmission through the pad.

These very large plants need at least 15 ft (4.5 m) of pool space. They grow best when water temperatures are 75°F (24°C) or above.

Victoria amazonica is much more tender than *V. cruziana* and *V.* 'Longwood Hybrid' and yet can be planted successfully at any time of the year in conservatories and greenhouses if water temperatures can be maintained at 85–90°F (29–32°C). Plant *V. cruziana* and 'Longwood Hybrid' in outside pools when water temperatures reach 65–70°F (18–21°C) or above. Refer to the hardiness zone maps in Appendix A and follow this general planting timetable:

IN NORTH AMERICA

Zone 10	late March/April, *V. cruziana*, *V.* 'Longwood Hybrid'; May, *V. amazonica*
Zone 9	May/June, *V. cruziana*, *V.* 'Longwood Hybrid'; late May/June, *V. amazonica*
Zone 8	May/June, *V. cruziana*, *V.* 'Longwood Hybrid'; late May/June, *V. amazonica*
Zone 7	25 May through 1 July, *V. cruziana*, *V.* 'Longwood Hybrid'; 10 June through 1 July, *V. amazonica*
Zone 6	1 June through 1 July, *V. cruziana*, *V.* 'Longwood Hybrid'; conservatory planting, *V. amazonica*
Zone 5	10 June though 10 July, *V. cruziana*, *V.* 'Longwood Hybrid'
Zone 4	heated or sheltered pools, where water will remain at correct temperature

IN EUROPE

Zone 10	May/June, *V. cruziana*, *V.* 'Longwood Hybrid'; June, *V. amazonica*
Zone 9	June, *V. cruziana*, *V.* 'Longwood Hybrid', in areas where water temperatures average 70°F (21°C) or above; conservatory planting, water temperature 85–90°F (29–32°C), *V. amazonica*
Zones 8–4	conservatory planting, water temperature 70°F (21°C) or above, *V. cruziana*, *V.* 'Longwood Hybrid'; conservatory planting, water temperature 85–90°F (29–32°C) or above, *V. amazonica*

In the following descriptions of *Victoria*, color references are to the Royal Horticultural Society (R.H.S.) Color Chart. Note that "Flower size" is a diameter measurement, "Leaf size" refers to the diameter of a mature leaf, and "Leaf spread" is the area on the water's surface covered by all the leaves of a mature plant.

Victoria amazonica (Poeppig) Sowerby [*V. regia* Lindley]. Giant water lily, Amazon water lily. Native to the Amazon River region of Brazil, Guiana, Bolivia. Characteristics: Night blooming, nonviviparous, very free flowering in warm climates; propagates by seed, seeds elliptical; smooth, sharp spines on all stems, on underside of leaves, outside of rims, and outer surface of sepals. Plates 42, 433–436.

PETAL COLOR: Creamy white then pink. *R.H.S. Chart*: Fan 4, Yellow-White Group, No. 158D; second day, Fan 1, Red Group, No. 37D. Sepal color: Creamy white then yellow, flushed pink. *R.H.S. Chart*: Fan 4, Yellow-White Group, No. 158D; second day, Fan 1, Yellow Group, No. 8C; flush, Red Group, No. 38D. Anther color: Pink. *R.H.S. Chart*: Fan 2, Red-Purple Group, No. 63B. Stamen color: White then pink. Flower shape: Very full, double. Flower size: 9–12 in (23–30 cm). Fragrance: Strong, pineapplelike. Number of petals: 58. Number of sepals: 4.

LEAF COLOR: Top, yellowish green, rim exterior pink, veined red; underside, reddish purple. Leaf and sinus: Leaves round, initially flat, rim developing, 3–6 in (8–15 cm) in height, exterior sharply spined; leaf undersides sharply spined. No true

sinus. Leaf size: 4–6 ft (1.2–2 m). Leaf spread: 15–20 ft (4.5–6 m), somewhat smaller when crowded. Stem color: Brownish green. Pubescence on peduncle or petiole: None.

COMMENTS: *Victoria amazonica* is the plant that Paxton brought to flower and much acclaim at Chatsworth, England, in the mid-19th century. As *V. amazonica* requires a water temperature of 85–90°F (29–32°C), Paxton had a special conservatory and tank built in order to grow it. High winds may severely damage pads. Leaves also tend to become distorted when grown in crowded conditions. In northern latitudes this plant is suited only for a large, warm, heated pool in a conservatory or greenhouse.

Victoria cruziana d'Orbigny. Santa Cruz water lily. Native to Paraguay, northern Argentina, Bolivia. Characteristics: Night blooming, nonviviparous, very free blooming; propagates by seed, seeds round or spherical, seed surface rough; short, sharp spines on all stems, underside of leaves, outside of rims, but none on sepals. Plate 437; Figure 70.

PETAL COLOR: Creamy white then pink. *R.H.S. Chart*: Fan 1, White Group, No. 155A; second day,

Red Group, No. 56C. Sepal color: Creamy white then pink. *R.H.S. Chart*: Fan 1, White Group, No. 155A; second day, Red Group, No. 56C. Anther color: Pink. *R.H.S. Chart*: Fan 2, Red-Purple Group, No. 63B. Stamen color: White then pink. Flower shape: Full, double. Flower size: 9–11 in (23–28 cm). Fragrance: Strong, pineapplelike. Number of petals: 65. Number of sepals: 4.

LEAF COLOR: Top, yellowish green, rim exterior green, veined red; new leaves rim exterior veined pinkish; underside, violet-purple. Leaf and sinus: Leaves round, rims 5–8 in (13–20 cm) high, frequently flared; no true sinus. Leaf size: 4–5.5 ft (1.2–1.7 m). Leaf spread: 15–18 ft (4.5–5.5 m). Stem color: Bronzy green. Pubescence on peduncle or petiole: None.

COMMENTS: *Victoria cruziana* is slightly less free flowering than *V. amazonica*, usually producing two or three new blooms weekly once blooming begins. *V. cruziana* is probably a more practical choice than *V. amazonica* for northern water gardeners, as it will take 10–15°F (9–12°C) more cold. It grows well in warm climates either in pools or conservatories. *V.*

cruziana needs water temperatures of at least 65–70°F (18–21°C). Optimum water temperatures are 75–90°F (24–32°C).

Victoria 'Longwood Hybrid' Patrick Nutt 1961. Parentage: *V. cruziana* × *V. amazonica*. Characteristics: Night blooming, nonviviparous, free flowering; stout sharp purple, black, or brown spines on all stems, on underside of leaves, on outside of rims, and on outside of sepals; seeds globose, 0.3 in (0.8 cm) long, seed surface rough. Plates 438–440.

PETAL COLOR: White then rose-pink or purplish. *R.H.S. Chart*: Fan 4, White Group, No. 155A; second day, Fan 2, Red-Purple Group, No. 63A. Sepal color: White then rosy pink. *R.H.S. Chart*: Fan 4, White Group, No. 155A; second day, Fan 2, Red-Purple Group, No. 62C. Anther color: Rose-pink. *R.H.S. Chart*: Fan 2, Red-Purple Group, No. 63A. Stamen color: White then pink. Flower shape: Huge, round, full. Flower size: 10–16 in (25–40 cm). Fragrance: Very wonderful, pineapplelike. Number of petals: 73–75. Number of sepals: 4.

LEAF COLOR: Top, yellowish green, rim exterior

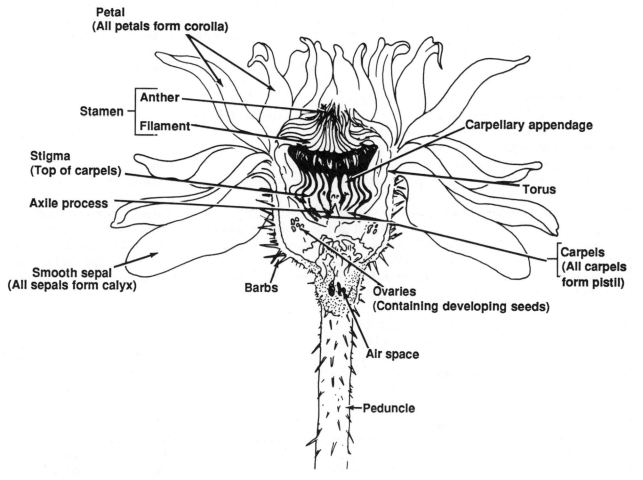

FIGURE 70. Cross section of a *Victoria cruziana* flower.

red, spiny; underside, purple, spiny. Leaf and sinus: Leaves round, initially flat, 2.5–4 in (6–10 cm) rim developing; no true sinus. Leaf size: 4–8 ft (1.2–2.5 m). Leaf spread: 12–40 ft (3.5–12 m). Stem color: Greenish brown. Pubescence on peduncle or petiole: None.

COMMENTS: 'Longwood Hybrid' is a true giant among aquatic plants and in many respects is superior to its parents. Increased vigor is reflected in its larger pads, better ability to withstand higher winds and lower water and air temperatures, its flowering 3 to 11 days earlier, and producing 11 to 16 more flowers in a season. Blooms open earlier in the evening, and once the plant begins to bloom there is a new blossom every second or third day.

On large leaves, trusses can be several inches in height under the center of the pad. Spines, characteristic of *Victoria*, develop on the outside of sepals and flowers as well as on stems. Hybrid seeds germinate quite readily once water temperature nears 70°F (21°C). Most seed propagation is done at Longwood Gardens though other sources are now available. 'Longwood Hybrid' requires a growing area at least 12 ft (3.5 m) wide, so is appropriate only for large, warm pools and conservatories.

'Longwood Hybrid' was crossed on 17 September 1960 at 9:30 p.m., eastern daylight saving time, by Patrick Nutt, Longwood Gardens. Mr. Nutt used a first-day bloom from *V. cruziana* as the seed parent and a second-day bloom from *V. amazonica* as the pollen parent. (The reverse scenario did not produce viable seed.) The first seed was collected on 25 October 1960 and stored moist for 12 weeks—six weeks in moist sand at 65°F (18°C) and six weeks in water at 50°F (10°C). 'Longwood Hybrid' first flowered in 1961.

THE GENUS *EURYALE*

The genus *Euryale* (prickly water lily, Gorgon plant) has a single species, *Euryale ferox*, originating in tropical East Africa, Southeast Asia, and China. A perennial in warm climates, it is cultivated in the same manner as the victorias. The leaves, which float on the water surface, are large, spiny, and veined, somewhat similar to those of *Victoria* but lacking rimmed edges. Plants have sharp spines on the exterior surface of the sepals, on the stems, and on both sides of the leaves. Neither the pads nor the flowers are considered as attractive as those of the victorias.

In its native habitat people highly prize *Euryale ferox* as part of the diet, sometimes baking the pea-sized starchy seeds, known as fox nuts. In Japan the young stems and the roots are eaten as vegetables. The Chinese reputedly have cultivated *E. ferox* for 3000 years.

Large botanic gardens in the United States, such as the Missouri Botanical Garden and Longwood Gardens, usually have one of these unusual plants on display. I have also seen one growing in a conservatory at Kew Gardens in London. I am always impressed by the large purple-veined leaves covered with spines and the deep violet flowers. *Euryale* plants are not widely available, and I know of no listing in any commercial aquatic nursery. A few commercial water gardens do have them for sale, however, even though they do not list them.

Plant *Euryale ferox* outside when water temperature averages 75°F (24°C) or above. Optimum water temperature range is 70–80°F (21–27°C). For maximum bloom number, set planter about 3–10 in (8–25 cm) below the water surface. I have seen plants bloom in 3 ft (1 m) of water in a natural pond in North Carolina (USDA zone 7), but they seem to come into flower later when grown in deeper water. Seeds germinate readily if they have not been allowed to dry out during storing or shipping. Refer to the hardiness zone maps in Appendix A and follow this general planting timetable:

IN NORTH AMERICA
Zone 10	late March/April
Zone 9	April/May
Zone 8	late May/June
Zone 7	25 May through 1 July
Zone 6	1 June through 1 July
Zone 5	10 June through 10 July
Zone 4	heated or sheltered pools, where water temperatures average 75°F (24°C) or above

IN EUROPE
Zone 10	May/June

Zone 9   late May/June, where water temperatures average 75°F (24°C) or above
Zones 8–4   conservatory planting, where water can be heated to 75°F (24°C) or above

Euryale ferox Salisbury. Prickly water lily, Gorgon plant. Native to tropical East Africa, Southeast Asia, China. Characteristics: Day blooming, nonviviparous, fairly free flowering; sharp spines on all stems, both sides of leaves, and on outside of sepals; propagates readily from seed. Plates 441–443; Figure 71.

PETAL COLOR: Inside row, white; outer rows, deep violet. *R.H.S. Chart*: Fan 4, White Group, No. 155D; outer, Fan 2, Violet Group, Nos. 86B–C. Sepal color: Reddish purple. *R.H.S. Chart*: Fan 2, Red-Purple Group, No. 70A. Anther color: Yellow. *R.H.S. Chart*: Fan 1, Yellow Group, No. 3C. Stamen color: White. Flower shape: Cuplike. Flower size: 1.5–3 in (4–8 cm). Fragrance: Slight. Number of petals: 23–24. Number of sepals: 4.

LEAF COLOR: Top, dark green, numerous purple-red veins, purple barbs; underside, purple-violet, numerous purple barbs. Leaf and sinus: Leaf nearly round, sharply barbed, purple-red veins, small bulges over surface. Leaf edge indented (usually rounded) 0.25–1 in (0.6–2.5 cm) toward plant center. Occasional sinus, 1 in (2.5 cm). Leaf size: 4–5 ft (1.2–1.5 m). Leaf spread: 10–15 ft (3–4.5 m). Stem color: Burgundy-red. Pubescence on peduncle or petiole: None.

COMMENTS: I find this plant to be an attractive

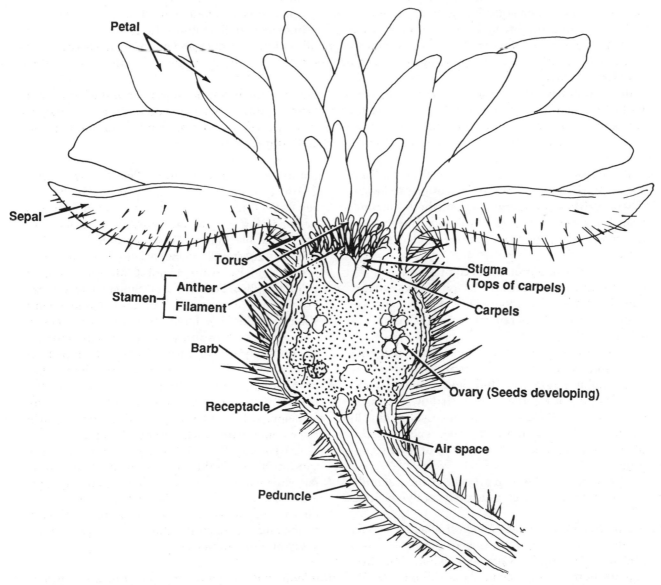

FIGURE 71. Cross section of a *Euryale ferox* flower.

addition to the medium and large water garden. For maximum growth *E. ferox* needs a growing area 8–15 ft (2.5–4.5 m) with 3–8 in (8–20 cm) of water over the planter. I have seen this plant adapt to a 5–8 ft (1.5–2.5 m) wide space and produce blooms. In the larger area, however, flowers are double the size of those grown in the smaller area, with two to three blooms produced at a time. Although I have seen many blooms develop with only 1–2 in (2.5–5 cm) of water over the planter, a depth of 3–8 in (8–20 cm) allows maximum bloom formation. This species is easily propagated from seed. It is very important that seed be stored moist.

THE GENUS *BARCLAYA*

The genus *Barclaya* is named in honor of G. W. Barclay, English gardener and plant collector. *Barclaya* plants develop from egg-shaped tubers that produce short runners and a basal leaf rosette. Plants require water temperatures of 78°F (26°C) or above. As such it is not suitable for pools or outdoor culture in either North America or Europe, but it can be planted in aquaria or deep tanks as long as the water temperature requirement can be maintained. Since all leaves are submerged, *Barclaya* makes a desirable show plant for aquarium use.

Leaves are wavy, linear, narrow toward the apex, blunt, up to 20 in (50 cm) long and 1.5 in (4 cm) wide, though smaller when aquarium grown. Upperside of leaf is olive green, usually with darker diagonal lines; underside is reddish green. Under optimum growing conditions the stellate flower bud comes to the top of the water to open. Under less than ideal conditions the buds will stay underwater and remain closed. Flowers have four or five divided sepals and eight or more petals. See Figure 72 for a representative cross section of a *Barclaya* flower.

In the following descriptions, note that "Flower size" is either a diameter measurement or the length and width, in that order, of the bloom. "Leaf size" is the length and width, in that order, of a submerged mature leaf, and "Leaf spread" is the diameter of the underwater leaf growth of a mature plant. Color references to the R.H.S. chart are omitted since I have not been able to make direct comparisons.

Barclaya kunstleri (King) Ridley [*B. motleyi* var. *kunstleri* King]. Native to Singapore, western Malaysia. Characteristics: Submerged aquatic herb, rhizome branching, petiole 6 in (15 cm) long, flowers submerged or emergent depending on depth of stream. Figure 73.

PETAL COLOR: Claret. Sepal color: Green. Anther color: White. Stamen color: Claret. Flower shape: Cuplike. Flower size: 1 × 2 in (2.5 × 5 cm). Fragrance: Slight to none. Number of petals: 12–15. Number of sepals: 5.

LEAF COLOR: Top, dark olive green, magenta dots; underside, magenta. Leaf and sinus: Leaves ovate to elliptic, glabrous, thin, apex rounded to obtuse, base usually cordate; sinus shallow. Leaf size: 3.5 × 2.5–2.75 in (9 × 6–7 cm). Leaf spread: 12 in (30 cm). Stem color: Light brown to white. Pubescence on peduncle or petiole: Occasional short fuzz on peduncle.

COMMENTS: This is a rare species of the water lily family and seldom seen outside its native habitat.

Barclaya longifolia Wallich [*Hydrostemma longifolium* (Wallich) Mabberley]. Native to Southeast Asia (Burma, Thailand, Malaysia). Characteristics: Aquatic herb with egg-shaped tuber about 1–1.25 × 0.5–0.75 in (2.5–3 × 1.3–2 cm), short runners, new plants develop at runner tips. Petiole length varies 2–3 in (5–8 cm), peduncle 12–16 in (30–40 cm), sepals 0.4–1 in (1–2.5 cm), flowers either emerging or remaining as buds under water. Plate 444; Figure 74; see also Figure 37 in Chapter 6.

PETAL COLOR: Claret. Sepal color: Greenish pink, green near base. Anther color: Claret-pink. Stamen color: Purplish. Flower shape: Stellate. Flower size: 1–3 × 1.5 in (2.5–8 × 4 cm). Fragrance: None or very slight. Number of petals: 8–10. Number of sepals: 5.

LEAF COLOR: Top, brownish green, darker diagonal lines; underside, purple. Leaf and sinus: Leaf long, wavy, straplike, base cordate, apex blunt, lobes rounded; sinus not present. Leaf size: Up to 20 × 1–3 in (50 × 2.5–8 cm); average length 6–12 in (15–30 cm). Leaf spread: 2–3 ft (0.6–1 m). Stem color: Brownish. Pubescence on peduncle or petiole: None.

COMMENTS: *Barclaya longifolia* can make a fine specimen plant for the large aquarium. It requires a fairly deep tank, 18 in (45 cm) or deeper, a temperature of approximately 78–85°F (26–29°C), and plenty of nutrients. It is not a desirable pool plant. Propagate it by dividing the young slips that develop on short runners.

Barclaya motleyi Hooker f. [*Hydrostemma motleyi* (Hooker f.) Mabberley]. Native to Sumatra, Borneo,

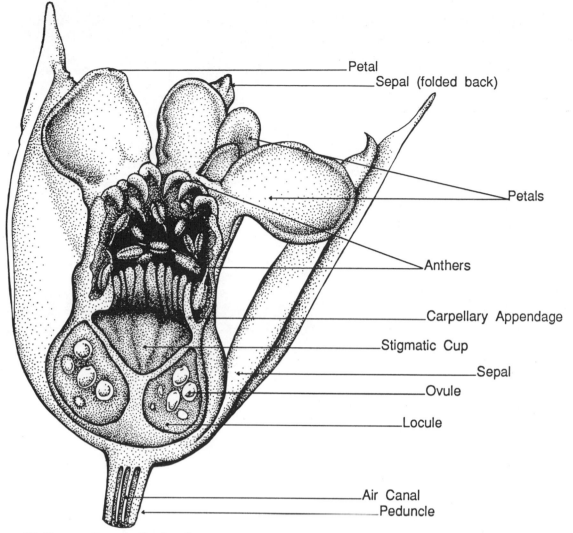

FIGURE 72. Cross section of a *Barclaya* flower.

New Guinea; sea level to 5000 ft (1525 m). Found growing in shallow (often muddy) pools and (often gravelly) streams. Characteristics: Egg-shaped tuber similar to that of *B. longifolia*, petiole usually 2.75–6.5 in (7–16 cm) long, peduncle 2–5.5 in (5–14 cm) long; flowers emergent. Sepals 1–1.75 in (2.5–4.5 cm) long, woolly yellow-brown or gray hairs on exterior surface; anthers oblong, curving in and down. Dense pubescence on lower blade surface. Figure 75.

PETAL COLOR: Pink to red. Sepal color: Green. Anther color: Yellow. Stamen color: Yellow. Flower shape: Stellate. Flower size: 1.5 × 3 in (4 × 8 cm). Fragrance: None or slight. Number of petals: 8–20. Number of sepals: 4–5.

LEAF COLOR: Top, olive green, tinted reddish pink; underside, green. Leaf and sinus: Leaf widely obovate, sometimes oblong, apex rounded, base cordate; no sinus present. Leaf size: 2.75–6.5 × 1.25–5.5 in (7–16 × 3–14 cm). Leaf spread: 24 in (60 cm).

Stem color: Brownish. Pubescence on peduncle or petiole: Yes.

COMMENTS: *Barclaya motleyi* is rarely available to the aquarium plant trade in the United States. I have contacted three of the largest growers and importers of rare aquarium plants and they do not know of anybody importing it. Occasionally Florida Aquatic Nurseries or Suwannee Laboratories (see Appendix B) has *B. motleyi*. It is not a desirable pool plant, however, due to its high water-temperature requirements of 78–85°F (26–29°C).

Barclaya rotundifolia Hotta. Native to Sarawak (Malaysia). Characteristics: Tuber resembles a small *Nuphar* rhizome, petioles thick, 2.75–6 in (7–15 cm) long, peduncles 2–5 in (5–13 cm) long, sepals 1–1.75 in (2.5–4.5 cm), round leaves have dense, short pubescence on underside. Figure 76.

PETAL COLOR: Pink to claret. Sepal color: Green. Anther color: Claret to yellow. Stamen color: Claret

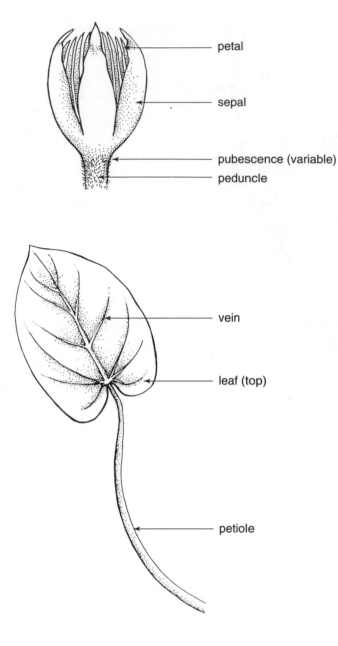

petal

sepal

pubescence (variable)

peduncle

vein

leaf (top)

petiole

FIGURE 73. *Barclaya kunstleri*, flower and leaf.

to yellow. Flower shape: Cuplike. Flower size: 2–3 in (5–8 cm). Fragrance: Slight. Number of petals: 4–5. Number of sepals: 5.

LEAF COLOR: Top, glossy green; underside, light green. Leaf and sinus: Round leaf, base deeply cordate; lobes overlap at sinus. Leaf size: 2.5–3.5 in (6–9 cm). Leaf spread: 2–3 ft (0.6–1 m). Stem color: Red-

dish brown to brown. Pubescence on peduncle or petiole: Thick short fuzz on both.

COMMENTS: *Barclaya rotundifolia* is rare in its native habitat. Partially due to this scarcity, it does not seem to have a commercial future for either aquarium or water garden use.

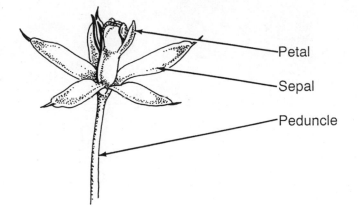

Petal

Sepal

Peduncle

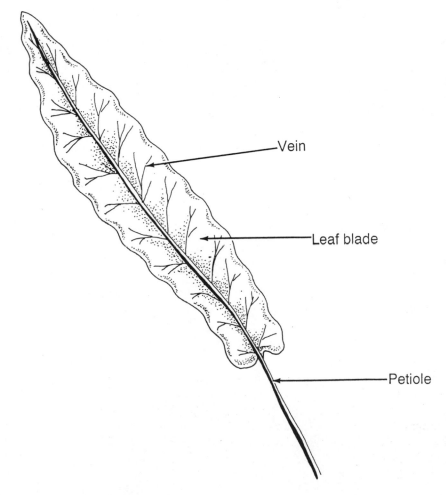

Vein

Leaf blade

Petiole

FIGURE 74. *Barclaya longifolia*, flower and leaf.

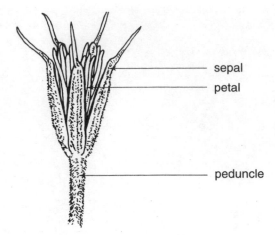

sepal

petal

peduncle

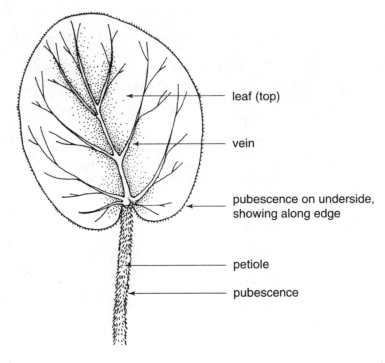

FIGURE 75. *Barclaya motleyi*, flower and leaf.

leaf (top)

vein

pubescence on underside,
showing along edge

petiole

pubescence

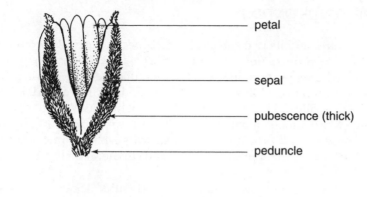

— petal

— sepal

— pubescence (thick)

— peduncle

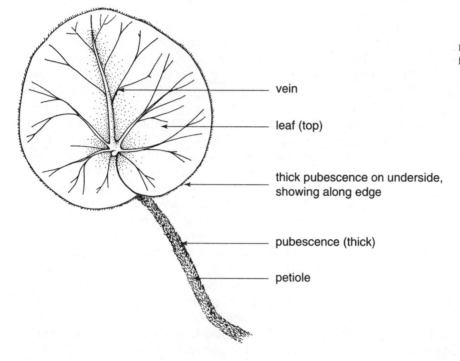

— vein

— leaf (top)

— thick pubescence on underside, showing along edge

— pubescence (thick)

— petiole

FIGURE 76. *Barclaya rotundifolia*, flower and leaf.

THE GENUS *ONDINEA*

The genus *Ondinea* is represented by *O. purpurea* and its two subspecies. Subspecies *purpurea* produces flowers without petals, while subspecies *petaloidea* produces flowers with petals. *Ondinea* is native to the remote Kimberley District of Western Australia, where the aborigines consider its tubers edible. During the winter dry season (June through November) the thumb-sized tubers can be found lodged in the sand of dry streambeds. The streambed soil is composed principally of sand, with 10 to 30 percent humus. With the onset of the summer wet season (December through May), tubers initiate growth. The tubers, about 1 in (2.5 cm) long and 0.5 in (1.3 cm) thick, are roundish, brown, with protruding wartlike scars where former leaves, roots, and flowers were attached (Plate 445). Initially the tuber produces roots and submerged, thin, translucent leaves with wavy, undulating margins.

In the following descriptions standardized color references are to the Royal Horticultural Society (R.H.S.) Color Chart. "Leaf size" is the length and width, in that order, of the leaf of the mature plant. "Leaf spread" is the area covered by the leaves of the mature plant either on the water's surface or underwater.

Ondinea purpurea Hartog 1970. Native to the Kimberley District, Western Australia; found growing in sun or partial shade in small, clear sandstone streams in a water depth of 1–5 ft (0.3–1.5 m), with a water temperature usually above 78°F (26°C). Characteristics: Day blooming, flowers with petals.

PETAL COLOR: Blue-violet to purple-pink. Flowers bloom for three consecutive days and are solitary and held above the water. On the first day a small quantity of weak sugar solution develops in the stigmatic cup in the flower center. Major insect pollinators are small *Trigona* bees. Pollen is shaken from the anthers and transported to the pool of nectar on the stigmatic disk, thereby achieving pollination. Numerous small brown seeds are produced from fleshy fruits. Field observations indicate that germination and tuber formation occur before the arrival of the dry season. No field data exist concerning seed germination and dormancy.

LEAF COLOR: Light to dark green above, light green to purple below. Submerged leaves are narrowly egg-shaped to arrow-shaped, ranging 8–24 in (20–60 cm) in length. In slow-moving or standing water, floating leaves (similar to the floating leaves of small-flowered *Nymphaea*) are also produced. Floating leaves are leathery, narrowly ovate to arrow-shaped, 0.75–4 in (2–10 cm) in length, green above and green to purple on the underside.

COMMENTS: A colleague, Don Bryne of Suwannee Laboratories, Lake City, Florida, has tried growing *Ondinea purpurea* commercially for the aquarium trade. Mr. Bryne reports that in both northern Florida and Jamaica in the fall, after the blooming season, plants develop tubers and go dormant. He does not predict much of a commercial future for it.

Ondinea purpurea **subsp.** *petaloidea* Kenneally & Schneider 1983. Native to the Kimberley District, Western Australia; found growing in clear sandy streams. Characteristics: Day blooming, flowers with petals, 27–34 stamens, sepals 0.6–1.5 × 0.25–0.5 in (1.5–4 × 0.6–1.3 cm), plant-forming tuber. Plate 446.

PETAL COLOR: Lavender-purple. *R.H.S. Chart*: Fan 2, Purple Group, No. 75C. Sepal color: Purplish violet-pink; exterior light green. *R.H.S. Chart*: Fan 2, Purple Group, No. 75D. Anther color: Purple-red. *R.H.S. Chart*: Fan 2, Red-Purple Group, No. 70C. Stamen color: Lavender-purple. Flower shape: Cuplike, pyramidal when calyx and corolla reflex. Flower size: 1.5–1.75 in (4–4.5 cm); after reflex, 0.75–1 in (2–2.5 cm). Fragrance: None or slight. Number of petals: 1–5. Number of sepals: 4.

LEAF COLOR: Surface leaves: top, green; underside, green to purplish. Submerged leaves: top, light to dark green; underside, light green to purplish. Leaf and sinus: Surface leaves arrow-shaped, lobe tips rounded, sinus narrow. Submerged leaves longer than wide, thin, base cordate, margins undulate, translucent, nestling on vertical stem, no sinus. Leaf size: Surface leaves 4 × 0.75 in (10 × 2 cm); submerged leaves 4–7 × 0.75–1.5 in (10–18 × 2–4 cm). Leaf spread: Surface leaves 8–10 in (20–25 cm); submerged leaves 8–16 in (20–40 cm). Stem color: Petioles light green; peduncles light greenish yellow. Pubescence on peduncle or petiole: None.

COMMENTS: Although this plant is a member of the water lily family, I do not see any commercial future for it, either for pools or aquaria, as it is very susceptible to aquatic bacteria and fungi. Dr. Schneider suggests that the pollen may be valuable for intergeneric crosses with *Nymphaea* species.

Ondinea purpurea **subsp.** *purpurea* Hartog 1970. Native to the Kimberley District, Western Australia; found growing in clear sandy streams. Characteristics: Day blooming, flower without petals, 14–23 stamens, sepals 0.3–0.6 × 0.06–0.1 in (0.8–1.5 × 0.15–0.3 cm), plant-forming tuber.

PETAL COLOR: No petals produced. Sepal color: Violet-pink; exterior light green. *R.H.S. Chart*: Fan 2, Purple Group, No. 75D. Anther color: Purple-red. *R.H.S. Chart*: Fan 2, Red-Purple Group, No. 70C. Stamen color: Lavender-purple. Flower shape: Pyramidal when sepals reflexed. Flower size: 0.4–0.6 in (1–1.5 cm). Fragrance: None or slight. Number of petals: 0. Number of sepals: 4.

LEAF COLOR: Surface leaves, top, green; underside, green to purplish. Submerged leaves, top, light to dark green; underside, light green to purplish. Leaf and sinus: Surface leaves narrowly ovate; sinus open. Submerged leaves longer than wide, thin, wavy, translucent, leaf bases closely spaced on vertical stem; no sinus. Leaf size: Surface leaves, 3.5 × 0.75 in (9 × 2 cm); submerged leaves, 2.75–5 × 0.75–1.25 in (7–13 × 2–3 cm). Leaf spread: Surface leaves, 8–16 in (20–40 cm); submerged leaves, 8–12 in (20–30 cm). Stem color: Petioles light green; peduncles light greenish yellow. Pubescence on peduncle or petiole: None.

COMMENTS: I do not see any commercial future for this member of the water lily family, either for pools or aquaria.

Appendix A

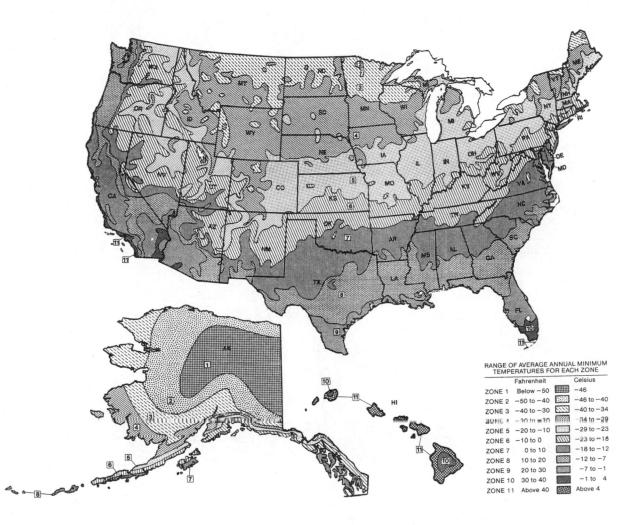

Hardiness Zone Map: USDA

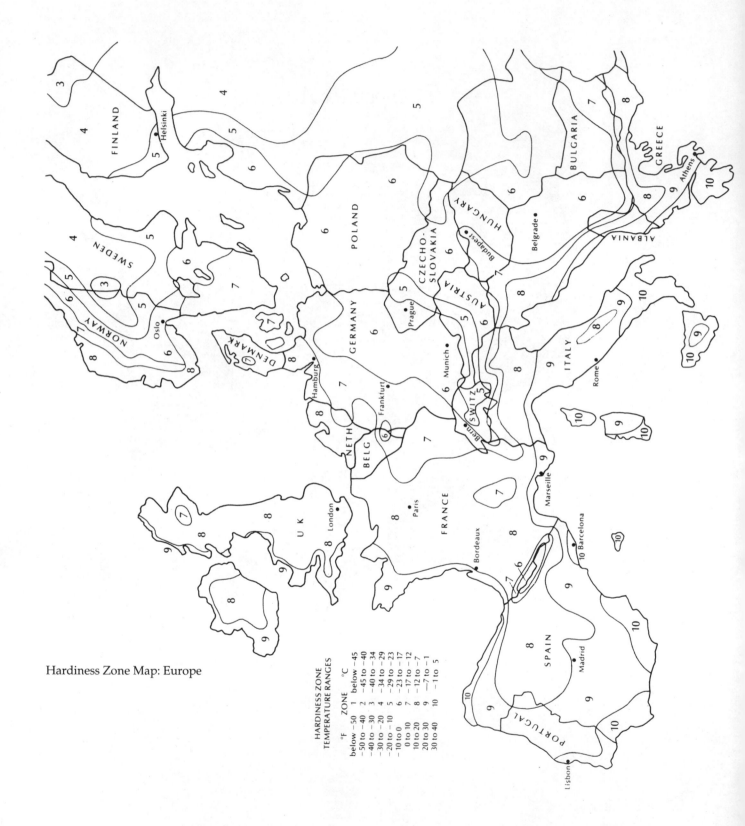

Hardiness Zone Map: Europe

Appendix B

Sources

The businesses listed in this appendix are likely sources of water gardening supplies. All offer products at retail (unless otherwise noted) in the following categories: plants; fish; pools; biological filters; and pumps, fountains, and other equipment.

PLANTS

United States

Aloha Lilies
123 N. Regency Place
Tucson, AZ 85711
local sales only

American Aquatic Gardens
621 Elysian Fields
New Orleans, LA 70117
tel. 504-944-0410

Aquatic Gardens and Koi Co.
Box 57, Highway 537
Jobstown, NJ 08041
wholesale and retail

Aquavirons
Box 1417
De Soto, TX 75115
tel. 214-212-4970

Arboretum Park, Inc.
8651 Old State Road 37 S.
Bloomington, IN 47403
tel. 812-824-6004

Bee Fork Water Garden
Box 71
Bunker, MO 63629

Bijou Water Gardens
26121 150th Avenue E.
Graham, WA 98338-8604
tel. 206-893-6988

Bittersweet Hill Nursery
1274 Governor Bridge Road
Davidsonville, MD 21035
tel. 401-798-0231

C & C Aquatics
2635 Steel Drive
Colorado Springs, CO 80907
tel. 719-471-7222

Carmona Nursery
1801 S. Central Avenue
Visalia, CA 93277

Charleston Aquatic Nursery
3095 Canal Bridge Road
John's Island, SC 29455
tel. 803-559-3151

Eagle Lake Farm, Inc.
627 W. Warfaker Road
Corpeville, WA 98239

Florida Aquatic Nurseries
700 S. Flamingo Road
Ft. Lauderdale, FL 33325
tel. 305-472-5120

Gilberg Perennial Farm
2906 Ossenfort Road
Glencoe, MO 63038
tel. 314-458-2033

Lilies of the Valley
26585 Rancho San Carlos
Carmel, CA 93923

299

The Lily Pond
3635 East Palm Lane
Phoenix, AZ 85008
tel. 602-273-1805

Lilypons Water Gardens
6800 Lilypons Road
Buckeystown, MD 21717
tel. 301-874-5133

Lilypons Water Gardens
Box 188
Brookshire, TX 77423
tel. 713-391-0076

Lilypons Water Gardens
Box 1130
Thermal, CA 92274
tel. 619-397-4258

Maryland Aquatic Nurseries
3218 Suffolk Lane
Fallston, MD 21047
tel. 301-557-7615

Matterhorn Nursery
227 Summit Pk. Road
Spring Valley, NY 10977
tel. 914-354-5986

Mayo Culp
5967 Noel Lane
Katy, TX 77493
tel. 713-371-9049

McAllister Water Gardens
1470 Whitehall Lane
St. Helena, CA 94574

McDonald's Aquatic Nurseries
18164 Arminta Street
Reseda, CA 91335
tel. 818-345-7525

Miami Water Gardens
22150 SW 147 Avenue
Miami, FL 33170
tel. 305-258-2664

Oliver Nurseries
1159 Bronson Road
Fairfield, CT 06430
tel. 203-259-5609

Paradise Ponds
7102 E. Sunnyvale Road
Paradise Valley, AZ 85253
tel. 617-447-4711
fax 617-447-4591

Paradise Water Gardens
14 May Street
Whitman, MA 02382
tel. 617-447-3803

Patio Garden Ponds
8317 S. Linn
Oklahoma City, OK 73159
tel. 405-682-1514

Perry's Water Gardens
191 Leatherman Gap Road
Franklin, NC 28734
tel. 704-524-3264

Pond-Around
176 Mulberry Drive
Mechanicsburg, PA 17055
tel. 717-697-6838

Pondo. Mondo
Box 946
Norwood, NC 28128
tel. 704-474-3362
fax 704-474-3361

Road Nursery
12511 Central Valley Road NW
Poulsbo, WA 98370
tel. 206-779-9589

Robert Steinbach
RR2, Box 75
Elgin, IL 60120

S. Scherer & Son's
104 Waterside Road
Northport, NY 11768
tel. 516-261-7432

Santa Barbara Water Gardens
Box 4353
Santa Barbara, CA 93140
tel. 805-969-5129

Shady Lakes Water Lily Gardens
11033 Highway 85 NW
Alameda, NM 87114
tel. 505-898-2568

Slocum Water Gardens
1101 Cypress Gardens Blvd.
Winter Haven, FL 33880
tel. 813-293-7151

Strawn Water Gardens
Route 4, Box 142
College Station, TX 77840
tel. 409-696-6644

Suwannee Laboratories, Inc.
Box 1823
Lake City, FL 32056

TetraPond
201 Tabor Road
Morris Plains, NJ 07950
tel. 201-540-4285
wholesale

Tranquil Water Lily
4761 Olive Street
San Diego, CA 92105
tel. 619-263-9965

Tropical Pond and Garden
17888 61 Place
N. Loxahatchee, FL 33470
tel. 407-791-8994
fax 407-795-4564

Valley View Farms
11035 York Road
Cockeysville, MD 21030
tel. 410-527-0700

Van Ness Water Gardens
2460 N. Euclid Avenue
Upland, CA 91786-1199
tel. 714-982-2425

W. Rolfe Ltd.
443 Paso Del Norte
Escondido, CA 92026

Walter's Aquatic Plants
6073 Lancaster Drive
San Diego, CA 92120
tel. 619-582-5408

Water Garden Gems
Route 2, Box 65
Marion, TX 78124

The Water Works
Tilley's Nursery, Inc.
111 E. Fairmount Street
Coopersburg, PA 18036
tel. 215-282-4784

Waterford Gardens
74 E. Allendale Road
Saddle River, NJ 07458
tel. 201-327-0721

Water's Edge
1200 Mississippi Street
Lawrence, KS 66044
tel. 913-842-1122

Waterville Water Gardens
224 Maumee Drive
Waterville, OH 43566

Wickleins Aquatic Farm and
    Nursery
1820 Cromwell Bridge Road
Baltimore, MD 21234

William Tricker, Inc.
Box 31267
7125 Tanglewood Drive
Independence, OH 44131
tel. 216-524-3491

Canada

A Fleur d'Eau Inc.
C.P. 120, 6 Rd. 237
Stanbridge East, PQ J0J 2H0
tel. 514-248-7008
fax 514-248-4623

Island Specialty Nursery
8797 Chemainus Road
Chemainus, BC V0R 1K0
tel. 604-246-6355

Moore Water Gardens
Box 340
Port Stanley, ON N0L 2A0
tel. 519-782-4052

Reimer Waterscapes
RR3, Box 34
Tillsonburg, ON N4G 4H3
tel. 519-842-6049

T-D Enterprises
865 Millgrove Sideroad
Millgrove, ON

United Kingdom

Ampthill Aquatics Ltd.
Abridge Road
Theydon Bois
Essex CM16 7NR

Anglo Aquarium Plant Co. Ltd.
Strayfield Road
Enfield
Middlesex EN2 9JE
tel. 0181-363-8548
wholesale

Beaver Water Plant and Fish
    Farm Ltd.
Eastbourne Road (A 22)
New Chapel, Lingfield
Surrey RH7 6Hl

Bennett's Water Lily and Fish
    Farm
Chickerell
Weymouth
Dorset DT3 4AF
wholesale and retail

Blagdon Water Gardens
Walrow Industrial Estate
Commerce Way
Highbridge
Somerset TA9 4AG
wholesale

Dorset Water Lily Company
101 W. Coker Road
Yeovil
Somerset
wholesale

Egmont Water Gardens
132 Tolworth Rise South
Surbiton
Surrey KT6 5LR

H. Tisbury and Sons
Spice Pitts Farm
Church Road, Noak Hill
Romford
Essex RM4 1LD

Hertfordshire Fisheries
North Orbital Road
St. Albans
Hertfordshire

London Aquatics Co. Ltd.
Greenwood Nurseries
Theobalds Park Road
Enfield
Middlesex EN2 9BW
wholesale

Lotus Water Garden Products
    Ltd.
Berkhampsted Road
Chesham
Buckinghamshire HP5 3EZ
wholesale

Newlake Gardens
West Park Road
Copthorne, Crawley
West Sussex RH10 3HQ

Prestopets Ltd.
Weald Bridge Nursery
Kent Lane
North Weald
Essex CM16 6AX

Rutland Water Garden Nursery
  Ltd.
Folly Farm
Uffington, Stanford
Lincolnshire PE9 4TE

Shirley Aquatics Ltd.
Stratford Road
Shirley, Solihull
West Midlands B90 4EF

Solesbridge Mill Water Gardens
Tropical Marine Center Ltd.
Solesbridge Lane
Chorleywood, Richmansworth
Hertfordshire WD3 5SX

Stapeley Water Gardens
72 London Road
Stapeley, Nantwich
Cheshire CW5 7LH
tel. 01270-623868
wholesale and retail

Surbiton Aquaria Co. Ltd.
27-29 Brighton Road
Surbiton
Surrey KT6 5LR

Wildwoods Water Gardens Ltd.
Theobalds Park Road
Crews Hill, Enfield
Middlesex EN2 9BW

Europe

Aqua Production SPRL
Chemin du Seucha 20
B-1300
Limal
Belgium
tel. 32-10-411256

Aquaflora Vinkeveen BV
Uitweg 25
3645 TA Vinkeveen
The Netherlands
tel. 31-2979-86709
fax 31-2979-89256

Aquatic D.C.
Chemin des Crahauts 16
B-5980
Boiceau
Belgium

Eberhard Schuster
Garten Baubetrieb
Post Gadebehn
2711 Augustenhof
Germany

Giardini di Marignolle
Via di Marignolle 69
50124 Florence
Italy

J. Hoogendoorn
Vitvercentrum De Plomp B.V.
Klapwijkseweg 8
2641 RC
The Netherlands

Latour-Marliac
Le Temple-sur-Lot
47110 Sainte Livrade sur Lot
France

Petrowsky, Jorg
Aschauteiche
3106 Eschede
Germany
tel. 05142-803
fax 05142-4030

R. Bezancon
15 Avenue du Raincy
94 Saint Maur
France

Wachter-Wasserpflanzen
Rollarg
2081 Appen-ETZ
Germany
tel. 4101-62511
fax 4101-61026

Israel

Noaa Lavid
Kibbutz
Hazorea 30060

Australia

Arcadia Lily Ponds
151 Arcadia Road
Arcadia 2159
New South Wales

Austral Watergardens
Pacific Highway
Cowan 2252
Queensland

Gedye's Water Gardens
37 Elizabeth Street
Doncaster East 3109
Victoria

Ledora Farm
Pacific Highway
Mt. Kgai (near Sydney)

Pisces Enterprises Aquatic Plant
Box 200
Kenmore 4069
Queensland

Sherringhams Nursery
299a Lane Cove Road
North Ryde
New South Wales

New Zealand

Haumoana Fish and Water
    Plant Farm
5 Haumoana Road
Haumoana, Hawke's Bay
Napier

Rapaura Water Gardens
Rapaura Falls Park (near Tapu)
Coromandel Peninsula

Waihi Water Gardens
RD 2, Pukeauri Road
Waihi
North Island

Singapore

Oriental Aquariums PTE Ltd.
Eu IT Hai
652 Lim Chu Kang Road
Singapore 2471
tel. 6566-90506

FISH

United States

   Practically all plant suppliers in the United States sell ornamental pool fish at retail also. If at all possible, drive to the aquatic nursery and make your own selections, or write for a catalog and have them shipped. Most aquatic nurseries in the United States ship via UPS now, which is quite reasonably priced. The following U.S. businesses are wholesale fish suppliers unless otherwise noted.

Aquatic Gardens and Koi Co.
Box 57, Highway 537
Jobstown, NJ 08041
wholesale and retail

Billy Blands Fishery
Route 1
Taylor, AR 71861
tel. 501-694-4811
wholesale

Blue Ridge Fish Hatchery, Inc.
4536 Kernersville Road
Kernersville, NC 27284
tel. 919-788-6770
wholesale

Golden Pond, Inc.
Box 251
Oakville, WA 98568
wholesale

Hunting Creek Fisheries, Inc.
6916 Black's Mill Road
Thurmont, MD 21788
tel. 301-271-7475
wholesale

Mt. Parnell Fisheries, Inc.
1574 Ft. Loudon Road
Mercersburg, PA 17236
tel. 717-369-3018
wholesale

Ozark Fisheries, Inc.
Stoutland, MO 65567
tel. 314-765-3227
wholesale

Canada

Moore Water Gardens
Box 340
Port Stanley, ON N0L 2A0
tel. 519-782-4052

Reimer Waterscapes
RR3, Box 34
Tillsonburg, ON N4G 4H3
tel. 519-842-6049

United Kingdom

Ampthill Aquatics Ltd.
Abridge Road
Theydon Bois
Essex CM16 7NR

Beaver Water Plant and Fish
  Farm Ltd.
Eastbourne Road (A 22)
New Chapel, Lingfield
Surrey RH7 6Hl

Bennett's Water Lily and Fish
  Farm
Chickerell
Weymouth
Dorset DT3 4AF
wholesale and retail

Blagdon Water Gardens
Walrow Industrial Estate
Commerce Way
Highbridge
Somerset TA9 4AG
wholesale

Egmont Water Gardens
132 Tolworth Rise South
Surbiton
Surrey KT6 5LR

H. Tisbury and Sons
Spice Pitts Farm
Church Road, Noak Hill
Romford
Essex RM4 1LD

Hertfordshire Fisheries
North Orbital Road
St. Albans
Hertfordshire

London Aquatics Co. Ltd.
Greenwood Nurseries
Theobalds Park Road
Enfield
Middlesex EN2 9BW
wholesale

Lotus Water Garden Products
  Ltd.
Berkhampsted Road
Chesham
Buckinghamshire HP5 3EZ
wholesale

Newlake Gardens
West Park Road
Copthorne, Crawley
West Sussex RH10 3HQ

Shirley Aquatics Ltd.
Stratford Road
Shirley, Solihull
West Midlands B90 4EF

Solesbridge Mill Water Gardens
Tropical Marine Center Ltd.
Solesbridge Lane
Chorleywood, Richmansworth
Hertfordshire WD3 5SX

Stapeley Water Gardens
72 London Road
Stapeley, Nantwich
Cheshire CW5 7LH
tel. 01270-623868
wholesale and retail

Surbiton Aquaria Co. Ltd.
27-29 Brighton Road
Surbiton
Surrey KT6 5LR

Wessex Fish Farms
Burton Bradstock
Bridport
Dorset DT6 4NE

Wildwoods Water Gardens Ltd.
Theobalds Park Road
Crews Hill, Enfield
Middlesex EN2 9BW

Wychwood Carp Farm
Farnham Road
Odiham, near Basingtoke
Hampshire RG25 1HS

Israel

Dag Noy Ornamental Fish
Hazorea Fisheries
Hazorea 30060

Australia

Gedye's Water Gardens
37 Elizabeth Street
Doncaster East 3109
Victoria

New Zealand

Haumoana Fish and Water Plant Farm
5 Haumoana Road
Haumoana, Hawke's Bay
Napier

POOLS

United States

Aqualite Pool Co.
430 Bedford Street
Whitman, MA 02382
tel. 617-447-4711

Atlantic Water Gardens
105 Kathy's Lane
May's Landing, NJ 08330
tel. 609-927-8972

Fiber Tech, Inc.
833 Main Street
Southbridge, MA 01550

Hecht Rubber Corporation
6161 Phillips Highway
Jacksonville, FL 32216
tel. 1-800-872-3401

Lerio Corporation
1501 Telegraph Road
Mobile, AL 36652
tel. 334-457-7661
tel. 1-800-457-8112
fax 334-452-7538

Lilypons Water Gardens
6800 Lilypons Road
Buckeystown, MD 21717
tel. 301-874-5133

Lilypons Water Gardens
Box 188
Brookshire, TX 77423
tel. 713-391-0076

Lilypons Water Gardens
Box 1130
Thermal, CA 92274
tel. 619-397-4258

Liquid Pond Liner
C.I.M. Industries Inc.
Peterborough, NH 03458
tel. 1-800-543-3458
fax 603-924-9482

MacCourt
111 S. Virginia Street
Crystal Lake, IL 60014
tel. 815-455-6300
tel. 1-800-552-5473
fax 815-455-6410

Pondo. Mondo
Box 946
Norwood, NC 28128
tel. 704-474-3362
fax 704-474-3361

Redmond Pond Seal
RCS Co. Inc.
Redmond, UT 84652
tel. 1-800-367-7258

Resource Conservation
  Technology
2633 N. Calvert Street
Baltimore, MD 21218
tel. 410-366-1146

Slocum Water Gardens
1101 Cypress Gardens Blvd.
Winter Haven, FL 33880
tel. 813-293-7151

TetraPond
201 Tabor Road
Morris Plains, NJ 07950
tel. 201-540-4285
wholesale

Van Ness Water Gardens
2460 N. Euclid Avenue
Upland, CA 91786-1199
tel. 714-982-2425

Waterford Gardens
74 E. Allendale Road
Saddle River, NJ 07458
tel. 201-327-0721

William Tricker, Inc.
Box 31267
7125 Tanglewood Drive
Independence, OH 44131
tel. 216-524-3491

Canada

Moore Water Gardens
Box 340
Port Stanley, ON N0L 2A0
tel. 519-782-4052

Reimer Waterscapes
RR3, Box 34
Tillsonburg, ON N4G 4H3
tel. 519-842-6049

United Kingdom

Ampthill Aquatics Ltd.
Abridge Road
Theydon Bois
Essex CM16 7NR

Bennett's Water Lily and Fish
    Farm
Chickerell
Weymouth
Dorset DT3 4AF
wholesale and retail

Blagdon Water Gardens
Walrow Industrial Estate
Commerce Way
Highbridge
Somerset TA9 4AG
wholesale

Deepools
Box 26
St. Austell
Cornwall PL25 4XF

Egmont Water Gardens
132 Tolworth Rise South
Surbiton
Surrey KT6 5LR

H. Tisbury and Sons
Spice Pitts Farm
Church Road, Noak Hill
Romford
Essex RM4 1LD

Hertfordshire Fisheries
North Orbital Road
St. Albans
Hertfordshire

Glass Art Ltd.
Stewkley
Leighton Buzzard
Beds. LU7 0TX
wholesale

Lotus Water Garden Products
    Ltd.
Berkhampsted Road
Chesham
Buckinghamshire HP5 3EZ
wholesale

Newlake Gardens
West Park Road
Copthorne, Crawley
West Sussex RH10 3HQ

Oasis Water Garden Products
    Ltd.
Deacon Industrial Estate, Unit
    C1
Chickenhall Lane
Eastleigh
Hants. SO5 5RP
wholesale

Remanoid Ltd.
No. 1 Industrial Estate, Unit 44
Medomsley Road, Consett
Durham DH8 6SZ
wholesale

Shirley Aquatics Ltd.
Stratford Road
Shirley, Solihull
West Midlands B90 4EF

Solesbridge Mill Water Gardens
Tropical Marine Center Ltd.
Solesbridge Lane
Chorleywood, Richmansworth
Hertfordshire WD3 5SX

Stapeley Water Gardens
72 London Road
Stapeley, Nantwich
Cheshire CW5 7LH
tel. 01270-623868
wholesale and retail

Surbiton Aquaria Co. Ltd.
27-29 Brighton Road
Surbiton
Surrey KT6 5LR

Wildwoods Water Gardens Ltd.
Theobalds Park Road
Crews Hill, Enfield
Middlesex EN2 9BW

Germany

Tetra Werke Dr. rer. nat. Ulrich
    Baensch Gmbtt.
Box 1580
4520 Melle

Australia

Gedye's Water Gardens
37 Elizabeth Street
Doncaster East 3109
Victoria

New Zealand

Haumoana Fish and Water
    Plant Farm
5 Haumoana Road
Haumoana, Hawke's Bay
Napier

BIOLOGICAL FILTERS

United States

Aqua-Bacta-Aid
Water Quality Science, Inc.
Box 532
Bolivar, MO 65613
wholesale

Aquatic Gardens and Koi Co.
Box 57, Highway 537
Jobstown, NJ 08041
wholesale and retail

Clear-Pond
Creative Sales West CP-32
Box 768
Oxnard, CA 93032
wholesale

United Kingdom

Lotus Water Garden Products
    Ltd.
Berkhampsted Road
Chesham
Buckinghamshire HP5 3EZ
wholesale

Stapeley Water Gardens
72 London Road
Stapeley, Nantwich
Cheshire CW5 7LH
tel. 01270-623868
wholesale and retail

PUMPS, FOUNTAINS, AND OTHER EQUIPMENT

United States

Practically all plant suppliers in the United States sell equipment at retail also. If at all possible, drive to the aquatic nursery and pick up the equipment, or write for a catalog and have it shipped. Most aquatic nurseries in the United States ship via UPS now, which is quite reasonably priced. The following U.S. businesses are wholesale suppliers of water gardening equipment.

Beckett Company
2521 Willowbrook Road
Dallas, TX 75220
tel. 214-357-6421
wholesale

Calvert Engineering, Inc.
Cal Pump Division
7051 Hayvenhurst Avenue
Van Nuys, CA 91406
tel. 818-781-6029
wholesale

Cyprio USA
2507 E. 21st Street
Des Moines, IA 50317
wholesale

Little Giant Pump Company
3810 N. Tulsa
Oklahoma City, OK 73112
tel. 405-497-2511
wholesale

TetraPond
201 Tabor Road
Morris Plains, NJ 07950
tel. 201-540-4285
wholesale

Canada

Moore Water Gardens
Box 340
Port Stanley, ON N0L 2A0
tel. 519-782-4052

Reimer Waterscapes
RR3, Box 34
Tillsonburg, ON N4G 4H3
tel. 519-842-6049

United Kingdom

Ampthill Aquatics Ltd.
Abridge Road
Theydon Bois
Essex CM16 7NR

Bennett's Water Lily and Fish
  Farm
Chickerell
Weymouth
Dorset DT3 4AF
wholesale and retail

Beresford Pumps Ltd.
Sir Henry Parks Road
Canley
Coventry CV5 6BN

Blagdon Water Gardens
Walrow Industrial Estate
Commerce Way
Highbridge
Somerset TA9 4AG
wholesale

Cotswold Pump Supplies Ltd.
1 John Rushout Court
Northwick Park
Blockley
Moreton-in-March
Gloucestershire GL56 9RJ
wholesale

Cougar Pumps Ltd.
19/20 Empire Centre
Imperial Way
Watford
Hertfordshire WD2 4YH
wholesale

Cyprio Ltd.
Hards Road
Frognall
Peterborough PE6 8RR
wholesale

Egmont Water Gardens
132 Tolworth Rise South
Surbiton
Surrey KT6 5LR

H. Tisbury and Sons
Spice Pitts Farm
Church Road, Noak Hill
Romford
Essex RM4 1LD

Hertfordshire Fisheries
North Orbital Road
St. Albans
Hertfordshire

Hozelock Ltd.
Haddenham
Aylesbury
Buckinghamshire HP17 8JD

Lotus Water Garden Products
 Ltd.
Berkhampsted Road
Chesham
Buckinghamshire HP5 3EZ
wholesale

Newlake Gardens
West Park Road
Copthorne, Crawley
West Sussex RH10 3HQ

Oasis Water Garden Products
 Ltd.
Deacon Industrial Estate, Unit
 C1
Chickenhall Lane
Eastleigh
Hants. SO5 5RP
wholesale

Obart Ltd.
Alforest Works
Kent House Lane
Beckenham
Kent
wholesale

Remanoid Ltd.
No. 1 Industrial Estate, Unit 44
Medomsley Road, Consett
Durham DH8 6SZ
wholesale

Shirley Aquatics Ltd.
Stratford Road
Shirley, Solihull
West Midlands B90 4EF

Stapeley Water Gardens
72 London Road
Stapeley, Nantwich
Cheshire CW5 7LH
tel. 01270-623868
wholesale and retail

Stuart Turner Ltd.
Henley-on-Thames
Oxon RG9 2AD

Surbiton Aquaria Co. Ltd.
27-29 Brighton Road
Surbiton
Surrey KT6 5LR

Water Techniques
Dawes Court Works
High Street
Esher
Surrey
wholesale

Wildwoods Water Gardens Ltd.
Theobalds Park Road
Crews Hill, Enfield
Middlesex EN2 9BW

Australia

Gedye's Water Gardens
37 Elizabeth Street
Doncaster East 3109
Victoria

New Zealand

Haumoana Fish and Water Plant Farm
5 Haumoana Road
Haumoana, Hawke's Bay
Napier

Glossary

adventitious. Added from outside; not inherent.

anther. Pollen-bearing part of stamen.

apical. Of, at, or constituting the apex.

awn. A group of sharp, bristly fibers.

carpel. A single pistil or single unit of a compound pistil.

changeable water lily. One with flowers opening up lighter colored, deepening on second and third days.

cordate. Heart-shaped; frequently used to describe leaf shape.

corymb. A broad, flat-topped cluster of flowers in which the outer flower stalks are long and those toward the center are progressively shorter.

crenate. Having a notched or scalloped edge; frequently used to describe leaf edges.

cultivar. Contraction of "cultivated variety"; an induced result of hybridizing or a natural hybrid that has been named.

dentate. Having a toothed margin; frequently used to describe leaf edges.

emersed. Having emerged above the surface; standing above the surface water level.

filament. The basal stalk of the stamen bearing the anthers.

finger rhizome. Refers to size of rhizome; small finger or thumb-sized rhizome, grows erect.

glaucous. Glowing or covered with a whitish "bloom" that can be rubbed off; usually refers to stem or leaf surfaces.

hardy water lily. A perennial aquatic herb.

hastate. Having a triangular shape like a spearhead; frequently used to describe leaf shape.

internode. The plant section found between two successive nodes or joints.

lanceolate. Narrow and tapering toward the end like a lance, several times longer than broad; frequently used to describe leaf shape.

mainstem. The vertical center of a flower.

Marliac rhizome. A thick type of hardy water lily rhizome developed by Joseph B. L. Marliac; plants with this type of rhizome are notable for freedom of bloom.

mutant. A plant with inheritable characteristics that differ from those of the parents.

obovate. Egg-shaped, the broad end is located at the top; frequently used to describe leaf shape. See also **ovate**.

odorata rhizome. A slender type of rhizome common to hardy water lily species, particularly in eastern North America.

ovate. Egg-shaped, the broad end is at the base; frequently used to describe leaf shape. See also **obovate**.

peduncle. The stalk of a single flower or the stalk of a cluster flower.

peltate. Shaped like a shield; frequently used to describe leaf shape.

perfoliate. Having a base surrounding the leaf stem; base appears perforated by the stem.

perianth. The outer part of the flower, including the calyx and corolla.

perigynous. Refers to flower structure; having the sepals, petals, and stamens attached to the rim surrounding the ovary, unattached to the ovary itself.

petiole. The leaf stalk.

pineapple rhizome. A thick, upright-growing rhizome typical of certain hardy water lilies.

pubescence. Surface fuzz, hairs, or down; sometimes present on peduncle or petiole of water lilies.

raceme. An unbranched flower cluster consisting of a single central stem; individual flowers grow on small stems off the central stem.

radical. In reference to leaves, of or coming from the root.

recurved. To curve or bend back; often used in reference to flower parts or leaves.

reniform. Kidney-shaped; frequently used to describe leaf shape.

rhizome. Modified underground stem from which the plant makes growth.

rosulate. Forming a rosette; sometimes used to describe leaf arrangement.

sessile. Lacking pedicel or peduncle, attachment is direct to main stem.

sinus. Area between the lobes of the water lily leaf.

spadix. Fleshy spike found in tiny flowers, usually enclosed in a **spathe** (which see).

spathe. A large leaflike part or pair of such parts enclosing a flower cluster.

stamen. The pollen-bearing organ in a flower; includes the slender stalk known as the filament at the base and a pollen sac, the anther, at the tip.

staminodes. The colored, petal-like organs located just outside the stamens in water lilies and lotuses; characterized by broad bases and anther-like sacs at the tips.

star lily. Tropical perennial herb, mostly resulting from crosses of *Nymphaea flavovirens* (syn. *N. gracilis*) with its own variations or with *N. capensis* var. *zanzibariensis*.

stigma. The upper tip of the flower pistil that receives pollen; plural, **stigmata**.

stellate. Star-shaped; usually used in reference to flowers.

stolon. A runner, especially a stem running underground.

stoma. A microscopic opening in the epidermis of plants; it is surrounded by guard cells and serves in gaseous exchange. Plural, **stomata**.

style. The slender stalklike part of a carpel located between the stigma and ovary.

terminal. Usually used in reference to the growth at the end of a stem.

thumb rhizome. Same as **finger rhizome** (which see).

tip. The staminal appendage in tropical day-blooming water lilies.

tomentose. Hairy; covered with hairs.

tuber. A short, thickened, fleshy part of an underground stem.

tuberosa rhizome. A slender hardy water lily rhizome in which young (new) tubers are attached to the parent tuber only by very fragile, thin pieces; the young tubers usually break off and remain underground when the parent tuber is pulled.

tropical water lily. Also known as tender water lily. Species forming an underwater herb, native to warmer countries; may also refer to a cultivar resulting from crossing two tropical water lily species or crossing a tropical water lily species and tropical water lily cultivar.

turion. A terminal overwintering bud, sometimes scaly, often thick and fleshy, growing from a submerged rootstock.

upright rhizome. A hardy water lily rhizome that grows upright.

variant. A plant displaying variation from the species.

viviparous. Germination that takes place while new plant is still attached to the parent plant.

Recommended Reading

Books and articles

Axelrod, Herbert, and William Vorderwinkler. 1984. *Goldfish and Koi in Your Home*. Neptune City, New Jersey: T.F.H. Publications, Inc. Ltd.

Bailey, Liberty Hyde, and Ethel Zoe Bailey. 1976. *Hortus Third*. New York: MacMillan Publishing Co., Inc.; London: Collier MacMillan Publishers.

Caillet, Marie, and Joseph K. Mertzweiller. 1988. *The Louisiana Iris*. The Society for Louisiana Irises/Texas Gardener Press.

Clifford, Derek. 1963. *A History of Garden Design*. Frederick A. Praeger.

Conard, Henry S. 1905. *The Waterlilies: A Monograph of the Genus Nymphaea*. Washington, D.C.: Carnegie Institution of Washington.

Fox, Shirley, ed. 1986. *Aquatic and Wetland Plants of Florida*. 3d ed. Bureau of Aquatic Plant Research and Control, Florida State Department of Natural Resources.

Gorer, Richard. 1978. *The Growth of Gardens*. London and Boston: Faber and Faber Limited.

Graf, Alfred B. 1980. *Exotica Series 3*. 10th ed. Roehrs Company, Inc.

Hadfield, Miles. 1979. *A History of British Gardening*. London: John Murray (Publishers) Ltd.

Henkel, Friedrich, F. Rehnelt, and L. Dittman. 1907. *Das Buch der Nymphaeaceen oder Seerosengewächse*. Darmstadt-Neuwiese: Friedrich Henkel.

Heritage, Bill. 1980. *The Lotus Book of Water Gardening*. Chesham, Buckinghamshire: Lotus Water Garden Products Ltd.

———. 1986. *Ponds and Water Gardens*. Rev. 2d ed. Poole, New York, and Sydney: Blandford Press Ltd.

International Water Lily Society. 1993. *Identification of Hardy Nymphaea*. Stapeley Water Gardens Ltd.

Jacobs, S. W. L. 1992. New species, lectotypes and synonyms of Australasian *Nymphaea*. *Telopea* 4(4): 635–641.

Kuck, Loraine. 1968. *The World of the Japanese Garden*. New York and Tokyo: Walker/Weatherhill.

Ladiges, W. 1983. *Cold-Water Fish in the Home and Garden*. Tetra Press.

Ledbetter, Gordon T. 1979. *Water Gardens*. Sherborne, Dorset, England: Alpha Books; New York: W. W. Norton & Company, Inc.

———. 1982. *The Better Water Gardens Book of Patio Ponds*. Blagdon, Avon, England: Better Water Gardens.

Masson, Georgina. 1966. *Italian Gardens*. New York: Harry N. Abrams, Inc.

Masters, Charles O. 1974. *Encyclopaedia of the Water-Lily*. Neptune City, New Jersey: T. F. H. Publications, Inc. Ltd.

McHoy, Peter. 1986. *Water Gardening*. Poole, New York, and Sydney: Blandford Press Ltd.

Mitchell, Robert T., and Herbert S. Zim. 1987. *Butterflies and Moths*. Rev. ed. New York: Golden Press/Western Publishing Co., Inc.

Mühlberg, Helmut. 1982. *The Complete Guide to Water Plants*. E. P. Publishing Ltd.

Ni Xueming, ed. 1987. *Lotus of China*. Wuhan, China: Wuhan Botanical Institute.

Niering, William A. 1985. *Wetlands*, The Audubon Society Nature Guides. New York: Alfred A. Knopf, Inc.

Perry, Frances. 1981. *The Water Garden*. New York: Van Nostrand Reinhold Company.

Reid, George K., and Herbert S. Zim. 1967. *Pond Life*. New York: Golden Press/Western Publishing Co., Inc.

Robinson, Peter. 1987. *Pool and Waterside Gardening*. Portland, Oregon: Timber Press; London: Collingridge Books, in association with the Royal Botanic Gardens, Kew.

Russell, Stanley. 1985. *The Stapeley Book of Water Gardens*. London: David & Charles.

Siren, Oswald. 1949. *Gardens of China*. New York: The Ronald Press Co.

Swindells, Philip. 1983. *Waterlilies*. Portland, Oregon: Timber Press; London: Croom Helm Ltd.

———. 1985. *Salem House Book of the Water Garden*. Salem House.

Thomas, Charles B. 1988. *Water Gardens for Plants and Fish*. Neptune City, New Jersey: T.F.H. Publications, Inc. Ltd.

Thomas, Graham Stuart. 1979. *Gardens of the National Trust*. The National Trust/Weidenfeld and Nicolson.

Uber, William C. 1988. *Water Gardening Basics*. Upland, California: Dragonfly Press.

Wiersema, John H. 1987. *A Monograph of Nymphaea Subgenus Hydrocallis (Nymphaeaceae)*. Vol. 16 of *Systematic Botany Monographs*. Ann Arbor, Michigan: The American Society of Plant Taxonomists.

Wiser, K. H., and P. V. Loiselle. 1986. *Your Garden Pond*. Tetra Press.

Zim, Herbert S., and Hobart M. Smith. 1953. *Reptiles and Amphibians*. New York: Golden Press/Western Publishing Co., Inc.

Journals

Pondscapes (the magazine of the National Pond Society)
Box 449
Acworth, GA 30101
U.S.A.

Water Garden Journal (the official publication of the International Water Lily Society, Inc.)
Santa Barbara Botanic Garden
1212 Mission Canyon Road
Santa Barbara, CA 93105
U.S.A.

Index